Machine Learning Solutions

Expert techniques to tackle complex machine learning problems using Python

Jalaj Thanaki

BIRMINGHAM - MUMBAI

Machine Learning Solutions

Commissioning Editor: Sunith Shetty
Acquisition Editor: Aman Singh
Content Development Editors: Snehal Kolte
Technical Editor: Danish Shaikh
Copy Editor: Safis Editing
Project Coordinator: Manthan Patel
Proofreader: Safis Editing
Indexers: Pratik Shirodkar
Graphics: Tania Dutta
Production Coordinator: Arvindkumar Gupta

First published: April 2018

Production reference: 1250418

Published by Packt Publishing Ltd.
Livery Place
35 Livery Street
Birmingham B3 2PB, UK.

ISBN 978-1-78839-004-0

www.packtpub.com

With the blessings of God, and all my love for Shetul, parents, and in-laws

Foreword

I have known Jalaj Thanaki for more than 1 year. Jalaj comes across as a passionate techno-analytical expert who has the rigor one requires to achieve excellence. Her points of view on big data analytics, NLP, machine learning, and AI are well informed and carry her own analysis and appreciation of the landscape of problems and solutions. I'm glad to be writing this foreword in my capacity as the CEO and MD of SMEcorner.

Machine Learning solutions are rapidly changing the world and the way we do business, be it retail, banking, financial services, publication, pharmaceutical, or manufacturing industry. Data of all forms is growing exponentially—quantitative, qualitative, structured, unstructured, speech, video, and so on. It is imperative to make use of this data to leverage all functions, avoid risk and frauds, enhance customer experience, increase revenues, and streamline operations.

Organizations are moving fast to embrace data science and investing largely to build high-end data science teams. Having spent more than 30 years in the finance domain as a leader and managing director of various organizations such as Barclays Bank, Equifax, Hinduja Leyland, and SMECorner, I get overwhelmed with the transition that the financial industry has seen in embracing machine learning solutions as a business and no longer as a support function.

In this book, Jalaj takes us through an exciting and insightful journey to develop the best possible machine learning solutions for data science applications. With all the practical examples covered and with solid explanations, in my opinion, this is one of the best practical books for readers who want to become proficient in machine learning and deep learning.

Wishing Jalaj and this book a roaring success, which they deserve.

Samir Bhatia
MD/CEO and Founder of SMECorner
Mumbai, India

Contributors

About the author

Jalaj is an experienced data scientist with a demonstrated history of working in the information technology, publishing, and finance industries. She is author of the book "Python Natural Language Processing".

Her research interest lies in Natural Language Processing, Machine Learning, Deep Learning, and Big Data Analytics. Besides being a data scientist, Jalaj is also a social activist, traveler, and nature-lover.

I would like to dedicate this book to my husband, Shetul, for his constant support and encouragement. I give deep thanks and gratitude to my parents and my in-laws who help me at every stage of my life. I would like to thank my reviewers for providing valuable suggestions towards the improvement of this book.

Thank you, God, for being kind to me...!

About the reviewer

Niclas has been using computers for fun and profit since he got his first computer (a C64) at age four. After a prolonged period of combining a start-up with university studies, he graduated from Åbo Akademi University with an M.Sc. in Computer Engineering in 2015.

His hobbies include long walks, lifting heavy metal objects at the gym and spending quality time with his wife and daughter.

Niclas currently works at Walkbase - a company he founded together with some of his class mates from university. At Walkbase, he leads the engineering team, building the next generation of retail analytics.

Mayur Narkhede has good blend of experience in Data Science and Industry domain. He is researcher with educational qualification of B.Tech in Computer Science and M.Tech. in CSE with Artificial Intelligence specialization.

Data Scientist with core experience in building automated end to end solutions, Proficient at applying technology, AI, ML, Data Mining and Design thinking for better understanding and prediction in improving business functions and desired requirements with growth profitability.

He has worked on multiple advanced solutions such as ML and Predictive model development for Oil and Gas, Financial Services, Road Traffic and Transport, Life Science and Big Data platform for asset intensive industries.

Shetul Thanaki has a bachelor degree in computer engineering from Sardar vallabhbhai patel University,Gujarat. He has 10 years of experience in IT industries. He is currently working with investment bank and provides IT solutions to its global market applications.

He has good knowledge on java technologies,rule based system and database systems. AI technologies in fintech space are one of his key interest areas.

Table of Contents

Preface

This book, titled Machine Learning Solutions, gives you a broad idea about the topic. As a reader, you will get the chance to learn how to develop cutting-edge data science applications using various Machine Learning (ML) techniques. This book is practical guide that can help you to build and optimize your data science applications.

We learn things by practically doing them. Practical implementations of various Machine Learning techniques, tips and tricks, optimization techniques, and so on will enhance your understanding in the ML and data science application development domains.

Now let me answer one of the most common questions I have heard from my friends and colleagues so frequently about ML and the data science application development front. This question is what really inspired me to write this book. For me, it's really important that all my readers get an idea of why am I writing this book. Let's find out that question...!

The question is, "How can I achieve the best possible accuracy for a machine learning application?" The answer includes lots of things that people should take care of:

- Understand the goal of the application really well. Why does your organization want to build this application?
- List down the expected output of the application and how this output helps the organization. This will clarify to you the technical aspect and business aspect of the application.
- What kind of dataset do you have? Is there anything more you need in order to generate the required output?
- Explore the dataset really well. Try to get an insight from the dataset.

- Check whether the dataset is having labels or not. If it is a labeled dataset, then you can apply supervised algorithms; if it is not labeled, then apply unsupervised algorithms. Your problem statement is a regression problem or classification problem.
- Build the very simple base line approach using simple ML techniques. Measure the accuracy.
- Now you may think, "I haven't chosen the right algorithm and that is the reason the accuracy of the base line approach is not good." It's ok!
- Try to list down all the possible problems that you can think your base-line approach has. Be honest about the problems.
- Now solve the problems one by one and measure the accuracy. If the accuracy is improving, then move forward in that direction; otherwise try out other solutions that eventually solve the shortcomings of the base line approach and improve the accuracy.
- You can repeat the process number of times. After every iteration, you will get a new and definite direction, which will lead you to the best possible solution as well as accuracy.

I have covered all the specified aspects in this book. Here, the major goal is how readers will get a state-of-the-art result for their own data science problem using ML algorithms, and in order to achieve that, we will use only the bare necessary theory and many hands-on examples of different domains.

We will cover the analytics domain, NLP domain, and computer vision domain. These examples are all industry problems and readers will learn how to get the best result. After reading this book, readers will apply their new skills to any sort of industry problem to achieve best possible for their machine learning applications.

Who this book is for

A typical reader will have a basic to intermediate knowledge of undergraduate mathematics, such as probabilities, statistics, calculus, and linear algebra. No advanced mathematics is required as the book will be mostly self-contained. Basic to intermediate knowledge of Machine Learning (ML) algorithms is required. No advance concepts of machine learning are required as the book will be mostly self-contained. A decent knowledge in Python is required too as it would be out-of-scope to go through an introduction to Python but each procedure will be explained step-by-step to be reproducible.

This book is full if practical examples. The reader wants to know about how to apply the Machine Learning (ML) algorithms for real life data science applications efficiently. This book starts from the basic ML techniques which can be used to develop base-line approach. After that readers learn how to apply optimization techniques for each application in order to achieve the state-of-the-art result. For each application, I have specified the basic concepts, tips and tricks along with the code.

What this book covers

Chapter 1, Credit Risk Modeling, builds the predictive analytics model to help us to predict whether the customer will default the loan or not. We will be using outlier detection, feature transformation, ensemble machine learning algorithms, and so on to get the best possible solution.

Chapter 2, Stock Market Price Prediction, builds a model to predict the stock index price based on a historical dataset. We will use neural networks to get the best possible solution.

Chapter 3, Customer Analytics, explores how to build customer segmentation so that marketing campaigns can be done optimally. Using various machine learning algorithms such as K-nearest neighbor, random forest, and so on, we can build the base-line approach. In order to get the best possible solution, we will be using ensemble machine learning algorithms.

Chapter 4, Recommendation Systems for E-commerce, builds a recommendation engine for e-commerce platform. It can recommend similar books. We will be using concepts such as correlation, TF-IDF, and cosine similarity to build the application.

Chapter 5, Sentiment Analysis, generates sentiment scores for movie reviews. In order to get the best solution, we will be using recurrent neural networks and Long short-term memory units.

Chapter 6, Job Recommendation Engine, is where we build our own dataset, which can be used to make a job recommendation engine. We will also use an already available dataset. We will be using basic statistical techniques to get the best possible solution.

Chapter 7, Text Summarization, covers an application to generate the extractive summary of a medical transcription. We will be using Python libraries for our base line approach. After that we will be using various vectorization and ranking techniques to get the summary for a medical document. We will also generate a summary for Amazon's product reviews.

Chapter 8, Developing Chatbots, develops a chatbot using the rule-based approach and deep learning-based approach. We will be using TensorFlow and Keras to build chatbots.

Chapter 9, Building a Real-Time Object Recognition App, teaches transfer learning. We learn about convolutional networks and YOLO (You Only Look Once) algorithms. We will be using pre-trained models to develop the application.

Chapter 10, Face Recognition and Face Emotion Recognition, covers an application to recognize human faces. During the second half of this chapter, we will be developing an application that can recognize facial expressions of humans. We will be using OpenCV, Keras, and TensorFlow to build this application.

Chapter 11, Building Gaming Bots, teaches reinforcement learning. Here, we will be using the gym or universe library to get the gaming environment. We'll first understand the Q-learning algorithm, and later on we will implement the same to train our gaming bot. Here, we are building bot for Atari games.

Appendix A, List of Cheat Sheets, shows cheat sheets for various Python libraries that we frequently use in data science applications.

Appendix B, Strategy for Wining Hackathons, tells you what the possible strategy for winning hackathons can be. I have also listed down some of the cool resources that can help you to update yourself.

To get the most out of this book

Basic to intermediate knowledge of mathematics, probability, statistics, and calculus is required.

Basic to intermediate knowledge of Machine Learning (ML) algorithms is also required.

Decent knowledge of Python is required.

While reading the chapter, please run the code so that you can understand the flow of the application. All the codes are available on GitHub. The link is: `https://github.com/jalajthanaki/Awesome_Machine_Learning_Solutions`.

Links of code are specified in the chapters. Installation instructions for each application are also available on GitHub.

You need minimum 8 GB of RAM to run the applications smoothly. If you can run code on GPU, then it would great; otherwise you can use pre-trained models. You can download pre-trained models using the GitHub link or Google drive link. The links are specified in the chapters.

Download the example code files

You can download the example code files for this book from your account at `http://www.packtpub.com`. If you purchased this book elsewhere, you can visit `http://www.packtpub.com/support` and register to have the files emailed directly to you.

You can download the code files by following these steps:

1. Log in or register at `http://www.packtpub.com`.
2. Select the **SUPPORT** tab.
3. Click on **Code Downloads & Errata**.
4. Enter the name of the book in the **Search** box and follow the on-screen instructions.

Once the file is downloaded, please make sure that you unzip or extract the folder using the latest version of:

- WinRAR / 7-Zip for Windows
- Zipeg / iZip / UnRarX for Mac
- 7-Zip / PeaZip for Linux

The code bundle for the book is also hosted on GitHub at `https://github.com/PacktPublishing/Machine-Learning-Solutions`. In case there's an update to the code, it will be updated on the existing GitHub repository.

We also have other code bundles from our rich catalog of books and videos available at `https://github.com/PacktPublishing/`. Check them out!

Conventions used

There are a number of text conventions used throughout this book.

`CodeInText`: Indicates code words in text, database table names, folder names, filenames, file extensions, pathnames, dummy URLs, user input, and Twitter handles. For example; "Mount the downloaded `WebStorm-10*.dmg` disk image file as another disk in your system."

A block of code is set as follows:

```
from __future__ import print_function
import pandas as pd
import numpy as np
import seaborn as sns
import matplotlib.pyplot as plt
```

When we wish to draw your attention to a particular part of a code block, the relevant lines or items are set in bold:

```
from __future__ import print_function
import pandas as pd
import numpy as np
import seaborn as sns
import matplotlib.pyplot as plt
```

Any command-line input or output is written as follows:

```
# cp /usr/src/asterisk-addons/configs/cdr_mysql.conf.sample
     /etc/asterisk/cdr_mysql.conf
```

Bold: Indicates a new term, an important word, or words that you see on the screen, for example, in menus or dialog boxes, also appear in the text like this. For example: "Select **System info** from the **Administration** panel."

Warnings or important notes appear in a box like this.

Tips and tricks appear like this.

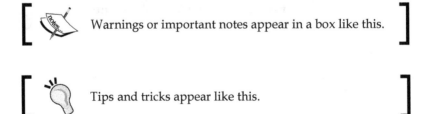

Get in touch

Feedback from our readers is always welcome.

General feedback: Email `feedback@packtpub.com`, and mention the book's title in the subject of your message. If you have questions about any aspect of this book, please email us at `questions@packtpub.com`.

Errata: Although we have taken every care to ensure the accuracy of our content, mistakes do happen. If you have found a mistake in this book we would be grateful if you would report this to us. Please visit, `http://www.packtpub.com/submit-errata`, selecting your book, clicking on the Errata Submission Form link, and entering the details.

Piracy: If you come across any illegal copies of our works in any form on the Internet, we would be grateful if you would provide us with the location address or website name. Please contact us at `copyright@packtpub.com` with a link to the material.

If you are interested in becoming an author: If there is a topic that you have expertise in and you are interested in either writing or contributing to a book, please visit `http://authors.packtpub.com`.

Reviews

Please leave a review. Once you have read and used this book, why not leave a review on the site that you purchased it from? Potential readers can then see and use your unbiased opinion to make purchase decisions, we at Packt can understand what you think about our products, and our authors can see your feedback on their book. Thank you!

For more information about Packt, please visit `packtpub.com`.

1
Credit Risk Modeling

All the chapters in this book are practical applications. We will develop one application per chapter. We will understand about the application, and choose the proper dataset in order to develop the application. After analyzing the dataset, we will build the base-line approach for the particular application. Later on, we will develop a revised approach that resolves the shortcomings of the baseline approach. Finally, we will see how we can develop the best possible solution using the appropriate optimization strategy for the given application. During this development process, we will learn necessary key concepts about Machine Learning techniques. I would recommend my reader run the code which is given in this book. That will help you understand concepts really well.

In this chapter, we will look at one of the many interesting applications of predictive analysis. I have selected the finance domain to begin with, and we are going to build an algorithm that can predict loan defaults. This is one of the most widely used predictive analysis applications in the finance domain. Here, we will look at how to develop an optimal solution for predicting loan defaults. We will cover all of the elements that will help us build this application.

We will cover the following topics in this chapter:

- Introducing the problem statement
- Understanding the dataset
    - Understanding attributes of the dataset
    - Data analysis
- Features engineering for the baseline model
- Selecting an ML algorithm
- Training the baseline model
- Understanding the testing matrix

- Testing the baseline model
- Problems with the existing approach
- How to optimize the existing approach
    - Understanding key concepts to optimize the approach
    - Hyperparameter tuning
- Implementing the revised approach
    - Testing the revised approach
    - Understanding the problem with the revised approach
- The best approach
- Implementing the best approach
- Summary

Introducing the problem statement

First of all, let's try to understand the application that we want to develop or the problem that we are trying to solve. Once we understand the problem statement and it's use case, it will be much easier for us to develop the application. So let's begin!

Here, we want to help financial companies, such as banks, NBFS, lenders, and so on. We will make an algorithm that can predict to whom financial institutes should give loans or credit. Now you may ask *what is the significance of this algorithm?* Let me explain that in detail. When a financial institute lends money to a customer, they are taking some kind of risk. So, before lending, financial institutes check whether or not the borrower will have enough money in the future to pay back their loan. Based on the customer's current income and expenditure, many financial institutes perform some kind of analysis that helps them decide whether the borrower will be a good customer for that bank or not. This kind of analysis is manual and time-consuming. So, it needs some kind of automation. If we develop an algorithm, that will help financial institutes gauge their customers efficiently and effectively.Your next question may be *what is the output of our algorithm?* Our algorithm will generate probability. This probability value will indicate the chances of borrowers defaulting. Defaulting means borrowers cannot repay their loan in a certain amount of time. Here, probability indicates the chances of a customer not paying their loan EMI on time, resulting in default. So, a higher probability value indicates that the customer would be a bad or inappropriate borrower (customer) for the financial institution, as they may default in the next 2 years. A lower probability value indicates that the customer will be a good or appropriate borrower (customer) for the financial institution and will not default in the next 2 years.

Here, I have given you information regarding the problem statement and its output, but there is an important aspect of this algorithm: its input. So, let's discuss what our input will be!

Understanding the dataset

Here, we are going to discuss our input dataset in order to develop the application. You can find the dataset at `https://github.com/jalajthanaki/credit-risk-modelling/tree/master/data`.

Let's discuss the dataset and its attributes in detail. Here, in the dataset, you can find the following files:

- `cs-training.csv`
  - Records in this file are used for training, so this is our training dataset.
- `cs-test.csv`
  - Records in this file are used for testing our machine learning models, so this is our testing dataset.
- `Data Dictionary.xls`
  - This file contains information about each of the attributes of the dataset. So, this file is referred to as our data dictionary.
- `sampleEntry.csv`
  - This file gives us an idea about the format in which we need to generate our end output for our testing dataset. If you open this file, then you will see that we need to generate the probability of each of the records present in the testing dataset. This probability value indicates the chances of borrowers defaulting.

Understanding attributes of the dataset

The dataset has 11 attributes, which are shown as follows:

Variable Name	Description	Type
SeriousDlqin2yrs	Person experienced 90 days past due delinquency or worse	Y/N
RevolvingUtilizationOfUnsecuredLines	Total balance on credit cards and personal lines of credit except real estate and no installment debt like car loans divided by the sum of credit limits	percentage
age	Age of borrower in years	integer
NumberOfTime30-59DaysPastDueNotWorse	Number of times borrower has been 30-59 days past due but no worse in the last 2 years.	integer
DebtRatio	Monthly debt payments, alimony,living costs divided by monthy gross income	percentage
MonthlyIncome	Monthly income	real
NumberOfOpenCreditLinesAndLoans	Number of Open loans (installment like car loan or mortgage) and Lines of credit (e.g. credit cards)	integer
NumberOfTimes90DaysLate	Number of times borrower has been 90 days or more past due.	integer
NumberRealEstateLoansOrLines	Number of mortgage and real estate loans including home equity lines of credit	integer
NumberOfTime60-89DaysPastDueNotWorse	Number of times borrower has been 60-89 days past due but no worse in the last 2 years.	integer
NumberOfDependents	Number of dependents in family excluding themselves (spouse, children etc.)	integer

Figure 1.1: Attributes (variables) of the dataset

We will look at each of the attributes one by one and understand their meaning in the context of the application:

1. **SeriousDlqin2yrs**:
    - In the dataset, this particular attribute indicates whether the borrower has experienced any past dues until 90 days in the previous 2 years.
    - The value of this attribute is Yes if the borrower has experienced past dues of more than 90 days in the previous 2 years. If the EMI was not paid by the borrower 90 days after the due date of the EMI, then this flag value is Yes.
    - The value of this attribute is No if the borrower has not experienced past dues of more than 90 days in the previous 2 years. If the EMI was paid by the borrower before 90 days from the due date of the EMI, then this flag value is No.
    - This attribute has target labels. In other words, we are going to predict this value using our algorithm for the test dataset.
2. **RevolvingUtilizationOfUnsecuredLines**:
    - This attribute indicates the credit card limits of the borrower after excluding any current loan debt and real estate.
    - Suppose I have a credit card and its credit limit is $1,000. In my personal bank account, I have $1,000. My credit card balance is $500 out of $1,000.

- So, the total maximum balance I can have via my credit card and personal bank account is $1,000 + $1,000 = $2,000; I have used $500 from my credit card limit, so the total balance that I have is $500 (credit card balance) + $1,000 (personal bank account balance) = $1,500.
- If account holder have taken home loan or other property loan and paying EMIs for those loan then we are not considering EMI value for property loan. Here, for this data attribute we have considered account holder's credit card balance and personal account balance.
- So, the RevolvingUtilizationOfUnsecuredLines value is = $1,500 / $2,000 = 0.7500

3. **Age**:
    - This attribute is self-explanatory. It indicates the borrower's age.
4. **NumberOfTime30-59DaysPastDueNotWorse**:
    - The number of this attribute indicates the number of times borrowers have paid their EMIs late but have paid them 30 days after the due date or 59 days before the due date.
5. **DebtRatio**:
    - This is also a self-explanatory attribute, but we will try and understand it better with an example.
    - If my monthly debt is $200 and my other expenditure is $500, then I spend $700 monthly. If my monthly income is $1,000, then the value of the DebtRatio is $700/$1,000 = 0.7000
6. **MonthlyIncome**:
    - This attribute contains the value of the monthly income of borrowers.
7. **NumberOfOpenCreditLinesAndLoans**:
    - This attribute indicates the number of open loans and/or the number of credit cards the borrower holds.
8. **NumberOfTimes90DaysLate**:
    - This attribute indicates how many times a borrower has paid their dues 90 days after the due date of their EMIs.
9. **NumberRealEstateLoansOrLines**:
    - This attribute indicates the number of loans the borrower holds for their real estate or the number of home loans a borrower has.

10. **NumberOfTime60-89DaysPastDueNotWorse**:
    - This attribute indicates how many times borrowers have paid their EMIs late but paid them 60 days after their due date or 89 days before their due date.
11. **NumberOfDependents**:
    - This attribute is self-explanatory as well. It indicates the number of dependent family members the borrowers have. The dependent count is excluding the borrower.

These are basic attribute descriptions of the dataset, so you have a basic idea of the kind of dataset we have. Now it's time to get hands-on. So from the next section onward, we will start coding. We will begin exploring our dataset by performing basic data analysis so that we can find out the statistical properties of the dataset.

Data analysis

This section is divided into two major parts. You can refer to the following figure to see how we will approach this section:

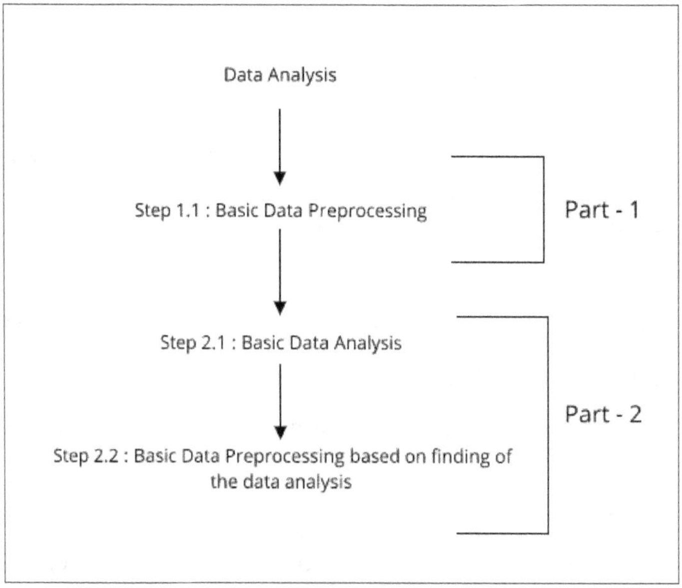

Figure 1.2: Parts and steps of data analysis

In the first part, we have only one step. In the preceding figure, this is referred to as step 1.1. In this first step, we will do basic data preprocessing. Once we are done with that, we will start with our next part.

The second part has two steps. In the figure, this is referred to as step 2.1. In this step, we will perform basic data analysis using statistical and visualization techniques, which will help us understand the data. By doing this activity, we will get to know some statistical facts about our dataset. After this, we will jump to the next step, which is referred to as step 2.2 in *Figure 1.2*. In this step, we will once again perform data preprocessing, but, this time, our preprocessing will be heavily based on the findings that we have derived after doing basic data analysis on the given training dataset. You can find the code at this GitHub Link: `https://github.com/jalajthanaki/credit-risk-modelling/blob/master/basic_data_analysis.ipynb`.

So let's begin!

Data preprocessing

In this section, we will perform a minimal amount of basic preprocessing. We will look at the approaches as well as their implementation.

First change

If you open the `cs-training.csv` file, then you will find that there is a column without a heading, so we will add a heading there. Our heading for that attribute is `ID`. If you want to drop this column, you can because it just contains the `sr.no` of the records.

Second change

This change is not a mandatory one. If you want to skip it, you can, but I personally like to perform this kind of preprocessing. The change is related to the heading of the attributes, we are removing "-" from the headers. Apart from this, I will convert all the column heading into lowercase. For example, the attribute named `NumberOfTime60-89DaysPastDueNotWorse` will be converted into `numberoftime6089dayspastduenotworse`. These kinds of changes will help us when we perform in-depth data analysis. We do not need to take care of this hyphen symbols while processing.

Implementing the changes

Now, you may ask *how will I perform the changes described?* Well, there are two ways. One is a manual approach. In this approach, you will open the `cs-training.csv` file and perform the changes manually. This approach certainly isn't great. So, we will take the second approach. With the second approach, we will perform the changes using Python code. You can find all the changes in the following code snippets.

Refer to the following screenshot for the code to perform the first change:

```
In [5]: # Rename "Unnamed: 0" column name to "ID"
        training_data.rename(columns= {"Unnamed: 0":"ID"},inplace=True)

        # Print first 5 records of the data frame
        training_data.head()
```

Out[5]:

	ID	SeriousDlqin2yrs	RevolvingUtilizationOfUnsecuredLines	age	NumberOfTime30-59DaysPastDueNotWorse	DebtRatio	MonthlyIncor
0	1	1	0.766127	45	2	0.802982	9120.0
1	2	0	0.957151	40	0	0.121876	2600.0
2	3	0	0.658180	38	1	0.085113	3042.0
3	4	0	0.233810	30	0	0.036050	3300.0
4	5	0	0.907239	49	1	0.024926	63588.0

```
In [6]: # Drop the column with Unnamed: 0 heading
        training_data_drop_col = pd.read_csv('./data/cs-training.csv',sep=',').drop('Unnamed: 0',axis =
        1)

In [7]: # Print first 5 records of the data frame
        training_data_drop_col.head()
```

Out[7]:

	SeriousDlqin2yrs	RevolvingUtilizationOfUnsecuredLines	age	NumberOfTime30-59DaysPastDueNotWorse	DebtRatio	MonthlyIncome
0	1	0.766127	45	2	0.802982	9120.0
1	0	0.957151	40	0	0.121876	2600.0
2	0	0.658180	38	1	0.085113	3042.0
3	0	0.233810	30	0	0.036050	3300.0
4	0	0.907239	49	1	0.024926	63588.0

Figure 1.3: Code snippet for implementing the renaming or dropping of the index column

For the second change, you can refer to *Figure 1.4:*

```
In [8]: # Replacing the "-" to "" as well as converting all the columns heading into lower case

        cleancolumns = []
        for i in range(len(training_data_drop_col.columns)):
            cleancolumns.append(training_data_drop_col.columns[i].replace('-','').lower())
        training_data_drop_col.columns = cleancolumns

In [9]: # Print first 5 records of the data frame
        training_data_drop_col.head()

Out[9]:
```

	seriousdlqin2yrs	revolvingutilizationofunsecuredlines	age	numberoftime3059dayspastduenotworse	debtratio	mont
0	1	0.766127	45	2	0.802982	9120.
1	0	0.957151	40	0	0.121876	2600.
2	0	0.658180	38	1	0.085113	3042.
3	0	0.233810	30	0	0.036050	3300.
4	0	0.907239	49	1	0.024926	6358

Figure 1.4: Code snippet for removing "-" from the column heading and converting all the column headings into lowercase

The same kind of preprocessing needs to be done on the `cs-test.csv` file. This is because the given changes are common for both the training and testing datasets.

You can find the entire code on GitHub by clicking on this link: `https://github.com/jalajthanaki/credit-risk-modelling/blob/master/basic_data_analysis.ipynb`.

You can also move hands-on along with reading.

I'm using Python 2.7 as well as a bunch of different Python libraries for the implementation of this code. You can find information related to Python dependencies as well as installation in the *README* section. Now let's move on to the basic data analysis section.

Basic data analysis followed by data preprocessing

Let's perform some basic data analysis, which will help us find the statistical properties of the training dataset. This kind of analysis is also called exploratory data analysis (EDA), and it will help us understand how our dataset represents the facts. After deriving some facts, we can use them in order to derive feature engineering. So let's explore some important facts!

From this section onward, all the code is part of one iPython notebook. You can refer to the code using this GitHub Link: `https://github.com/jalajthanaki/credit-risk-modelling/blob/master/Credit%20Risk%20Analysis.ipynb`.

The following are the steps we are going to perform:

1. Listing statistical properties
2. Finding the missing values
3. Replacing missing values
4. Correlation
5. Detecting Outliers

Listing statistical properties

In this section, we will get an idea about the statistical properties of the training dataset. Using pandas' describe function, we can find out the following basic things:

- `count`: This will give us an idea about the number of records in our training dataset.
- `mean`: This value gives us an indication of the mean of each of the data attributes.
- `std`: This value indicates the standard deviation for each of the data attributes. You can refer to this example: `http://www.mathsisfun.com/data/standard-deviation.html`.
- `min`: This value gives us an idea of what the minimum value for each of the data attributes is.
- `25%`: This value indicates the 25th percentile. It should fall between 0 and 1.
- `50%`: This value indicates the 50th percentile. It should fall between 0 and 1.
- `75%`: This value indicates the 75th percentile. It should fall between 0 and 1.
- `max`: This value gives us an idea of what the maximum value for each of the data attributes is.

Take a look at the code snippet in the following figure:

```
In [4]: # Describe the all statistical properties of the training dataset
        training_data[training_data.columns[1:]].describe()

Out[4]:
```

	revolvingutilizationofunsecuredlines	age	numberoftime3059dayspastduenotworse	debtratio	monthlyincome	numberofopencreditlinesandl
count	150000.000000	150000.000000	150000.000000	150000.000000	1.202690e+05	150000.00
mean	6.048438	52.295207	0.421033	353.005076	6.670221e+03	8.45
std	249.755371	14.771866	4.192781	2037.818523	1.438467e+04	5.14
min	0.000000	0.000000	0.000000	0.000000	0.000000e+00	0.00
25%	0.029867	41.000000	0.000000	0.175074	3.400000e+03	5.00
50%	0.154181	52.000000	0.000000	0.366508	5.400000e+03	8.00
75%	0.559046	63.000000	0.000000	0.868254	8.249000e+03	11.00
max	50708.000000	109.000000	98.000000	329664.000000	3.008750e+06	58.00

Figure 1.5: Basic statistical properties using the describe function of pandas

We need to find some other statistical properties for our dataset that will help us understand it. So, here, we are going to find the median and mean for each of the data attributes. You can see the code for finding the median in the following figure:

```
training_data[training_data.columns[1:]].median()

revolvingutilizationofunsecuredlines        0.154181
age                                        52.000000
numberoftime3059dayspastduenotworse         0.000000
debtratio                                   0.366508
monthlyincome                            5400.000000
numberofopencreditlinesandloans             8.000000
numberoftimes90dayslate                     0.000000
numberrealestateloansorlines                1.000000
numberoftime6089dayspastduenotworse         0.000000
numberofdependents                          0.000000
dtype: float64

training_data[training_data.columns[1:]].mean()

revolvingutilizationofunsecuredlines        6.048438
age                                        52.295207
numberoftime3059dayspastduenotworse         0.421033
debtratio                                 353.005076
monthlyincome                            6670.221237
numberofopencreditlinesandloans             8.452760
numberoftimes90dayslate                     0.265973
numberrealestateloansorlines                1.018240
numberoftime6089dayspastduenotworse         0.240387
numberofdependents                          0.757222
dtype: float64
```

Figure 1.6: Code snippet for generating the median and the mean for each data attribute

Now let's check out what kind of data distribution is present in our dataset. We draw the frequency distribution for our target attribute, `seriousdlqin2yrs`, in order to understand the overall distribution of the target variable for the training dataset. Here, we will use the `seaborn` visualization library. You can refer to the following code snippet:

```
total_len = len(training_data['seriousdlqin2yrs'])
percentage_labels = (training_data['seriousdlqin2yrs'].value_counts()/total_len)*100
percentage_labels

0    93.316
1     6.684
Name: seriousdlqin2yrs, dtype: float64

sns.countplot(training_data.seriousdlqin2yrs).set_title('Data Distribution')
ax = plt.gca()
for p in ax.patches:
    height = p.get_height()
    ax.text(p.get_x() + p.get_width()/2.,
            height + 2,
            '{:.2f}%'.format(100*(height/total_len)),
            fontsize=14, ha='center', va='bottom')
sns.set(font_scale=1.5)
ax.set_xlabel("Labels for seriousdlqin2yrs attribute")
ax.set_ylabel("Numbers of records")
sns.plt.show()
```

Figure 1.7: Code snippet for understanding the target variable distribution as well as the code snippet for the visualization of the distribution

You can refer to the visualization chart in the following figure:

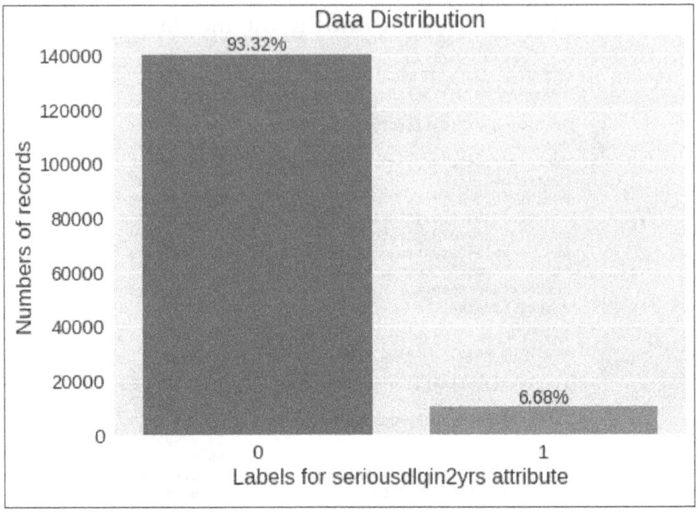

Figure 1.8: Visualization of the variable distribution of the target data attribute

From this chart, you can see that there are many records with the target label *0* and fewer records with the target label *1*. You can see that the data records with a *0* label are about 93.32%, whereas 6.68% of the data records are labeled *1*. We will use all of these facts in the upcoming sections. For now, we can consider our outcome variable as imbalanced.

Finding missing values

In order to find the missing values in the dataset, we need to check each and every data attribute. First, we will try to identify which attribute has a missing or null value. Once we have found out the name of the data attribute, we will replace the missing value with a more meaningful value. There are a couple of options available for replacing the missing values. We will explore all of these possibilities.

Let's code for our first step. Here, we will see which data attribute has missing values as well count how many records there are for each data attribute with a missing value. You can see the code snippet in the following figure:

```
training_data.isnull().sum()

seriousdlqin2yrs                              0
revolvingutilizationofunsecuredlines          0
age                                           0
numberoftime3059dayspastduenotworse           0
debtratio                                     0
monthlyincome                             29731
numberofopencreditlinesandloans               0
numberoftimes90dayslate                       0
numberrealestateloansorlines                  0
numberoftime6089dayspastduenotworse           0
numberofdependents                         3924
dtype: int64
```

Figure 1.9: Code snippet for identifying which data attributes have missing values

As displayed in the preceding figure, the following two data attributes have missing values:

- `monthlyincome`: This attribute contains 29,731 records with a missing value.
- `numberofdependents`: This attribute contains 3,924 records with a missing value.

You can also refer to the code snippet in the following figure for the graphical representation of the facts described so far:

```
x = training_data.columns
y = training_data.isnull().sum()
sns.barplot(x,y)
ax = plt.gca()
for p in ax.patches:
    height = p.get_height()
    ax.text(p.get_x() + p.get_width()/2.,
            height + 2,
            int(height),
            fontsize=12, ha='center', va='bottom')
ax.set_xlabel("Data Attributes")
ax.set_ylabel("count of missing records for each attribute")
plt.xticks(rotation=90)
sns.plt.show()
```

Figure 1.10: Code snippet for generating a graph of missing values

You can view the graph itself in the following figure:

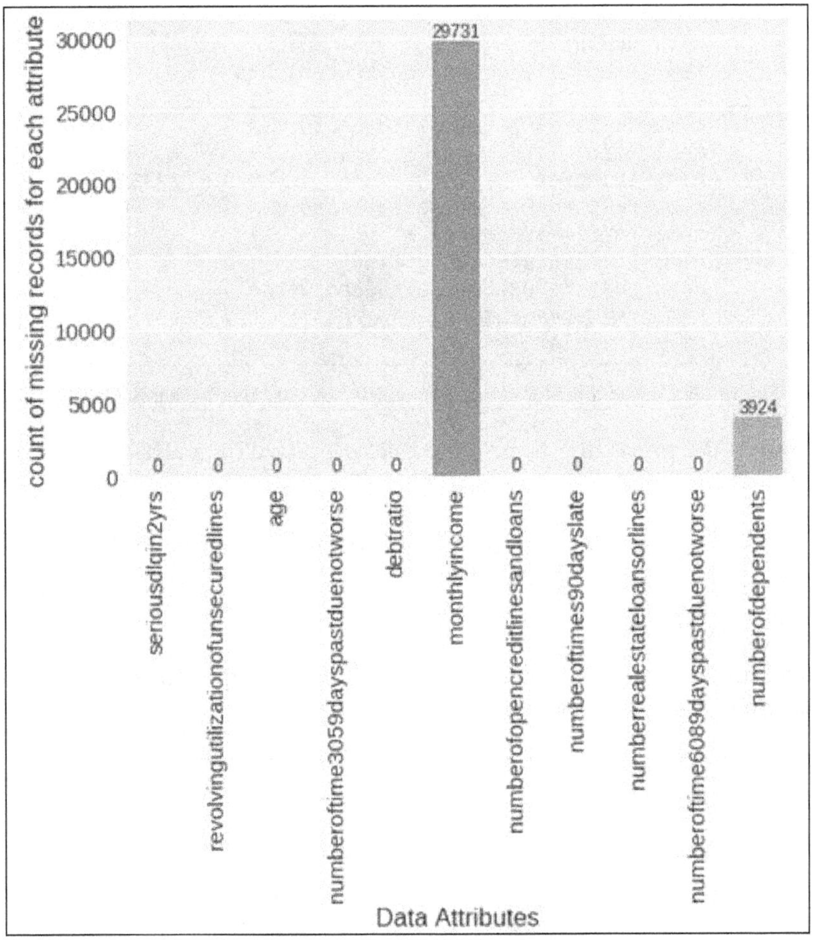

Figure 1.11: A graphical representation of the missing values

In this case, we need to replace these missing values with more meaningful values. There are various standard techniques that we can use for that. We have the following two options:

- Replace the missing value with the mean value of that particular data attribute
- Replace the missing value with the median value of that particular data attribute

In the previous section, we already derived the mean and median values for all of our data attributes, and we will use them. Here, our focus will be on the attributes titled `monthlyincome` and `numberofdependents` because they have missing values. We have found out which data attributes have missing values, so now it's time to perform the actual replacement operation. In the next section, you will see how we can replace the missing values with the mean or the median.

Replacing missing values

In the previous section, we figured out which data attributes in our training dataset contain missing values. We need to replace the missing values with either the mean or the median value of that particular data attribute. So in this section, we will focus particularly on how we can perform the actual replacement operation. This operation of replacing the missing value is also called imputing the missing data.

Before moving on to the code section, I feel you guys might have questions such as these: *should I replace missing values with the mean or the median? Are there any other options available?* Let me answer these questions one by one.

The answer to the first question, practically, will be a trial and error method. So you first replace missing values with the mean value, and during the training of the model, measure whether you get a good result on the training dataset or not. Then, in the second iteration, we need to try to replace the values with the median and measure whether you get a good result on the training dataset or not.

In order to answer the second question, there are many different imputation techniques available, such as the deletion of records, replacing the values using the KNN method, replacing the values using the most frequent value, and so on. You can select any of these techniques, but you need to train the model and measure the result. Without implementing a technique, you can't really say with certainty that a particular imputation technique will work for the given training dataset. Here, we are talking in terms of the credit-risk domain, so I would not get into the theory much, but just to refresh your concepts, you can refer to the following articles:

- `https://machinelearningmastery.com/handle-missing-data-python/`
- `http://scikit-learn.org/stable/modules/generated/sklearn.preprocessing.Imputer.html`
- `https://www.analyticsvidhya.com/blog/2016/01/guide-data-exploration/`

We can see the code for replacing the missing values using the attribute's mean value and its median value in the following figure:

```
# Actual replacement of the missing value using mean value.
training_data_mean_replace = training_data.fillna((training_data.mean()))
training_data_mean_replace.head()
```

	seriousdlqin2yrs	revolvingutilizationofunsecuredlines	age	numberoftime3059dayspastduenotworse	debtratio
0	1	0.766127	45	2	0.802982
1	0	0.957151	40	0	0.121876
2	0	0.658180	38	1	0.085113
3	0	0.233810	30	0	0.036050
4	0	0.907239	49	1	0.024926

```
training_data_mean_replace.isnull().sum()
```

```
seriousdlqin2yrs                        0
revolvingutilizationofunsecuredlines    0
age                                     0
numberoftime3059dayspastduenotworse     0
debtratio                               0
monthlyincome                           0
numberofopencreditlinesandloans         0
numberoftimes90dayslate                 0
numberrealestateloansorlines            0
numberoftime6089dayspastduenotworse     0
numberofdependents                      0
dtype: int64
```

Figure 1.12: Code snippet for replacing the mean values

In the preceding code snippet, we replaced the missing value with the mean value, and in the second step, we verified that all the missing values have been replaced with the mean of that particular data attribute.

In the next code snippet, you can see the code that we have used for replacing the missing values with the median of those data attributes. Refer to the following figure:

```
# Actual replacement of the missing value using median value.
training_data_median_replace = training_data.fillna((training_data.median()))
training_data_median_replace.head()
```

	seriousdlqin2yrs	revolvingutilizationofunsecuredlines	age	numberoftime3059dayspastduenotworse	debtratio
0	1	0.766127	45	2	0.802982
1	0	0.957151	40	0	0.121876
2	0	0.658180	38	1	0.085113
3	0	0.233810	30	0	0.036050
4	0	0.907239	49	1	0.024926

```
training_data_median_replace.isnull().sum()
```

```
seriousdlqin2yrs                        0
revolvingutilizationofunsecuredlines    0
age                                     0
numberoftime3059dayspastduenotworse     0
debtratio                               0
monthlyincome                           0
numberofopencreditlinesandloans         0
numberoftimes90dayslate                 0
numberrealestateloansorlines            0
numberoftime6089dayspastduenotworse     0
numberofdependents                      0
dtype: int64
```

Figure 1.13: Code snippet for replacing missing values with the median

In the preceding code snippet, we have replaced the missing value with the median value, and in second step, we have verified that all the missing values have been replaced with the median of that particular data attribute.

In the first iteration, I would like to replace the missing value with the median.

In the next section, we will see one of the important aspects of basic data analysis: finding correlations between data attributes. So, let's get started with correlation.

Correlation

I hope you basically know what correlation indicates in machine learning. The term correlation refers to a mutual relationship or association between quantities. If you want to refresh the concept on this front, you can refer to `https://www.investopedia.com/terms/c/correlation.asp`.

So, here, we will find out what kind of association is present among the different data attributes. Some attributes are highly dependent on one or many other attributes. Sometimes, values of a particular attribute increase with respect to its dependent attribute, whereas sometimes values of a particular attribute decrease with respect to its dependent attribute. So, correlation indicates the positive as well as negative associations among data attributes. You can refer to the following code snippet for the correlation:

```
training_data.fillna((training_data.median()), inplace=True)
# Get the correlation of the training dataset
training_data[training_data.columns[1:]].corr()
```

	revolvingutilizationofunsecuredlines	age
revolvingutilizationofunsecuredlines	1.000000	-0.005898
age	-0.005898	1.000000
numberoftime3059dayspastduenotworse	-0.001314	-0.062995
debtratio	0.003961	0.024188
monthlyincome	0.006513	0.027581
numberofopencreditlinesandloans	-0.011281	0.147705
numberoftimes90dayslate	-0.001061	-0.061005
numberrealestateloansorlines	0.006235	0.033150
numberoftime6089dayspastduenotworse	-0.001048	-0.057159
numberofdependents	0.001193	-0.215693

Figure 1.14: Code snippet for generating correlation

You can see the code snippet of the graphical representation of the correlation in the following figure:

```
sns.set()
sns.heatmap(training_data[training_data.columns[1:]].corr(),annot=True,fmt=".1f",
            cmap=(sns.cubehelix_palette(8, start=.5, rot=-.75)))
plt.show()
```

Figure 1.15: Code snippet for generating a graphical snippet

You can see the graph of the correlation in the following figure:

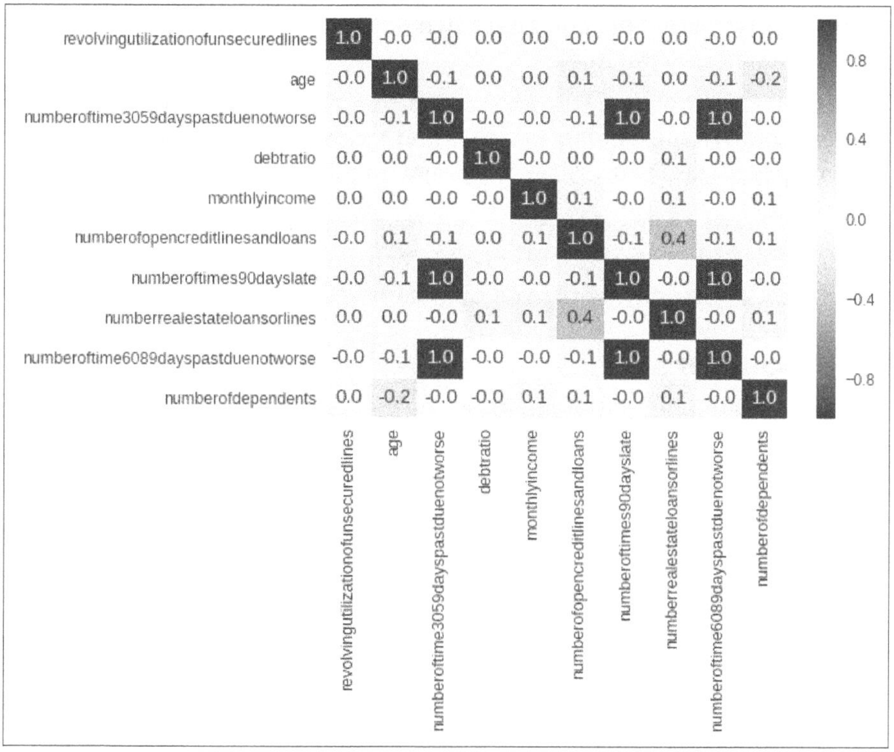

Figure 1.16: Heat map for correlation

Let's look at the preceding graph because it will help you understand correlation in a great way. The following facts can be derived from the graph:

- Cells with 1.0 values are highly associated with each other.
- Each attribute has a very high correlation with itself, so all the diagonal values are 1.0.
- The data attribute **numberoftime3059dayspastduenotworse** (refer to the data attribute given on the vertical line or on the *y axis*) is highly associated with two attributes, **numberoftimes90dayslate** and **numberoftime6089dayspastduenotworse**. These two data attributes are given on the *x axis* (or on the horizontal line).
- The data attribute numberoftimes90dayslate is highly associated with numberoftime3059dayspastduenotworse and numberoftime6089dayspastduenotworse. These two data attributes are given on the *x* axis (or on the horizontal line).

- The data attribute numberoftime6089dayspastduenotworse is highly associated with numberoftime3059dayspastduenotworse and numberoftimes90dayslate. These two data attributes are given on the *x* axis (or on the horizontal line).
- The data attribute **numberofopencreditlinesandloans** also has an association with **numberrealestateloansorlines** and vice versa. Here, the data attribute numberrealestateloansorlines is present on the *x* axis (or on the horizontal line).

Before moving ahead, we need to check whether these attributes contain any outliers or insignificant values. If they do, we need to handle these outliers, so our next section is about detecting outliers from our training dataset.

Detecting outliers

In this section, you will learn how to detect outliers as well as how to handle them. There are two steps involved in this section:

- Outliers detection techniques
- Handling outliers

First, let's begin with detecting outliers. Now you guys might have wonder *why should we detect outliers*. In order to answer this question, I would like to give you an example. Suppose you have the weights of 5-year-old children. You measure the weight of five children and you want to find out the average weight. The children weigh 15, 12, 13, 10, and 35 kg. Now if you try to find out the average of these values, you will see that the answer 17 kg. If you look at the weight range carefully, then you will realize that the last observation is out of the normal range compared to the other observations. Now let's remove the last observation (which has a value of 35) and recalculate the average of the other observations. The new average is 12.5 kg. This new value is much more meaningful in comparison to the last average value. So, the outlier values impact the accuracy greatly; hence, it is important to detect them. Once that is done, we will explore techniques to handle them in upcoming section named handling outlier.

Outliers detection techniques

Here, we are using the following outlier detection techniques:

- Percentile-based outlier detection
- Median Absolute Deviation (MAD)-based outlier detection
- Standard Deviation (STD)-based outlier detection
- Majority-vote-based outlier detection
- Visualization of outliers

Percentile-based outlier detection

Here, we have used percentile-based outlier detection, which is derived based on the basic statistical understanding. We assume that we should consider all the data points that lie under the percentile range from 2.5 to 97.5. We have derived the percentile range by deciding on a threshold of 95. You can refer to the following code snippet:

```
# Percentile based outlier detection
def percentile_based_outlier(data, threshold=95):
    diff = (100 - threshold) / 2.0
    (minval, maxval) = np.percentile(data, [diff, 100 - diff])
    return ((data < minval) | (data > maxval))
```

Figure 1.17: Code snippet for percentile-based outlier detection

We will use this method for each of the data attributes and detect the outliers.

Median Absolute Deviation (MAD)-based outlier detection

MAD is a really simple statistical concept. There are four steps involved in it. This is also known as modified Z-score. The steps are as follows:

1. Find the median of the particular data attribute.
2. For each of the given values for the data attribute, subtract the previously found median value. This subtraction is in the form of the absolute value. So, for each data point, you will get the absolute value.
3. In the third step, generate the median of the absolute values that we derived in the second step. We will perform this operation for each data point for each of the data attributes. This value is called the MAD value.
4. In the fourth step, we will use the following equation to derive the modified Z-score:

$$\frac{0.6745 \times \left(x_i - \tilde{x}\right)}{MAD}$$

$$MAD = median\left(\left|Y_i - \tilde{Y}\right|\right)$$

$$\tilde{Y} \text{ is the median of the data and } \left|Y\right| \text{ is the absolute value of points } Y$$

Now it's time to refer to the following code snippet:

```
def mad_based_outlier(points, threshold=3.5):
    if len(points.shape) == 1:
        points = points[:,None]
    median_y = np.median(points)
    median_absolute_deviation_y = np.median([np.abs(y - median_y) for y in points])
    modified_z_scores = [0.6745 * (y - median_y) / median_absolute_deviation_y
                         for y in points]

    return np.abs(modified_z_scores) > threshold
```

Figure 1.18: Code snippet for MAD-based outlier detection

Standard Deviation (STD)-based outlier detection

In this section, we will use standard deviation and the mean value to find the outlier. Here, we select a random threshold value of 3. You can refer to the following code snippet:

```
def std_div(data, threshold=3):
    std = data.std()
    mean = data.mean()
    isOutlier = []
    for val in data:
        if val/std > threshold:
            isOutlier.append(True)
        else:
            isOutlier.append(False)
    return isOutlier
#std_div(data=training_data.age)
```

Figure 1.19: Standard Deviation (STD) based outlier detection code

Majority-vote-based outlier detection:

In this section, we will build the voting mechanism so that we can simultaneously run all the previously defined methods—such as percentile-based outlier detection, MAD-based outlier detection, and STD-based outlier detection—and get to know whether the data point should be considered an outlier or not. We have seen three techniques so far. So, if two techniques indicate that the data should be considered an outlier, then we consider that data point as an outlier; otherwise, we don't. So, the minimum number of votes we need here is two. Refer to the following figure for the code snippet:

```
def outlierVote(data):
    x = percentile_based_outlier(data)
    y = mad_based_outlier(data)
    z = std_div(data)
    temp = zip(data.index, x, y, z)
    final = []
    for i in range(len(temp)):
        if temp[i].count(False) >= 2:
            final.append(False)
        else:
            final.append(True)
    return final
```

Figure 1.20: Code snippet for the voting mechanism for outlier detection

Visualization of outliers

In this section, we will plot the data attributes to get to know about the outliers visually. Again, we are using the `seaborn` and `matplotlib` library to visualize the outliers. You can find the code snippet in the following figure:

```
def plotOutlier(x):
    fig, axes = plt.subplots(nrows=4)
    for ax, func in zip(axes, [percentile_based_outlier, mad_based_outlier, std_div, outlierVote]):
        sns.distplot(x, ax=ax, rug=True, hist=False)
        outliers = x[func(x)]
        ax.plot(outliers, np.zeros_like(outliers), 'ro', clip_on=False)

    kwargs = dict(y=0.95, x=0.05, ha='left', va='top', size=20)
    axes[0].set_title('Percentile-based Outliers', **kwargs)
    axes[1].set_title('MAD-based Outliers', **kwargs)
    axes[2].set_title('STD-based Outliers', **kwargs)
    axes[3].set_title('Majority vote based Outliers', **kwargs)
    fig.suptitle('Comparing Outlier Tests with n={}'.format(len(x)), size=20)
    fig = plt.gcf()
    fig.set_size_inches(15,10)
```

Figure 1.21: Code snippet for the visualization of the outliers

Refer to the preceding figure for the graph and learn how our defined methods detect the outlier. Here, we chose a sample size of 5,000. This sample was selected randomly.

```
plotOutlier(training_data.revolvingutilizationofunsecuredlines.sample(5000))
```

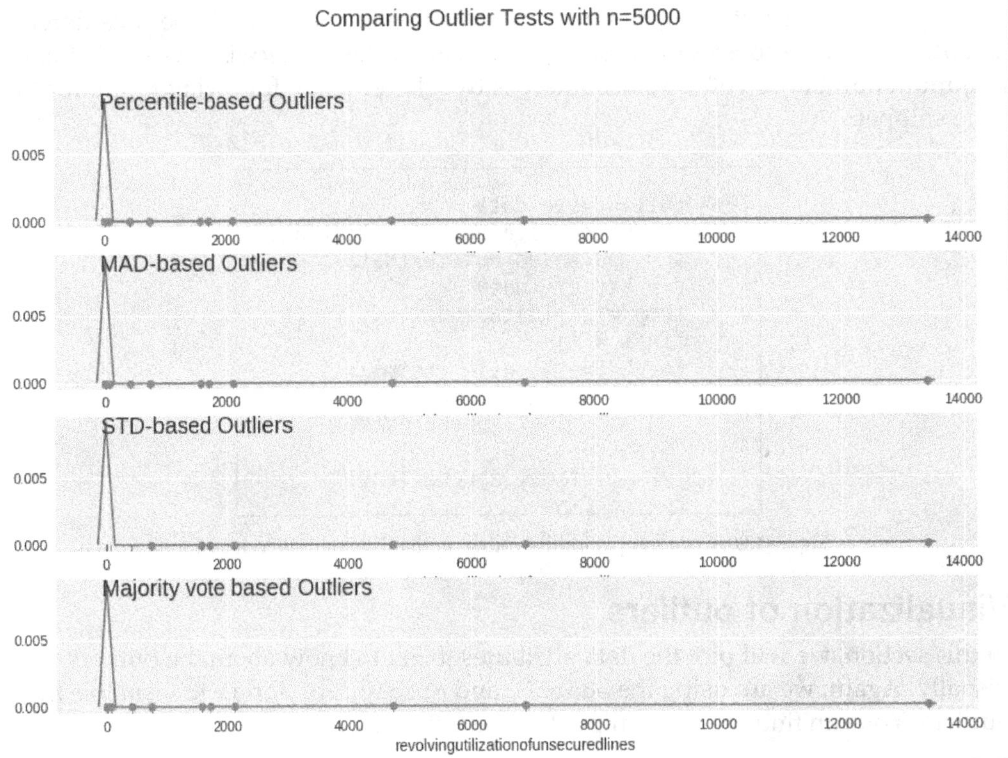

Figure 1.22: Graph for outlier detection

Here, you can see how all the defined techniques will help us detect outlier data points from a particular data attribute. You can see all the attribute visualization graphs on this GitHub link at `https://github.com/jalajthanaki/credit-risk-modelling/blob/master/Credit%20Risk%20Analysis.ipynb`.

So far, you have learned how to detect outliers, but now it's time to handle these outlier points. In the next section, we will look at how we can handle outliers.

Handling outliers

In this section, you will learn how to remove or replace outlier data points. This particular step is important because if you just identify the outlier but aren't able to handle it properly, then at the time of training, there will be a high chance that we over-fit the model. So, let's learn how to handle the outliers for this dataset. Here, I will explain the operation by looking at the data attributes one by one.

Revolving utilization of unsecured lines

In this data attribute, when you plot an outlier detection graph, you will come to know that values of more than 0.99999 are considered outliers. So, values greater than 0.99999 can be replaced with 0.99999. So for this data attribute, we perform the replacement operation. We have generated new values for the data attribute `revolvingutilizationofunsecuredlines`.

For the code, you can refer to the following figure:

```
revNew = []
training_data.revolvingutilizationofunsecuredlines
for val in training_data.revolvingutilizationofunsecuredlines:
    if val <= 0.99999:
        revNew.append(val)
    else:
        revNew.append(0.99999)
training_data.revolvingutilizationofunsecuredlines = revNew
```

Figure 1.23: Code snippet for replacing outlier values with 0.99999

Age

In this attribute, if you explore the data and see the percentile-based outlier, then you see that there is an outlier with a value of 0 and the youngest age present in the data attribute is 21. So, we replace the value of 0 with 22. We code the condition such that the age should be more than 22. If it is not, then we will replace the age with 22. You can refer to the following code and graph.

The following figure shows how the frequency distribution of age is given in the dataset. By looking at the data, we can derive the fact that 0 is the outlier value:

```
import collections
collections.Counter(training_data.age)

Counter({0: 1,
         21: 183,
         22: 434,
         23: 641,
         24: 816,
         25: 953,
         26: 1193,
         27: 1338,
         28: 1560,
         29: 1702,
         30: 1937,
         31: 2038,
         32: 2050,
         33: 2239,
```

Figure 1.24: Frequency for each data value shows that 0 is an outlier

Refer to the following box graph, which gives us the distribution indication of the age:

```
training_data.age.plot.box()

<matplotlib.axes._subplots.AxesSubplot at 0x7fcf93b48d90>
```

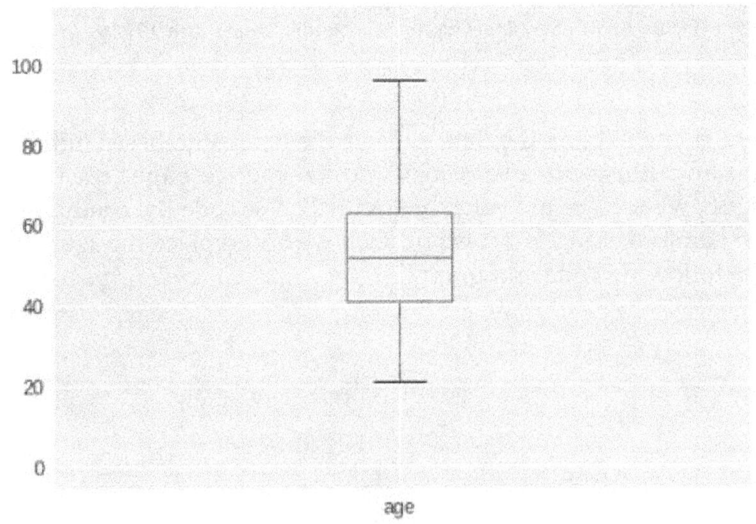

Figure 1.25: Box graph for the age data attribute

Before removing the outlier, we got the following outlier detection graph:

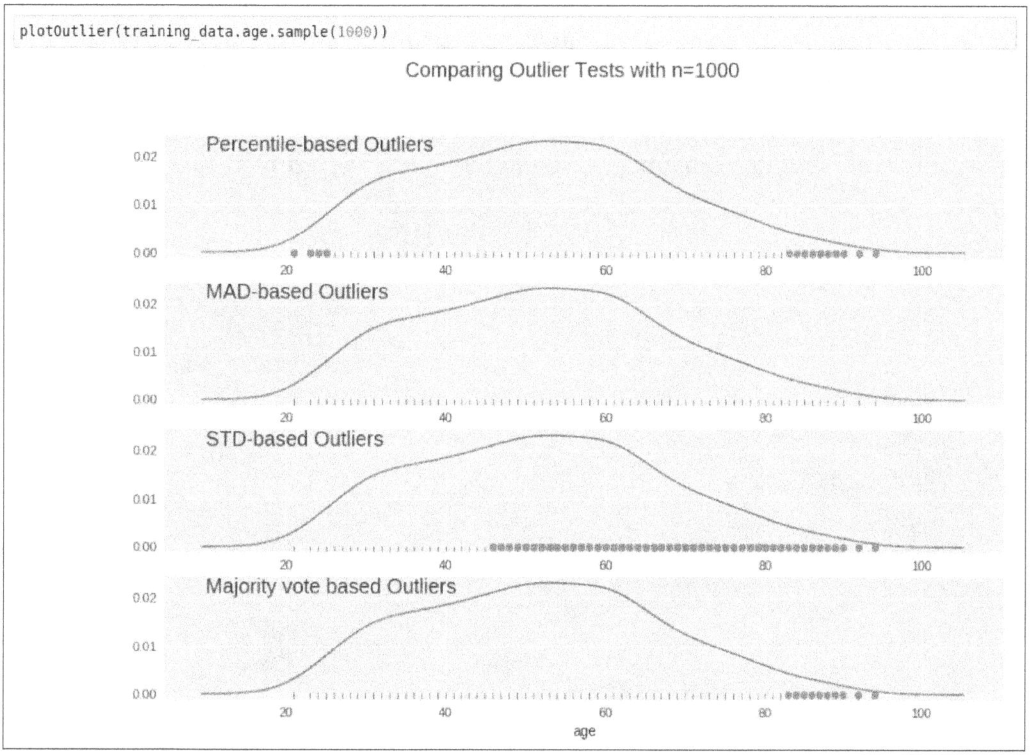

Figure 1.26: Graphical representation of detecting outliers for data attribute age

The code for replacing the outlier is as follows:

```
ageNew = []
for val in training_data.age:
    if val > 21:
        ageNew.append(val)
    else:
        ageNew.append(21)

training_data.age = ageNew
```

Figure 1.27: Replace the outlier with the minimum age value 21

In the code, you can see that we have checked each data point of the age column, and if the age is greater than 21, then we haven't applied any changes, but if the age is less than 21, then we have replaced the old value with 21. After that, we put all these revised values into our original dataframe.

Number of time 30-59 days past due not worse

In this data attribute, we explore the data as well as referring to the outlier detection graph. Having done that, we know that values 96 and 98 are our outliers. We replace these values with the media value. You can refer to the following code and graph to understand this better.

Refer to the outlier detection graph given in the following figure:

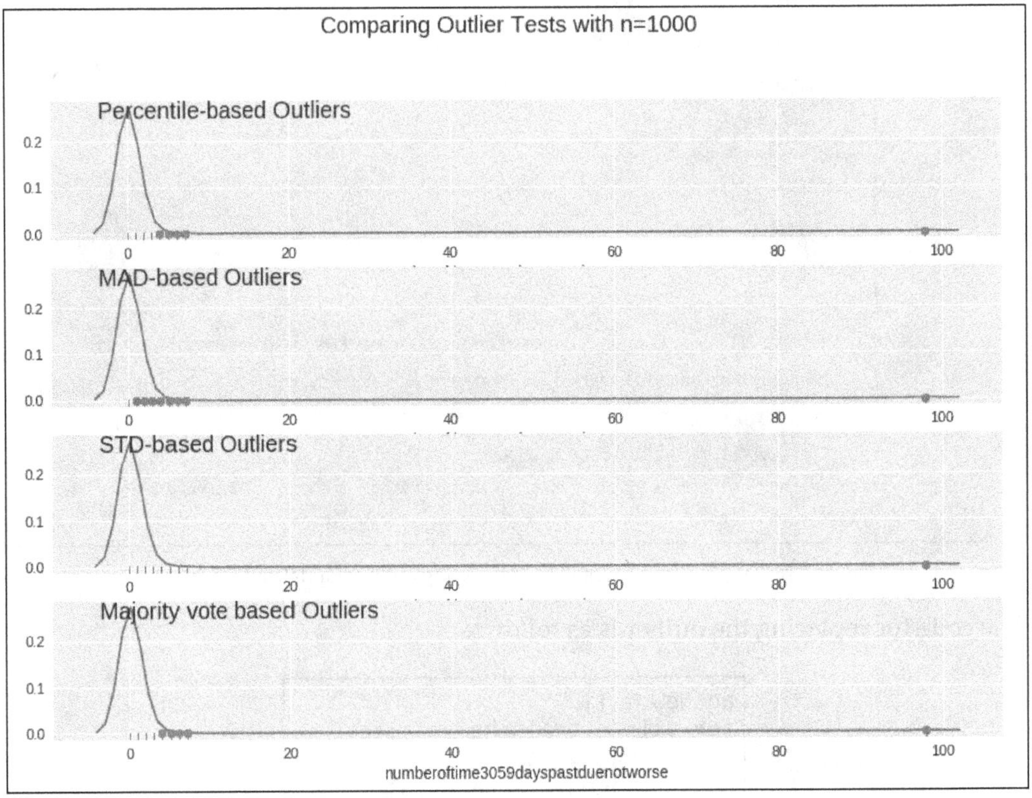

Figure 1.28: Outlier detection graph

Refer to the frequency analysis of the data in the following figure:

```
collections.Counter(training_data.numberoftime3059dayspastduenotworse)

Counter({0: 126018,
         1: 16033,
         2: 4598,
         3: 1754,
         4: 747,
         5: 342,
         6: 140,
         7: 54,
         8: 25,
         9: 12,
         10: 4,
         11: 1,
         12: 2,
         13: 1,
         96: 5,
         98: 264})
```

Figure 1.29: Outlier values from the frequency calculation

The code snippet for replacing the outlier values with the median is given in the following figure:

```
New = []
med = training_data.numberoftime3059dayspastduenotworse.median()
for val in training_data.numberoftime3059dayspastduenotworse:
    if ((val == 98) | (val == 96)):
        New.append(med)
    else:
        New.append(val)

training_data.numberoftime3059dayspastduenotworse = New
```

Figure 1.30: Code snippet for replacing outliers

Debt ratio

If we look at the graph of the outlier detection of this attribute, then it's kind of confusing. Refer to the following figure:

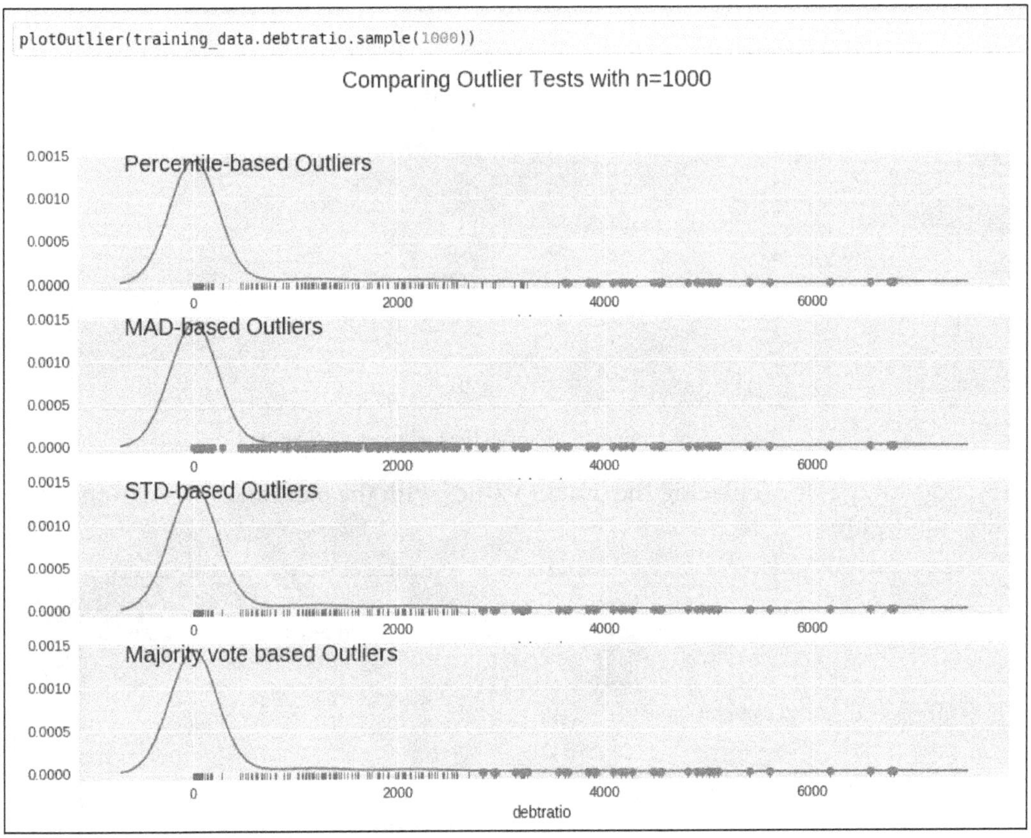

Figure 1.31: Graph of outlier detection for the debt ratio column

Why? It's confusing because we are not sure which outlier detection method we should consider. So, here, we do some comparative analysis just by counting the number of outliers derived from each of the methods. Refer to the following figure:

```
def outlierRatio(data):
    functions = [percentile_based_outlier, mad_based_outlier, std_div, outlierVote]
    outlierDict = {}
    for func in functions:
        funcResult = func(data)
        count = 0
        for val in funcResult:
            if val == True:
                count += 1
        outlierDict[str(func)[10:].split()[0]] = [count, '{:.2f}%'.format((float(count)/len(data))*100)]

    return outlierDict
outlierRatio(training_data.debtratio)

{'mad_based_outlier': [31727, '21.15%'],
 'outlierVote': [3750, '2.50%'],
 'percentile_based_outlier': [3750, '2.50%'],
 'std_div': [779, '0.52%']}
```

Figure 1.32: Comparison of various outlier detection techniques

The maximum number of outliers was detected by the MAD-based method, so we will consider that method. Here, we will find the minimum upper bound value in order to replace the outlier values. The minimum upper bound is the minimum value derived from the outlier value. Refer to the following code snippet:

```
minUpperBound = min([val for (val, out) in zip(training_data.debtratio, mad_based_outlier(training_data.debtratio))

newDebtRatio = []
for val in training_data.debtratio:
    if val > minUpperBound:
        newDebtRatio.append(minUpperBound)
    else:
        newDebtRatio.append(val)

training_data.debtratio = newDebtRatio
```

Figure 1.33: The code for the minimum upper bound

Monthly income

For this data attribute, we will select the voting-based outlier detection method, as shown in the following figure:

```
plotOutlier(training_data.monthlyincome.sample(1000))
```

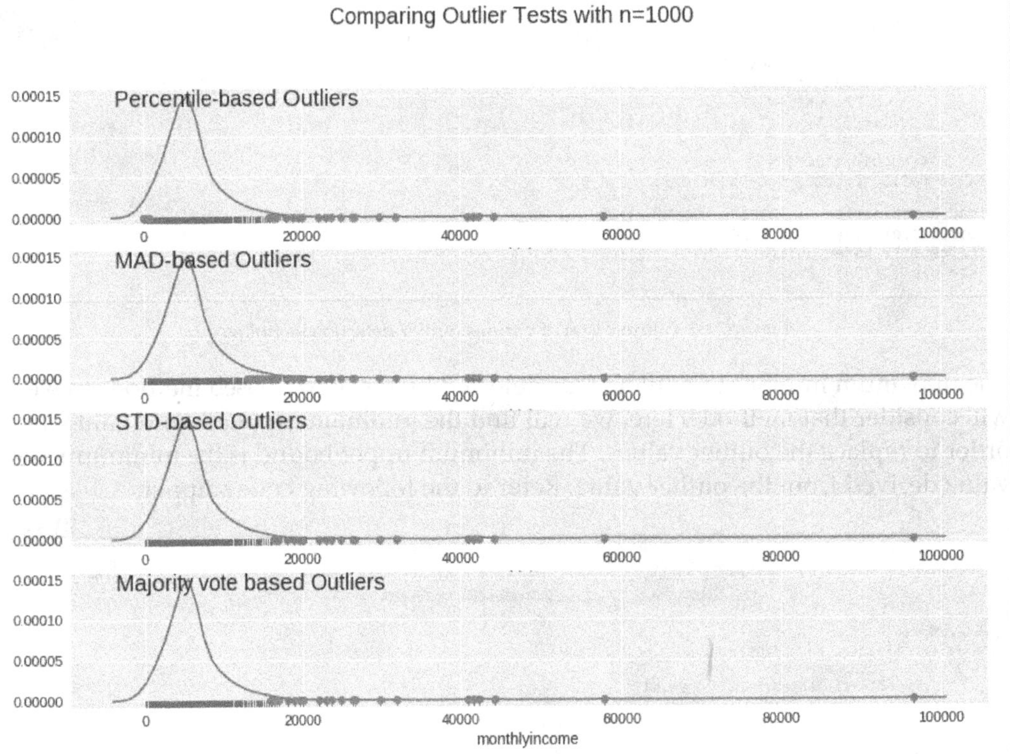

Figure 1.34: Outlier detection graph

In order to replace the outlier, we will use the same logic that we have for the `debt ratio` data attribute. We replace the outliers by generating a minimum upper bound value. You can refer to the code given in the following figure:

```
def replaceOutlier(data, method = outlierVote, replace='median'):
    '''replace: median (auto)
                'minUpper' which is the upper bound of the outlier detection'''
    vote = outlierVote(data)
    x = pd.DataFrame(zip(data, vote), columns=['debt', 'outlier'])
    if replace == 'median':
        replace = x.debt.median()
    elif replace == 'minUpper':
        replace = min([val for (val, vote) in zip(data, vote) if vote == True])
        if replace < data.mean():
            return 'There are outliers lower than the sample mean'
    debtNew = []
    for i in range(x.shape[0]):
        if x.iloc[i][1] == True:
            debtNew.append(replace)
        else:
            debtNew.append(x.iloc[i][0])

    return debtNew
```

```
incomeNew = replaceOutlier(training_data.monthlyincome, replace='minUpper')
```

```
training_data.monthlyincome = incomeNew
```

Figure 1.35: Replace the outlier value with the minimum upper bound value

Number of open credit lines and loans

If you refer to the graph given in the following figure, you will see that there are no highly deviated outlier values present in this column:

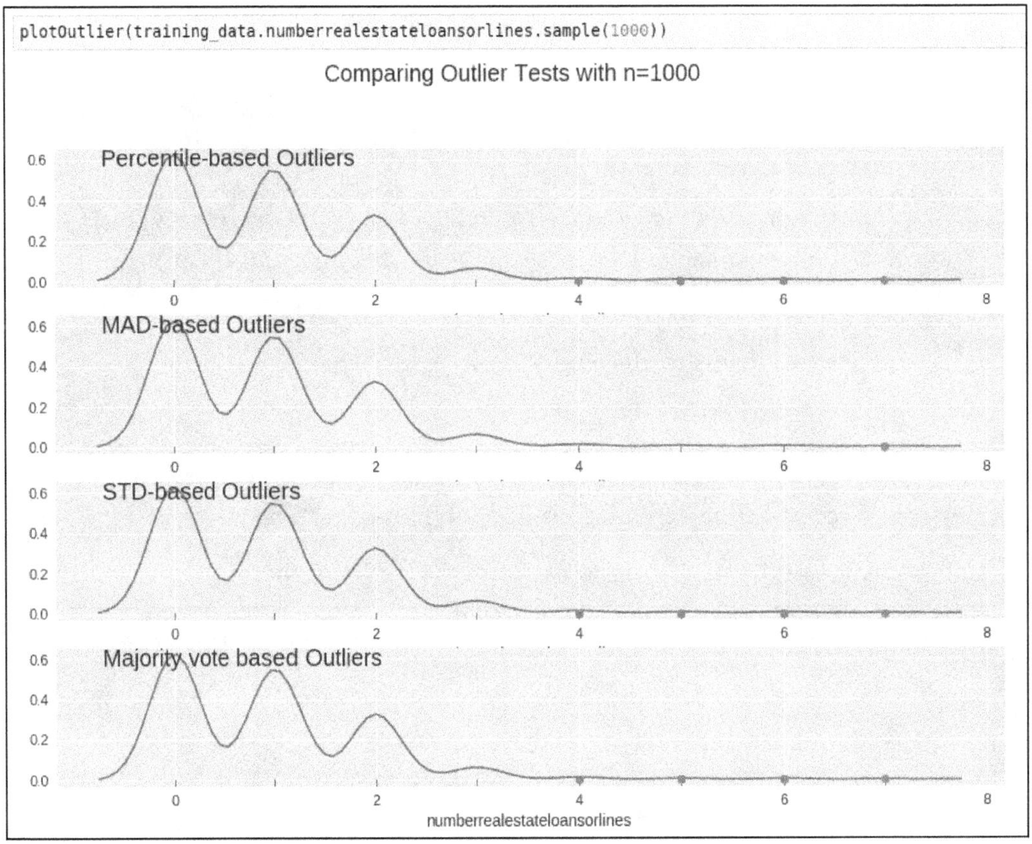

Figure 1.36: Outlier detection graph

So, we will not perform any kind of replacement operation for this data attribute.

Number of times 90 days late

For this attribute, when you analyze the data value frequency, you will immediately see that the values 96 and 98 are outliers. We will replace these values with the median value of the data attribute.

Refer to the frequency analysis code snippet in the following figure:

```
collections.Counter(training_data.numberoftimes90dayslate)

Counter({0: 141662,
         1: 5243,
         2: 1555,
         3: 667,
         4: 291,
         5: 131,
         6: 80,
         7: 38,
         8: 21,
         9: 19,
         10: 8,
         11: 5,
         12: 2,
         13: 4,
         14: 2,
         15: 2,
         17: 1,
         96: 5,
         98: 264})
```

Figure 1.37: Frequency analysis of the data points

The outlier replacement code snippet is shown in the following figure:

```
def removeSpecificAndPutMedian(data, first = 98, second = 96):
    New = []
    med = data.median()
    for val in data:
        if ((val == first) | (val == second)):
            New.append(med)
        else:
            New.append(val)

    return New

new = removeSpecificAndPutMedian(training_data.numberoftimes90dayslate)

training_data.numberoftimes90dayslate = new
```

Figure 1.38: Outlier replacement using the median value

Number of real estate loans or lines

When we see the frequency of value present in the data attribute, we will come to know that a frequency value beyond 17 is too less. So, here we replace every value less than 17 with 17.

You can refer to the code snippet in the following figure:

```
realNew = []
for val in training_data.numberrealestateloansorlines:
    if val > 17:
        realNew.append(17)
    else:
        realNew.append(val)
training_data.numberrealestateloansorlines = realNew
```

Figure 1.39: Code snippet for replacing outliers

Number of times 60-89 days past due not worse

For this attribute, when you analyze the data value frequency, you will immediately see that the values 96 and 98 are outliers. We will replace these values with the median value of the data attribute.

Refer to the frequency analysis code snippet in the following figure:

```
collections.Counter(training_data.numberoftime6089dayspastduenotworse)

Counter({0: 142396,
         1: 5731,
         2: 1118,
         3: 318,
         4: 105,
         5: 34,
         6: 16,
         7: 9,
         8: 2,
         9: 1,
         11: 1,
         96: 5,
         98: 264})
```

Figure 1.40: Frequency analysis of the data

The outlier replacement code snippet is shown in the following figure:

```
new = removeSpecificAndPutMedian(training_data.numberoftime6089dayspastduenotworse)
training_data.numberoftime6089dayspastduenotworse = new
```

Figure 1.41: Code snippet for replacing outliers using the median value

You can refer to the `removeSpecificAndPutMedian` method code from *Figure 1.38*.

Number of dependents

For this attribute, when you see the frequency value of the data points, you will immediately see that data values greater than 10 are outliers. We replace values greater than 10 with 10.

Refer to the code snippet in the following figure:

```
collections.Counter(training_data.numberofdependents)

Counter({0.0: 90826,
         1.0: 26316,
         2.0: 19522,
         3.0: 9483,
         4.0: 2862,
         5.0: 746,
         6.0: 158,
         7.0: 51,
         8.0: 24,
         9.0: 5,
         10.0: 5,
         13.0: 1,
         20.0: 1})

depNew = []
for var in training_data.numberofdependents:
    if var > 10:
        depNew.append(10)
    else:
        depNew.append var

training_data.numberofdependents = depNew
```

Figure 1.42: Code snippet for replacing outlier values

This is the end of the outlier section. In this section, we've replaced the value of the data points in a more meaningful way. We have also reached the end of our basic data analysis section. This analysis has given us a good understanding of the dataset and its values. The next section is all about feature engineering. So, we will start with the basics first, and later on in this chapter, you will learn how feature engineering will impact the accuracy of the algorithm in a positive manner.

Feature engineering for the baseline model

In this section, you will learn how to select features that are important in order to develop the predictive model. So right now, just to begin with, we won't focus much on deriving new features at this stage because first, we need to know which input variables / columns / data attributes / features give us at least baseline accuracy. So, in this first iteration, our focus is on the selection of features from the available training dataset.

Finding out Feature importance

We need to know which the important features are. In order to find that out, we are going to train the model using the Random Forest classifier. After that, we will have a rough idea about the important features for us. So let's get straight into the code. You can refer to the code snippet in the following figure:

```
from sklearn.ensemble import RandomForestClassifier
```

```
training_data.columns[1:]
```

```
Index([u'revolvingutilizationofunsecuredlines', u'age',
       u'numberoftime3059dayspastduenotworse', u'debtratio', u'monthlyincome',
       u'numberofopencreditlinesandloans', u'numberoftimes90dayslate',
       u'numberrealestateloansorlines', u'numberoftime6089dayspastduenotworse',
       u'numberofdependents'],
      dtype='object')
```

```
X = training_data.drop('seriousdlqin2yrs', axis=1)
y = training_data.seriousdlqin2yrs
features_label = training_data.columns[1:]
forest = RandomForestClassifier (n_estimators = 10000, random_state=0, n_jobs = -1)
forest.fit(X,y)
importances = forest.feature_importances_
indices = np. argsort(importances)[::-1]
for i in range(X.shape[1]):
    print ("%2d) %-*s %f" % (i + 1, 30, features_label[i],importances[indices[i]]))
```

```
 1) revolvingutilizationofunsecuredlines 0.189053
 2) age                            0.154817
 3) numberoftime3059dayspastduenotworse 0.150809
 4) debtratio                      0.141929
 5) monthlyincome                  0.098143
 6) numberofopencreditlinesandloans 0.088968
 7) numberoftimes90dayslate        0.050406
 8) numberrealestateloansorlines   0.044934
 9) numberoftime6089dayspastduenotworse 0.044333
10) numberofdependents             0.036607
```

Figure 1.43: Derive the importance of features

In this code, we are using Random Forest Classifier from scikit-learn. We use the `fit()` function to perform training, and then, in order to generate the importance of the features, we will use the `feature_importances_` function, which is available in the scikit-learn library. Then, we will print the features with the highest importance value to the lowest importance value.

Let's draw a graph of this to get a better understanding of the most important features. You can find the code snippet in the following figure:

```
plt.title('Feature Importances')
plt.bar(range(X.shape[1]),importances[indices], color="green", align="center")
plt.xticks(range(X.shape[1]),features_label, rotation=90)
plt.xlim([-1, X.shape[1]])
plt.show()
```

Figure 1.44: Code snippet for generating a graph for feature importance

In this code snippet, we are using the matplotlib library to draw the graph. Here, we use a bar graph and feed in the values of all the data attributes and their importance values, which we previously derived. You can refer to the graph in the following figure:

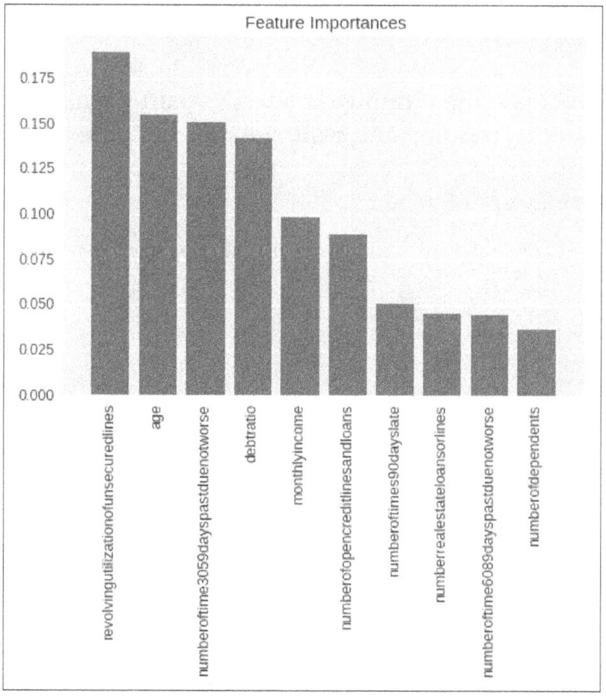

Figure 1.45: Graph of feature importance

For the first iteration, we did this quite some work on the feature engineering front. We will surely revisit feature engineering in the upcoming sections. Now it's time to implement machine learning algorithms to generate the baseline predictive model, which will give us an idea of whether a person will default on a loan in the next 2 years or not. So let's jump to the next section.

Selecting machine learning algorithms

This section is the most important one. Here, we will try a couple of different ML algorithms in order to get an idea about which ML algorithm performs better. Also, we will perform a training accuracy comparison.

By this time, you will definitely know that this particular problem is considered a classification problem. The algorithms that we are going to choose are as follows (this selection is based on intuition):

- K-Nearest Neighbor (KNN)
- Logistic Regression
- AdaBoost
- GradientBoosting
- RandomForest

Our first step is to generate the training data in a certain format. We are going to split the training dataset into a training and testing dataset. So, basically, we are preparing the input for our training. This is common for all the ML algorithms. Refer to the code snippet in the following figure:

```
from sklearn.linear_model import LogisticRegression
from sklearn.ensemble import AdaBoostClassifier, GradientBoostingClassifier, RandomForestClassifier
from sklearn.neighbors import KNeighborsClassifier
from sklearn.model_selection import train_test_split
from sklearn.metrics import roc_auc_score

X = training_data.drop('seriousdlqin2yrs', axis=1)
y = training_data.seriousdlqin2yrs

X_train, X_test, y_train, y_test = train_test_split(X, y, test_size=0.25)
```

Figure 1.46: Code snippet for generating a training dataset in the key-value format for training

As you can see in the code, variable x contains all the columns except the target column entitled `seriousdlqin2yrs`, so we have dropped this column. The reason behind dropping this attribute is that this attribute contains the answer/target/label for each row. ML algorithms need input in terms of a key-value pair, so a target column is key and all other columns are values. We can say that a certain pattern of values will lead to a particular target value, which we need to predict using an ML algorithm.

Here, we also split the training data. We will use 75% of the training data for actual training purposes, and once training is completed, we will use the remaining 25% of the training data to check the training accuracy of our trained ML model. So, without wasting any time, we will jump to the coding of the ML algorithms, and I will explain the code to you as and when we move forward. Note that here, I'm not get into the mathematical explanation of the each ML algorithm but I am going to explain the code.

K-Nearest Neighbor (KNN)

In this algorithm, generally, our output prediction follows the same tendency as that of its neighbor. K is the number of neighbors that we are going to consider. If K=3, then during the prediction output, check the three nearest neighbor points, and if one neighbor belongs to *X* category and two neighbors belongs to *Y* category, then the predicted label will be *Y*, as the majority of the nearest points belongs to the *Y* category.

Let's see what we have coded. Refer to the following figure:

```
knMod = KNeighborsClassifier(n_neighbors=5, weights='uniform', algorithm='auto', leaf_size=30, p=2,
                             metric='minkowski', metric params=None)
```

Figure 1.47: Code snippet for defining the KNN classifier

Let's understand the parameters one by one:

- As per the code, K=5 means our prediction is based on the five nearest neighbors. Here, `n_neighbors=5`.
- Weights are selected uniformly, which means all the points in each neighborhood are weighted equally. Here, weights='uniform'.
- algorithm='auto': This parameter will try to decide the most appropriate algorithm based on the values we passed.
- leaf_size = 30: This parameter affects the speed of the construction of the model and query. Here, we have used the default value, which is 30.

- p=2: This indicates the power parameter for the Minkowski metric. Here, p=2 uses `euclidean_distance`.
- metric='minkowski': This is the default distance metric, which helps us build the tree.
- metric_params=None: This is the default value that we are using.

Logistic regression

Logistic regression is one of most widely used ML algorithms and is also one of the oldest. This algorithm generates probability for the target variable using sigmod and other nonlinear functions in order to predict the target labels.

Let's refer to the code and the parameter that we have used for Logistic regression. You can refer to the code snippet given in the following figure:

```
glmMod = LogisticRegression(penalty='l1', dual=False, tol=0.0001, C=1.0, fit_intercept=True,
                            intercept_scaling=1, class_weight=None,
                            random_state=None, solver='liblinear', max_iter=100,
                            multi_class='ovr', verbose=2)
```

Figure 1.48: Code snippet for the Logistic regression ML algorithm

Let's understand the parameters one by one:

- penalty='l1': This parameter indicates the choice of the gradient descent algorithm. Here, we have selected the Newton-Conjugate_Gradient method.
- dual=False: If we have number of sample > number of features, then we should set this parameter as false.
- tol=0.0001: This is one of the stopping criteria for the algorithm.
- c=1.0: This value indicates the inverse of the regularization strength. This parameter must be a positive float value.
- fit_intercept = True: This is a default value for this algorithm. This parameter is used to indicate the bias for the algorithm.
- solver='liblinear': This algorithm performs well for small datasets, so we chose that.
- intercept_scaling=1: If we select the liblinear algorithm and fit_intercept = True, then this parameter helps us generate the feature weight.
- class_weight=None: There is no weight associated with the class labels.
- random_state=None: Here, we use the default value of this parameter.
- max_iter=100: Here, we iterate 100 times in order to converge our ML algorithm on the given dataset.

- multi_class='ovr': This parameter indicates that the given problem is the binary classification problem.
- verbose=2: If we use the liblinear in the solver parameter, then we need to put in a positive number for verbosity.

AdaBoost

The AdaBoost algorithm stands for Adaptive Boosting. Boosting is an ensemble method in which we will build strong classifier by using multiple weak classifiers. AdaBoost is boosting algorithm giving good result for binary classification problems. If you want to learn more about it then refer this article `https://machinelearningmastery.com/boosting-and-adaboost-for-machine-learning/`.

This particular algorithm has N number of iterations. In the first iteration, we start by taking random data points from the training dataset and building the model. After each iteration, the algorithm checks for data points in which the classifier doesn't perform well. Once those data points are identified by the algorithm based on the error rate, the weight distribution is updated. So, in the next iteration, there are more chances that the algorithm will select the previously poorly classified data points and learn how to classify them. This process keeps running for the given number of iterations you provide.

Let's refer to the code snippet given in the following figure:

```
adaMod = AdaBoostClassifier(base_estimator=None, n_estimators=200, learning_rate=1.0)
```

Figure 1.49: Code snippet for the AdaBosst classifier

The parameter-related description is given as follows:

- **base_estimator = None**: The base estimator from which the boosted ensemble is built.
- **n_estimators=200**: The maximum number of estimators at which boosting is terminated. After 200 iterations, the algorithm will be terminated.
- **learning_rate=1.0**: This rate decides how fast our model will converge.

GradientBoosting

This algorithm is also a part of the ensemble of ML algorithms. In this algorithm, we use basic regression algorithm to train the model. After training, we will calculate the error rate as well as find the data points for which the algorithm does not perform well, and in the next iteration, we will take the data points that introduced the error and retrain the model for better prediction. The algorithm uses the already generated model as well as a newly generated model to predict the values for the data points.

You can see the code snippet in the following figure:

```
gbMod = GradientBoostingClassifier(loss='deviance', learning_rate=0.1, n_estimators=200, subsample=1.0,
                                   min_samples_split=2, min_samples_leaf=1, min_weight_fraction_leaf=0.0,
                                   max_depth=3,
                                   init=None, random_state=None, max_features=None, verbose=0)
```

Figure 1.50: Code snippet for the Gradient Boosting classifier

Let's go through the parameters of the classifier:

- **loss='deviance'**: This means that we are using logistic regression for classification with probabilistic output.
- **learning_rate = 0.1**: This parameter tells us how fast the model needs to converge.
- **n_estimators = 200**: This parameter indicates the number of boosting stages that are needed to be performed.
- **subsample = 1.0**: This parameter helps tune the value for bias and variance. Choosing subsample < 1.0 leads to a reduction in variance and an increase in bias.
- **min_sample_split=2**: The minimum number of samples required to split an internal node.
- **min_weight_fraction_leaf=0.0**: Samples have equal weight, so we have provided the value 0.
- **max_depth=3**: This indicates the maximum depth of the individual regression estimators. The maximum depth limits the number of nodes in the tree.
- **init=None**: For this parameter, loss.init_estimator is used for the initial prediction.
- **random_state=None**: This parameter indicates that the random state is generated using the `numpy.random` function.
- **max_features=None**: This parameter indicates that we have N number of features. So, `max_features=n_features`.
- **verbose=0**: No progress has been printed.

RandomForest

This particular ML algorithm generates the number of decision trees and uses the voting mechanism to predict the target label. In this algorithm, there are a number of decision trees generated, creating a forest of trees, so it's called RandomForest.

In the following code snippet, note how we have declared the RandomForest classifier:

```
rfMod = RandomForestClassifier(n_estimators=10, criterion='gini', max_depth=None, min_samples_split=2,
                               min_samples_leaf=1, min_weight_fraction_leaf=0.0, max_features='auto',
                               max_leaf_nodes=None, bootstrap=True, oob_score=False, n_jobs=1,
                               random_state=None, verbose=0)
```

Figure 1.51: Code snippet for Random Forest Classifier

Let's understand the parameters here:

- `n_estimators=10`: This indicates the number of trees in the forest.
- `criterion='gini'`: Information gained will be calculated by gini.
- `max_depth=None`: This parameter indicates that nodes are expanded until all leaves are pure or until all leaves contain less than min_samples_split samples.
- `min_samples_split=2`: This parameter indicates that there is a minimum of two samples required to perform splitting in order to generate the tree.
- `min_samples_leaf=1`: This indicates the sample size of the leaf node.
- `min_weight_fraction_leaf=0.0`: This parameter indicates the minimum weighted fraction of the sum total of weights (of all the input samples) required to be at a leaf node. Here, weight is equally distributed, so a sample weight is zero.
- `max_features='auto'`: This parameter is considered using the auto strategy. We select the auto value, and then we select max_features=sqrt(n_features).
- `max_leaf_nodes=None`: This parameter indicates that there can be an unlimited number of leaf nodes.
- `bootstrap=True`: This parameter indicates that the bootstrap samples are used when trees are being built.
- `oob_score=False`: This parameter indicates whether to use out-of-the-bag samples to estimate the generalization accuracy. We are not considering out-of-the-bag samples here.
- `n_jobs=1`: Both fit and predict job can be run in parallel if `n_job = 1`.

- `random_state=None`: This parameter indicates that random state is generated using the `numpy.random` function.
- `verbose=0`: This controls the verbosity of the tree building process. 0 means we are not printing the progress.

Up until now, we have seen how we declare our ML algorithm. We have also defined some parameter values. Now, it's time to train this ML algorithm on the training dataset. So let's discuss that.

Training the baseline model

In this section, we will perform actual training using the following ML algorithms. This step is time-consuming as it needs more computation power. We use 75% of the training dataset for actual training and 25% of the dataset for testing in order to measure the training accuracy.

You can find the code snippet in the following figure:

```
knMod.fit(X_train, y_train)

KNeighborsClassifier(algorithm='auto', leaf_size=30, metric='minkowski',
           metric_params=None, n_jobs=1, n_neighbors=5, p=2,
           weights='uniform')

glmMod.fit(X_train, y_train)

[LibLinear]

LogisticRegression(C=1.0, class_weight=None, dual=False, fit_intercept=True,
          intercept_scaling=1, max_iter=100, multi_class='ovr', n_jobs=1,
          penalty='l1', random_state=None, solver='liblinear', tol=0.0001,
          verbose=2, warm_start=False)

adaMod.fit(X_train, y_train)

AdaBoostClassifier(algorithm='SAMME.R', base_estimator=None,
          learning_rate=1.0, n_estimators=200, random_state=None)

gbMod.fit(X_train, y_train)

GradientBoostingClassifier(criterion='friedman_mse', init=None,
              learning_rate=0.1, loss='deviance', max_depth=3,
              max_features=None, max_leaf_nodes=None,
              min_impurity_split=1e-07, min_samples_leaf=1,
              min_samples_split=2, min_weight_fraction_leaf=0.0,
              n_estimators=200, presort='auto', random_state=None,
              subsample=1.0, verbose=0, warm_start=False)

rfMod.fit(X_train, y_train)

RandomForestClassifier(bootstrap=True, class_weight=None, criterion='gini',
            max_depth=None, max_features='auto', max_leaf_nodes=None,
            min_impurity_split=1e-07, min_samples_leaf=1,
            min_samples_split=2, min_weight_fraction_leaf=0.0,
            n_estimators=10, n_jobs=1, oob_score=False, random_state=None,
            verbose=0, warm_start=False)
```

Figure 1.52: Code snippet for performing training

In the preceding code snippet, you can see that we performed the actual training operation using the `fit()` function from the scikit-learn library. This function uses the given parameter and trains the model by taking the input of the target data attribute and other feature columns.

Once you are done with this step, you'll see that our different ML algorithms generate different trained models. Now it's time to check how good our trained model is when it comes to prediction. There are certain techniques that we can use on 25% of the dataset. In the next section, we will understand these techniques.

Understanding the testing matrix

In this section, we will look at some of the widely used testing matrices that we can use in order to get an idea about how good or bad our trained model is. This testing score gives us a fair idea about which model achieves the highest accuracy when it comes to the prediction of the 25% of the data.

Here, we are using two basic levels of the testing matrix:

- The mean accuracy of the trained models
- The ROC-AUC score

The Mean accuracy of the trained models

In this section, we will understand how scikit-learn calculates the accuracy score when we use the scikit-learn function `score()` to generate the training accuracy. The function score() returns the mean accuracy. More precisely, it uses residual standard error. Residual standard error is nothing but the positive square root of the mean square error. Here, the equation for calculating accuracy is as follows:

$$R^2_{Residule\ Standard\ Error} = 1 - \frac{u}{v}$$

$$u = \sum_{i=0}^{N} \left(Y_{True\ Lables} - Y_{Predicted\ Labels} \right)^2$$

$$v = \sum_{i=0}^{N} \left(Y_{True\ Lables} - \overline{Y}_{Mean\ of\ true\ labels} \right)^2$$

The best possible score is 1.0 and the model can have a negative score as well (because the model can be arbitrarily worse). If a constant model always predicts the expected value of y, disregarding the input features, it will get a residual standard error score of 0.0.

The ROC-AUC score

The ROC-AUC score is used to find out the accuracy of the classifier. ROC and AUC are two different terms. Let's understand each of the terms one by one.

ROC

ROC stands for *Receiver Operating Characteristic*. It's is a type of curve. We draw the ROC curve to visualize the performance of the binary classifier. Now that I have mentioned that ROC is a curve, you may want to know which type of curve it is, right? The ROC curve is a 2-D curve. It's *x axis* represents the *False Positive Rate* (FPR) and its y *axis* represents the *True Positive Rate* (TPR). TPR is also known as sensitivity, and FPR is also known as specificity (SPC). You can refer to the following equations for FPR and TPR.

TPR = True Positive / Number of positive samples = TP / P

FPR = False Positive / Number of negative samples = FP / N = 1 - SPC

For any binary classifier, if the predicted probability is ≥ 0.5, then it will get the class label X, and if the predicted probability is < 0.5, then it will get the class label Y. This happens by default in most binary classifiers. This cut-off value of the predicted probability is called the threshold value for predictions. For all possible threshold values, FPR and TPR have been calculated. This FPR and TPR is an x,y value pair for us. So, for all possible threshold values, we get the x,y value pairs, and when we put the points on an ROC graph, it will generate the ROC curve. If your classifier perfectly separates the two classes, then the ROC curve will hug the upper-right corner of the graph. If the classifier performance is based on some randomness, then the ROC curve will align more to the diagonal of the ROC curve. Refer to the following figure:

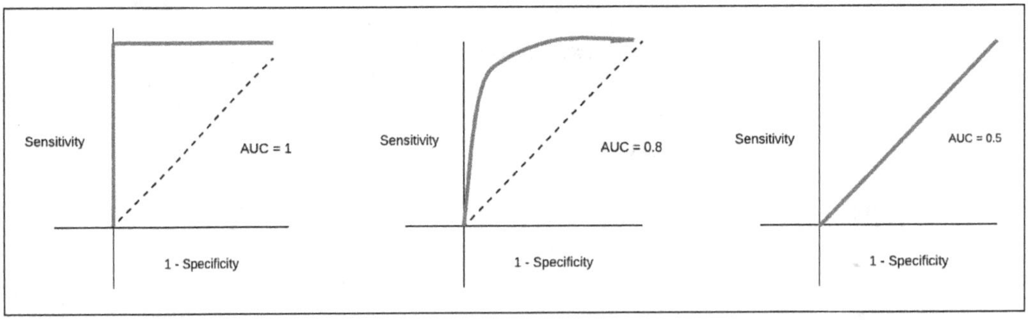

Figure 1.53: ROC curve for different classification scores

In the preceding figure, the leftmost ROC curve is for the perfect classifier. The graph in the center shows the classifier with better accuracy in real-world problems. The classifier that is very random in its guess is shown in the rightmost graph. When we draw an ROC curve, how can we quantify it? In order to answer that question, we will introduce AUC.

AUC

AUC stands for Area Under the Curve. In order to quantify the ROC curve, we use the AUC. Here, we will see how much area has been covered by the ROC curve. If we obtain a perfect classifier, then the AUC score is 1.0, and if we have a classifier that is random in its guesses, then the AUC score is 0.5. In the real world, we don't expect an AUC score of 1.0, but if the AUC score for the classifier is in the range of 0.6 to 0.9, then it will be considered a good classifier. You can refer to the following figure:

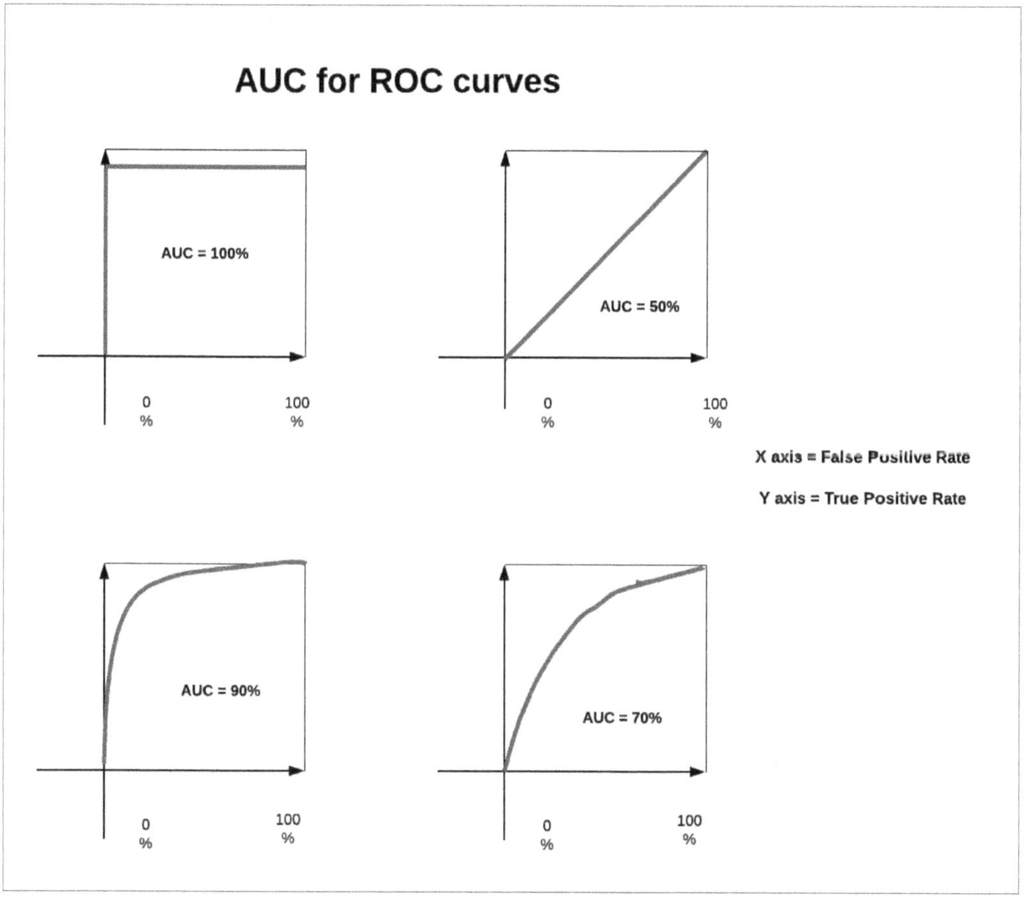

Figure 1.54: AUC for the ROC curve

In the preceding figure, you can see how much area under the curve has been covered, and that becomes our AUC score. This gives us an indication of how good or bad our classifier is performing.

These are the two matrices that we are going to use. In the next section, we will implement actual testing of the code and see the testing matrix for our trained ML models.

Testing the baseline model

In this section, we will implement the code, which will give us an idea about how good or how bad our trained ML models perform in a validation set. We are using the mean accuracy score and the AUC-ROC score.

Here, we have generated five different classifiers and, after performing testing for each of them on the validation dataset, which is 25% of held-out dataset from the training dataset, we will find out which ML model works well and gives us a reasonable baseline score. So let's look at the code:.

```
knMod.score(X_test, y_test)
0.93090666666666666

test_labels=knMod.predict_proba(np.array(X_test.values))[:,1]

roc_auc_score(y_test,test_labels , average='macro', sample_weight=None)
0.60489625790796775

glmMod.score(X_test, y_test)
0.93690666666666667

test_labels=glmMod.predict_proba(np.array(X_test.values))[:,1]

roc_auc_score(y_test,test_labels , average='macro', sample_weight=None)
0.84413030121899479

adaMod.score(X_test, y_test)
0.93562666666666672

test_labels=adaMod.predict_proba(np.array(X_test.values))[:,1]

roc_auc_score(y_test,test_labels , average='macro', sample_weight=None)
0.85348539902575915
```

Figure 1.55: Code snippet to obtain a test score for the trained ML model

In the preceding code snippet, you can see the scores for three classifiers.

Refer to the code snippet in the following figure:

```
gbMod.score(X_test, y_test)
0.93669333333333338

test_labels=gbMod.predict_proba(np.array(X_test.values))[:,1]

roc_auc_score(y_test,test_labels , average='macro', sample_weight=None)
0.85994964765550574

rfMod.score(X_test, y_test)
0.93240000000000001

test_labels=rfMod.predict_proba(np.array(X_test.values))[:,1]

roc_auc_score(y_test,test_labels , average='macro', sample_weight=None)
0.78200046765301123
```

Figure 1.56: Code snippet to obtain the test score for the trained ML model

In the code snippet, you can see the score of the two classifiers.

Using the `score()` function of scikit-learn, you will get the mean accuracy score, whereas, the `roc_auc_score()` function will provide you with the ROC-AUC score, which is more significant for us because the mean accuracy score considers only one threshold value, whereas the ROC-AUC score takes into consideration all possible threshold values and gives us the score.

As you can see in the code snippets given above, the AdaBoost and GradientBoosting classifiers get a good ROC-AUC score on the validation dataset. Other classifiers, such as logistic regression, KNN, and RandomForest do not perform well on the validation set. From this stage onward, we will work with AdaBoost and GradientBoosting classifiers in order to improve their accuracy score.

In the next section, we will see what we need to do in order to increase classification accuracy. We need to list what can be done to get good accuracy and what are the current problems with the classifiers. So let's analyze the problem with the existing classifiers and look at their solutions.

Problems with the existing approach

We got the baseline score using the AdaBoost and GradientBoosting classifiers. Now, we need to increase the accuracy of these classifiers. In order to do that, we first list all the areas that can be improvised but that we haven't worked upon extensively. We also need to list possible problems with the baseline approach. Once we have the list of the problems or the areas on which we need to work, it will be easy for us to implement the revised approach.

Here, I'm listing some of the areas, or problems, that we haven't worked on in our baseline iteration:

- Problem: We haven't used cross-validation techniques extensively in order to check the overfitting issue.
    - Solution: If we use cross-validation techniques properly, then we will know whether our trained ML model suffers from overfitting or not. This will help us because we don't want to build a model that can't even be generalized properly.
- Problem: We also haven't focused on hyperparameter tuning. In our baseline approach, we mostly use the default parameters. We define these parameters during the declaration of the classifier. You can refer to the code snippet given in *Figure 1.52*, where you can see the classifier taking some parameters that are used when it trains the model. We haven't changed these parameters.
    - Solution: We need to tune these hyperparameters in such a way that we can increase the accuracy of the classifier. There are various hyperparameter-tuning techniques that we need to use.

In the next section, we will look at how these optimization techniques actually work as well as discuss the approach that we are going to take. So let's begin!

Optimizing the existing approach

In this section, we will gain an understanding of the basic technicality regarding cross-validation and hyperparameter tuning. Once we understand the basics, it will be quite easy for us to implement them. Let's start with a basic understanding of cross-validation and hyperparameter tuning.

Understanding key concepts to optimize the approach

In this revised iteration, we need to improve the accuracy of the classifier. Here, we will cover the basic concepts first and then move on to the implementation part. So, we will understand two useful concepts:

- Cross-validation
- Hyperparameter tuning

Cross-validation

Cross-validation is also referred to as rotation estimation. It is basically used to track a problem called overfitting. Let me start with the overfitting problem first because the main purpose of using cross-validation is to avoid the overfitting situation.

Basically, when you train the model using the training dataset and check its accuracy, you find out that your training accuracy is quite good, but when you apply this trained model on an as-yet-unseen dataset, you realize that the trained model does not perform well on the unseen dataset and just mimics the output of the training dataset in terms of its target labels. So, we can say that our trained model is not able to generalize properly. This problem is called overfitting, and in order to solve this problem, we need to use cross-validation.

In our baseline approach, we didn't use cross-validation techniques extensively. The good part is that, so far, we generated our validation set of 25% of the training dataset and measured the classifier accuracy on that. This is a basic technique used to get an idea of whether the classifier suffers from overfitting or not.

There are many other cross validation techniques that will help us with two things:

- Tracking the overfitting situation using CV: This will give us a perfect idea about the overfitting problem. We will use K-fold CV.
- Model selection using CV: Cross-validation will help us select the classification models. This will also use K-fold CV.

Now let's look at the single approach that will be used for both of these tasks. You will find the implementation easy to understand.

The approach of using CV

The scikit-learn library provides great implementation of cross-validation. If we want to implement cross-validation, we just need to import the cross-validation module. In order to improvise on accuracy, we will use K-fold cross-validation. What this K-fold cross-validation basically does is explained here.

When we use the train-test split, we will train the model by using 75% of the data and validate the model by using 25% of the data. The main problem with this approach is that, actually, we are not using the whole training dataset for training. So, our model may not be able to come across all of the situations that are present in the training dataset. This problem has been solved by K-fold CV.

In K-fold CV, we need to provide the positive integer number for K. Here, you divide the training dataset into the K sub-dataset. Let me give you an example. If you have 125 data records in your training dataset and you set the value as k = 5, then each subset of the data gets 25 data records. So now, we have five subsets of the training dataset with 25 records each.

Let's understand how these five subsets of the dataset will be used. Based on the provided value of K, it will be decided how many times we need to iterate over these subsets of the data. Here we have taken K=5. So, we iterate over the dataset K-1 = 5-1 =4 times. Note that the number of iterations in K-fold CV is calculated by the equation K-1. Now let's see what happens to each of the iterations:

- **First iteration**: We take one subset for testing and the remaining four subsets for training.
- **Second iteration**: We take two subsets for testing and the remaining three subsets for training.
- **Third iteration**: We take three subsets for testing and the remaining two subsets for training.
- **Fourth iteration**: We take four subsets for testing and the remaining subset for training. After this fourth iteration, we don't have any subsets left for training or testing, so we stop after iteration K-1.

This approach has the following advantages:

K-fold CV uses all the data points for training, so our model takes advantage of getting trained using all of the data points.

- After every iteration, we get the accuracy score. This will help us decide how models perform.

- We generally consider the mean value and standard deviation value of the cross-validation after all the iterations have been completed. For each iteration, we track the accuracy score, and once all iterations have been done, we take the mean value of the accuracy score as well as derive the standard deviation (std) value from the accuracy scores. This CV mean and standard deviation score will help us identify whether the model suffers from overfitting or not.
- If you perform this process for multiple algorithms then based on this mean score and the standard score, you can also decide which algorithm works best for the given dataset.

The disadvantage of this approach is as follows:

- This k-fold CV is a time-consuming and computationally expensive method.

So after reading this, you hopefully understand the approach and, by using this implementation, we can ascertain whether our model suffers from overfitting or not. This technique will also help us select the ML algorithm. We will check out the implementation of this in the Implementing the Revised Approach section.

Now let's check out the next optimization technique, which is hyperparameter tuning.

Hyperparameter tuning

In this section, we will look at how we can use a hyperparameter-tuning technique to optimize the accuracy of our model. There are some kind of parameters whose value cannot be learnt during training process. These parameters are expressing higher-level properties of the ML model. These higher-level parameters are called hyperparameters. These are tuning nobs for ML model. We can obtain the best value for hyperparameter by trial and error. You can refer more on this by using this link: `https://machinelearningmastery.com/difference-between-a-parameter-and-a-hyperparameter/`, If we come up with the optimal value of the hyperparameters, then we will able to achieve the best accuracy for our model, but the challenging part is that we don't know the exact values of these parameters over our head. These parameters are the tuning knobs for our algorithm. So, we need to apply some techniques that will give us the best possible value for our hyperparameter, which we can use when we perform training.

In scikit-learn, there are two functions that we can use in order to find these hyperparameter values, which are as follows:

- Grid search parameter tuning
- Random search parameter tuning

Grid search parameter tuning

In this section, we will look at how grid search parameter tuning works. We specify the parameter values in a list called grid. Each value specified in grid has been taken in to consideration during the parameter tuning. . The model has been built and evaluated based on the specified grid value. This technique exhaustively considers all parameter combinations and generates the final optimal parameters.

Suppose we have five parameters that we want to optimize. Using this technique, if we want to try 10 different values for each of the parameters, then it will take 10^5 evaluations. Assume that, on average, for each parameter combination, 10 minutes are required for training; then, for the evaluation of 10^5, it will take years. Sounds crazy, right? This is the main disadvantage of this technique. This technique is very time consuming. So, a better solution is random search. '

Random search parameter tuning

The intuitive idea is the same as grid search, but the main difference is that instead of trying out all possible combinations, we will just randomly pick up the parameter from the selected subset of the grid. If I want to add on to my previous example, then in random search, we will take a random subset value of the parameter from 10^5 values. Suppose that we take only 1,000 values from 10^5 values and try to generate the optimal value for our hyperparameters. This way, we will save time.

In the revised approach, we will use this particular technique to optimize the hyperparameters.

From the next section, we will see the actual implementation of K-fold cross-validation and hyperparameter tuning. So let's start implementing our approach.

Implementing the revised approach

In this section, we will see the actual implementation of our revised approach, and this revised approach will use K-fold cross-validation and hyperparameter optimization. I have divided the implementation part into two sections so you can connect the dots when you see the code. The two implementation parts are as follows:

- Implementing a cross-validation based approach
- Implementing hyperparameter tuning

Implementing a cross-validation based approach

In this section, we will see the actual implementation of K-fold CV. Here, we are using the scikit-learn cross-validation score module. So, we need to choose the value of K-fold. By default, the value is 3. I'm using the value of K = 5. You can refer to the code snippet given in the following figure:

```
from sklearn.model_selection import cross_val_score
def cvDictGen(functions, scr, X_train=X, y_train=y, cv=5, verbose=1):
    cvDict = {}
    for func in functions:
        cvScore = cross_val_score(func, X_train, y_train, cv=cv, verbose=verbose, scoring=scr)
        cvDict[str(func).split('(')[0]] = [cvScore.mean(), cvScore.std()]

    return cvDict

def cvDictNormalize(cvDict):
    cvDictNormalized =
    for key in cvDict.keys():
        for i in cvDict[key]:
            cvDictNormalized[key] = ['{:0.2f}'.format((cvDict[key][0]/cvDict[cvDict.keys()[0]][0])),
                                     '{:0.2f}'.format((cvDict[key][1]/cvDict[cvDict.keys()[0]][1]))]
    return cvDictNormalized
```

Figure 1.57: Code snippet for the implementation of K-fold cross validation

As you can see in the preceding figure, we obtain `cvScore.mean()` and `cvScore.std()` scores to evaluate our model performance. Note that we have taken the whole training dataset into consideration. So, the values for these parameters are `X_train = X` and `y_train = y`. Here, we define the `cvDictGen` function , which will track the mean value and the standard deviation of the accuracy. We have also implemented the `cvDictNormalize` function, which we can use if we want to obtain a normalized mean and a standard deviation (std) score. For the time being, we are not going to use the `cvDictNormalize` function.

Now it's time to run the `cvDictGen` method. You can see the output in the following figure:

```
cvD = cvDictGen(functions=[knMod, glmMod, adaMod, gbMod, rfMod], scr='roc_auc')
cvD

[Parallel(n_jobs=1)]: Done   5 out of   5 | elapsed:    6.2s finished

[LibLinear][LibLinear][LibLinear][LibLinear][LibLinear]

[Parallel(n_jobs=1)]: Done   5 out of   5 | elapsed:    1.8s finished
[Parallel(n_jobs=1)]: Done   5 out of   5 | elapsed:   57.1s finished
[Parallel(n_jobs=1)]: Done   5 out of   5 | elapsed:   54.4s finished
[Parallel(n_jobs=1)]: Done   5 out of   5 | elapsed:    6.7s finished

{'AdaBoostClassifier': [0.85863701255476743, 0.0020946319753293269],
 'GradientBoostingClassifier': [0.86390715340406421, 0.002629919837334762],
 'KNeighborsClassifier': [0.5952570076118191, 0.0023729926242542316],
 'LogisticRegression': [0.84930027022880594, 0.0036900431896093847],
 'RandomForestClassifier': [0.7771107259458645, 0.0053331630813484377]}
```

Figure 1.58: Code snippet for the output of K-fold cross validation

We have performed cross-validation for five different ML algorithms to check which ML algorithm works well. As we can see, in our output given in the preceding figure, GradietBoosting and Adaboot classifier work well. We have used the cross-validation score in order to decide which ML algorithm we should select and which ones we should not go with. Apart from that, based on the mean value and the std value, we can conclude that our ROC-AUC score does not deviate much, so we are not suffering from the overfitting issue.

Now it's time to see the implementation of hyperparameter tuning.

Implementing hyperparameter tuning

In this section, we will look at how we can obtain optimal values for hyperparameters. Here, we are using the `RandomizedSearchCV` hyperparameter tuning method. We have implemented this method for the AdaBoost and GradientBossting algorithms. You can see the implementation of hyperparameter tuning for the Adaboost algorithm in the following figure:

```
adaHyperParams = {'n_estimators': [10,50,100,200,420]}

gridSearchAda = RandomizedSearchCV(estimator=adaMod, param_distributions=adaHyperParams, n_iter=5,
                                   scoring='roc_auc', fit_params=None, cv=None, verbose=2).fit(X_train, y_train)

...

gridSearchAda.best_params_, gridSearchAda.best_score_

({'n_estimators': 100}, 0.85619227253371544)
```

Figure 1.59: Code snippet of hyperparameter tuning for the Adaboost algorithm

After running the `RandomizedSearchCV` method on the given values of parameters, it will generate the optimal parameter value. As you can see in the preceding figure, we want the optimal value for the parameter; `n_estimators.RandomizedSearchCV` obtains the optimal value for `n_estimators`, which is 100.

You can see the implementation of hyperparameter tuning for the GradientBoosting algorithm in the following figure:

```
gbHyperParams = {'loss' : ['deviance', 'exponential'],
                 'n_estimators': randint(10, 500),
                 'max_depth': randint(1,10)}

gridSearchGB = RandomizedSearchCV(estimator=gbMod, param_distributions=gbHyperParams, n_iter=10,
                                   scoring='roc_auc', fit_params=None, cv=None, verbose=2).fit(X_train, y_train)

...

gridSearchGB.best_params_, gridSearchGB.best_score_

({'loss': 'deviance', 'max_depth': 2, 'n_estimators': 449},
 0.85989355047978822)
```

Figure 1.60: Code snippet of hyperparameter tuning for the GradientBoosting algorithm

As you can see in the preceding figure, the `RandomizedSearchCV` method obtains the optimal value for the following hyperparameters:

- 'loss': 'deviance'
- 'max_depth': 2
- 'n_estimators': 449

Now it's time to test our revised approach. Let's see how we will test the model and what the outcome of the testing will be.

Implementing and testing the revised approach

Here, we need to plug the optimal values of the hyperparameters, and then we will see the ROC-AUC score on the validation dataset so that we know whether there will be any improvement in the accuracy of the classifier or not.

You can see the implementation and how we have performed training using the best hyperparameters by referring to the following figure:

```
bestGbModFitted = gridSearchGB.best_estimator_.fit(X_train, y_train)

bestAdaModFitted = gridSearchAda.best_estimator_.fit(X_train, y_train)
```

Figure 1.61: Code snippet for performing training by using optimal hyperparameter values

Once we are done with the training, we can use the trained model to predict the target labels for the validation dataset. After that, we can obtain the ROC-AUC score, which gives us an idea of how much we are able to optimize the accuracy of our classifier. This score also helps validate our direction, so if we aren't able to improve our classifier accuracy, then we can identify the problem and improve accuracy in the next iteration. You can see the ROC-AUC score in the following figure:

```
test_labels=bestGbModFitted.predict_proba(np.array(X_test.values))[:,1]

roc_auc_score(y_test,test_labels , average='macro', sample_weight=None)

0.86999235296222088

test_labels=bestAdaModFitted.predict_proba(np.array(X_test.values))[:,1]

roc_auc_score(y_test,test_labels , average='macro', sample_weight=None)

0.8657238524971379
```

Figure 1.62: Code snippet of the ROC-AUC score for the revised approach

As you can see in the output, after hyperparameter tuning, we have an improvement in the ROC-AUC score compared to our baseline approach. In our baseline approach, the ROC-AUC score for AdaBoost is 0.85348539, whereas after hyperparameter tuning, it is 0.86572352. In our baseline approach, the ROC-AUC score for GradientBoosting is 0.85994964, whereas after hyperparameter tuning, it is 0.86999235. These scores indicate that we are heading in the right direction.

The question remains: *can we further improve the accuracy of the classifiers?* Sure, there is always room for improvement, so we will follow the same approach. We list all the possible problems or areas we haven't touched upon yet. We try to explore them and generate the best possible approach that can give us good accuracy on the validation dataset as well as the testing dataset.

So let's see what our untouched areas in this revised approach will be.

Understanding problems with the revised approach

Up until the revised approach, we did not spend a lot of time on feature engineering. So in our best possible approach, we spent time on the transformation of features engineering. We need to implement a voting mechanism in order to generate the final probability of the prediction on the actual test dataset so that we can get the best accuracy score.

These are the two techniques that we need to apply:

- Feature transformation
- An ensemble ML model with a voting mechanism

Once we implement these techniques, we will check our ROC-AUC score on the validation dataset. After that, we will generate a probability score for each of the records present in the real test dataset. Let's start with the implementation.

Best approach

As mentioned in the previous section, in this iteration, we will focus on feature transformation as well as implementing a voting classifier that will use the AdaBoost and GradientBoosting classifiers. Hopefully, by using this approach, we will get the best ROC-AUC score on the validation dataset as well as the real testing dataset. This is the best possible approach in order to generate the best result. If you have any creative solutions, you can also try them as well. Now we will jump to the implementation part.

Implementing the best approach

Here, we will implement the following techniques:

- Log transformation of features
- Voting-based ensemble model

Let's implement feature transformation first.

Log transformation of features

We will apply log transformation to our training dataset. The reason behind this is that we have some attributes that are very skewed and some data attributes that have values that are more spread out in nature. So, we will be taking the natural log of one plus the input feature array. You can refer to the code snippet shown in the following figure:

```
import numpy as np
from sklearn.preprocessing import FunctionTransformer

transformer = FunctionTransformer(np.log1p)
X_train_1 = np.array(X_train)
X_train_transform = transformer.transform(X_train_1)

bestGbModFitted_transformed = gridSearchGB.best_estimator_.fit(X_train_transform, y_train)

bestAdaModFitted_transformed = gridSearchAda.best_estimator_.fit(X_train_transform, y_train)

cvDictbestpara_transform = cvDictGen(functions=[bestGbModFitted_transformed, bestAdaModFitted_transformed],
                                     scr='roc_auc')

[Parallel(n_jobs=1)]: Done   5 out of   5 | elapsed:   59.4s finished
[Parallel(n_jobs=1)]: Done   5 out of   5 | elapsed:   28.1s finished

cvDictbestpara_transform

{'AdaBoostClassifier': [0.85917740828466138, 0.0026272442965240275],
 'GradientBoostingClassifier': [0.86388892996674593, 0.0027147060401564809]}
```

Figure 1.63: Code snippet for log(p+1) transformation of features.

I have also tested the ROC-AUC accuracy on the validation dataset, which gives us a minor change in accuracy.

Voting-based ensemble ML model

In this section, we will use a voting-based ensemble classifier. The scikit-learn library already has a module available for this. So, we implement a voting-based ML model for both untransformed features as well as transformed features. Let's see which version scores better on the validation dataset. You can refer to the code snippet given in the following figure:

Voting based ensamble model

```
from sklearn.ensemble import VotingClassifier
votingMod = VotingClassifier(estimators=[('gb', bestGbModFitted_transformed),
                                         ('ada', bestAdaModFitted_transformed)], voting='soft',weights=[2,1])
votingMod = votingMod.fit(X_train_transform, y_train)
```

```
test_labels=votingMod.predict_proba(np.array(X_test_transform))[:,1]
```

```
votingMod.score(X_test_transform, y_test)
```

```
0.93762666666666672
```

```
roc_auc_score(y_test,test_labels , average='macro', sample_weight=None)
```

```
0.86828513403077934
```

```
from sklearn.ensemble import VotingClassifier
votingMod_old = VotingClassifier(estimators=[('gb', bestGbModFitted), ('ada', bestAdaModFitted)],
                                 voting='soft',weights=[2,1])
votingMod_old = votingMod.fit(X_train, y_train)
```

```
test_labels=votingMod_old.predict_proba(np.array(X_test.values)) :,1
```

```
roc_auc_score(y_test,test_labels , average='macro', sample_weight=None)
```

```
0.86832347818671751
```

Figure 1.64: Code snippet for a voting based ensemble classifier

Here, we are using two parameters: weight 2 for GradientBoosting and 1 for the AdaBoost algorithm. I have also set the voting parameter as soft so classifiers can be more collaborative.

We are almost done with trying out our best approach using a voting mechanism. In the next section, we will run our ML model on a real testing dataset. So let's do some real testing!

Running ML models on real test data

Here, we will be testing the accuracy of a voting-based ML model on our testing dataset. In the first iteration, we are not going to take log transformation for the test dataset, and in the second iteration, we are going to take log transformation for the test dataset. In both cases, we will generate the probability for the target class. Here, we are generating probability because we want to know how much of a chance there is of a particular person defaulting on their loan in the next 2 years. We will save the predicted probability in a `csv` file.

You can see the code for performing testing in the following figure:

Testing on Real Test Dataset

```
# Read Training dataset as well as drop the index column
test_data = pd.read_csv('./data/cs-test.csv').drop('Unnamed: 0', axis = 1)
# For each column heading we replace "-" and convert the heading in lowercase
cleancolumn = []
for i in range(len(test_data.columns)):
    cleancolumn.append(test_data.columns[i].replace('-', '').lower())
test_data.columns = cleancolumn
```

```
test_data.drop(['seriousdlqin2yrs'], axis=1, inplace=True)
test_data.fillna (training_data.median()), inplace=True
```

...

```
test_labels_votingMod_old = votingMod_old.predict_proba(np.array(test_data.values))[:,1]
print (len(test_labels_votingMod_old))
```

```
101503
```

```
output = pd.DataFrame({'ID':test_data.index, 'probability':test_labels_votingMod_old})
```

```
output.to_csv("./predictions.csv", index=False)
```

```
import numpy as np
from sklearn.preprocessing import FunctionTransformer

transformer = FunctionTransformer(np.log1p)
test_data_temp = np.array(test_data)
test_data_transform = transformer.transform(test_data_temp)
```

```
test_labels_votingMod = votingMod.predict_proba(np.array(test_data.values))[:,1]
print (len(test_labels_votingMod_old))
```

```
101503
```

```
output = pd.DataFrame({'ID':test_data.index, 'probability':test_labels_votingMod})
```

```
output.to_csv("./predictions_voting_Feature_transformation.csv", index=False)
```

Figure 1.65: Code snippet for testing

If you can see *Figure 1.64* then you come to know that here, we have achieved 86% accuracy. This score is by far the most efficient accuracy as per industry standards.

Summary

In this chapter, we looked at how to analyze a dataset using various statistical techniques. After that, we obtained a basic approach and, by using that approach, we developed a model that didn't even achieve the baseline. So, we figured out what had gone wrong in the approach and tried another approach, which solved the issues of our baseline model. Then, we evaluated that approach and optimized the hyper parameters using cross-validation and ensemble techniques in order to achieve the best possible outcome for this application. Finally, we found out the best possible approach, which gave us state-of-the-art results. You can find all of the code for this on GitHub at `https://github.com/jalajthanaki/credit-risk-modelling`. You can find all the installation related information at `https://github.com/jalajthanaki/credit-risk-modelling/blob/master/README.md`.

In the next chapter, we will look at another very interesting application of the analytics domain: predicting the stock price of a given share. Doesn't that sound interesting? We will also use some modern machine learning (ML) and deep learning (DL) approaches in order to develop stock price prediction application, so get ready for that as well!

2
Stock Market Price Prediction

In this chapter, we will cover an amazing application that belongs to predictive analysis. I hope the name of the chapter has already given you a rough idea of what this chapter is going to be all about. We will try to predict the price of the stock index. We will apply some modern machine learning techniques as well as deep learning techniques.

We will cover the following topics in this chapter:

- Introducing the problem statement
- Collecting the dataset
- Understanding the dataset
- Data preprocessing and data analysis
- Feature engineering
- Selecting the Machine Learning (ML) algorithm
- Training the baseline model
- Understanding the testing matrix
- Testing the baseline model
- Exploring problems with the existing approach
- Understanding the revised approach
    - Understanding concepts and approaches

- Implementing the revised approach
    - Testing the revised approach
    - Understanding problems with the revised approach
- The best approach
- Summary

So, let's get started!

Introducing the problem statement

The stock market is a place where you can buy and sell units of ownership in the company, which we call **stocks**. If the company performs well and increases its profit, then you will earn some profit as well because you have the stocks of the company, but if the company's profit goes down, then you will lose the money you have with the company. So if you invest your money in the right company at the right time, it could lead to you earning quite a lot of money. The question is which company's stock should you buy? Is there any way we can predict the future prices of the stock of any company given the historical prices of the company's stock so that we can have higher chances of getting good returns? The answer is yes. This is what we will explore in this chapter.

If you invest in the stock market, then you may have heard that stock prices are completely random and unpredictable. This is called the *efficient market hypothesis,* but a majority of the big financial firms, such as JP Morgan, Citigroup, and Goldman Sachs, have mathematical and quantitative analysts who are trying to develop predictive models to help these big firms decide when to invest and in which stock.

Before investing in any stock, we do some basic research regarding the company's profile. We try to understand its business model. We also check the balance sheets of the company to get to know what the profit and loss of the company is. What are the products that the company will launch in the next couple of months? What kind of news is coming in about the company? What are the current industry trends? After researching all these parameters, we will invest our money in a particular company's stock if we feel we will gain some profit; otherwise, we won't invest in that company.

We depend on various sources of information to get an idea about whether we need to buy stocks or sell stocks. Don't you think all this analysis takes a lot of our time? I want to put two questions in front of you. First, can we use some of the data points discussed here and build a system that will help us find out future stock prices? And can we use historical stock prices to predict future stock prices? The answer to both of these questions is yes, definitely: we can build a system that will use historical stock prices and some of the other data points so that we can predict the future prices of stock. As per the efficient market hypothesis, by using historical prices of stock and various other data points, we can obtain the future prices of the stock, which will be better than a random guess. In this chapter, we will build a predictive model, which will predict the close price of the stock. In the next section, we will look at how to collect the dataset in order to build the model. So, let's get started!

Collecting the dataset

In order to build the model, first we need to collect the data. We will use the following two data points:

- **Dow Jones Industrial Average** (**DJIA**) index prices
- News articles

DJIA index prices give us an overall idea about the stock market's movements on a particular day, whereas news articles help us find out how news affects the stock prices. We will build our model using these two data points. Now let's collect the data.

Collecting DJIA index prices

In order to collect the DJIA index prices, we will use Yahoo Finance. You can visit this link: `https://finance.yahoo.com/quote/%5EDJI/history?period1=1196706600&period2=1512325800&interval=1d&filter=history&frequency=1d`. Once you click on this link, you can see that the price data shows up. You can change the time period and click on the **Download Data** link and that's it; you can have all the data in `.csv` file format. Refer to the following screenshot of the Yahoo finance DJIA index price page:

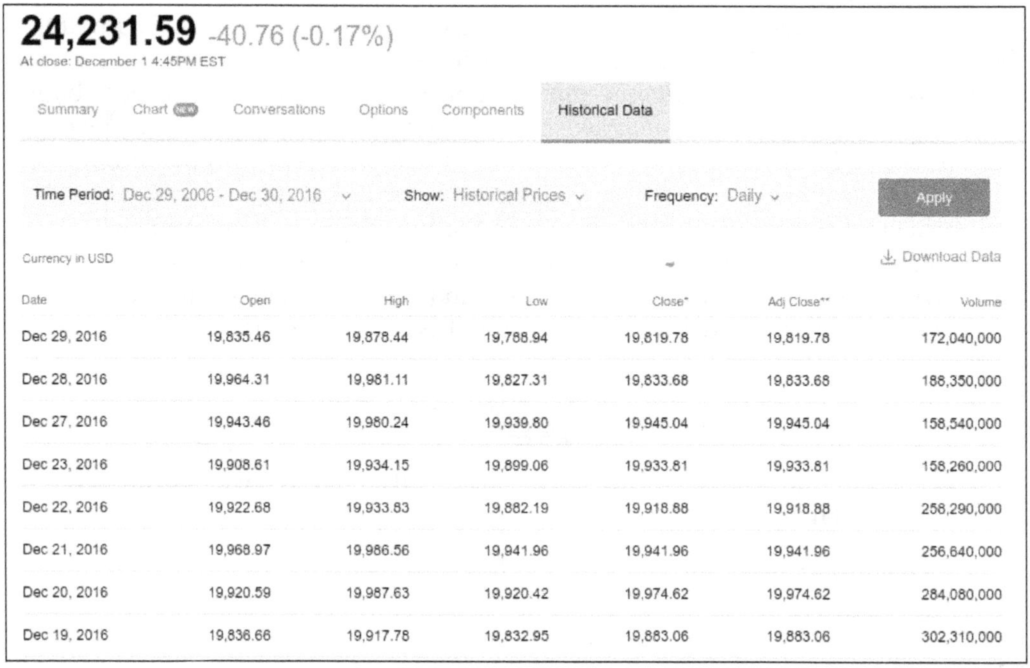

Date	Open	High	Low	Close*	Adj Close**	Volume
Dec 29, 2016	19,835.46	19,878.44	19,788.94	19,819.78	19,819.78	172,040,000
Dec 28, 2016	19,964.31	19,981.11	19,827.31	19,833.68	19,833.68	188,350,000
Dec 27, 2016	19,943.46	19,980.24	19,939.80	19,945.04	19,945.04	158,540,000
Dec 23, 2016	19,908.61	19,934.15	19,899.06	19,933.81	19,933.81	158,260,000
Dec 22, 2016	19,922.68	19,933.83	19,882.19	19,918.88	19,918.88	258,290,000
Dec 21, 2016	19,968.97	19,986.56	19,941.96	19,941.96	19,941.96	256,640,000
Dec 20, 2016	19,920.59	19,987.63	19,920.42	19,974.62	19,974.62	284,080,000
Dec 19, 2016	19,836.66	19,917.78	19,832.95	19,883.06	19,883.06	302,310,000

Figure 2.1: Yahoo Finance page for DJIA index price

Here, we have downloaded the dataset for the years 2007-2016, which means we have 10 years of data for DJIA index prices. You can see this in *Figure 2.1*, as well. You can find this dataset using this GitHub link: `https://github.com/jalajthanaki/stock_price_prediction/blob/master/data/DJIA_data.csv`.

Just bear with me for a while; we will understand the meaning of each of the data attributes in the *Understand the dataset* section in this chapter. Now, let's look at how we can collect the news articles.

Collecting news articles

We want to collect news articles so that we can establish the correlation between how news affects the DJIA index value. We are going to perform a sentiment analysis on the news articles. You may wonder why we need to perform sentiment analysis. If any news has a negative effect on the financial market, then it is likely that the prices of stocks will go down, and if news about the financial market is positive, then it is likely that prices of the stocks will go up. For this dataset, we will use news articles from the New York Times (NYTimes). In order to collect the dataset of news articles, we will use the New York Times' developer API. So, let's start coding!

First of all, register yourself on the NYTimes developer website and generate your API key. The link is `https://developer.nytimes.com/signup`. I have generated the API key for the Archive API. Here, we are using *newsapi, JSON, requests*, and *sys* dependencies. You can also refer to the NYTimes developer documentation using this link: `https://developer.nytimes.com/archive_api.json#/Documentation/GET/%7Byear%7D/%7Bmonth%7D.json`.

You can find the code at this GitHub link: `https://github.com/jalajthanaki/stock_price_prediction/blob/master/getdata_NYtimes.py`. You can see the code snippet in the following screenshot:

```python
from newsapi.articles import Articles
import sys,json
import requests

key = '522497f7b4b940b7946eeed6909ed817'
params = {}
api = Articles(API_KEY=key)
reload(sys)
sys.setdefaultencoding('utf8')


class APIKeyException(Exception):
    def __init__(self, message): self.message = message


class InvalidQueryException(Exception):
    def __init__(self, message): self.message = message


class ArchiveAPI(object):
    def __init__(self, key=None):
        self.key = key
        self.root = 'http://api.nytimes.com/svc/archive/v1/{}/{}.json?api-key={}'
        if not self.key:
            nyt_dev_page = 'http://developer.nytimes.com/docs/reference/keys'
            exception_str = 'Warning: API Key required. Please visit {}'
            raise APIKeyException(exception_str.format(nyt_dev_page))

    def query(self, year=None, month=None, key=None, ):
        if not key: key = self.key
        if (year < 1882) or not (0 < month < 13):
            # currently the Archive API only supports year >= 1851
            exception_str = 'Invalid query: See http://developer.nytimes.com/archive_api.json'
            raise InvalidQueryException(exception_str)
        url = self.root.format(year, month, key)
        print url
        r = requests.get(url)
        return r.json()
```

Figure 2.2: Code snippet for getting the news article data from the New York Times

As you can see in the code, there are three methods. The first two methods are for exceptions and the third method checks for the validation and requests the URL that can generate the news article data for us. This NYTimes API URL takes three parameters, which are given as follows:

- Year
- Month
- API key

After this step, we will call the third function and pass the year value from 2007 to 2016. We will save the data in the *JSON* format. You can refer to the code snippet in the following screenshot:

```
years = [2016, 2015, 2014, 2013, 2012, 2011, 2010, 2009, 2008, 2007]
months = [1, 2, 3, 4, 5, 6, 7, 8, 9, 10, 11, 12]
api = ArchiveAPI('522497f7b4b940b7946eeed6909ed817')
for year in years:
    for month in months:
        mydict = api.query(year, month)
        file_str = './data/nytimes' + str(year) + '-' + '{:02}'.format(
            month) + '.json'
        with open(file_str, 'w') as fout:
            json.dump(mydict, fout)
        fout.close()
```

Figure 2.3: Code snippet for getting news article data from the New York Times

You can find the raw JSON dataset using this GitHub link: `https://github.com/jalajthanaki/stock_price_prediction/blob/master/data/2016-01.json`.

Now let's move on to the next section, in which we will understand the dataset and the attributes that we have collected so far.

Understanding the dataset

In this section, we will understand the meaning of data attributes, which will help us understand what kind of dataset we are going to deal with and what kind of preprocessing is needed for the dataset. We understand our dataset in two sections, and those sections are given as follows:

- Understanding the DJIA dataset
- Understanding the NYTimes news article dataset

Understanding the DJIA dataset

In the DJIA dataset, we have seven data attributes. They are quite easy to understand, so let's look at each of them one by one:

- `Date`: The first column indicates the date in the YYYY-MM-DD format when you see data in the .csv file.
- `Open`: This indicates the price at which the market opens, so it is the opening value for the DJIA index for that particular trading day.
- `High`: This is the highest price for the DJIA index for a particular trading day.
- `Low`: This is the lowest price for DJIA index for a particular trading day.
- `Close`: The price of DJIA index at the close of the trading day.
- `Adj close`: The adjusted closing price (adj close price) uses the closing price as a starting point and takes into account components such as dividends, stock splits, and new stock offerings. The adj close price represents the true reflection of the DJIA index. Let me give you an example so that you can understand the adj close price better: if a company offers a dividend of $5 per share, and if the closing price of that company share is $100, then the adj close price will become $95. So, the adj close price considers various factors and, based on them, generates the true value of the company's stock. Here, we are looking at the DJIA index value so, most of the time, the closing price and the adj close price are the same.
- `Volume`: These values indicate the number of index traded on exchange for a particular trading day.

These are the basic details of the DJIA index dataset. We use historical data and try to predict future movement in the DJIA index.

In the next section, we will look at the NYTimes news article dataset.

Understanding the NYTimes news article dataset

We have used the NYTimes developer API and collected the news articles in a JSON form, so, here, we will look at the JSON response so we can identify the data attributes that are the most important and that we can focus on. In the next figure, you can see the JSON response that we get from the NYTimes:


```
{
    "response": {
        "docs": [
            {
                "type_of_material": "Blog",
                "blog": [],
                "news_desk": null,
                "lead_paragraph": "The Jets hardly had the most challenging schedule this season, but they did beat the Patriots at New England, where they'll return Sunday for a playoff game.",
                "headline": {
                    "main": "The View From Boston",
                    "kicker": "The Fifth Down"
                },
                "abstract": "The Jets hardly had the most challenging schedule this season, but they did beat the Patriots at New England, where they'll return Sunday for a playoff game. It was
                the Jets' most impressive victory of the season. A seemingly gleeful Ron Borges of The Boston Globe described it this way. (Borges has been a fierce [...]",
                "print_page": null,
                "word_count": 488,
                "_id": "4fd367788eb7c8105d8b78bd",
                "snippet": "The Jets hardly had the most challenging schedule this season, but they did beat the Patriots at New England, where they'll return Sunday for a playoff game. It was
                the Jets' most impressive victory of the season. A seemingly gleeful Ron Borges of...",
                "source": "The New York Times",
                "slideshow_credits": null,
                "web_url": "https://fifthdown.blogs.nytimes.com/2007/01/01/the-view-from-boston/",
                "multimedia": [],
                "subsection_name": null,
                "keywords": [
                    {
                        "value": "News",
                        "name": "type_of_material",
                        "rank": "1"
                    }
                ],
                "byline": {
                    "person": [
                        {
                            "organization": "",
                            "role": "reported",
                            "rank": 1,
                            "firstname": "Toni",
                            "lastname": "MONKOVIC"
                        }
                    ],
                    "original": "By TONI MONKOVIC"
                },
                "document_type": "blogpost",
                "pub_date": "2007-01-01T17:52:17Z",
                "section_name": "Sports"
            }
        ]
    }
}
```


Figure 2.4: JSON response for news articles using the NYTimes developer tool

In this figure, we can see the JSON response for a single news article. As you can see, there is a main data attribute response that carries all other data attributes. We will focus on the data attributes that are given inside the docs array. Don't worry; we will not use all the data attributes. Here, we will focus on the following data attributes:

- `type_of_material`: This attribute indicates that a particular news article is derived from a particular kind of source, whether it's a blog, a news article, analysis, and so on.
- `headlines`: The headline data attribute has the two sub-data attributes. The main data attribute contains the actual headline of the news and the kicker data attribute is convey the highlight of the article.
- `pub_date`: This data attribute indicates the publication of the news article. You can find this attribute in the second-last section of the doc array.
- `section_name`: This data attribute appeared in the preceding image in the last section. It provides the category of the news article.
- `news_desk`: This data attribute also indicates the news category. When `section_name` is absent in a response, we will refer to this attribute.

As we understand data attributes properly, we should move on to the next section, which is the data preprocessing and data analysis part.

Data preprocessing and data analysis

In this section, we will mainly cover data preprocessing and data analysis. As a part of data preprocessing, we are preparing our training dataset. You may be wondering what kind of data preparation I'm talking about, considering we already have the data. Allow me to tell you that we have two different datasets and both datasets are independent. So, we need to merge the DJIA dataset and NYTimes news article dataset in order to get meaningful insights from these datasets. Once we prepare our training dataset, we can train the data using different machine learning (ML) algorithms.

Now let's start the coding to prepare the training dataset. We will be using `numpy`, `csv`, `JSON`, and `pandas` as our dependency libraries. Here, our code is divided into two parts. First, we will prepare the dataset for the DJIA index dataset and then we will move to the next part, which is preparing the NYTimes news article dataset. During the preparation of the training dataset, we will code the basic data analysis steps as well.

Preparing the DJIA training dataset

You can see the code snippet in the following screenshot. You can find the code at this GitHub link: `https://github.com/jalajthanaki/stock_price_prediction/blob/master/datapreparation.ipynb`.

Import dependancies

```
import numpy as np
import csv,json
import pandas as pd
```

Prepare DJIA training dataset

```
# Reading DJIA index prices csv file
with open('./data/DJIA_data.csv', 'rb') as csvfile:
    spamreader = csv.reader(csvfile, delimiter=',')
    # Converting the csv file reader to a lists
    data_list = list(spamreader)

# Separating header from the data
header = data_list[0]
data_list = data_list[1:]
data_list = np.asarray(data_list)

# Selecting date and close value for each day
selected_data = data_list[:, [0, 4, 5]]
df = pd.DataFrame(data=selected_data[0:,1:],
                                index=selected_data[0:,0],
                                columns=['close', 'adj close'],
                                        dtype='float64')
```

Figure 2.5: Code snippet for preparing the DJIA dataset

As you can see in the preceding code snippet, we are reading the csv file that we downloaded from the Yahoo Finance page earlier. After that, we convert the data into a list format. We also separated the header and actual data from the list. Once we have the data in list format, we convert the data into a numpy array. We have selected only three columns from the DIJA dataset, as follows:

- Date
- Close price
- Adj close price

You may have one question in mind: why have we considered only close price and Adj close price from the DJIA csv file? Let me clarify: as we know that open price is mostly a nearby value of the last day's close price, we haven't considered the open price. We haven't considered the high price and low price because we don't know in which particular timestamp these high and low prices occurred. For the first iteration, it is quite complicated to predict when the stock index reach a high or low value, so, in the meantime, we ignore these two columns. We are mainly interested in the overall trend for the DJIA index. If we figure out the trend precisely, we can predict the high and low price values later on. Here, we restrict our goal to predicting the closing prices for the DJIA index for future trading days.

Now back to the coding part: we built the pandas dataframe in such a way that the date column acts as the index column, and close price and adj close price are the two other columns of the dataset. You can see the output of the dataframe defined in the form of the `df` variable in the code snippet given in *Figure 2.5*. You can see the output of dataframe df in the following figure:

```
df.head()
```

	close	adj close
2006-12-28	12501.519531	12501.519531
2006-12-29	12463.150391	12463.150391
2007-01-03	12474.519531	12474.519531
2007-01-04	12480.690430	12480.690430
2007-01-05	12398.009766	12398.009766

Figure 2.6: Output of pandas dataframe, which is defined as the *df* variable in the code snippet in Figure 2.5

Hopefully now you have a clear understanding of the kind of steps we have followed so far. We have created the basic dataframe, so now we will move on to the basic data analysis part for a DJIA dataset.

Basic data analysis for a DJIA dataset

In this section, we will perform basic data analysis on a DJIA dataset. This dataset has the date value, but if you look at the values of the date carefully, then you will see that there are some missing dates. Suppose data is missing for 30-12-2006, 31-12-2006, 1-1-2007, and many other dates. In such cases, we will add the date values that are missing. You can refer to the code snippet given in *Figure 2.7*, as well as find the code for this on this GitHub: `https://github.com/jalajthanaki/stock_price_prediction/blob/master/datapreparation.ipynb`.

Basic Data analysis for DJIA dataset

```
# copy the data to the new dataframe df1 which is temporary dataframe
df1 = df

#idx contains all the data value between given date range
idx = pd.date_range('12-29-2006', '12-31-2016')

# Adding missing dates to the dataframe
df1.index = pd.DatetimeIndex(df1.index)
df1 = df1.reindex(idx, fill_value=np.NaN)
df1.head()
```

	close	adj close
2006-12-29	12463.150391	12463.150391
2006-12-30	NaN	NaN
2006-12-31	NaN	NaN
2007-01-01	NaN	NaN
2007-01-02	NaN	NaN

Figure 2.7: Code snippet for adding all the missing date values in the DJIA dataset

As you can see in the preceding figure, we come across another challenge after adding these missing date values. We have added the date value, but there is no close price or adj close price available corresponding to each of them, so we need to replace the NaN values logically, not randomly.

In order to replace the NaN values of close price and adj close price, we will use the pandas interpolation functionality. We use linear interpolation to generate the missing values for NaN. There are many types of interpolation available, but here we are using linear interpolation, and the mathematical equation for linear interpolation is as follows:

$$x_2 = \frac{(y_2 - y_1) * (x_3 - x_1)}{(y_3 - y_1)} + x_1$$

$$y_2 = \frac{(x_2 - x_1) * (y_3 - y_1)}{(x_3 - x_1)} + x_1$$

Equation 2.1: Linear interpolation math formula

If the two known points are given by the coordinates (x1,y_1) and (x_3,y_3), the linear interpolant is the straight line between these points.

You can refer to the code snippet in the following screenshot:

```
# Reference for pandas interpolation http://pandas.pydata.org/pandas-docs/stable/missing_data.html

interpolated_df = df1.interpolate()
#print interpolated_df.count() # gives 3656 count

# Removing extra date rows added in data for calculating interpolation
interpolated_df = interpolated_df[3:]
```

```
interpolated_df.head()
```

	close	adj close
2007-01-01	12469.971875	12469.971875
2007-01-02	12472.245703	12472.245703
2007-01-03	12474.519531	12474.519531
2007-01-04	12480.690430	12480.690430
2007-01-05	12398.009766	12398.009766

Figure 2.8: Code snippet for basic data analysis and interpolation implementation

The code for this is available on GitHub at `https://github.com/jalajthanaki/stock_price_prediction/blob/master/datapreparation.ipynb`.

As you can see in the code snippet, we haven't defined which type of interpolation should be performed on our dataset; in this case, linear interpolation has been performed by default. So after applying the linear interpolation, we can replace the NaN values with the actual logical values. We have also removed three records from the year 2006. So now, we have a total of 3653 records.

This is the kind of basic data preprocessing and data analysis we did for the DJIA index dataset. Now let's move on to the NYTimes news article dataset. We need to prepare the training dataset first, so let's begin with it.

Preparing the NYTimes news dataset

In this section, we will see how we can prepare the NYTimes news dataset. We have downloaded the whole news article dataset but we have not put in a filtering mechanism for choosing news article categories. Perform the following steps when preparing the NYTimes dataset:

1. Converting publication date into the YYYY-MM-DD format.
2. Filtering news articles by their category.
3. Implementing the filter functionality and merge the dataset.
4. Saving the merged dataset in the pickle file format.

So, let's start coding for each of these steps.

Converting publication date into the YYYY-MM-DD format

First, we will convert the publication date of the news articles into the YYYY-MM-DD format so that we can merge DJIA and NYTimes news article datasets later on. In order to achieve this, you can refer to the following code snippet:

```
# we will convert the date format in YYYY-MM-DD format from the existing date format in json response.
date_format = ["%Y-%m-%dT%H:%M:%SZ", "%Y-%m-%dT%H:%M:%S+%f"]
def try_parsing_date(text):
    for fmt in date_format:
        #return datetime.strptime(text, fmt)
        try:
            return datetime.strptime(text, fmt).strftime('%Y-%m-%d')
        except ValueError:
            pass
    raise ValueError('no valid date format found')
```

Figure 2.9: Code snippet for converting the date format of the publication date of the news article

Here, we have written a function that can parse and convert the publication date format into the necessary YYYY-MM-DD format. We will call this function later on when we read the JSON files in which we have stored the JSON response.

Filtering news articles by category

The other thing that we are going to do here is filter our news article dataset by news category. We have downloaded all types of news articles, but for the stock market price prediction application, we need news articles that belong to specific news categories. So, we need to implement filters that will help us extract the necessary subset of news articles. You can refer to the following code snippet:

```
years = [2016, 2015, 2014, 2013, 2012, 2011, 2010, 2009, 2008, 2007]
months = [1, 2, 3, 4, 5, 6, 7, 8, 9, 10, 11, 12]
dict_keys = ['pub_date', 'headline'] #, 'lead_paragraph']
articles_dict = dict.fromkeys(dict_keys)

# Filtering list for type_of_material
type_of_material_list = ['blog', 'brief', 'news', 'editorial', 'op-ed', 'list','analysis']

# Filtering list for section_name
section_name_list = ['business', 'national', 'world', 'u.s.' , 'politics', 'opinion', 'tech', 'science',  'health']
news_desk_list = ['business', 'national', 'world', 'u.s.' , 'politics', 'opinion', 'tech', 'science',  'health',
                  'foreign']

current_date = '2016-01-01'
from datetime import datetime
current_article_str = ''
```

Figure 2.10: Code snippet for filtering news articles by their categories

You can refer to the code provided at this GitHub link: `https://github.com/jalajthanaki/stock_price_prediction/blob/master/datapreparation.ipynb`.

As shown in the preceding figure, we are extracting news articles that belong to the following news categories:

- Business
- National
- World
- U.S.A.
- Politics
- Opinion
- Tech
- Science
- Health
- Foreign

Implementing the filter functionality and merging the dataset

Now, we need to iterate each of the JSON files and extract the news articles that have one of the news categories defined in the previous section. You can refer to the code snippet for the implementation of the filter functionality. In the upcoming code snippet, you can also find the implementation for merging the DJIA dataset and the NYTimes news articles dataset. To merge the two datasets, we are adding each of the news article headlines to the pandas dataframe,and from this we will generate our final training dataset. This functionality is shown in the following screenshot:

```
## Adding article column to dataframe
interpolated_df["articles"] = ''
count_articles_filtered = 0
count_total_articles = 0
count_main_not_exist = 0
count_unicode_error = 0
count_attribute_error = 0
for year in years:
    for month in months:
        file_str = './data/nytimes/' + str(year) + '-' + '{:02}'.format(month) + '.json'
        with open(file_str) as data_file:
            NYTimes_data = json.load(data_file)
        count_total_articles = count_total_articles + len(NYTimes_data["response"]["docs"][:])
        for i in range(len(NYTimes_data["response"]["docs"][:])):
            try:
                if any(substring in NYTimes_data["response"]["docs"][:][i]['type_of_material'].lower()
                       for substring in type_of_material_list):
                    if any(substring in NYTimes_data["response"]["docs"][:][i]['section_name'].lower()
                           for substring in section_name_list):
                        #count += 1
                        count_articles_filtered += 1
                        #print 'i: ' + str(i)
                        articles_dict = { your_key: NYTimes_data["response"]["docs"][:][i][your_key]
                                         for your_key in dict_keys }
                        # Selecting just 'main' from headline
                        articles_dict['headline'] = articles_dict['headline']['main']

                        # Selecting lead paragraph
                        #articles_dict['headline'] = articles_dict['lead_paragraph']
                        date = try_parsing_date(articles_dict['pub_date'])
                        #print 'article_dict: ' + articles_dict['headline']
                        if date == current_date:
                            current_article_str = current_article_str + '. ' + articles_dict['headline']
                        else:
                            interpolated_df.set_value(current_date, 'articles',
                                                      interpolated_df.loc[current_date,'articles']
                                                      + '. ' + current_article_str)
                            current_date = date
                            #interpolated_df.set_value(date, 'articles', current_article_str)
                            #print str(date) + current_article_str
                            current_article_str = articles_dict['headline']
                        # For last condition in a year
                        if (date == current_date) and (i == len(NYTimes_data["response"]["docs"][:]) - 1):
                            interpolated_df.set_value(date, 'articles', current_article_str)
```

Figure 2.11: Code snippet for the filtering and merging functionalities

We have also coded a bit of the exceptional handling functionality. This is done so that if any JSON response does not have the value for the data attributes section_name, news_desk, or type_of_material, then this code will throw an exception. You can refer to the code snippet in the following screenshot:

```
    #Exception for section_name or type_of_material absent
    except AttributeError:
        #print 'attribute error'
        #print NYTimes_data["response"]["docs"][:][i]
        count_attribute_error += 1
        # If article matches news_desk_list if none section_name found
        try:
            if any(substring in NYTimes_data["response"]["docs"][:][i]['news_desk'].lower()
                   for substring in news_desk_list):
                    #count += 1
                    count_articles_filtered += 1
                    #print 'i: ' + str(i)
                    articles_dict = { your_key: NYTimes_data["response"]["docs"][:][i][your_key]
                                     for your_key in dict_keys }
                    # Selecting just 'main' from headline
                    articles_dict['headline'] = articles_dict['headline']['main']
                    # Selecting lead_paragraph
                    #articles_dict['headline'] = articles_dict['lead_paragraph']
                    date = try_parsing_date(articles_dict['pub_date'])
                    #print 'article_dict: ' + articles_dict['headline']
                    if date == current_date:
                        current_article_str = current_article_str + '. ' + articles_dict['headline']
                    else:
                        interpolated_df.set_value(current_date, 'articles',
                                                  interpolated_df.loc[current_date, 'articles']
                                                  + '. ' + current_article_str)
                        current_date = date
                        #interpolated_df.set_value(date, 'articles', current_article_str)
                        #print str(date) + current_article_str
                        current_article_str = articles_dict['headline']
                    # For last condition in a year
                    if (date == current_date) and (i == len(NYTimes_data["response"]["docs"][:]) - 1):
                        interpolated_df.set_value(date, 'articles', current_article_str)

        except AttributeError:
            pass
        pass
    except KeyError:
        print 'key error'
        #print NYTimes_data["response"]["docs"][:][i]
        count_main_not_exist += 1
        pass
    except TypeError:
        print "type error"
        #print NYTimes_data["response"]["docs"][:][i]
        count_main_not_exist += 1
        pass
```

Figure 2.12: Implementation of exception handling

We will consider news articles that have no `section_name` and `news_desk` as well. We will add all the news article headlines to our dataset and put them into the pandas dataframe. You can see the code snippet in the following screenshot:

```
# Putting all articles if no section_name or news_desk not found
for date, row in interpolated_df.T.iteritems():
    if len(interpolated_df.loc[date, 'articles']) <= 400:
        #print interpolated_df.loc[date, 'articles']
        #print date
        month = date.month
        year = date.year
        file_str = './data/nytimes/' + str(year) + '-' + '{:02}'.format(month) + '.json'
        with open(file_str) as data_file:
            NYTimes_data = json.load(data_file)
        count_total_articles = count_total_articles + len(NYTimes_data["response"]["docs"][:])
        interpolated_df.set_value(date.strftime('%Y-%m-%d'), 'articles', '')
        for i in range(len(NYTimes_data["response"]["docs"][:])):
            try:

                articles_dict = { your_key: NYTimes_data["response"]["docs"][:][i][your_key]
                                  for your_key in dict_keys }
                articles_dict['headline'] = articles_dict['headline']['main'] # Selecting just 'main' from headline
                #articles_dict['headline'] = articles_dict['lead_paragraph'] # Selecting lead_paragraph
                pub_date = try_parsing_date(articles_dict['pub_date'])
                #print 'article_dict: ' + articles_dict['headline']
                if date.strftime('%Y-%m-%d') == pub_date:
                    interpolated_df.set_value(pub_date, 'articles', interpolated_df.loc[pub_date, 'articles']
                                              + '. ' + articles_dict['headline'])

            except KeyError:
                print 'key error'
                #print NYTimes_data["response"]["docs"][:][i]
                #count_main_not_exist += 1
                pass
            except TypeError:
                print "type error"
                #print NYTimes_data["response"]["docs"][:][i]
                #count_main_not_exist += 1
                pass
```

Figure 2.13: Handling news articles that have no section_name and news_desk

You can see the final merged dataset in the form of the pandas dataframe, as shown in the following screenshot:

```
interpolated_df.head()
```

	close	adj close	articles
2007-01-01	12469.971875	260944000.0	. Estimates of Iraqi Civilian Deaths. Romania ...
2007-01-02	12472.245703	294072000.0	. For Dodd, Wall Street Looms Large. Ford's Lo...
2007-01-03	12474.519531	327200000.0	. Ethics Changes Proposed for House Trips, K S...
2007-01-04	12480.690430	259060000.0	. I Feel Bad About My Face. Bush Recycles the ...
2007-01-05	12398.009766	235220000.0	. Macworld Bingo. Anti-Surge Protests Against ...

Figure 2.14: Final merged training dataset

Here, for each date, we correspond all the news headlines that belong to the business, national, world, U.S.A., politics, opinion, technology, science, and heath categories. We have downloaded 1,248,084 news articles, and from these articles, we have considered 461,738 news articles for our model.

You can access the code using this GitHub link: `https://github.com/jalajthanaki/stock_price_prediction/blob/master/datapreparation.ipynb`.

Saving the merged dataset in the pickle file format

Once we merge the data, we need to save the data objects, so we will use the pickle module of Python. Pickle helps us serialize and de-serialize the data. The pickle dependency library is fast because the bulk of it is written in C, like the Python interpreter itself. Here, we save our training dataset as a `.pkl` file format. You can refer to the following code snippet:

```
# Saving the data as pickle file
interpolated_df.to_pickle('./data/pickled_ten_year_filtered_lead_para.pkl')


# Save pandas frame in csv form
interpolated_df.to_csv('./data/sample_interpolated_df_10_years_filtered_lead_para.csv',
                       sep='\t', encoding='utf-8')



# Reading the data as pickle file
# dataframe_read = pd.read_pickle('./data/pickled_ten_year_filtered_lead_para.pkl')
```

Figure 2.15: Code snippet for saving data in the pickle format

We have saved the dataset as the `pickled_ten_year_filtered_lead_para.pkl` file. You can find the code on GitHub at `https://github.com/jalajthanaki/stock_price_prediction/blob/master/datapreparation.ipynb`.

In the next section, we will mainly focus on the feature engineering part. We will also perform some minor data cleaning steps. So let's jump to the next section.

Feature engineering

As discussed earlier, we want to predict the close price for the DJIA index for a particular trading day. In this section, we will do feature selection based on our intuition for our basic prediction model for stock prices. We have already generated the training dataset. So, now we will load the saved .pkl format dataset and perform feature selection as well as minor data processing. We will also generate the sentiment score for each of the filtered NYTimes news articles and will use this sentiment score to train our baseline model. We will use the following Python dependencies:

- numpy
- pandas
- nltk

This section has the following steps:

1. Loading the dataset
2. Minor preprocessing
3. Feature selection
4. Sentiment analysis

So, let's begin coding!

Loading the dataset

We have saved the data in the pickle format, and now we need to load data from it. You can refer to the following code snippet:

Import dependencies

```
import numpy as np
import pandas as pd
from nltk.classify import NaiveBayesClassifier
from nltk.corpus import subjectivity
from nltk.sentiment import SentimentAnalyzer
from nltk.sentiment.util import *
import matplotlib.pyplot as plt
%matplotlib inline
```

Load dataset

```
# Reading the saved data pickle file
df_stocks = pd.read_pickle('./data/pickled_ten_year_filtered_lead_para.pkl')
```

Figure 2.16: Code snippet for loading the dataset from the pickle file

You can refer to the code by clicking on this GitHub link: `https://github.com/jalajthanaki/stock_price_prediction/blob/master/Stock_Price_Prediction.ipynb`.

As you can see, in the dataframe output, there is a dot (.) before every article headline in the entire dataset, so we need to remove these dots. We will execute this change in the next section.

Minor preprocessing

As a part of minor preprocessing, we will be performing the following two changes:

- Converting the adj close prices into the integer format
- Removing the leftmost dot (.) from news headlines

Converting adj close price into the integer format

We know that the adj close price is in the form of a float format. So, here we will convert float values into the integer format as well as store the converted values as *price* attributes in our pandas dataframe. Now, you may wonder why we consider only the adj close prices. Bear with me for a while, and I will give you the reason for that. You can find the convergence code snippet in the following screenshot:

```
df_stocks['prices'] = df_stocks['adj close'].apply(np.int64)

# selecting the prices and articles
df_stocks = df_stocks[['prices', 'articles']]

df_stocks.head()
```

	prices	articles
2007-01-01	12469	. Estimates of Iraqi Civilian Deaths. Romania ...
2007-01-02	12472	. For Dodd, Wall Street Looms Large. Ford's Lo...
2007-01-03	12474	. Ethics Changes Proposed for House Trips, K S...
2007-01-04	12480	. I Feel Bad About My Face. Bush Recycles the ...
2007-01-05	12398	. Macworld Bingo. Anti-Surge Protests Against ...

Figure 2.17: Code snippet for converting the adj close price into the integer format

[You can refer to the code at this GitHub link: `https://github.com/jalajthanaki/stock_price_prediction/blob/master/Stock_Price_Prediction.ipynb`.]

Now, let's move on to the second change.

Removing the leftmost dot from news headlines

In this section, we will see the implementation for removing the leftmost dot. We will be using the `lstrip()` function to remove the dot. You can refer to the code snippet in the following screenshot:

```
df_stocks['articles'] = df_stocks['articles'].map(lambda x: x.lstrip('.-'))
```

```
df_stocks.head()
```

	prices	articles
2007-01-01	12469	Estimates of Iraqi Civilian Deaths. Romania a...
2007-01-02	12472	For Dodd, Wall Street Looms Large. Ford's Los...
2007-01-03	12474	Ethics Changes Proposed for House Trips, K St...
2007-01-04	12480	I Feel Bad About My Face. Bush Recycles the T...
2007-01-05	12398	Macworld Bingo. Anti-Surge Protests Against M...

Figure 2.18: Code snippet for removing *dot* from the news article headlines

[You can refer to the code at this GitHub link: `https://github.com/jalajthanaki/stock_price_prediction/blob/master/Stock_Price_Prediction.ipynb`.]

Now, let's move on to our next section, which is feature engineering.

Feature engineering

Feature selection is one of the most important aspects of feature engineering and any **Machine Learning** (**ML**) application. So, here we will focus on feature selection. In the previous section, I raised the question of why we select only the *adj close price* and not the *close price*. The answer to this question lies in the feature selection. We select the *adj close prices* because these prices give us a better idea about what the last price of the DJIA index is, including the stock, mutual funds, dividends, and so on. In our dataset, *close prices* are mostly the same as the *adj close price* and in future, if we consider the *close price* for unseen data records, we can't derive the *adj close price* because it may be equal to the *close price* or higher than the *close price,* The *adj close price* for DJIA index may higher than the *close price* because it will include stocks, mutual funds, dividend and so on. but we don't know how much higher it will be for unseen dataset where we have just considered *close price*. So if we consider the *adj close price,* then we will know that the *close price* may be less than or equal to the *adj close price*, but not more than the *adj close price*. The *adj close price* is kind of maximum possible value for closing price. So, we have considered the *adj close price* for the development. For the baseline model, we will be considering the *adj close price*. We have renamed the column to *price*. You can refer to the following code snippet:

```
df = df_stocks[['prices']].copy()
df.head
```

	prices
2007-01-01	12469
2007-01-02	12472
2007-01-03	12474
2007-01-04	12480
2007-01-05	12398

Figure 2.19: Code snippet for considering the adj close price as a part of feature selection

As a next step, we will now perform sentiment analysis on the news article dataset. We can use the sentiment score when we train our model. So, let's move on to the sentiment analysis part.

Sentiment analysis of NYTimes news articles

In order to implement sentiment analysis, we are using the nltk inbuilt sentiment analysis module. We will obtain negative, positive, and compound sentiment scores. We have used a lexicon-based approach. In the lexicon-based approach, words of each sentence are analyzed, and based on the `sentiwordnet` score, each word is given a specific sentiment score; then, the aggregate sentence level score is decided.

> Sentiwordnet is the dictionary which contain sentiment score for words.

We will cover details related to sentiment analysis in *Chapter 5, Sentiment Analysis*. You can refer to the following sentiment analysis code snippet:

```
from nltk.sentiment.vader import SentimentIntensityAnalyzer
nltk.download('vader_lexicon')
import unicodedata
sid = SentimentIntensityAnalyzer()
for date, row in df_stocks.T.iteritems():
    try:
        sentence = unicodedata.normalize('NFKD', df_stocks.loc[date, 'articles']).encode('ascii','ignore')
        ss = sid.polarity_scores(sentence)
        df.set_value(date, 'compound', ss['compound'])
        df.set_value(date, 'neg', ss['neg'])
        df.set_value(date, 'neu', ss['neu'])
        df.set_value(date, 'pos', ss['pos'])
    except TypeError:
        print df_stocks.loc[date, 'articles']
        print date
```

```
[nltk_data] Downloading package vader_lexicon to
[nltk_data]     /home/jalaj/nltk_data...
[nltk_data]   Package vader_lexicon is already up-to-date!

2007-04-20 00:00:00
```

Figure 2.20: Sentiment analysis code snippet

All scores generated by the preceding code are stored in the dataframe, so you can see the aggregate score of news article headlines in the following screenshot:

```
df.head()
```

	prices	compound	neg	neu	pos
2007-01-01	12469	-0.9881	0.176	0.723	0.102
2007-01-02	12472	-0.9834	0.131	0.772	0.097
2007-01-03	12474	-0.9995	0.204	0.745	0.051
2007-01-04	12480	-0.9975	0.112	0.835	0.053
2007-01-05	12398	-0.9882	0.118	0.8	0.082

Figure 2.21: Aggregate sentiment analysis score stored in the dateframe

By the end of this section, we will obtain the sentiment score for the NYTimes news articles dataset and combine these sentiment scores as part of the training dataset. So far, we have done minor preprocessing, selected the data attribute as per our intuition, and generated the sentiment score. Now, we will select the machine learning algorithm and try to build the baseline model. So, let's move on to the next section.

Selecting the Machine Learning algorithm

In this section, we will choose the Machine Learning (ML) algorithm based on our intuition and then perform training using our training dataset. This is the first model for this particular chapter, so the trained model is our baseline model, which we will improve later on. So, let's decide which kind of ML algorithm suits this stock price prediction application.

The stock price prediction application is a time-series analysis problem, where we need to predict the next point in the time series. This prediction activity is similar to linear regression, so we can say that this application is a kind of regression problem and any algorithm from the regression family should work. Let's select the ensemble algorithm, which is *RandomForestRegressor*, in order to develop our baseline model. So let's train our baseline model, and, based on the result of that model, we will modify our approach.

Training the baseline model

As you know, we have selected the **RandomForestRegressor** algorithm. We will be using the scikit learn library to train the model. These are the steps we need to follow:

1. Splitting the training and testing dataset
2. Splitting prediction labels for the training and testing dataset
3. Converting sentiment scores into the numpy array
4. Training the ML model

So, let's implement each of these steps one by one.

Splitting the training and testing dataset

We have 10 years of data values. So for training purposes, we will be using 8 years of the data, which means the dataset from 2007 to 2014. For testing purposes, we will be using 2 years of the data, which means data from 2015 and 2016. You can refer to the code snippet in the following screenshot to implement this:

Split training and testing data

```
train_start_date = '2007-01-01'
train_end_date = '2014-12-31'
test_start_date = '2015-01-01'
test_end_date = '2016-12-31'
train = df.loc[train_start_date : train_end_date]
test = df.loc[test_start_date:test_end_date]
```

Figure 2.22: Splitting the training and testing dataset

As you can see from the preceding screenshot, our training dataset has been stored in the train dataframe and our testing dataset has been stored in the test dataframe.

Splitting prediction labels for the training and testing datasets

As we split the training and testing dataset, we also need to store the adj close price separately because we need to predict these *adj close prices* (indicated in the code as `prices`); these price values are labels for our training data, and this training becomes supervised training as we will provide the actual price in the form of labels. You can refer to the following code for the implementation:

Split prediction labels for training and testing dataset

```
y_train = pd.DataFrame(train['prices'])
y_test = pd.DataFrame(test['prices'])
```

Figure 2.23: Splitting the prediction labels for training and testing datasets

Here, all attributes except the price are given in a feature vector format and the price is in the form of labels. The ML algorithm takes this feature vector, labels the pair, learns the necessary pattern, and predicts the price for the unseen data.

Converting sentiment scores into the numpy array

Before we start the training, there is one last, necessary point that we need to keep in mind: we are converting the sentiment analysis scores into the numpy array format. This is because once we set the price attribute as a prediction label, our features vector will contain only the sentiment scores and date. So in order to generate a proper feature vector, we have converted the sentiment score into a numpy array. The code snippet to implement this is provided in the following screenshot:

```
sentiment_score_list = []
for date, row in train.T.iteritems():
    #sentiment_score = np.asarray([df.loc[date, 'compound'],
                                   #df.loc[date, 'neg'],df.loc[date, 'neu'],df.loc[date, 'pos']])
    sentiment_score = np.asarray([df.loc[date, 'neg'],df.loc[date, 'pos']])
    sentiment_score_list.append(sentiment_score)
numpy_df_train = np.asarray(sentiment_score_list)
```

```
sentiment_score_list = []
for date, row in test.T.iteritems():
    #sentiment_score = np.asarray([df.loc[date, 'compound'],
                                   #df.loc[date, 'neg'],df.loc[date, 'neu'],df.loc[date, 'pos']])
    sentiment_score = np.asarray([df.loc[date, 'neg'],df.loc[date, 'pos']])
    sentiment_score_list.append(sentiment_score)
numpy_df_test = np.asarray(sentiment_score_list)
```

Figure 2.24: Code snippet for converting sentiment analysis score into the numpy array

As you can see from the code snippet, we have performed the same conversion operation for both training the dataset and testing the dataset.

> Note that if you get a value error, check the dataset because there may be a chance that a column in the dataset has a blank or null value.

Now, let's train our model!

Training of the ML model

In the first iteration, we use the RandomForestRegressor algorithm, which is provided as part of the scikit-learn dependency. You can find the code for this in the following screenshot:

```
from treeinterpreter import treeinterpreter as ti
from sklearn.tree import DecisionTreeRegressor
from sklearn.ensemble import RandomForestRegressor
from sklearn.metrics import classification_report,confusion_matrix

rf = RandomForestRegressor()
rf.fit(numpy_df_train, y_train)

/usr/local/lib/python2.7/dist-packages/ipykernel_launcher.py:7: DataConversionWarning: A column-vector y was passed
when a 1d array was expected. Please change the shape of y to (n_samples,), for example using ravel().
  import sys

RandomForestRegressor(bootstrap=True, criterion='mse', max_depth=None,
           max_features='auto', max_leaf_nodes=None,
           min_impurity_split=1e-07, min_samples_leaf=1,
           min_samples_split=2, min_weight_fraction_leaf=0.0,
           n_estimators=10, n_jobs=1, oob_score=False, random_state=None,
           verbose=0, warm_start=False)
```

Figure 2.25: Code snippet for training using RandomForestRegressor

As you can see from the preceding screenshot, we have used all the default values for our hyperparameters. For a more detailed description regarding hyperparameters, you can refer to `http://scikit-learn.org/stable/modules/generated/sklearn.ensemble.RandomForestRegressor.html`.

Now that our model has been trained, we need to test it using our testing dataset. Before we test, let's discuss the approach we will take to test our model.

Understanding the testing matrix

In this section, we will understand the testing matrix and visualization approaches to evaluate the performance of the trained ML model. So let's understand both approaches, which are as follows:

- The default testing matrix
- The visualization approach

The default testing matrix

We are using the default score API of scikit-learn to check how well the ML is performing. In this application, the score function is the coefficient of the sum of the squared error. It is also called the coefficient of R2, which is defined by the following equation:

$$1-\frac{u}{v}$$

Here, *u* indicates the residual sum of squares. The equation for *u* is as follows:

$$u=\left(\left(y_{true}-y_{prediction}\right)^{2}\right).sum(\ )$$

The variable *v* indicates the total sum of squares. The equation for *v* is as follows:

$$u=\left(\left(y_{true}-y_{true}.mean(\ )\right)^{2}\right).sum(\ )$$

The best possible score is 1.0, and it can be a negative score as well. A negative score indicates that the trained model can be arbitrarily worse. A constant model that always predicts the expected value for label *y*, disregarding the input features, will produce an R2 score of 0.0.

In order to obtain the score, we just need to call the score function. The code for testing will be the same as that in the *Test baseline model* section. Now let's take a look at another testing approach that is quite helpful in understanding the output with respect to true testing labels. So, let's check that out!

The visualization approach

In this section, we will be exploring an effective and intuitive approach, which is the **visualization** of the predicted output versus real output. This approach gives you a lot of insight as the graphs are easy to understand and you can decide the next steps to improve the model.

In this application, we will be using the actual prices from the testing dataset and the predicted prices for the testing dataset, which will indicate how good or bad the predictions are. You will find the code and graph for this process in the next section, named *Testing the baseline model.*

Testing the baseline model

In this section, we will be implementing our testing approach so that we can evaluate our model's accuracy. We will first generate the output prediction and then we'll start testing it. We will be implementing the following steps here:

1. Generating and interpreting the output
2. Generating the score
3. Visualizing the output

Generating and interpreting the output

To generate the prediction, we are using the `treeinterpreter` library. We are predicting the price value for each of our testing dataset records using the following code:

```
prediction, bias, contributions = ti.predict(rf, numpy_df_test)
print prediction
#print contributions
```

```
[ 14375.5          15544.9          13681.5          13322.2          11868.1
  12379.9           9534.8          12996.3          12992.8          13468.7
  13851.9          10898.16583333  13191.3          13651.8          11418.2
  13789.           11855.9          11009.93833333  13529.8          11548.5
  11513.9          12917.5          12618.36666667  11767.4          15437.3
  11756.2          12535.6          13381.14166667  11130.55         12949.06
  10225.5          14899.3          12566.7          12495.53333333  13998.4
  13371.6          13818.53333333  13088.           12582.63333333  13640.8
  11828.41666667  11248.25         12962.9          12065.5          14768.5
  13955.3          13168.16666667  13072.8          14048.325        12649.3
  13288.75         12715.96666667   9876.7          12388.2          14269.7
  13369.6          13825.2          12609.6          13389.16666667  14620.45
  10390.6          12211.           13521.2          12311.6          14263.
  14884.6          11286.8          14526.5          13752.8          12199.595
  13843.1          13002.6          12275.2           9574.9          12354.18333333
  13081.7          12144.           13402.15         12249.69333333  10138.3
  10208.1          12153.77666667  10600.41666667  12176.3          14180.2
  11610.4          13910.8          10236.8          13552.05833333  14305.21
  11992.7          13800.83333333  11208.93333333  12703.7           9232.9
```

Figure 2.26: Code snippet for generating the prediction

Here, *prediction* is the array in which we have elements that are the corresponding predicted *adj close price* for all records of the testing dataset. Now, we will compare this predicted output with the actual *adj close price* of the testing dataset. By doing this, we will get to know how accurately our first model is predicting the *adj close price*. In order to evaluate further, we will generate the accuracy score.

Generating the accuracy score

In this section, we will generate the accuracy score as per the equations provided in the *default testing matrix* section. The code for this is as follows:

```
rf.score(numpy_df_test,y_test)
-43.74194279056055
```

Figure 2.27: Code snippet for generating the score for the test dataset

As you can see from the preceding code snippet, our model is not doing too well. At this point, we don't know what mistakes we've made or what went wrong. This kind of situation is common when you are trying to solve or build an ML model. We can grasp the problem better using visualization techniques.

Visualizing the output

We will be using the visualization graph in this section. Using the graph, we will identify the kind of error we have committed so that we can fix that error in the next iteration. We will plot a graph where the *y-axis* represents the *adj close prices* and the *x-axis* represent the *dates*. We plot the *actual prices* and *predicted prices* on the graph so that we will get a brief idea about how our algorithm is performing. We will use the following code snippet to generate the graph:

```
idx = pd.date_range(test_start_date, test_end_date)
predictions_df = pd.DataFrame(data=prediction[0:], index = idx, columns=['prices'])
```

```
predictions_df.head()
```

	prices
2015-01-01	14737.3
2015-01-02	13901.8
2015-01-03	14009.4
2015-01-04	13098.6
2015-01-05	9541.3

```
ax = predictions_df.rename(columns=
                    {"prices": "predicted_price"}).plot(title=
                    'Random Forest predicted prices 8-2 years')
ax.set_xlabel("Dates")
ax.set_ylabel("Adj Close Prices")
fig = y_test.rename(columns={"prices": "actual_price"}).plot(ax = ax).get_figure()
fig.savefig("./graphs/random forest without smoothing.png")
```

```
# colors = ['332288', '88CCEE', '44AA99', '117733', '999933', 'DDCC77', 'CC6677', '882255', 'AA4499']
```

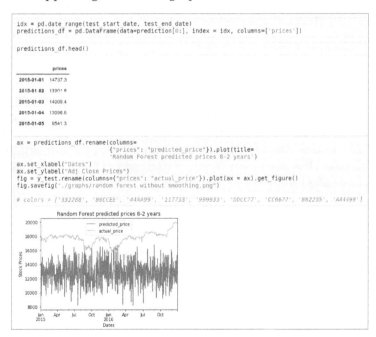

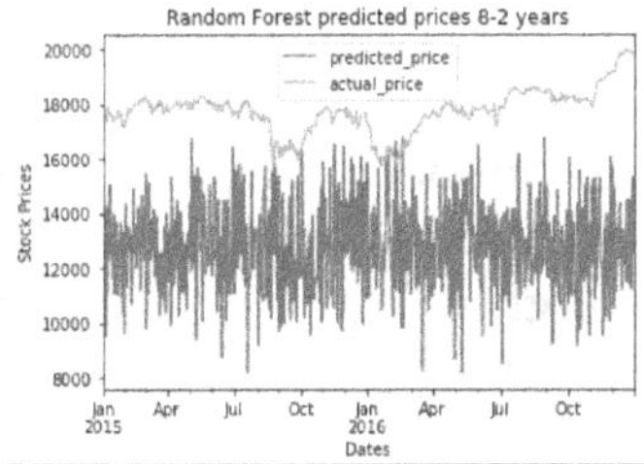

Figure 2.28: Code snippet for generating graph for predicted prices vs actual prices.

As you can see from the preceding graph, the top single line (orange color) represents the actual price and the messy spikes (blue color) below the line represent the predicted prices. From this plot, we can summarize that our model can't predict the proper prices. Here, you can see that the actual prices and predicted prices are not aligned with each other. We need to fix this issue. There are some techniques that we can try, such as alignment, smoothing, and trying a different algorithm. So, let's cover the problems of this approach in the next section.

> You can access the entire code on this topic from the GitHub link at `https://github.com/jalajthanaki/stock_price_prediction/blob/master/Stock_Price_Prediction.ipynb`.

Exploring problems with the existing approach

In this section, we will be discussing the problems of the existing approach. There are mainly three errors we could have possibly committed, which are listed as follows:

- Alignment
- Smoothing
- Trying a different ML algorithm

Let's discuss each of the points one by one.

Alignment

As we have seen in the graph, our actual price and predicted prices are not aligned with each other. This becomes a problem. We need to perform alignment on the price of the stocks. We need to consider the average value of our dataset, and based on that, we will generate the alignment. You can understand more about alignment in upcoming section called *Alignment-based approach*.

Smoothing

The second problem I feel we have with our first model is that we haven't applied any smoothing techniques. So for our model, we need to apply smoothing techniques as well. We will be using the **Exponentially Weighted Moving Average** (**EWMA**) technique for smoothing. This technique is used to adjust the variance of the dataset.

Trying a different ML algorithm

For our model, we have used the `RandomForestRegressor` algorithm. But what if we try the same thing with our model using a different algorithm, say *Logistic Regression*? In the next section, you will learn how to implement this algorithm—after applying the necessary alignment and smoothing, of course.

We have seen the possible problems with our first baseline approach. Now, we will try to understand the approach for implementing the alignment, smoothing, and `Logistic Regression` algorithms.

Understanding the revised approach

In this section, we will be looking at the key concepts and approaches for alignment and smoothing. It is not that difficult to implement the *Logistic Regression* algorithm; we will be using the scikit-learn API. So, we will start with understanding the concepts and approaches for implementation.

Understanding concepts and approaches

Here, we will discuss how alignment and smoothing will work. Once we understand the technicality behind alignment and smoothing, we will focus on the Logistic Regression-based approach.

Alignment-based approach

Using this approach, we will be increasing the prices using a constant value so that our predicted price and actual price in testing the dataset will be aligned. Suppose we take 10 days into consideration. We will generate the average of the value of the prices. After that, we generate the average value for the prices that have been predicted by the first ML model. Once we generate both average values, we need to subtract the values, and the answer is the alignment value for those `10` days.

Let's take an intuitive working example that will help clear your vision. Consider 10 days from January 2, 2015, to January 11, 2015. For each record, you will take the average value for the actual price. Suppose the number will come to 17,676 and the average of predicted price value will be 13,175. In this case, you will get a difference of 4,501, which is the value for the alignment. We will add this value to our testing dataset so that testing price values and predicted price values will be aligned. You will find the code implementation in the *Implement revised approach* section.

Smoothing-based approach

In this approach, we will be using EWMA. **EWMA** stands for **Exponentially Weighted Moving Average**. The smoothing approach is based on the weighted average concept. In general, a weighted moving average is calculated by the following equation:

$$y_t = \frac{\sum_{i=0}^{t} w_i x_{t-i}}{\sum_{i=0}^{t} w_i}$$

Here, x_t is the input and y_t is the output. Weights are calculated using the following equations:

The EW functions support two variants of exponential weights. The default, `adjust=True`, uses the weights $w_i = (1-\alpha)^i$ which gives

$$y_t = \frac{x_t + (1-\alpha)x_{t-1} + (1-\alpha)^2 x_{t-2} + \ldots + (1-\alpha)^t x_0}{1 + (1-\alpha) + (1-\alpha)^2 + \ldots + (1-\alpha)^t}$$

When `adjust=False` is specified, moving averages are calculated as

$$y_0 = x_0$$
$$y_t = (1-\alpha)y_{t-1} + \alpha x_t,$$

which is equivalent to using weights

$$w_i = \begin{cases} \alpha(1-\alpha)^i & \text{if } i < t \\ (1-\alpha)^i & \text{if } i = t. \end{cases}$$

Figure 2.29: Equation for calculating the weight for EWMA

Image source: http://pandas.pydata.org/pandas-docs/stable/computation.html#exponentially-weighted-windows

Here, α is the smoothing constant. If the value of the smoothing constant is high, then it will be close to the actual value, and if the smoothing constant is low, then it will be smoother but not close to the actual value. Typically, in statistics the smoothing constant ranges between 0.1 and 0.3. Therefore, we can generate the smoothed value using the smoothing constant.

Let's take a working example. Take a smoothing constant = 0.3; if the actual value is 100 and the predicted value is 110, then the smoothed value can be obtain using this equation, which is (smoothing constant * actual value) + (1- smoothing constant) * predicted value. The value that we will obtain is *(0.3* 100) + (1-0.3)*110 = 107*. For more information, you can refer to `http://pandas.pydata.org/pandas-docs/stable/computation.html#exponentially-weighted-windows`.

We will see the actual code-level implementation in the Implement revised approach section. pandas already has an API, so we can easily implement EWMA.

Logistic Regression-based approach

Implementing the Logistic Regression algorithm is a simple task because we just need to use the scikit-learn API. For the testing dataset, we will apply alignment and smoothing. After evaluating accuracy, we will decide whether we need to change the ML algorithm or not. We started with our intuition and slowly we improved our approaches. I don't really need to explain the Logistic Regression algorithm itself, but during the implementation, we will discuss the important points.

Now, it is time to move on to the implementation part of our revised approach. So, let's take a look at the next section.

Implementing the revised approach

In this section, we will discuss the three parts of implementation, which are as follows:

- Implementation
- Testing the revised approach
- Understanding the problem with the revised approach

Implementation

Here, we are implementing the following:

- Alignment
- Smoothing
- Logistic Regression

We have already discussed the approach and key concepts, so now we just focus on the code part here. You can find all the code at this GitHub link: `https://github.com/jalajthanaki/stock_price_prediction/blob/master/Stock_Price_Prediction.ipynb`.

Implementing alignment

The alignment is performed on the testing dataset. You can refer to the following code snippet:

Alignment of the testing dataset price value and pridicted values

```
from datetime import datetime, timedelta
temp_date = test_start_date
average_last_5_days_test = 0
total_days = 10
for i in range(total_days):
    average_last_5_days_test += test.loc[temp_date, 'prices']
    # Converting string to date time
    temp_date = datetime.strptime(temp_date, "%Y-%m-%d").date()
    # Reducing one day from date time
    difference = temp_date + timedelta(days=1)
    # Converting again date time to string
    temp_date = difference.strftime('%Y-%m-%d')
    #print temp_date
average_last_5_days_test = average_last_5_days_test / total_days
print average_last_5_days_test

temp_date = test_start_date
average_upcoming_5_days_predicted = 0
for i in range(total_days):
    average_upcoming_5_days_predicted += predictions_df.loc[temp_date, 'prices']
    # Converting string to date time
    temp_date = datetime.strptime(temp_date, "%Y-%m-%d").date()
    # Adding one day from date time
    difference = temp_date + timedelta(days=1)
    # Converting again date time to string
    temp_date = difference.strftime('%Y-%m-%d')
    #print temp_date
average_upcoming_5_days_predicted = average_upcoming_5_days_predicted / total_days
print average_upcoming_5_days_predicted
#average train.loc['2013-12-31', 'prices'] - advpredictions_df.loc['2014-01-01', 'prices']
difference_test_predicted_prices = average_last_5_days_test - average_upcoming_5_days_predicted
print difference_test_predicted_prices
```

```
17679
12582.01
5096.99
```

Figure 2.30: Code snippet for alignment on the test dataset

As you can see in the preceding code snippet, we obtain a difference of 10 days *adj close price* using the average price of the last 5 days and the average price of the predicted upcoming 5 days in order to align the test data. Here, we also convert the date from the string into the date format. As you can see, 5096.99 is the difference in the test prediction price, which we will add to our predicted *adj close price* value. We have generated the graph again so we can easily understand that the alignment approach is implemented nicely. You can refer to the following code snippet:

```
predictions_df['prices'] = predictions_df['prices'] + difference_test_predicted_prices
predictions_df.head()
```

	prices
2015-01-01	18210.99
2015-01-02	18984.84
2015-01-03	18867.79
2015-01-04	17426.19
2015-01-05	16273.99

```
ax = predictions_df.rename(columns={"prices": "predicted_price"}).plot(title='Random Forest predicted prices 8-2 yea
ax.set_xlabel("Dates")
ax.set_ylabel("Stock Prices")
fig = y_test.rename(columns={"prices": "actual_price"}).plot(ax = ax).get_figure()
fig.savefig("./graphs/random forest with aligning.png")
```

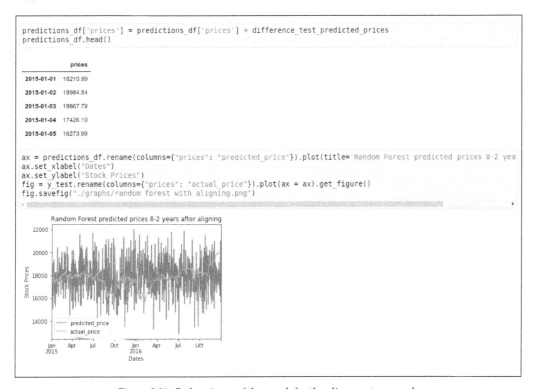

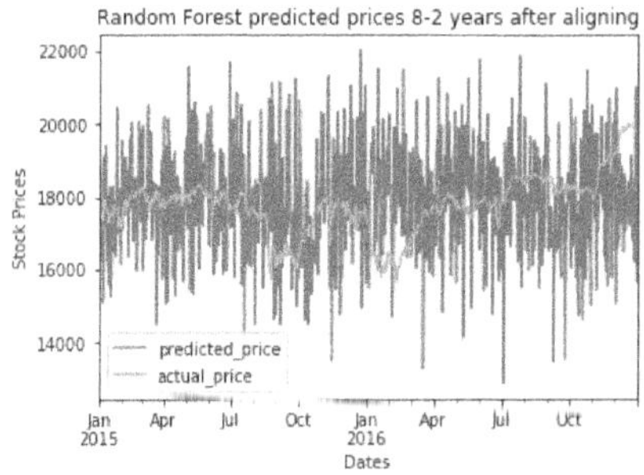

Figure 2.31: Code snippet of the graph for the alignment approach

As you can see in the preceding code snippet, the alignment graph shows that our testing dataset price and predicted prices are aligned. The benefit of the aligned graph is that now we can define in a precise manner that `RandomForestRegressor` didn't do its job with high accuracy as its performance was not great for all data records. The alignment graph gave us a crystal clear picture of our previous iteration. So when we train the logistic regression now, we will evaluate the predicted prices using alignment.

Implementing smoothing

We are using the pandas EWMA API using 60 days' time span and frequency time *D*. This "D" indicates that we are dealing with the datetime format in our dataset. You can see the code implementation in the following code snippet:

Smoothing based approach

Applying EWMA pandas to smooth the stock prices

```
predictions_df['ewma'] = predictions_df["prices"].ewm(span=60, freq="D").mean()
```

```
predictions_df.head()
```

	prices	ewma
2015-01-01	18210.99	18210.990000
2015-01-02	18984.84	18604.363750
2015-01-03	18867.79	18695.115447
2015-01-04	17426.19	18361.849263
2015-01-05	16273.99	17915.983279

```
predictions_df['actual_value'] = test['prices']
predictions_df['actual_value_ewma'] = predictions_df["actual_value"].ewm(span=60, freq="D").mean()
```

```
predictions_df.head()
```

	prices	ewma	actual_value	actual_value_ewma
2015-01-01	18210.99	18210.990000	17828	17828.000000
2015-01-02	18984.84	18604.363750	17832	17830.033333
2015-01-03	18867.79	18695.115447	17722	17792.815295
2015-01-04	17426.19	18361.849263	17612	17745.326592
2015-01-05	16273.99	17915.983279	17501	17693.150223

Figure 2.32: Code snippet for EWMA smoothing

We are also generating the graph in which we put the *predicted price, average predicted price, actual price,* and *average actual price.* You can refer to the following code and graph:

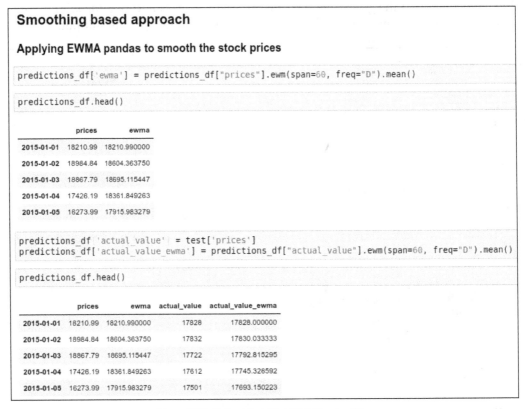

```
# Changing column names
predictions_df.columns = ['predicted_price', 'average_predicted_price', 'actual_price', 'average_actual_price']

# Now plotting test predictions after smoothing
predictions_plot = predictions_df.plot(title='Random Forest predicted prices 8-2 years after aligning & smoothing')
predictions_plot.set_xlabel("Dates")
predictions_plot.set_ylabel("Stock Prices")
fig = predictions_plot.get_figure()
fig.savefig("./graphs/random forest after smoothing.png")
```

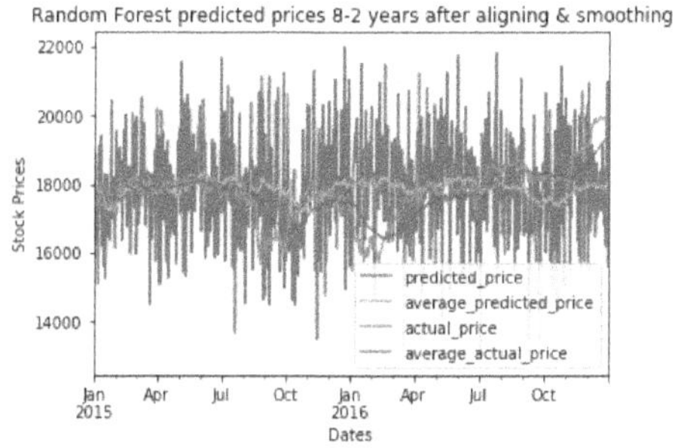

Figure 2.33: Code snippet for generating the graph after smoothing

In this graph, you can see that after smoothing the *average predicted price,* the curve follows the *actual price* trend. Although the accuracy is not great, we will move toward a positive direction. The smoothing technique will be useful for us if we want to tune our algorithm. You can refer to the following graph for the *average predicted price versus actual price:*

```
# Plotting just predict and actual average curves
predictions_df_average = predictions_df[['average_predicted_price', 'actual_price']]
predictions_plot = predictions_df_average.plot(title='Random Forest 8-2 years after aligning & smoothing')
predictions_plot.set_xlabel("Dates")
predictions_plot.set_ylabel("Stock Prices")
fig = predictions_plot.get_figure()
fig.savefig("./graphs/random forest after smoothing 2.png")
```

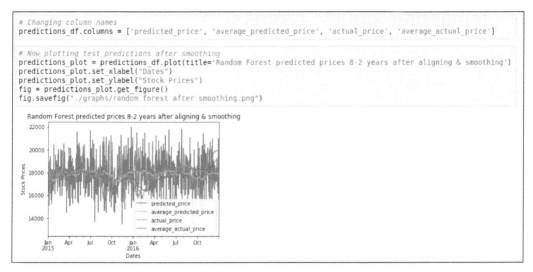

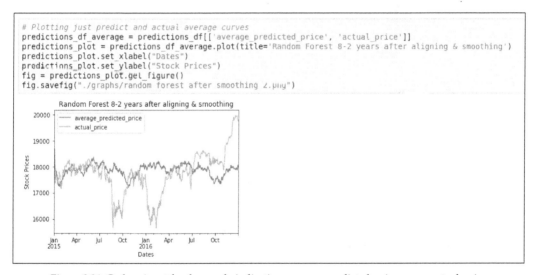

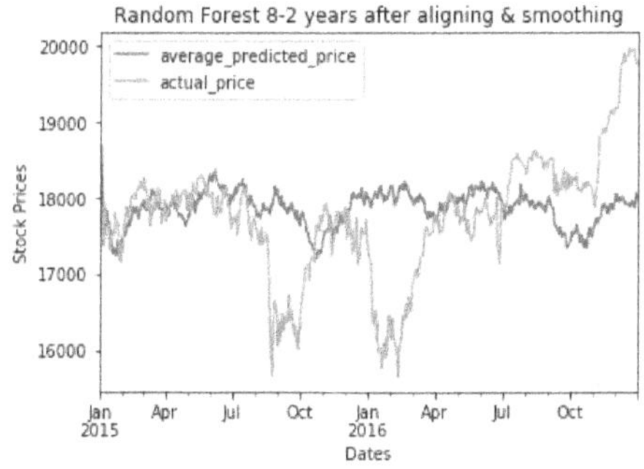

Figure 2.34: Code snippet for the graph, indicating average_predicted_price versus actual_price

By referring to the preceding graph, we can indicate that we apply alignment and smoothing because it helps tune our ML model for the next iteration.

Implementing logistic regression

In this section, we will be implementing logistic regression. Take a look at the following screenshot:

```
years = [2007, 2008, 2009, 2010, 2011, 2012, 2013, 2014, 2015, 2016]
prediction_list = []
for year in years:
    # Splitting the training and testing data
    train_start_date = str(year) + '-01-01'
    train_end_date = str(year) + '-10-31'
    test_start_date = str(year) + '-11-01'
    test_end_date = str(year) + '-12-31'
    train = df.ix[train_start_date : train_end_date]
    test = df.ix[test_start_date:test_end_date]

    # Calculating the sentiment score
    sentiment_score_list = []
    for date, row in train.T.iteritems():
        sentiment_score = np.asarray([df.loc[date, 'compound'],df.loc[date, 'neg'],df.loc[date, 'neu'],df.loc[date, '
        #sentiment_score = np.asarray([df.loc[date, 'neg'],df.loc[date, 'pos']])
        sentiment_score_list.append(sentiment_score)
    numpy_df_train = np.asarray(sentiment_score_list)
    sentiment_score_list = []
    for date, row in test.T.iteritems():
        sentiment_score = np.asarray([df.loc[date, 'compound'],df.loc[date, 'neg'],df.loc[date, 'neu'],df.loc[date, '
        #sentiment_score = np.asarray([df.loc[date, 'neg'],df.loc[date, 'pos']])
        sentiment_score_list.append(sentiment_score)
    numpy_df_test = np.asarray(sentiment_score_list)

    # Generating models
    lr = LogisticRegression()
    lr.fit(numpy_df_train, train['prices'])

    prediction = lr.predict(numpy_df_test)
    prediction_list.append(prediction)

    #print train_start_date + ' ' + train_end_date + ' ' + test_start_date + ' ' + test_end_date
    idx = pd.date_range(test_start_date, test_end_date)
    #print year
    predictions_df_list = pd.DataFrame(data=prediction[0:], index = idx, columns=['prices'])

    difference_test_predicted_prices = offset_value(test_start_date, test, predictions_df_list)
    # Adding offset to all the advpredictions_df price values
    predictions_df_list['prices'] = predictions_df_list['prices'] + difference_test_predicted_prices
    predictions_df_list

    # Smoothing the plot
    predictions_df_list['ewma'] = pd.ewma(predictions_df_list["prices"], span=10, freq="D")
    predictions_df_list['actual_value'] = test['prices']
    predictions_df_list['actual_value_ewma'] = pd.ewma(predictions_df_list["actual_value"], span=10, freq="D")
    # Changing column names
    predictions_df_list.columns = ['predicted_price', 'average_predicted_price', 'actual_price', 'average_actual_pri
    predictions_df_list.plot()
    predictions_df_list_average = predictions_df_list[['average_predicted_price', 'average_actual_price']]
    predictions_df_list_average.plot()
    print lr.score numpy_df_test,test['prices']
```

Figure 2.35: Code snippet for logistic regression

Here, we have trained the model again using the logistic regression ML algorithm. We have also implemented alignment and smoothing for the test dataset. Now, let's evaluate the logistic regression model.

Testing the revised approach

We have tested the logistic regression model. You can refer to the visualization in the form of graphs that show that this revised approach is certainly better than *RandomForesRegressor (without alignment and smoothing)*, but it is not up to the mark:

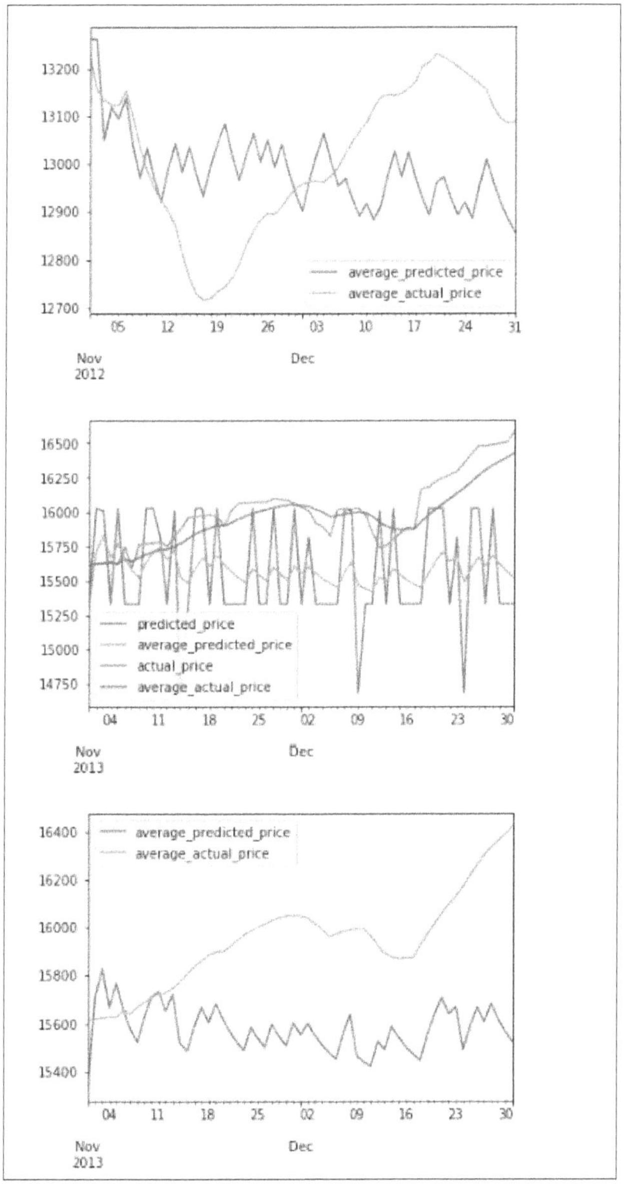

Figure 2.36: Year-wise prediction graph

As you can see in the preceding screenshot, we have generated a year-wise graph for *logistic Regression*; we can see a slight improvement using this model. We have also used alignment and smoothing, but they are not too effective.

Now, let's discuss what the problems with this revised approach are, and then we can implement the best approach.

Understanding the problem with the revised approach

In this section, we will discuss why our revised approach doesn't give us good results. ML models don't work because datasets are not normalized. The second reason is that even after alignment and smoothing, the *RandomForestRegression* ML model faces an overfitting issue. For the best approach, we need to handle normalization and overfitting. We can solve this issue using a neural network-based ML algorithm. So in our last iteration, we will develop the neural network that can give us the best accuracy.

The best approach

Here, we are going to implement the neural network-based algorithm **multilayer perceptron** (**MLP**). You can refer to the following code snippet:

```
years = [2007, 2008, 2009, 2010, 2011, 2012, 2013, 2014, 2015, 2016]
prediction_list = []
for year in years:
    # Splitting the training and testing data
    train_start_date = str(year) + '-01-01'
    train_end_date = str(year) + '-10-31'
    test_start_date = str(year) + '-11-01'
    test_end_date = str(year) + '-12-31'
    train = df.ix[train_start_date : train_end_date]
    test = df.ix[test_start_date:test_end_date]

    # Calculating the sentiment score
    sentiment_score_list = []
    for date, row in train.T.iteritems():
        sentiment_score = np.asarray([df.loc[date, 'compound'],df.loc[date, 'neg'],df.loc[date, 'neu'],df.loc[date, '
        #sentiment_score = np.asarray([df.loc[date, 'neg'],df.loc[date, 'pos']])
        sentiment_score_list.append(sentiment_score)
    numpy_df_train = np.asarray(sentiment_score_list)
    sentiment_score_list = []
    for date, row in test.T.iteritems():
        sentiment_score = np.asarray([df.loc[date, 'compound'],df.loc[date, 'neg'],df.loc[date, 'neu'],df.loc[date, '
        #sentiment_score = np.asarray([df.loc[date, 'neg'],df.loc[date, 'pos']])
        sentiment_score_list.append(sentiment_score)
    numpy_df_test = np.asarray(sentiment_score_list)

    # Generating models
    rf = MLPClassifier(hidden_layer_sizes=(100, 200, 100), activation='relu',
                       solver='adam', alpha=0.0001, learning_rate_init = 0.0001, shuffle=False) # span = 20 # best
    rf.fit(numpy_df_train, train['prices'])
    prediction = rf.predict(numpy_df_test)
    prediction_list.append(prediction)
    #print train_start_date + ' ' + train_end_date + ' ' + test_start_date + ' ' + test_end_date
    idx = pd.date_range(test_start_date, test_end_date)
    #print year
    predictions_df_list = pd.DataFrame(data=prediction[0:], index = idx, columns=['prices'])

    difference_test_predicted_prices = offset_value(test_start_date, test, predictions_df_list)
    # Adding offset to all the advpredictions_df price values
    predictions_df_list['prices'] = predictions_df_list['prices'] + difference_test_predicted_prices
    predictions_df_list

    # Smoothing the plot
    predictions_df_list['ewma'] = pd.ewma(predictions_df_list["prices"], span=20, freq="D")
    predictions_df_list['actual_value'] = test['prices']
    predictions_df_list['actual_value_ewma'] = pd.ewma(predictions_df_list["actual_value"], span=20, freq="D")
    # Changing column names
    predictions_df_list.columns = ['predicted_price', 'average_predicted_price', 'actual_price', 'average_actual_pric
    predictions_df_list.plot()
    predictions_df_list_average = predictions_df_list[['average_predicted_price', 'average_actual_price']]
    predictions_df_list_average.plot()
#    predictions_df_list.show()
```

Figure 2.37: Code snippet for multilayer perceptron

Here, you can see that we are using the Relu activation function, and the gradient descent solver function is ADAM. We are using a learning rate of 0.0001. You can evaluate the result by referring to the following graph:

```
predictions_df1 = pd.DataFrame data=prediction[0:], index = idx, columns=['prices']
predictions_df1.plot()
train['prices'].plot()
```

```
<matplotlib.axes._subplots.AxesSubplot at 0x7fe56523e790>
```

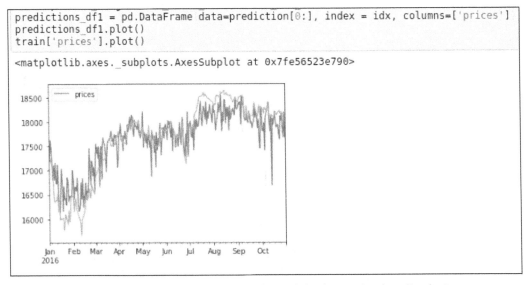

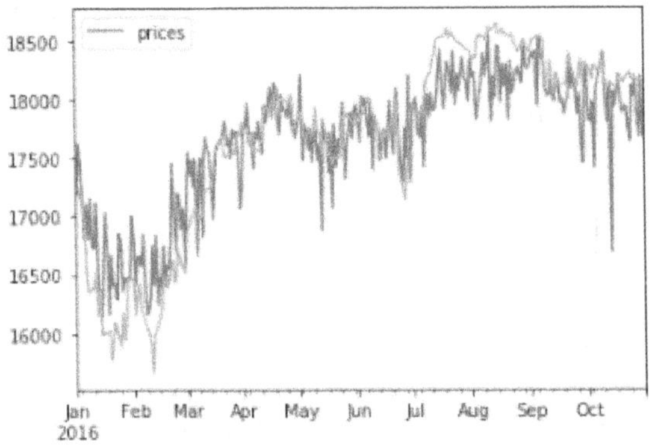

Figure 2.38: Code snippet for generating the graph for the actual and predicted prices

This graph shows that all the data records' predicted prices follow the actual price pattern. You can say that our MLP model works well to predict the stock market prices. You can find the code at this GitHub link: `https://github.com/jalajthanaki/stock_price_prediction/blob/master/Stock_Price_Prediction.ipynb`.

Summary

In this chapter, you learned how to predict stock prices. We covered the different machine learning algorithms that can help us in this. We tried Random Forest Regressor, Logistic Regression, and multilayer perceptron. We found out that the multilayer perceptron works really well. I really want to discuss something beyond what we have done so far. If you are under the impression that using the sentiment analysis of news and predictive methods, we can now correctly predict the stock market price with a hundred percent accuracy, then you would be wrong. We can't predict stock prices with a hundred percent accuracy. Many communities, financial organizations, and academic researchers are working in this direction in order to make a stock market price predictive model that is highly accurate. This is an active research area.

So if you are interested in research and freelancing, then you can join some pretty cool communities. There are two communities that are quite popular. One of these is quantopian (`https://www.quantopian.com/`). In this community, you can submit your stock price prediction algorithm, and if it outperforms other competitors' algorithms, then you will win a cash price, and if you get the license for your algorithm, then you get some profit from transactions that will be done through your licensed algorithm. The second community is numer.ai (`https://numer.ai/`). This community is similar to quantopian. So, the possibilities of this application are limitless. Both communities offer some great tutorials. So try something different, and hopefully you will come up with a great algorithm.

In the next chapter, we will tap the retail or e-commerce domain and try to figure out some interesting facts about the user behavior dataset and users' social footprint. This will help us understand how the company should change their website or some functionality on the website. What are the chances of the email campaign going well and which type of users will respond to this campaign? Keep reading this book! We will discuss all these things in the next chapter.

3
Customer Analytics

Customer analytics is a process in which we use the data of customer behavior to derive the most important business decisions using market segmentation and predictive analytics. Market segmentation is the process of dividing the user base into subgroups based on their behavior and other types of shared characteristics. This will help companies in providing customized products for each user segment. The result of this kind of analysis will lead the company to grow their business in an effective manner. Companies also make more profit. There are a lot of advantages. I know this is only a brief discussion about market segmentation, but just bear with me for a while. I will give you all the necessary information in the upcoming sections.

Companies can use the result generated by market segmentation and predictive models for direct marketing, site selection, customer acquisition, and customer relationship management. In short, with the help of customer analytics, the company can decide the most optimal and effective marketing strategy as well as growth strategy. The company can achieve great results with a limited amount of marking expenditure. Customer analytics include various methods. You can refer to the names of these methods in the following diagram:

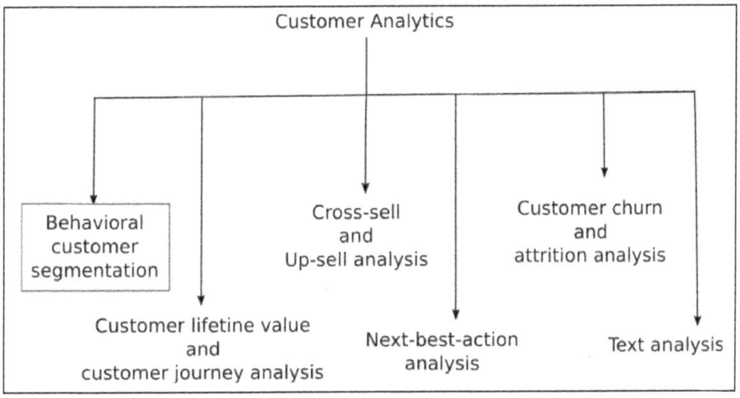

Figure 3.1: Variety of methods for customer analytics

In this chapter, we won't be covering all the methods given in the previous figure, but we will cover the methods that are most widely used in the industry. We will build a customer segmentation application. In this chapter, we will cover the following topics:

- Introducing customer segmentation:
    - Introducing the problem statement
- Understanding the datasets
- Building the baseline approach for customer segmentation:
    - Implementing the baseline approach
    - Understanding the testing matrix
    - Testing the result of the baseline approach
    - Problems with the baseline approach
    - Optimizing the baseline approach
- Building the revised approach for customer segmentation:
    - Implementing the revised approach
    - Testing the revised approach
    - Problems with the revised approach
    - Understanding how to improve the revised approach
- The best approach for customer segmentation:
    - Implementing the best approach
- Testing the best approach
- Customer segmentation for various domains
- Summary

We will start with customer segmentation.

Introducing customer segmentation

In this section, we will cover customer segmentation in detail. Initially, I provided just a brief introduction of customer segmentation so that you could understand the term a bit. Here, we will understand a lot more about customer segmentation, which will help us further when we build the customer segmentation analysis.

As mentioned earlier, customer segmentation is a process where we divide the consumer base of the company into subgroups. We need to generate the subgroups by using some specific characteristics so that the company sells more products with less marketing expenditure. Before moving forward, we need to understand the basics, for example, what do I mean by customer base? What do I mean by segment? How do we generate the consumer subgroup? What are the characteristics that we consider while we are segmenting the consumers? Let's answers these questions one by one.

Basically, the consumer base of any company consists of two types of consumers:

1. Existing consumers
2. Potential consumers

Generally, we need to categorize our consumer base into subgroups. These subgroups are called segments. We need to create the groups in such a way that each subgroup of customers has some shared characteristics. In order to explain how to generate the subgroup, let me give you an example.

Suppose a company is selling baby products. Then, it needs to come up with a consumer segment (consumer subgroup) that includes the consumers who want to buy the baby products. We can build the first segment (subgroup) with the help of a simple criterion. We will include consumers who have one baby in their family and bought a baby product in the last month. Now, the company launches a baby product that is too costly or premium. In that case, we can further divide the first subgroup into monthly income and socio-economic status. Based on these new criteria, we can generate the second subgroup of consumers. The company will target the consumers of the second subgroup for the costly and premium products, and for general products, the company will target consumers who are part of the first subgroup.

When we have different segments, we can design a customized marketing strategy as well as customized products that suit the customer of the particular segment. This segment-wise marketing will help the company sell more products with lower marketing expenses. Thus, the company will make more profit. This is the main reason why companies use customer segmentation analysis nowadays. Customer segmentation is used among other domain such as the retail domain, finance domain, and in customer relationship management (CRM)-based products. I have provided a list of the basic features that can be considered during the segmentation. You can refer to them in the following screenshot:

Segmentation base	Brief explanation of base and examples
Demographic	Quantifiable population characteristics. (e.g. age, gender, income, education, socioeconomic status, family size or situation)
Geographic	Physical location or region. (e.g. country, state, region, city, suburb, postcode).
Geo-demographic or geoclusters	Combination of geographic & demographic variables. (e.g. Rural farmers, Urban professionals)
Psychographics	Lifestyle, social or personality characteristics. (e.g. Socially Aware; Traditionalists, Conservatives, Active 'club-going' young professionals)
Behavioural	Purchasing, consumption or usage behaviour. (e.g. Needs-based, benefit-sought, usage occasion, purchase frequency, customer loyalty, buyer readiness).
Contextual and situational	The same consumer changes in their attractiveness to marketers based on context and situation. This is particularly used in digital targeting via programmatic bidding approaches (e.g. Actively shopping, just entering into a life change event, being physically in a certain location or at a particular retailer which is known from GPS data via smart phones.)

Figure 3.2: List of basic features used in customer segmentation

You may wonder how companies are making marketing strategies based on the customer segmentation analysis. The answer is companies are using the STP approach to make the marketing strategy firm. What is the STP approach? First of all, STP stands for Segmentation-Targeting-Positioning. In this approach, there are three stages. The points that we handle in each stage are explained as follows:

- **Segmentation**: In this stage, we create segments of our customer base using their profile characteristics as well as consider features provided in the preceding figure. Once the segmentation is firm, we move on to the next stage.
- **Targeting**: In this stage, marketing teams evaluate segments and try to understand which kind of product is suited to which particular segment(s). The team performs this exercise for each segment, and finally, the team designs customized products that will attract the customers of one or many segments. They will also select which product should be offered to which segment.

- **Positioning**: This is the last stage of the STP process. In this stage, companies study the market opportunity and what their product is offering to the customer. The marketing team should come up with a unique selling proposition. Here, the team also tries to understand how a particular segment perceives the products, brand, or service. This is a way for companies to determine how to best position their offering. The marketing and product teams of companies create a value proposition that clearly explains how their offering is better than any other competitors. Lastly, the companies start their campaign representing this value proposition in such a way that the consumer base will be happy about what they are getting.

I have summarized all the preceding points in the following diagram:

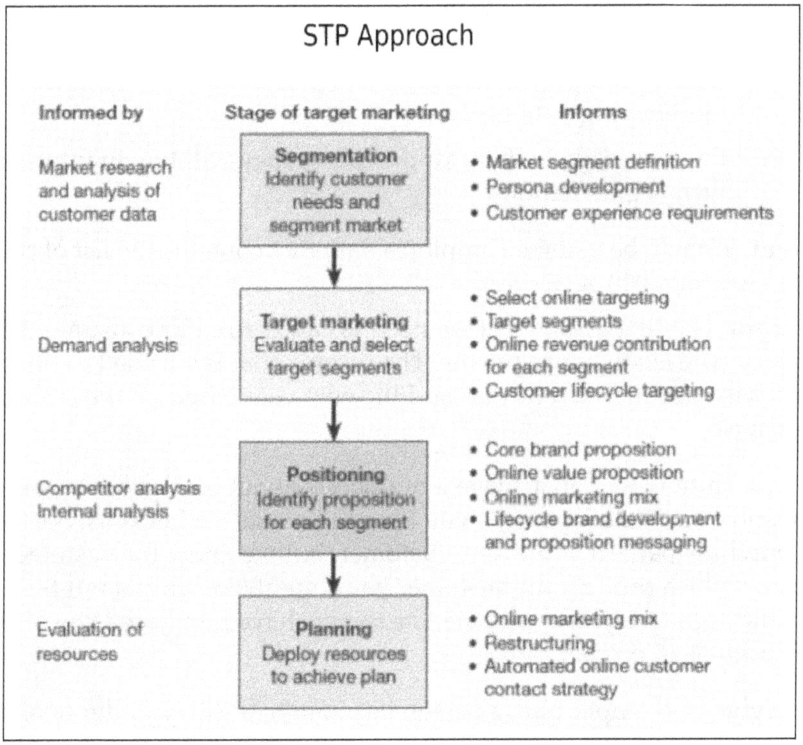

Figure 3.3: Summarization of the STP approach

We have covered most of the basic parts of customer segmentation. Now it's time to move on to the problem statement.

Introducing the problem statement

As you know, customer segmentation helps companies retain existing customers as well as acquire new potential customers. Based on the segmentation, companies can create customized products for a particular customer segment, but so far, we don't know how to generate the segments. This is the point that we will focus on in this chapter. You need to learn how to create customer segmentation. There are many domains for which we can build customer segmentation, such as e-commerce, travel, finance, telecom, and so on. Here, we will focus only on the e-commerce domain.

Here is a detailed explanation of the problem statement, input, and output for the e-commerce customer segmentation application that we will be building:

- **Problem statement**: The goal of our customer segmentation application is to come up with a solution for the given questions:
    - Can we categorize the customers in a particular segment based on their buying patterns?
    - Can we predict which kind of items they will buy in future based on their segmentation?
- **Input**: We will be using e-commerce data that contains the list of purchases in 1 year for 4,000 customers.
- **Output**: The first goal is that we need to categorize our consumer base into appropriate customer segments. The second goal is we need to predict the purchases for the current year and the next year based on the customers' first purchase.

You may wonder how we can achieve a prediction about the upcoming purchases using segmentation. Well, let me tell you how segmentation helps us! So, we don't know the purchase pattern of the new customer, but we know the customer profile. We also know which product the customer has bought. So, we can put the customer into one of the segments where all other customers have purchased similar items and share similar kinds of profile.

Let me give you an example. Say, a person has bought a Harry Potter book and that person lives in the UK. The age group of the customer is from 13-22. If we have already generated a customer segment that satisfies these characteristics, then we will put this new customer in that particular subgroup. We will derive the list of items that the customer may buy in future. We will also offer similar services that other customers in the subgroup have.

The approach that we will be using in order to develop customer segmentation for the e-commerce domain can also be used in other domains, but data points (features) will differ for each domain. Later on in the chapter, we will discuss what kind of data points you may consider for other domains, such as travelling, finance, and so on. I will provide the list of data points for other domains that will help you build the customer segmentation application from scratch.

Now it is time to understand the dataset for building customer segmentation for the e-commerce domain.

Understanding the datasets

Finding out an appropriate dataset is a challenging task in data science. Sometimes, you find a dataset but it is not in the appropriate format. Our problem statement will decide what type of dataset and data format we need. These kinds of activities are a part of data wrangling.

> Data wrangling is defined as the process of transforming and mapping data from one data form into another. With transformation and mapping, our intention should be to create an appropriate and valuable dataset that can be useful in order to develop analytics products. Data wrangling is also referred to as data munging and is a crucial part of any data science application.

Generally, e-commerce datasets are proprietary datasets, and it's rare that you get transactions of real users. Fortunately, *The UCI Machine Learning Repository* hosts a dataset named *Online Retail*. This dataset contains actual transactions from UK retailers.

Description of the dataset

This Online Retail dataset contains the actual transactions between December 1, 2010 and December 9, 2011. All the transactions are taken from the registered non-store online retail platform. These online retail platforms are mostly based in the UK. The online retail platforms are selling unique all-occasion gifts. Many consumers of these online retail platforms are wholesalers. There are 532610 records in this dataset.

Downloading the dataset

You can download this dataset by using either of the following links:

1. `http://archive.ics.uci.edu/ml/datasets/online+retail`
2. `https://www.kaggle.com/fabiendaniel/customer-segmentation/data`

Attributes of the dataset

These are the attributes in this dataset. We will take a look at a short description for each of them:

1. InvoiceNo: This data attribute indicates the invoice numbers. It is a six-digit integer number. The records are uniquely assigned for each transaction. If the invoice number starts with the letter 'c', then it indicates a cancellation.
2. StockCode: This data attribute indicates the product (item) code. It is a five-digit integer number. All the item codes are uniquely assigned to each distinct product.
3. Description: This data attribute contains the description about the item.
4. Quantity: This data attribute contains the quantities for each product per transaction. The data is in a numeric format.
5. InvoiceDate: The data attribute contains the invoice date and time. It indicates the day and time when each transaction was generated.
6. UnitPrice: The price indicates the product price per unit in sterling.
7. CustomerID: This column has the customer identification number. It is a five-digit integer number uniquely assigned to each customer.
8. Country: This column contains the geographic information about the customer. It records the country name for the customers.

You can refer to the sample of the dataset given in the following screenshot:

InvoiceNo	StockCode	Description	Quantity	InvoiceDate	UnitPrice	CustomerID	Country
536365	85123A	WHITE HANGING HEART T-LIGHT HOLDER	6	12/1/2010 8:26	2.55	17850	United Kingdom
536365	71053	WHITE METAL LANTERN	6	12/1/2010 8:26	3.39	17850	United Kingdom
536365	84406B	CREAM CUPID HEARTS COAT HANGER	8	12/1/2010 8:26	2.75	17850	United Kingdom
536365	84029G	KNITTED UNION FLAG HOT WATER BOTTLE	6	12/1/2010 8:26	3.39	17850	United Kingdom
536365	84029E	RED WOOLLY HOTTIE WHITE HEART.	6	12/1/2010 8:26	3.39	17850	United Kingdom
536365	22752	SET 7 BABUSHKA NESTING BOXES	2	12/1/2010 8:26	7.65	17850	United Kingdom
536365	21730	GLASS STAR FROSTED T-LIGHT HOLDER	6	12/1/2010 8:26	4.25	17850	United Kingdom
536366	22633	HAND WARMER UNION JACK	6	12/1/2010 8:28	1.85	17850	United Kingdom
536366	22632	HAND WARMER RED POLKA DOT	6	12/1/2010 8:28	1.85	17850	United Kingdom
536367	84879	ASSORTED COLOUR BIRD ORNAMENT	32	12/1/2010 8:34	1.69	13047	United Kingdom
536367	22745	POPPY'S PLAYHOUSE BEDROOM	6	12/1/2010 8:34	2.1	13047	United Kingdom

Figure 3.4: Sample recodes from the dataset

Now we will start building the customer segmentation application.

Building the baseline approach

In this section, we will start implementing the basic model for the customer segmentation application. Furthermore, we will improve this baseline approach. While implementing, we will cover the necessary concepts, technical aspects, and significance of performing that particular step. You can find the code for the customer-segmentation application at this GitHub link: `https://github.com/jalajthanaki/Customer_segmentation`

The code related to this chapter is given in a single iPython notebook. You can access the notebook using this GitHub link: `https://github.com/jalajthanaki/Customer_segmentation/blob/master/Cust_segmentation_online_retail.ipynb`.

Refer to the code given on GitHub because it will help you understand things better. Now let's begin the implementation!

Implementing the baseline approach

In order to implement the customer segmentation model, our implementation will have the following steps:

1. Data preparation
2. Exploratory data analysis (EDA)
3. Generating customer categories
4. Classifying customers

Let's begin with data preparation!

Data preparation

This is a basic step when you try to build any analytics application. First, we need to be sure that the format of the data is in an appropriate form. If it is not, then we need to prepare our dataset in such a way that we can build our application easily. In this step, we will find out whether we have a good quality dataset or not. We can also find out some basic facts about the dataset.

Luckily, we don't need to change the format of our e-commerce dataset, but we will be exploring the dataset in such a way that we can find out the quality of the dataset. If format of the dataset is not proper then you need to decide the format of the dataset in such a way that any kind of analysis can be performed using the dataset. You can convert the data records either in CSV format or in JSON format or in XML format. In addition, we can derive general facts about the dataset, such as whether our dataset is biased or not, whether the dataset contains any null values, the mapping of the customers with `Customer_ID` is proper or not, whether their purchases are properly recorded in dataset or not, and so on.

Loading the dataset

In order to load the dataset, we will use the pandas `read_csv` API. You can find the code snippet given in the following screenshot:

```
# read the datafile
df_initial = pd.read_csv('./input_data/data.csv',encoding="ISO-8859-1",
                         dtype={'CustomerID': str,'InvoiceID': str})
print('Dataframe dimensions:', df_initial.shape)
df_initial['InvoiceDate'] = pd.to_datetime(df_initial['InvoiceDate'])
```

```
('Dataframe dimensions:', (541909, 8))
```

```
# show first lines
display(df_initial[:5])
```

	InvoiceNo	StockCode	Description	Quantity	InvoiceDate	UnitPrice	CustomerID	Country
0	536365	85123A	WHITE HANGING HEART T-LIGHT HOLDER	6	2010-12-01 08:26:00	2.55	17850	United Kingdom
1	536365	71053	WHITE METAL LANTERN	6	2010-12-01 08:26:00	3.39	17850	United Kingdom
2	536365	84406B	CREAM CUPID HEARTS COAT HANGER	8	2010-12-01 08:26:00	2.75	17850	United Kingdom
3	536365	84029G	KNITTED UNION FLAG HOT WATER BOTTLE	6	2010-12-01 08:26:00	3.39	17850	United Kingdom
4	536365	84029E	RED WOOLLY HOTTIE WHITE HEART.	6	2010-12-01 08:26:00	3.39	17850	United Kingdom

Figure 3.5: Code snippet for loading the dataset

As you can see, the dimensions of the dataset are (541909, 8). This means that there are 541,909 records in the dataset and eight data attributes. We have already covered these eight data attributes.

Now we need to perform exploratory data analysis (EDA), which can help us preprocess our dataset.

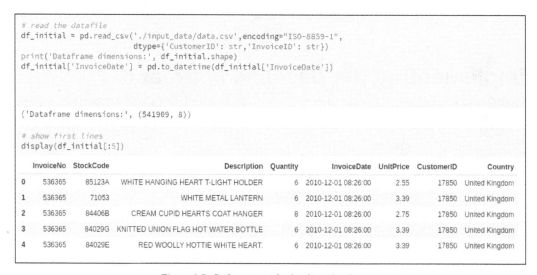

Exploratory data analysis (EDA)

In this section, we need to check the statistical properties of the dataset and perform some preprocessing steps:

1. Removing null data entries
2. Removing duplicate data entries
3. EDA for various data attributes

Removing null data entries

First, we need to check the data type of each of the attributes as well as find out which column has a null value. You can refer to the code snippet shown in the following screenshot:

Identify null values

```
# gives some infomation on columns types and number of null values
tab_info=pd.DataFrame(df_initial.dtypes).T.rename(index={0:'column type'})
tab_info=tab_info.append(pd.DataFrame(df_initial.isnull().sum()).T.rename(index={0:'null values (nb)'}))
tab_info=tab_info.append(pd.DataFrame(df_initial.isnull().sum()/df_initial.shape[0]*100).T.
                         rename(index={0:'null values (%)'}))
print ('-' * 10 + " Display information about column types and number of null values " + '-' * 10 )
print
display(tab_info)
```

```
---------- Display information about column types and number of null values ----------
```

	InvoiceNo	StockCode	Description	Quantity	InvoiceDate	UnitPrice	CustomerID	Country
column type	object	object	object	int64	datetime64[ns]	float64	object	object
null values (nb)	0	0	1454	0	0	0	135080	0
null values (%)	0	0	0.268311	0	0	0	24.9267	0

Figure 3.6: Code snippet for exploring the dataset

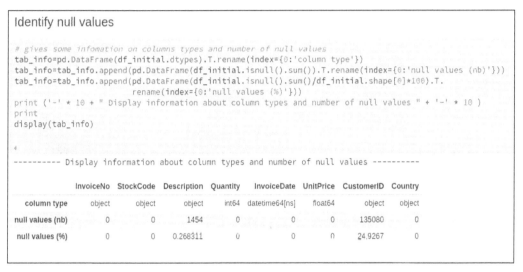

As you can see in the code, we have generated the total number of null values for each data attribute. We have also generated the percentage of null values for each data attribute. We can observe that for the `CustomerID` column, there are ~25% data entries that are null. That means there is no `CustomerID` value available for ~25% of the dataset. This indicates that there are many entries that do not belong to any customer. These are abended data entries. We cannot map them to the existing CustomerIDs. As a result, we need to delete them. You can find the code snippet for deleting null data entries from the dataset in the following screenshot:

```
df_initial.dropna(axis = 0, subset = ['CustomerID'], inplace = True)
print('Dataframe dimensions:', df_initial.shape)
# gives some information on columns types and number of null values
tab_info=pd.DataFrame(df_initial.dtypes).T.rename(index={0:'column type'})
tab_info=tab_info.append(pd.DataFrame(df_initial.isnull().sum()).T.rename(index={0:'null values (nb)'}))
tab_info=tab_info.append(pd.DataFrame(df_initial.isnull().sum()/df_initial.shape[0]*100).T.
                         rename(index={0:'null values (%)'}))
display(tab_info)
```

```
('Dataframe dimensions:', (406829, 8))
```

	InvoiceNo	StockCode	Description	Quantity	InvoiceDate	UnitPrice	CustomerID	Country
column type	object	object	object	int64	datetime64[ns]	float64	object	object
null values (nb)	0	0	0	0	0	0	0	0
null values (%)	0	0	0	0	0	0	0	0

Figure 3.7: Deleting null data entries

Removing duplicate data entries

After this step, we will check whether there are any duplicate data entries present in the dataset. In order to answer this question, we will use the pandas `duplicate()` function. You can refer to the code snippet shown in the following screenshot:

```
print('Duplicate data entries: {}'.format(df_initial.duplicated().sum()))
df_initial.drop_duplicates(inplace = True)
```

```
Duplicate data entries: 5225
```

Figure 3.8: Removing duplicate data entries

As you can see, we found 5,225 duplicate data entries. Therefore, we have removed them.

Now let's analyze each data attribute in detail.

EDA for various data attributes

EDA for each data attribute will help us get more insight into the dataset. Later on, we will use these facts to build an accurate customer segmentation application.

We will start exploring data attributes in the following order:

1. Country
2. Customer and products
3. Product categories
4. Defining product categories

Country

We need to find out facts such as how many countries there are in our dataset. In order to answer this question, we need to execute the code shown in the following screenshot:

Exploring the data attribute : Country

```
temp = df_initial[['CustomerID', 'InvoiceNo', 'Country']].groupby(
    ['CustomerID', 'InvoiceNo', 'Country']).count()
temp = temp.reset_index(drop = False)
countries = temp['Country'].value_counts()
print('No. of cuntries in dataframe: {}'.format(len(countries)))

No. of cuntries in dataframe: 37
```

Figure 3.9: Code snippet for generating the number of counties present in the dataset

We also need to find the country from which we receive the maximum number of orders. We can find that out by using the pandas `groupby()` and `count()` functions. We sort the number of orders in descending order. You can refer to the code snippet in the following screenshot:

```
temp_no_of_order_per_count = df_initial[['CustomerID','Country']].groupby(['Country']).count()
#temp_no_of_order_per_count = temp_no_of_order_per_count.reset_index(drop = False)

print('-' * 10 + " Contry-wise order calculation "+ '-' * 10)
print
print (temp_no_of_order_per_count.sort_values(
    by='CustomerID', ascending=False).rename(index=str,
                                    columns={"CustomerID": "Country wise number of order"}))
---------- Contry-wise order calculation ----------

                     Country wise number of order
Country
United Kingdom                             361878
Germany                                      9495
France                                       8491
EIRE                                         7485
Spain                                        2533
Netherlands                                  2371
Belgium                                      2069
Switzerland                                  1877
Portugal                                     1480
Australia                                    1259
Norway                                       1086
Italy                                         803
Channel Islands                               758
Finland                                       695
Cyprus                                        622
Sweden                                        462
Austria                                       401
Denmark                                       389
Japan                                         358
Poland                                        341
USA                                           291
Israel                                        250
Unspecified                                   244
Singapore                                     229
Iceland                                       182
Canada                                        151
Greece                                        146
Malta                                         127
```

Figure 3.10: Code snippet for generating country-wise number of orders

As you can see in the preceding snippet, there are a majority of orders from UK-based customers. Now we need to explore the customer and products variables.

Customer and products

Here, we have approximately 400,000 data items. We need to know the number of users and products that are present in these data entries. We will be using the `value_counts()` function from the `pandas` library. Take a look at the code snippet in the following screenshot:

The dataframe contains ~400,000 entries. What are the number of users and products in these entries ?

```
pd.DataFrame([{'products': len(df_initial['StockCode'].value_counts()),
               'transactions': len(df_initial['InvoiceNo'].value_counts()),
               'customers': len(df_initial['CustomerID'].value_counts()),
              }], columns = ['products', 'transactions', 'customers'],
              index = ['quantity'])
```

	products	transactions	customers
quantity	3684	22190	4372

Figure 3.11: Code for exploring customer and products

As you can see in the above screen shot that this dataset contains the records of 4372 users who bought 3684 different items

We have derived some interesting facts. In the given dataset, there are 4,372 customers who have bought 3,684 different products. The total number of transactions is 22,190.

We should also find out how many products have been purchased for each transaction. For that, we will use the `InvoiceNo` and `InvoiceDate` data attributes, and we will calculate the number of products purchased for every transaction. You can refer to the code snippet shown in the following screenshot:

Now we need to explore the number of products purchased in every transaction

```
temp = df_initial.groupby(by=['CustomerID', 'InvoiceNo'], as_index=False)['InvoiceDate'].count()
nb_products_per_basket = temp.rename(columns = {'InvoiceDate':'Number of products'})
nb_products_per_basket[:10].sort_values('CustomerID')
```

	CustomerID	InvoiceNo	Number of products
0	12346	541431	1
1	12346	C541433	1
2	12347	537626	31
3	12347	542237	29
4	12347	549222	24
5	12347	556201	18
6	12347	562032	22
7	12347	573511	47
8	12347	581180	11
9	12348	539318	17

Figure 3.12: Code snippet for exploring the number of products per transaction

As shown in the preceding code snippet, we can make the following observations:

- There are some users who have made a purchase only once on the e-commerce platform and bought one item. An example of this kind of user is `customerID 12346`.
- There are some users who frequently buy a large number of items per order. An example of this kind of user is `customerID 12347`.
- If you look at the InvoiceNo data attribute, then you can see that there is the prefix `C` for one invoice. This `'C'` indicates that the particular transaction has been canceled.

As we know, there can be a couple of canceled orders present in our dataset, and we need to count the number of transactions corresponding to the canceled orders. We have used a simple check condition using the lambda expression. Now we will calculate the percentage of canceled orders. You can refer to the code snippet given in the following screenshot:

Analysis of cancelled orders

We need to count the number of transactions corresponding to cancelled orders

```
nb_products_per_basket['order_cancelled'] = nb_products_per_basket['InvoiceNo'].apply(
    lambda x:int('C' in x))
display(nb_products_per_basket[:5])

n1 = nb_products_per_basket['order_cancelled'].sum()
n2 = nb_products_per_basket.shape[0]
percentage = (n1/n2)*100
print('Number of orders cancelled: {}/{} ({:.2f}%) '.format(n1, n2, percentage))
```

	CustomerID	InvoiceNo	Number of products	order_cancelled
0	12346	541431	1	0
1	12346	C541433	1	1
2	12347	537626	31	0
3	12347	542237	29	0
4	12347	549222	24	0

```
Number of orders cancelled: 3654/22190 (16.47%)
```

Note that the number of cancelled transactions are quite large (~16% of the total number of transactions).

Figure 3.13: Code snippet for generating the percentage of canceled orders

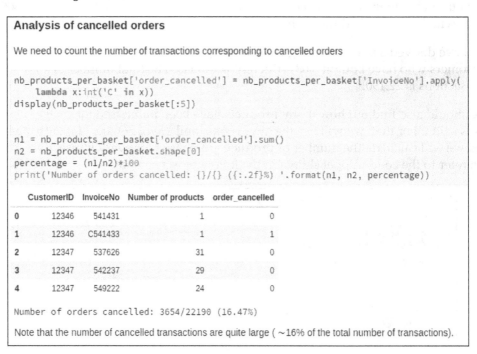

Let's list down some of the canceled order entries so that we can find out how to handle them. Take a look at the following screenshot:

```
display(df_initial.sort_values('CustomerID')[:5])
```

	InvoiceNo	StockCode	Description	Quantity	InvoiceDate	UnitPrice	CustomerID	Country
61619	541431	23166	MEDIUM CERAMIC TOP STORAGE JAR	74215	2011-01-18 10:01:00	1.04	12346	United Kingdom
61624	C541433	23166	MEDIUM CERAMIC TOP STORAGE JAR	-74215	2011-01-18 10:17:00	1.04	12346	United Kingdom
286623	562032	22375	AIRLINE BAG VINTAGE JET SET BROWN	4	2011-08-02 08:48:00	4.25	12347	Iceland
72260	542237	84991	60 TEATIME FAIRY CAKE CASES	24	2011-01-26 14:30:00	0.55	12347	Iceland
14943	537626	22772	PINK DRAWER KNOB ACRYLIC EDWARDIAN	12	2010-12-07 14:57:00	1.25	12347	Iceland

Figure 3.14: List of canceled orders

Basically, in order to handle the canceled orders, we will need to take the following steps:

- As you can observe, if the order is canceled, then there is another transaction that will mostly have an identical transaction except for the quantity and invoice date. First, we need to check whether this is true for all entries.
- We can perform this checking operation by using simple logic. Mostly, the canceled order has a negative quantity, so we will check whether there is an order indicating the same quantity (but positive), with the same description values.
- There are some discount entries as well, and we need to handle them. We will discard the discount entries.

You can refer to the code for this, as shown in the following screenshot:

```
df_check = df_initial[(df_initial['Quantity'] < 0) & (df_initial['Description'] != 'Discount')]
                                 ['CustomerID','Quantity','StockCode',
                                  'Description','UnitPrice']]

for index, col in  df_check.iterrows():
    if df_initial[(df_initial['CustomerID'] == col[0]) & (df_initial['Quantity'] == -col[1])
                & (df_initial['Description'] == col[2])].shape[0] == 0:
        print(index, df_check.loc[index])
        print(15*'-'+'>'+' HYPOTHESIS NOT FULFILLED')
        break
```

```
(154, CustomerID                              15311
Quantity                                     -1
StockCode                                350004C
Description     SET OF 3 COLOURED  FLYING DUCKS
UnitPrice                                  4.65
Name: 154, dtype: object)
---------------> HYPOTHESIS NOT FULFILLED
```

Once more, we find that the initial hypothesis is not verified. Hence, cancellations do not necessarily correspond to orders that would have been made beforehand.

Figure 3.15: Code for handelling cancel orders

When we run the preceding code, we find out that there are no similar entries present in our dataset for all canceled transactions. In order to overcome this situation, we will create a new variable in our dataframe, which indicates whether the transaction has been canceled or not. There are three possibilities for canceled orders:

- There are some transactions that were canceled without counterparts. A few of them are probably due to the fact that the buy orders were performed before December 2010. We have the dataset from December 2010 to December 2011.
- There are some orders that were canceled with exactly one counterpart. We will consider them as well.
- There are some entries that are doubtful. We will check whether there is at least one counterpart with the exact same quantity available. If available, then we can mark those entries as doubtful.

You can refer to the code shown in the following screenshot:

```
df_cleaned = df_initial.copy(deep = True)
df_cleaned['QuantityCanceled'] = 0

entry_to_remove = [] ; doubtfull_entry = []

for index, col in  df_initial.iterrows():
    if (col['Quantity'] > 0) or col['Description'] == 'Discount': continue
    df_test = df_initial[(df_initial['CustomerID'] == col['CustomerID']) &
                         (df_initial['StockCode']  == col['StockCode']) &
                         (df_initial['InvoiceDate'] < col['InvoiceDate']) &
                         (df_initial['Quantity']   > 0)].copy()

    # Cancelation WITHOUT counterpart
    if (df_test.shape[0] == 0):
        doubtfull_entry.append(index)

    # Cancelation WITH a counterpart
    elif (df_test.shape[0] == 1):
        index_order = df_test.index[0]
        df_cleaned.loc[index_order, 'QuantityCanceled'] = -col['Quantity']
        entry_to_remove.append(index)

    # Various counterparts exist in orders: we delete the last one
    elif (df_test.shape[0] > 1):
        df_test.sort_index(axis=0 ,ascending=False, inplace = True)
        for ind, val in df_test.iterrows():
            if val['Quantity'] < -col['Quantity']: continue
            df_cleaned.loc[ind, 'QuantityCanceled'] = -col['Quantity']
            entry_to_remove.append(index)
            break

print("entry_to_remove: {}".format(len(entry_to_remove)))
print("doubtfull_entry: {}".format(len(doubtfull_entry)))

entry_to_remove: 7521
doubtfull_entry: 1226
```

Figure 3.16: Code snippet for generating flags for canceled orders

As we can see in the preceding code snippet, there are 7,521 entries that show the canceled orders with their counterpart. There are 1,226 entries that show canceled orders without their counterpart. For the sake of simplicity, we are going to delete all the entries related to the canceled orders. The code for deleting these records is given in the following screenshot:

```
df_cleaned.drop(entry_to_remove, axis = 0, inplace = True)
df_cleaned.drop(doubtfull_entry, axis = 0, inplace = True)
remaining_entries = df_cleaned[(df_cleaned['Quantity'] < 0) & (df_cleaned['StockCode'] != 'D')]
print("nb of entries to delete: {}".format(remaining_entries.shape[0]))
remaining_entries[:5]
```

```
nb of entries to delete: 48
```

	InvoiceNo	StockCode	Description	Quantity	InvoiceDate	UnitPrice	CustomerID	Country	QuantityCanceled
77598	C542742	84535B	FAIRY CAKES NOTEBOOK A6 SIZE	-94	2011-01-31 16:26:00	0.65	15358	United Kingdom	0
90444	C544038	22784	LANTERN CREAM GAZEBO	-4	2011-02-15 11:32:00	4.95	14659	United Kingdom	0
111968	C545852	22464	HANGING METAL HEART LANTERN	-5	2011-03-07 13:49:00	1.65	14048	United Kingdom	0
116064	C546191	47566B	TEA TIME PARTY BUNTING	-35	2011-03-10 10:57:00	0.70	16422	United Kingdom	0
132642	C547675	22263	FELT EGG COSY LADYBIRD	-49	2011-03-24 14:07:00	0.66	17754	United Kingdom	0

Figure 3.17: Code snippet for deleting canceled orders

Now let's analyze the entries based on the stock code because we know that during the identification of the canceled order, we discover discount items based on the *stock code D*. So first of all, we will be listing down all the stock codes and their meaning. You can refer to the following screenshot:

Analysis of the StockCode

Above, it has been seen that some values of the **StockCode** variable indicate a particular transaction (i.e. D for *Discount*). I check the contents of this variable by looking for the set of codes that would contain only letters:

```
list_special_codes = df_cleaned[df_cleaned['StockCode'].str.contains('^[a-zA-Z]+', regex=True)]
list_special_codes
```

```
array([u'POST', u'D', u'C2', u'M', u'BANK CHARGES', u'PADS', u'DOT'],
      dtype=object)
```

```
for code in list_special_codes:
    print("{:<15} -> {:<30}".format(code, df_cleaned[df_cleaned['StockCode'] == code]['Descript
```

```
POST            -> POSTAGE
D               -> Discount
C2              -> CARRIAGE
M               -> Manual
BANK CHARGES    -> Bank Charges
PADS            -> PADS TO MATCH ALL CUSHIONS
DOT             -> DOTCOM POSTAGE
```

We see that there are several types of peculiar transactions, connected e.g. to port charges or bank charges.

Figure 3.18: Code snippet for stock code

Now let's focus on the pricing of the individual order. In the given dataset, the order from a single customer has been split into several lines. What do I mean by several lines? In order to understand that, refer to the following screenshot:

	InvoiceNo	StockCode	Description	Quantity	InvoiceDate	UnitPrice	CustomerID	Country	QuantityCanceled
61619	541431	23166	MEDIUM CERAMIC TOP STORAGE JAR	74215	2011-01-18 10:01:00	1.04	12346	United Kingdom	74215
148288	549222	22375	AIRLINE BAG VINTAGE JET SET BROWN	4	2011-04-07 10:43:00	4.25	12347	Iceland	0
428971	573511	22698	PINK REGENCY TEACUP AND SAUCER	12	2011-10-31 12:25:00	2.95	12347	Iceland	0
428970	573511	47559B	TEA TIME OVEN GLOVE	10	2011-10-31 12:25:00	1.25	12347	Iceland	0
428969	573511	47567B	TEA TIME KITCHEN APRON	6	2011-10-31 12:25:00	5.95	12347	Iceland	0

Single order containing multiple products
and
that is the reason dataset is having multiple data entries for a single order.

Figure 3.19: Understanding data entries for orders

Each entry in our dataset indicates prizes for a single kind of product. If the order including different products is placed by a single customer, then there are multiple entries for that particular order. The number of data entries depends on how many different products that order has. As you can see in the preceding figure, there were three different products included in one order. We need to obtain the total price for each order. In order to achieve that, we will add a column named *TotalPrice*, which gives us the total value of the order or the basket price for a single order. The main logic for deriving *TotalPrice* is that we are multiplying *UnitPrice* with the net quantity. We obtain the net quantity by deducting the canceled quantity from the total quantity. Take a look at the code snippet shown in the following screenshot:

```
df_cleaned['TotalPrice'] = df_cleaned['UnitPrice'] * (df_cleaned['Quantity'] - df_cleaned['QuantityCanceled'])
df_cleaned.sort_values('CustomerID')[:5]
```

	InvoiceNo	StockCode	Description	Quantity	InvoiceDate	UnitPrice	CustomerID	Country	QuantityCanceled	TotalPrice
61619	541431	23166	MEDIUM CERAMIC TOP STORAGE JAR	74215	2011-01-18 10:01:00	1.04	12346	United Kingdom	74215	0.0
148288	549222	22375	AIRLINE BAG VINTAGE JET SET BROWN	4	2011-04-07 10:43:00	4.25	12347	Iceland	0	17.0
428971	573511	22698	PINK REGENCY TEACUP AND SAUCER	12	2011-10-31 12:25:00	2.95	12347	Iceland	0	35.4
428970	573511	47559B	TEA TIME OVEN GLOVE	10	2011-10-31 12:25:00	1.25	12347	Iceland	0	12.5
428969	573511	47567B	TEA TIME KITCHEN APRON	6	2011-10-31 12:25:00	5.95	12347	Iceland	0	35.7

Figure 3.20: Code for obtaining TotalPrice

Once we obtain the total price, we will generate the sum for individual orders and then group our entries based on the invoice data. We will list only those data entries that have a basket price greater than 0. The code to achieve this is given in the following screenshot:

```
# sum of purchases / user & order
temp = df_cleaned.groupby(by=['CustomerID', 'InvoiceNo'], as_index=False)['TotalPrice'].sum()
basket_price = temp.rename(columns = {'TotalPrice':'Basket Price'})

# date of the order
df_cleaned['InvoiceDate_int'] = df_cleaned['InvoiceDate'].astype('int64')
temp = df_cleaned.groupby(by=['CustomerID', 'InvoiceNo'], as_index=False)['InvoiceDate_int'].mean()
df_cleaned.drop('InvoiceDate_int', axis = 1, inplace = True)
basket_price.loc[:, 'InvoiceDate'] = pd.to_datetime(temp['InvoiceDate_int'])

# selection of significant entries
basket_price = basket_price[basket_price['Basket Price'] > 0]
basket_price.sort_values('CustomerID')[:6]
```

	CustomerID	InvoiceNo	Basket Price	InvoiceDate
1	12347	537626	711.79	2010-12-07 14:57:00.000001024
2	12347	542237	475.39	2011-01-26 14:29:59.999999744
3	12347	549222	636.25	2011-04-07 10:42:59.999999232
4	12347	556201	382.52	2011-06-09 13:01:00.000000256
5	12347	562032	584.91	2011-08-02 08:48:00.000000000
6	12347	573511	1294.32	2011-10-31 12:25:00.000001280

Figure 3.21: Code for generating the basket price based on the invoice date

Now it's time to get an idea about the distribution of the orders' amounts for the given dataset. What do I mean by distribution of the orders' amounts? Well, we should be aware about the prices for all the orders present in the dataset, and we need to put in the ranges based on the amount of all the orders. This will help us derive the number of orders in the dataset that are above £200. It will also help us identify the number of orders that are below £100. This kind of information helps us know the data distribution based on the number of orders. This will give us a basic picture about sales on the e-commerce platform. The code snippet for generating data distribution based on the orders' amounts is displayed in the following screenshot:

```
# Purchase count
price_range = [0, 50, 100, 200, 500, 1000, 5000, 50000]
count_price = []
for i, price in enumerate(price_range):
    if i == 0: continue
    val = basket_price[(basket_price['Basket Price'] < price) &
                       (basket_price['Basket Price'] > price_range[i-1])]['Basket Price'].count()
    count_price.append(val)

# Representation of the number of purchases / amount
plt.rc('font', weight='bold')
f, ax = plt.subplots(figsize=(11, 6))
colors = ['yellowgreen', 'gold', 'wheat', 'c', 'violet', 'royalblue','firebrick']
labels = [ '{}<.<{}'.format(price_range[i-1], s) for i,s in enumerate(price_range) if i != 0]
sizes  = count_price
explode = [0.0 if sizes[i] < 100 else 0.0 for i in range(len(sizes))]
ax.pie(sizes, explode = explode, labels=labels, colors = colors,
       autopct = lambda x:'{:1.0f}%'.format(x) if x > 1 else '',
       shadow = False, startangle=0)
ax.axis('equal')
f.text(0.5, 1.01, "Distribution of order amounts", ha='center', fontsize = 18);
```

Figure 3.22: Code snippet for generating data distribution based on orders' amounts

You can see the pictorial representation of this data distribution as follows:

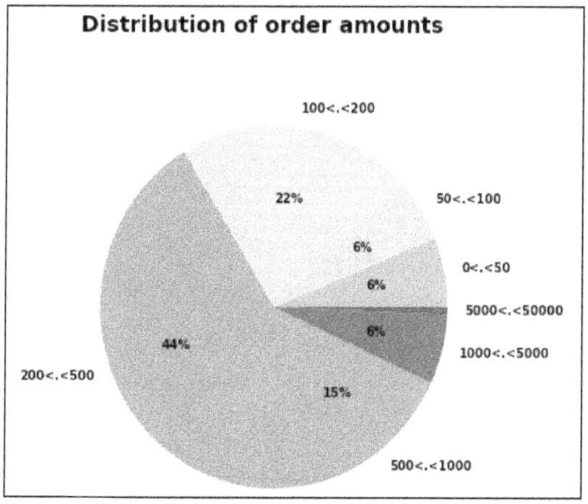

Figure 3.23: Pictorial representation of the data distribution

As we can see, approximately 65% of the orders are above £200. We have explored orders in great detail. Now let's begin with the analysis of product categories.

Product categories

In this section, we will be doing an EDA of the product-related data attribute. We will include the following kinds of analysis in this section:

- Analyzing the product description
- Defining the product categories
- Characterizing the content of clusters

Analyzing the product description

In this section, we will be using two data attributes. We will use the `StockCode` data attribute, which contains a unique ID for each product. We will also use the `Description` data attribute in order to group the products in different categories. Let's start with the product description.

First, we will define the function that will take the dataframe as input, and then we will perform the the following operations:

- We will extract names (nouns) from the product description.
- Then, we will generate the root form of the extracted names. We will store the root of the name as the key and all associated names as its value. We will use a stemmer from the NLTK library for this step. A stemmer basically generates the root form of the words by removing suffixes and prefixes.
- We will count the frequency of the roots of the names, which means we will count how many times the root form of each name appears.
- If various names have the same root, then we consider the root form as the keyword tag.

You can see the code for this function in the following screenshot:

```
is_noun = lambda pos: pos[:2] == 'NN'

def keywords_inventory(dataframe, colonne = 'Description'):
    stemmer = nltk.stem.SnowballStemmer("english")
    keywords_roots  = dict()  # collect the words / root
    keywords_select = dict()  # association: root <-> keyword
    category_keys   = []
    count_keywords  = dict()
    icount = 0
    for s in dataframe[colonne]:
        if pd.isnull(s): continue
        lines = s.lower()
        tokenized = nltk.word_tokenize(lines)
        nouns = [word for (word, pos) in nltk.pos_tag(tokenized) if is_noun(pos)]

        for t in nouns:
            t = t.lower() ; racine = stemmer.stem(t)
            if racine in keywords_roots:
                keywords_roots[racine].add(t)
                count_keywords[racine] += 1
            else:
                keywords_roots[racine] = {t}
                count_keywords[racine] = 1

    for s in keywords_roots.keys():
        if len(keywords_roots[s]) > 1:
            min_length = 1000
            for k in keywords_roots[s]:
                if len(k) < min_length:
                    clef = k ; min_length = len(k)
            category_keys.append(clef)
            keywords_select[s] = clef
        else:
            category_keys.append(list(keywords_roots[s])[0])
            keywords_select[s] = list(keywords_roots[s])[0]

    print("number of keywords in variable '{}': {}".format(colonne,len(category_keys)))
    return category_keys, keywords_roots, keywords_select, count_keywords
```

Figure 3.24: Code snippet of the function for generating keywords from the product description

Now we need to call this function and feed the input dataframe. You can take a look at the code snippet given in the following screenshot:

```
df_produits = pd.DataFrame(df_initial['Description'].unique()).rename(columns = {0:'Description'})

keywords, keywords_roots, keywords_select, count_keywords = keywords_inventory(df_produits)

Nb of keywords in variable 'Description': 1483
```

Figure 3.25: Code snippet that actually generates keywords

Here, we are returning three variables:

- `Keyword`: This is the list of extracted names
- `Keywords_roots`: This is a dictionary where the keys are the root of the name and values are the list of names associated with root name.
- `Count_keywords`: This is a dictionary that keeps track of the frequency of each name. The count indicates the number of times a particular name appeared in the description. Later on, we will convert the dictionary into a list.

Now let's plot the keywords versus their frequency graphs. The code is given in the following screenshot:

```
liste = sorted(list_products, key = lambda x:x[1], reverse = True)

plt.rc('font', weight='normal')
fig, ax = plt.subplots(figsize=(7, 25))
y_axis = [i[1] for i in liste[:125]]
x_axis = [k for k,i in enumerate(liste[:125])]
x_label = [i[0] for i in liste[:125]]
plt.xticks(fontsize = 15)
plt.yticks(fontsize = 13)
plt.yticks(x_axis, x_label)
plt.xlabel("Number of occurences", fontsize = 18, labelpad = 10)
ax.barh(x_axis, y_axis, align = 'center')
ax = plt.gca()
ax.invert_yaxis()

plt.title("Words occurence",bbox={'facecolor':'k', 'pad':5}, color='w',fontsize = 25)
plt.show()
```

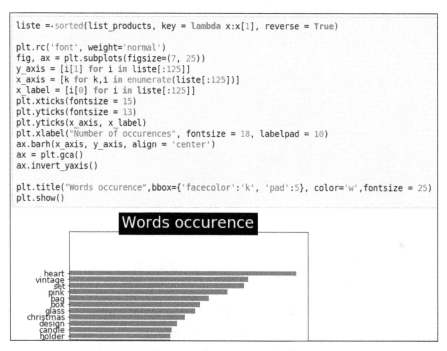

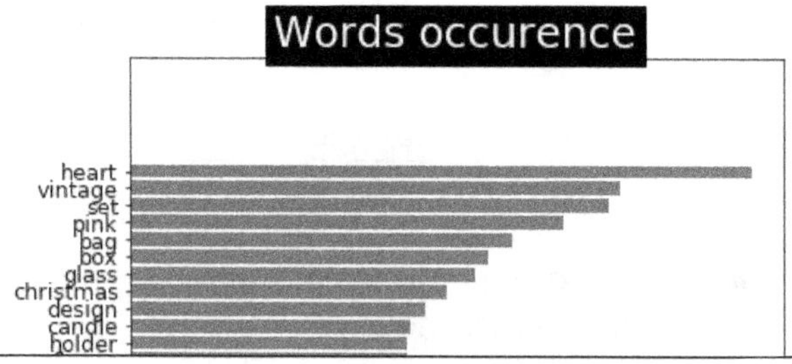

Figure 3.26: Code snippet for generating the frequency graph

As you can see in the preceding figure, the word (meaning the noun or the name) heart has appeared the maximum number of times in the product description. You might wonder what the significance of generating this word frequency is. Well, we are using this to categorize products. Now it's time to look into how to come up with product categories.

Defining product categories

Here we will obtain the product categories. We have obtained more than 1,400 keywords, and the most frequent names have appeared in more than 200 products. Now we need to remove words that are less important. We can observe some useless words, such as names of colors and discard them. So, we will consider words that appear in the dataset more than 13 times. You can refer to the code snippet shown in the following screenshot:

```
list_products = []
for k,v in count_keywords.items():
    word = keywords_select[k]
    if word in ['pink', 'blue', 'tag', 'green', 'orange']: continue
    if len(word) < 3 or v < 13: continue
    if ('+' in word) or ('/' in word): continue
    list_products.append([word, v])

list_products.sort(key = lambda x:x[1], reverse = True)
print('Preserved words:', len(list_products))
```

```
Preserved words: 193
```

Figure 3.27: Code snippet for preserving important words

Now we need to encode the data. Here, we have textual data and we need to convert it into a numerical format. For this, we will use one-hot encoding. One-hot encoding is a simple concept. In order to understand it, refer to the given matrix x. Take a look at the following screenshot:

	word 1	...	word j	...	word N
product 1	$a_{1,1}$				$a_{1,N}$
...			...		
product i	...		$a_{i,j}$		...
...			...		
product M	$a_{M,1}$				$a_{M,N}$

where the $a_{i,j}$ coefficient is 1 if the description of the product i contains the word j, and 0 otherwise.

Figure 3.28: Table for understanding one-hot data encoding

If a particular word is present in the product description, then the value of the coefficient is 1, and if the word is not present in the product description, then the value of the coefficient is 0. You can refer to the the following screenshot:

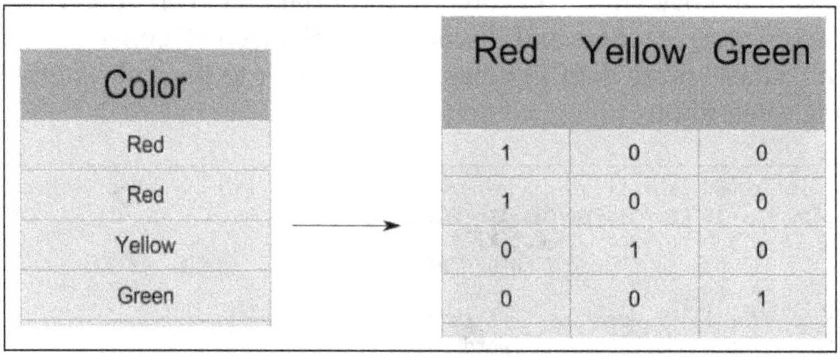

Figure 3.29: Intuitive example for one-hot data encoding

As you can see, this data encoding is a binary kind of vectorization because we are placing either zero or one. We will get a sparse vector for each word after encoding. In layman's terms, we can say that this kind of vectorization indicates the presence of the word in the product description.

Now let's create the groups or cluster for the product based on the price range. For that, we will be using the keyword list that we have generated, check whether the product description has the words that are present in the keywords, and take the mean value of `UnitPrice`. You can refer to the code given in the following screenshot:

```
threshold = [0, 1, 2, 3, 5, 10]
label_col = []
for i in range(len(threshold)):
    if i == len(threshold)-1:
        col = '.>{}'.format(threshold[i])
    else:
        col = '{}<.<{}'.format(threshold[i],threshold[i+1])
    #print(i)
    #print(col)
    label_col.append(col)
    X.loc[:, col] = 0

for i, prod in enumerate(liste_produits):
    prix = df_cleaned[ df_cleaned['Description'] == prod]['UnitPrice'].mean()
    #print (prix)
    j = 0
    while prix > threshold[j]:
        j+=1
        if j == len(threshold): break
    X.loc[i, label_col[j-1]] = 1
```

and to choose the appropriate ranges, I check the number of products in the different groups:

```
print("{:<8} {:<20} \n".format('range', 'number of products') + 20*'-')
for i in range(len(threshold)):
    if i == len(threshold)-1:
        col = '.>{}'.format(threshold[i])
    else:
        col = '{}<.<{}'.format(threshold[i],threshold[i+1])
    print("{:<10}  {:<20}".format(col, X.loc[:, col].sum()))
```

```
range    number of products
--------------------
0<.<1       964
1<.<2       1009
2<.<3       673
3<.<5       606
5<.<10      470
.>10        156
```

Figure 3.30: Code snippet for generating the product group based on the price range

Now we will create clusters of the products. We will be using the k-means clustering algorithm. We will also be using the scikit-learn library to implement the K-means clustering algorithm. The algorithm from scikit-learn uses Euclidean distance. In our case, this is not the best choice. We should use Hamming distance. The most suitable library for that is `Kmods`, but this library is not available for all operating systems, so we have to use the scikit-learn library. We need to define the number of clusters that can represent the data perfectly. We will come up with the ideal number of clusters, and then we will use the silhouette score.

You can take a look at how the k-means clustering algorithm works by using the link of this book: `https://www.packtpub.com/big-data-and-business-intelligence/python-natural-language-processing`, Refer section K-means clustering form *Chapter 8, Machine Learning for NLP problems.*

Let's take a step back and understand the silhouette score first. The silhouette coefficient is calculated using two things. The first is the mean intra-cluster distance (a) and the second is the mean nearest-cluster distance (b) for each sample in our dataset. So, the equation is as follows:

$$(b-a) / max\ (a, b)$$

The b indicates the distance between a sample and the nearest cluster that the sample is not a part of. This score works if the number of labels is $2 <= n\_labels <= n\_samples - 1$. The best possible value for this score is 1, and worst value is -1. Value 0 shows that we have overlapping clusters. Negative values indicate that the sample has been assigned to the wrong cluster. Refer to the code snippet shown in the following screenshot:

```
matrix = X.as_matrix()
for n_clusters in range(3,10):
    kmeans = KMeans(init='k-means++', n_clusters = n_clusters, n_init=30)
    kmeans.fit(matrix)
    clusters = kmeans.predict(matrix)
    silhouette_avg = silhouette_score(matrix, clusters)
    print("For n_clusters =", n_clusters, "The average silhouette_score is :", silhouette_avg)

For n_clusters = 3 The average silhouette_score is : 0.10071681758064248
For n_clusters = 4 The average silhouette_score is : 0.12098716952963189
For n_clusters = 5 The average silhouette_score is : 0.1452148389646187
For n_clusters = 6 The average silhouette_score is : 0.15541467786864369
For n_clusters = 7 The average silhouette_score is : 0.15961172545889715
For n_clusters = 8 The average silhouette_score is : 0.14781633357176888
For n_clusters = 9 The average silhouette_score is : 0.1420248111579961
```

Figure 3.31: Code snippet for choosing the ideal number of clusters using silhouette score

Here, we have implemented the code using the scikit-learn API. As we can see, beyond five clusters, a cluster may contain very few elements, so we choose to categorize the products into five clusters. We will try to increase the value of the silhouette score. For that, we will iterate through the dataset. You can refer to the code shown in the following screenshot:

```
n_clusters = 5
silhouette_avg = -1
while silhouette_avg < 0.145:
    kmeans = KMeans(init='k-means++', n_clusters = n_clusters, n_init=30)
    kmeans.fit(matrix)
    clusters = kmeans.predict(matrix)
    silhouette_avg = silhouette_score(matrix, clusters)

    #km = kmodes.KModes(n_clusters = n_clusters, init='Huang', n_init=2, verbose=0)
    #clusters = km.fit_predict(matrix)
    #silhouette_avg = silhouette_score(matrix, clusters)
    print("For n_clusters =", n_clusters, "The average silhouette_score is :", silhouette_avg)

For n_clusters = 5 The average silhouette_score is : 0.14631355248870398
```

Figure 3.32: Code snippet to improvise the silhouette score

Now let's move on to characterizing the content of the clusters section, which can help us understand how well the products have been classified into particular clusters.

Characterizing the content of clusters

In this section, we will analyze the properties of the product cluster. There will be three subsections here:

- Silhouette intra-cluster score analysis
- Analysis using a word cloud
- Principal component analysis (PCA)

Before we jump into this analysis, we need to check the number of products in each cluster. For that, we will be using the code snippet given in the following screenshot:

```
pd.Series(clusters).value_counts()

3    1009
2     964
1     829
0     606
4     470
dtype: int64
```

Figure 3.33: Code snippet for counting the number of products for each cluster

As you can see in the output, there are 1,009 products that belong to cluster number 3, whereas there are only 470 products that belong to cluster number 4. We will start an in-depth analysis of these five clusters and their elements. First, we will start with the silhouette intra-cluster score analysis.

Silhouette intra-cluster score analysis

Basically, in this section, we will be checking the intra-cluster score for each element. We will sort the silhouette intra-cluster score. After sorting, we will draw a graph where the *x axis* represents the silhouette coefficient value and the *y axis* represents the cluster label. We generate the silhouette intra-cluster score for all the samples. We are building this graph because we want to choose an optimal value for `n_clusters` based on the silhouette intra-cluster score.

As we have generated the silhouette intra-cluster score earlier, we know `n_clusters = 5` is the ideal choice for us, so we will represent the clusters in a pictorial manner. You can refer to the function that generates graphs in the following screenshot:

```
def graph_component_silhouette(n_clusters, lim_x, mat_size, sample_silhouette_values, clusters):
    #plt.rcParams["patch.force_edgecolor"] = True
    plt.style.use('fivethirtyeight')
    mpl.rc('patch', edgecolor = 'dimgray', linewidth=1)

    fig, ax1 = plt.subplots(1, 1)
    fig.set_size_inches(8, 8)
    ax1.set_xlim([lim_x[0], lim_x[1]])
    ax1.set_ylim([0, mat_size + (n_clusters + 1) * 10])
    y_lower = 10
    for i in range(n_clusters):

        # Aggregate the silhouette scores for samples belonging to cluster i, and sort them
        ith_cluster_silhouette_values = sample_silhouette_values[clusters == i]
        ith_cluster_silhouette_values.sort()
        size_cluster_i = ith_cluster_silhouette_values.shape[0]
        y_upper = y_lower + size_cluster_i
        #color = cm.spectral(float(i) / n_clusters) facecolor=color, edgecolor=color,
        ax1.fill_betweenx(np.arange(y_lower, y_upper), 0, ith_cluster_silhouette_values, alpha=0.8)

        # Label the silhouette plots with their cluster numbers at the middle
        ax1.text(-0.03, y_lower + 0.5 * size_cluster_i, str(i), color = 'red', fontweight = 'bold',
                bbox=dict(facecolor='white', edgecolor='black', boxstyle='round, pad=0.3'))

        # Compute the new y_lower for next plot
        y_lower = y_upper + 10
```

Figure 3.34: Code snippet of the function for silhouette intra-cluster score analysis

After executing and calling this function, we can obtain the graph displayed in the following screenshot:

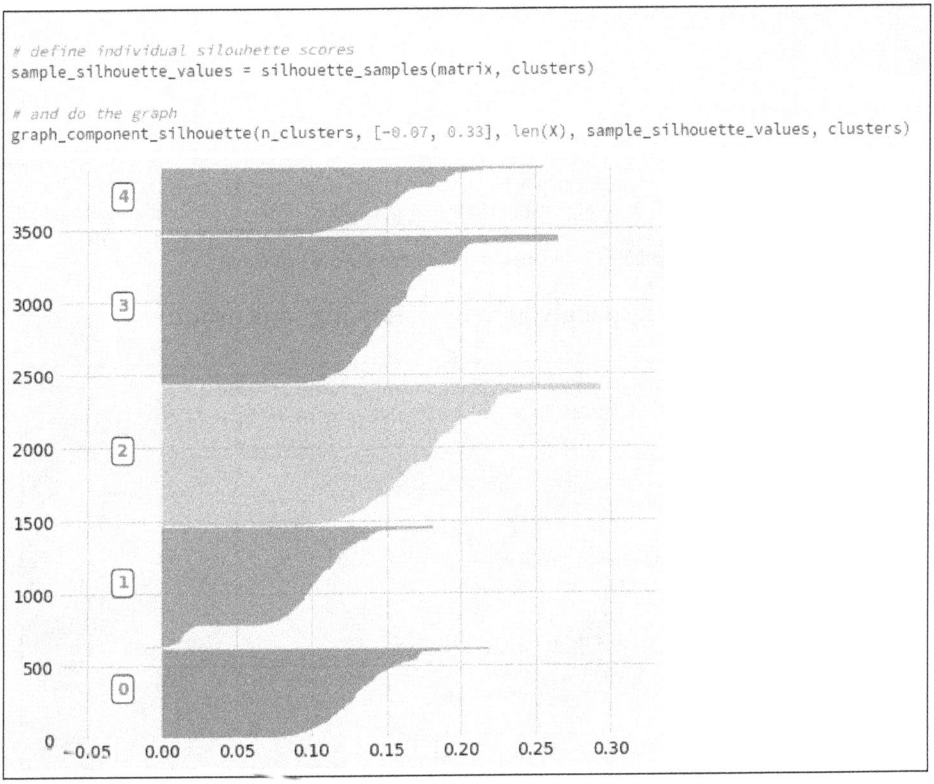

# define individual silouhette scores
sample_silhouette_values = silhouette_samples(matrix, clusters)
# and do the graph
graph_component_silhouette(n_clusters, [-0.07, 0.33], len(X), sample_silhouette_values, clusters)
4
3
2
1
0
3500
3000
2500
2000
1500
1000
500
0
-0.05
0.00
0.05
0.10
0.15
0.20
0.25
0.30

Figure 3.35: Code snippet and graph for silhouette intra-cluster analysis

> Note that here, we obtain the graph for the optimal `n_cluster` value. This value is 5 in our case.

Analysis using a word cloud

In this section, we will analyze the clusters based on the keywords. We will check what words each cluster has. For this analysis, we will be using the word cloud library. You must be wondering why we are using this type of analysis. In our clusters, we are expecting similar kinds of products to belong to one cluster. We, as humans, know the language. When we see the words for the entire cluster, we can easily conclude whether our clusters have similar kinds of products or not. We will generate graphs that are intuitive enough for us to judge the accuracy of clustering.

You can refer to the code snippet given in the following screenshot:

```
liste = pd.DataFrame(liste_produits)
liste_words = [word for (word, occurence) in list_products]

occurence = [dict() for _ in range(n_clusters)]

for i in range(n_clusters):
    liste_cluster = liste.loc[clusters == i]
    for word in liste_words:
        if word in ['art', 'set', 'heart', 'pink', 'blue', 'tag']: continue
        occurence[i][word] = sum(liste_cluster.loc[:, 0].str.contains(word.upper()))
```

Figure 3.36: Code snippet for generating a word cloud

You can refer to the code snippet given in the following screenshot:

```
def random_color_func(word=None, font_size=None, position=None,
                      orientation=None, font_path=None, random_state=None):
    h = int(360.0 * tone / 255.0)
    s = int(100.0 * 255.0 / 255.0)
    l = int(100.0 * float(random_state.randint(70, 120)) / 255.0)
    return "hsl({}, {}%, {}%)".format(h, s, l)

def make_wordcloud(liste, increment):
    ax1 = fig.add_subplot(4,2,increment)
    words = dict()
    trunc_occurences = liste[0:150]
    for s in trunc_occurences:
        words[s[0]] = s[1]

    wordcloud = WordCloud(width=1000,height=400, background_color='lightgrey',
                          max_words=1628,relative_scaling=1,
                          color_func = random_color_func,
                          normalize_plurals=False)
    wordcloud.generate_from_frequencies(words)
    ax1.imshow(wordcloud, interpolation="bilinear")
    ax1.axis('off')
    plt.title('cluster n{}'.format(increment-1))

fig = plt.figure(1, figsize=(14,14))
color = [0, 160, 130, 95, 280, 40, 330, 110, 25]
for i in range(n_clusters):
    list_cluster_occurences = occurence[i]

    tone = color[i] # define the color of the words
    liste = []
    for key, value in list_cluster_occurences.items():
        liste.append([key, value])
    liste.sort(key = lambda x:x[1], reverse = True)
    make_wordcloud(liste, i+1)
```

Figure 3.37: Code snippet for generating word cloud graphs

You can refer to the graphs given in the following screenshot:

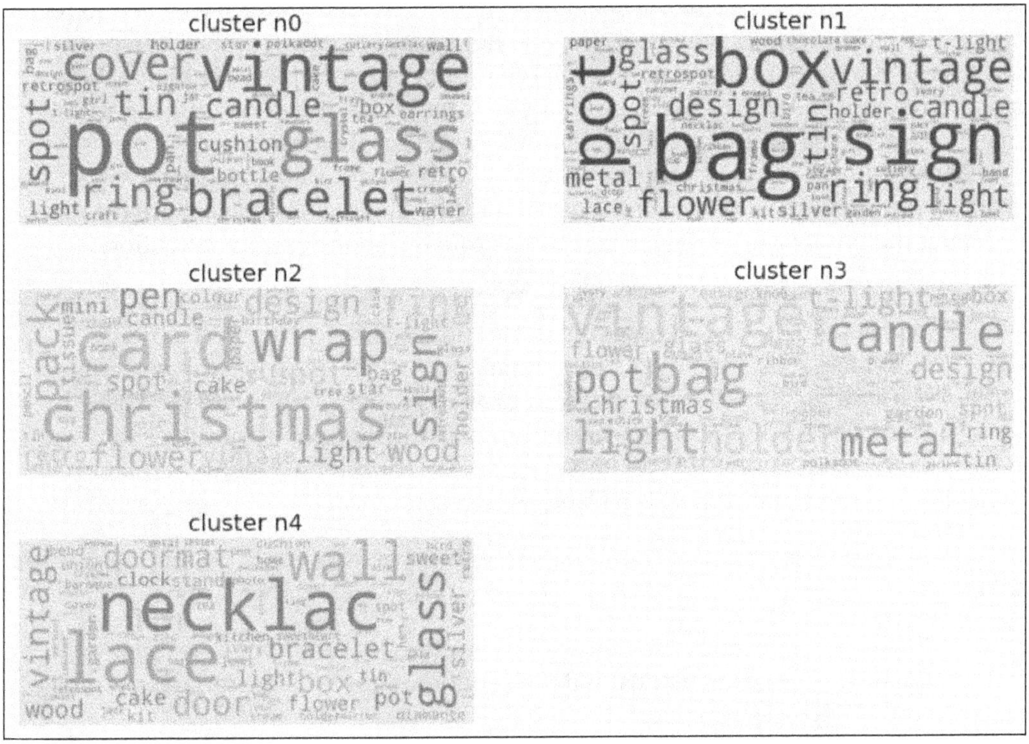

Figure 3.38: Word cloud graphs for all five clusters

From the preceding graphs, we can conclude the following points:

- Cluster number 2 contains all the words related to gifts, such as Christmas, packaging, gift, cards, and so on.
- Cluster number 4 contains all the words related to luxury items and jewelry. So, keywords such as necklace, silver, lace, and so on are present in this cluster.
- There are some words that are present in every cluster, so it is difficult to clearly distinguish them.

Now let's jump to the next section, where we will perform principal component analysis.

Principal component analysis (PCA)

In order to check whether all the clusters have truly distinct values, we need to focus on their composition. As we know, the one-hot encoded matrix of the keywords has a large number of dimensions or a large number of variables. There may be a situation where because of the large number of variables, our clustering algorithm may over-fit the dataset. First of all, we need to reduce the number of variables, but we cannot reduce them randomly. We need to choose the most important variables that can represent most of the characteristics of the dataset. The procedure for reducing the number of variables logically is called dimensionality reduction.

In order to achieve this, we will be using PCA, which is a statistical technique in which we will perform orthogonal transformation in order to convert a highly correlated set of data samples into a set of values that are linearly uncorrelated variables, and these variables are referred to as principal components. So basically, we will be using PCA because we want to reduce the number of variables that we have considered so far. PCA is a famous technique for dimensionality reduction. By using PCA, we can avoid the over-fitting issue.

Now, you might want to know situations in which you can use PCA, and they are as follows:

- If we want to reduce the number of variables (the number of features or the number of dimensions) but we cannot identify which variables can be considered and which can't
- If we want to ensure that our variables are independent of each other
- If we are comfortable making our independent variables less interpretable

In our case, we need to reduce the number of variables. For that, we are going to implement the code given in the following screenshot:

```
pca = PCA()
pca.fit(matrix)
pca_samples = pca.transform(matrix)
```

and then check for the amount of variance explained by each component:

```
fig, ax = plt.subplots(figsize=(14, 5))
sns.set(font_scale=1)
plt.step(range(matrix.shape[1]), pca.explained_variance_ratio_.cumsum(), where='mid',
         label='cumulative explained variance')
sns.barplot(np.arange(1,matrix.shape[1]+1), pca.explained_variance_ratio_, alpha=0.5, color = 'g',
            label='individual explained variance')
plt.xlim(0, 100)

ax.set_xticklabels([s if int(s.get_text())%2 == 0 else '' for s in ax.get_xticklabels()])

plt.ylabel('Explained variance', fontsize = 14)
plt.xlabel('Principal components', fontsize = 14)
plt.legend(loc='upper left', fontsize = 13);
```

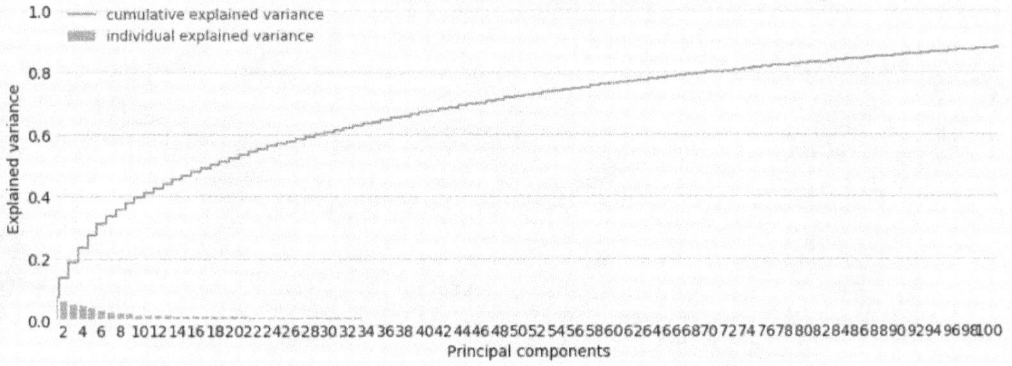

Figure 3.39: Code snippet for implementing PCA

As you can see in the preceding code, we are checking the amount of variance explained by each component. We need to consider more than 100 components to explain 90% of the variance of our dataset.

Here, I will consider a limited number of components because this decomposition is performed only to visualize the data. You can refer to the code shown in the following screenshot:

```
pca = PCA(n_components=50)
matrix_9D = pca.fit_transform(matrix)
mat = pd.DataFrame(matrix_9D)
mat['cluster'] = pd.Series(clusters)

import matplotlib.patches as mpatches

sns.set_style("white")
sns.set_context("notebook", font_scale=1, rc={"lines.linewidth": 2.5})

LABEL_COLOR_MAP = {0:'r', 1:'gold', 2:'b', 3:'k', 4:'c', 5:'g'}
label_color = [LABEL_COLOR_MAP[l] for l in mat['cluster']]

fig = plt.figure(figsize = (12,10))
increment = 0
for ix in range(4):
    for iy in range(ix+1, 4):
        increment += 1
        ax = fig.add_subplot(3,3,increment)
        ax.scatter(mat[ix], mat[iy], c= label_color, alpha=0.4)
        plt.ylabel('PCA {}'.format(iy+1), fontsize = 12)
        plt.xlabel('PCA {}'.format(ix+1), fontsize = 12)
        ax.yaxis.grid(color='lightgray', linestyle=':')
        ax.xaxis.grid(color='lightgray', linestyle=':')
        ax.spines['right'].set_visible(False)
        ax.spines['top'].set_visible(False)

        if increment == 9: break
    if increment == 9: break


comp_handler = []
for i in range(5):
    comp_handler.append(mpatches.Patch(color = LABEL_COLOR_MAP[i], label = i))

plt.legend(handles=comp_handler, bbox_to_anchor=(1.1, 0.97),
           title='Cluster',
           shadow = True, frameon = True, framealpha = 1,fontsize = 13,
           bbox_transform = plt.gcf().transFigure) #facecolor = 'lightgrey',

plt.tight_layout()
```

Figure 3.40: Code snippet for generating PCA decomposition graphs

As you can see, we have used PCA components using `PCA(n_components=50)`, and we have stored the values in dataframe `mat`, which we can use in future.

The output of the preceding code is in the form of graphs. So, you can refer to the following screenshot:

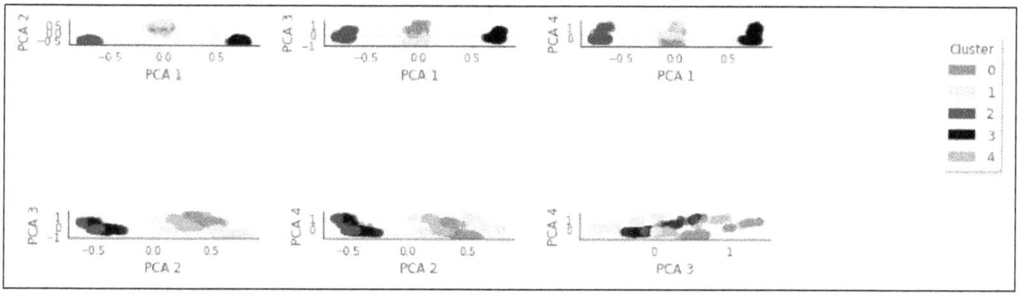

Figure 3.41: Graphs for the PCA for each cluster

Here, we have used `tight_layout`, which is the reason why the graphs shrank a bit.

So far, we have performed enough EDA to help us generate a basic insight into the dataset. Now we will move on to the next section, where we will start building customer categories or customer segmentation. We will take into account all the findings that we have implemented so far.

Generating customer categories

As you know, our first goal is to develop customer segmentation. From this section onward, we will focus mainly on how we can come up with customer segmentation. So far, we have done an analysis of orders, products, prices, and so on. Here, our main focus is on generating customer categories based on the insights that we got during EDA.

These are the steps that we are going to follow in order to develop the customer categories:

- Formatting data:
    - Grouping products
    - Splitting the dataset
    - Grouping orders
- Creating customer categories:
    - Data encoding
    - Generating customer categories

Now let's see what we are going to do in each of these steps.

Formatting data

As mentioned earlier, we will be using the findings that we generated during EDA. In the previous section, we generated five clusters for products. In order to perform the rest of the analysis, we will use this already generated list of keywords, matrices, and clusters. By using them, we will be generating a new categorical variable, `categ_product`. This variable indicates the cluster of each product. You can refer to the code snippet shown in the following screenshot:

```
corresp = dict()
for key, val in zip (liste_produits, clusters):
    corresp[key] = val

df_cleaned['categ_product'] = df_cleaned.loc[:, 'Description'].map(corresp)
df_cleaned[['InvoiceNo', 'Description',
            'categ_product']][:10]
```

	InvoiceNo	Description	categ_product
0	536365	WHITE HANGING HEART T-LIGHT HOLDER	1
1	536365	WHITE METAL LANTERN	0
2	536365	CREAM CUPID HEARTS COAT HANGER	0
3	536365	KNITTED UNION FLAG HOT WATER BOTTLE	0
4	536365	RED WOOLLY HOTTIE WHITE HEART.	0
5	536365	SET 7 BABUSHKA NESTING BOXES	4
6	536365	GLASS STAR FROSTED T-LIGHT HOLDER	0
7	536366	HAND WARMER UNION JACK	1
8	536366	HAND WARMER RED POLKA DOT	3
9	536367	ASSORTED COLOUR BIRD ORNAMENT	3

Figure 3.42: Code snippet for generating new categorical variable categ_product

As you can see, the new variable indicates the cluster number for each data entry. Now let's group the products.

Grouping products

You might wonder that if we have already developed the categories of the product, then why are we performing the grouping step here. Well, here, we will perform grouping in such a way that we can know what amount has been spent in each product category. For this, we will add five new variables, for example, categ_0, categ_1, categ_2, categ_3, and categ_4. You can refer to the code snippet displayed in the following screenshot:

```
for i in range(5):
    col = 'categ_{}'.format(i)
    df_temp = df_cleaned[df_cleaned['categ_product'] == i]
    price_temp = df_temp['UnitPrice'] * (df_temp['Quantity'] - df_temp['QuantityCanceled'])
    price_temp = price_temp.apply(lambda x:x if x > 0 else 0)
    df_cleaned.loc[:, col] = price_temp
    df_cleaned[col].fillna(0, inplace = True)


df_cleaned[['InvoiceNo', 'Description',
            'categ_product', 'categ_0', 'categ_1', 'categ_2', 'categ_3','categ_4']][:10]
```

	InvoiceNo	Description	categ_product	categ_0	categ_1	categ_2	categ_3	categ_4
0	536365	WHITE HANGING HEART T-LIGHT HOLDER	1	0.00	15.3	0.0	0.00	0.0
1	536365	WHITE METAL LANTERN	0	20.34	0.0	0.0	0.00	0.0
2	536365	CREAM CUPID HEARTS COAT HANGER	0	22.00	0.0	0.0	0.00	0.0
3	536365	KNITTED UNION FLAG HOT WATER BOTTLE	0	20.34	0.0	0.0	0.00	0.0
4	536365	RED WOOLLY HOTTIE WHITE HEART.	0	20.34	0.0	0.0	0.00	0.0
5	536365	SET 7 BABUSHKA NESTING BOXES	4	0.00	0.0	0.0	0.00	15.3
6	536365	GLASS STAR FROSTED T-LIGHT HOLDER	0	25.50	0.0	0.0	0.00	0.0
7	536366	HAND WARMER UNION JACK	1	0.00	11.1	0.0	0.00	0.0
8	536366	HAND WARMER RED POLKA DOT	3	0.00	0.0	0.0	11.10	0.0
9	536367	ASSORTED COLOUR BIRD ORNAMENT	3	0.00	0.0	0.0	54.08	0.0

Figure 3.43: Code snippet for generating the amount spent in each product category

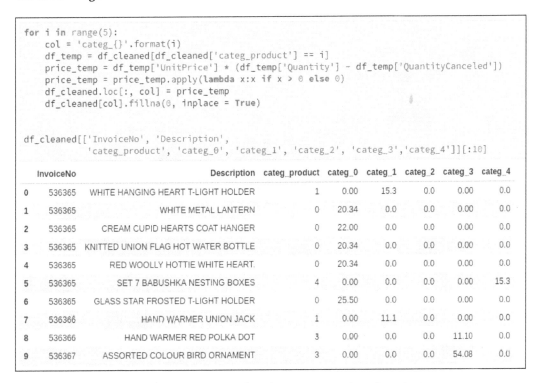

Orders are split into multiple entries, so we need to use the basket price. This time, we will merge the basket price as well as the way it is distributed over five product categories. We will put all this information into the new dataframe. Refer to the following screenshot:

```
# sum of purchases / user & order
temp = df_cleaned.groupby(by=['CustomerID', 'InvoiceNo'], as_index=False)['TotalPrice'].sum()
basket_price = temp.rename(columns = {'TotalPrice':'Basket Price'})

# percentage of the price of the order / product category
for i in range(5):
    col = 'categ_{}'.format(i)
    temp = df_cleaned.groupby(by=['CustomerID', 'InvoiceNo'], as_index=False)[col].sum()
    basket_price.loc[:, col] = temp

# date of the order

df_cleaned['InvoiceDate_int'] = df_cleaned['InvoiceDate'].astype('int64')
temp = df_cleaned.groupby(by=['CustomerID', 'InvoiceNo'], as_index=False)['InvoiceDate_int'].mean()
df_cleaned.drop('InvoiceDate_int', axis = 1, inplace = True)
basket_price.loc[:, 'InvoiceDate'] = pd.to_datetime(temp['InvoiceDate_int'])

# selection of significant entries:
basket_price = basket_price[basket_price['Basket Price'] > 0]
basket_price.sort_values('CustomerID', ascending = True)[:5]
```

	CustomerID	InvoiceNo	Basket Price	categ_0	categ_1	categ_2	categ_3	categ_4	InvoiceDate
1	12347	537626	711.79	293.35	83.40	23.40	187.2	124.44	2010-12-07 14:57:00.000001024
2	12347	542237	475.39	169.20	91.35	84.34	130.5	0.00	2011-01-26 14:29:59.999999744
3	12347	549222	636.25	115.00	109.35	81.00	330.9	0.00	2011-04-07 10:42:59.999999232
4	12347	556201	382.52	168.76	78.06	41.40	74.4	19.90	2011-06-09 13:01:00.000000256
5	12347	562032	584.91	158.16	157.95	61.30	109.7	97.80	2011-08-02 08:48:00.000000000

Figure 3.44: Code snippet for obtaining the distribution of basket prices for five clusters

Finally, we have the basket price for each order, and we also know the price distribution over five clusters. The new dataframe is `basket_price`. Now let's move on to the next section.

Splitting the dataset

In this section, we will be using the dataframe `basket_price`, which contains data entries for the past 12 months. The second goal of this application is to predict the customer purchase behavior based on their first site visit or purchase. So, in order to achieve that goal right now, we will split the dataset. We will use 10 months' dataset for training and 2 months' dataset for testing. I'm including this step here because later on, we can use these training and testing datasets and you can easily get to use the new dataframe. You can refer to the code given in the following screenshot:

```
print(basket_price['InvoiceDate'].min(), '->', basket_price['InvoiceDate'].max())

2010-12-01 08:26:00 -> 2011-12-09 12:50:00

set_entrainement = basket_price[basket_price['InvoiceDate'] < datetime.date(2011,10,1)]
set_test         = basket_price[basket_price['InvoiceDate'] >= datetime.date(2011,10,1)]
basket_price = set_entrainement.copy(deep = True)
```

Figure 3.45: Code snippet for splitting the dataset using time

Now we will group the customers and their orders along with the basket price distribution.

Grouping orders

Here, we will merge the customers and their orders so that we can learn which customer placed how many orders. We will also generate the minimum order amount, the maximum order amount, and the mean order amount. Refer to the code given in the following screenshot:

```
# of visits and stats on cart amount / users
transactions_per_user=basket_price.groupby(by=['CustomerID'])['Basket Price'].agg(['count','min',
                                                                                    'max','mean','sum'])
for i in range(5):
    col = 'categ_{}'.format(i)
    transactions_per_user.loc[:,col] = basket_price.groupby(by=['CustomerID'])[col].sum() /\
                                            transactions_per_user['sum']*100

transactions_per_user.reset_index(drop = False, inplace = True)
basket_price.groupby(by=['CustomerID'])['categ_0'].sum()
transactions_per_user.sort_values('CustomerID', ascending = True)[:5]
```

	CustomerID	count	min	max	mean	sum	categ_0	categ_1	categ_2	categ_3	categ_4
0	12347	5	382.52	711.79	558.172000	2790.86	29.836681	18.636191	32.408290	8.676179	10.442659
1	12348	4	227.44	892.00	449.310000	1797.24	41.953217	20.030714	0.000000	0.000000	38.016069
2	12350	1	334.40	334.40	334.400000	334.40	48.444976	39.862440	0.000000	0.000000	11.692584
3	12352	6	144.35	840.30	345.663333	2073.98	12.892120	56.603728	15.711338	14.301006	0.491808
4	12353	1	89.00	89.00	89.000000	89.00	13.033708	64.606742	0.000000	22.359551	0.000000

Figure 3.46: Code snippet for generating order-wise stats for each customer

We will also generate two variables that indicate the number of days elapsed since the last purchase and the first purchase. The names of these variables are `FirstPurchase` and `LastPurchase`. Refer to the code snippet given in the following screenshot:

```
last_date = basket_price['InvoiceDate'].max().date()

first_registration = pd.DataFrame(basket_price.groupby(by=['CustomerID'])['InvoiceDate'].min())
last_purchase      = pd.DataFrame(basket_price.groupby(by=['CustomerID'])['InvoiceDate'].max())

test  = first_registration.applymap(lambda x:(last_date - x.date()).days)
test2 = last_purchase.applymap(lambda x:(last_date - x.date()).days)

transactions_per_user.loc[:, 'LastPurchase'] = test2.reset_index(drop = False)['InvoiceDate']
transactions_per_user.loc[:, 'FirstPurchase'] = test.reset_index(drop = False)['InvoiceDate']

transactions_per_user[:5]
```

	CustomerID	count	min	max	mean	sum	categ_0	categ_1	categ_2	categ_3	categ_4	LastPurchase	FirstPurchase
0	12347	5	382.52	711.79	558.172000	2790.86	29.836681	18.636191	32.408290	8.676179	10.442659	59	297
1	12348	4	227.44	892.80	449.310000	1797.24	41.953217	20.030714	0.000000	0.000000	38.016069	5	288
2	12350	1	334.40	334.40	334.400000	334.40	48.444976	39.862440	0.000000	0.000000	11.692584	240	240
3	12352	6	144.35	840.30	345.663333	2073.98	12.892120	56.603728	15.711338	14.301006	0.491808	2	226
4	12353	1	89.00	89.00	89.000000	89.00	13.033708	64.606742	0.000000	22.359551	0.000000	134	134

Figure 3.47: Code snippet for generating elapsed days for the last and first purchase

The customer categories in which we are interested are the ones that make only one order. One of our main objectives is to target these customers in such a way that we can retain them. We need to obtain the data for the number of customers that belong to this category. For that, refer to the code given in the following screenshot:

```
n1 = transactions_per_user[transactions_per_user['count'] == 1].shape[0]
n2 = transactions_per_user.shape[0]
print("No. customers with single purchase: {:<2}/{:<5} ({:<2.2f}%)".format(n1,n2,n1/n2*100))

No. customers with single purchase: 1445/3608  (40.05%)
```

Figure 3.48: Code snippet for generating the number of customers with one purchase

From the preceding code, we can find out that 40% of the customer base has placed only one order, and we need to retain them.

Now let's build the customer categories.

Creating customer categories

Basically, we will be generating the customer segmentation here. So, we will work on achieving the first goal of the chapter in this section. We will build customer segmentation based on the customers' purchase pattern. There are two steps in this section:

- Data encoding
- Generating customer categories or customer segmentation

We will start with data encoding.

Data encoding

We will be generating the dataframe that contains the summary of all operations we have performed so far. Each record of this dataframe is associated with a single client. We can use this information to characterize various types of customers.

The dataframe that we have generated has different variables. All these variables have different ranges and variations. So, we need to generate a matrix where these data entries are standardized. You can refer to the code given in the following screenshot:

```
list_cols = ['count','min','max','mean','categ_0','categ_1','categ_2','categ_3','categ_4']
#_____________________________________________________________
selected_customers = transactions_per_user.copy(deep = True)
matrix = selected_customers[list_cols].as_matrix()
```

In practice, the different variables I selected have quite different ranges of variation and before continuing the analysis, I create a matrix where these data are standardized:

```
scaler = StandardScaler()
scaler.fit(matrix)
print('variables mean values: \n' + 90*'-' + '\n' , scaler.mean_)
scaled_matrix = scaler.transform(matrix)

variables mean values:
------------------------------------------------------------------------------------------
 [  3.62305987 259.93189634 556.26687999 377.06036244  25.22916919
  28.73795868  16.37327913  15.67936332  13.98907929]
```

Figure 3.49: Code snippet for generating summary data entries for each client

Before creating customer segmentation, we need to create the base. This base should include important variables. We need to include a small number of important variables. In order to select the important variables, we will be using principal component analysis. So, that we can describe the segmentation accurately. We will use PCA for this task. The code snippet is given in the following screenshot:

```
pca = PCA()
pca.fit(scaled_matrix)
pca_samples = pca.transform(scaled_matrix)
```

and I represent the amount of variance explained by each of the components:

```
fig, ax = plt.subplots(figsize=(14, 5))
sns.set(font_scale=1)
plt.step(range(matrix.shape[1]), pca.explained_variance_ratio_.cumsum(), where='mid',
        label='cumulative explained variance')
sns.barplot(np.arange(1,matrix.shape[1]+1), pca.explained_variance_ratio_, alpha=0.5, color = 'g',
            label='individual explained variance')
plt.xlim(0, 10)

ax.set_xticklabels([s if int(s.get_text())%2 == 0 else '' for s in ax.get_xticklabels()])

plt.ylabel('Explained variance', fontsize = 14)
plt.xlabel('Principal components', fontsize = 14)
plt.legend(loc='best', fontsize = 13);
```

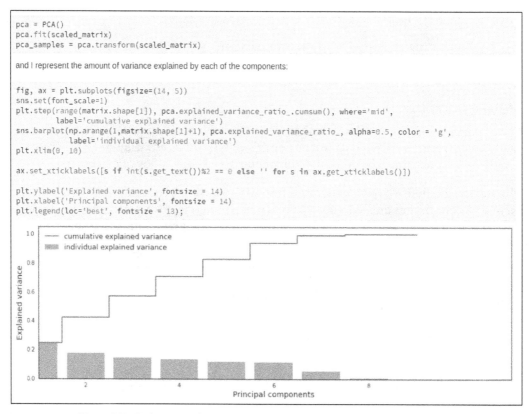

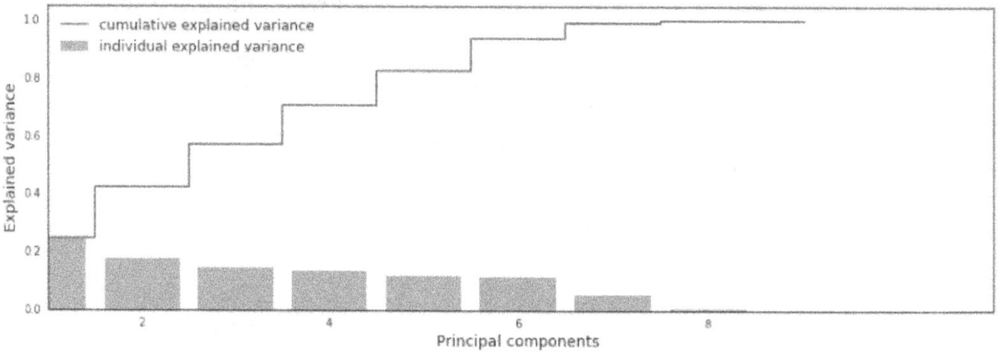

Figure 3.50: Code snippet for PCA in order to generate the customer segmentation

Here, we can see that there are eight principal components. Now let's move on to the next section, where we will generate the customer segmentation.

Generating customer categories

We will be using the k-means clustering algorithm to generate segmentation. The number of clusters will be derived by using the silhouette score. We have used the silhouette score earlier, and by using the same method, we can derive the number of clusters. Here, we obtain 11 clusters based on the silhouette score. You can refer to the following screenshot:

```
n_clusters = 11
kmeans = KMeans(init='k-means++', n_clusters = n_clusters, n_init=100)
kmeans.fit(scaled_matrix)
clusters_clients = kmeans.predict(scaled_matrix)
silhouette_avg = silhouette_score(scaled_matrix, clusters_clients)
print('silhouette score: {:<.3f}'.format(silhouette_avg))
```

```
silhouette score: 0.217
```

At first, I look at the number of customers in each cluster:

```
pd.DataFrame(pd.Series(clusters_clients).value_counts(), columns = ['number of clients']).T
```

	0	5	8	3	4	9	7	6	1	2	10
number of clients	1489	487	390	348	291	233	188	152	12	11	7

Figure 3.51: Code snippet for generating customer segmentations

As you can see, there is a large difference in the size of the segmentation, so we need to analyze the components of the clusters using PCA.

PCA analysis

We will use six components here. The code snippet and graphical representation of PCA for 11 clusters are given in the following screenshot:

```
pca = PCA(n_components=6)
matrix_3D = pca.fit_transform(scaled_matrix)
mat = pd.DataFrame(matrix_3D)
mat['cluster'] = pd.Series(clusters_clients)
```

in order to create a representation of the various clusters:

```
import matplotlib.patches as mpatches

sns.set_style("white")
sns.set_context("notebook", font_scale=1, rc={"lines.linewidth": 2.5})

LABEL_COLOR_MAP = {0:'r', 1:'tan', 2:'b', 3:'k', 4:'c', 5:'g', 6:'deeppink', 7:'skyblue', 8:'darkcyan',
                   9:'orange',
                   10:'yellow', 11:'tomato', 12:'seagreen'}
label_color = [LABEL_COLOR_MAP[l] for l in mat['cluster']]

fig = plt.figure(figsize = (12,10))
increment = 0
for ix in range(6):
    for iy in range(ix+1, 6):
        increment += 1
        ax = fig.add_subplot(4,3,increment)
        ax.scatter(mat[ix], mat[iy], c= label_color, alpha=0.5)
        plt.ylabel('PCA {}'.format(iy+1), fontsize = 12)
        plt.xlabel('PCA {}'.format(ix+1), fontsize = 12)
        ax.yaxis.grid(color='lightgray', linestyle=':')
        ax.xaxis.grid(color='lightgray', linestyle=':')
        ax.spines['right'].set_visible(False)
        ax.spines['top'].set_visible(False)

        if increment == 12: break
    if increment == 12: break

#_______________________________________________
# I set the legend: abreviation -> airline name
comp_handler = []
for i in range(n_clusters):
    comp_handler.append(mpatches.Patch(color = LABEL_COLOR_MAP[i], label = i))

plt.legend(handles=comp_handler, bbox_to_anchor=(1.1, 0.9),
           title='Cluster',
           shadow = True, frameon = True, framealpha = 1,
           fontsize = 13, bbox_transform = plt.gcf().transFigure) #facecolor = 'lightgrey',

plt.tight_layout()
```

Figure 3.52: Code snippet for implementing PCA and generating graphs

As an output, the following graphs have been generated:

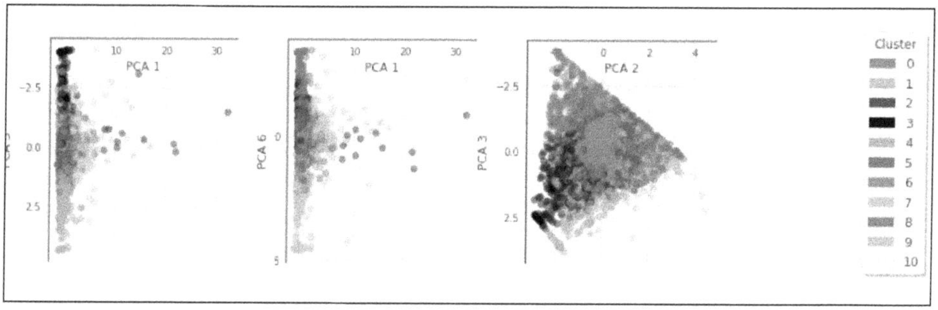

Figure 3.53: Graphs of PCA for customer segmentation

I have displayed only three graphs here. In the code, there are nine graphs. When you run the code, you can see them all. Note that the first component separates the tiniest cluster from the rest. For this dataset, we can say that there will always be a representation in which two segments will appear to be distinct. Now let's obtain silhouette scores.

Analyzing the cluster using silhouette scores

In this section, we will generate the silhouette score for each cluster. This will indicate the quality of the separation of data samples. You can refer to the code snippet and graph shown in the following screenshot:

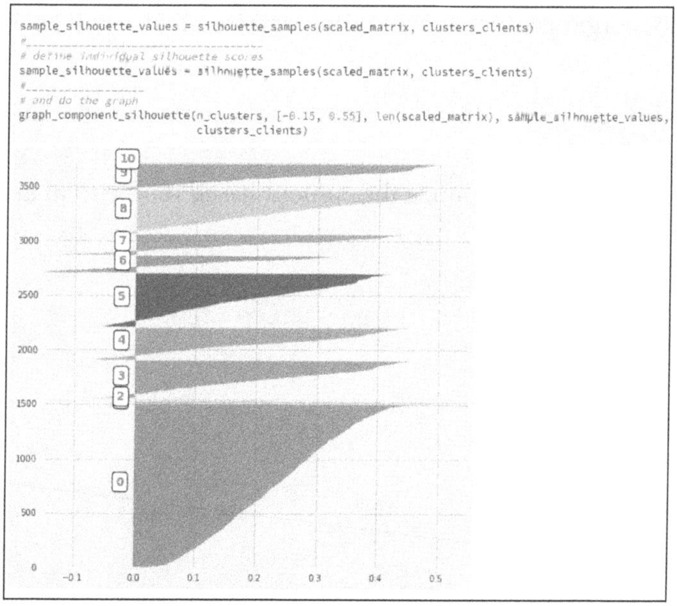

Figure 3.54: Code snippet for generating graphs for silhouette scores

From the preceding graphs, we can ensure that all the clusters are disjointed. Now we need to learn more about the habits of the customers of each cluster. To do that, we will add variables that define the cluster to which each customer belongs.

For this, we will be generating a new dataframe, `selected_customers`. After generating the new dataframe, we will average the content of the dataframe. This will provide us with the average basket price, total visits, and so on. You can refer to the code shown in the following screenshot:

```
selected_customers.loc[:, 'cluster'] = clusters_clients

merged_df = pd.DataFrame()
for i in range(n_clusters):
    test = pd.DataFrame(selected_customers[selected_customers['cluster'] == i].mean())
    test = test.T.set_index('cluster', drop = True)
    test['size'] = selected_customers[selected_customers['cluster'] == i].shape[0]
    merged_df = pd.concat([merged_df, test])
#_____________________________________________________
merged_df.drop('CustomerID', axis = 1, inplace = True)
print('number of customers:', merged_df['size'].sum())

merged_df = merged_df.sort_values('sum')

number of customers: 3608
```

Figure 3.55: Code snippet for storing the habits of the customers

Now we need to reorganize the content of the dataframe. We will be considering two points here:

1. We need to reorganize the data based on the amount spent in each product category
2. After that, we will reorganize the content based on the total amount spent

You can take a look at the implementation shown in the following screenshot:

```
liste_index = []
for i in range(5):
    column = 'categ_{}'.format(i)
    liste_index.append(merged_df[merged_df[column] > 45].index.values[0])

liste_index_reordered = liste_index
liste_index_reordered += [ s for s in merged_df.index if s not in liste_index]

merged_df = merged_df.reindex(index = liste_index_reordered)
merged_df = merged_df.reset_index(drop = False)
display(merged_df[['cluster', 'count', 'min', 'max', 'mean', 'sum', 'categ_0',
                   'categ_1', 'categ_2', 'categ_3', 'categ_4', 'size']])
```

	cluster	count	min	max	mean	sum	categ_0	categ_1	categ_2	categ_3	categ_4	size
0	4.0	2.158076	201.563814	335.191924	262.058036	657.302646	51.285434	17.683058	6.611438	13.688688	10.784610	291
1	8.0	2.366667	204.284026	350.932897	271.285802	701.958718	6.960057	67.243626	5.249333	10.862250	9.684735	390
2	9.0	2.227468	192.907468	319.542876	247.378087	594.252403	6.016855	13.036688	57.385765	18.089334	5.471358	233
3	5.0	2.427105	217.226982	333.360864	272.118091	672.683965	8.037816	16.447660	13.129836	56.334283	6.053461	487
4	3.0	2.488506	192.640865	308.972845	244.623993	622.081382	13.055303	18.042451	5.250963	11.415390	52.252108	348
5	0.0	3.320349	218.424420	464.717321	332.127937	1112.598308	17.086875	29.126731	13.671240	25.524655	14.594479	1489
6	7.0	1.691489	1048.068351	1370.794686	1196.428458	2086.226867	16.956104	31.472654	11.965345	25.958524	13.647733	188
7	1.0	1.666667	3480.920833	3966.812500	3700.139306	5949.600000	15.171169	23.557001	22.890736	20.102624	18.278470	12
8	6.0	18.263158	87.963158	1554.952237	565.621205	9748.711513	16.281496	31.764704	12.268306	24.041071	15.665037	152
9	10.0	92.000000	10.985714	1858.250000	374.601553	34845.105714	13.402971	29.951729	13.117583	25.832531	17.721038	7
10	2.0	22.909091	385.752727	16513.428182	4601.666146	83676.573636	17.813890	34.754173	6.520520	20.206767	20.704650	11

Figure 3.56: Code snippet for reorganizing the dataset

As you can see, we have obtained the behavior of the customer for each segment. Now we can recommend the items based on these characteristics. We can design the marketing campaign based on the generated facts.

The particular marketing strategy can be applied to customers who belong to cluster 4 and cluster 8. We should recommend the premium products to the cluster 1 clients.

So far, we have achieved our first goal. Now it's time to aim for the second goal. So let's begin!

Classifying customers

Before we begin, let's have a refresher on what our goal is. This helps you understand things in a clearer manner. The objective is that we are going to build a classifier that will classify the customers into different customer segments that were established in the previous section. We also need one more feature. Our classifier should generate this classification result when the customer visits the platform for the first time. In order to implement this kind of functionality, we will be using various supervised machine learning algorithms. We will use the scikit-learn API.

In order to develop the baseline classifier, we need to perform the following steps:

- Defining the helper functions
- Splitting the data into training and testing
- Implementing the Machine Learning (ML) algorithm

Defining helper functions

Basically, we define a class named `class_fit` and then we define various functions that can help us when we train the ML model. These are the helper functions that we will be using:

1. The `train` function helps us train the model
2. The `predict` function helps us predict the result for the test dataset or the new data sample
3. The `grid_search` function helps us find out appropriate hyperparameters and the value of cross-validation(CV) folds
4. The `grid_fit` function helps us train the model using cross-validation and generate the optimal hyperparameters .
5. The `grid_predict` function helps us generate prediction as well as the accuracy score.

You can refer to the code snippet shown in the following screenshot:

```
class Class_Fit(object):
    def __init__(self, clf, params=None):
        if params:
            self.clf = clf(**params)
        else:
            self.clf = clf()

    def train(self, x_train, y_train):
        self.clf.fit(x_train, y_train)

    def predict(self, x):
        return self.clf.predict(x)

    def grid_search(self, parameters, Kfold):
        self.grid = GridSearchCV(estimator = self.clf, param_grid = parameters, cv = Kfold)

    def grid_fit(self, X, Y):
        self.grid.fit(X, Y)

    def grid_predict(self, X, Y):
        self.predictions = self.grid.predict(X)
        print("Precision: {:.2f} % ".format(100*metrics.accuracy_score(Y, self.predictions)))
```

Figure 3.57: Code snippet for the helper function

Now let's move on to the next section.

Splitting the data into training and testing

We will be using the data that we have stored in the `selected_customers` dataframe. You can see some entries of the dataset on which we will apply the ML algorithm. Take a look at the following screenshot:

```
selected_customers.head()
```

	CustomerID	count	min	max	mean	sum	categ_0	categ_1	categ_2	categ_3	categ_4	LastPurchase	FirstPurchase	cluster
0	12347	5	382.52	711.79	558.172000	2790.86	32.408290	18.636191	10.442659	29.836681	8.676179	59	297	0
1	12348	4	227.44	892.80	449.310000	1797.24	0.000000	20.030714	38.016069	41.953217	0.000000	5	288	5
2	12350	1	334.40	334.40	334.400000	334.40	0.000000	39.862440	11.692584	48.444976	0.000000	240	240	5
3	12352	6	144.35	840.30	345.663333	2073.98	15.711338	56.603728	0.491808	12.892120	14.301006	2	226	8
4	12353	1	89.00	89.00	89.000000	89.00	0.000000	64.606742	0.000000	13.033708	22.359551	134	134	8

```
columns = ['mean', 'categ_0', 'categ_1', 'categ_2', 'categ_3', 'categ_4' ]
X = selected_customers[columns]
Y = selected_customers['cluster']
```

Figure 3.58: Sample entries in the dataset

As you can see, we will predict the cluster number for the new customer, so we have stored that value as `Y`, and columns such as `mean, categ_0 to categ_4` are used as input features for the ML model, so we have stored them in the `X` variable. Now we need to split this data into training and testing. For that, we use the sklearn API `train_test_split()`. We are using 80% of the data for training and 20% of data for testing. Take a look at the following screenshot:

```
X_train, X_test, Y_train, Y_test = model_selection.train_test_split(X, Y, train_size = 0.8)
```

Figure 3.59: Code snippet for splitting the dataset into training and testing

We have the training and testing datasets with us. Now, we need to start implementing the ML algorithm.

Implementing the Machine Learning (ML) algorithm

For the baseline approach, we will be implementing the Support Vector machine (SVM) classifier. We will be using helper functions that we have previously defined. Here, I will create an instance of the class and call the methods that we have declared previously. Take a look at the code snippet shown in the following screenshot:

```
svc = Class_Fit(clf = svm.LinearSVC)
svc.grid_search(parameters = [{'C':np.logspace(-2,2,10)}], Kfold = 5)
```

Once this instance is created, I adjust the classifier to the training data:

```
svc.grid_fit(X = X_train, Y = Y_train)
```

Figure 3.60: Code snippet for training the model using the SVM classifier

As you can see in the code snippet, `svc` is the class instance. We are using linear SVM. We have used `grid_search` to search optimal hyperparameters as well as obtain the number of CV folds. After that, we have called the `grid_fit` method, which is used to train the ML model using our training dataset.

This is the way we have implemented our baseline approach. Now let's test the result.

Understanding the testing matrix

We will be using the confusion matrix and the learning curve to evaluate the ML models. So before starting with the testing, we need to understand what the confusion matrix and the learning curve are. We will cover these concepts one by one.

Confusion matrix

When we are implementing a multi-class classifier, naturally, we have multiple classes and the number of data entries belonging to all the classes is different, so during testing, we need to know whether the classifier performs equally well for all the classes or whether it is biased toward some classes. This analysis can be done using the confusion matrix. It will have a count of how many data entries are correctly classified and how many are misclassified.

Let's take an example. Say, there is a total of 10 data entries that belong to a class, and the label for that class is 1. Now when we generate the prediction from our ML model, we will check how many data entries out of the 10 entries get the predicted class label 1. Suppose six data entries are correctly classified and get the class label 1. In this case, for six entries, the *predicted label* and *True label* is the same, so the accuracy is 60%, whereas for the remaining data entries, the ML model misclassifies them. The ML model predicts class labels other than 1.

From the preceding example, you can see that the confusion matrix gives us an idea about how many data entries are classified correctly and how many are misclassified. We can explore the class-wise accuracy of the classifier. Take a look at the following screenshot:

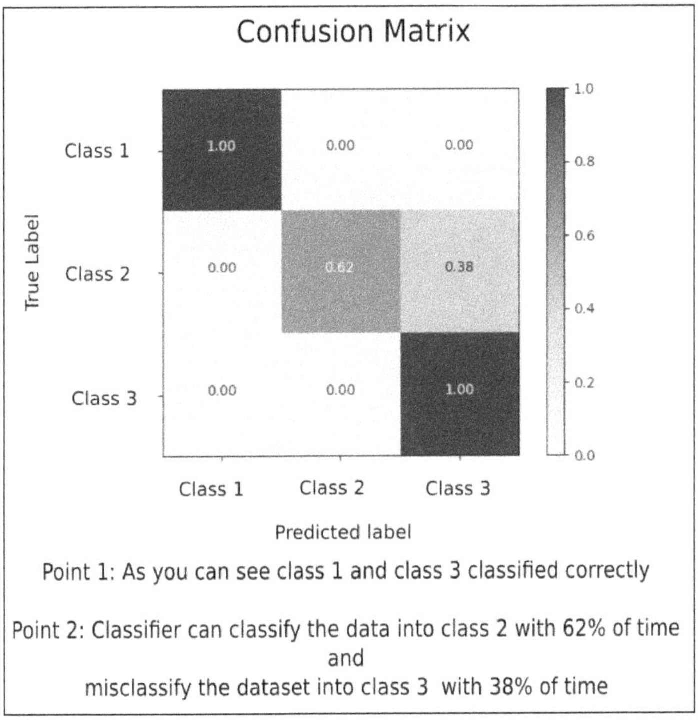

Figure 3.61: Example of confusion matrix

Now let's take a look at the learning curve.

Learning curve

We are plotting two lines here. One line indicates the training score, and the other line indicates the testing score. Here, the training and testing scores determine cross-validated training and testing scores for different training dataset sizes. By using this learning curve, we can monitor whether the ML model is converging properly or not. Both the CV score and the training score will help us determine whether training is going in the right direction or the ML model is suffering from over-fitting or under-fitting. With the increased size of dataset, if the CV score and training scores achieve a low score, then it means that the training was not performed in a proper manner. However, if the CV score and training score increase with the increased size of dataset, then it means that the training is moving in the right direction. Refer to the following screenshot:

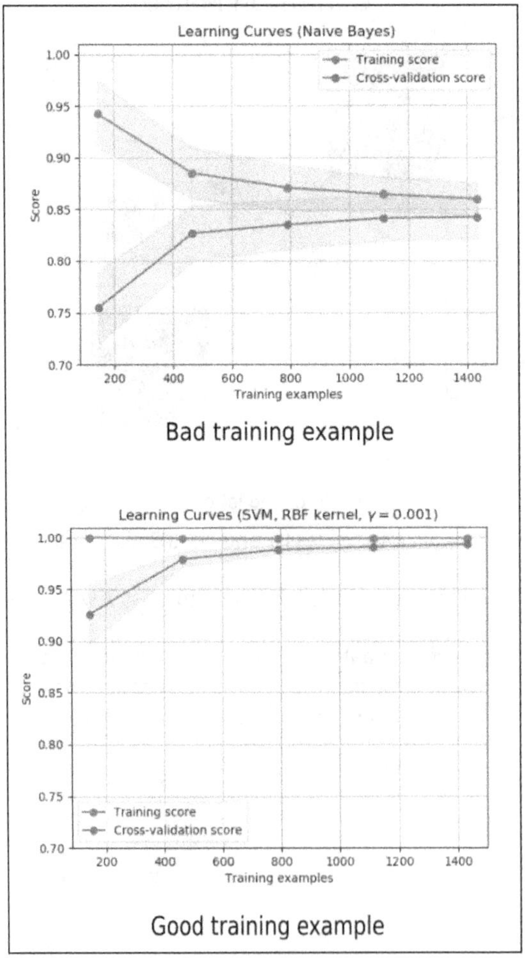

Figure 3.62: Bad and good examples for the learning curve

Now that we have understood the basic intuition behind the testing matrix, we can start testing our baseline approach.

Testing the result of the baseline approach

In this section, we will test the baseline model using the following approaches:

- Generating the accuracy score for the classifier
- Generating the confusion matrix for the classifier
- Generating the learning curve for the classifier

Generating the accuracy score for classifier

First, we will use `grid_predict` to generate the accuracy score for testing the dataset. We will check the accuracy of the SVM algorithm. For that, the code snippet is given in the following screenshot:

```
svc.grid_predict(X_test, Y_test)

Precision: 79.50 %
```

Figure 3.63: Code snippet for generating the accuracy score

We got a 79.50% precision for the baseline approach. Now let's look at the quality of the prediction using the confusion matrix.

Generating the confusion matrix for the classifier

Now we will generate the confusion matrix, which will give us a fair idea about which class is classified correctly and which classes have misclassified the data most of the time. To generate the confusion matrix, refer to the code given in the following screenshot:

```
def plot_confusion_matrix(cm, classes, normalize=False, title='Confusion matrix', cmap=plt.cm.Blues):
    if normalize:
        cm = cm.astype('float') / cm.sum(axis=1)[:, np.newaxis]
        print("Normalized confusion matrix")
    else:
        print('Confusion matrix, without normalization')

    plt.imshow(cm, interpolation='nearest', cmap=cmap)
    plt.title(title)
    plt.colorbar()
    tick_marks = np.arange(len(classes))
    plt.xticks(tick_marks, classes, rotation=0)
    plt.yticks(tick_marks, classes)

    fmt = '.2f' if normalize else 'd'
    thresh = cm.max() / 2.
    for i, j in itertools.product(range(cm.shape[0]), range(cm.shape[1])):
        plt.text(j, i, format(cm[i, j], fmt),
                 horizontalalignment="center",
                 color="white" if cm[i, j] > thresh else "black")
    #------------------------------------------------
    plt.tight_layout()
    plt.ylabel('True label')
    plt.xlabel('Predicted label')
```

from which I create the following representation:

```
class_names = [i for i in range(11)]
cnf_matrix = confusion_matrix(Y_test, svc.predictions)
np.set_printoptions(precision=2)
plt.figure(figsize = (8,8))
plot_confusion_matrix(cnf_matrix, classes=class_names, normalize = False, title='Confusion matrix')
```

Figure 3.64: Code snippet for generating the confusion matrix

We have used the `confusion_matrix` API for sklearn. To draw the plot, we will define a method with the name `plot_confusion_matrix`. With the help of the preceding code, we have generated the confusion matrix given in the following screenshot:

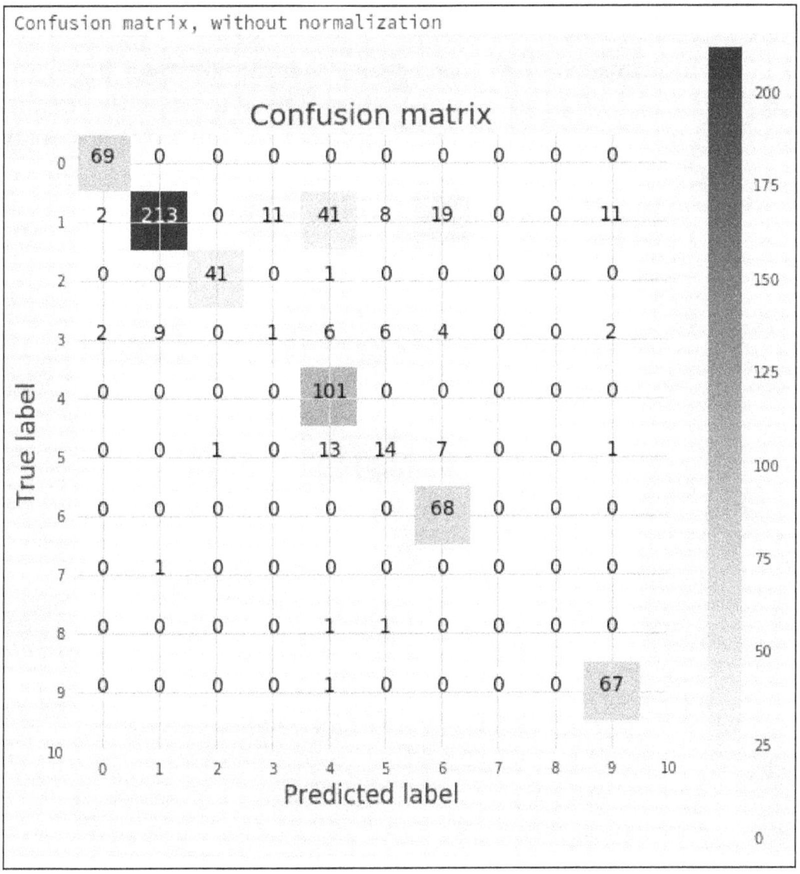

Figure 3.65: Confusion matrix for the baseline approach

As you can see, the classifier was able to classify the data into class labels 0, 2, 4, 6, and 10 accurately, whereas for class labels 1, 5, 7, and 8, the classifier is not performing so well.

Let's draw the learning curve for the baseline approach.

Generating the learning curve for the classifier

A learning curve indicates whether the classifier is facing the over-fitting or under-fitting issue. The `plot_learning_curve` method is used to draw the learning curve for the classifier. You can refer to the code snippet in the following screenshot:

```
def plot_learning_curve(estimator, title, X, y, ylim=None, cv=None,
                        n_jobs=-1, train_sizes=np.linspace(.1, 1.0, 10)):
    """Generate a simple plot of the test and training learning curve"""
    plt.figure()
    plt.title(title)
    if ylim is not None:
        plt.ylim(*ylim)
    plt.xlabel("Training examples")
    plt.ylabel("Score")
    train_sizes, train_scores, test_scores = learning_curve(
        estimator, X, y, cv=cv, n_jobs=n_jobs, train_sizes=train_sizes)
    train_scores_mean = np.mean(train_scores, axis=1)
    train_scores_std = np.std(train_scores, axis=1)
    test_scores_mean = np.mean(test_scores, axis=1)
    test_scores_std = np.std(test_scores, axis=1)
    plt.grid()

    plt.fill_between(train_sizes, train_scores_mean - train_scores_std,
                     train_scores_mean + train_scores_std, alpha=0.1, color="r")
    plt.fill_between(train_sizes, test_scores_mean - test_scores_std,
                     test_scores_mean + test_scores_std, alpha=0.1, color="g")
    plt.plot(train_sizes, train_scores_mean, 'o-', color="r", label="Training score")
    plt.plot(train_sizes, test_scores_mean, 'o-', color="g", label="Cross-validation score")

    plt.legend(loc="best")
    return plt
```

from which I represent the leanring curve of the SVC classifier:

```
g = plot_learning_curve(svc.grid.best_estimator_,
                        "SVC learning curves", X_train, Y_train, ylim = [1.01, 0.6],
                        cv = 5,  train_sizes = [0.05, 0.1, 0.2, 0.3, 0.4, 0.5,
                                                0.6, 0.7, 0.8, 0.9, 1])
```

Figure 3.66: Code snippet for generating the learning curve for the baseline approach

The learning curve is displayed in the following screenshot:

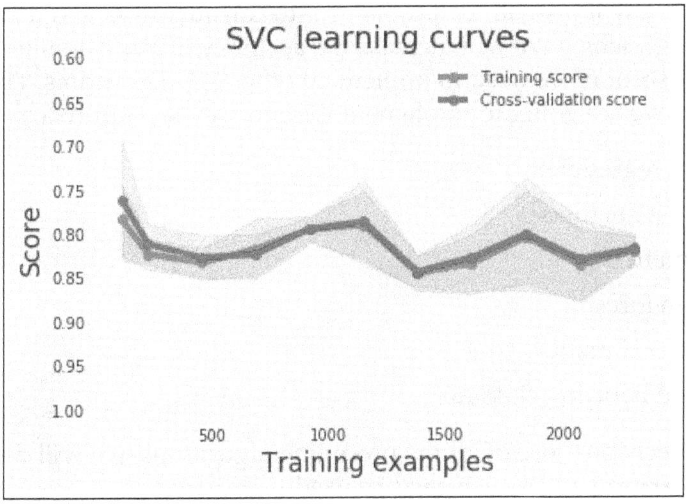

Figure 3.67: Learning curve for the baseline approach

As you can see, the CV curve converges at the same limit when we increase the sample size. This means that we have low variance and we are not suffering from over-fitting. Variance is the value that indicates how much our target function will change if we will provide different training dataset. Ideally the value of the target function is derived from the training dataset by Machine Learning algorithm however the value of estimated function should not change too much if we use another training dataset. Minor change (minor variance) in the estimated function is expected. Here, the accuracy score has a low bias, which means the model is not facing the under-fitting issue as well.

Problems with the baseline approach

In this section, we will be discussing the problems we are facing with the baseline approach so that we can optimize the current approach. The problems are as follows:

- The precision score is low. There is scope for improvement.
- We need to try other ML algorithms so that we can compare the results. Later on, if there is a need, then we can build the voting mechanism.

Basically, in the revised approach, we need to try out various ML algorithms so that we will be sure which algorithm we can use and which ones we should not use.

Optimizing the baseline approach

In this section, we will take all the problems into consideration and discuss the approach through which we will increase the accuracy of our classifier. As discussed in the previous section, we need to implement other ML algorithms. These are the six algorithms that we are going to implement with the revised approach:

- Logistic regression
- K-nearest neighbor
- Decision tree
- Random forest
- Adaboost classifier
- Gradient boosting classifier

Based on the precision score of all the preceding algorithms, we will decide which algorithm can be used and which can't be used.

Without wasting time, let's start implementing the revised approach.

Building the revised approach

In this section, we will implement the various ML algorithms, check their precision score, and monitor their learning curve. There is a total of six ML algorithms that will be used to identify which one is the best suited for our application.

Implementing the revised approach

In this section, we will be implementing logistic regression, K-nearest neighbor, decision tree, random forest, Adaboost, and gradient descent. In order to implement this, we will be using the helper class that we built earlier. You can take a look at the code snippet given in the following screenshot:

```
#Logistic Regression
lr = Class_Fit(clf = linear_model.LogisticRegression)
lr.grid_search(parameters = [{'C':np.logspace(-2,2,20)}], Kfold = 5)
lr.grid_fit(X = X_train, Y = Y_train)
lr.grid_predict(X_test, Y_test)

Precision: 88.23 %

# K -nearest neighbour
knn = Class_Fit(clf = neighbors.KNeighborsClassifier)
knn.grid_search(parameters = [{'n_neighbors': np.arange(1,50,1)}], Kfold = 5)
knn.grid_fit(X = X_train, Y = Y_train)
knn.grid_predict(X_test, Y_test)

Precision: 80.47 %

# decision tree
tr = Class_Fit(clf = tree.DecisionTreeClassifier)
tr.grid_search(parameters = [{'criterion' : ['entropy', 'gini'], 'max_features' :['sqrt', 'log2']}], Kfold = 5)
tr.grid_fit(X = X_train, Y = Y_train)
tr.grid_predict(X_test, Y_test)

Precision: 86.84 %

# random forest classifier
rf = Class_Fit(clf = ensemble.RandomForestClassifier)
param_grid = {'criterion' : ['entropy', 'gini'], 'n_estimators' : [20, 40, 60, 80, 100],
               'max_features' :['sqrt', 'log2']}
rf.grid_search(parameters = param_grid, Kfold = 5)
rf.grid_fit(X = X_train, Y = Y_train)
rf.grid_predict(X_test, Y_test)

Precision: 91.00 %

#Adaboost classifier
ada = Class_Fit(clf = AdaBoostClassifier)
param_grid = {'n_estimators' : [10, 20, 30, 40, 50, 60, 70, 80, 90, 100]}
ada.grid_search(parameters = param_grid, Kfold = 5)
ada.grid_fit(X = X_train, Y = Y_train)
ada.grid_predict(X_test, Y_test)

Precision: 54.43 %

# gradient boosting classifier
gb = Class_Fit(clf = ensemble.GradientBoostingClassifier)
param_grid = {'n_estimators' : [10, 20, 30, 40, 50, 60, 70, 80, 90, 100]}
gb.grid_search(parameters = param_grid, Kfold = 5)
gb.grid_fit(X = X_train, Y = Y_train)
gb.grid_predict(X_test, Y_test)

Precision: 91.41 %
```

Figure 3.68: Code snippet for performing training using various ML classifiers

We have already generated a precision score for all the classifiers. We can see random forest and gradient-boosting classifiers with great precision. However, we have still not checked their learning curve. First, we will check their learning curve and then conclude whether any classifier has been facing the over-fitting or under-fitting issue.

Testing the revised approach

In this section, we will be checking the learning curves for all the classifiers. You can refer to the learning curves in the following screenshot:

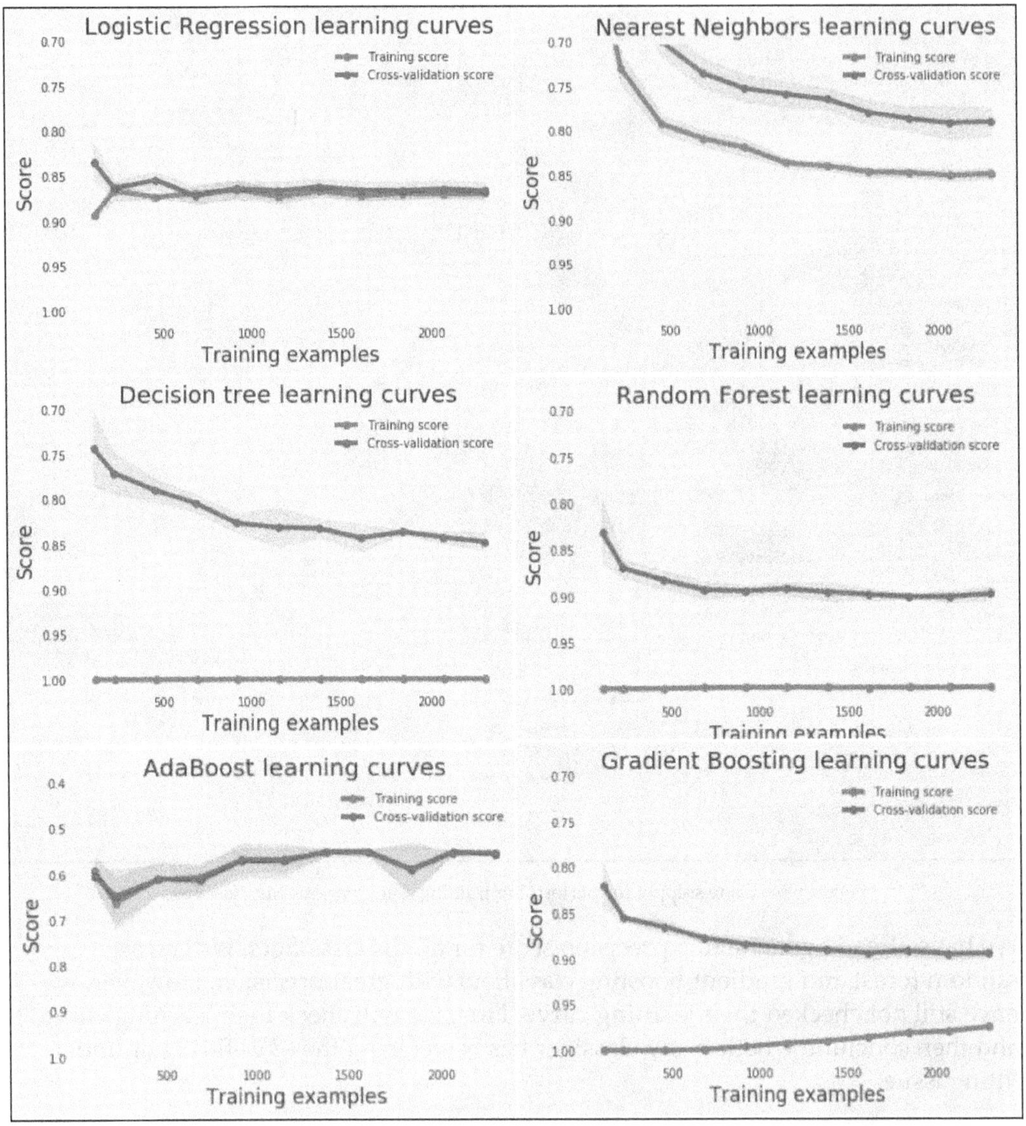

Figure 3.69: Learning curve for various ML classifiers

You can see that all the classifiers are trained appropriately. There is no under-fitting or over-fitting issue. With the increase data size, the scores are improving as well.

Problems with the revised approach

The major problem with this approach is that we need to decide which algorithm we need to use and which one we should stop using. We will discard the Adaboost classifier as its precision score is too low.

There is another catch that I need to highlight here. There is no single classifier that works well for all class labels. There may be a classifier that works well for class label 0, whereas another may work well for class label 8. I believe, we should not discard any other classifier. We need to come up with a voting mechanism. In more technical terms, we need to develop an ensemble model so that the quality of our prediction is great and accurate.

Now we will take a look at what our approach will be in order to build a voting classifier that can give us the best possible accuracy.

Understanding how to improve the revised approach

As discussed, in order to improve the revised approach, we will be using a voting mechanism. For that, we will be using scikit-learn voting classifier APIs. First of all, we will use grid searching in order to generate appropriate hyperparameters for each classifier. After that, we will use voting-classifier APIs of scikit-learn and train the model. The approach is simple, so let's start implementing it.

The best approach

The classifier model that we will be generating in this approach should give us the best possible accuracy. We have already discussed this approach. If you are new to ensemble ML models, then let me give you a basic intuitive idea behind it. In layman's terms, ensemble ML models basically use a combination of various ML algorithms. What is the benefit of combining various ML models together? Well, we know there is no single classifier that can perfectly classify all the samples, so if we combine more than one classifier, then we can get more accuracy because the problem with one classifier can be overcome by another classifier. Due to this reason, we will use a voting classifier that is a type of ensemble classifier.

Implementing the best approach

As you know, we use grid search and voting classifier APIs to implement the best approach. As discussed, first, we will use grid search to obtain the best possible hyperparameters and then use the voting classifier API. The step-by-step implementation is given in the following screenshot:

```
rf_best  = ensemble.RandomForestClassifier(**rf.grid.best_params_)
gb_best  = ensemble.GradientBoostingClassifier(**gb.grid.best_params_)
svc_best = svm.LinearSVC(**svc.grid.best_params_)
tr_best  = tree.DecisionTreeClassifier(**tr.grid.best_params_)
knn_best = neighbors.KNeighborsClassifier(**knn.grid.best_params_)
lr_best  = linear_model.LogisticRegression(**lr.grid.best_params_)
```

Then, I define a classifier that merges the results of the various classifiers:

```
votingC = ensemble.VotingClassifier(estimators=[('rf', rf_best),('gb', gb_best),
                                                ('knn', knn_best)], voting='soft')
```

and train it:

```
votingC = votingC.fit(X_train, Y_train)
```

Finally, we can create a prediction for this model:

```
predictions = votingC.predict(X_test)
print("Precision: {:.2f} % ".format(100*metrics.accuracy_score(Y_test, predictions)))

Precision: 90.86 %
```

Figure 3.70: Code snippet for the best approach

As you can see, we get 90% precision for this approach. This time, we need to test the approach on our hold out corpus of two months so that we can find out how the voting classifier is performing on the unseen dataset.

In the next section, we will be testing this approach.

Testing the best approach

We test our ML model on 20% of the dataset, which we put aside before even starting the training. This dataset is kind of a dev dataset for us. For training, we have considered 10 months' dataset. Now it is time to test the model on the hold out corpus. Here, our hold-out corpus consists of 2 months' data entries. These are the steps that we need to implement:

- Transforming the hold-out corpus in the form of the training dataset
- Converting the transformed dataset into a matrix form
- Generating the predictions

So let's start with the first step.

Transforming the hold-out corpus in the form of the training dataset

First of all, we need to convert the data that resides in the `set_test` dataframe in the form of the training dataset. For that, we will store the copy in the new dataframe with the name `basket_price`.

Now we will generate the user characteristic data with the help of the same operation that we perform for the baseline approach. Don't worry. When you see the code, you will remember the steps that we performed earlier. After transforming the dataset, we will store it in the dataframe, `transactions_per_user`. You can refer to the code snippet shown in the following screenshot:

```
basket_price = set_test.copy(deep = True)

transactions_per_user=basket_price.groupby(by=['CustomerID'])['Basket Price'].agg(['count',
                                                                                    'min','max',
                                                                                    'mean','sum'])
for i in range(5):
    col = 'categ_{}'.format(i)
    transactions_per_user.loc[:,col] = basket_price.groupby(by=['CustomerID'])[col].sum() /\
                                            transactions_per_user['sum']*100

transactions_per_user.reset_index(drop = False, inplace = True)
basket_price.groupby(by=['CustomerID'])['categ_0'].sum()

#__________________________
# Correcting time range
transactions_per_user['count'] = 5 * transactions_per_user['count']
transactions_per_user['sum']   = transactions_per_user['count'] * transactions_per_user['mean']

transactions_per_user.sort_values('CustomerID', ascending = True)[:5]
```

	CustomerID	count	min	max	mean	sum	categ_0	categ_1	categ_2	categ_3	categ_4
0	12347	10	224.82	1294.32	759.57	7595.70	25.053649	12.696657	32.343299	5.634767	24.271627
1	12349	5	1757.55	1757.55	1757.55	8787.75	52.138488	4.513101	12.245455	20.389178	10.713778
2	12352	5	311.73	311.73	311.73	1558.65	60.084047	6.672441	8.735123	17.290604	7.217785
3	12356	5	58.35	58.35	58.35	291.75	100.000000	0.000000	0.000000	0.000000	0.000000
4	12357	5	6207.67	6207.67	6207.67	31038.35	26.686341	5.089832	14.684737	25.189000	28.350089

Figure 3.71: Code snippet for transforming the test dataset into the same form of training dataset

Now let's convert the dataset into a matrix form.

Converting the transformed dataset into a matrix form

Our classifiers take the matrix as an input, so we need to convert the transformed dataset into the matrix format. For that, we will use the code snippet shown in the following screenshot:

```
list_cols = ['count','min','max','mean','categ_0','categ_1','categ_2','categ_3','categ_4']
#_______________________________________________________________
matrix_test = transactions_per_user[list_cols].as_matrix()
scaled_test_matrix = scaler.transform(matrix_test)
```

Figure 3.72: Code snippet for converting the test dataset into the matrix format

We are using a basic type conversion here.

Generating the predictions

In this section, we will be generating the precision score using voting classifiers. So, in order to generate the prediction for the test dataset, we need to use the code snippet given in the following screenshot:

```
predictions = votingC.predict(X)
print("Precision: {:.2f} % ".format(100*metrics.accuracy_score(Y, predictions)))

Precision: 76.83 %
```

Figure 3.73: Code snippet for generating the precision score for the test dataset

As you can see, we will achieve 76% of accuracy on our hold-out corpus. This is nice because we just use 10 months of data to build this model. By using 10 months' dataset, we achieve the best possible accuracy for this domain. If we consider more number of datarecords, then we can still improve the results. This can be an exercise for you guys to consider more datasets and improvise the result.

Customer segmentation for various domains

Note that we are considering e-commerce data here, but you can consider other datasets of various domains. You can build customer segmentation for a company providing travel services, financial services, and so on. The data points will vary from domain to domain.

For travel services, you could consider how frequently a user is booking flights or rooms using the traveling platform. Demographic and professional information helps a great deal, say, how many times a user uses promotional offers. The data for user activity is important as well.

If you are building a segmentation application for the financial domain, then you can consider the data points such as: the transaction history of the account holder, for example, the frequency of using a debit card or a credit card, per-month income, per-month expenditure, the average balance the customer is maintaining in their bank account(s), the type of account user have, professional information of the customer, and so on. There are other common data points that you can consider for both the domains, such as the time spent on the website or the mobile app.

Right now, I will limit myself to these two domains, but you can perform customer segmentation for the telecom domain, the marketing domain, the educational domain, the entertainment domain, and so on.

Summary

All the given analytics models we have developed so far are critical for running a successful business. In this chapter, we developed customer segmentation based on the behavior of the customers. In order to do that, we used various algorithms, such as SVM, linear regression, decision tree, random forest, gradient boosting, voting-based models, and so on. By using the voting-based model, we achieved the best possible accuracy. Customer segmentation analysis is important for small and midsized organizations because these analysis help them optimize their marketing strategy as well as significantly improve the customer acquisition cost. I developed the code for the customer churn analysis, available at: `https://github.com/jalajthanaki/Customer_churn_analysis`, and for customer life-time value analysis at: `https://github.com/jalajthanaki/Customer_lifetime_value_analysis` . You can refer to them to learn more about customer analytics. You can read about customer analytics at: `https://github.com/Acrotrend/Awesome-Customer-Analytics`.

In the upcoming chapter, we will build a recommendation system that is specific to e-commerce products. We will build a recommendation application that will recommend books to users based on their browsing and purchasing activities on the platform. We will implement various techniques to build the best possible recommendation engine. So keep reading!

4
Recommendation Systems for E-Commerce

In the previous three chapters, we have covered a lot of tips and tricks that can be used to build various types of analytics products. In this chapter, we are going to build a recommendation engine for the e-commerce domain. Let's go over some background of recommendation systems. Then, we will discuss the problem statement that we are trying to solve in this chapter.

Let's take a relatable example from real life. We surf videos on YouTube almost every day, right? Suppose you saw some videos related to rock music on YouTube last night. This morning, when you open your YouTube, you may find that there are a couple of suggested YouTube channels with good videos on rock music. YouTube actually changes its suggestions based on your watching habits. Do you want to know how that algorithm works? Let's take another example that might be useful to us in this chapter. Most of us buy stuff from various e-commerce sites. Suppose you are trying to purchase a book from Amazon. When you search for a book there is a section that suggests other books in the same genre. The title of this section is *Customers who bought this item also bought*; you may find these suggestions useful and buy another book as well. Take a look at the following screenshot:

Figure 4.1: Book suggestions on Amazon

All these suggestions you find on e-commerce websites use a specific algorithm, and this algorithm is referred to as the recommendation algorithm. This chapter is all about how to build the recommendation system using different types of Machine Learning (ML) algorithms. Other than e-commerce, there are many domains in which the recommendation system has been used; for example, Netflix and YouTube use the recommendation algorithm to suggest videos we may like, Airbnb provides a recommendation based on our activities on their website. The retail banking domain too uses the logic of the recommendation engine to offer various types of credit cards and offers to their customers. The list is never-ending, so now let's learn how to build a recommendation system.

In this chapter, we will cover the following topics:

- Introducing the problem statement
- Understanding the datasets
- Building the baseline approach:
    - Understanding the basic concepts
    - Implementing the baseline approach
    - Understanding the testing matrix
    - Testing the result of the baseline approach
    - Problems with the baseline approach
    - Optimizing the baseline approach
- Building the revised approach:
    - Implementing the revised approach
    - Testing the revised approach
    - Problems with the revised approach
    - Understanding how to improve the revised approach
- The best approach:
    - Understanding the key concepts
    - Implementing the best approach
- Summary

So let's discuss the problem statement as well as start with the basic concepts of the recommendation system.

Introducing the problem statement

As you know, in this chapter, we are trying to build a recommendation system. A domain that mainly uses the recommendation system is e-commerce. So, in our basic version of the recommendation engine specifically, we will be building an algorithm that can suggest the name of the products based on the category of the product. Once we know the basic concepts of the recommendation engine, we will build a recommendation engine that can suggest books in the same way as the Amazon website.

We will be building three versions of the recommendation algorithm. The baseline approach is simple but intuitive so that readers can learn what exactly the recommendation algorithm is capable of doing. Baseline is easy to implement. In the second and third approach, we will be building the book recommendation engine using ML algorithms.

Let's look at the basic methods or approaches that are used to build the recommendation system. There are two main approaches, which you can find in the following figure:

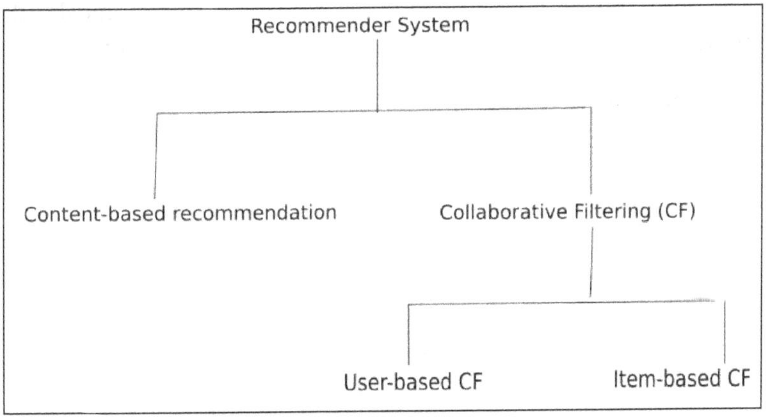

Figure 4.2: Approaches for the recommendation engine

We will be using these two approaches although there are other approaches as well, such as a knowledge-based approach or a hybrid approach. But in this chapter, we will be focusing on the given two approaches.

Now let's look at the dataset that we are going to use.

Understanding the datasets

In this chapter, we are using two datasets, as follows:

- E-commerce item data
- Book-Crossing dataset

e-commerce Item Data

This dataset contains data items taken from actual stock keeping units (SKUs). It is from an outdoor apparel brand's product catalog. We are building the recommendation engine for this outdoor apparel brand's product catalog. You can access the dataset by using this link: `https://www.kaggle.com/cclark/product-item-data/data`.

This dataset contains 500 data items. There are two columns in the dataset.

- **ID**: This column indicates the indexing of the data item. In layman's terms, it is the serial number of the dataset.
- **Description**: This column has all the necessary descriptions about the products, and we need to use this data to build the recommendation engine.

You can refer to the following figure:

id	description
1	Active classic boxers - There's a reason why our boxers are a cult favorite - they keep their cool, especially in sticky situations. The quick-drying, lightweight underwear takes up minimal space in a travel pack. An exposed, brushed waistband offers next-to-skin softness, five-panel construction with a traditional boxer back for a classic fit, and a functional fly. Made of 3.7-oz 100% recycled polyester with moisture-wicking performance. Inseam (size M) is 4 1/2". Recyclable through the Common Threads Recycling Program. <b>Details:</b><ul> <li>"Silky Capilene 1 fabric is ultralight, breathable and quick-to-dry"</li> <li>"Exposed, brushed elastic waistband for comfort"</li> <li>5-panel construction with traditional boxer back</li> <li>"Inseam (size M) is 4 1/2"""</li></ul> <b>Fabric: </b>3.7-oz 100% all-recycled polyester with Gladiodor natural odor control for the garment. Recyclable through the Common Threads Recycling Program <b>Weight: </b>99 g (3.5 oz) Made in Mexico.
2	Active sport boxer briefs - Skinning up Glory requires enough movement without your boxers deciding to poach their own route. The form-fitting Active Sport Boxer Briefs are made from breathable 93% polyester (71% recycled) fabric that's fast-wicking, dries quickly and has 7% spandex for stretch; the seamless waistband and soft leg edges won't roll or bind. The gusseted, flat-sewn 6" inseam (size M) is offset to prevent inner-thigh chafe. Fly-free with a smooth front panel. Recyclable through the Common Threads Recycling Program. <b>Details:</b><ul> <li>"Stretch mesh provides support, open-weave mesh for airflow, wicks efficiently, dries fast"</li> <li>Seamless construction</li> <li>"Flat-sewn, gusseted inseam is set forward to prevent inner-thigh chafe"</li> <li>Fly-free support</li> <li>"Inseam (size M) is 6"""</li></ul> <b>Fabric: </b>"4.6-oz 93% polyester (71% recycled)/7% spandex, with moisture-wicking performance. Recyclable through the Common Threads Recycling Program" <b>Weight: </b>(60 g 2.1 oz) Made in Israel.

Figure 4.3: Snippet of the e-commerce item data

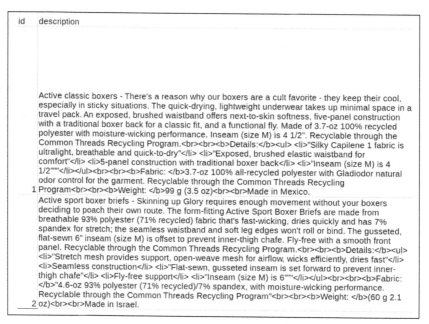

As you can see, the description column has textual data, and we need to process this textual dataset in order to build the recommendation engine. Now let's move to the next dataset.

The Book-Crossing dataset

The Book-Crossing dataset is widely used to build recommendation systems. You can access it at `http://www2.informatik.uni-freiburg.de/~cziegler/BX/`. This dataset is available in two formats, as follows:

- SQL dump
- CSV dump

We are using the CSV dump of the dataset. Both formats have three tables with different data attributes. The names of these three files are as follows:

- `BX-Book-Ratings.csv`
- `BX-Books.csv`
- `BX-Users.csv`

Let's explore the data given in each of the data tables.

BX-Book-Ratings.csv

This CSV file contains data related to the rating of the book. This table contains three data attributes, which are as follows:

- **User-ID**: This data attribute indicates the unique user ID. This column has a numeric value. The length of the user ID is six.
- **ISBN**: The full form of ISBN is International Standard Book Number. This data attribute indicates the unique identification number of the book.
- **Book rating**: This data attribute indicates the user rating for the book. The rating of the book varies from 0 to 10. 0, with 0 indicating less appreciation and 10.0 indicating the highest appreciation.

BX-Books.csv

This file contains all the details regarding the books. The table contains the following data attributes:

- **ISBN**: The ISBN is provided to identify the book. All invalid ISBNs have already been deleted. This data table contains only valid ISBNs.
- **Book-Title**: This data attribute contains the name of the book.

- **Book-Author**: This data attribute contains the name of the author of the book.
- **Year-Of-Publication**: This indicates the year of publication of the book and is in the YYYY format.
- **Publisher**: This data column has the name of the publisher who has published the book.
- **Image-URL-S**: This data attribute has the URL for the image of the book's cover page. S indicates a small size of cover page image.
- **Image-URL-M**: This data attribute has the URL for the image of the book's cover page. M indicates a medium size of cover image.
- **Image-URL-L**: This data attribute has the URL for the image of the book's cover page. L indicates a large size of cover image.

Now let's look at the details of the previous data table.

BX-Users.csv

This is the third data table of the Book-Crossing dataset. This file contains information about the users.

This particular data file contains the following data attributes:

- **User-ID**: This data column indicates the user ID, which is a six-digit integer number.
- **Location**: This data is the part of the demographic details regarding the user. The location indicates the name and abbreviation of the city. The location details for all users are not available, so you will find the `null` value for those users whose locations haven't been found.
- **Age**: This is also a demographic data point. If the user's age is tracked, then it is present in the dataset; if not, then the value of the age is `null`.

We have gathered basic information about the two datasets. We will be moving toward building the basic version of the recommendation engine.

Building the baseline approach

From this section onward, we will focus on how to build the basic version of the recommendation engine (which means the recommendation system in the context of this chapter). In order to develop the baseline approach, we will be using the content-based approach. These are the topics that we will be covering:

- Understanding the basic concepts
- Implementing the baseline approach
- Understanding the testing matrix
- Testing the result of the baseline approach
- Problems with the baseline approach
- Learning optimization tricks for the baseline approach

Without wasting any time, let's look at how the content-based approach has been used to build the recommendation engine.

Understanding the basic concepts

As I've specified earlier, we are using the content-based approach. You must be wondering what this approach is and how I have decided to use it. In order to find the answers to these questions, we need to understand the approach first, and then we can discuss why I chose it.

Understanding the content-based approach

The intuition behind this algorithm is simple. If you are buying or are interested in one type of item, then you will probably like a similar product(s) as well. Let's take an example. If you are buying a pair of jeans, then there is a high chance that you will also like to buy t-shirts or tops, as well as formal trousers or other types of trousers. Basically, the recommendation for the products is based on the content that you have explored, bought, or are interested in. This approach works well when the context and properties of each of the item can be determined easily. This kind of recommendation system is used to recommend video and audio content to users.

When you watch a comedy video on YouTube you might notice there are suggestions for other funny clips and comedy videos. This is because there is a high chance that you will like similar kinds of content based on your watching and browsing history. You can understand this example with the help of the following figure:

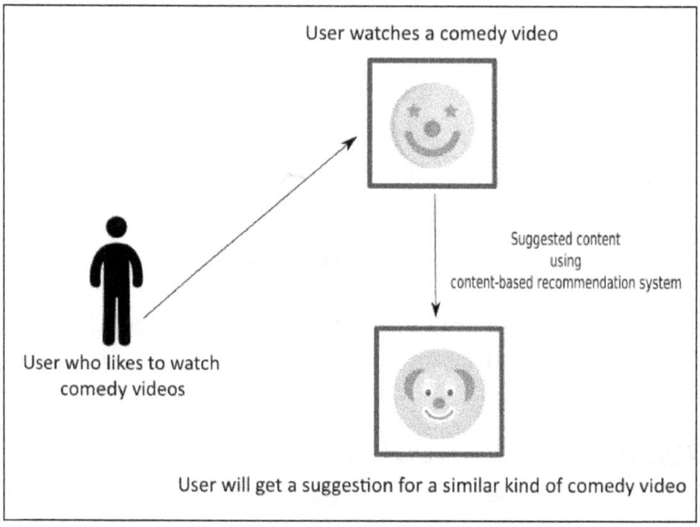

Figure 4.4: Pictorial representation of the idea of the content-based approach

So, when we need to build a system that can recommend items or products that are similar to the user's buying pattern or browsing pattern, we use this approach. The reason for choosing this approach is that this type of recommendation is not influenced by choices of other users. This will provide a personalized experience for users. A recommendation is totally based on the items and its features that users like. This approach helps the e-commerce company increase their sales with less effort. It needs less manual work, which is a good point to note here. We can also use products that have been newly introduced by e-commerce platforms.

In order to implement this approach, we need to focus on the architecture part of it as well as look at basic concepts, such as TF-IDF and cosine similarity. We will explore all these topics in the next section.

Implementing the baseline approach

In this section, we will be designing the architecture of the content-based recommendation system. After that, we will look at how we can build a simple recommendation system. So, there are two subtopics that we will be covering here:

- Architecture of the recommendation system
- Steps for implementing the baseline approach

Architecture of the recommendation system

In this section, we will cover the basic architecture for the content-based recommendation system. Refer to the following figure, which explains the components in more detail:

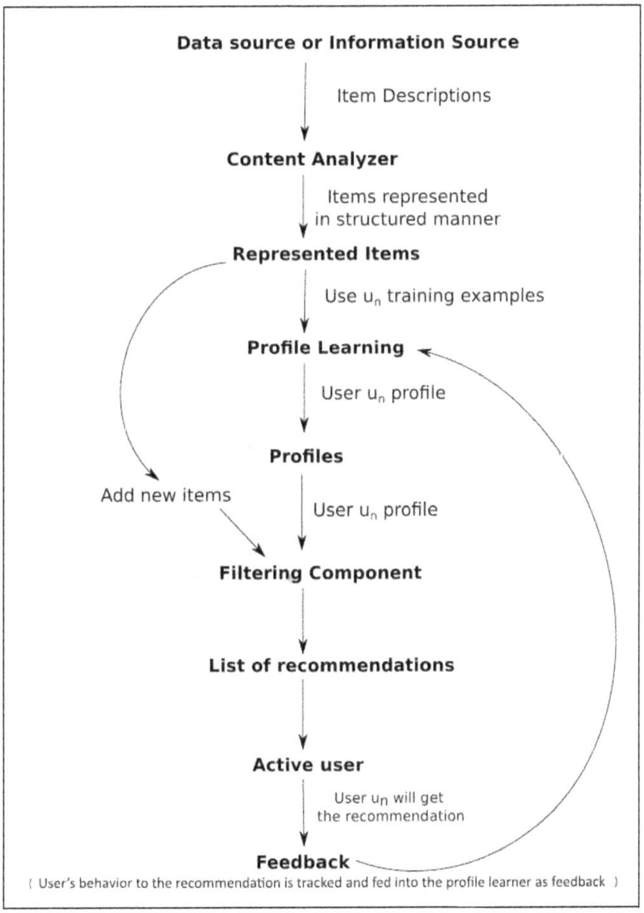

Figure 4.5: Architecture of the content-based recommendation system

As you can see, there are a number of components that we need to use in order to build the recommendation system. We are using the data source or the information source to store details about the items or products. The content analyzer converts the item description into a certain format so that the recommendation engine can consume this information. We have all the products or item-related information with us. Now we need to know what the user is browsing, buying, or searching for on the e-commerce platform. This user-related information is used as a training example for the recommendation system. These training examples are the input of the profile learning module that actual analyzes the age, gender, time spent on website, as well as other demographics and user-activity-based information.

This collective information will be passed on to the filtering component. Based on the information of the products available on the e-commerce platform and user's activities, we will recommend the list of items to the customer.

The logic of the recommendation engine comes into picture here. We will push the recommendations to the active users of the e-commerce platform. Here, active users are those who have bought the product in last month or who have browsed the platform more frequently. We need to track the activity of the users, which acts as the feedback for our recommendation engine.

In the feedback, we can track the number of items the user clicked on from the list of recommendations. Did they buy any items that were a part of the recommendation list? This kind of feedback is useful because based on this feedback, we can fine-tune the logic of the recommendation engine. We will send the feedback to the profile learner, and using that, we will update the interest area for each user so that in future we can give them more suggestions regarding sport clothes, if the person previously browsed sport shoes. Now that you understand the components and their workings, let's take a look at the step-by-step implementation of the baseline approach.

Steps for implementing the baseline approach

In this section, we will cover the coding of the basic recommendation engine. You can refer to the code by using this GitHub link: `https://github.com/jalajthanaki/Basic_Ecommerce_Recomendation_System`

These are the steps that we need to follow:

1. Loading the dataset
2. Generating the feature using TF-IDF the cosine similarity matrix
3. Generating the prediction

Loading the dataset

We are using the e-commerce item dataset here. In this dataset, there is an item description that we need to use. We will use the `pandas` library to load the dataset. You can refer to the following screenshot:

```
#Load dataset using pandas
ds = pd.read_csv("./data/sample-data.csv")
```

Figure 4.6: Code snippet for loading the dataset

Generating features using TF-IDF

We will be using the concept of TF-IDF, which is a simple but effective statistical feature technique. TF-IDF stands for Term Frequency-Inverse Document Frequency. I will explain this briefly.

TF-IDF has two parts: Term Frequency and Inverse Document Frequency. Let's begin with term frequency. The term is self-explanatory, but we will walk through the concept anyway. Term frequency indicates the frequency of each of the words present in the document or dataset. The equation for TF is given in the following formula:

$$TF_{(t_i)} = \frac{Number\ of\ times\ term\ t_i\ appears\ in\ a\ document}{Total\ number\ of\ terms\ in\ the\ document}$$

Figure 4.7: Equation for TF

Now let's talk about inverse document frequency. IDF indicates how important the word is to the document. This is because when we calculate TF, we give equal importance to every single word. If the word *the* appears in the dataset more frequently, then its term frequency (TF) value is high but that word does not carry much importance for the document. If the word *the* appears in the document 100 times, then it means that it does not carry that much information compared to words that are less frequent in the dataset. Thus, we need to define some weighing down of frequent terms while scaling up the rare ones, which is what decides the importance of each word. We will achieve this by using the equation given in the following formula:

$$IDF_{(t_i)} = \log_{10} \frac{Total\ number\ of\ documents}{Number\ of\ documents\ with\ term\ t_i\ in\ it}$$

Figure 4.8: Equation for IDF

So, the final equation to calculate TF-IDF is given in the following formula:

$$TF \times IDF = \left[\left(\frac{Number\ of\ times\ term\ t_i\ appears\ in\ a\ document}{Total\ number\ of\ terms\ in\ the\ document} \right) \times \left(\log_{10} \frac{Total\ number\ of\ documents}{Number\ of\ documents\ with\ term\ t_i\ in\ it} \right) \right]$$

Figure 4.9: Equation for TF-IDF

If you want to read this in detail, then I would recommend that you read this topic from this book: *Chapter 5, Python Natural Language Processing*. For that, you can refer to this link:

`https://www.packtpub.com/big-data-and-business-intelligence/python-natural-language-processing`

The practical implementation of this concept is quite easy. We use the scikit-learn library to code this up. You can refer to the following screenshot:

```
tf = TfidfVectorizer(analyzer='word', ngram_range=(1, 3), min_df=0, stop_words='english')
tfidf_matrix = tf.fit_transform(ds['description'])
```

Figure 4.10: Code snippet for generating features using TF-IDF

Here, we have used the `TfidfVectorizer` API and generated the TF-IDF vectors for the item description. We have removed the English stop words using the `stop_words` parameter. Here, we have provided `ngram_range` from 1 to 3. Now let's build the cosine similarity matrix.

Building the cosine similarity matrix

In this section, we will build the cosine similarity matrix, which is actually the main step required in order to build the content-based recommendation engine. This matrix indicates how similar the description of one product is to the other product. Here, we will check the cosine similarity between the TF-IDF vectors of all the products. We need to find the angle between two TF-IDF vectors. This angle represents how close or how far apart the TF-IDF vectors are. For that, we need to obtain the dot product between TF-IDF vectors by using the following equation:

$$\vec{a} \cdot \vec{b} = \sum_{i=1}^{n} a_i b_i = a_1 b_1 + a_2 b_2 + \cdots + a_n b_n$$

Figure 4.11: Equation for the dot product

Now, with the help of the given cosine equation, we can generate the angle between these vectors. You can refer to the equations in the following formula:

$$\cos\theta = \frac{\vec{a}\cdot\vec{b}}{\|\vec{a}\|\|\vec{b}\|}$$

$$\|\vec{a}\| = \sqrt{a_1^2 + a_2^2 + a_3^2 + \cdots + a_n^2}$$

$$\|\vec{b}\| = \sqrt{b_1^2 + b_2^2 + b_3^2 + \cdots + b_n^2}$$

Figure 4.12: Equation for cosine similarity and norm for vectors

Now let's look at a basic example so that you can understand the basic math behind it. For that, you need to refer to the following equation:

$$\textit{Consider following vectors}$$

$$a : [1,1,0]$$

$$b : [1,0,1]$$

$$\textit{Norm of vector a is} = \|\vec{a}\| = \sqrt{1^2 + 1^2 + 0^2} = \sqrt{2}$$

$$\textit{Norm of vector b is} = \|\vec{b}\| = \sqrt{1^2 + 2^2 + 1^2} = \sqrt{2}$$

$$\vec{a}\cdot\vec{b} = \sum_{i=1}^{n} a_i b_i = a_1 b_1 + a_2 b_2 + a_3 b_3 = 1\times1 + 1\times0 + 0\times1 = 1 + 0 + 0 = 1$$

$$\cos\theta = \frac{1}{\sqrt{2}\times\sqrt{2}} = \frac{1}{2} = 0.5$$

$$\theta = \cos^{-1} 0.5 = 60^\circ$$

Figure 4.13: Basic cosine similarity example

As you can see in the preceding figure, there are two vectors; each of them has three elements. First, we calculated their norms and then we performed the dot product on them. After that, we used the cosine similarity formula and found the angle between these vectors. Note that we can measure the cosine similarity for two nonzero vectors. The interval for the cosine angle is *[0,2π)*.

The coding implementation for this is pretty easy. You can refer to the code snippet shown in the following screenshot:

```
cosine_similarities = linear_kernel(tfidf_matrix, tfidf_matrix)

results = {}

for idx, row in ds.iterrows():
    similar_indices = cosine_similarities[idx].argsort()[:-100:-1]
    similar_items = [(cosine_similarities[idx][i], ds['id'][i]) for i in similar_indices]

    # First item is the item itself, so remove it.
    # Each dictionary entry is like: [(1,2), (3,4)], with each tuple being (score, item_id)
    results[row['id']] = similar_items[1:]

print('done!')
```

Figure 4.14: Code snippet for generating the cosine similarity

Here, we have stored all the recommendations in a dictionary, where each item and its corresponding recommendation have been stored. There are 500 items in our dataset, and for each and every item, we have generated a list of items that can be recommended to the users. Now it's time to generate the prediction.

Generating the prediction

In this section, we will be generating the recommendation list for the given `item_id`. We need to pass any `item_id` from 1 to 500. The system will obtain five different suggestions, which are referred to as recommended items. These recommended items are similar to the item whose `item_id` we have passed to the algorithm. You can see the code snippet in the following screenshot:

```
# hacky little function to get a friendly item name from the description field, given an item ID
def item(id):
    return ds.loc[ds['id'] == id]['description'].tolist()[0].split(' - ')[0]

# Just reads the results out of the dictionary. No real logic here.
def recommend(item_id, num):

    print("Recommending " + str(num) + " products similar to " + item(item_id) + "...")
    print("-------")
    recs = results[item_id][:num]
    for rec in recs:
        print("Recommended: " + item(rec[1]) + " (score:" + str(rec[0]) + ")")

# Just plug in any item id here (1-500), and the number of recommendations you want (1-99)
# You can get a list of valid item IDs by evaluating the variable 'ds', or a few are listed below

recommend(item_id=4, num=5)

Recommending 5 products similar to Alpine guide pants...
-------
Recommended: Alpine guide pants (score:0.8253856759948807)
Recommended: Guide jkt (score:0.20769755384994865)
Recommended: Guide jkt (score:0.18827991801713173)
Recommended: Rock guide pants (score:0.1657402682869924)
Recommended: Lw guide pants (score:0.16373827536275273)
```

Figure 4.15: Code snippet for generating prediction

As you can see, we retrieve the results from the dictionary. We have printed the value of cos θ as our scoring values. If the score is close to one, then it can be said that these items are more similar and there is a higher chance that the user will like the recommendation. If the score is closer to 0 or –1, then items appear less attractive to the users. So just note that here, the score indicates the value of cos θ and not the angle directly.

Now let's look at the testing matrix, which can help us evaluate this approach as well as other approaches that we will be implementing in this chapter.

Understanding the testing matrix

In this section, we will be exploring the testing or evolution matrix for the content-based recommendation engine. Here, the cosine similarity score is the biggest testing score for us. That is because with the help of that score, we can easily come to learn whether the algorithm can suggest the items whose cosine similarity score is close to 1 close to 0.

For some items, we will obtain a score that is close to 1, and for other items, we obtain a score that is close to 0. So, we need to focus on this cosine score in order to get an idea of how well or badly the recommendation engine is doing. You can refer to the following figure:

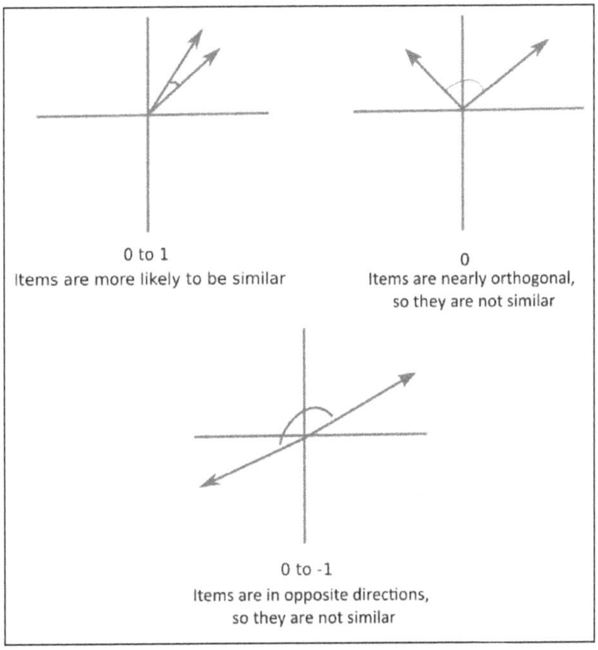

Figure 4.16: Understanding of the cosine similarity score and angle

As we can see in the preceding figure, we need to use the cosine score in order to test this approach. We can perform the following steps for testing. We need to count the number of items with more than a certain score, which means that we can decide the threshold value for the cosine similarity score and count how many items the recommendation engine is suggesting above that threshold value. Let me give you an example. Suppose we decide a cut-off score of 0.15. In this case, all items whose cosine score is above 0.15 are considered a good recommendation. Here, the trick is that you need to experiment with this threshold value because based on the user's activity, you may change it later on. This parameter will be a tunable parameter for us. In the next section, we will look at the code for the testing.

Testing the result of the baseline approach

In this section, we will see how we can implement the logic of the threshold value. After that, we will compare the results for different items. You can refer to the code snippet shown in the following screenshot:

```
#### Start testign logic
        if rec[0] >0.15:
            i+=1
    print ("Recommendation score: "+ str(i))
    score_count.append(str(i))
    return Counter(score_count)
#### End Testing logic

# Just plug in any item id here (1-500), and the number of recommendations you want (1-99)
# You can get a list of valid item IDs by evaluating the variable 'ds', or a few are listed below
# If you wnat to generate recommendtion for single item then uncommend the following line
# recommend(item_id=3, num=5)


## Testing on all items so generate recommendation for all items

for i in range(1,501):
    # print
    score_counter_variable = recommend(item_id=i, num=5)
    print("-----------Recommendation for a single item ends here-----------")
    print()

## Generate test score in percentage
score_dict = dict(score_counter_variable)
score_0 = (score_dict.get("0")/500)*100
score_1 = (score_dict.get("1")/500)*100
score_2 = (score_dict.get("2")/500)*100
score_3 = (score_dict.get("3")/500)*100
score_4 = (score_dict.get("4")/500)*100
score_5 = (score_dict.get("5")/500)*100

score_0 =round((score_0),2)
score_1 =round((score_1),2)
score_2 =round((score_2),2)
score_3 =round((score_3),2)
score_4 =round((score_4),2)
score_5 =round((score_5),2)


print ("0 useful recommendation: "+ str(score_0)+'%')
print ("1 useful recommendation: "+ str(score_1)+'%')
print ("2 useful recommendation: "+ str(score_2)+'%')
print ("3 useful recommendation: "+ str(score_3)+'%')
print ("4 useful recommendation: "+ str(score_4)+'%')
print ("5 useful recommendation: "+ str(score_5)+'%')
```

Figure 4.17: Code snippet for testing

Now you can see the results for different `item_ids`. You can find the result of the three items. I have picked up `item_id` randomly. Take a look at the following screenshot:

```
Recommending ----->>>>>>> 5 products similar to Active classic boxers...
Recommended items: Cap 1 boxer briefs (score:0.22037921472617453)
Recommended items: Active boxer briefs (score:0.16938950913002357)
Recommended items: Cap 1 bottoms (score:0.16769458065321555)
Recommended items: Cap 1 t-shirt (score:0.16485527745622977)
Recommended items: Cap 3 bottoms (score:0.148126154605864)
Recommendation score: 4
-----------Recommendation for a single item ends here-----------
Recommending ----->>>>>>> 5 products similar to Active sport boxer briefs...
Recommended items: Active sport briefs (score:0.4181663992161579)
Recommended items: Cap 1 boxer briefs (score:0.11546382098627586)
Recommended items: Active boxer briefs (score:0.11303392245400203)
Recommended items: Active briefs (score:0.11247854521091638)
Recommended items: Active boy shorts (score:0.11147017924424424)
Recommendation score: 1
-----------Recommendation for a single item ends here-----------
Recommending ----->>>>>>> 5 products similar to Active sport briefs...
Recommended items: Active sport boxer briefs (score:0.4181663992161579)
Recommended items: Active boy shorts (score:0.1140184812203876)
Recommended items: Active briefs (score:0.11053729446572895)
Recommended items: Active briefs (score:0.1091764001658287)
Recommended items: Active mesh bra (score:0.10172320448715239)
Recommendation score: 1
-----------Recommendation for a single item ends here-----------
Recommending ----->>>>>>> 5 products similar to Alpine guide pants...
Recommended items: Alpine guide pants (score:0.8253856759948807)
Recommended items: Guide jkt (score:0.20769755384994865)
Recommended items: Guide jkt (score:0.18827991801713173)
Recommended items: Rock guide pants (score:0.1657402682869924)
Recommended items: Lw guide pants (score:0.16373827536275273)
Recommendation score: 5
-----------Recommendation for a single item ends here-----------
Recommending ----->>>>>>> 5 products similar to Alpine wind jkt...
Recommended items: Alpine wind jkt (score:0.9550036493156216)
Recommended items: Nine trails jkt (score:0.18304420089101783)
Recommended items: Nine trails jkt (score:0.18039926859231437)
Recommended items: Houdini full-zip jkt (score:0.15754217002277993)
Recommended items: Nine trails vest (score:0.15209799272552918)
Recommendation score: 5
```

Figure 4.18: Result of items

Take a look at the following code snippet:

```
0 useful recommendation: 3.2%
1 useful recommendation: 6.0%
2 useful recommendation: 7.4%
3 useful recommendation: 6.4%
4 useful recommendation: 7.2%
5 useful recommendation: 69.8%
```

Figure 4.19: Analysis based on useful recommendations

As you can see in the preceding figure, this approach gives us useful recommendations 69.8% of the time, and it provides four useful suggestions 7.2% of the time. After looking at the analysis of the result, we can say that the baseline approach is doing well, and we can definitely improve the results with the help of the other approach.

In the next section, we will discuss the problems this baseline approach has and how we can solve them.

Problems with the baseline approach

In this section, we will be discussing the problems that are a part of the baseline approach. We need to understand the problems so that we can take care of them in the revised approach. The problems with this approach are as follows:

- **Limited content analysis**: If we do not have enough information in order to differentiate the items more accurately, then the recommendation engine won't be giving useful or more precise suggestions.
- **Over-specialization**: Content-based systems are based on the user profile and the items they are browsing, so the user will get the same kind of suggestion if they are browsing the same thing again and again. There is no different or novel item that the user can find. This is bad because if we provide the same recommendation more often, then there is no element of surprise for the user and they won't be motivated to buy things. This problem is called over-specialization.
- **New-user**: If there is a new user who is exploring the e-commerce platform and we have a very limited amount of information about the user, then we cannot give them a good recommendation initially. This situation occurs due to the lack of a solid profile.

All the preceding problems are well known for their content-based recommendation engine. In order to solve these problems, we can try out some other approach. The details related to this are given in the next section.

Optimizing the baseline approach

Here, we will have an overview of how we can resolve the problems that we encountered in the previous section. In the baseline approach, we are basically dependent on the user profile and the item description, but this approach did not turn out well. In order to improve that we will be using two approaches. In the revised approach, we will be using the correction-based approach. After that, we will try the collaborative-filtering-based approach.

This correlation-based approach depends on the users' activities and is not dependent on the content or the description of the item. This helps us resolve the issues of new users, over-specialization, and limited content analysis. We are using a correlation coefficient to build the recommendation engine. This is a simple statistical technique that can be quite helpful. The basic concepts that are important for implementation will be described as and when we start building the revised approach.

So let's build the revised approach.

Building the revised approach

In this iteration, we will be building the recommendation engine using a statistical concept called correlation. We will be looking at how users' activities and choices are correlated to one another. We try to find out the pattern from the users' activities and behavior on the e-commerce platform.

Here, we will be using the Book-Crossing dataset. One of the critical parameters for building the recommendation system is the book rating attribute. I will explain the concepts along with the implementation part, so it will be easy for you to understand.

Implementing the revised approach

In order to implement the revised approach, we will need to perform the following steps. You can refer to the code on GitHub at: `https://github.com/jalajthanaki/Book_recommendation_system/blob/master/correlation_based_recommendation_system.ipynb`

1. Loading the dataset
2. **Exploratory Data Analysis** (**EDA**) of book-rating datafile
3. Exploring the book datafile
4. EDA of user datafile
5. Implementing the logic of correlation for the recommendation engine

Loading dataset

As a first step, we will use the `pandas` library to load our Book-Crossing dataset. As you already know, this dataset has three datafiles. We are loading all of them. You can refer to the following code snippet:

```
import pandas as pd
import numpy as np
import matplotlib.pyplot as plt

books = pd.read_csv('./data/BX-Books.csv', sep=';', error_bad_lines=False, encoding="latin-1")
books.columns = ['ISBN', 'bookTitle', 'bookAuthor', 'yearOfPublication', 'publisher', 'imageUrlS', 'imageUrlM', 'imageUrlL']
users = pd.read_csv('./data/BX-Users.csv', sep=';', error_bad_lines=False, encoding="latin-1")
users.columns = ['userID', 'Location', 'Age']
ratings = pd.read_csv('./data/BX-Book-Ratings.csv', sep=';', error_bad_lines=False, encoding="latin-1")
ratings.columns = ['userID', 'ISBN', 'bookRating']
```

Figure 4.20: Code snippet for loading the data

Our data separator is a semicolon, and we are using latin-1 as encoding. We have defined three `pandas` dataframes.

Now let's jump to the next step, which is the EDA step for all three datafiles.

EDA of the book-rating datafile

For this datafile, we have generated the ratings dataframe. We need to know what kind of data distribution this datafile has. That means we need to check how many books are getting a 10 out of 10 score, how many books are getting a 5 out of 10 score, and how many books do not have any rating at all. Refer to the following code snippet to generate this information for us:

```
print(ratings.shape)
print(list(ratings.columns))

(1149780, 3)
['userID', 'ISBN', 'bookRating']

ratings.head()
```

	userID	ISBN	bookRating
0	276725	034545104X	0
1	276726	0155061224	5
2	276727	0446520802	0
3	276729	052165615X	3
4	276729	0521795028	6

```
plt.rc("font", size=15)
print(ratings.bookRating.value_counts(sort=False))
ratings.bookRating.value_counts(sort=False).plot(kind='bar')
plt.title('Rating Distribution\n')
plt.xlabel('Rating')
plt.ylabel('Count')
plt.savefig('system1.png', bbox_inches='tight')
plt.show()

0     716109
1       1770
2       2759
3       5996
4       8904
5      50974
6      36924
7      76457
8     103736
9      67541
10     78610
```

Figure 4.21: Code snippet for EDA of book-rating datafile

You can find the bar chart for this in the following figure:

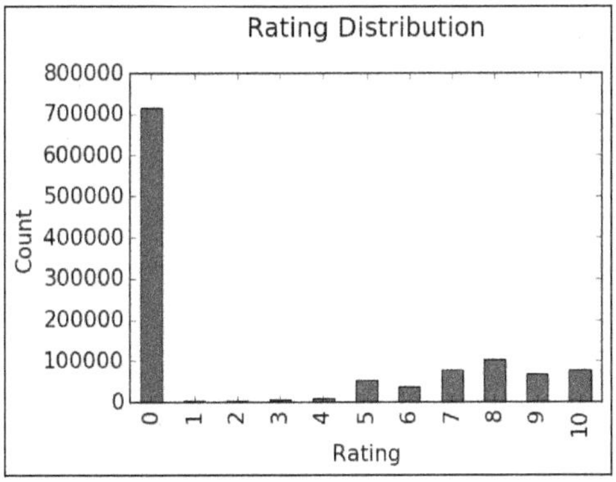

Figure 4.22: Bar chart for book-rating score distribution

As we can see, there are 7,16,109 books with a zero rating, whereas 1,03,736 books have a rating of eight. Based on this analysis, we can deduce that there are many books whose rating is zero, so the data distribution is biased here. We need to keep this point in mind.

Exploring the book datafile

In this section, we will perform the EDA of the book datafile. We also need to check the data attributes and format the data. No other trick needs to be applied for this datafile. Take a look at the code snippet shown in the following screenshot:

```
print(books.shape)
print(list(books.columns))

(271360, 8)
['ISBN', 'bookTitle', 'bookAuthor', 'yearOfPublication', 'publisher', 'imageUrlS', 'imageUrlM', 'imageUrlL']

books.head()
```

	ISBN	bookTitle	bookAuthor	yearOfPublication	publisher	imageUrlS
0	0195153448	Classical Mythology	Mark P. O. Morford	2002	Oxford University Press	http://images.amazon.com/images/P/0195153448.0...
1	0002005018	Clara Callan	Richard Bruce Wright	2001	HarperFlamingo Canada	http://images.amazon.com/images/P/0002005018.0...
2	0060973129	Decision in Normandy	Carlo D'Este	1991	HarperPerennial	http://images.amazon.com/images/P/0060973129.0...
3	0374157065	Flu: The Story of the Great Influenza Pandemic...	Gina Bari Kolata	1999	Farrar Straus Giroux	http://images.amazon.com/images/P/0374157065.0...
4	0393045218	The Mummies of Urumchi	E. J. W. Barber	1999	W. W. Norton & Company	http://images.amazon.com/images/P/0393045218.0...

Figure 4.23: Code snippet for exploring the book datafile

You can see that we have checked the shape and columns list for the book datafile. There is nothing that critical we need to consider in order to build the recommendation engine.

EDA of the user datafile

Here, we need to perform an analysis of the users' datafile. This datafile is important as we will be using it often to derive some important facts for this approach. First, we need to obtain the age distribution. The age distribution is one of the critical data points when we are building a recommendation system because users of a similar age group have similar reading patterns, and if we obtain this pattern, then we can generate more effective recommendations for our users. You can refer to the code snippet shown in the following screenshot:

```
print(users.shape)
print(list(users.columns))

(278858, 3)
['userID', 'Location', 'Age']

users.head()
```

	userID	Location	Age
0	1	nyc, new york, usa	NaN
1	2	stockton, california, usa	18.0
2	3	moscow, yukon territory, russia	NaN
3	4	porto, v.n.gaia, portugal	17.0
4	5	farnborough, hants, united kingdom	NaN

```
users.Age.hist(bins=[0, 10, 20, 30, 40, 50, 100])
plt.title('Age Distribution\n')
plt.xlabel('Age')
plt.ylabel('Count')
plt.savefig('system2.png', bbox_inches='tight')
plt.show()
```

Figure 4.24: Code snippet for generating the age distribution

You can refer to the box chart, which indicates the age distribution shown in the following figure:

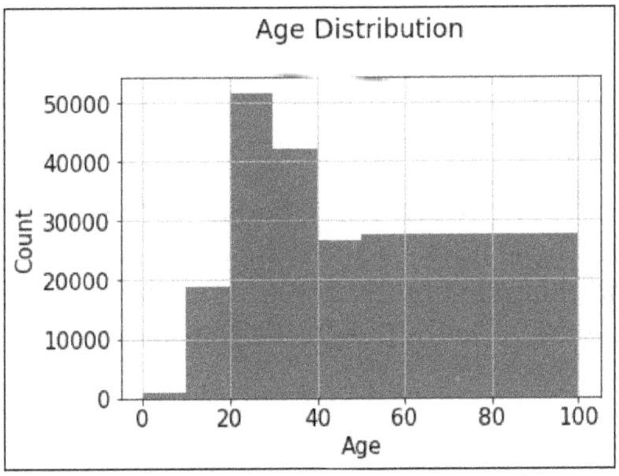

Figure 4.25: Box graph for the age distribution

Based on the distribution, we can derive the fact that we have a majority of the users whose age falls between 20 and 40. So if we focus on their reading and browsing pattern, then our work will get easier.

Implementing the logic of correlation for the recommendation engine

In this section, we will cover the core logic of the recommendation engine. The logic can be divided into two parts:

- Recommendations based on the rating of the books
- Recommendations based on correlations

So let's start!

Recommendations based on the rating of the books

In order to build a book recommendation system that is based on the rating of the book, all the ratings are provided by the readers. So, for the implementation of this approach, we will be extracting the top five books with the highest ratings, which means we need to obtain a list of the books with the most ratings from the reader. The code snippet for that is shown in the following figure:

```
rating_count = pd.DataFrame(ratings.groupby('ISBN')['bookRating'].count())
rating_count.sort_values('bookRating', ascending=False).head()
```

ISBN	bookRating
0971880107	2502
0316666343	1295
0385504209	883
0060928336	732
0312195516	723

Figure 4.26: Code snippet for generating the top five books based on book rating

We have generated the ISBN of the top five books on the book rating count, but we also need to check what those books' names are and what the average rating for each of them is. You can find the name of the books by merging the book and book-rating data frame. You can see the code for this in the following screenshot:

```
most_rated_books = pd.DataFrame(['0971880107', '0316666343', '0385504209', '0060928336', '03121
95516'], index=np.arange(5), columns = ['ISBN'])
most_rated_books_summary = pd.merge(most_rated_books, books, on='ISBN')
most_rated_books_summary
```

	ISBN	bookTitle	bookAuthor	yearOfPublication	publisher	imageUrlS
0	0971880107	Wild Animus	Rich Shapero	2004	Too Far	http://images.amazon.com/images/P/0971880107.0...

Figure 4.27: Code snippet for generating the names of the top 5 books

Now, you may wonder what the benefit of this approach is. Let me tell you, we have a list of the books in descending order based on the book rating. If a user buys the book based on the rating of the book, then we can suggest other books that have the same rating. This way, users get suggestions that are more accurate than the previous approach.

If you look at the results of the top five books, then you will learn that the maximum rating is for Rich Shapero's book `Wild Animus`. All five books are novels. If someone wants to buy `Wild Animus`, then the user may also buy `The Lovely Bones: A Novel`. That is the reason this approach makes sense.

Now let's see the correlation-based recommendation engine.

Recommendations based on correlations

We are using the bivariant correlation and the **Pearson correlation coefficient** (**PCC**). This is also referred to as `Person's r`. This correlation provides a measure of the linear correction between the two variables `a and b`. Here, we are considering the rating of two books and applying the PCC technique to them. The value of Person's `r` is in the range of `+1 to -1`. The interpretation for this correlation value is as follows:

- **+1**: This value indicates the total positive linear correlation. This means that if there is an increment in the value of the variable 1, then variable 2 is incremented as well.
- **0**: This value indicates that there is no linear correlation. This means that the two variables are not related.
- **-1**: This value indicates that there is a total negative linear correlation. This means that if there is an increment in the value of variable 1, then variable 2 is decremented.

The equation for the PCC is shown in the following equation:

$$r = \textit{Pearson correlation coefficient} = \frac{\sum XY - \frac{(\sum X)(\sum Y)}{n}}{\sqrt{\left(\sum X^2 - \frac{(\sum X)^2}{n}\right)\left(\sum Y^2 - \frac{(\sum Y)^2}{n}\right)}}$$

Figure 4.28: Equation for PCC or Person's r

Let's consider a simple math example so you know how we have calculated Person's r. Take a look at the following equation:

Value of X and Y data points

X	Y
1	2
3	5
4	5
4	8

The formula for Pearson's r is given below

$$r = Pearson\ correlation\ coefficient = \frac{\sum XY - \frac{(\sum X)(\sum Y)}{n}}{\sqrt{\left(\sum X^2 - \frac{(\sum X)^2}{n}\right)\left(\sum Y^2 - \frac{(\sum Y)^2}{n}\right)}}$$

We need to do the necessary calculations

$$\sum XY = (1)(2)+(3)(5)+(4)(5)+(4)(8) = 69$$
$$\sum X = 1+3+4+4 = 12$$
$$\sum Y = 2+5+5+8 = 20$$
$$\sum X^2 = 1^2+3^2+4^2+4^2 = 42$$
$$\sum Y^2 = 2^2+5^2+5^2+8^2 = 118$$

We need to add the previous calculations into the formula

$$r = \frac{69 - \frac{(12)(20)}{4}}{\sqrt{42 - \frac{(12)^2}{4}\left(118 - \frac{(20)^2}{4}\right)}} = .866$$

Figure 4.29: Math example for Person's r

[Note: we are considering the ratings of the two books in order to find the correlation between them.]

First of all, we need to obtain the average rating for all books. The code snippet is given in the following screenshot:

```
average_rating = pd.DataFrame(ratings.groupby('ISBN')['bookRating'].mean())
average_rating['ratingCount'] = pd.DataFrame(ratings.groupby('ISBN')['bookRating'].count())
average_rating.sort_values('ratingCount', ascending=False).head()
```

ISBN	bookRating	ratingCount
0971880107	1.019584	2502
0316666343	4.468726	1295
0385504209	4.652322	883
0060928336	3.448087	732
0312195516	4.334716	723

Figure 4.30: Code snippet for generating an average book rating

Note that the books that received the most rating counts are not the ones that are highly rated. This means there are some books for which readers share their feedback more often, but that doesn't mean those books are highly rated. Maybe some books were rated by 100 users but the score for the book is 4.3. This is the most important point that I need to highlight because this is where mistakes can happen. For making a better system, we need to consider the book-rating count and the book-rating score.

Here, we will be excluding users who have provided less than 200 ratings as well as books that have received less than 100 ratings. This means we are setting up a threshold so that we can make a better system. We can achieve this by using the code snippet given in the following screenshot:

```
counts1 = ratings['userID'].value_counts()
ratings = ratings[ratings['userID'].isin(counts1[counts1 >= 200].index)]
counts = ratings['bookRating'].value_counts()
ratings = ratings[ratings['bookRating'].isin(counts[counts >= 100].index)]
```

Figure 4.31: Code snippet for setting up threshold for considering users and books

Now we are converting the ratings dataframe into a 2D matrix. This matrix is a sparse matrix because not every user has provided a rating for every book. You can see the code in the following screenshot:

```
ratings_pivot = ratings.pivot(index='userID', columns='ISBN').bookRating
userID = ratings_pivot.index
ISBN = ratings_pivot.columns
print(ratings_pivot.shape)
ratings_pivot.head()
```

```
(905, 207699)
```

ISBN	0330299891	0375404120	0586045007	9022906116	9032803328	9044922564	9044922572	9044922718	9044923161
userID									
254	NaN	NaN	NaN	NaN	NaN	NaN	NaN	NaN	NaN
2276	NaN	NaN	NaN	NaN	NaN	NaN	NaN	NaN	NaN
2766	NaN	NaN	NaN	NaN	NaN	NaN	NaN	NaN	NaN
2977	NaN	NaN	NaN	NaN	NaN	NaN	NaN	NaN	NaN
3363	NaN	NaN	NaN	NaN	NaN	NaN	NaN	NaN	NaN

5 rows × 207699 columns

Figure 4.32: Code snippet for generating a sparse matrix for rating

We have completed some basic work, now it's time to find out about books that correlate with the second most-rated book, *The Lovely Bones: A Novel.* I want to quote the summary of this book, which is taken from Wikipedia: `https://en.wikipedia.org/wiki/The_Lovely_Bones`

> "*It is the story of a teenage girl who, after being raped and murdered, watches from her personal Heaven as her family and friends struggle to move on with their lives while she comes to terms with her own death*".

Now we need to obtain a book that can be recommended to a user if they are trying to buy this book. The code that can help us get the recommendation is given in the following screenshot:

```
bones_ratings = ratings_pivot['0316666343']
similar_to_bones = ratings_pivot.corrwith(bones_ratings)
corr_bones = pd.DataFrame(similar_to_bones, columns=['pearsonR'])
corr_bones.dropna(inplace=True)
corr_summary = corr_bones.join(average_rating['ratingCount'])
corr_summary[corr_summary['ratingCount']>=300].sort_values('pearsonR', ascending=False).head(10)

/usr/local/lib/python2.7/dist-packages/numpy/lib/function_base.py:3175: RuntimeWarning: Degrees c
  c = cov(x, y, rowvar)
/usr/local/lib/python2.7/dist-packages/numpy/lib/function_base.py:3109: RuntimeWarning: divide by
  c *= 1. / np.float64(fact)
```

	pearsonR	ratingCount
ISBN		
0316666343	1.000000	1295
0312291639	0.471872	354
0316601950	0.434248	568
0446610038	0.429712	391
0446672211	0.421478	585
0385265700	0.351635	319
0345342968	0.316922	321
0060930535	0.309860	494
0375707972	0.308145	354
0684872153	0.272480	326

Figure 4.33: Code snippet for generating a correlation-based recommendation

Here, you can see that we are using a sparse matrix and have applied the `corrwith` API to generate a correlation. There may be some runtime warnings. They are related to the float data type. Apart from that, we have coded the condition we need in order to recommend books that have received more than or equal to 300 user-rating counts. We have obtained the ISBN using the preceding code. So, we need to obtain the names of the books as well. For that, we need to use the code snippet given in the following screenshot:

```
books_corr_to_bones = pd.DataFrame(['0312291639', '0316601950',
                                    '0446610038', '0446672211',
                                    '0385265700', '0345342968',
                                    '0060930535', '0375707972',
                                    '0684872153'],
                                   index=np.arange(9), columns=['ISBN'])
corr_books = pd.merge(books_corr_to_bones, books, on='ISBN')
corr_books
```

	ISBN	bookTitle	bookAuthor	yearOfPublication	publisher	imageUrlS
0	0312291639	The Nanny Diaries: A Novel	Emma McLaughlin	2003	St. Martin's Griffin	http://images.amazon.com/images/P/0312291639.0...
1	0316601950	The Pilot's Wife : A Novel	Anita Shreve	1999	Back Bay Books	http://images.amazon.com/images/P/0316601950.0...
2	0446610038	1st to Die: A Novel	James Patterson	2002	Warner Vision	http://images.amazon.com/images/P/0446610038.0...
3	0446672211	Where the Heart Is (Oprah's Book Club (Paperba...	Billie Letts	1998	Warner Books	http://images.amazon.com/images/P/0446672211.0...
4	0385265700	The Book of Ruth (Oprah's Book Club (Paperback))	Jane Hamilton	1990	Anchor	http://images.amazon.com/images/P/0385265700.0...
5	0345342968	Fahrenheit 451	RAY BRADBURY	1987	Del Rey	http://images.amazon.com/images/P/0345342968.0...
6	0060930535	The Poisonwood Bible: A Novel	Barbara Kingsolver	1999	Perennial	http://images.amazon.com/images/P/0060930535.0...
7	0375707972	The Reader	Bernhard Schlink	1999	Vintage Books USA	http://images.amazon.com/images/P/0375707972.0...
8	0684872153	Angela's Ashes (MMP) : A Memoir	Frank McCourt	1999	Scribner	http://images.amazon.com/images/P/0684872153.0...

Figure 4.34: Code snippet for generating the name of the book

Let's select the top three recommendations for the book, which are, *The Nanny Diaries: A Novel, The Pilot's Wife: A Novel, and 1st to Die: A Novel.* The Nanny Diaries criticizes the upper-class society of Manhattan as seen through the eyes of their children's caregivers. The Pilot's Wife: A Novel is written by the same author who wrote The Lovely Bones. 1st to Die is the first book of a women's murder club series.

If you actually look at the content of these three books, then we can see that all these recommendations make sense.

Testing the revised approach

We have already obtained the recommendation, and if we check the suggested books using this revised approach, then we see that this simple correlation-based approach works rather well. We performed manual testing and evaluated the quality of the recommendations and the suggestions were surprisingly more sensible and useful for the users.

In the next section, we will be discussing the problems with this approach and how we can improvise the approach further. Before implementing optimization, we need to discuss the points on which we will be focusing. So, let's list down all the problems or areas of improvements.

Problems with the revised approach

In this section, we need to list down the problems or areas of improvement so that we can improve the revised approach. Here are the points for areas of improvement:

- The correlation-based approach is not generalized for all kinds of situations, so we need a more sophisticated approach. Basically, the correlation-based approach performs really well if the model has seen a similar kind of data example during training. For unseen data examples, it may not generate good results.
- We can't always do manual testing, so we need a recommendation engine that is easy to develop, build, and test. The new approach can also adopt future changes, which means new approaches should be easy for us to change or modify as and when required.

Now let's see how we can improve this revised approach.

Understanding how to improve the revised approach

In order to improve the revised approach, we will be using the well-known recommendation algorithm, collaborative filtering (CF). We will be using the Machine Learning (ML) algorithm K-nearest neighbors (KNN). This is a basic outline for how we can improve the revised approach.

With the help of the CF algorithm and the ML algorithm, it will be easy for us to test the algorithm as well as modify the algorithm based on our requirements. You may know how KNN works, so we are not going to dive into the KNN algorithm in detail, but we will definitely try to understand the intuition behind the KNN algorithm. We will also understand how the CF-based recommendation engine works in detail so that all your concepts are clear during the implementation. With the help of these algorithms, we will build the best possible book recommendation system. We will compare the results of our algorithm with Amazon.

In the next section, we will cover the algorithms first and then start implementing our approach.

The best approach

In this section, we are trying to build the best possible recommendation engine. There are two parts to this section:

- Understanding the key concepts
- Implementing the best approach

Our first part covers the basic concepts, such as how the CF and KNN algorithms work, what kind of features we need to choose, and so on. In the second part, we will be implementing the recommendation engine using the KNN and CF algorithm. We will generate the accuracy score as well as the recommendation for books. So let's begin!

Understanding the key concepts

In this section, we will understand the concepts of collaborative filtering. This covers a lot of aspects of the recommendation system. So, let's explore CF.

Collaborative filtering

There are two main types of collaborative filtering, as follows:

- Memory-based CF:
  - User-user collaborative filtering
  - Item-item collaborative filtering
- Model-based CF:
  - Matrix-factorization-based algorithms
  - Deep learning

We will begin with memory-based CF and then move on to the model-based CF.

Memory-based CF

Memory-based CF is further divided into two sections. I have defined these sections earlier. Refer to the *Introducing the problem statement* section. Here, we need to understand the concepts. We will begin with user-user CF and then look into item-item CF.

User-user collaborative filtering

In user-user CF, we consider a particular user. Now we need to find users that are similar to our particular user. We find similar users by observing their buying pattern and rating pattern for the items. Based on the similarity in the ratings and buying patterns, we recommend products to similar types of users. In order to understand user-user CF, you can refer to the following figure:

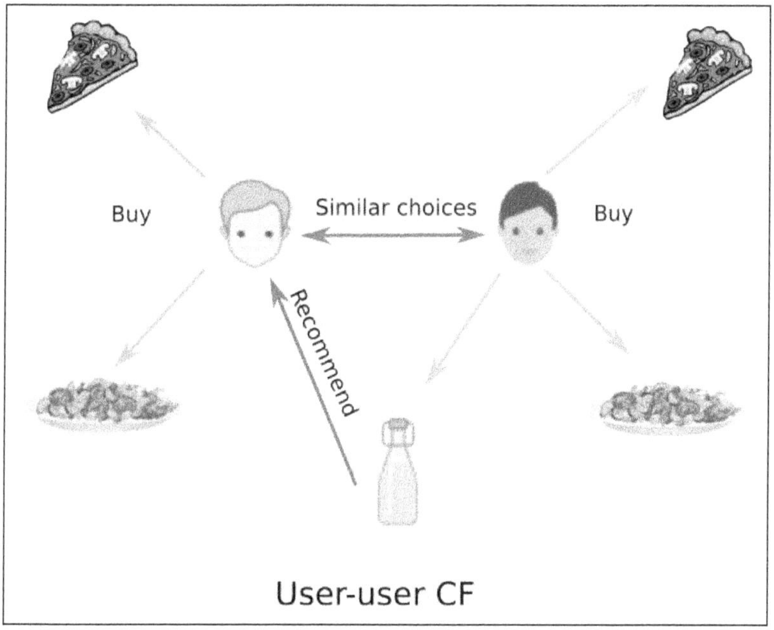

Figure 4.35: Pictorial representation of user-user CF

Item-item CF works differently, however.

Item-item collaborative filtering

In item-item CF, we consider items. We find users who like a particular item and other items that the user or similar users also liked and bought. So, we recommend the item along with the particular item the user is looking for. Here, we need to take items as the input and generate the list of items as a recommendation. You can refer to the following figure:

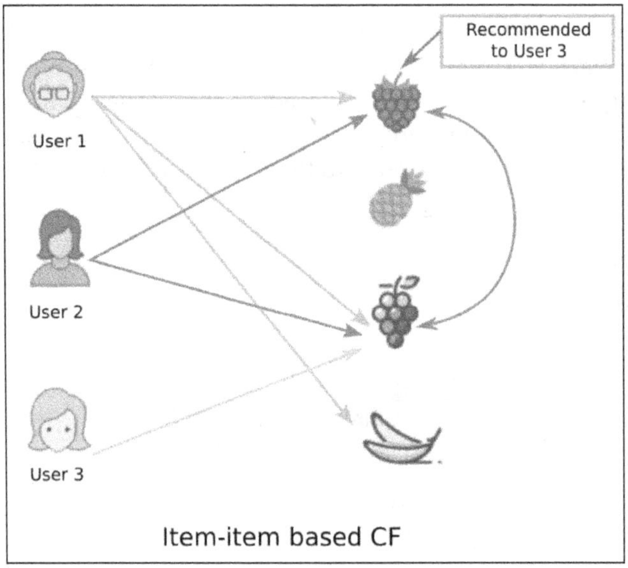

Figure 4.36: Image representing item-item CF

These two approaches can be summarized as follows:

- **Item-item CF**: We consider users who have liked x item as well as y
- **User-user CF**: We consider users who, similar to you, also liked x and y items

Memory-based models use similarity-based techniques. In this approach, there are no optimization techniques, such as a gradient descent, involved so it will be easy to implement. We can use the KNN ML algorithm as it doesn't use a gradient descent-based optimization strategy. So, during the implementation, we will be using the KNN algorithm.

The idea behind the KNN algorithm is simple. We need to obtain the weight for each user or item. We can generate this weight by a cosine similarity or a person's correlation coefficient. We use the similarity values, but we need to limit the number of similar users because we cannot consider all users to be similar. This number is denoted by K. Here, K indicates the number of similar neighbors or users we need to consider. This is the reason why the algorithm is called K-nearest neighbors (KNN). If you want more details on the KNN algorithm, then you can refer to this article: `https://www.analyticsvidhya.com/blog/2018/03/introduction-k-neighbours-algorithm-clustering/`

Model-based CF

In this approach, we will be using ML-based techniques to predict the recommendation for users, especially for those items that are unrated. For that, we can use the matrix factorization method or the Deep-Learning-based approach. We will focus on the matrix factorization method here.

So, let's look at matrix factorization.

Matrix-factorization-based algorithms

The main idea behind the matrix-factorization-based algorithm is that preferences of the user can be determined by the matrix operation. We need to define the small number of hidden or latent factors. We can refer to this matrix as factors or embeddings. Let's take an example to understand it better.

We need to define the embedding matrix. Here, the values are randomly initialized and then we perform a dot product of this embedding matrix and the book embedding matrix. The resultant matrix is generated in such a way that we can predict which book can be recommended to which user. For matrix factorization, we need nonnegative elements in our resultant matrix. We will use singular value decomposition (SVD) models to identify latent factors. There are some other techniques that can be used as well, such as probabilistic matrix factorization, nonnegative matrix factorization, and so on. We will implement this matrix factorization technique.

Difference between memory-based CF and model-based CF

The main difference between memory-based CF and model-based CF is that in the memory-based approach, there are no optimization techniques involved, whereas in the model-based approach, there is an optimization strategy and other optimization functions involved that improve accuracy of the model over a period of time. Now we will implement the CF-based approach.

Implementing the best approach

We will be implementing this approach by using the following steps. You can refer to the code on GitHub at: `https://github.com/jalajthanaki/Book_recommendation_system/blob/master/KNN_based_recommendation_system.ipynb`.

1. Loading the dataset
2. Merging the data frames
3. EDA for the merged data frame
4. Filtering data based on geolocation
5. Applying the KNN algorithm
6. Recommendation using the KNN algorithm
7. Applying matrix factorization
8. Recommendation using matrix factorization

Loading the dataset

Just like we loaded the dataset in the revised approach, we need to implement it here as well. Take a look at the following screenshot:

```
import pandas as pd
import numpy as np
from scipy.sparse import csr_matrix
import sklearn
from sklearn.decomposition import TruncatedSVD

books = pd.read_csv('./data/BX-Books.csv', sep=';', error_bad_lines=False, encoding="latin-1",low_memory=False)
books.columns = ['ISBN', 'bookTitle', 'bookAuthor', 'yearOfPublication', 'publisher', 'imageUrlS', 'imageUrlM', 'imageUrlL']
users = pd.read_csv('./data/BX-Users.csv', sep=';', error_bad_lines=False, encoding="latin-1",low_memory=False)
users.columns = ['userID', 'Location', 'Age']
ratings = pd.read_csv('./data/BX-Book-Ratings.csv', sep=';', error_bad_lines=False, encoding="latin-1",low_memory=False)
ratings.columns = ['userID', 'ISBN', 'bookRating']
```

Figure 4.37: Code snippet for loading the dataset

Merging the data frames

We need to merge the books and ratings data frames. We will be generating the total rating each book has received to date. The code snippet for this is as follows:

```
combine_book_rating = pd.merge(ratings,books,on='ISBN')
columns = ['yearOfPublication', 'publisher', 'bookAuthor','imageUrlS','imageUrlM','imageUrlL']
combine_book_rating = combine_book_rating.drop(columns,axis=1)
combine_book_rating.head()
```

	userID	ISBN	bookRating	bookTitle
0	276725	034545104X	0	Flesh Tones: A Novel
1	2313	034545104X	5	Flesh Tones: A Novel
2	6543	034545104X	0	Flesh Tones: A Novel
3	8680	034545104X	5	Flesh Tones: A Novel
4	10314	034545104X	9	Flesh Tones: A Novel

```
combine_book_rating = combine_book_rating.dropna(axis = 0, subset = ['bookTitle'])

book_ratingCount = (combine_book_rating.
     groupby(by = ['bookTitle'])['bookRating'].
     count().
     reset_index().
     rename(columns = {'bookRating': 'totalRatingCount'})
     [['bookTitle', 'totalRatingCount']]
    )
book_ratingCount.head()
```

	bookTitle	totalRatingCount
0	A Light in the Storm: The Civil War Diary of ...	4
1	Always Have Popsicles	1
2	Apple Magic (The Collector's series)	1
3	Ask Lily (Young Women of Faith: Lily Series, ...	1
4	Beyond IBM: Leadership Marketing and Finance ...	1

Figure 4.38: Code snippet for generating the rating count

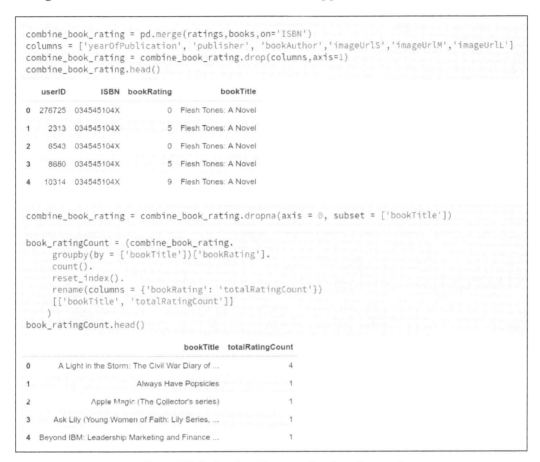

After that, we will be generating the book-rating score as well. Refer to the following screenshot:

```
rating_with_totalRatingCount = combine_book_rating.merge(book_ratingCount,
                                                          left_on = 'bookTitle',
                                                          right_on = 'bookTitle',
                                                          how = 'left')
rating_with_totalRatingCount.head()
```

	userID	ISBN	bookRating	bookTitle	totalRatingCount
0	276725	034545104X	0	Flesh Tones: A Novel	60
1	2313	034545104X	5	Flesh Tones: A Novel	60
2	6543	034545104X	0	Flesh Tones: A Novel	60
3	8680	034545104X	5	Flesh Tones: A Novel	60
4	10314	034545104X	9	Flesh Tones: A Novel	60

Figure 4.39: Code snippet for generating the book-rating score

EDA for the merged data frames

Here, we will perform data analysis for the total rating count. After that, we need to obtain the quantile value for the rating of the book. That quantile value gives us a good idea about the data distribution. You can refer to the code snippet shown in the following screenshot:

```
pd.set_option('display.float_format', lambda x: '%.3f' % x)
print(book_ratingCount['totalRatingCount'].describe())
```

```
count    241071.000
mean          4.277
std          16.739
min           1.000
25%           1.000
50%           1.000
75%           3.000
max        2502.000
Name: totalRatingCount, dtype: float64
```

```
print(book_ratingCount['totalRatingCount'].quantile(np.arange(.9, 1, .01)))
```

```
0.900    7.000
0.910    8.000
0.920    9.000
0.930   10.000
0.940   11.000
0.950   13.000
0.960   16.000
0.970   20.000
0.980   29.000
0.990   50.000
Name: totalRatingCount, dtype: float64
```

```
popularity_threshold = 50
rating_popular_book = rating_with_totalRatingCount.query('totalRatingCount >= @popularity_threshold')
rating_popular_book.head()
```

	userID	ISBN	bookRating	bookTitle	totalRatingCount
0	276725	034545104X	0	Flesh Tones: A Novel	60
1	2313	034545104X	5	Flesh Tones: A Novel	60
2	6543	034545104X	0	Flesh Tones: A Novel	60
3	8680	034545104X	5	Flesh Tones: A Novel	60
4	10314	034545104X	9	Flesh Tones: A Novel	60

Figure 4.40: Code snippet for EDA on total-book-rating

As you can see, only 1% of the books received a user rating of 50 or more. There are many books in this dataset, but we will consider only 1% of these books. The total number of unique books is 2,713.

Filtering data based on geolocation

We will limit our user data to the USA and Canada regions. This filter speeds up the computation. We need to combine the user data and the total book-rating count data. For that, the code is shown in the following screenshot:

```
combined = rating_popular_book.merge(users, left_on = 'userID', right_on = 'userID', how = 'left')

us_canada_user_rating = combined[combined['Location'].str.contains("usa|canada")]
us_canada_user_rating=us_canada_user_rating.drop('Age', axis=1)
us_canada_user_rating.head()
```

	userID	ISBN	bookRating	bookTitle	totalRatingCount	Location
0	276725	034545104X	0	Flesh Tones: A Novel	60	tyler, texas, usa
1	2313	034545104X	5	Flesh Tones: A Novel	60	cincinnati, ohio, usa
2	6543	034545104X	0	Flesh Tones: A Novel	60	strafford, missouri, usa
3	8680	034545104X	5	Flesh Tones: A Novel	60	st. charles county, missouri, usa
4	10314	034545104X	9	Flesh Tones: A Novel	60	beaverton, oregon, usa

```
us_canada_user_rating_pivot = us_canada_user_rating.pivot(index = 'bookTitle', columns = 'userID', values = 'bookRating').fillna(0)
us_canada_user_rating_matrix = csr_matrix(us_canada_user_rating_pivot.values)
```

Figure 4.41: Code snippet for geolocation-based filtering

As you can see, now we have users that are from the USA and Canada.

Applying the KNN algorithm

It's time to apply the main logic. We will be applying the KNN algorithm using the `sklearn` library. Our main goal is to determine the closeness of the data instances. You can take a look at the code snippet shown in the following screenshot:

```
from sklearn.neighbors import NearestNeighbors

model_knn = NearestNeighbors(metric = 'cosine', algorithm = 'brute')
model_knn.fit(us_canada_user_rating_matrix)

NearestNeighbors(algorithm='brute', leaf_size=30, metric='cosine',
         metric_params=None, n_jobs=1, n_neighbors=5, p=2, radius=1.0)
```

Figure 4.42: Code snippet for implementing the KNN algorithm

We have used cosine similarity as the KNN matric parameter and we are considering the five nearest neighbors. This means that the value for K=5. After the model is trained, we need to obtain the recommendation using them.

Recommendation using the KNN algorithm

Here, we need to obtain the recommendation using the KNN algorithm that has been trained just now. The code is shown in the following screenshot:

```
query_index = np.random.choice(us_canada_user_rating_pivot.shape[0])
#distances, indices = model_knn.kneighbors(us_canada_user_rating_pivot.iloc[query_index, :].values.reshape(1, -1), n_neighbors = 6)
distances, indices = model_knn.kneighbors(us_canada_user_rating_pivot.iloc[1907, :].values.reshape(1, -1), n_neighbors = 6)

for i in range(0, len(distances.flatten())):
    if i == 0:
        print('Recommendations for {0}:\n'.format(us_canada_user_rating_pivot.index[1907]))
    else:
        print('{0}: {1}, with distance of {2}:'.format(i, us_canada_user_rating_pivot.index[indices.flatten()[i]], distances.flatten()[i]))

Recommendations for The Green Mile: Night Journey (Green Mile Series):

1: The Two Dead Girls (Green Mile Series), with distance of 0.2413022186886533:
2: The Green Mile: Coffey's Hands (Green Mile Series), with distance of 0.26063737394209996:
3: The Green Mile: The Mouse on the Mile (Green Mile Series), with distance of 0.26952377054292587:
4: The Green Mile: The Bad Death of Eduard Delacroix (Green Mile Series), with distance of 0.3212787692847636:
5: The Green Mile: Coffey on the Mile (Green Mile Series), with distance of 0.34034250405531474:
```

Figure 4.43: Code snippet for obtaining a recommendation using KNN

For recommendation purposes, we have chosen the value of K = 6, which means we are considering the six nearest neighbors to recommend the book to any user. Here, we have chosen the book randomly from the `us_canada_user_rating_pivot` data frame.

The suggestions look great. All of The Green Mile series books are recommended here.

Applying matrix factorization

Now let's implement the matrix factorization method. We will convert the USA and Canada user rating data frame into a 2D matrix. This matrix is also referred to as a utility matrix. We have replaced the missing value with 0. You can refer to the code given in the following screenshot:

```
us_canada_user_rating_pivot2 = us_canada_user_rating.pivot(index = 'userID', columns = 'bookTitle', values = 'bookRating').fillna(0)

us_canada_user_rating_pivot2.head()
```

bookTitle	10 Lb. Penalty	16 Lighthouse Road	1984	1st to Die: A Novel	2010: Odyssey Two	204 Rosewood Lane	2061: Odyssey Three	24 Hours	2nd Chance	3rd Degree	...	YOU BELONG TO ME	Year of Wonders	You Belong To Me	You Shall Know Our Velocity	Young Wives	Zen and the Art of Motorcycle Maintenance: An Inquiry into Values	Zoya	\O\" Is for Outlaw"	\Surely You're Joking, Mr. Feynman!\": Adventures of a Curious Character"	stardust
userID																					
8	0.000	0.000	0.000	0.000	0.000	0.000	0.000	0.000	0.000	0.000	...	0.000	0.000	0.000	0.000	0.000	0.000	0.000	0.000	0.000	0.000
9	0.000	0.000	0.000	0.000	0.000	0.000	0.000	0.000	0.000	0.000	...	0.000	0.000	0.000	0.000	0.000	0.000	0.000	0.000	0.000	0.000
14	0.000	0.000	0.000	0.000	0.000	0.000	0.000	0.000	0.000	0.000	...	0.000	0.000	0.000	0.000	0.000	0.000	0.000	0.000	0.000	0.000
16	0.000	0.000	0.000	0.000	0.000	0.000	0.000	0.000	0.000	0.000	...	0.000	0.000	0.000	0.000	0.000	0.000	0.000	0.000	0.000	0.000
17	0.000	0.000	0.000	0.000	0.000	0.000	0.000	0.000	0.000	0.000	...	0.000	0.000	0.000	0.000	0.000	0.000	0.000	0.000	0.000	0.000

5 rows × 2442 columns

Figure 4.44: Code snippet for generating the utility matrix

Now we need to transpose the utility matrix. The `bookTitles` become rows and `userID` is converted into columns. After that, we will apply `TruncatedSVD` for dimensionality reduction. This operation is performed on columns—on `userID`—because we need to use the book's title afterward. You can refer to the code shown in the following screenshot:

```
us_canada_user_rating_pivot2.shape

(40017, 2442)

X = us_canada_user_rating_pivot2.values.T
X.shape

(2442, 40017)

import sklearn
from sklearn.decomposition import TruncatedSVD

SVD = TruncatedSVD(n_components=12, random_state=17)
matrix = SVD.fit_transform(X)
matrix.shape

(2442, 12)
```

Figure 4.45: Code snippet for SVD dimensionality reduction

Here, we have chosen the value of `n_components` as 12. So as you can see, the dimensionality of our data frame has reduced a lot. Earlier, the dimensions of the data frame were 40017 x 2442, which has now become 2442 x 12.

Now we perform Pearson's correlation coefficient for every book pair in our final matrix. We will compare the results with the KNN algorithm. Basically, we should get the suggestion we got previously using the KNN algorithm for this approach as well.

Recommendation using matrix factorization

Here, we need to generate a recommendation using the matrix factorization technique. We will list down all the recommendations for The Green Mile: Night Journey (Green Mile Series). The algorithm should suggest highly correlated books. We have applied a threshold for the correlation. Only those books that have a correlation score of more than 0.9 to less than 1 are listed using this approach. You can refer to the code snippet given in the following screenshot:

```
us_canada_book_title = us_canada_user_rating_pivot2.columns
us_canada_book_list = list(us_canada_book_title)
coffey_hands = us_canada_book_list.index("The Green Mile: Night Journey (Green Mile Series)")
#Green Mile: Night Journey (Green Mile Series)
#The Green Mile: Coffey's Hands (Green Mile Series)
print(coffey_hands)

1907

corr_coffey_hands  = corr[coffey_hands]

list(us_canada_book_title[(corr_coffey_hands<1.0) & (corr_coffey_hands>0.9)])

['Carrie',
 'Desperation',
 'Four Past Midnight',
 'Hearts In Atlantis : New Fiction',
 'It',
 'Needful Things',
 'Needful Things: The Last Castle Rock Story',
 'Rose Madder',
 'The Bachman Books: Rage, the Long Walk, Roadwork, the Running Man',
 'The Dark Half',
 'The Dead Zone',
 'The Green Mile: Coffey on the Mile (Green Mile Series)',
 "The Green Mile: Coffey's Hands (Green Mile Series)",
 'The Green Mile: The Bad Death of Eduard Delacroix (Green Mile Series)',
 'The Green Mile: The Complete Serial Novel',
 'The Green Mile: The Mouse on the Mile (Green Mile Series)',
 'The Shining',
 'The Two Dead Girls (Green Mile Series)']
```

Figure 4.46: Code snippet for generating a recommendation using matrix factorization

As you can see, the recommendation for all the books that have been recommended using the KNN-based approach appear here as well. So, this CF-based recommendation system works in the best manner. You can find the same kind of recommendations on Amazon as well. Refer to the following screenshot:

Figure 4.47: Recommendation on Amazon

We can confirm that our recommendation engine works well.

Summary

This is the last chapter of the analytics domain. So far, you have learned a lot of concepts that can help us build amazing analytics applications. In this chapter, you learned how to make a recommendation engine for an e-commerce product. In the baseline approach, we used the concept of TF-IDF and cosine similarity. In the revised approach, we built a book recommendation system that used the concept of correlation. In the best approach, we used the KNN algorithm to build a recommendation engine that used a collaborative-filtering-based approach. We looked at the advantages and disadvantages of all the approaches. You also learned about the architecture of the recommendation system. All these topics will help you understand and build your own recommendation system. You can also build a computer vision-based recommendation engine. This kind of recommendation engine really changes the way content is recommended to the users. So don't hesitate to build new types of recommendation systems.

From the next chapter onward, we will be addressing the applications that belong to the natural language processing domain or the natural language generation domain. The next chapter is all about sentiment analysis, which is a well-known and simple NLP application. We will be using a variety of Machine Learning algorithms to achieve the best possible result.

5
Sentiment Analysis

So far, we have explored some really cool applications in the analytics domain. In this chapter, we will explore the famous Natural Language Processing (NLP) technique, which you may have already guessed because of the name of the chapter. Absolutely right; we will build a sentiment analysis-based application. In general, everyone is familiar with sentiment analysis-based applications. If you aren't, then don't worry. We will discuss and understand all the necessary details.

First of all, I want to give you a basic idea about sentiment analysis. I will provide an example so it will be easy for you to understand. Regardless of where we live, we all watch movies. Nowadays, we read reviews or others' opinions on various social media platforms. After that, if a majority of the opinions about the movie are good, then we watch that movie. If the opinions are not impressive, we might not watch the movie. So during this entire process, our mind analyzes these opinions and categorizes them into either positive opinions, negative opinions, or neutral opinions. In this chapter, we will be performing the same kind of analysis.

Let me introduce the formal definition of sentiment analysis. Sentiment analysis is a technique where we consider a sentence, paragraph, document, or any information that is in the form of a natural language and determine whether that text's emotional tone is positive, negative, or neutral. We will be applying machine learning and Deep Learning to build a sentiment analysis application.

We will be covering the following topics in this chapter:

- Introducing the problem statement
- Understanding the dataset
- Building training and testing datasets for the baseline model
- Feature engineering for the baseline model
- Selecting the Machine Learning (ML) algorithm
- Training the baseline model

- Understanding the testing matrix
- Testing the baseline model
- Problems with the existing approach
- How to optimize the existing approach
    - Understanding key concepts for optimizing the approach
- Implementing the revised approach
    - Testing the revised approach
    - Understanding problems with the revised approach
- Best approach
    - Implementing the best approach
- Summary

Introducing problem statements

We are living in a competitive world. Before buying any product and investing our time or money in anything, we try to find out what others think about that product(s) or service(s). We try to analyze their reviews or opinions. If we find them positive and trustworthy, then we buy the product and invest our money or time in that particular service. On the other hand, if we find these opinions or reviews negative, then we might not buy the product and not invest our money or time in that particular service. In the current era of the internet, it is easy to find reviews on social media platforms, blogs, news sources, and so on. This activity of analyzing reviews will be useful for consumers as well as makers of products or service providers. This is because, based on the reviews of their customer, they can change their product effectively, providing more satisfaction to their customers and make a good profit from that product or service. I have already given you the formal definition of sentiment analysis, so I'm not going to bore you with it again. Let's try to understand what the main focus of this chapter will be.

We will be developing a sentiment analysis application for movie reviews. During training, we will consider labels associated with each of the movie reviews so that we can train our machine learning algorithm based on the given labels. After training, when we pass any unseen movie reviews, then our trained machine learning algorithm will predict the sentiment, which means whether the provided movie review indicates a positive sentiment or a negative sentiment.

We will be considering an IMDb (Internet Movie Database) movie review dataset to develop sentiment analysis for movie reviews. We will look at the details regarding the dataset in the next section.

Understanding the dataset

In this section, we will look into our dataset. We have considered an IMDb dataset, which you can download at: `http://ai.stanford.edu/~amaas/data/sentiment/`. After clicking on this link, you can see that there is a link provided on the page. This link is titled `Large Movie Review Dataset v1.0`; we need to click on it. This way, we can download the IMDb dataset. Once you have downloaded the dataset, you need to extract the .tar.gz file. Once you extract the `.tar.gz` file, you can see that there are two folders inside the extracted folder and some other files. Let's look at each of them in the following section.

Understanding the content of the dataset

After extracting the dataset file, we'll see that there are some folders and files inside it. We will be discussing all of the content's meaning and what we will be using for our training purposes. This dataset has two folders and three files:

- train folder
- test folder
- `imdb.vocab` file
- `imdbEr.txt`
- README

Train folder

This folder contains data for training. Inside this folder, there are two main folders. The `pos` folder contains positive movie reviews and the `neg` folder contains negative movie reviews. Inside the `pos` folder, there are 12,500 positive movie reviews. Inside the `neg` folder, there are 12,500 negative movie reviews. So in total, we have 25,000 movie reviews; by using them, we will train our Machine Learning (ML) model. For testing purposes, we can use movie reviews provided inside the `unsup` folder. These movie reviews are unlabeled, so we can use them for testing purposes or divide our labeled data into training and testing groups so it will be easy for us to find out how our trained ML model works.

There are other files inside the train folder but we are not going to use them. Those files carry data that already has tokenized bag-of-word (BOW) features. In order to get a clear picture of the folder structure, you can refer to the code snippet provided in the following figure:

```
jalaj@jalaj:~/Downloads/aclImdb/train$ tree -L 1 ./
./
├── labeledBow.feat
├── neg
├── pos
├── unsup
├── unsupBow.feat
├── urls_neg.txt
├── urls_pos.txt
└── urls_unsup.txt

3 directories, 5 files
jalaj@jalaj:~/Downloads/aclImdb/train$
```

Figure 5.1: Folder structure of the train folder

If you want to explore the dataset in more detail, then you can refer to the documentation provided at: `http://www.paddlepaddle.org/docs/0.10.0/documentation/en/tutorials/sentiment_analysis/index_en.html`.

Test folder

This folder contains data for testing. Inside this folder, there are `pos` and `neg` folders, which contain positive and negative movie reviews, respectively. Each of the folders contains 12,500 movie reviews, so in total, we have 25,000 movie reviews for testing. These movie reviews are labeled one so we can use this dataset to test our trained model. There are other `BOW` files and `url` files, which we will not be using. You can see the folder structure of the test folder in the following figure:

```
jalaj@jalaj:~/Downloads/aclImdb/test$ tree -L 1 ./
./
├── labeledBow.feat
├── neg
├── pos
├── urls_neg.txt
└── urls_pos.txt

2 directories, 3 files
jalaj@jalaj:~/Downloads/aclImdb/test$
```

Figure 5.2: Folder structure of the test folder

imdb.vocab file

This file contains the unique words used in all movie reviews, so it is the vocabulary file for the `IMDb` dataset. If you open this file, then you can see words and observe that all of them are unique. You can see the contents of this file in the following figure:

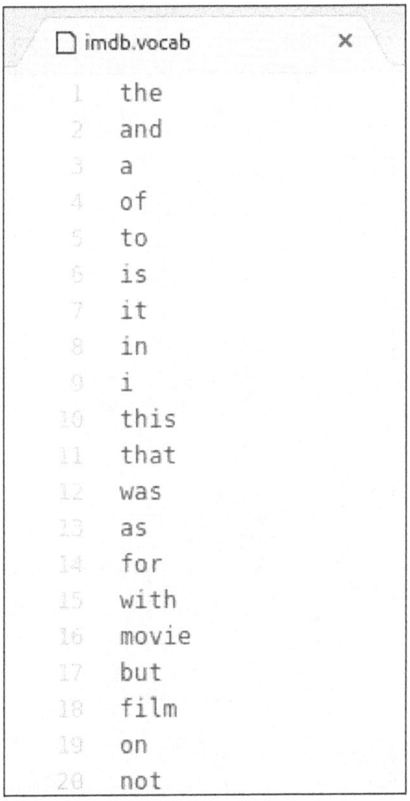

Figure 5.3: Contents of the imdb.vocab file

imdbEr.txt file

This file indicates the expected rating for each token in the `imdb.vocab` file. This means that all these numerical values indicate the score for each individual word provided in the `imdb.vocab` file. If the word is positive, then the numerical value is a positive float number. If the word is negative, then the numerical value is a negative float value. You can see the contents of the file in the following figure:

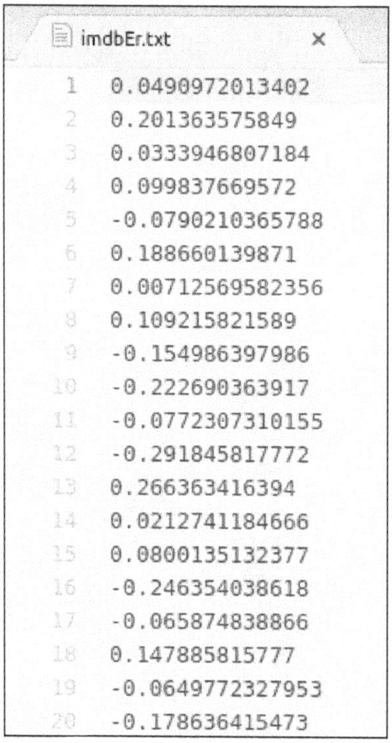
imdbEr.txt

```
0.0490972013402
0.201363575849
0.0333946807184
0.099837669572
-0.0790210365788
0.188660139871
0.00712569582356
0.109215821589
-0.154986397986
-0.222690363917
-0.0772307310155
-0.291845817772
0.266363416394
0.0212741184666
0.0800135132377
-0.246354038618
-0.065874838866
0.147885815777
-0.0649772327953
-0.178636415473
```

Figure 5.4: The imdbEr.txt file, which has a score for each of the words given in the imdb.vocab file

README

This file contains the documentation regarding the dataset. You can get a hold of the basic information using this file.

Note that for developing this sentiment analysis application, we will consider data from only the `train` folder because processing up to 50,000 movie reviews takes a lot of computation power, so instead of 50,000 movie reviews, we will be considering only 25,000 movie reviews from the `train` folder, and we will hold out some movie reviews for testing. Now let's try to understand how the content of the movie review files has been provided.

Understanding the contents of the movie review files

Inside the `pos` and `neg` folders, there are `.txt` files that contain the movie reviews. All the `.txt` files inside the `pos` folder are positive movie reviews. You can refer to the sample content provided in the following figure:

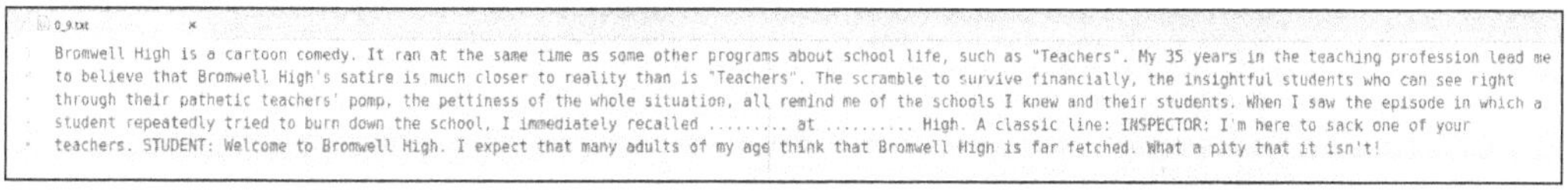
0_9.txt

Bromwell High is a cartoon comedy. It ran at the same time as some other programs about school life, such as "Teachers". My 35 years in the teaching profession lead me to believe that Bromwell High's satire is much closer to reality than is "Teachers". The scramble to survive financially, the insightful students who can see right through their pathetic teachers' pomp, the pettiness of the whole situation, all remind me of the schools I knew and their students. When I saw the episode in which a student repeatedly tried to burn down the school, I immediately recalled .... at .... High. A classic line: INSPECTOR: I'm here to sack one of your teachers. STUDENT: Welcome to Bromwell High. I expect that many adults of my age think that Bromwell High is far fetched. What a pity that it isn't!

Figure 5.5: Sample movie review from the pos folder; the filename is 0_9.txt

The movie reviews are provided in simple plain text. Here, we will be performing only a small preprocessing change, in which we rename the `pos` and `neg` folder names to `positiveReviews` and `negativeReviews`, respectively. This `IMDb` dataset had already been preprocessed, so we are not performing any extensive preprocessing. You can download the final training dataset by using this GitHub link: `https://github.com/jalajthanaki/Sentiment_Analysis/blob/master/data.tar.gz`.

Now we need to start building the ML model for our sentiment analysis application. We will perform the following steps:

- Building the training and testing datasets
- Feature engineering for the baseline model
- Selecting the Machine Learning algorithm
- Training the baseline model
- Understanding the testing matrix
- Testing the baseline model

So let's try to understand all these steps.

Building the training and testing datasets for the baseline model

In this section, we will be generating the training dataset as well as the testing dataset. We will iterate over the files of our dataset and consider all files whose names start with the digit 12 as our test dataset. So, roughly 90% of our dataset is considered the training dataset and 10 % of our dataset is considered the testing dataset. You can refer to the code for this in the following figure:

Import dependencies

```
import os
import time

from sklearn.feature_extraction.text import TfidfVectorizer
from sklearn.naive_bayes import MultinomialNB
from sklearn import svm
from sklearn.metrics import classification_report
from sklearn.metrics import accuracy_score
```

Build training dataset and testing dataset

```
data_dir = "/home/jalaj/PycharmProjects/Sentiment_Analysis/data"
classes = ['positiveReviews', 'negativeReviews']

# Read the data
train_data = []
train_labels = []
test_data = []
test_labels = []
for curr_class in classes:
    dirname = os.path.join(data_dir, curr_class)
    for fname in os.listdir(dirname):
        with open(os.path.join(dirname, fname), 'r') as f:
            content = f.read()
            if fname.startswith('12'):
                test_data.append(content)
                test_labels.append(curr_class)
            else:
                train_data.append(content)
                train_labels.append(curr_class)
```

Figure 5.6: Code snippet for building the training and testing dataset

As you can see, if the filename starts with 12 then we consider the content of those files as the testing dataset. All files apart from these are considered the training dataset. You can find the code at this GitHub link: `https://github.com/jalajthanaki/Sentiment_Analysis/blob/master/Baseline_approach.ipynb`.

Feature engineering for the baseline model

For this application, we will be using a basic statistical feature extraction concept in order to generate the features from raw text data. In the NLP domain, we need to convert raw text into a numerical format so that the ML algorithm can be applied to that numerical data. There are many techniques available, including indexing, count based vectorization, **Term Frequency - Inverse Document Frequency** (**TF-IDF**), and so on. I have already discussed the concept of TF-IDF in *Chapter 4, Generate features using TF-IDF*:

> Indexing is basically used for fast data retrieval. In indexing, we provide a unique identification number. This unique identification number can be assigned in alphabetical order or based on frequency. You can refer to this link: `http://scikit-learn.org/stable/modules/generated/sklearn.preprocessing.LabelEncoder.html`
>
> Count-based vectorization sorts the words in alphabetical order and if a particular word is present then its vector value becomes 1, otherwise 0. The size of the vector is the same as the vocabulary size of our training dataset. You can refer to the simple code by using this link: `https://github.com/jalajthanaki/NLPython/blob/6c74ddecac03b9aec740ae2e11dd8b52f11c0623/ch5/bagofwordsdemo/BOWdemo.py`

Here, we are using the TF-IDF vectorizer technique from scikit-learn. The `TfidfVectorizer` function converts a collection of raw documents into a matrix of TF-IDF features. If you are new to TF-IDF, then I would recommend that you refer to `http://www.tfidf.com/` or `https://www.packtpub.com/mapt/book/big_data_and_business_intelligence/9781787121423/5`.

You can refer to the code snippet provided in the following figure:

Generate feature vector by using TfidfVectorizer

```
# Create feature vectors
vectorizer = TfidfVectorizer(min_df=5,
                             max_df = 0.8,
                             sublinear_tf=True,
                             use_idf=True)
train_vectors = vectorizer.fit_transform(train_data)
test_vectors = vectorizer.transform(test_data)
```

Figure 5.7: Code snippet for generating feature vectors by using TF-IDF

As you see in the preceding code snippet for generating feature vectors by using TF-IDF, we have defined some parameters, which I want to explain properly:

- `min_df`: This parameter provides a strict lower limit for document frequency. We have set this parameter to 5. So terms that appear fewer than 5 times in the dataset will not be considered for generating the TF-IDF vector.
- `max_df`: This parameter ignores terms that have a document frequency strictly higher than the given threshold. If the value of this parameter is float, then it represents a proportion of the document. We have set the parameter value to 0.8, which means we are considering 80% of the dataset.
- `sublinear_tf`: This parameter is used to apply scaling. The value of this parameter is False by default . If its value is True, then the value of tf will be replaced with the *1+log(tf)* formula. This formula will help us perform scaling on our vocabulary.
- `use_idf`: This parameter indicates whether the IDF reweighting mechanism is enabled or not. By default, IDF reweighting is enabled and hence the flag value for this parameter is True.

Two methods are used here, as follows:

- `fit_transform()`: By using this method, you have learned vocabulary and IDF, and this method returns the term-document matrix.
- `transform()`: This method transforms documents into a document-term matrix. This method uses vocabulary and document frequency learned from the fit_transform method.

You can find the preceding code at this GitHub link: `https://github.com/jalajthanaki/Sentiment_Analysis/blob/master/Baseline_approach.ipynb`.

Now let's see which algorithm is best suited to building the baseline model.

Selecting the machine learning algorithm

Sentiment analysis is a classification problem. There are some algorithms that can be really helpful for us. In movie reviews, you may discover that there are some phrases that appear quite frequently. If these frequently used phrases indicate some kind of sentiment, most likely, they are phrases that indicate a positive sentiment or a negative sentiment. We need to find phrases that indicate a sentiment. Once we find phrases that indicate sentiment, we just need to classify the sentiment either in a positive sentiment class or a negative sentiment class. In order to find out the actual sentiment class, we need to identify the probability of the most likely positive phrases and most likely negative phrases so that based on a higher probability value, we can identify that the given movie review belongs to a positive or a negative sentiment. The probabilities we will be taking into account are the prior and posterior probability values. This is the fundamental base of the naive Bayes algorithm. So, we will be using the multinomial naive Bayes algorithm. Apart from this, we will be using the **Support Vector Machine** (**SVM**) algorithm. We will be implementing it with different types of kernel tricks.

If you want to learn more about naive Bayes, then you can refer to `http://www.saedsayad.com/naive_bayesian.html`, and if you want to learn more about SVM, then you can refer to: `https://www.analyticsvidhya.com/blog/2017/09/understaing-support-vector-machine-example-code/` or `https://www.packtpub.com/mapt/book/big_data_and_business_intelligence/9781787121423/8/ch08lvl1sec77/understanding-ml-algorithms-and-other-concepts`.

In the next section, we will look at the code that helps us perform training.

Training the baseline model

In this section, we will look at the code that helps us perform actual training on the training dataset. We will look at the implementation first, and then I will explain the code step by step. Here, we will be implementing Naive Bayes and SVM algorithms. For implementation, we will be using the scikit-learn library. You can find the code at this GitHub link: `https://github.com/jalajthanaki/Sentiment_Analysis/blob/master/Baseline_approach.ipynb`.

Implementing the baseline model

In order to understand the implementation of the baseline model, you can refer to the following code snippet:

Perform training using different ML algos

```
# Perform classification with MultinomialNB
clf = MultinomialNB()
clf.fit(train_vectors, train_labels)
prediction = clf.predict(test_vectors)

# Perform classification with SVM, kernel=rbf
classifier_rbf = svm.SVC()
classifier_rbf.fit(train_vectors, train_labels)
prediction_rbf = classifier_rbf.predict(test_vectors)

# Perform classification with SVM, kernel=linear
classifier_linear = svm.SVC(kernel='linear')
classifier_linear.fit(train_vectors, train_labels)
prediction_linear = classifier_linear.predict(test_vectors)

# Perform classification with SVM, kernel=linear
classifier_liblinear = svm.LinearSVC()
classifier_liblinear.fit(train_vectors, train_labels)
prediction_liblinear = classifier_liblinear.predict(test_vectors)
```

Figure 5.8: Code snippet for performing training using naive Bayes and SVM

We have implemented the following four algorithms here:

- Multinomial naive Bayes
- C-support vector classification with kernel rbf
- C-support vector classification with kernel linear
- Linear support vector classification

Multinomial naive Bayes

As you can see in the preceding code snippet, we have used Multinomial naive Bayes. The multinomial naive Bayes classifier is suitable for classification with discrete features, which means that if the features are word counts or TF-IDF vectors, then we can use this classifier. The multinomial distribution normally requires integer feature counts. However, fractional counts such as TF-IDF might work as well. So, we have to apply this algorithm to `train_vectors`. The `fit()` method is the step where the actual training is performed. Here, we have used all hyper parameters by default.

C-support vector classification with kernel rbf

We have also implemented SVM with the *rbf* kernel. Kernel is a function that will help train the algorithm. The equation for the *rbf* kernel function is as follows:

$$rbf\ kernel = \exp\left(-\gamma \left\|x - x'\right\|^2\right)$$

$$Where\ \gamma\ is\ specified\ by\ keyword\ gamma,\ must\ be\ greater\ than\ 0.$$

C-support vector classification with kernel linear

We have also implemented SVM with the linear kernel. The equation for the linear kernel function is as follows:

$$linear\ kernel = \left\langle x, x' \right\rangle$$

Linear support vector classification

We have also used linear support vector classification. We will use the `LinearSVC()` method type for implementing this classification. This is similar to SVC with the parameter kernel=*linear* but implemented in terms of liblinear rather than `libsvm`, so it has more flexibility in the choice of penalties and loss functions, and should scale better to a large number of samples.

For all the preceding ML algorithms, we have provided input, which are `train_vectors` and `train_labels`. We will test the ML model accuracy by using the test vectors and comparing predicted labels with actual `test_labels`. Before performing testing, we will decide which kind of testing parameters we will be using. So let's look at the testing matrix.

Understanding the testing matrix

In this section, we will look at the testing matrix that we should consider in order to evaluate the trained ML models. For the baseline approach, we will be using the following five testing matrices:

- Precision
- Recall
- F1-score
- Support
- Training accuracy

Before we understand these terms, let's cover some basic terms that will help us to understand the preceding terms.

- **True Positive** (TP)—If the classifier predicts that the given movie review carries a positive sentiment and that movie review has a positive sentiment in an actual scenario, then these kinds of test cases are considered TP. So, you can define the TP as if the test result is one that detects the condition when the condition is actually present.
- **True Negative** (TN)—If the classifier predicts that the given movie review carries a negative sentiment and that movie review has a negative sentiment in an actual scenario, then those kinds of test cases are considered True Negative(TN). So, you can define the TN as if the test result is one that does not detect the condition when the condition is actually absent.
- **False Positive** (FP)—If the classifier predicts that the given movie review carries a positive sentiment and that movie review has a negative sentiment in an actual scenario, then those kinds of test cases are considered False Positive (FP). So, you can define the FP as if the test result is one that detects the condition when the condition is actually absent. This is like a flase alram.
- **False Negative** (FN)—If the classifier predicts that the given movie review carries a negative sentiment and that movie review has a positive sentiment in an actual scenario, then those kinds of test cases are considered False Negative (FN). So, you can define the FN as if the test result is one that does not detect the condition when the condition is actually present. This is the situation where certain conditions have been overlooked.

Now we will look at all five main testing matrices that use TP, TN, FP, and FN terms.

Precision

Precision is the ability of the classifier to assign a positive class label for samples that originally belong to a positive class label. Precision does not assign a positive class for a given sample that originally belongs to a negative class. The equation for generating the precision score is as follows:

$$Precision = \frac{TP}{TP + FP}$$

Recall

Recall is the ability of the classifier to find all the positive samples. The equation for generating recall score is as follows:

$$Recall = \frac{TP}{TP + FN}$$

F1-Score

F1-score is the harmonic means of precision and recall. So you can find the equation as follows:

$$F1 - Score = 2 \times \frac{precision.recall}{precision + recall}$$

Support

Support is the number of occurrences of each class in true target labels. The value of support helps when it comes to calculating the average value for precision, recall, and F1-score. You can see the equations for calculating the average value of precision, recall, and F1-Score as follows:

$$Avg.Precision = \frac{\left(Precision_{class_1} \times Support_{class1} + Precision_{class_2} \times Support_{class2} + \ldots + Precision_{class_n} \times Support_{classn}\right)}{Total\ value\ of\ support}$$

$$Avg.Recall = \frac{\left(Recall_{class_1} \times Support_{class1} + Recall_{class_2} \times Support_{class2} + \ldots + Recall_{class_n} \times Support_{classn}\right)}{Total\ value\ of\ support}$$

$$Avg.F1 = score = \frac{\left(F1 - score_{class_1} \times Support_{class1} + F1 - score_{class_2} \times Support_{class2} + \ldots + F1 - score_{class_n} \times Support_{classn}\right)}{Total\ value\ of\ support}$$

Actual calculation using the preceding formula will be provided in the *Testing the baseline mode* section. So bear with me for a while and we will see the actual testing result.

Training accuracy

Training accuracy guides us in order to obtain the correct direction for developing any ML application. We test the trained ML model on the testing dataset. When we perform this testing, we have actual labels of the sentiment class for each of the testing records, and we also have the predicted sentiment class for all testing records so we can compare the results. So, the set of labels predicted for a testing dataset must exactly match the corresponding set of labels in the actual testing dataset. We count the records where our predicted labels are the same as actual labels, and then we convert this count to a percentage.

We will see all the testing matrices for each of the implemented ML algorithms in the next section, and then we will decide which algorithm performs well. So let's look at the implementation of testing the baseline model.

Testing the baseline model

Here, we will look at the code snippet that performs the actual testing. We will be obtaining all the testing matrices that have been explained so far. We are going to test all the different ML algorithms so that we can compare the accuracy score.

Testing of Multinomial naive Bayes

You can see the testing result for the multinomial naive Bayes algorithm in the following figure:

Test the result of MultinomialNB

```
# Print results in a nice table for MultinomialNB
print("\nResults for NaiveBayes (MultinomialNB) ")
print(classification_report(test_labels, prediction))
print "\nAccuracy score of Multinomial naive bayes algorithm -----> " + str(accuracy_score(test_labels, prediction))

print "\n\n\n"

print "Reviews Prediction"
print "\nPredicted label is------> "+prediction[10]
print "\nMovie Review is ------> \n"+test_data[10]
```

```
Results for NaiveBayes (MultinomialNB)
                 precision    recall  f1-score   support

negativeReviews       0.79      0.87      0.82       611
positiveReviews       0.85      0.77      0.81       611

    avg / total       0.82      0.82      0.82      1222


Accuracy score of Multinomial naive bayes algorithm -----> 0.815875613748



Reviews Prediction

Predicted label is------> positiveReviews

Movie Review is ------>
- After their sons are sentenced to life in prison, Adelle (Debbie Reynolds) and Helen (Shirley Winters) begin rece
iving threatening phone calls because someone fells their sons got off easy. The pair decides to move to California
to escape the publicity of the trial and to start a new life. They start a dance school that is soon very successfu
l. One of the students has a rich unmarried father with whom Adelle quickly falls in love. In the meantime, Helen i
s busy raising rabbits and becoming a little too infatuated with an evangelist on the radio. It's only a mater of t
ime before everything falls apart and the women enter a world of madness and murder.<br /><br />- I can't help but
compare What's the Matter with Helen? to Whoever Slew Auntie Roo?, also starring Shelly Winters. Where that movie s
eemed almost restrained in its presentation of Auntie Roo's madness, there's nothing holding Helen back in this mov
ie. It may take a good deal of the movie's running time, but once she snaps, Helen is one Bad Mad Mutha. You don't
want to mess with her. Winters is so delightfully demented that it was impossible for me not to enjoy her performan
ce. I'm not going to spoil the movie, but the things Helen is capable of are totally over-the-top.<br /><br />- As
good as Winters is, Reynolds is totally ridiculous in her role as the gold-digging tap dancer. I got the impression
that she thought she was in a movie that would get her nominated for some award. This ain't Citizen Kane! Quit acti
ng so serious. Hey, Debbie, don't you realize that you're main purpose is to be a victim of Winters' insanity.<br /
><br />- I just love these former-female-stars-in-the-twilight-of-their-career horror movies. What's the Matter wit
h Helen? is as fun as any.
```

Figure 5.9: Code snippet for testing multinomial naive Bayes algorithm

As you can see, using this algorithm we have achieved an accuracy score of 81.5%.

Testing of SVM with rbf kernel

You can see the testing result for SVM with the rbf kernel algorithm in the following figure:

Test the result of SVM with rbf kernel

```
# Print results in a nice table for SVM algorithm with rbf kernel
print("\nResults for SVM algorithm with rbf kernel")
print(classification_report(test_labels, prediction_rbf))
print "\nAccuracy score of SVM algorithm with rbf kernel-----> " + str(accuracy_score(test_labels, prediction_rbf))

print "\n\n\n"

print "Reviews Prediction"
print "\nPredicted label is------> "+prediction[10]
print "\nMovie Review is ------> \n"+test_data[10]
```

```
Results for SVM algorithm with rbf kernel
                 precision    recall  f1-score   support

negativeReviews       0.98      0.31      0.48       611
positiveReviews       0.59      1.00      0.74       611

    avg / total       0.79      0.65      0.61      1222

Accuracy score of SVM algorithm with rbf kernel-----> 0.654664484452



Reviews Prediction

Predicted label is------> positiveReviews

Movie Review is ------>
- After their sons are sentenced to life in prison, Adelle (Debbie Reynolds) and Helen (Shirley Winters) begin rece
iving threatening phone calls because someone fells their sons got off easy. The pair decides to move to California
to escape the publicity of the trial and to start a new life. They start a dance school that is soon very successfu
l. One of the students has a rich unmarried father with whom Adelle quickly falls in love. In the meantime, Helen i
s busy raising rabbits and becoming a little too infatuated with an evangelist on the radio. It's only a mater of t
ime before everything falls apart and the women enter a world of madness and murder.<br /><br />- I can't help but
compare What's the Matter with Helen? to Whoever Slew Auntie Roo?, also starring Shelly Winters. Where that movie s
eemed almost restrained in its presentation of Auntie Roo's madness, there's nothing holding Helen back in this mov
ie. It may take a good deal of the movie's running time, but once she snaps, Helen is one Bad Mad Mutha. You don't
want to mess with her. Winters is so delightfully demented that it was impossible for me not to enjoy her performan
ce. I'm not going to spoil the movie, but the things Helen is capable of are totally over-the-top.<br /><br />- As
good as Winters is, Reynolds is totally ridiculous in her role as the gold-digging tap dancer. I got the impression
that she thought she was in a movie that would get her nominated for some award. This ain't Citizen Kane! Quit acti
ng so serious. Hey, Debbie, don't you realize that you're main purpose is to be a victim of Winters' insanity.<br /
><br />- I just love these former-female-stars-in-the-twilight-of-their-career horror movies. What's the Matter wit
h Helen? is as fun as any.
```

Figure 5.10: Code snippet for testing SVM with rbf kernel

As you can see, we have performed a test on the testing dataset and obtained an accuracy of 65.4%.

Testing SVM with the linear kernel

You can see the testing result for SVM with the linear kernel algorithm in the following figure:

Test the result of SVM with linear kernel

```
# Print results in a nice table for SVM algorithm with linear kernel
print("\nResults for SVM algorithm with linear kernel")
print(classification_report(test_labels, prediction_linear))
print "\nAccuracy score of SVM algorithm with linear kernel-----> " + str(accuracy_score(test_labels, prediction_lin

print "\n\n\n"

print "Reviews Prediction"
print "\nPredicted label is------> "+prediction[10]
print "\nMovie Review is ------> \n"+test_data[10]
```

```
Results for SVM algorithm with linear kernel
                 precision    recall  f1-score   support

negativeReviews       0.82      0.86      0.84       611
positiveReviews       0.85      0.81      0.83       611

    avg / total       0.84      0.84      0.84      1222

Accuracy score of SVM algorithm with linear kernel-----> 0.836333878887



Reviews Prediction

Predicted label is------> positiveReviews

Movie Review is ------>
- After their sons are sentenced to life in prison, Adelle (Debbie Reynolds) and Helen (Shirley Winters) begin rece
iving threatening phone calls because someone fells their sons got off easy. The pair decides to move to California
to escape the publicity of the trial and to start a new life. They start a dance school that is soon very successfu
l. One of the students has a rich unmarried father with whom Adelle quickly falls in love. In the meantime, Helen i
s busy raising rabbits and becoming a little too infatuated with an evangelist on the radio. It's only a mater of t
ime before everything falls apart and the women enter a world of madness and murder.<br /><br />- I can't help but
compare What's the Matter with Helen? to Whoever Slew Auntie Roo?, also starring Shelly Winters. Where that movie s
eemed almost restrained in its presentation of Auntie Roo's madness, there's nothing holding Helen back in this mov
ie. It may take a good deal of the movie's running time, but once she snaps, Helen is one Bad Mad Mutha. You don't
want to mess with her. Winters is so delightfully demented that it was impossible for me not to enjoy her performan
ce. I'm not going to spoil the movie, but the things Helen is capable of are totally over-the-top.<br /><br />- As
good as Winters is, Reynolds is totally ridiculous in her role as the gold-digging tap dancer. I got the impression
that she thought she was in a movie that would get her nominated for some award. This ain't Citizen Kane! Quit acti
ng so serious. Hey, Debbie, don't you realize that you're main purpose is to be a victim of Winters' insanity.<br /
><br />- I just love these former-female-stars-in-the-twilight-of-their-career horror movies. What's the Matter wit
h Helen? is as fun as any.
```

Figure 5.11: Code snippet for testing SVM with linear kernel

As you can see, we have performed a test on the testing dataset and obtained an accuracy of 83.6%.

Testing SVM with linearSVC

You can see the testing result for SVM with the linearSVC kernel algorithm in the following figure:

Test the result of SVM with linearSVC

```
# Print results in a nice table for SVM algorithm with liblinear kernel
print("\nResults for SVM algorithm with liblinear kernel")
print(classification_report(test_labels, prediction_liblinear))
print "\nAccuracy score of SVM algorithm with liblinear kernel-----> " + str(accuracy_score(test_labels, prediction_


print "\n\n\n"

print "Reviews Prediction"
print "\nPredicted label is------> "+prediction[10]
print "\nMovie Review is ------> \n"+test_data[10]
```

```
Results for SVM algorithm with liblinear kernel
                 precision    recall  f1-score   support

negativeReviews       0.82      0.86      0.84       611
positiveReviews       0.85      0.81      0.83       611

    avg / total       0.84      0.84      0.84      1222


Accuracy score of SVM algorithm with liblinear kernel-----> 0.836333878887



Reviews Prediction

Predicted label is------> positiveReviews

Movie Review is ------>
- After their sons are sentenced to life in prison, Adelle (Debbie Reynolds) and Helen (Shirley Winters) begin rece
iving threatening phone calls because someone fells their sons got off easy. The pair decides to move to California
to escape the publicity of the trial and to start a new life. They start a dance school that is soon very successfu
l. One of the students has a rich unmarried father with whom Adelle quickly falls in love. In the meantime, Helen i
s busy raising rabbits and becoming a little too infatuated with an evangelist on the radio. It's only a mater of t
ime before everything falls apart and the women enter a world of madness and murder.<br /><br />- I can't help but
compare What's the Matter with Helen? to Whoever Slew Auntie Roo?, also starring Shelly Winters. Where that movie s
eemed almost restrained in its presentation of Auntie Roo's madness, there's nothing holding Helen back in this mov
ie. It may take a good deal of the movie's running time, but once she snaps, Helen is one Bad Mad Mutha. You don't
want to mess with her. Winters is so delightfully demented that it was impossible for me not to enjoy her performan
ce. I'm not going to spoil the movie, but the things Helen is capable of are totally over-the-top.<br /><br />- As
good as Winters is, Reynolds is totally ridiculous in her role as the gold-digging tap dancer. I got the impression
that she thought she was in a movie that would get her nominated for some award. This ain't Citizen Kane! Quit acti
ng so serious. Hey, Debbie, don't you realize that you're main purpose is to be a victim of Winters' insanity.<br /
><br />- I just love these former-female-stars-in-the-twilight-of-their-career horror movies. What's the Matter wit
h Helen? is as fun as any.
```

Figure 5.12: Code snippet for testing SVM with linearSVC kernel

We have performed a test on the testing dataset here and obtained an accuracy of 83.6%.

So, after seeing the accuracy score of each of the implemented algorithms, we can say that SVM with linear kernel and linearSVC is performing really well. Now, you may wonder whether we can improve the accuracy. We can do that for sure. So let's discuss the problems that exist in this baseline approach.

Problem with the existing approach

In the baseline approach, we got great accuracy. However, we ignored the following points, which we can be implemented in our revised approach:

- We did not focus on word embedding-based techniques
- **Deep learning** (**DL**) algorithms such as CNN can be helpful for us

We need to focus on these two points because word embedding-based techniques really help retain the semantics of the text. So we should use these techniques as well as the DL-based-algorithm, which helps us provide more accuracy because DL algorithms perform well when a nested data structure is involved. What do I mean by a nested data structure? Well, that means any written sentence or spoken sentence made up of phrases, phrases made of words, and so on. So, natural language has a nested data structure. DL algorithms help us understand the nested structure of the sentences from our text dataset.

How to optimize the existing approach

There are certain techniques that can help us improve this application. The key techniques that can help us improvise the baseline approach are as follows:

- We can use word embedding-based techniques such as Word2Vec, glove, and so on
- We should also implement **Convolution Neural Networks** (**CNN**) to get an idea about how a deep learning algorithm can help us

So in the revised approach, we will be focusing on word embedding techniques and the Deep Learning algorithm. We will be using Keras with the TensorFlow backend. Before implementation, let's understand the revised approach in detail.

Understanding key concepts for optimizing the approach

In this section, we will understand the revised approach in detail, so we know what steps we should implement. We are using Keras, a Deep Learning library that provides us with high-level APIs so we can implement CNN easily. The following steps are involved:

- **Importing the dependencies**: In this step, we will be importing different dependencies such as Numpy and Keras with the TensorFlow backend. We will be using different APIs belonging to the Keras library.

- **Downloading and loading the IMDb dataset**: In this step, we will be downloading the IMDb dataset and loading this dataset by using Keras APIs
- **Choosing top words and maximum text length**: In this stage, we will set the value of our vocabulary, which we can use during the word embedding stage. So, we have selected the top 10,000 words. After that, we have restricted the length of movie reviews to 1600.
- **Implementing word embedding**: At this stage of the code, we will be using default embedding techniques from Keras and generate the word vector with a length of 300.
- **Building a CNN**: In this stage, we will be making three-layer neural networks, where the first layer has 64 neurons, the second layer has 32 neurons, and the last layer has 16 neurons. Here, we are using sigmoid as an activation function. The Activation function introduces non-linearity to the neural network so that we can generate a probability score for each class using mathematical functions.
- **Training and obtaining the accuracy**: Finally, we train the model and generate the accuracy score. We have set the epoch value to 3 and set adam as the optimization function and our loss function is `binary_crossentropy`. Epoch basically indicates how many times we need to perform training on our whole dataset. Cross-entropy loss measures the performance of a classifier whose output is a probability value between 0 and 1. Cross-entropy loss increases as the predicted probability differs from the actual label. After training, we will generate the accuracy of the model. This training stage may take time as well as a great amount of computation power.

Now let's see the code in the next section.

Implementing the revised approach

In this section, we will see the implementation in the form of a code snippet. We will be following the same step that we saw in the previous section. So, without any delay, let's look at the code. You can refer to this code by using this GitHub link: `https://github.com/jalajthanaki/Sentiment_Analysis/blob/master/Revised_approach.ipynb`.

Importing the dependencies

You can refer to the code snippet in the following figure, where you can find the imported dependencies as well:

Revised approach

Import dependencies

```
import numpy
from keras.datasets import imdb
from keras.models import Sequential
from keras.layers import Dense
from keras.layers import LSTM, Convolution1D, Flatten, Dropout
from keras.layers.embeddings import Embedding
from keras.preprocessing import sequence
from keras.callbacks import TensorBoard
```

```
Using TensorFlow backend.
```

Figure 5.13: Code snippet where we can see the imported dependencies

As you can see, we have used the TensorFlow backend with the Keras library.

Downloading and loading the IMDb dataset

You can refer to the code snippet in the following figure, where you can also find the code for downloading and loading the IMDb dataset:

Load datset and Load top 10000 words from Imdb dataset

```
# Using keras to load the dataset with the top_words
top_words = 10000
(X_train, y_train), (X_test, y_test) = imdb.load_data(nb_words=top_words)
```

```
/usr/local/lib/python2.7/dist-packages/keras/datasets/imdb.py:45: UserWarning: The `nb_words` argument in `load_dat
a` has been renamed `num_words`.
  warnings.warn('The `nb_words` argument in `load_data` '

Downloading data from https://s3.amazonaws.com/text-datasets/imdb.npz
17448960/17464789 [============================>.] - ETA: 0s
```

Figure 5.14: Code snippet for downloading and loading the IMDb dataset

We have also set the value of the vocabulary.

Choosing the top words and the maximum text length

At this stage, we have set the top word values as well as the maximum text length value. You can refer to the code snippet in the following figure:

Load datset and Load top 10000 words from Imdb dataset

```
# Using keras to load the dataset with the top words
top_words = 10000
(X_train, y_train), (X_test, y_test) = imdb.load_data(nb_words=top_words)
```

```
/usr/local/lib/python2.7/dist-packages/keras/datasets/imdb.py:45: UserWarning: The `nb_words` argument in `load_dat
a` has been renamed `num_words`.
  warnings.warn('The `nb_words` argument in `load_data` '

Downloading data from https://s3.amazonaws.com/text-datasets/imdb.npz
17448960/17464789 [============================>.] - ETA: 0s
```

Set the maximum movie review length

```
# Pad the sequence to the same length
max_review_length = 1600
X_train = sequence.pad_sequences(X_train, maxlen=max_review_length)
X_test = sequence.pad_sequences(X_test, maxlen=max_review_length)
```

Figure 5.15: Code snippet to set the vocabulary value and the maximum text length value

In the first part of code, we have set the top_word parameter to 10,000, and in the second part of the code, we have set the length of the movie review to 1,600. The top_word indicates the vocabulary size. From our dataset, we have picked the top 10,000 unique words. Most of the movie reviews have words that are present in our word vocabulary. Here, we are not processing very long movie reviews, because of that reason we have set the length of the movie review.

Implementing word embedding

At this stage, we have implemented the default Keras word embedding method in order to obtain a feature vector with a size of 300. You can refer to the following code snippet:

Default Word embedding based on word2vec

```
# Using embedding from Keras
embedding_vecor_length = 300
model = Sequential()
model.add(Embedding(top_words, embedding_vecor_length, input_length=max_review_length))
```

Figure 5.16: Code snippet for obtaining word feature vector based on the word embedding technique

Building a convolutional neural net (CNN)

In this section you can refer to the code, which will help you understand the architecture of a neural net. Here, we have used CNN because it handles higher level features or a nested structure of the dataset really well. You can refer to the code snippet in the following figure:

Build Convolution Neural Net (CNN)

```
# Convolutional model (3x conv, flatten, 2x dense)
model.add(Convolution1D(64, 3, border_mode='same'))
model.add(Convolution1D(32, 3, border_mode='same'))
model.add(Convolution1D(16, 3, border_mode='same'))
model.add(Flatten())
model.add(Dropout(0.2))
model.add(Dense(180,activation='sigmoid'))
model.add(Dropout(0.2))
model.add(Dense(1,activation='sigmoid'))
```

```
/usr/local/lib/python2.7/dist-packages/ipykernel_launcher.py:2: UserWarning: Update your `Conv1D` call to the Keras
2 API: `Conv1D(64, 3, padding="same")`

/usr/local/lib/python2.7/dist-packages/ipykernel_launcher.py:3: UserWarning: Update your `Conv1D` call to the Keras
2 API: `Conv1D(32, 3, padding="same")`
  This is separate from the ipykernel package so we can avoid doing imports until
/usr/local/lib/python2.7/dist-packages/ipykernel_launcher.py:4: UserWarning: Update your `Conv1D` call to the Keras
2 API: `Conv1D(16, 3, padding="same")`
  after removing the cwd from sys.path.
```

Figure 5.17: Code snippet for building CNN

Here, we have built the neural network with two dense layers in it.

Training and obtaining the accuracy

At this stage, we have performed the training. You can refer to the code in the following figure:

Train on training datset

```
# Log to tensorboard
tensorBoardCallback = TensorBoard(log_dir='./logs', write_graph=True)
model.compile(loss='binary_crossentropy', optimizer='adam', metrics=['accuracy'])

model.fit(X_train, y_train, nb_epoch=3, callbacks=[tensorBoardCallback], batch_size=64)
```

```
/usr/local/lib/python2.7/dist-packages/keras/models.py:848: UserWarning: The `nb_epoch` argument in `fit` has been
renamed `epochs`.
  warnings.warn('The `nb_epoch` argument in `fit` '

Epoch 1/3
25000/25000 [==============================] - 20s - loss: 0.3767 - acc: 0.8226
Epoch 2/3
25000/25000 [==============================] - 18s - loss: 0.1758 - acc: 0.9324
Epoch 3/3
25000/25000 [==============================] - 18s - loss: 0.0624 - acc: 0.9782

<keras.callbacks.History at 0x7fed3616bbd0>
```

Figure 5.18: Code snippet for performing training on the training dataset

Here, we will be performing training three times as our epoch value is set to 3. As sentiment analysis is a binary problem, we have used `binary_crossentropy` as loss function. If you have a GPU-based computer, then the training time will be less; otherwise, this step is time consuming and the computation power consuming.

Once training is done, we can obtain training accuracy. For training accuracy, you can refer to the following figure:

Obtain training accuracy score

```
# Evaluation on the test set
scores = model.evaluate(X_train, y_train, verbose=0)
print("Accuracy: %.2f%%" % (scores[1]*100))
```

```
Accuracy: 99.42%
```

Figure 5.19: Code snippet for obtaining training accuracy

Here, the accuracy is the training accuracy. Now we need to obtain testing accuracy because that will give us an actual idea about how well the train model is performing on unseen data. So let's see what the testing accuracy is.

Testing the revised approach

In this section, we will obtain the accuracy of the testing dataset. You can refer to the code snippet in the following figure:

Obtain testing accuracy score

```
# Evaluation on the test set
scores = model.evaluate(X_test, y_test, verbose=0)
print("Accuracy: %.2f%%" % (scores[1]*100))
```

```
Accuracy: 86.45%
```

Figure 5.20: Code snippet for obtaining testing accuracy

After obtaining the testing accuracy, we got an accuracy value of 86.45%. This testing accuracy is better than our baseline approach. Now let's see what points we can improve in order to come up with the best approach.

Understanding problems with the revised approach

In this section, we will discuss what points of the revised approach we can improve. These are the points that we can implement in order to obtain the best possible approach:

- We can use pretrained Word2Vec or glove models to generate the word vector
- We should use a recurrent neural network with LSTM to get better output

In this section, we will understand and implement the best approach, where we will load the pretrained glove (global word vector) model and use an RNN and LSTM network.

The best approach

There are some steps that we can follow in order to obtain the best possible approach. In this approach, we have used a glove pretrained model and have trained the model using the RNN and LSTM networks. The glove model has been pretrained on a large dataset so that it can generate more accurate vector values for words. That is the reason we are using glove here. In the next section, we will look at the implementation of the best approach. You can find all the code at this GitHub link: `https://github.com/jalajthanaki/Sentiment_Analysis/blob/master/Best_approach_sentiment_analysis.ipynb`.

Implementing the best approach

In order to implement the best approach, we will be performing the following steps:

- Loading the glove model
- Loading the dataset
- Preprocessing
- Loading the precomputed ID matrix
- Splitting the train and test datasets
- Building a neural network
- Training the neural network
- Loading the trained model
- Testing the trained model

Loading the glove model

In order to get the best performance, we will be using the pretrained glove model. You can download it at `https://nlp.stanford.edu/projects/glove/`. We have already generated the binary file and saved that file as an `.npy` extension. This file is with the `wordsList.npy` file. You can refer to the code snippet in the following figure:

Import data and binary glove model saved in form of .npy format

```
import numpy as np
wordsList = np.load('./data/wordsList.npy')
print('Loaded the word list!')
wordsList = wordsList.tolist() #Originally loaded as numpy array
wordsList = [word.decode('UTF-8') for word in wordsList] #Encode words as UTF-8
wordVectors = np.load('./data/wordVectors.npy')
print ('Loaded the word vectors!')
```

```
Loaded the word list!
Loaded the word vectors!
```

```
print(len(wordsList))
print(wordVectors.shape)
```

```
400000
(400000, 50)
```

```
baseballIndex = wordsList.index('baseball')
wordVectors[baseballIndex]
```

```
array([-1.93270004,  1.04209995, -0.78514999,  0.91033   ,  0.22711   ,
       -0.62158   , -1.64929998,  0.07686   , -0.58679998,  0.058831  ,
        0.35628   ,  0.68915999, -0.50598001,  0.70472997,  1.26639998,
       -0.40031001, -0.020687  ,  0.80862999, -0.90565997, -0.074054  ,
       -0.87674999, -0.62910002, -0.12684999,  0.11524   , -0.55685002,
       -1.68260002, -0.26291001,  0.22632   ,  0.713     , -1.08280003,
        2.12310004,  0.49869001,  0.066711  , -0.48225999, -0.17896999,
        0.47699001,  0.16384   ,  0.16537   , -0.11506   , -0.15962   ,
       -0.94926   , -0.42833   , -0.59456998,  1.35660005, -0.27506   ,
        0.19918001, -0.36008   ,  0.55667001, -0.70314997,  0.17157   ], dtype=float32)
```

```
import tensorflow as tf
maxSeqLength = 10 #Maximum length of sentence
numDimensions = 300 #Dimensions for each word vector
firstSentence = np.zeros((maxSeqLength), dtype='int32')
firstSentence[0] = wordsList.index("i")
firstSentence[1] = wordsList.index("thought")
firstSentence[2] = wordsList.index("the")
firstSentence[3] = wordsList.index("movie")
firstSentence[4] = wordsList.index("was")
firstSentence[5] = wordsList.index("incredible")
firstSentence[6] = wordsList.index("and")
firstSentence[7] = wordsList.index("inspiring")
#firstSentence[8] and firstSentence[9] are going to be 0
print(firstSentence.shape)
print(firstSentence) #Shows the row index for each word
```

Figure 5.21: Code snippet for loading the glove pretrained model

Dimensionality of the word vector is 50 and this model contains word vectors for 400,000 words.

Loading the dataset

You can refer to the following code snippet:

Load dataset

```
from os import listdir
from os.path import isfile, join
positiveFiles = ['./data/positiveReviews/' + f for f in listdir('./data/positiveReviews/')
                 if isfile(join('./data/positiveReviews/', f))]
negativeFiles = ['./data/negativeReviews/' + f for f in listdir('./data/negativeReviews/')
                 if isfile(join('./data/negativeReviews/', f))]
numWords = []
for pf in positiveFiles:
    with open(pf, "r") as f:
        line=f.readline()
        counter = len(line.split())
        numWords.append(counter)
print('Positive files finished')

for nf in negativeFiles:
    with open(nf, "r") as f:
        line=f.readline()
        counter = len(line.split())
        numWords.append(counter)
print('Negative files finished')

numFiles = len(numWords)
print('The total number of files is', numFiles)
print('The total number of words in the files is', sum(numWords))
print('The average number of words in the files is', sum(numWords)/len(numWords))
```

```
Positive files finished
Negative files finished
('The total number of files is', 25000)
('The total number of words in the files is', 5844464)
('The average number of words in the files is', 233)
```

Figure 5.22: Code snippet for loading the dataset

We have considered 25,000 movie reviews in total.

Preprocessing

You can refer to the code snippet in the following figure:

```
# Removes punctuation, parentheses, question marks, etc., and leaves only alphanumeric characters
import re
strip_special_chars = re.compile("[^A-Za-z0-9 ]+")

def cleanSentences(string):
    string = string.lower().replace("<br />", " ")
    return re.sub(strip_special_chars, "", string.lower())
```

Figure 5.23: Code snippet for performing pre-processing

Loading precomputed ID matrix

In this section, we are generating the index for each word. This process is computationally expensive, so I have already generated the index matrix and made it ready for loading. You can refer to the code snippet in the following figure:

Load in a pre-computed IDs matrix

```
# ids = np.zeros((numFiles, maxSeqLength), dtype='int32')
# fileCounter = 0
# for pf in positiveFiles:
#    with open(pf, "r") as f:
#        indexCounter = 0
#        line=f.readline()
#        cleanedLine = cleanSentences(line)
#        split = cleanedLine.split()
#        for word in split:
#            try:
#                ids[fileCounter][indexCounter] = wordsList.index(word)
#            except ValueError:
#                ids[fileCounter][indexCounter] = 399999 #Vector for unkown words
#            indexCounter = indexCounter + 1
#            if indexCounter >= maxSeqLength:
#                break
#        fileCounter = fileCounter + 1

# for nf in negativeFiles:
#    with open(nf, "r") as f:
#        indexCounter = 0
#        line=f.readline()
#        cleanedLine = cleanSentences(line)
#        split = cleanedLine.split()
#        for word in split:
#            try:
#                ids[fileCounter][indexCounter] = wordsList.index(word)
#            except ValueError:
#                ids[fileCounter][indexCounter] = 399999 #Vector for unkown words
#            indexCounter = indexCounter + 1
#            if indexCounter >= maxSeqLength:
#                break
#        fileCounter = fileCounter + 1
# #Pass into embedding function and see if it evaluates.
# np.save('idsMatrix', ids)
```

```
ids = np.load('./data/idsMatrix.npy')
```

Figure 5.24: Code snippet for generating matrix for word IDs

Splitting the train and test datasets

In this section, we will see the code snippet for generating the training and testing datasets. You can refer to the code snippet in the following figure:

Prepare Train and Test dataset

```
from random import randint

def getTrainBatch():
    labels = []
    arr = np.zeros([batchSize, maxSeqLength])
    for i in range(batchSize):
        if (i % 2 == 0):
            num = randint(1,11499)
            labels.append([1,0])
        else:
            num = randint(13499,24999)
            labels.append([0,1])
        arr[i] = ids[num-1:num]
    return arr, labels

def getTestBatch():
    labels = []
    arr = np.zeros([batchSize, maxSeqLength])
    for i in range(batchSize):
        num = randint(11499,13499)
        if (num <= 12499):
            labels.append([1,0])
        else:
            labels.append([0,1])
        arr[i] = ids[num-1:num]
    return arr, labels
```

Figure 5.25: Code snippet for splitting dataset into training and testing dataset

Building a neural network

We have used a **recurrent neural net** (**RNN**) with **Long-Short Term Memory Unit** (**LSTMs**) cells as a part of their hidden states. LSTM cells are used to store sequential information. If you have multiple sentences, then LSTM stores the context of the previous or previous to previous sentences, which helps us improve this application. If you want to understand LSTM in detail, then you can refer to `http://colah.github.io/posts/2015-08-Understanding-LSTMs/`.

You can refer to the code snippet in the following figure:

Define the hyper parameters

```
batchSize = 24
lstmUnits = 64
numClasses = 2
iterations = 100000
```

Start building neural network

```
import tensorflow as tf
tf.reset_default_graph()

labels = tf.placeholder(tf.float32, [batchSize, numClasses])
input_data = tf.placeholder(tf.int32, [batchSize, maxSeqLength])
```

```
data = tf.Variable(tf.zeros([batchSize, maxSeqLength, numDimensions]),dtype=tf.float32)
data = tf.nn.embedding_lookup(wordVectors,input_data)
```

```
lstmCell = tf.contrib.rnn.BasicLSTMCell(lstmUnits)
lstmCell = tf.contrib.rnn.DropoutWrapper(cell=lstmCell, output_keep_prob=0.75)
value, _ = tf.nn.dynamic_rnn(lstmCell, data, dtype=tf.float32)
```

```
weight = tf.Variable(tf.truncated_normal([lstmUnits, numClasses]))
bias = tf.Variable(tf.constant(0.1, shape=[numClasses]))
value = tf.transpose(value, [1, 0, 2])
last = tf.gather(value, int(value.get_shape()[0]) - 1)
prediction = (tf.matmul(last, weight) + bias)
```

```
correctPred = tf.equal(tf.argmax(prediction,1), tf.argmax(labels,1))
accuracy = tf.reduce_mean(tf.cast(correctPred, tf.float32))
```

```
loss = tf.reduce_mean(tf.nn.softmax_cross_entropy_with_logits(logits=prediction, labels=labels))
optimizer = tf.train.AdamOptimizer().minimize(loss)
```

```
import datetime

tf.summary.scalar('Loss', loss)
tf.summary.scalar('Accuracy', accuracy)
merged = tf.summary.merge_all()
logdir = "tensorboard/" + datetime.datetime.now().strftime("%Y%m%d-%H%M%S") + "/"
writer = tf.summary.FileWriter(logdir, sess.graph)
```

Figure 5.26: Code snippet for building RNN with LSTM

First, we define the hyper parameters. We set the batch size to 64, LSTM units to 64, the number of classes to 2, and then we perform 100,000 iterations.

Training the neural network

In this section, you can refer to the code snippet in the following figure, which is used for performing training:

Train model

```
sess = tf.InteractiveSession()
saver = tf.train.Saver()
sess.run(tf.global_variables_initializer())

for i in range(iterations):
    #Next Batch of reviews
    nextBatch, nextBatchLabels = getTrainBatch();
    sess.run(optimizer, {input_data: nextBatch, labels: nextBatchLabels})

    #Write summary to Tensorboard
    if (i % 50 == 0):
        summary = sess.run(merged, {input_data: nextBatch, labels: nextBatchLabels})
        writer.add_summary(summary, i)

    #Save the network every 10,000 training iterations
    if (i % 10000 == 0 and i != 0):
        save_path = saver.save(sess, "models/pretrained_lstm.ckpt", global_step=i)
        print("saved to %s" % save_path)
writer.close()

# After running this cell use the following command to see the training progres on tensorboard.
# Step 1: go to the directory where you save this ipython notebook and execute this command
# Step 2: $tensorboard --logdir=tensorboard
# Step 3: there is one link is coming where tensorboard running usually it is http://localhost:6006/
# After sept 2 in my case the link is poping with the following message.
            # this will Starting TensorBoard 54 at http://jalaj:6006
```

```
saved to models/pretrained_lstm.ckpt-10000
saved to models/pretrained_lstm.ckpt-20000
saved to models/pretrained_lstm.ckpt-30000
saved to models/pretrained_lstm.ckpt-40000
saved to models/pretrained_lstm.ckpt-50000
saved to models/pretrained_lstm.ckpt-60000
saved to models/pretrained_lstm.ckpt-70000
saved to models/pretrained_lstm.ckpt-80000
saved to models/pretrained_lstm.ckpt-90000
```

Figure 5.27: Code snippet for performing training

After each 10,000 iterations, we save the model. During the training, you can monitor the progress by using TensorBoard. You can refer to the following figure, which shows the progress over the period of training. You can monitor the accuracy and loss percentage during training, so you find out how the DL model is converging during training:

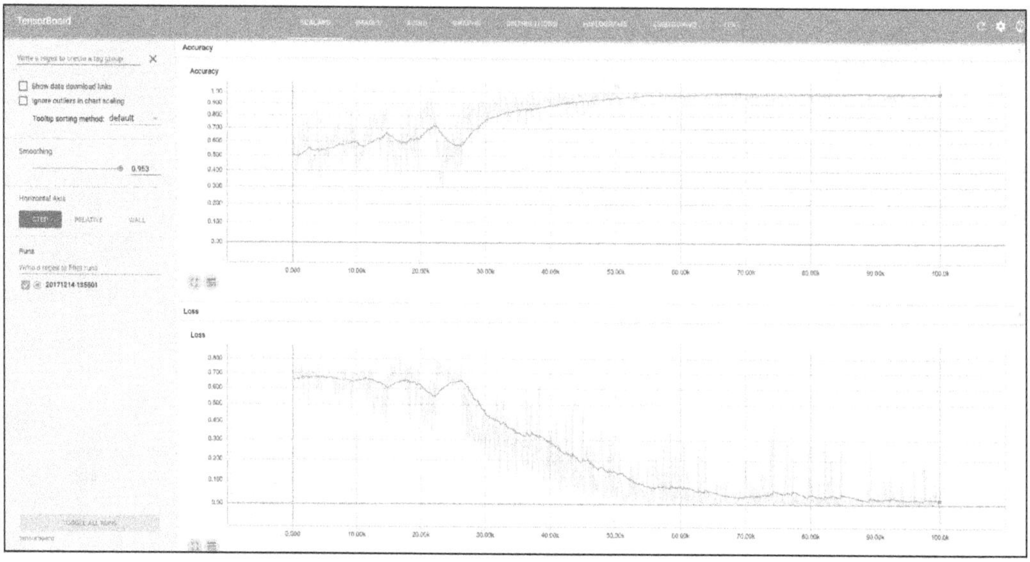

Figure 5.28: Accuracy and loss graph generated during training on TensorBoard

Training is time consuming and computationally expensive, so with a GPU it may take 2- 3 hours to train the model. Therefore, you can use the pretrained model by downloading it from GitHub at: `https://github.com/jalajthanaki/Sentiment_Analysis/blob/master/models.tar.gz`.

Loading the trained model

Once training is done, we can save the trained model. After loading this model, we can check its accuracy as well. You can refer to the code snippet in the following figure:

Load trained model

```
sess = tf.InteractiveSession()
saver = tf.train.Saver()
saver.restore(sess, tf.train.latest_checkpoint('models'))
```

```
INFO:tensorflow:Restoring parameters from models/pretrained_lstm.ckpt-90000
```

Generate test accuracy for testing dataset

```
iterations = 10
for i in range(iterations):
    nextBatch, nextBatchLabels = getTestBatch();
    print("Accuracy for this batch:", (sess.run(accuracy, {input_data: nextBatch, labels: nextBatchLabels})) * 100)
```

```
('Accuracy for this batch:', 87.5)
('Accuracy for this batch:', 83.333337306976318)
('Accuracy for this batch:', 75.0)
('Accuracy for this batch:', 91.666668653488159)
('Accuracy for this batch:', 87.5)
('Accuracy for this batch:', 83.333337306976318)
('Accuracy for this batch:', 91.666668653488159)
('Accuracy for this batch:', 83.333337306976318)
('Accuracy for this batch:', 79.166668653488159)
('Accuracy for this batch:', 91.666668653488159)
```

Figure 5.29: Code snippet for generating testing accuracy

Here we have generated a testing accuracy of 91.66%.

Testing the trained model

In this section, we will be passing new movie reviews, and by loading the trained model, we will generate the prediction of sentiment. You can refer to the code snippet in the following figure:

```
sess = tf.InteractiveSession()
saver = tf.train.Saver()
saver.restore(sess, tf.train.latest_checkpoint('models'))
```

```
INFO:tensorflow:Restoring parameters from models/pretrained_lstm.ckpt-90000
```

```
# Removes punctuation, parentheses, question marks, etc., and leaves only alphanumeric characters
import re
strip_special_chars = re.compile("[^A-Za-z0-9 ]+")

def cleanSentences(string):
    string = string.lower().replace("<br />", " ")
    return re.sub(strip_special_chars, "", string.lower())

def getSentenceMatrix(sentence):
    arr = np.zeros([batchSize, maxSeqLength])
    sentenceMatrix = np.zeros([batchSize,maxSeqLength], dtype='int32')
    cleanedSentence = cleanSentences(sentence)
    split = cleanedSentence.split()
    for indexCounter,word in enumerate(split):
        try:
            sentenceMatrix[0,indexCounter] = wordsList.index(word)
        except ValueError:
            sentenceMatrix[0,indexCounter] = 399999 #Vector for unkown words
    return sentenceMatrix
```

```
inputText = "That movie was terrible."
inputMatrix = getSentenceMatrix(inputText)
```

```
predictedSentiment = sess.run(prediction, {input_data: inputMatrix})[0]
# predictedSentiment[0] represents output score for positive sentiment
# predictedSentiment[1] represents output score for negative sentiment

if (predictedSentiment[0] > predictedSentiment[1]):
    print "Positive Sentiment"
else:
    print "Negative Sentiment"
```

```
Negative Sentiment
```

Figure 5.30: Code snippet for loading trained model and generating sentiment for a given sentence of the movie review

In this snippet, we have passed one sentence as part of a movie review, and our trained model identifies it as a negative sentiment. You can also refer to the code snippet in the following figure, which generates a sentiment for the sentence carrying a negative word in it:

```
secondInputText = "That movie was the best one I have ever seen."
secondInputMatrix = getSentenceMatrix(secondInputText)

predictedSentiment = sess.run(prediction, {input_data: secondInputMatrix})[0]
if (predictedSentiment[0] > predictedSentiment[1]):
    print "Positive Sentiment"
else:
    print "Negative Sentiment"

Positive Sentiment

thirdInputText = "That movie was not that grate."
thirdInputMatrix = getSentenceMatrix(thirdInputText)

predictedSentiment = sess.run(prediction, {input_data: thirdInputMatrix})[0]
if (predictedSentiment[0] > predictedSentiment[1]):
    print "Positive Sentiment"
else:
    print "Negative Sentiment"

Negative Sentiment
```

Figure 5.31: Code snippet for loading trained model and generating sentiment for given sentence of the movie review

This approach gives you great results.

Summary

In this chapter, we looked at how to build a sentiment analysis model that gives us state-of-the-art results. We used an IMDb dataset that had positive and negative movie reviews and understood the dataset. We applied the machine learning algorithm in order to get the baseline model. After that, in order to optimize the baseline model, we changed the algorithm and applied deep-learning-based algorithms. We used glove, RNN, and LSTM techniques to achieve the best results. We learned how to build sentiment analysis applications using Deep Learning. We used TensorBoard to monitor our model's training progress. We also touched upon modern machine learning algorithms as well as Deep Learning techniques for developing sentiment analysis, and the Deep Learning approach works best here.

We used a GPU to train the neural network, so if you discover that it needs more computation power from your end to train the model, then you can use the Google cloud or **Amazon Web Services** (**AWS**) GPU-based instances. I have already uploaded the pretrained model, so you can directly use that as well. You can find the pretrained model at this GitHub link: `https://github.com/jalajthanaki/Sentiment_Analysis/blob/master/models.tar.gz`.

In the next chapter, we will build a job recommendation system that will help people find jobs, especially related to the job profiles in which they are interested. For a job recommendation system, we will be using various resources for linking resumes, job search queries, and so on. Again, we will be developing this system using machine learning and Deep Learning systems.

6
Job Recommendation Engine

We have already seen how to develop a recommendation system for the e-commerce product in *Chapter 4, Recommendation Systems for e-Commerce*, Now, we will apply the same concepts that you learned in *Chapter 4, Recommendation Systems for e-Commerce* but the type and format of the dataset is different. Basically, we will build a job recommendation engine. For this application, we have taken into account the text dataset. The main concept of building the recommendation engine will not change, but this chapter gives you a fair idea of how to apply the same concepts to different types of datasets.

In this chapter, we will cover the following topics:

- Introducing the problem statement
- Understanding the datasets
- Building the baseline approach
    - Implementing the baseline approach
    - Understanding the testing matrix
    - Problems with the baseline approach
    - Optimizing the baseline approach
- Building the revised approach
    - Implementing the revised approach
    - Testing the revised approach
    - Problems with the revised approach
    - Understanding how to improve the revised approach
- The best approach
    - Implementing the best approach
- Summary

So, let's discuss the problem statement.

Introducing the problem statement

In this chapter, we will build an engine that can recommend jobs to any user. This is the simplest goal we want to achieve. How we are going to build it? In order to answer this question, let me give you an idea about what kind of approaches we will take in order to build a job recommendation system.

For our baseline approach, we will scrape resumes of dummy users and try to build a job recommendation engine based on the scraped dataset. The reason we are scraping the dataset is that, most of the time, there will not be any dataset available for many data science applications. Suppose you are in a position where you have not found any dataset. What you will do then? I want to provide a solution for these kinds of scenarios. So, you will learn how to scrape the data and build the baseline solution.

In the revised approach, we will be using a dataset hosted by Kaggle. Using the content-based approach, we will be building a job recommendation engine. For the best approach, we will be using the concept of user-based collaborative filtering for this domain, and build the final job recommendation system.

Now, let's look into the datasets.

Understanding the datasets

Here, we are using two datasets. The two datasets are as follows:

- The scraped dataset
- The job recommendation challenge dataset

Let's start with the scraped dataset.

Scraped dataset

For this dataset, we have scraped the dummy resume from indeed.com (we are using this data just for learning and research purposes). We will download the resumes of users in PDF format. These will become our dataset. The code for this is given at this GitHub link: `https://github.com/jalajthanaki/Basic_job_recommendation_engine/blob/master/indeed_scrap.py`.

Take a look at the code given in the following screenshot:

```
def download_file(download_url,idx):
    response = urllib2.urlopen(download_url)
    file = open("./resume_scrap/"+sys.argv[1]+ "/"+str(idx)+".pdf", 'w')
    file.write(response.read())
    file.close()


indeed = "http://www.indeed.com"
url_prefix = "http://www.indeed.com/resumes?q="+sys.argv[1]+"&co=US&start="

target_idx = 10000

idx = int(sys.argv[2])
file_no = idx
while(idx < target_idx):
    url = url_prefix + str(idx)
    page = requests.get(url).content
    all_links = re.findall(r"/r/[^\?]*", page)
    for link in all_links:
        time.sleep(1)
        url = indeed + link
        page = requests.get(url).content
        print file_no
        print ' files downloaded'
        try:
            download_link = re.search(r"/r/[^\"]*pdf", page).group(0)
            url = indeed + download_link
            download_file(url,file_no)
            file_no = file_no + 1
        except:
            continue

    idx = idx + 50
```

Figure 6.1: Code snippet for scraping the data

Using the preceding code, we can download the resumes. We have used the `requests` library and `urllib` to scrape the data. All these downloaded resumes are in PDF form, so we need to parse them. To parse the PDF document, we will use a Python library called `PDFminer`. We need to extract the following data attributes from the PDF documents:

- Work experience
- Education
- Skills
- Awards
- Certifications
- Additional information

You can take a look at the code snippet shown in the following screenshot:

```
class Experience:
    company = ''
    title = ''
    descripton = ''

    def __init__(self, doc):
        self.title = re.findall(r'^.*', doc)[0].strip()
        self.company = re.split(r'[\n-]', doc)[1].strip()
        self.description = doc[len(re.findall(r'.*\n.*\s-\s.*', doc)[0]):].strip()


def get_fields(doc):
    fields = [''] * (len(parse_fields) + 1)
    last_index = len(doc)
    for i in range(len(fields)):
        field_index = len(fields) - 2 - i
        if field_index == -1:
            fields[0] = doc[0:last_index].strip()
            break
        doc_pos = string.find(doc, '\n' + parse_fields[field_index] + '\n')
        if doc_pos != -1:
            fields[field_index + 1] = doc[doc_pos + len(parse_fields[field_index]) + 2:last_index].strip()
            last_index = doc_pos
    return fields
```

Figure 6.2: Code snippet to parse PDF documents

Basically, `PDFminer` is converting the content of PDF into text. Once we have the text data using regular expressions, we can fetch the necessary details. You can see the entire code by using this GitHub link: `https://github.com/jalajthanaki/Basic_job_recommendation_engine/blob/master/pdf_parse.py`.

Once we fetch all the necessary information, we will save the data in a pickle format. Now, you don't need to scrap the data and fetch all necessary information. I have uploaded the data into a pickle file format at this GitHub link: `https://github.com/jalajthanaki/Basic_job_recommendation_engine/blob/master/resume_data.pkl`

We will use the `resume_data.pkl` file for our baseline approach.

Job recommendation challenge dataset

This dataset is provided by `www.careerbuilder.com` and is hosted on Kaggle. You can download the dataset using this link: `https://www.kaggle.com/c/job-recommendation/data`. These are the data files that we are going to use for our revised and best approach. All the values given in these datafiles are tab-separated:

- `apps.tsv`
- `users.tsv`
- `jobs.zip`
- `user_history.tsv`

apps.tsv

This datafile contains the records of users' job applications. It indicates job positions that a particular user has applied for. The job position is described by the JobID column. All the necessary information about this datafile is given in the following screenshot:

```
apps.head()
```

	UserID	WindowID	Split	ApplicationDate	JobID
0	47	1	Train	2012-04-04 15:56:23.537	169528
1	47	1	Train	2012-04-06 01:03:00.003	284009
2	47	1	Train	2012-04-05 02:40:27.753	2121
3	47	1	Train	2012-04-05 02:37:02.673	848187
4	47	1	Train	2012-04-05 22:44:06.653	733748

```
apps.columns

Index(['UserID', 'WindowID', 'Split', 'ApplicationDate', 'JobID'], dtype='object')

apps.shape

(1603111, 5)

apps.info()

<class 'pandas.core.frame.DataFrame'>
RangeIndex: 1603111 entries, 0 to 1603110
Data columns (total 5 columns):
UserID             1603111 non-null int64
WindowID           1603111 non-null int64
Split              1603111 non-null object
ApplicationDate    1603111 non-null object
JobID              1603111 non-null int64
dtypes: int64(3), object(2)
memory usage: 61.2+ MB
```

Figure 6.3: Data information about apps.tsv

There are five data columns:

- `UserId`: This indicates the unique ID for a given user. By using this ID, we can access the user's profile.
- `WindowsID`: This is the mask data attribute with the constant value of 1. This data attribute is not important for us.
- `Split`: This data attribute indicates which data records we should consider for training and testing.

- `Application date`: This is the timestamp at which the user applied for the job.
- `JobID`: This attribute indicates the `JobIds` for which the user nominates themselves. Using this `JobId`, we can access other information about a particular job.

users.tsv

This datafile contains the user profile and all user-related information. You can find all the necessary information displayed in the following screenshot:

```
users.head()
```

	UserID	WindowID	Split	City	State	Country	ZipCode	DegreeType	Major	GraduationDate	WorkHist
0	47	1	Train	Paramount	CA	US	90723	High School	NaN	1999-06-01 00:00:00	3
1	72	1	Train	La Mesa	CA	US	91941	Master's	Anthropology	2011-01-01 00:00:00	10
2	80	1	Train	Williamstown	NJ	US	08094	High School	Not Applicable	1985-06-01 00:00:00	5
3	98	1	Train	Astoria	NY	US	11105	Master's	Journalism	2007-05-01 00:00:00	3
4	123	1	Train	Baton Rouge	LA	US	70808	Bachelor's	Agricultural Business	2011-05-01 00:00:00	1

```
users.columns
```

```
Index(['UserID', 'WindowID', 'Split', 'City', 'State', 'Country', 'ZipCode',
       'DegreeType', 'Major', 'GraduationDate', 'WorkHistoryCount',
       'TotalYearsExperience', 'CurrentlyEmployed', 'ManagedOthers',
       'ManagedHowMany'],
      dtype='object')
```

```
users.shape
```

```
(389708, 15)
```

Figure 6.4 Data information about users.tsv

These are the data attributes:

- `UserID`: This data attribute indicates the user's unique identification number.
- `WindowID`: This is the mask data attribute with a constant value of 1. This data attribute is not important for us.
- `Split`: This data attribute indicates which data records we should consider for training and testing.
- `City`: This attribute indicates the user's current city.
- `State`: This attribute indicates the user's state.
- Country: This attribute indicates the user's country.
- `ZipCode`: This data attribute indicates the user's ZIP code.
- `DegreeType`: This data column indicates the user's degree; whether the user is a high school pass-out or has a bachelor's degree.
- `Major`: This data attribute indicates the major subject in which the user has a degree.
- `GraduationDate`: This data attribute indicates the graduation date of the user.
- `WorkHistoryCount`: This data attribute indicates the number of companies the user has worked for.
- `TotalYearsExperience`: This data column indicates the user's total years of experience.
- `CurrentlyEmployed`: This data attribute has a binary value. If the user is currently employed, then the value is *Yes*; if not, then the value is *No*.
- `ManagedOthers`: This data attribute has a binary value as well. If the user is managing other people, then the value of this column is *Yes*; if the user is not managing other people, then the value of this column is *No*.
- `ManagedHowMany`: This data attribute has a numerical value. The value of this column indicates the number of people that are managed by the user. If the user is not managing anyone, then the value is 0.

Jobs.zip

When you extract this ZIP file, you can get the `jobs.tsv` file. There is more information available in the following screenshot:

```
jobs_US.columns
```

```
Index(['JobID', 'WindowID', 'Title', 'Description', 'Requirements', 'City',
       'State', 'Country', 'Zip5', 'StartDate', 'EndDate'],
      dtype='object')
```

```
jobs_US.head().transpose()
```

	0	1	2
JobID	1	4	7
WindowID	1	1	1
Title	Security Engineer/Technical Lead	SAP Business Analyst / WM	P/T HUMAN RESOURCES ASSISTANT
Description	<p>Security Clearance Required: Top Secr...	<strong>NO Corp. to Corp resumes are bein...	<b> <b> P/T HUMAN RESOURCES ASSISTANT</b> <...
Requirements	<p>SKILL SET</p>\r<p> </p>\r<p>Network Se...	<p><b>WHAT YOU NEED: </b></p>\r<p>Four year co...	Please refer to the Job Description to view th...
City	Washington	Charlotte	Winter Park
State	DC	NC	FL
Country	US	US	US
Zip5	20531	28217	32792
StartDate	2012-03-07 13:17:01.643	2012-03-21 02:03:44.137	2012-03-02 16:36:55.447
EndDate	2012-04-06 23:59:59	2012-04-20 23:59:59	2012-04-01 23:59:59

Figure 6.5: Data information about jobs.tsv

- `JobID`: This is the unique ID for each job present in the dataset.
- `WindowID`: This is the mask data attribute that has a constant value of 1. This data attribute is not important for us.
- `Title`: This data attribute indicates the job title.
- `Description`: This data attribute indicates the job description.
- `Requirements`: This data attribute indicates the job requirements.
- `City`: This data field indicates the job location in terms of the city.
- `State`: This data field indicates the job location in terms of the state.

- `Country`: This data field indicates the job location in terms of the country.
- `Zip5`: This data field indicates the ZIP code of the job location.
- `StartDate`: This date indicates when the job is posted or is open for applications.
- `EndDate`: This date is the deadline for the job application.

user_history.tsv

The `user_history.tsv` file contains the user's job history. There is more information available on this in the following screenshot:

```
user_history.head()
```

	UserID	WindowID	Split	Sequence	JobTitle
0	47	1	Train	1	National Space Communication Programs-Special ...
1	47	1	Train	2	Detention Officer
2	47	1	Train	3	Passenger Screener, TSA
3	72	1	Train	1	Lecturer, Department of Anthropology
4	72	1	Train	2	Student Assistant

```
user_history.columns
Index(['UserID', 'WindowID', 'Split', 'Sequence', 'JobTitle'], dtype='object')

user_history.shape
(1753901, 5)
```

Figure 6.6: Data information about user_history.tsv

There are only two new columns for this datafile.

- `Sequence`: This sequence is a numerical field. The number indicates the sequential order of the user's job.
- `JobTitle`: This data field indicates the job title of the user.

We have covered all the attributes in our datafiles; now let's start building the baseline approach.

Building the baseline approach

In this section, we will be building the baseline approach. We will use the scraped dataset. The main approach we will be using is TF-IDF (Term-frequency, Inverse Document Frequency) and cosine similarity. Both of these concepts have already been described in *Chapter 4, Recommendation System for e-commerce.* The name of the pertinent sections are *Generating features using TF-IDF* and *Building the cosine similarity matrix.*

As this application has more textual data, we can use TF-IDF, CountVectorizers, cosine similarity, and so on. There are no ratings available for any job. Because of this, we are not using other matrix decomposition methods, such as SVD, or correlation coefficient-based methods, such as Pearsons'R correlation.

For the baseline approach, we are trying to find out the similarity between the resumes, because that is how we will know how similar the user profiles are. By using this fact, we can recommend jobs to all the users who share a similar kind of professional profile. For the baseline model, our context is to generate the similarity score between the resumes.

Implementing the baseline approach

In order to develop a simple job recommendation system, we need to perform the following steps:

- Defining constants
- Loading the dataset
- Defining the helper function
- Generating TF-IDF vectors and cosine similarity

Defining constants

We will define some constant values. These values are based on the dataset we have scraped. In our dataset, we have scraped the dummy resumes for seven companies, and there are seven data attributes that we have generated by parsing the resumes. We consider 100 resumes as our first training dataset and 50 resumes as our testing dataset. The size of our second training dataset is 50. You can refer to the code snippet shown in the following screenshot:

```
from sklearn.feature_extraction.text import CountVectorizer
from sklearn.metrics.pairwise import cosine_similarity
from sklearn.feature_extraction.text import TfidfVectorizer
import pickle
import dill
import math
from math import log

parse_fields = ['WORK EXPERIENCE', 'EDUCATION', 'SKILLS', 'AWARDS', 'CERTIFICATIONS', 'ADDITIONAL INFORMATION']
companies = ['amazon', 'apple', 'facebook', 'ibm', 'microsoft', 'oracle', 'twitter']

num_category = 7
num_company = 7
train1_size = 100
train2_size = 50
test_size = 50
```

Figure 6.7: Code snippet for defining constants

After this step, we will load the dataset.

Loading the dataset

As you know, we have already parsed the resumes that are in the PDF file format. We store the parsed data into the pickle format, and we need to load that pickle file. We will use the `dill` library to load the pickle file. You can refer to the code snippet shown in the following screenshot:

```
with open('resume_data.pkl', 'rb') as input:
    all_resumes = dill.load(input)

for i in range(num_category):
    for j in range(num_company):
        for d in range(len(all_resumes[i][j])):
            all_resumes[i][j][d] = all_resumes[i][j][d].lower().replace(companies[j], '')
```

Figure 6.8: Code snippet for loading the dataset

We have restored the dataset. As the next step, we need to define the functions so that we can build a basic job recommendation system.

Defining the helper function

There are various helper functions that will be useful for us. There are a total of three helper functions for this approach:

- `my_normalize`
- `get_sim_vector`
- `get_class`

The first function is used to normalize the testing score. We will get the testing score in the form of a matrix. You can take a look at the code snippet shown in the following screenshot:

```
def my_normalize(m):
    for i in range(num_category):
        for j in range(num_company):
            m[i][j] = m[i][j] + 0.001

    for i in range(num_category):
        sum = 0
        for j in range(num_company):
            sum = sum + m[i][j]
        for j in range(num_company):
            m[i][j] = m[i][j] / sum
```

Figure 6.9: Code snippet for helper function my_normalize

This normalization is nothing but the weighted average of the testing score matrix. So, it takes the testing score matrix and generates the normalized testing score matrix. Bear with me for a while; we will see what the testing score matrix looks like when we generate the result of this baseline approach.

The second function basically takes the TF-IDF vector matrix and dataset as an input. As an output, it generates the cosine similarity score. You can refer to the code snippet given in the following screenshot:

```
def get_sim_vector(tfidf, tfidf_matrix, doc):
    response = tfidf.transform([doc])
    sim = cosine_similarity(response, tfidf_matrix)
    return sim[0]
```

Figure 6.10: Code snippet for helper function get_sim_vector

The third function basically takes the cosine similarity array as an input and iterates through it in order to get the maximum cosine value from the cosine similarity array. You can find the code snippet given in the following screenshot:

```
def get_class(sim):
    cur_max = -1
    max_index = 0
    for j in range(num_company):
        if sim[j] > cur_max:
            cur_max = sim[j]
            max_index = j
    return max_index
```

Figure 6.11: Code snippet for helper function get_class

We have understood the input, output, and work of our helper functions. Now, it's time to see their usage when we generate TF-IDF vectors and the cosine similarity. So, let's move on to the next section.

Generating TF-IDF vectors and cosine similarity

In this section, we will be developing the core logic of the baseline approach. We will be using a simple TF-IDF concept. In order to build the job recommendation engine using simple TF-IDF, we need to perform the following steps:

- Building the training dataset
- Generating IF-IDF vectors for the training dataset
- Building the testing dataset
- Generating the similarity score

Let's build the training dataset.

Building the training dataset

Basically, we have not divided our dataset into training and testing. So, for training, we need to generate the training dataset by using the code snippet that is shown in the following screenshot:

```
train_set = []
for c in range(num_company):
    doc = ''
    for i in range(num_category):
        for d in range(train1_size):
            doc = doc + all_resumes[c][d][i]
    train_set.append(doc)
```

Figure 6.12: Code snippet for generating the training dataset

The code is simple to understand. As you can see, we have used the `train1_size` constant value, which we have defined earlier, so that we can generate 100 resumes that can be used for training purposes.

Now, let's move on to the next step.

Generating IF-IDF vectors for the training dataset

In order to generate TF-IDF vectors, we will be using scikit-learn's `TfidfVectorizer` API. This basically converts our text data into a numerical format. You can take a look at the code snippet given in the following screenshot:

```
tfidf_vectorizer = TfidfVectorizer()
tfidf_matrix_train = tfidf_vectorizer.fit_transform(train_set
```

Figure 6.13: Code snippet for generating TF-IDF

By using the preceding code, we can convert our textual training dataset into a vectorized format. The matrix of the TF-IDF is used when we generate the predictions for testing the dataset. Now, let's build the testing dataset.

Building the testing dataset

We have trained the model. Now, we need to build the test dataset so that we can check how well or how badly our trained model is performing on the test dataset. We have used 100 resumes from our dataset for training purposes, so now, we need to use the resumes that are not the part of the training dataset. In order to generate the testing dataset, we will execute the following code so that we can generate the test dataset. You can refer to the code snippet shown in the following screenshot:

```
for c in range(num_company):

    for d in range(test_size):

        doc = ''

        for i in range(num_category):
            idx = train1_size + train2_size + d
            doc = doc + all_resumes[c][idx][0]
```

Figure 6.14: Code snippet for generating the testing dataset

As you can see, we have generated the test dataset using the index of the resume, and have taken only those documents that are not a part of the training.

Generating the similarity score

In this section, first, we will take the test dataset as an input and generate the TF-IDF vectors for them. Once the TF-IDF vector matrix has been generated, we will use the cosine similarity API in order to generate the similarity score. For this API, we will pass the two TF-IDF matrices. One matrix is what we recently generated using the testing dataset, and the second matrix is what we generated using the training dataset. When we pass these two matrices, we will get the cosine similarity array as the output. You can refer to the code snippet given in the following screenshot:

```
for c in range(num_company):

    for d in range(test_size):

        doc = ''

        for i in range(num_category):
            idx = train1_size + train2_size + d
            doc = doc + all_resumes[c][idx][0]

        response = tfidf_vectorizer.transform([doc])
        sim = cosine_similarity(response, tfidf_matrix_train)
        final_score = sim[0]
```

Figure 6.15: Code snippet for generating a cosine similarity for the testing dataset

As an output, we can generate the cosine similarity array displayed in the following screenshot:

```
--------- Simple TF-IDF approach----------
Cosine similarity [0.61707904 0.58249633 0.59366155 0.53968523 0.55128595 0.47689279
 0.58443591]
Cosine similarity [0.4685434  0.41961969 0.43911285 0.35710199 0.36045035 0.31405082
 0.42677321]
Cosine similarity [0.36425037 0.30881501 0.32317222 0.26277949 0.2664471  0.22644886
 0.31827208]
```

Figure 6.16: Cosine similarity array

The array shown in the preceding screenshot has seven elements. Each element indicates the similarity of that resume for seven companies. So, if the highest cosine value appears in the 0th index, then it means that the given resume is more similar to resumes of other users who are working at Amazon. So, we will recommend a job opening at Amazon to that particular user, as their resume is more similar to other employees who are working at Amazon.

Now, let's explore some facts related to the testing matrix.

Understanding the testing matrix

When we build a recommendation engine using TF-IDF, count vectorizer, and cosine similarity, we are actually building the content-based recommendation engine. There is no predefined testing matrix available for generating the accuracy score. In this case, either we need to check our recommendations relevance manually, or we can take a heuristic to get the basic intuitive score. In *Chapter 4, Recommendation Systems for E-Commerce,* for the baseline approach, we implemented some basic threshold-based heuristics to get a basic idea of how well the recommendation engine was working. I suggest that you refer to the *Test the result of baseline approach* section in *Chapter 4, Recommendation Engine for e-commerce.*

Problems with the baseline approach

There are a number of problems with the baseline approach. I will list all of them one by one:

- There are not enough data attributes available in the dataset to build a good job recommendation system.

- The baseline approach can't really provide accurate job recommendations, because we have the dataset of user resumes only, and based on that, we can just say something like "your resume will look like other employees at Amazon, so please apply for job openings at Amazon". Now, the problem is identifying the kind of jobs we need to recommend to the user: whether we should recommend all job openings at Amazon, or some of them.
- In my opinion, the baseline solution is not able to provide us the complete picture, because of the quality and quantity of the dataset.

The solution for these problems will be discussed in the next section.

Optimizing the baseline approach

In the previous section, we listed the shortcomings of the baseline approach. In this section, we will look at how we can overcome these shortcomings. We are facing a major problem because we did not use appropriate quality and quantity for the dataset. So, first of all, we need to use the dataset in which we have information about users' profiles as well as information about the job openings. Here, we are not scraping more resumes or posting information about jobs anymore. We are using the dataset released by the career builder. We have already seen basic information about this dataset earlier in this chapter.

To build the revised approach, we will use this new dataset. Now, let's start building the revised approach.

Building the revised approach

In this section, we will be using the readily available job recommendation challenge dataset. We have already covered the data attributes of this dataset. We will be using a context-based approach to build the recommendation engine. In order to build the revised approach, we need to perform the following steps. The code for the revised approach is given at this GitHub link: `https://github.com/jalajthanaki/Job_recommendation_engine/blob/master/Job_recommendation_engine.ipynb`

Let's implement the following steps:

- Loading the dataset
- Splitting the training and testing datasets
- Exploratory data analysis
- Building the recommendation engine using the jobs datafile

Loading the dataset

As you know, the dataset is in various files. We need to load all these files. Remember that all the datafiles are in a `.tsv` format, so we need to use the `\t` delimiter as a parameter. You can refer to the code snippet shown in the following screenshot:

Import dependencies

```
%matplotlib inline
import matplotlib.pyplot as plt
import seaborn as sns
import pandas as pd
import numpy as np
import ast
from scipy import stats
from ast import literal_eval
from sklearn.feature_extraction.text import TfidfVectorizer, CountVectorizer
from sklearn.metrics.pairwise import linear_kernel, cosine_similarity
# from nltk.stem.snowball import SnowballStemmer
# from nltk.stem.wordnet import WordNetLemmatizer
# from nltk.corpus import wordnet
# from surprise import Reader, Dataset, SVD, evaluate

import warnings; warnings.simplefilter('ignore')
```

Load dataset

```
!ls ./input_data/*.tsv
```

```
./input_data/apps.tsv  ./input_data/test_users.tsv    ./input_data/users.tsv
./input_data/jobs.tsv  ./input_data/user_history.tsv
```

```
apps = pd.read_csv('./input_data/apps.tsv', delimiter='\t',encoding='utf-8')
user_history = pd.read_csv('./input_data/user_history.tsv', delimiter='\t',encoding='utf-8')
jobs = pd.read_csv('./input_data/jobs.tsv', delimiter='\t',encoding='utf-8', error_bad_lines=False)
users = pd.read_csv('./input_data/users.tsv' ,delimiter='\t',encoding='utf-8')
test_users = pd.read_csv('./input_data/test_users.tsv', delimiter='\t',encoding='utf-8')
```

Figure 6.17: Code snippet for loading the dataset

As you can see, we have used the pandas `read_csv` method with the delimiter as a parameter, and loaded the dataset in the form of five different dataframes.

Splitting the training and testing datasets

There are three data files in which training and testing both types of data records is present. These dataframes are as follows:

- apps
- user_history
- users

In the preceding dataframes, some records are tagged as `Train` and some records are tagged as `Test`. The data attribute `Split` indicates which data records are considered a part of the training dataset and which ones are used for testing. So, we need to filter our dataset. You can take a look at the code snippet given in the following screenshot:

```
user_history_training = user_history.loc[user_history['Split'] =='Train']
user_history_testing = user_history.loc[user_history['Split'] =='Test']
apps_training = apps.loc[apps['Split'] == 'Train']
apps_testing = apps.loc[apps['Split'] == 'Test']
users_training = users.loc[users['Split']=='Train']
users_testing = users.loc[users['Split']=='Test']
```

Figure 6.18: Code snippet for splitting the training and testing datasets

We have applied a simple filter operation for all three dataframes and stored their output in new dataframes.

Now, let's move on to the **Exploratory Data Analysis** (**EDA**) section.

Exploratory Data Analysis

In this section, we will be performing some basic analysis so that we can find out what kind of data is present in our dataset. For the revised approach, we are building the recommendation system using data attributes given in the jobs dataframe. So, before using it to build the recommendation engine, we will check the quality of the data records. We need to check whether any blank values are present in the dataset. Apart from that, we also need to check the data distribution of this dataframe.

We will perform EDA specifically on geo-location data attributes. Here, we have performed grouping by operation on three data columns: City, State, and Country. You can take a look at the code snippet given in the following screenshot:

```
jobs.groupby(['City','State','Country']).size().reset_index(name='Locationwise')
```

	City	State	Country	Locationwise
0	</b> Brno <b>		CZ	1
1	</b> Praha <b>		CZ	1
2	- Any		CZ	13
3	29 Palms	CA	US	1
4	<		HU	1
5	<		TR	2
6	AMF O'Hare	IL	US	2
7	APAC-Australia		AU	68
8	Aaron	IN	US	6
9	Abanaka	OH	US	1
10	Abbeville	LA	US	34
11	Abbeville	SC	US	10

Figure 6.19: Grouping by operation on City, State, and Country

As you can see in the code snippet, there are many records where the state name is not present. We need to take care of them.

Apart from this, we also need to count the data records country-wise so that we can find out how many data records are present for each country. You can refer to the code snippet shown in the following screenshot:

```
jobs.groupby(['Country']).size().reset_index(name='Locationwise').sort_values('Locationwise',
                                                                              ascending=False).head()
```

	Country	Locationwise
59	US	1090462
4	AF	560
19	CZ	193
40	MX	93
52	TR	81

Figure 6.20: Code snippet for counting data records country-wise

As you can see in the preceding code snippet, there approximately 1 million jobs from the US region. We can say that in our dataset, the country location for most of the jobs is the US. To make our life easy, we are just considering jobs where the country is the US. You can refer to the code snippet given in the following screenshot:

```
jobs_US = jobs.loc[jobs['Country']=='US']
```

```
jobs_US[['City','State','Country']]
```

	City	State	Country
0	Washington	DC	US
1	Charlotte	NC	US
2	Winter Park	FL	US
3	Orlando	FL	US
4	Orlando	FL	US
5	Ormond Beach	FL	US
6	Orlando	FL	US
7	Orlando	FL	US
8	Orlando	FL	US
9	Winter Park	FL	US
10	Los Angeles	CA	US
11	Longwood	FL	US
12	Altamonte Springs	FL	US
13	Orlando	FL	US
14	Daytona Beach	FL	US
15	Oviedo	FL	US

Figure 6.21: Code snippet for all the data records where the country is the US

Here, we need to check whether there is an empty data value present for the city or state data columns. After observing the output of the preceding code, we can see that there are no data records where the city or state name is missing.

Now, let's look at the state for which we have maximum job openings. Remember that we have considered only those jobs where the country location is the US. In order to find out the number of jobs state-wise, you can refer to the code snippet given in the following screenshot:

```
jobs_US.groupby(['City','State','Country']).size().reset_index(name='Locationwise').sort_values('Locationwise',
                                                                                                ascending=False).head()
```

	City	State	Country	Locationwise
6601	Houston	TX	US	19306
9835	New York	NY	US	18395
2651	Chicago	IL	US	17806
3475	Dallas	TX	US	13139
610	Atlanta	GA	US	12352

```
State_wise_job_US = jobs_US.groupby(['State']).size().reset_index(name=
                                                                  'Locationwise'
                                                                 ).sort_values('Locationwise',ascending=False)
```

```
State_wise_job_US
```

	State	Locationwise
5	CA	109630
48	TX	98071
10	FL	71024
16	IL	58743
38	NY	53998
42	PA	48999
39	OH	45048
34	NJ	35175
30	NC	34553
11	GA	33453

Figure 6.22: Code snippet for generating state-wise number of jobs

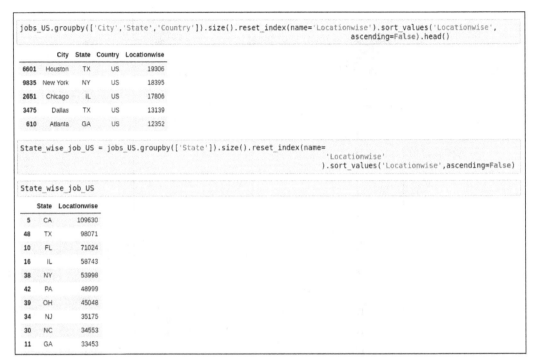

You can also refer to the graph shown in the following screenshot:

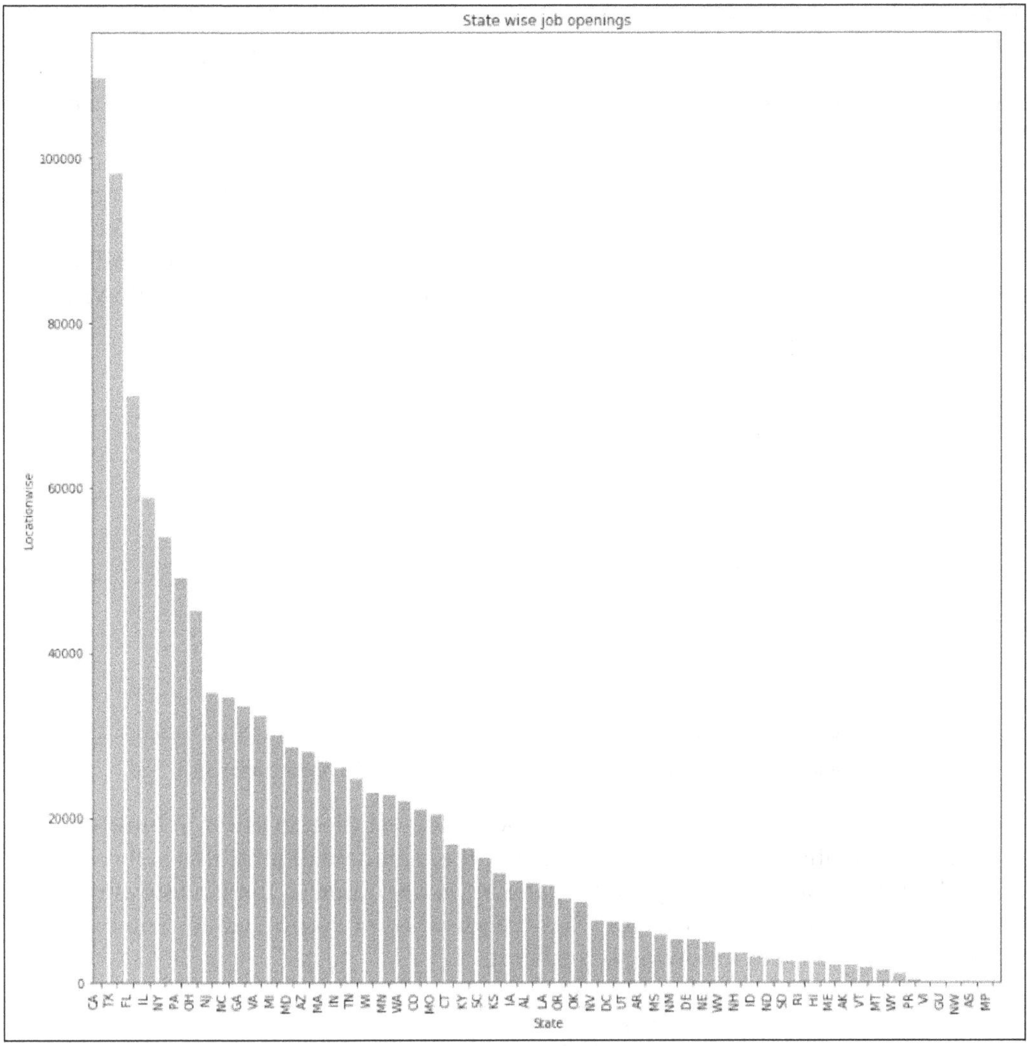

Figure 6.23: Graph for state-wise number of jobs

As you can see, maximum job opportunities are available in California, Texas, Florida, Illinois, and New York. We have done enough EDA for the revised approach. Now, we are going to start building the recommendation engine.

Building the recommendation engine using the jobs datafile

In this section, we will explore the code to see how we can build a job recommendation engine. We will use TF-IDF and cosine similarity concepts in order to build the recommendation engine.

We have taken the `jobs_US dataframe` into account here. This dataframe contains jobs where the country is the US. So, we don't have any junk data records. We will be considering only 10,000 data records for training because training for 1 million data records is time consuming. You can refer to the code shown in the following screenshot:

```
jobs_US.columns

Index(['JobID', 'WindowID', 'Title', 'Description', 'Requirements', 'City',
       'State', 'Country', 'Zip5', 'StartDate', 'EndDate'],
      dtype='object')

jobs_US.head().transpose()

...

jobs_US_base_line = jobs_US.iloc[0:10000,0:8]

jobs_US_base_line.head()
```

Figure 6.24: Code snippet of the jobs dataset to build the revised approach

Here, we will be focusing on the job title and job description in order to build the recommendation engine. As we are using the metadata of jobs, this is the content-based approach. We apply concatenation operation to the job title and job descriptions, as well as replace `nan value` with an empty string value. You can refer to the code given in the following screenshot:

```
jobs_US_base_line['Title'] = jobs_US_base_line['Title'].fillna('')
jobs_US_base_line['Description'] = jobs_US_base_line['Description'].fillna('')
#jobs_US_base_line['Requirements'] = jobs_US_base_line['Requirements'].fillna('')

jobs_US_base_line['Description'] = jobs_US_base_line['Title'] + jobs_US_base_line['Description']
```

Figure 6.25: Code snippet for applying the concatenation operation

Now, we will generate the TF-IDF vectors for the concatenated string. We will use the TF-IDF vector matrix in order to generate the cosine similarity score. We will be using the `linear_kernel` function from scikit-learn in order to generate the cosine similarity. This function can generate the cosine similarity in less time compared to the `cosine_similarity` function of scikit-learn, which takes longer. You can refer to the code snippet shown in the following screenshot:

```
tf = TfidfVectorizer(analyzer='word',ngram_range=(1, 2),min_df=0, stop_words='english')
tfidf_matrix = tf.fit_transform(jobs_US_base_line['Description'])

tfidf_matrix.shape

(10000, 515343)

# http://scikit-learn.org/stable/modules/metrics.html#linear-kernel
cosine_sim = linear_kernel(tfidf_matrix, tfidf_matrix)

cosine_sim[0]

array([1.        , 0.04300443, 0.00643851, ..., 0.03807697, 0.03807697,
       0.03807697])

jobs_US_base_line = jobs_US_base_line.reset_index()
titles = jobs_US_base_line['Title']
indices = pd.Series(jobs_US_base_line.index, index=jobs_US_base_line['Title'])
#indices.head(2)
```

Figure 6.26: Code snippet for generating TF-IDF and cosine similarity

As you can see, we have generated a high-dimensional TF-IDF matrix here. By using `linear_kernel`, we have generated the cosine similarity score as well.

As we are done with the implementation of the revised approach, we need to test the recommendation now.

Testing the revised approach

In this section, we will generate a similar kind of job recommendation based on any given job title. We are passing the job title as the input here, and with the help of the cosine similarity score, we can generate the top 10 similar kinds of jobs that any user can apply for.

For example, suppose a person is an SAP business analyst. That person may want to apply to a similar kind of job, so here, our function will take the job title as the input and generate the top 10 similar kinds of jobs for that particular user. The code for generating the top 10 job recommendations is given in the following screenshot:

```
def get_recommendations(title):
    idx = indices[title]
    #print (idx)
    sim_scores = list(enumerate(cosine_sim[idx]))
    #print (sim_scores)
    sim_scores = sorted(sim_scores, key=lambda x: x[1], reverse=True)
    job_indices = [i[0] for i in sim_scores]
    return titles.iloc[job_indices]
```

```
get_recommendations('SAP Business Analyst / WM').head(10)
```

```
1                            SAP Business Analyst / WM
6051                     SAP FI/CO Business Consultant
5868                        SAP FI/CO Business Analyst
5159                           SAP Basis Administrator
5351    SAP Sales and Distribution Solution Architect
4796       Senior Specialist - SAP Configuration - SD
5117                        SAP Integration Specialist
5409             Senior Business Systems Analyst - SAP
5244                                  Business Analyst
4728            SAP ABAP Developer with PRA experience
Name: Title, dtype: object
```

```
get_recommendations('Security Engineer/Technical Lead').head(10)
```

```
0                Security Engineer/Technical Lead
5906                     Senior Security Engineer
3771                       Director of Admissions
6293    3 Network Architects needed - immediate
3557                            Assistant Manager
401          National Sales & Marketing Manager
2606                  Inventory Analyst/ Scheduler
3757                         CLINICAL PHARMACIST
3478             Customer Service Representatives
3558                                Store Manager
Name: Title, dtype: object
```

Figure 6.27: Code snippet for generating the top 10 job recommendations

When we see the output, the recommendations start making sense. The person who is an SAP business analyst will get jobs recommendations, such as SAP FI/Co-business analyst. The result of the revised approach is satisfying for us, and the recommendations seem relevant.

Problems with the revised approach

In this section, we will be discussing the problems with the revised approach. In the best approach, we can resolve this problem. In the revised approach, we have used only the jobs data attribute. We haven't considered the user's profile or the user's preferences. During the implementation of the best approach, we will also consider the user's profile, and based on the user's profile, we will suggest the jobs to them.

In the next section, we will take a look at an intuitive idea for how to optimize the revised approach.

Understanding how to improve the revised approach

Until now, we have used data attributes given in the jobs datafile, but we haven't used the data attributes from the `users` datafile and the `apps` datafile. The `users` datafile contains the user's profile information, and the `apps` datafile contains information about which user applied for which jobs.

The best approach has three simple steps:

1. First, with the help of user's profile, we will find and generate the top 10 similar users.
2. We will try to find out the jobs these 10 people applied for. We can then generate `JobIDs`.
3. Now, we will generate the job title using `JobIDs`.

Here, we have taken the user's profile into account, so the recommendations are more specific to the particular user base. Now, let's start implementing it.

The best approach

We have already seen the intuitive approach for how we will build the best possible approach. Here, we will use the same techniques as the ones we used in the revised approach. In this approach, we are adding more data attributes to make the recommendation engine more accurate. You can refer to the code by using this GitHub link: `https://github.com/jalajthanaki/Job_recommendation_engine/blob/master/Job_recommendation_engine.ipynb`.

Implementing the best approach

These are the steps we need to take in order to implement the best possible approach:

- Filtering the dataset
- Preparing the training dataset
- Applying the concatenation operation
- Generating the TF-IDF and cosine similarity score
- Generating recommendations

Let's start implementing each of these listed steps.

Filtering the dataset

In this step, we need to filter the user's dataframe. We are applying the filter on the country data column. We need to consider the US-based users because there are around 300K users based outside of the US, and other users are from elsewhere in the world. The code to filter the user dataframe is given in the following screenshot:

```
users_training.head()
```

	UserID	WindowID	Split	City	State	Country	ZipCode	DegreeType	Major	GraduationDate	WorkHistoryCount	TotalYearsExperience	Currentl
0	47	1	Train	Paramount	CA	US	90723	High School	NaN	1999-06-01 00:00:00	3	10.0	
1	72	1	Train	La Mesa	CA	US	91941	Master's	Anthropology	2011-01-01 00:00:00	10	8.0	
2	80	1	Train	Williamstown	NJ	US	08094	High School	Not Applicable	1985-06-01 00:00:00	5	11.0	
3	98	1	Train	Astoria	NY	US	11105	Master's	Journalism	2007-05-01 00:00:00	3	3.0	
4	123	1	Train	Baton Rouge	LA	US	70808	Bachelor's	Agricultural Business	2011-05-01 00:00:00	1	9.0	

```
user_based_approach_US = users_training.loc[users_training['Country']=='US']
```

Figure 6.28: Code snippet to filter the user's dataframe

Now, let's prepare the training dataset.

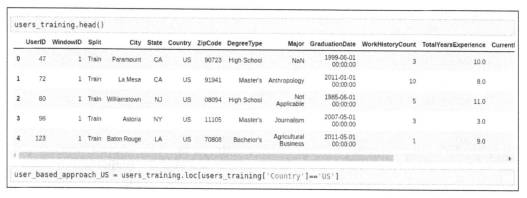

Preparing the training dataset

There are 300K users, but we are not considering all of them because of the limited training time and computational power. Here, we are considering only 10,000 users. If you have more computational resources, then you can consider a higher number of users. You can refer to the code snipp.et shown in the following screenshot:

```
user_based_approach = user_based_approach_US.iloc[0:10000,:]
```

```
user_based_approach.head()
```

	UserID	WindowID	Split	City	State	Country	ZipCode	DegreeType	Major	GraduationDate	WorkHistoryCount	TotalYearsExperience	Currentl
0	47	1	Train	Paramount	CA	US	90723	High School	NaN	1999-06-01 00:00:00	3	10.0	
1	72	1	Train	La Mesa	CA	US	91941	Master's	Anthropology	2011-01-01 00:00:00	10	8.0	
2	80	1	Train	Williamstown	NJ	US	08094	High School	Not Applicable	1985-06-01 00:00:00	5	11.0	
3	98	1	Train	Astoria	NY	US	11105	Master's	Journalism	2007-05-01 00:00:00	3	3.0	
4	123	1	Train	Baton Rouge	LA	US	70808	Bachelor's	Agricultural Business	2011-05-01 00:00:00	1	9.0	

Figure 6.29: Code snippet for selecting data records for training

Now, let's move on to the next step.

Applying the concatenation operation

In this step, we are basically performing the concatenation operation. In order to find a similar user profile, we will concatenate the user's degree type, major, and years of experience. We will generate the TF-IDF and cosine similarity for this concatenated data value. You can refer to the code snippet given in the following screenshot:

```
user_based_approach['DegreeType'] = user_based_approach['DegreeType'].fillna('')
user_based_approach['Major'] = user_based_approach['Major'].fillna('')
user_based_approach['TotalYearsExperience'] = str(user_based_approach['TotalYearsExperience'].fillna(''))

user_based_approach['DegreeType'] = user_based_approach['DegreeType'] + user_based_approach['Major'] +
                                    user_based_approach['TotalYearsExperience']
```

Figure 6.30: Code snippet for applying the concatenation operation

Now, we will generate the TF-IDF and cosine similarity score using this concatenated data value.

Generating the TF-IDF and cosine similarity score

In this section, we will generate the TF-IDF and cosine similarity score using the scikit-learn API. We are using the same API that we used in the revised approach. Here, we haven't changed the technique, but we will change the data attributes. You can refer to the code snippet shown in the following screenshot:

```
tf = TfidfVectorizer(analyzer='word',ngram_range=(1, 2),min_df=0, stop_words='english')
tfidf_matrix = tf.fit_transform(user_based_approach['DegreeType'])

tfidf_matrix.shape

(10000, 7337)

# http://scikit-learn.org/stable/modules/metrics.html#linear-kernel
cosine_sim = linear_kernel(tfidf_matrix, tfidf_matrix)

cosine_sim[0]

array([1.        , 0.67053882, 0.84759861, ..., 0.43990417, 0.79335895,
       0.69670809])

user_based_approach = user_based_approach.reset_index()
userid = user_based_approach['UserID']
indices = pd.Series(user_based_approach.index, index=user_based_approach['UserID'])
#indices.head(2)
```

Figure 6.31: Code snippet for generating TF-IDF and cosine similarity

As you can see, we have generated the cosine similarity score, so based on that, we can generate a similar user profile and give them a job recommendation based on their job-application track records.

Generating recommendations

In order to generate the job recommendation, we need to perform the following steps:

- **Step 1**: In order to generate the top 10 similar user profiles, we need to pass the UserID, and as an output, we get the 10 UserIDs that are the most similar with respect to the input UserID. You can refer to the following screenshot:

```
def get_recommendations_userwise(userid):
    idx = indices[userid]
    #print (idx)
    sim_scores = list(enumerate(cosine_sim[idx]))
    #print (sim_scores)
    sim_scores = sorted(sim_scores, key=lambda x: x[1], reverse=True)
    user_indices = [i[0] for i in sim_scores]
    #print (user_indices)
    return user_indices[0:11]

print ("-----Top 10 Similar users with userId: 123------")
get_recommendations_userwise(123)

-----Top 10 Similar users with userId: 123------
[4, 150, 1594, 5560, 2464, 2846, 7945, 8125, 1171, 11, 24]
```

Figure 6.32: Code snippet for generating the top 10 similar users

- **Step 2**: We will take the list of `userIDs` that we generated in step 1 and try to find out the same `UserIDs` in the apps dataframe. The purpose of this kind of search operation is that we need to know which user applied for which job position. By using the apps data frame, we get `JobIDs`.
- **Step 3**: Once we obtain `JobIDs`, we will obtain job titles using the jobs dataframe.

The code snippet for step 2 and step 3 is given in the following screenshot:

```
print ("-----Top 10 Similar users with userId: 47------")
get_recommendations_userwise(47)

-----Top 10 Similar users with userId: 47------
[0, 79, 126, 182, 345, 366, 393, 423, 434, 490, 544]

get_job_id(get_recommendations_userwise(47))
```

	JobID	Title	Description	City	State
905894	428902	Aircraft Servicer	<b>Job Classification: </b> Direct Hire \r\n\r...	Memphis	TN
975525	1098447	Automotive Service Advisor	<div>\r<div>Briggs Nissan in Lawrence Kansas h...	Lawrence	KS
980507	37309	Medical Lab Technician - High Volume Lab	<span>Position Title: <span> &...	Fort Myers	FL
986244	83507	Nurse Tech (CNA/STNA)	<p align="center"><b>Purpose of Your Job Posit...	Englewood	FL
987452	93883	Nurse Tech II (CNA/STNA)	<B>Nurse Tech II (CNA/STNA)</B> \r \rTh...	Fort Myers	FL
1000910	228284	REGISTERED NURSE – ICU	<p><strong><span><font face="">Registered Nurs...	Punta Gorda	FL
1007140	284840	Certified Nursing Assistant / CNA	<hr>\r<p style="text-align: center"> <strong>Ce...	Saint Petersburg	FL
1007141	284841	Home Health Aide / HHA	<hr>\r<p style="text-align: center"> <strong>Ho...	Saint Petersburg	FL
1009455	312536	Secretary II	 <b>Department: </b>COMM Maryland Cardi...	Baltimore	MD
1011978	341662	Medical Assistant	Certified Medical Assistant for busy Pain Clin...	Fort Myers	FL
1034578	551375	Phlebotomist	<p>Every day All Medical Personnel helps excep...	Clearwater	FL
1048060	684278	Sales Representative / Customer Service / Acco...	<P>Central Payment offers limitless opportunit...	Bonita Springs	FL
1066952	867194	Hospital Liaison and Pharmaceutical	Hospital Liaison with Pharmaceutical exp ...	Fort Myers	FL
1070785	910932	Nursing: CNA (PRN)	<p> </p>\r<p>Take advantage of this great...	Fort Myers	FL
1076051	960285	All college grads apply! Entry level sales and...	<div> <span>\r<div>\r<div><strong>All college ...	Fort Myers	FL
1091311	1108709	Certified Nursing Assistant / CNA / HHA	<hr>\r<p style="text-align: center"> <strong>Ce...	Sarasota	FL

Figure 6.33: Code snippet to obtain JobIDs and Job title

As you can see, we have obtained similar users for `UserID 47`, and as we can see in the job recommendations, we get fairly relevant jobs based on the users' profile and their educational qualification. In the recommendation, we can see medical domain jobs in the Florida location. That is because, in our user base, a majority of the users' profiles are from a medical background. As we have considered both the user profile and job profile, we are able to get the most relevant job recommendations.

Summary

For this entire chapter, we used a content-based approach in order to develop a job recommendation engine, and you learned how to scrap the dataset and build the baseline job recommendation engine. After that, we explored another dataset. For the revised and best approach, we used the readily available dataset. During the course of the development of the revised approach, we considered the metadata of jobs, and built a recommendation system that works quite well. For the best approach, we tried to find out similar user profiles. Based on the user's profile, we suggested jobs to the group of users.

In the next chapter, we will be building a summarization application. There, we will take a look at documents for the medical domain and try to summarize them. We will use deep-learning algorithms in order to build an application. So, keep reading!

7
Text Summarization

In this chapter, we will be building the summarization application. We will specifically focus on the textual dataset. Our primary goal is to perform the summarization task on medical notes. Basically, the idea is to come up with a good solution to summarize medical transcription documents.

This kind of summarization application helps doctors a great manner. You ask how? Let's take an example. Suppose a patient has 10 years of history with a certain disease, and after 10 years, he consults a new doctor for better results. On the first day, the patient needs to hand over their last 10 years of medical prescriptions to this new doctor. After that, the doctor will need to study all these documents. The doctor also relies on the conversation he had with the patient. By using medical notes and conversations with the patient, the doctor can find out the patient's health status. This is quite a lengthy method.

However, what if we could generate a summary of the patient's medical notes and provide these summarized documents to the doctor? It seems like a promising solution because this way, we can save the doctor's time and efforts. Doctors can understand their patients' issues in an efficient and accurate way. Patients can start getting treatment from their first meeting with the doctor. This is a win-win situation for both parties, and this kind of solution is what we are trying to build here. So, in this chapter, we will cover the following topics:

- Understanding the basics of summarization
- Introducing the problem statement
- Understanding datasets
- Building the baseline approach:
    - Implementing the baseline approach
    - Problems with the baseline approach
    - Optimizing the baseline approach

- Building the revised approach:
    - Implementing the revised approach
    - Problems with the revised approach
    - Understanding how to improve the revised approach
- The best approach:
    - Implementing the best approach
- The best approach: building a summarization application for Amazon reviews
- Summary

Understanding the basics of summarization

In this section, we will be focusing on the basic concepts of summarization. In today's fast-growing information age, text summarization has become an important tool. It will be difficult for humans to generate a summary for large text documents. There are lots of documents available on the web today. So, we need a solution that can automatically generate a summary for documents efficiently, accurately, and intelligently. This task is referred to as automatic text summarization.

Automatic text summarization is all about finding relevant information from the large text document in a small amount of time. Basically, there are two types of summarization:

- Extractive summarization
- Abstractive summarization

Let's look at the types of summarization one by one.

Extractive summarization

In the extractive summarization method, we will be generating a summary of the document by selecting words, phrases, or sentences from the original document. We will be using concepts such as **Term-Frequency, Inverse-Document Frequency** (**TF-IDF**), Count vectorizers, Cosine similarity, and the ranking algorithm to generate this type of summary.

We have covered concepts such as TF-IDF, Count vectorizers, and Cosine similarity in *Chapter 4, Recommendation Systems for E-Commerce,* section *Understanding TF-IDF.* We will look at the ranking mechanism when we implement the code for it in this chapter.

Abstractive summarization

In the abstractive summarization method, we will try and make the machine learn internal language representation so that it can generate more human-like summaries by paraphrasing.

In order to implement this type of summarization, we will be using deep learning algorithms such as a sequence-to-sequence model with an attention mechanism. You will learn about the algorithm and concepts later on in this chapter.

Introducing the problem statement

At the beginning of the chapter, we already looked at an overview of the problem statement. Here, we will be delving into further details. We want to build an automatic text summarization application. We will be providing a medical transcription document as the input. Our goal is to generate the summary of this document. Note that here, we are going to provide a single document as the input, and as an output, we will be generating the summary of that single document. We want to generate an informative summary for the document. An informative summary is a type of summary where the summarization document is a substitute of the original document as far as the converging of information is concerned. This is because we are dealing with the medical domain.

Initially, we use extractive summarization methods in our approaches. We will be generating the extractive summary for a medical document. Later on in this chapter, we will be also developing a solution that can generate an abstractive summarization of Amazon reviews.

Now, it is time to explore the dataset and look at the challenges we have faced in accessing the dataset.

Understanding datasets

This section is divided into two parts. In the first part, we need to discuss the challenges we have faced in order to generate the dataset. In the later section, we will be discussing the attributes of the dataset.

Challenges in obtaining the dataset

As we all know, the health domain is a highly regulated domain when it comes to obtaining the dataset. These are some of the challenges I want to highlight:

- For summarization, ideally, we need to have a corpus that contains original text as well as a summary of that text. This is called parallel corpus. Unfortunately, there is no good, free parallel corpus available for medical document summarization. We need to obtain this kind of parallel dataset for the English language.
- There are some free datasets available, such as the MIMIC II and MIMIC III dataset, but they won't contain summaries of the medical transcription. We can access just the medical transcription from this dataset. Gaining access to this dataset is a lengthy and time-consuming process.

In order to solve the preceding challenges, professionals, researchers, academics, and big tech companies need to come forward and make good quality, freely available datasets for the medical domain. Now let's look at how to get the medical transcription dataset.

Understanding the medical transcription dataset

You might wonder if we do not have a parallel dataset with us, then how will we build the summarization application? There is a workaround here. I have a sample medical transcription from the MIMIC - II dataset. We will be using them and generating an extractive summary of the documents. Apart from that, we will be referring to `www.mtsamples.com` in order to get an idea about the different kind of medical transcriptions we could possibly have. With the help of a minimum number of documents, we are going to build the summarization application. You can see what these medical transcriptions will look like in the following figure:

Sample Type / Medical Specialty: Chiropractic
Sample Name: Chiropractic Progress Note

Description: Patient with hip pain, osteoarthritis, lumbar spondylosis, chronic sacroiliitis, etc.
(Medical Transcription Sample Report)

CHIEF COMPLAINT: Hip pain.

HISTORY OF PRESENTING ILLNESS: The patient is a very pleasant 41-year-old white female that is known to me previously from our work at the Pain Management Clinic, as well as from my residency training program, San Francisco. We have worked collaboratively for many years at the Pain Management Clinic and with her departure there, she has asked to establish with me for clinic pain management at my office. She reports moderate to severe pain related to a complicated past medical history. In essence, she was seen at a very young age at the clinic for bilateral knee and hip pain and diagnosed with bursitis at age 23. She was given nonsteroidals at that time, which did help with this discomfort. With time, however, this became inadequate and she was seen later in San Francisco in her mid 30s by Dr. V, an orthopedist who diagnosed retroverted hips at Hospital. She was referred for rehabilitation and strengthening. Most of this was focused on her SI joints. At that time, although she had complained of foot discomfort, she was not treated for it. This was in 1993 after which she and her new husband moved to the Boston area, where she lived from 1995-1996. She was seen at the Pain Center by Dr. R with similar complaints of hip and knee pain. She was seen by rheumatologists there and diagnosed with osteoarthritis as well as osteophytosis of the back. Medications at that time were salicylate and Ultram.

When she returned to Portland in 1996, she was then working for Dr. B. She was referred to a podiatrist by her local doctor who found several fractured sesamoid bones in her both feet, but this was later found not to be the case. Subsequently, nuclear bone scans revealed osteoarthritis. Orthotics were provided. She was given Paxil and Tramadol and subsequently developed an unfortunate side effect of grand mal seizure. During this workup of her seizure, imaging studies revealed a pericardial fluid-filled cyst adhered to her ventricle. She has been advised not to undergo any corrective or reparative surgery as well as to limit her activities since. She currently does not have an established cardiologist having just changed insurance plans. She is establishing care with Dr. S, of Rheumatology for her ongoing care. Up until today, her pain medications were being written by Dr. Y prior to establishing with Dr. L.

Figure 7.1: Sample medical transcription

Generally, in medical transcriptions, there are a couple of sections, and they are as follows:

- **Chief complaint**: This section describes the main problem or disease that the patient is facing
- **History of patient's illness**: This section has a detailed description of the patient's medical status and their history of a similar disease or other kinds of diseases
- **Past medical history**: This section describes the name of the diseases that the patient had in past
- **Past surgical history**: If the patient had any surgeries in the past, then the name of those surgeries is mentioned here

- **Family history**: If any family member has the same type of disease or a history of certain kinds of diseases in the family, then those are mentioned in this section
- **Medications**: This section describes the medicine names
- **Physical examination**: This section has all the descriptions related to physical examinations
- **Assessment**: This section contains the details about the potential disease the patient may have after taking all preceding parameters into consideration.
- **Recommendations**: This section describes the recommended solution for the patient's complaints
- **Keywords**: This section has the keywords that can describe the entire document properly so the dataset can be used for the topic modeling task as well

This kind of transcription is random in certain sections. Some transcriptions contain all the preceding sections, and some do not. So, the number of sections for this kind of document may vary a lot.

Now let's look at details related to the Amazon review dataset.

Understanding Amazon's review dataset

Later on in this chapter, we will be using the Amazon review dataset in order to generate the abstractive summary. So, it is better if you understand basic data attributes for this dataset. First of all, you can download that dataset by using this link: `https://www.kaggle.com/currie32/summarizing-text-with-amazon-reviews/data`. The name of the file you need to download is `Reviews.csv`.

You can look at the content of this dataset by referring to the following screenshot:

	Id	ProductId	UserId	ProfileName	HelpfulnessNumerator	HelpfulnessDenominator	Score	Time	Summary	Text
0	1	B001E4KFG0	A3SGXH7AUHU8GW	delmartian	1	1	5	1303862400	Good Quality Dog Food	I have bought several of the Vitality canned d...
1	2	B00813GRG4	A1D87F6ZCVE5NK	dll pa	0	0	1	1346976000	Not as Advertised	Product arrived labeled as Jumbo Salted Peanut...
2	3	B000LQOCH0	ABXLMWJIXXAIN	Natalia Corres "Natalia Corres"	1	1	4	1219017600	"Delight" says it all	This is a confection that has been around a fe...
3	4	B000UA0QIQ	A395BORC6FGVXV	Karl	3	3	2	1307923200	Cough Medicine	If you are looking for the secret ingredient i...
4	5	B006K2ZZ7K	A1UQRSCLF8GW1T	Michael D. Bigham "M. Wassir"	0	0	5	1350777600	Great taffy	Great taffy at a great price. There was a wid...

Figure 7.2: Data records from Amazon's review dataset

Let's understand each of the data attributes of this dataset:

- `ID`: This attribute indicates the serial number for data records.
- `ProductId`: This attribute indicates the unique ID for the particular product.
- `UserId`: This attribute indicates the unique user ID of the user who has shared their review for a particular product.
- `ProfileName`: This data attribute is the user's profile name. Using this profile name, the user will have submitted their review.
- `HelpfulnessNumerator`: This attribute indicates how many other users found this review useful in a positive way.
- `HelpfulnessDenominator`: This attribute indicates the total number of users who voted as to whether this review was useful or not useful.
- `Score`: This is the score for a particular product. Zero means the user didn't like it, and five means the user liked it a lot.
- `Time`: This attribute indicates the timestamp at which the review has been submitted.
- `Summary`: This attribute is quite useful as it indicates the summary for the entire review.
- `Text`: This attribute is the long text review for any given product.

Now we have looked at both the datasets. Let's move on to the next section.

Building the baseline approach

In this section, we will be implementing the baseline approach for the summarization application. We will be using medical transcriptions to generate the summary. Here we will be using a small trial MIMIC-II dataset which contains a few sample medical documents and `www.mtsamples.com` for getting medical transcriptions. You can find the code by using this GitHub link: `https://github.com/jalajthanaki/medical_notes_extractive_summarization/tree/master/Base_line_approach`.

Let's start building the baseline approach.

Implementing the baseline approach

Here, we will be performing the following steps in order to build the baseline approach:

- Install python dependencies
- Write code and generate summary

Installing python dependencies

We will be using two python dependencies, which are really easy to use, in order to develop the summarization application. One is `PyTeaser`, and the second one is `Sumy`. You need to execute the following commands in order to install these two dependencies:

```
$ sudo pip install pyteaser
$ sudo pip install sumy or $ sudo pip3 install sumy
```

> Note that the `PyTeaser` library works only with `python 2.7`. Sumy can work with `python 2.7` and `python 3.3+`.

Now let's write the code.

Writing the code and generating the summary

Both the `PyTeaser` and Sumy libraries have great features. They take any weburl as the input and generate the summary for the given weburl. You can refer to the code snippet given in the following screenshot:

```
from pyteaser import SummarizeUrl
url = 'http://mtsamples.com/site/pages/sample.asp?Type=6-Cardiovascular%20/%20Pulmonary&Sample=901-Angina'
summaries = SummarizeUrl(url)
for i in range(len(summaries)):
    print summaries[i]
```

Figure 7.3: Code snippet for generating summarization using PyTeaser

As you can see, we are passing the weburl of the sample medical transcription from `www.mtsample.com`. The `PyTeaser` library will generate the top five sentences of the document as the summary. To view the output, you can take a look at the the following screenshot:

ANGINA is chest pain due to a lack of oxygen to the heart most often occurring in men age 35 or older and postmenopausal women. It is usually located right under the breast bone. Physical and emotional stress, as well as eating heavy meals, can bring it on. In a healthy person, these stresses are easily handled. In a person with an underlying heart condition like coronary artery disease, heart valve problem, arrhythmias or high blood pressure, the heart doesn't get enough blood (i.e. not enough oxygen to the heart muscles). Other causes could be due to a hyperactive thyroid disorder or anemia. People more likely to have angina may also have diabetes mellitus, be overweight, smoke, have a poor diet with lots of salt and fat, fail to exercise, have a stressful workload or have a family history of coronary artery disease.

SIGNS AND SYMPTOMS:
* Pain in chest described as tightness, heavy pressure, aching or squeezing.
* The pain sometimes radiates to the jaw, left arm, teeth and/or outer ear.
* Possibly a left-sided numbness, tingling, or pain in the arm, shoulder, elbow or chest.
* Occasionally a sudden difficulty in breathing occurs.
* Pain may be located between the shoulder blades.

TREATMENT:
* Nitroglycerin relieves the immediate symptoms of angina in seconds. Carry it with you at all times.
* Other medications may be prescribed for the underlying heart problems. It is important to take them as prescribed by your doctor.
* Surgery may be necessary to open the blocked coronary arteries (balloon angioplasty) or to bypass them.
* Correct the contributing factors you have control over. Lose weight, don't smoke, eat a low-salt, low-fat diet and avoid physical and emotional stresses that cause angina. Such stressors include anger, overworking, going between extremes in hot and cold, sudden physical exertion and high altitudes (pressurized airplanes aren't a risk). Practice relaxation techniques.
* Exercise! Discuss first what you are able to do with your doctor and then go do it.
* Even with treatment, angina may result in a heart attack, congestive heart failure or a fatal abnormal heartbeat. Treatment decreases the odds that these will occur.
* Let your doctor know if your angina doesn't go away after 10 minutes, even when you have taken a nitroglycerin tablet. Call if you have repeated chest pains that awaken you from sleep regardless if the nitroglycerin helps. If your pain changes or feels different, call your doctor or call 911 if the pain is severe.

Keywords: cardiovascular / pulmonary, lack of oxygen, heart valve, arrhythmias, blood pressure, heart, tightness, nitroglycerin, coronary artery disease, oxygen, angina, coronary, chest,

Summary of the above document

```
View this sample in Blog format on MedicalTranscriptionSamples.com

 Description: A sample note on Angina.

 (Medical Transcription Sample Report)

 ANGINA is chest pain due to a lack of oxygen to the heart most often occurring in men age 35 or older
  and postmenopausal women.
A sample note on Angina.(Medical Transcription Sample Report)is chest pain due to a lack of oxygen to the
  heart most often occurring in men age 35 or older and postmenopausal women.
Keywords: cardiovascular / pulmonary, lack of oxygen, heart valve, arrhythmias, blood pressure, heart,
  tightness, nitroglycerin, coronary artery disease, oxygen, angina, coronary, chest, NOTE: These
  transcribed medical transcription sample reports and examples are provided by various users and are for
  reference purpose only.
These transcribed medical transcription sample reports may include some uncommon or unusual formats; this
  would be due to the preference of the dictating physician.
 If your pain changes or feels different, call your doctor or call 911 if the pain is severe
  .cardiovascular / pulmonary, lack of oxygen, heart valve, arrhythmias, blood pressure, heart, tightness,
   nitroglycerin, coronary artery disease, oxygen, angina, coronary, chest,
```

Figure 7.4: Summary for the medical transcription using PyTeaser

Now let's try out the `Sumy` library. You can refer to the code given in the following screenshot:

```
# -*- coding: utf-8 -*-

from __future__ import absolute_import
from __future__ import division, print_function, unicode_literals

from sumy.parsers.html import HtmlParser
from sumy.parsers.plaintext import PlaintextParser
from sumy.nlp.tokenizers import Tokenizer
from sumy.summarizers.lsa import LsaSummarizer as Summarizer
from sumy.nlp.stemmers import Stemmer
from sumy.utils import get_stop_words


LANGUAGE = "english"
SENTENCES_COUNT = 10


if __name__ == "__main__":
    url = "http://mtsamples.com/site/pages/sample.asp?Type=99-Chiropractic&Sample=230-Chiropractic%20Progress%20Note"
    parser = HtmlParser.from_url(url, Tokenizer(LANGUAGE))
    # or for plain text files
    # parser = PlaintextParser.from_file("document.txt", Tokenizer(LANGUAGE))
    stemmer = Stemmer(LANGUAGE)

    summarizer = Summarizer(stemmer)
    summarizer.stop_words = get_stop_words(LANGUAGE)

    for sentence in summarizer(parser.document, SENTENCES_COUNT):
        print(sentence)
```

Figure 7.5: Code snippet for generating summarization using Sumy

In the `Sumy` library, we need to pass the weburl as the input, but there is one difference. As you can see in the preceding code, we have provided `SENTENCES_COUNT = 10`, which means our summary or output has 10 sentences. We can control the number of statements by using the `SENTENCES_COUNT` parameter. You can refer to the output given in the following figure:

CHIEF COMPLAINT: Hip pain.

HISTORY OF PRESENTING ILLNESS: The patient is a very pleasant 41-year-old white female that is known to me previously from our work at the Pain Management Clinic, as well as from my residency training program, San Francisco. We have worked collaboratively for many years at the Pain Management Clinic and with her departure there, she has asked to establish with me for clinic pain management at my office. She reports moderate to severe pain related to a complicated past medical history. In essence, she was seen at a very young age at the clinic for bilateral knee and hip pain and diagnosed with bursitis at age 23. She was given nonsteroidals at that time, which did help with this discomfort. With time, however, this became inadequate and she was seen later in San Francisco in her mid 30s by Dr. V, an orthopedist who diagnosed retroverted hips at Hospital. She was referred for rehabilitation and strengthening. Most of this was focused on her SI joints. At that time, although she had complained of foot discomfort, she was not treated for it. This was in 1993 after which she and her new husband moved to the Boston area, where she lived from 1995-1996. She was seen at the Pain Center by Dr. R with similar complaints of hip and knee pain. She was seen by rheumatologists there and diagnosed with osteoarthritis as well as osteophytosis of the back. Medications at that time were salicylate and Ultram.

When she returned to Portland in 1996, she was then working for Dr. B. She was referred to a podiatrist by her local doctor who found several fractured sesamoid bones in her both feet, but this was later found not to be the case. Subsequently, nuclear bone scans revealed osteoarthritis. Orthotics were provided. She was given Paxil and Tramadol and subsequently developed an unfortunate side effect of grand mal seizure. During this workup of her seizure, imaging studies revealed a pericardial fluid-filled cyst adhered to her ventricle. She has been advised not to undergo any corrective or reparative surgery as well as to limit her activities since. She currently does not have an established cardiologist having just changed insurance plans. She is establishing care with Dr. S, of Rheumatology for her ongoing care. Up until today, her pain medications were being written by Dr. Y prior to establishing with Dr. L.

Pain management in town had been first provided by the office of Dr. F. Under his care, followup MRIs were done which showed ongoing degenerative disc disease, joint disease, and facet arthropathy in addition to previously described sacroiliitis. A number of medications were attempted there, including fentanyl patches with Flonase from 25 mcg titrated upwards to 50 mcg, but this caused oversedation. She then transferred her care to Ab Cd, FNP under the direction of Dr. K. Her care there was satisfactory, but because of her work schedule, the patient found this burdensome as well as the guidelines set forth in terms of monthly meetings and routine urine screens. Because of a previous commitment, she was unable to make one unscheduled request to their office in order to produce a random urine screen and was therefore discharged.

PAST MEDICAL HISTORY:
1. Attention deficit disorder.
2. TMJ arthropathy.
3. Migraines.
4. Osteoarthritis as described above.

PAST SURGICAL HISTORY:
1. Cystectomies.
2. Sinuses.
3. Left ganglia of the head and subdermally in various locations.
4. TMJ and bruxism.

FAMILY HISTORY: The patient's father also suffered from bilateral hip osteoarthritis.

Summary of the above document

```
Description: Patient with hip pain, osteoarthritis, lumbar spondylosis, chronic sacroiliitis, etc.
HISTORY OF PRESENTING ILLNESS: The patient is a very pleasant 41-year-old white female that is known
  to me previously from our work at the Pain Management Clinic, as well as from my residency
  training program, San Francisco.
With time, however, this became inadequate and she was seen later in San Francisco in her mid 30s by
  Dr. V, an orthopedist who diagnosed retroverted hips at Hospital.
She was given Paxil and Tramadol and subsequently developed an unfortunate side effect of grand mal
  seizure.
Because of a previous commitment, she was unable to make one unscheduled request to their office in
  order to produce a random urine screen and was therefore discharged.
PHYSICAL EXAMINATION: A well-developed, well-nourished white female in no acute distress, sitting
  comfortably and answering questions appropriately, making good eye contact, and no evidence of
  pain behavior.VITAL SIGNS: Blood pressure 110/72 with a pulse of 68.HEENT: Normocephalic.
Mucous membranes are moist without exudate.NECK: Free range of motion without thyromegaly.CHEST:
  Clear to auscultation without wheeze or rhonchi.HEART: Regular rate and rhythm without murmur,
  gallop, or rub.ABDOMEN: Soft, nontender.MUSCULOSKELETAL: There is musculoskeletal soreness and
  tenderness found at the ankles, feet, as well as the low back, particularly above the SI joints
  bilaterally.
Keywords: chiropractic, pain management, progress note, romberg's, si joints, toe-heel, chronic
  sacroiliitis, hip pain, ipsilateral, lumbar spondylosis, musculoskeletal, osteoarthritis,
  osteophytosis, tmj arthropathy, bilateral hip, NOTE : These
transcribed medical transcription sample reports and examples are provided by various users and
are for reference purpose only.
These transcribed medical transcription sample reports may include some uncommon or unusual formats;
this would be due to the preference of the dictating physician.
Any resemblance of any type of name or date or
place or anything else to real world is purely incidental.
```

Figure 7.6: Summary for medical transcription using Sumy

If you view and compare the output of the `Sumy` and `PyTeaser` libraries, then you could say that the `Sumy` library is performing really well compared to the `PyTeaser` library. As you can see, both these libraries obtain a basic summary of the given document. These libraries are using the ranking algorithm and the frequency of the words in order to obtain the summaries. We don't have control over their internal mechanisms. You might be wondering whether we can make our own summarization so that we can optimize the code as and when needed. The answer is yes; we can develop our code for this task. Before that, let's discuss the shortcomings of this approach, and then we will build our own code with the revised approach.

Problems with the baseline approach

Here, we will be discussing the shortcomings of the baseline approach so that we can take care of these disadvantages in the next iteration:

- As mentioned earlier, we do not have full ownership over the code of these libraries. So, we cannot change or add functionalities easily.
- We have obtained a basic kind of summary, so we need to improve the result of the summary.
- Because of the lack of a parallel corpus, we cannot build a solution that can generate an abstractive summary for medical documents.

These are three main shortcomings of the baseline approach, and we need to solve them. In this chapter, we will be focusing on first and second shortcomings. For the third shortcoming, we cannot do much about it. So, we have to live with that shortcoming.

Let's discuss how we will be optimizing this approach.

Optimizing the baseline approach

In this section, we will be discussing how to optimize the baseline approach. We will be implementing a simple summarization algorithm. The idea behind this algorithm is simple: This approach is also generating an extractive summary for the medical document. We need to perform the following steps:

1. First, we need to determine the frequencies of the words in the given document.
2. The, we split the document into a series of sentences.

3. In order to generate the summary, we select the sentences that have more frequent words.
4. Finally, we reorder summarize sentences so that the generated output is aligned with the original document.

The preceding algorithm can solve our two shortcomings, although we may need help with the third one because right now, there is no availability of the dataset that can be used in the summarization task, especially in the medical domain. For this chapter, we have to live with this shortcoming (unfortunately, we don't have any other option), but don't worry. This doesn't mean we will not learn how to generate the abstractive summary. In order to learn how to generate abstractive summaries, we will be using the Amazon review dataset later on this chapter.

Now let's implement the steps of the algorithms that we described in this section.

Building the revised approach

Now we will be coding the algorithm that we discussed in the previous section. After implementing it, we will check how well or badly our algorithm is performing. This algorithm is easy to implement, so let's begin with the code. You can find the code at this GitHub link: `https://github.com/jalajthanaki/medical_notes_extractive_summarization/tree/master/Revised_approach`.

Implementing the revised approach

In this section, we will be implementing the summarization algorithm step by step. These are the functions that we will be building here:

- The get_summarized function
- The reorder_sentences function
- The summarize function

Let's begin with the first one.

The get_summarized function

Basically, this function performs the summarization task. First, it will take the content of the document as input in the form of string. After that, this function generates the frequency of the words, so we need to tokenize the sentences into words. After that, we will be generating the top 100 most frequent words from the given document. For small of dataset, the top 100 most frequent words can describe the vocabulary of the given dataset really well so we are not considering more words. If you have large dataset, then you can consider the top 1,000 or top 10,000 most frequent words based on the size of the dataset. You can refer to the code given in the following figure:

```
def get_summarized(self, input, num_sentences ):
    # TODO: allow the caller to specify the tokenizer they want
    # TODO: allow the user to specify the sentence tokenizer they want

    tokenizer = RegexpTokenizer('\w+')

    # get the frequency of each word in the input
    base_words = [word.lower()
        for word in tokenizer.tokenize(input)]
    words = [word for word in base_words if word not in stopwords.words()]
    word_frequencies = FreqDist(words)

    # now create a set of the most frequent words
    most_frequent_words = [pair[0] for pair in
        word_frequencies.items()[:100]]
```

Figure 7.7: Code snippet for generating the most frequent words from the given input document

Now let's code the second step. We need to split the documents into sentences. We will convert the sentences into lowercase. We will use the NLTK sentence splitter here. You can refer to the code given in the following figure:

```
# break the input up into sentences.  working_sentences is used
# for the analysis, but actual_sentences is used in the results
# so capitalization will be correct.

sent_detector = nltk.data.load('tokenizers/punkt/english.pickle')
actual_sentences = sent_detector.tokenize(input)
working_sentences = [sentence.lower()
    for sentence in actual_sentences]
```

Figure 7.8: Code snippet for generating sentences from the input document

In the third step, we will iterate over the list of the most frequent words and find out the sentences that include a higher amount of frequent words. You can refer to the code shown in the following figure:

```
# iterate over the most frequent words, and add the first sentence
# that inclues each word to the result.
output_sentences = []

for word in most_frequent_words:
    for i in range(0, len(working_sentences)):
        if (word in working_sentences[i]
          and actual_sentences[i] not in output_sentences):
            output_sentences.append(actual_sentences[i])
            break
        if len(output_sentences) >= num_sentences: break
    if len(output_sentences) >= num_sentences: break
```

Figure 7.9: Code snippet for generating the sentence that has a higher amount of frequent words

Now it's time to rearrange the sentences so that the sentence order aligns with the original input document.

The reorder_sentences function

This function basically reorders the summarized sentence so that all the sentences align with the order of the sentences of the original document. We will take summarized sentences and sentences from the original document into consideration and perform the sorting operation. You can refer to the code given in the following figure:

Define the function

```
def reorder_sentences( self, output_sentences, input ):
    output_sentences.sort( lambda s1, s2:
        input.find(s1) - input.find(s2) )
    return output_sentences
```

Call this function inside the get_summarized function

```
# sort the output sentences back to their original order
return self.reorder_sentences(output_sentences, input)
```

Figure 7.10: Code snippet for reordering the summarized sentences

Now let's move on to the final step.

The summarize function

This function basically generates the summary. This is the method that we can call from any other file. Here, we need to pass the input data and the number of sentences we need in the summarized content. You can refer to the code that is displayed in the following figure:

```
def summarize(self, input, num_sentences):
    return " ".join(self.get_summarized(input, num_sentences))
```

Figure 7.11: Code snippet for defining the function that can be called outside of the class

Generating the summary

Now let's look at a demonstration of this this code and generate the summary for the document. We will pass the textual content from `www.mtsamples.com` and then try to generate a summary of the content. You can refer to the code snippet given in the following figure:

```
import summarize

ss = summarize.SimpleSummarizer()
input = "The patient is an 86-year-old female admitted for evaluation of abdominal pain and bloody stools. " \
        "The patient has colitis and also diverticulitis, undergoing treatment. " \
        "During the hospitalization, the patient complains of shortness of breath, which is worsening. " \
        "The patient underwent an echocardiogram, which shows severe mitral regurgitation and also large pleural effusio
        "This consultation is for further evaluation in this regard. As per the patient, she is an 86-year-old female, h
        "She has been having shortness of breath for many years. She also was told that she has a heart murmur, which wa

input_str = "Mr. ABC is a 60-year-old gentleman who had a markedly abnormal stress test earlier today in my office with
            "He required 3 sublingual nitroglycerin in total (please see also admission history and physical for full de
            "The patient underwent cardiac catheterization with myself today which showed mild-to-moderate left main dis
            "I discussed these results with the patient, and he had been relating to me that he was having rest anginal

input_str_2 = """ The patient is a very pleasant 41-year-old white female that is known to me previously from our work a

When she returned to Portland in 1996, she was then working for Dr. B. She was referred to a podiatrist by her local doc

Pain management in town had been first provided by the office of Dr. F. Under his care, followup MRIs were done which sh

    """
print "\n------- Output for first document --------\n"
print ss.summarize(input, 4)
print "\n------- Output for second document --------\n"
print ss.summarize(input_str, 3)
print "\n------- Output for third document --------\n"
print ss.summarize(input_str, 5)
```

Figure 7.12: Code snippet to call the summarized function

The output of the preceding code is given in the following figure:

```
------- Output for first document --------

The patient is an 86-year-old female admitted for evaluation of abdominal pain and bloody stools.
  The patient underwent an echocardiogram, which shows severe mitral regurgitation and also large
  pleural effusion.This consultation is for further evaluation in this regard. As per the patient,
  she is an 86-year-old female, has limited activity level. She also was told that she has a heart
  murmur, which was not followed through on a regular basis.

------- Output for second document --------

Mr. ABC is a 60-year-old gentleman who had a markedly abnormal stress test earlier today in my
  office with severe chest pain after 5 minutes of exercise on the standard Bruce with horizontal ST
  depressions and moderate apical ischemia on stress imaging only. He required 3 sublingual
  nitroglycerin in total (please see also admission history and physical for full details). The
  patient underwent cardiac catheterization with myself today which showed mild-to-moderate left
  main distal disease of 30%, moderate proximal LAD with a severe mid-LAD lesion of 99%, and a
  mid-left circumflex lesion of 80% with normal LV function and some mild luminal irregularities in
  the right coronary artery with some moderate stenosis seen in the mid to distal right PDA.I
  discussed these results with the patient, and he had been relating to me that he was having rest
  anginal symptoms, as well as nocturnal anginal symptoms, and especially given the severity of the
  mid left anterior descending lesion, with a markedly abnormal stress test, I felt he was best
  suited for transfer for PCI.

------- Output for third document --------

Mr. ABC is a 60-year-old gentleman who had a markedly abnormal stress test earlier today in my
  office with severe chest pain after 5 minutes of exercise on the standard Bruce with horizontal ST
  depressions and moderate apical ischemia on stress imaging only. He required 3 sublingual
  nitroglycerin in total (please see also admission history and physical for full details). The
  patient underwent cardiac catheterization with myself today which showed mild-to-moderate left
  main distal disease of 30%, moderate proximal LAD with a severe mid-LAD lesion of 99%, and a
  mid-left circumflex lesion of 80% with normal LV function and some mild luminal irregularities in
  the right coronary artery with some moderate stenosis seen in the mid to distal right PDA.I
  discussed these results with the patient, and he had been relating to me that he was having rest
  anginal symptoms, as well as nocturnal anginal symptoms, and especially given the severity of the
  mid left anterior descending lesion, with a markedly abnormal stress test, I felt he was best
  suited for transfer for PCI. I discussed the case with Dr. X at Medical Center who has kindly
  accepted the patient in transfer.
```

Figure 7.13: Output for the revised approach

As you can see, the output is more relevant than the baseline approach. We know the approach for the kind of steps we have been performing so far. This approach gives us clarity about how we can generate the extractive summary for the medical transcription. The good part of this approach is that we do not need any parallel summarization corpus.

Now let's discuss the shortcomings of the revised approach.

Problems with the revised approach

In this section, we will be discussing the shortcomings of the revised approach, as follows:

- The revised approach does not have the ranking mechanism to rank the sentences based on their importance.
- We have considered word frequencies so far; we have not considered their importance with respect to the other words. Suppose word *a* appears a thousand times in a document. That doesn't mean it carries more importance.

Now let's see how we can overcome these shortcomings.

Understanding how to improve the revised approach

In this section, we will be discussing the steps that we should take in order to improve the revised approach. To obtain the best result for extractive summarization, we need to use TF-IDF and the sentence ranking mechanism to generate the summary. We have covered TF-IDF in *Chapter 4, Recommendation Systems for E-Commerce*, in the *Generating features using TF-IDF* section. We will be building the ranking mechanism by using cosine similarity and LSA (Latent Semantic Analysis). We have already looked at cosine similarity in *Chapter 4, Recommendation Systems for E-Commerce*. Let's explore the LSA algorithm.

The LSA algorithm

The LSA algorithm is similar to the cosine similarity. We will generate the matrix by using the words present in the paragraphs of the document. The row of the matrix will represent the unique words present in each paragraph, and columns represent each paragraph. You can view the matrix representation for the LSA algorithm in the following figure:

Para 1:	The cat is on tree.			
Para 2:	The cat is eating mouse.			
Para 3:	The cat is beautiful.			
			Paragraphs	
	Words	Para 1	Para 2	Para 3
	the	1	0	0
	cat	1	1	1
	is	1	1	1
	on	1	0	0
	tree	1	0	0
	eating	0	1	0
	mouse	0	1	0
	beautiful	0	0	1

Figure 7.14: Matrix representation for the LSA algorithm

The basic assumption for the LSA algorithm is that words that are close in their meaning will occur in a similar piece of text. As you can see from the preceding example, if we say that the word pair (cat, is) occurs more frequently, it means that it carries higher semantic meaning than the (cat, mouse) word pair. This is the meaning of the assumption behind the algorithm. We generate the matrix that is given in the previous figure and then try to reduce the number of rows of the matrix by using the **single value decomposition** (**SVD**) method. SVD is basically a factorization of the matrix.

> You can read more on SVD by using this link: `https://en.wikipedia.org/wiki/Singular-value_decomposition`.

Here, we are reducing the number of rows (which means the number of words) while preserving the similarity structure among columns (which means paragraphs). In order to generate the similarity score between word pairs, we are using cosine similarity. This is more than enough to keep in mind in order to build the summarization application.

Now let's discuss the approach we are taking in order to build the best possible solution for generating an extractive summary for medical documents.

The idea behind the best approach

We will perform the following steps in order to build the best approach:

1. First of all, we will take the content of the document in the form of a string.
2. We will parse the sentence, and after that, we will remove the stop words and special characters. We will be converting the abbreviations into their full forms.

3. After that, we will generate the lemma of the words and their **Part-of-Speech (POS)** tags. Lemma is nothing but the root form of words and POS tags indicate whether the word is used as a verb, noun, adjective, or adverb. There are many POS tags available. You can find a list of POS tags at this site: `https://www.ling.upenn.edu/courses/Fall_2003/ling001/penn_treebank_pos.html`.
4. We will generate the matrix of the TF-IDF vectors for the words.
5. We will generate the SVD matrix using the `SciPy` library for the given TF-IDF matrix.
6. Finally, using cosine-similarity, we can rank the sentences and generate the summary.

Now let's look at the implementation of these steps.

The best approach

In this section, we will look at the implementation of the best approach. We will also discuss the structure of the code. So, without wasting time, let's begin with the implementation. You can find the code by using this GitHub link: `https://github.com/jalajthanaki/medical_notes_extractive_summarization/tree/master/Best_approach`.

Implementing the best approach

The steps you need to take in order to implement the code are provided in the following list:

1. Understanding the structure of the project
2. Understanding helper functions
3. Generating the summary

Let's start with the first step.

Understanding the structure of the project

The structure of the project is quite important here. There will be four different files in which we will be writing code. You can see the structure of the project in the following figure:

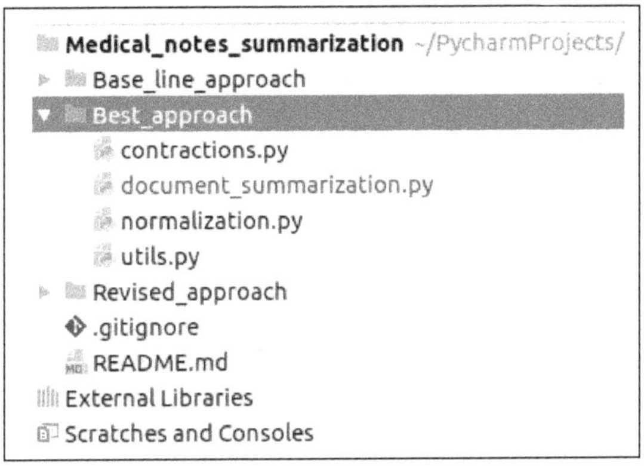

Figure 7.15: Structure of the project's code files

There are four code files. I will explain their usage one by one:

- `Contractions.py`: This file contains an extensive list of all of the abbreviations, especially grammatical abbreviations. You can take a look at the list abbreviations in the following figure:

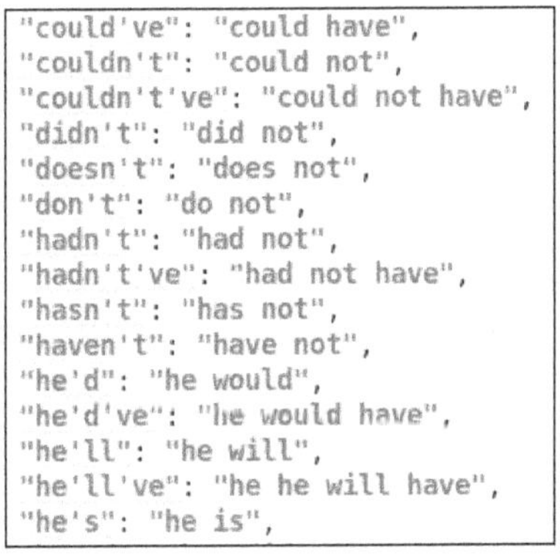

```
"could've": "could have",
"couldn't": "could not",
"couldn't've": "could not have",
"didn't": "did not",
"doesn't": "does not",
"don't": "do not",
"hadn't": "had not",
"hadn't've": "had not have",
"hasn't": "has not",
"haven't": "have not",
"he'd": "he would",
"he'd've": "he would have",
"he'll": "he will",
"he'll've": "he he will have",
"he's": "he is",
```

Figure 7.16: List of abbreviations and their full forms

- `Normalization.py`: This file contains various helper functions for the preprocessing step
- `Utils.py`: This file contains the helper function that is used to calculate TF-IDF and obtain the SVD matrix for the given TF-IDF matrix
- `Document_summarization.py`: This file uses the already defined helper function and generates a summary for the document

Now let's see what kind of helper functions we have defined in each file.

Understanding helper functions

We will discuss the helper function file-wise so you will get an idea as to which helper function is part of which file.

Normalization.py

This file contains many helper functions. I will explain each helper function based on the sequence of its usage:

- `parse_document`: This function takes the content of the document as the input and tokenizes it sentence-wise. This means we are splitting the string sentence by sentence. We will consider only the Unicode string here. You can refer to the code snippet given in the following figure:

```
def parse_document(document):
    document = re.sub('\n', ' ', document)
    if isinstance(document, str):
        document = document
    elif isinstance(document, unicode):
        return unicodedata.normalize('NFKD', document).encode('ascii', 'ignore')
    else:
        raise ValueError('Document is not string or unicode!')
    document = document.strip()
    sentences = nltk.sent_tokenize(document)
    sentences = [sentence.strip() for sentence in sentences]
    return sentences
```

Figure 7.17: Code snippet for parsing documents

- `remove_special_characters`: This function will remove the special characters from the strings. You can refer to the code snippet given in the following figure for a better idea:

```
def remove_special_characters(text):
    tokens = tokenize_text(text)
    pattern = re.compile('[{}]'.format(re.escape(string.punctuation)))
    filtered_tokens = filter(None, [pattern.sub(' ', token) for token in tokens])
    filtered_text = ' '.join(filtered_tokens)
    return filtered_text
```

Figure 7.18: Code snippet for removing special characters from the string

- `remove_stopwords`: This function will remove the stop words from the sentences. You can refer to the code snippet given in the following figure:

```
def remove_stopwords(text):
    tokens = tokenize_text(text)
    filtered_tokens = [token for token in tokens if token not in stopword_list]
    filtered_text = ' '.join(filtered_tokens)
    return filtered_text
```

Figure 7.19: Code snippet for removing stop words

- `unescape_html`: This function removes HTML tags from the sentences. You can refer to the code snippet given in the following figure:

```
def unescape_html(parser, text):

    return parser.unescape(text)
```

Figure 7.20: Code snippet for removing HTML tags

- `pos_tag_text`: This function tokenizes the sentences into words, after which it will provide POS tags to these words. You can refer to the code snippet given in the following figure:

```
# Annotate text tokens with POS tags
def pos_tag_text(text):

    def penn_to_wn_tags(pos_tag):
        if pos_tag.startswith('J'):
            return wn.ADJ
        elif pos_tag.startswith('V'):
            return wn.VERB
        elif pos_tag.startswith('N'):
            return wn.NOUN
        elif pos_tag.startswith('R'):
            return wn.ADV
        else:
            return None

    tagged_text = tag(text)
    tagged_lower_text = [(word.lower(), penn_to_wn_tags(pos_tag))
                         for word, pos_tag in
                         tagged_text]
    return tagged_lower_text
```

Figure 7.21: Code snippet for generating POS tags

- `lemmatize_text`: This function will tokenize the sentence into words and then generate the lemma of the words. You can refer to the code given in the following figure:

```
# lemmatize text based on POS tags
def lemmatize_text(text):

    pos_tagged_text = pos_tag_text(text)
    lemmatized_tokens = [wnl.lemmatize(word, pos_tag) if pos_tag
                         else word
                         for word, pos_tag in pos_tagged_text]
    lemmatized_text = ' '.join(lemmatized_tokens)
    return lemmatized_text
```

Figure 7.22: Code snippet for generating the lemma of the words

- `expand_contractions`: This function looks at the abbreviations. If there is any abbreviation that is present in our list in the given sentence, then we will replace that abbreviation with its full form. You can refer to the code displayed in the following figure:

```
def expand_contractions(text, contraction_mapping):

    contractions_pattern = re.compile('({})'.format('|'.join(contraction_mapping.keys())),
                                      flags=re.IGNORECASE|re.DOTALL)
    def expand_match(contraction):
        match = contraction.group(0)
        first_char = match[0]
        expanded_contraction = contraction_mapping.get(match)\
                               if contraction_mapping.get(match)\
                               else contraction_mapping.get(match.lower())
        expanded_contraction = first_char+expanded_contraction[1:]
        return expanded_contraction

    expanded_text = contractions_pattern.sub(expand_match, text)
    expanded_text = re.sub("'", "", expanded_text)
    return expanded_text
```

Figure 7.23: Code snippet for replacing abbreviations with full forms

- `normalize_corpus`: This function calls all the preceding helper functions and generates the preprocessed sentences. You can refer to the code given in the following figure:

```
def normalize_corpus(corpus, lemmatize=True, tokenize=False):

    normalized_corpus = []
    for text in corpus:
        text = html_parser.unescape(text)
        text = expand_contractions(text, CONTRACTION_MAP)
        if lemmatize:
            text = lemmatize_text(text)
        else:
            text = text.lower()
        text = remove_special_characters(text)
        text = remove_stopwords(text)
        if tokenize:
            text = tokenize_text(text)
            normalized_corpus.append(text)
        else:
            normalized_corpus.append(text)

    return normalized_corpus
```

Figure 7.24: Code snippet for generating preprocessed sentences

Now let's see what functions we have defined in the `utils.py` file.

Utils.py

In this file, there are only two helper functions. They are described here.

- `build_feature_matrixs`: This function generates the TF-IDF vectors using the scikit-learn `Tfidfvectorizer` API. We are providing the preprocessed text as the input, and as the output, we have the matrix. This matrix contains the vectorized value of the given words. You can refer to the code snippet for this, which is provided in the following figure:

```
from sklearn.feature_extraction.text import CountVectorizer, TfidfVectorizer

def build_feature_matrix(documents, feature_type='frequency'):

    feature_type = feature_type.lower().strip()

    if feature_type == 'binary':
        vectorizer = CountVectorizer(binary=True, min_df=1,
                                     ngram_range=(1, 1))
    elif feature_type == 'frequency':
        vectorizer = CountVectorizer(binary=False, min_df=1,
                                     ngram_range=(1, 1))
    elif feature_type == 'tfidf':
        vectorizer = TfidfVectorizer(min_df=1,
                                     ngram_range=(1, 1))
    else:
        raise Exception("Wrong feature type entered. Possible values: 'binary', 'frequency', 'tfidf'")

    feature_matrix = vectorizer.fit_transform(documents).astype(float)

    return vectorizer, feature_matrix
```

Figure 7.25: Code snippet for generating TF-IDF vectors

- `low_rank_svd`: This particular function uses the API from python's `SciPy` library. It performs the SVD on the TF-IDF matrix, and after that, we obtain the cosine similarity score. Based on the score, we will rank the sentences. Here, we just define the function that can generate the SVD for the TF-IDF matrix. You can refer to the code snippet given in the following figure:

```
from scipy.sparse.linalg import svds

def low_rank_svd(matrix, singular_count=2):

    u, s, vt = svds(matrix, k=singular_count)
    return u, s, vt
```

Figure 7.26: Code snippet for generating SVD

Now let's use all these helper functions in order to generate the summary.

Generating the summary

In this section, we will look at the code that is given in the `document_summarization.py` file. There are two methods that are responsible for generating the summary for the given document. They are as follows:

- `textrank_text_summarizer`: This method takes the preprocessed document as the input, and by using the `build_feature_matrix` helper function, we will generate the TF-IDF matrix. After that, we will generate the similarity score. Based on the similarity score, we will sort the sentences and provide them a rank. As an output, we will display these sorted sentences. Here, sentence sequence is aligned with the original document, so we don't need to worry about that. You can take a look at the code snippet given in the following figure:

```
def textrank_text_summarizer(documents, num_sentences=2,
                             feature_type='frequency'):

    vec, dt_matrix = build_feature_matrix(norm_sentences,
                                          feature_type='tfidf')
    similarity_matrix = (dt_matrix * dt_matrix.T)

    similarity_graph = networkx.from_scipy_sparse_matrix(similarity_matrix)
    scores = networkx.pagerank(similarity_graph)

    ranked_sentences = sorted(((score, index)
                               for index, score
                               in scores.items()),
                              reverse=True)

    top_sentence_indices = [ranked_sentences[index][1]
                            for index in range(num_sentences)]
    top_sentence_indices.sort()

    for index in top_sentence_indices:
        print sentences[index]
```

Figure 7.27: Code snippet in order to generate the summary using the textrank_text_summarizer method

- `lsa_text_summarizer`: This function takes the preprocessed text as the input and generates the TF-IDF matrix. After that, the `low_rank_svd` method is applied on the matrix, and we get our factorized matrix. We will generate the similarity score using these factorized matrices. After sorting sentences based on this similarity score, we can generate the summary. You can refer to the code snippet displayed in the following figure:

```
def lsa_text_summarizer(documents, num_sentences=2,
                        num_topics=2, feature_type='frequency',
                        sv_threshold=0.5):

    vec, dt_matrix = build_feature_matrix(documents,
                                          feature_type=feature_type)

    td_matrix = dt_matrix.transpose()
    td_matrix = td_matrix.multiply(td_matrix > 0)

    u, s, vt = low_rank_svd(td_matrix, singular_count=num_topics)
    min_sigma_value = max(s) * sv_threshold
    s[s < min_sigma_value] = 0

    salience_scores = np.sqrt(np.dot(np.square(s), np.square(vt)))
    top_sentence_indices = salience_scores.argsort()[-num_sentences:][::-1]
    top_sentence_indices.sort()

    for index in top_sentence_indices:
        print sentences[index]
```

Figure 7.28: Code snippet for generating the summary using lsa_text_summarizer

We will call these functions and generate the output. The code snippet for that is given in the following figure:

```
DOCUMENT_1 = """

The patient is an 86-year-old female admitted for evaluation of abdominal pain and bloody stools. The patient has coliti
During the hospitalization, the patient complains of shortness of breath, which is worsening. The patient underwent an e
This consultation is for further evaluation in this regard. As per the patient, she is an 86-year-old female, has limite
She has been having shortness of breath for many years. She also was told that she has a heart murmur, which was not fol

"""

DOCUMENT_2 = """ The patient is a very pleasant 41-year-old white female that is known to me previously from our work at

When she returned to Portland in 1996, she was then working for Dr. B. She was referred to a podiatrist by her local doc

Pain management in town had been first provided by the office of Dr. F. Under his care, followup MRIs were done which sh
"""

sentences = parse_document(DOCUMENT_1)
norm_sentences = normalize_corpus(sentences,lemmatize=True)
print "Total Sentences:", len(norm_sentences)

print ("\n---------lsa summarization for document 1--------")
lsa_text_summarizer(norm_sentences, num_sentences=4,
                    num_topics=2, feature_type='frequency',
                    sv_threshold=0.5)

print ("---------text-rank summarization for document 1--------\n")
textrank_text_summarizer(norm_sentences, num_sentences=4,
                         feature_type='tfidf')

sentences = parse_document(DOCUMENT_2)
norm_sentences = normalize_corpus(sentences,lemmatize=True)
print "Total Sentences:", len(norm_sentences)

print ("\n---------lsa summarization for document 2--------")
lsa_text_summarizer(norm_sentences, num_sentences=4,
                    num_topics=2, feature_type='frequency',
                    sv_threshold=0.5)

print ("---------text-rank summarization for document 2--------\n")
textrank_text_summarizer(norm_sentences, num_sentences=4,
                         feature_type='tfidf')
```

Figure 7.29: Code snippet for generating the output summary

You can take a look at the output shown in the following figure:

```
---------lsa summarization for document 1--------
The patient is an 86-year-old female admitted for evaluation of abdominal pain and bloody stools.
The patient has colitis and also diverticulitis, undergoing treatment.
The patient underwent an echocardiogram, which shows severe mitral regurgitation and also large
  pleural effusion.
As per the patient, she is an 86-year-old female, has limited activity level.
---------text-rank summarization for document 1--------

The patient is an 86-year-old female admitted for evaluation of abdominal pain and bloody stools.
The patient has colitis and also diverticulitis, undergoing treatment.
During the hospitalization, the patient complains of shortness of breath, which is worsening.
As per the patient, she is an 86-year-old female, has limited activity level.
Total Sentences: 26
```

Figure 7.30: Output summary for document_1

The output for another document is given in the following figure:

```
---------lsa summarization for document 2--------
The patient is a very pleasant 41-year-old white female that is known to me previously from our work
  at the Pain Management Clinic, as well as from my residency training program, San Francisco.
We have worked collaboratively for many years at the Pain Management Clinic and with her departure
  there, she has asked to establish with me for clinic pain management at my office.
Up until today, her pain medications were being written by Dr. Y prior to establishing with Dr. L.
  Pain management in town had been first provided by the office of Dr. F. Under his care, followup
  MRIs were done which showed ongoing degenerative disc disease, joint disease, and facet arthropathy
   in addition to previously described sacroiliitis.
She then transferred her care to Ab Cd, FNP under the direction of Dr. K. Her care there was
  satisfactory, but because of her work schedule, the patient found this burdensome as well as the
  guidelines set forth in terms of monthly meetings and routine urine screens.
---------text-rank summarization for document 2--------

We have worked collaboratively for many years at the Pain Management Clinic and with her departure
  there, she has asked to establish with me for clinic pain management at my office.
With time, however, this became inadequate and she was seen later in San Francisco in her mid 30s by
  Dr. V, an orthopedist who diagnosed retroverted hips at Hospital.
She was seen at the Pain Center by Dr. R with similar complaints of hip and knee pain.
Up until today, her pain medications were being written by Dr. Y prior to establishing with Dr. L.
  Pain management in town had been first provided by the office of Dr. F. Under his care, followup
  MRIs were done which showed ongoing degenerative disc disease, joint disease, and facet arthropathy
   in addition to previously described sacroiliitis.
```

Figure 7.31: Output summary for document_2

As you can see, compared to the revised approach, we will get a much more relevant extractive type of summary for the given document. Now let's build the abstractive summarization application using Amazon's product review dataset.

Building the summarization application using Amazon reviews

We are building this application so that you can learn how to use parallel corpus in order to generate the abstractive summary for the textual dataset. We have already explained basic stuff related to the dataset earlier in the chapter. Here, we will cover how to build an abstractive summarization application using the Deep Learning (DL) algorithm. You can refer to the code using this GitHub link: `https://github.com/jalajthanaki/Amazon_review_summarization/blob/master/summarize_reviews.ipynb`.

You can also download the pre-trained model using this link: `https://drive.google.com/open?id=1inExMtqR6Krddv7nHR4ldWTYY7_hMALg`.

For this application, we will perform the following steps:

- Loading the dataset
- Exploring the dataset
- Preparing the dataset
- Building the DL model
- Training the DL model
- Testing the DL model

Loading the dataset

In this section, we will see the code for how we can load the dataset. Our dataset is in the CSV file format. We will be using pandas to read our dataset. You can refer to the code snippet given in the following figure:

```
import pandas as pd
import numpy as np
import tensorflow as tf
import re
from nltk.corpus import stopwords
import time
from tensorflow.python.layers.core import Dense
from tensorflow.python.ops.rnn_cell_impl import _zero_state_tensors
print('TensorFlow Version: {}'.format(tf.__version__))
```

```
TensorFlow Version: 1.1.0
```

Insepcting the Data

```
reviews = pd.read_csv("Reviews.csv")
```

```
reviews.shape
```

```
(568454, 10)
```

```
reviews.head()
```

Figure 7.32: Code snippet for loading the dataset

Exploring the dataset

In this section, we will be doing some basic analysis of the dataset. We will check whether any null entries are present. If there are, then we will remove them. You can refer to the code snippet given in the following figure:

```
# Check for any nulls values
reviews.isnull().sum()

Id                         0
ProductId                  0
UserId                     0
ProfileName               16
HelpfulnessNumerator       0
HelpfulnessDenominator     0
Score                      0
Time                       0
Summary                   27
Text                       0
dtype: int64

# Remove null values and unneeded features
reviews = reviews.dropna()
reviews = reviews.drop(['Id','ProductId','UserId','ProfileName','HelpfulnessNumerator','HelpfulnessDenominator',
                        'Score','Time'], 1)
reviews = reviews.reset_index(drop=True)

reviews.head()
```

	Summary	Text
0	Good Quality Dog Food	I have bought several of the Vitality canned d...
1	Not as Advertised	Product arrived labeled as Jumbo Salted Peanut...
2	"Delight" says it all	This is a confection that has been around a fe...
3	Cough Medicine	If you are looking for the secret ingredient i...
4	Great taffy	Great taffy at a great price. There was a wid...

Figure 7.33: Code snippet for removing null data entries

Now let's prepare the dataset that can be used to train the model.

Preparing the dataset

These are the steps that we will perform in order to prepare the dataset:

- We will replace the abbreviations that appeared in the text with their full forms
- We will remove special characters, URLs, and HTML tags from the review data column
- We will remove stop words from the reviews

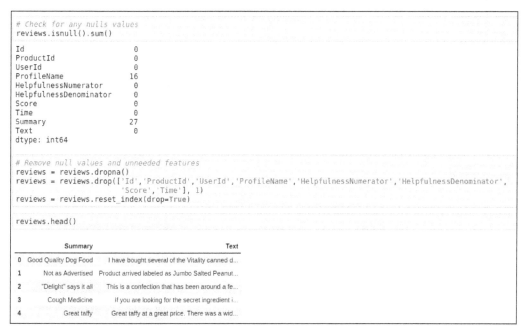

We have performed all the preceding steps and generated the junk-free review. You can refer to the code snippet given in the following figure:

```
# Clean the summaries and texts
clean_summaries = []
for summary in reviews.Summary:
    clean_summaries.append(clean_text(summary, remove_stopwords=False))
print("Summaries are complete.")

clean_texts = []
for text in reviews.Text:
    clean_texts.append(clean_text(text))
print("Texts are complete.")

Summaries are complete.
Texts are complete.

# Inspect the cleaned summaries and texts to ensure they have been cleaned well
for i in range(5):
    print("Clean Review #",i+1)
    print(clean_summaries[i])
    print(clean_texts[i])
    print()

Clean Review # 1
good quality dog food
bought several vitality canned dog food products found good quality product looks like stew processed meat smells be
tter labrador finicky appreciates product better

Clean Review # 2
not as advertised
product arrived labeled jumbo salted peanuts peanuts actually small sized unsalted sure error vendor intended repres
ent product jumbo
```

Figure 7.34: Code snippet for performing preprocessing of the reviews

Here, there are 132,884 unique words. You can find the size of the vocabulary when you run the code. These unique words are the vocabulary for this application, and we need to convert these words into a vector format. The vector format of the words is called word embeddings. You can use Word2vec, Numberbatch, or GloVe in order to generate word embeddings. Here, we will be using Numberbatch's embedding pre-trained model in order to generate word embedding for this application. The Numberbatch's pretrained model is more optimize and faster than GloVe so we are using Numberbatch's model. You can refer to the code snippet given in the following figure:

```
# Load Conceptnet Numberbatch's (CN) embeddings, similar to GloVe, but probably better
# (https://github.com/commonsense/conceptnet-numberbatch)
embeddings_index = {}
with open('./numberbatch-en-17.02.txt', encoding='utf-8') as f:
    for line in f:
        values = line.split(' ')
        word = values[0]
        embedding = np.asarray(values[1:], dtype='float32')
        embeddings_index[word] = embedding

print('Word embeddings:', len(embeddings_index))

Word embeddings: 484557
```

Figure 7.35: Code snippet for generating word embedding using Numberbatch's pre-trained model

If you want to learn more about word2vec, then you can refer to my previous book, *Python Natural Language Processing*, particularly *Chapter 6, Advance Feature Engineering and NLP Algorithms*. The link is `https://www.packtpub.com/mapt/book/big_data_and_business_intelligence/9781787121423/6`.

Building the DL model

In this section, we will be building the DL algorithm. We are using the seq2seq neural network. Basically, the seq2seq model is used to process the sequential data. Language or sentences are the sequence of words. In this algorithm, there is an encoder that accepts the word embedding and learns the language representation. The output of this layer is fed to the decoding layer. Here, we will also use the attention mechanism. The attention mechanism will focus on the most import part of the sentences. It will store the semantic representation of the sentences. For the attention mechanism, we will use the LSTM cell with the recurrent neural network architecture, which learns the complex semantic representation of the language and stores it in the LSTM network. When we generate the final output, we will be using the weight of the decoder cells as well as the weight of LSTM cells and will generate the final word embedding. Based on the word embedding, we will generate the summary.

In order to achieve this, we need to build seq2seq using a **Recurrent Neural Network (RNN)** with the attention mechanism. You can refer to the code given in the following figure:

```
def encoding_layer(rnn_size, sequence_length, num_layers, rnn_inputs, keep_prob):
    '''Create the encoding layer'''

    for layer in range(num_layers):
        with tf.variable_scope('encoder_{}'.format(layer)):
            cell_fw = tf.contrib.rnn.LSTMCell(rnn_size,
                                              initializer=tf.random_uniform_initializer(-0.1, 0.1, seed=2))
            cell_fw = tf.contrib.rnn.DropoutWrapper(cell_fw,
                                                    input_keep_prob = keep_prob)

            cell_bw = tf.contrib.rnn.LSTMCell(rnn_size,
                                              initializer=tf.random_uniform_initializer(-0.1, 0.1, seed=2))
            cell_bw = tf.contrib.rnn.DropoutWrapper(cell_bw,
                                                    input_keep_prob = keep_prob)

            enc_output, enc_state = tf.nn.bidirectional_dynamic_rnn(cell_fw,
                                                                    cell_bw,
                                                                    rnn_inputs,
                                                                    sequence_length,
                                                                    dtype=tf.float32)
    # Join outputs since we are using a bidirectional RNN
    enc_output = tf.concat(enc_output,2)

    return enc_output, enc_state

def training_decoding_layer(dec_embed_input, summary_length, dec_cell, initial_state, output_layer,
                            vocab_size, max_summary_length):
    '''Create the training logits'''

    training_helper = tf.contrib.seq2seq.TrainingHelper(inputs=dec_embed_input,
                                                        sequence_length=summary_length,
                                                        time_major=False)

    training_decoder = tf.contrib.seq2seq.BasicDecoder(dec_cell,
                                                       training_helper,
                                                       initial_state,
                                                       output_layer)

    training_logits, _ = tf.contrib.seq2seq.dynamic_decode(training_decoder,
                                                           output_time_major=False,
                                                           impute_finished=True,
                                                           maximum_iterations=max_summary_length)
    return training_logits
```

Figure 7.36: Code snippet for building the RNN encoding layer

You can refer to the code snippet given in the following figure:

```
def decoding_layer(dec_embed_input, embeddings, enc_output, enc_state, vocab_size, text_length, summary_length,
                   max_summary_length, rnn_size, vocab_to_int, keep_prob, batch_size, num_layers):
    '''Create the decoding cell and attention for the training and inference decoding layers'''

    for layer in range(num_layers):
        with tf.variable_scope('decoder_{}'.format(layer)):
            lstm = tf.contrib.rnn.LSTMCell(rnn_size,
                                           initializer=tf.random_uniform_initializer(-0.1, 0.1, seed=2))
            dec_cell = tf.contrib.rnn.DropoutWrapper(lstm,
                                                     input_keep_prob = keep_prob)

    output_layer = Dense(vocab_size,
                         kernel_initializer = tf.truncated_normal_initializer(mean = 0.0, stddev=0.1))

    attn_mech = tf.contrib.seq2seq.BahdanauAttention(rnn_size,
                                                     enc_output,
                                                     text_length,
                                                     normalize=False,
                                                     name='BahdanauAttention')

    #DynamicAttentionWrapper
    dec_cell = tf.contrib.seq2seq.DynamicAttentionWrapper(dec_cell,
                                                          attn_mech,
                                                          rnn_size)
    # DynamicAttentionWrapperState
    initial_state = tf.contrib.seq2seq.DynamicAttentionWrapperState(enc_state[0], zero_state_tensors(rnn_size,
                                                                    batch_size,
                                                                    tf.float32,
                                                                    #enc_output,
                                                                    ))
    with tf.variable_scope("decode"):
        training_logits = training_decoding_layer(dec_embed_input,
                                                  summary_length,
                                                  dec_cell,
                                                  initial_state,
                                                  output_layer,
                                                  vocab_size,
                                                  max_summary_length)
    with tf.variable_scope("decode", reuse=True):
        inference_logits = inference_decoding_layer(embeddings,
                                                    vocab_to_int['<GO>'],
                                                    vocab_to_int['<EOS>'],
                                                    dec_cell,
                                                    initial_state,
                                                    output_layer,
                                                    max_summary_length,
                                                    batch_size)

    return training_logits, inference_logits
```

Figure 7.37: Code snippet for building the RNN decoding layer

The code snippet for building the seq2seq model is given in the following figure:

```
def seq2seq_model(input_data, target_data, keep_prob, text_length, summary_length, max_summary_length,
                  vocab_size, rnn_size, num_layers, vocab_to_int, batch_size):
    '''Use the previous functions to create the training and inference logits'''

    # Use Numberbatch's embeddings and the newly created ones as our embeddings
    embeddings = word_embedding_matrix

    enc_embed_input = tf.nn.embedding_lookup(embeddings, input_data)
    enc_output, enc_state = encoding_layer(rnn_size, text_length, num_layers, enc_embed_input, keep_prob)

    dec_input = process_encoding_input(target_data, vocab_to_int, batch_size)
    dec_embed_input = tf.nn.embedding_lookup(embeddings, dec_input)

    training_logits, inference_logits  = decoding_layer(dec_embed_input,
                                                        embeddings,
                                                        enc_output,
                                                        enc_state,
                                                        vocab_size,
                                                        text_length,
                                                        summary_length,
                                                        max_summary_length,
                                                        rnn_size,
                                                        vocab_to_int,
                                                        keep_prob,
                                                        batch_size,
                                                        num_layers)

    return training_logits, inference_logits
```

Figure 7.38: Code snippet for building seq2seq

Now let's train the model.

Training the DL model

Basically, we have built the neural network, and now it's time to start the training. In this section, we will define the values for all hyperparameters, such as the learning rate, the batch size, and so on. You can refer to the code given in the following figure:

```
# Train the Model
learning_rate_decay = 0.95
min_learning_rate = 0.0005
display_step = 20 # Check training loss after every 20 batches
stop_early = 0
stop = 3 # If the update loss does not decrease in 3 consecutive update checks, stop training
per_epoch = 3 # Make 3 update checks per epoch
update_check = (len(sorted_texts_short)//batch_size//per_epoch)-1

update_loss = 0
batch_loss = 0
summary_update_loss = [] # Record the update losses for saving improvements in the model

checkpoint = "best_model.ckpt"
with tf.Session(graph=train_graph) as sess:
    sess.run(tf.global_variables_initializer())

    # If we want to continue training a previous session
    #loader = tf.train.import_meta_graph("./" + checkpoint + '.meta')
    #loader.restore(sess, checkpoint)

    for epoch_i in range(1, epochs+1):
        update_loss = 0
        batch_loss = 0
        for batch_i, (summaries_batch, texts_batch, summaries_lengths, texts_lengths) in enumerate(
                get_batches(sorted_summaries_short, sorted_texts_short, batch_size)):
            start_time = time.time()
            _, loss = sess.run(
                [train_op, cost],
                {input_data: texts_batch,
                 targets: summaries_batch,
                 lr: learning_rate,
                 summary_length: summaries_lengths,
                 text_length: texts_lengths,
                 keep_prob: keep_probability})

            batch_loss += loss
            update_loss += loss
            end_time = time.time()
            batch_time = end_time - start_time
```

Figure 7.39: Code snippet for training the model

During the training, we will be tracking the loss function and using the gradient descent algorithm, and we will try to minimize the value of our loss function. You can refer to the code snippet given in the following figure:

```
            if batch_i % update_check == 0 and batch_i > 0:
                print("Average loss for this update:", round(update_loss/update_check,3))
                summary_update_loss.append(update_loss)

                # If the update loss is at a new minimum, save the model
                if update_loss <= min(summary_update_loss):
                    print('New Record!')
                    stop_early = 0
                    saver = tf.train.Saver()
                    saver.save(sess, checkpoint)

                else:
                    print("No Improvement.")
                    stop_early += 1
                    if stop_early == stop:
                        break
                update_loss = 0


        # Reduce learning rate, but not below its minimum value
        learning_rate *= learning_rate_decay
        if learning_rate < min_learning_rate:
            learning_rate = min_learning_rate

        if stop_early == stop:
            print("Stopping Training.")
            break
```

```
Epoch   1/100 Batch   20/781 - Loss:  4.497, Seconds: 60.47
Epoch   1/100 Batch   40/781 - Loss:  2.833, Seconds: 63.95
Epoch   1/100 Batch   60/781 - Loss:  2.801, Seconds: 63.94
Epoch   1/100 Batch   80/781 - Loss:  2.795, Seconds: 59.97
Epoch   1/100 Batch  100/781 - Loss:  2.817, Seconds: 44.92
Epoch   1/100 Batch  120/781 - Loss:  2.768, Seconds: 54.55
Epoch   1/100 Batch  140/781 - Loss:  2.682, Seconds: 67.50
Epoch   1/100 Batch  160/781 - Loss:  2.643, Seconds: 52.61
```

Figure 7.40: Code snippet for tracing the loss function

Here, we have the trained the model on CPU for 6 to 8 hours, and we have the loss value 1.413. You can train the model for more amount time as well. Now let's test the trained model.

Testing the DL model

In this section, we load the trained model and generate the summary for a randomly selected review. You can refer to the code snippet given in the following figure:

```
def text_to_seq(text):
    '''Prepare the text for the model'''

    text = clean_text(text)
    return [vocab_to_int.get(word, vocab_to_int['<UNK>']) for word in text.split()]

# Create your own review or use one from the dataset
#input_sentence = "I have never eaten an apple before, but this red one was nice. \
                  #I think that I will try a green apple next time."
#text = text_to_seq(input_sentence)
random = np.random.randint(0,len(clean_texts))
input_sentence = clean_texts[random]
text = text_to_seq(clean_texts[random])

checkpoint = "./best_model.ckpt"

loaded_graph = tf.Graph()
with tf.Session(graph=loaded_graph) as sess:
    # Load saved model
    loader = tf.train.import_meta_graph(checkpoint + '.meta')
    loader.restore(sess, checkpoint)

    input_data = loaded_graph.get_tensor_by_name('input:0')
    logits = loaded_graph.get_tensor_by_name('predictions:0')
    text_length = loaded_graph.get_tensor_by_name('text_length:0')
    summary_length = loaded_graph.get_tensor_by_name('summary_length:0')
    keep_prob = loaded_graph.get_tensor_by_name('keep_prob:0')

    #Multiply by batch_size to match the model's input parameters
    answer_logits = sess.run(logits, {input_data: [text]*batch_size,
                                      summary_length: [np.random.randint(5,8)],
                                      text_length: [len(text)]*batch_size,
                                      keep_prob: 1.0})[0]

# Remove the padding from the tweet
pad = vocab_to_int["<PAD>"]

print('Original Text:', input_sentence)

print('\nText')
print('  Word Ids:    {}'.format([i for i in text]))
print('  Input Words: {}'.format(" ".join([int_to_vocab[i] for i in text])))

print('\nSummary')
print('  Word Ids:       {}'.format([i for i in answer_logits if i != pad]))
print('  Response Words: {}'.format(" ".join([int_to_vocab[i] for i in answer_logits if i != pad])))
```

Figure 7.41: Code snippet for generating the summary for the given review

The output for the preceding code is shown in the following figure:

```
INFO:tensorflow:Restoring parameters from ./best_model.ckpt
Original Text: tried many lindt chocolate bars best one thought cadbury raisin nuts best one tried one lindt lindt
milk chocolate one best industry size quantity raisins nuts proportional prefer eat chocolate bar fridge least 10 m
inutes snaps better mouth also taste great room temperature recommend chocolate bar anyone especially enjoy milk ch
ocolate

Text
  Word Ids:    [22515, 5069, 3564, 80, 21263, 25519, 943, 52152, 24991, 7684, 61285, 25519, 943, 22515, 943, 3564,
3564, 61577, 80, 943, 25519, 18647, 39818, 39999, 43912, 61285, 51856, 50955, 47085, 80, 33534, 1003, 51981, 45984,
33257, 35975, 61759, 8436, 34851, 53382, 61554, 630, 8045, 31750, 80, 33534, 56108, 54566, 3043, 61577, 80]
  Input Words: tried many lindt chocolate bars best one thought cadbury raisin nuts best one tried one lindt lindt
milk chocolate one best industry size quantity raisins nuts proportional prefer eat chocolate bar fridge least 10 m
inutes snaps better mouth also taste great room temperature recommend chocolate bar anyone especially enjoy milk ch
ocolate

Summary
  Word Ids:       [25519, 80, 33534]
  Response Words: best chocolate bar
```

Examples of reviews and summaries:

- Review(1): The coffee tasted great and was at such a good price! I highly recommend this to everyone!
- Summary(1): great coffee

- Review(2): This is the worst cheese that I have ever bought! I will never buy it again and I hope you won't either!
- Summary(2): omg gross gross

- Review(3): love individual oatmeal cups found years ago sam quit selling sound big lots quit selling found target expensive buy individually trilled get entire case time go anywhere need water microwave spoon know quaker flavor packets
- Summary(3): love it

Figure 7.42: Summary for the given review

This approach is great if we want to generate a one-line summary for the given textual data. In future, if we will have the parallel medical transcription dataset for the summarization task, then this approach will work well.

Summary

In this chapter, we built the summarization application for medical transcriptions. In the beginning, we listed the challenges in order to generate a good parallel corpus for the summarization task in the medical domain. After that, for our baseline approach, we used the already available Python libraries, such as `PyTeaser` and `Sumy`. In the revised approach, we used word frequencies to generate the summary of the medical document. In the best possible approach, we combined the word frequency-based approach and the ranking mechanism in order to generate a summary for medical notes.

In the end, we developed a solution, where we used Amazon's review dataset, which is the parallel corpus for the summarization task, and we built the deep learning-based model for summarization. I would recommend that researchers, community members, and everyone else come forward to build high-quality datasets that can be used for building some great data science applications for the health and medical domains.

In the next chapter, we will be building chatbots. Chatbots, or virtual assistants, have become a hot topic in the data science domain over the last couple of years. So, in the next chapter, we will take into consideration a movie dialog dataset and the Facebook `bAbI` dataset. With the help of these datasets and by using deep learning algorithms, we will build chatbots. So, if you want to learn how to build one for yourself, then keep reading!

8
Developing Chatbots

The year 2017 was all about chatbots, and that continues in 2018. Chatbots are not new at all. The concept of chatbots has been around since the 1970s. Sometimes, a chatbot application is also referred to as a question-answering system. This is a more specific technical term for a chatbot. Let's take a step into history. Lunar was the first rule-based question-answering system. Using this system, geologists could ask questions regarding the moon rock from the Apollo missions. In order to improvise the rule-based system that was used in the Apollo mission, we had to find out a way to encode pattern-based question and answers. For this purpose, **Artificial Intelligence Markup Language** was used, also called **AIML**. This helps the programmer code less lines of code in order to achieve the same result that we generated by using a hardcoded pattern-based system. With recent advances in the field of **Machine Learning** (**ML**), we can build a chatbot without hardcoded responses.

Chatbots are now used in apps because of the numerous benefits they have; for example, users don't need to install different varieties of apps on their mobile. If there is a chatbot that provides you the news, then you can ask for news that is on CNN or The Economic Times. Big tech giants such as Facebook, Hike, WeChat, Snapchat, Slack, and so on provide chatbots for better customer engagement. They achieve this by making a chatbot that one can guide their customers in order to perform some operations; it also provides useful information about the product and its platforms.

Chatbots provide different services. By using the Facebook chatbot platform you can order flowers and see the news as well. Doesn't it sound cool? Technically, these chatbots are the new apps of the current era. I have briefly discussed the benefits of the chatbot, but we will look at them in detail in this chapter.

In this chapter, we will be covering the following topics:

- Introducing the problem statement
- Understanding the datasets
- Building the basic version of chatbots:
    - Understanding rule-based systems
    - Understanding the approach
    - Understanding architecture
- Implementing the rule-based system of chatbots
- Testing rule-based chatbots
- Problem with the existing approach:
    - Understanding key concepts for optimizing the approach
- Implementing the revised approach:
    - Data preparation
    - Implementing the sequence-to-sequence (seq2seq) model
- Testing the revised approach:
    - Understanding the testing metrics
    - Testing the revised version of chatbots
- Problem with the revised approach:
    - Understanding key concepts for solving the existing problems
- The best approach:
    - Implementing the best approach
- Summary

Introducing the problem statement

In this chapter, our primary goal is to understand how to build a chatbot. Chatbots, or **question-answering systems (QA systems)**, are really helpful. Let's consider a fun example. Suppose you are a student and you have five books to read. Reading and understanding five books may take time. What if you could feed the content of all these five books to the computer and ask only relevant questions? By doing this, students could learn the concepts and new information faster. As we all know, major internet product companies are arranging information so it is easy to access. Chatbots or QA systems will help us understand the meaning behind this information. This is the main reason why chatbots are the buzzword for the year 2017. Whatever application you can think of, you can make a chatbot for it. Many messaging platforms now host chatbots built by developers, including Facebook Messenger, Slack, WeChat, and so on. Chatbots are the new app because they already live inside the installed apps that you probably use a dozen times in a day. Chatbots developed using Facebook chatbot APIs are inside the Facebook Messenger app. You might use Messenger a dozen times a day. So, users don't need to install a separate app for a specific functionality. This will help companies engage their customers even better.

Before we proceed, I want to introduce a couple of important terms that can help us understand which kind of chatbot development we are targeting in this chapter. First of all, let's understand what the different approaches for developing a chatbot are:

- Retrieval-based approach
- Generative-based approach

Retrieval-based approach

In a retrieval-based approach, we need to define the set of predefined responses, and we will apply some kind of heuristics on predefined responses so that the chatbot can generate the best possible answers for the given questions. The answers are very dependent on the input question and the context of that input question.

Earlier, during the development of the retrieval-based model, we used only expression matching, which can help us get the appropriate answer, but using only expression matching won't help us here. So recently, researchers and programmers have started using expression matching along with advanced machine learning (ML) classifier techniques. Let's take an example to understand how the machine learning classifier will be useful in order to build retrieval-based chatbots.

Suppose Alice needs to send flowers to her friends on their birthdays. One of her friends, Emma, likes roses and another friend, Lucy, likes lilies. Alice uses a flower-ordering chatbot to book her order. She writes, *I want to book one multicolor rose flower bouquet and one with lilies*. So, in this case, if we implement a basic ML classifier, the chatbot can easily identify that there are two different orders Alice is booking, and it is also able to interpret the quantity of each of them. The chatbot will also ask for the different addresses and so on. By using ML techniques, we can code more complex heuristics, which can help us to generate more appropriate chatbot answers. The Facebook messenger chatbot API is an example of this.

There is another interesting example that can be solved by using ML heuristics. Say, you ask a chatbot, *what day is it today? Or, today is what day?* If we have implemented advanced ML techniques, then it can recognize that both questions are worded differently but have the same intent. During the development of the chatbot, intent and context detection are more complex tasks, which can be implemented by ML techniques and using some heuristics.

Now let's move on to the harder approach, which is the generative-based approach.

Generative-based approach

In the generative-based approach, there aren't any predefined responses given to the chatbot. The chatbot generates the responses from scratch. In order to build the generative-based chatbot, we need to provide a lot of data and the machine will learn how to answer the questions asked by users just by seeing the data. In 2015, Google researchers Oriol Vinyals and Quoc V. Le proposed an approach called A *Neural Conversational Network*. You can refer to the paper at: `https://arxiv.org/pdf/1506.05869v2.pdf`.

In this paper, researchers have used a Cornell movie dialog dataset. This dataset has been fed to the machines so that it can learn the basic English language. For this, they have used the **Sequence-to-sequence** (**seq2seq**) neural network architecture. After that, they used the IT support dataset so that the machines have domain knowledge. Once a machine is trained on that, they have tested the chatbot in the IT support department, this chatbot will be able to answer questions with great accuracy. In the upcoming section, we will build our own Neural Conversational Network. This approach is less time consuming and overcomes the challenges we face in the retrieval-based model, such as intent identification, context identification, and so on.

There are some other important terms that we need to discuss here. There are some important constraints that we need to think about before developing a chatbot. The first one is related to the conversation domain:

- Open domain
- Closed domain

Open domain

First, let's understand what an open domain is. Conversations are fuzzy and uncertain sometimes. Let me give you an example. Suppose you meet an old school friend that you haven't seen for many years. During the course of the conversation, you don't know which particular topic you both are going to talk about. In this situation, the conversation can go anywhere. So, the domain of the conversation is not fixed. You can talk about life, jobs, travelling, family, and so on. There is an infinite number of topics that you can talk about. This kind of conversation, where we can't restrict the areas we are talking about, is called an open domain. Developing an open domain chatbot is difficult because ideally, this kind of chatbot can answer every question from any kind of domain with human-level accuracy.

Currently, these kinds of chatbots are not made. When we are able to make this kind of chatbot, it will have to pass the Turing Test. Let me give you a glimpse of the Turing Test so that you can understand the explanation better. This experiment was created by the great computer scientist Alan Turing in 1950. In this experiment, a person, called a judge, asks a series of questions to a person and a machine. Now, the judge won't know which answer is from the human and which one is from the machine. But after seeing or hearing the answers, if the judge can't differentiate which answers are coming from the human and which answers are coming from the machine, then the machine passes the Turing Test, and we can say that the machine exhibited human-level intelligence because it behaves as intelligently as humans. So far, there is not a single chatbot that has passed the Turing Test with human-level accuracy. You can read more about the Turing Test by visiting `https://en.wikipedia.org/wiki/Turing_test`. This segment of technology is growing rapidly, so the next five years could be exciting.

Google has been quite aggressive in making an open domain chatbot. It is building this product in the form of Google Assistance, but the accuracy levels and functionality in passing the Turing Test are still limited. Now let's understand the second type of domain.

Closed domain

A closed domain is the opposite of an open domain. For a closed domain, we need to restrict the conversation topics. Let's take an example: in the office, we sometimes have meetings. Before the meeting, the participants know the topics on which there's going to be a discussion. So during the meeting, we just focus on those topics. Here, we won't have an infinite number of topics and domains to talk about. This kind of conversation, where we have restricted the areas we can talk about, is called a closed domain.

If a financial institute such as a bank launches a chatbot for their customers, then the developed chatbot cannot answer questions such as *can you tell me what the weather in Singapore is today?* But it helps you check the procedure of applying for a credit card, and this is because a chatbot can understand questions related to a specific domain. A chatbot for a closed domain is definitely possible, and there are many companies that are building domain-specific chatbots as it is good for engaging with the customer base. So during the chapter, we will be focusing on the closed domain chatbot.

Let's try to understand the last constraint; the conversation length, which means the length of the answers we will be getting from the chatbot. Based on that, we need to understand the following terms:

- Short conversation
- Long conversation

Short conversation

This type of chatbot can generate short answers. During the development of the chatbot, we need to ask ourselves whether we expect a short conversation or not. If we expect a short answer then you should be glad because this short conversation-based chatbot can be easily built. An example of a short conversation is as follows:

Human: Hi

Machine: Hello

Human: How are you?

Machine: I'm fine

This example indicates short conversations generated by a chatbot.

Long conversation

This type of chatbot can generate long answers. It is hard for a machine to learn long conversations, so building a chatbot that can generate long conversations is difficult. Let's look at an example of a long conversation:

Human: I want to tell you a story.

Machine: Please go on.

Human: Here you go. John went to the market. Daniel is travelling to India. Siri has an apple. Siri is in the kitchen. So my question is, where is Siri?

Machine: Based on your story, I think Siri is in the kitchen.

As you can see in this example, in order to generate the right answer, the machine should also store and process the given facts so that it can generate the right answer. Therefore, long conversation and reasoning-based chatbots are a bit hard to develop.

So far, you have learned a lot of terms. Now let's see how they're going to affect us when we develop a chatbot. Based on the approaches and domain type, we can build different types of chatbots.

Open domain and generative-based approach

We want to build a chatbot using the generative-based approach, which operates on the open domain. This means that the chatbot needs to learn how to answer the questions from any domain from scratch. The conversation can go in any direction here. This type of chatbot is an example of **Artificial General Intelligence** (**AGI**), and we are not quite there yet

So, developing this type of chatbot is not a part of this chapter.

Open domain and retrieval-based approach

If we want to build a chatbot that can operate on an open domain using a retrieval-based approach, then as coders, we need to hardcode pretty much all the responses and possible questions as well as variations. This approach consumes a hell of a lot of time, so this type of chatbot is also not a part of this chapter.

Closed domain and retrieval-based approach

We have understood that we can't operate on the open domain, but what about the closed domain? We can surely work on the closed domain as there is a finite number of questions that can be asked by a user to a chatbot and that a chatbot can answer. If we use the retrieval-based approach for a closed domain, then we can code questions that are relatively easy. We can integrate some NLP tools, such as a parser, **Name Entity Recognition** (**NER**), and so on in order to generate the most accurate answer.

Let's take an example. Suppose we want to build a chatbot that can give us real-time weather information for any location. If we build the chatbot using a retrieval-based approach, then the user will definitely get an accurate answer for questions such as *What is the weather in Mumbai? What is the weather in California? Are there any chances of rainfall today?* The chatbot will give you answers to the first two questions really well, but during the third question, it will be confused because we don't provide a location for the chances of rainfall. If the chatbot has used some heuristics, then there will be a chance that you may get a response. Chatbot may ask you about the location for which you want to know the chances of rainfall, but mostly, this won't happen. The chatbot directly tells you the chances of rainfall in, say, California. In reality, I want to know the chances of rainfall in Mumbai. So, these kinds of context-related problems are common to the retrieval-based approach. We need to implement the generative-based approach to overcome context-related problems.

Closed domain and generative-based approach

When we use the generative-based approach for the closed domain, the development of this kind of chatbot takes less coding time, and the quality of the answers improves as well. If we want our chatbot to understand long contexts and intents over a series of questions from the user, then the generative-based approach is the right choice. After training on large corpus and optimization, the chatbot can understand the context and intent of questions as well as be able to ask reasoning types of questions. This space of chatbot development is exciting and interesting for research and implementing new ideas.

Let's take an example. Suppose we have built a chatbot to apply for a home loan from a bank. When the user runs this chatbot, it may ask these questions: what is the status of my home loan application? Are there any documents remaining from my side that I should upload? Will I get approval in the next 2 days or not? Have you received my tax sheets and salary slips? The context of the last question is dependent on the second question. These kinds of questions and their answers can be easily generated with the generative-based approach.

Refer to the following figure, which will help us summarize all the preceding discussions:

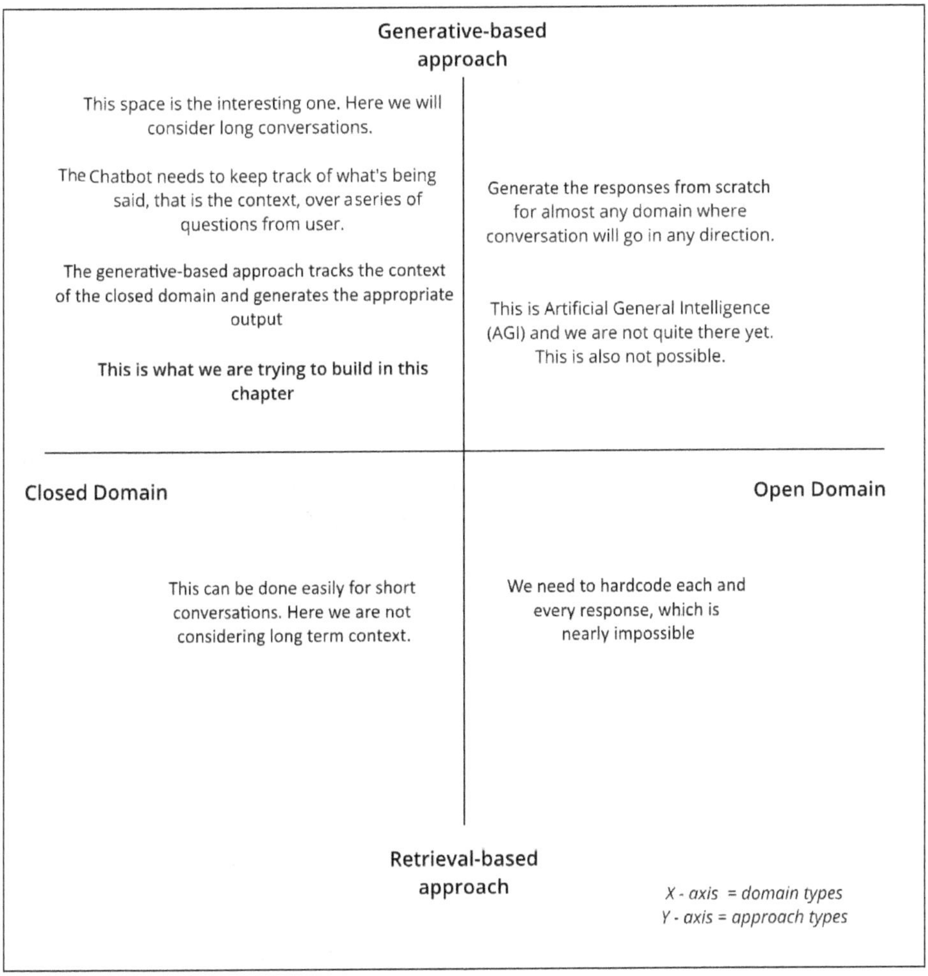

Figure 8.1: Pictorial representation of the approach to develop a chatbot

In this chapter, we will be building a chatbot that will be based on the closed domain and that uses retrieval-based and generative-based approaches.

Now let's look at the dataset that we will be using in this chapter.

Understanding datasets

In order to develop a chatbot, we are using two datasets. These datasets are as follows:

- Cornell Movie-Dialogs dataset
- bAbI dataset

Cornell Movie-Dialogs dataset

This dataset has been widely used for developing chatbots. You can download the Cornell Movie-Dialogs corpus from this link: `https://www.cs.cornell.edu/~cristian/Cornell_Movie-Dialogs_Corpus.html`. This corpus contains a large metadata-rich collection of fictional conversations extracted from raw movie scripts.

This corpus has 220,579 conversational exchanges between 10,292 pairs of movie characters. It involves 9,035 characters from 617 movies. In total, it has 304,713 utterances. This dataset also contains movie metadata. There are the following types of metadata:

- Movie-related metadata includes the following details:
    - Genre of the movie
    - Release year
    - IMDb rating
- Character-related metadata includes the following details:
    - Gender of 3,774 characters
    - Total number of characters in movies

When you download this dataset, you'll notice that there are two files we will be using throughout this chapter. The names of the files are `movie_conversations.txt` and `movie_lines.txt`. Let's look at the content details of each file.

Content details of movie_conversations.txt

This file contains `line_id` for the `movie_lines.txt` file. You can see the content of `movie_conversations.txt` in the following figure:

```
u0 +++$+++ u2 +++$+++ m0 +++$+++ ['L194', 'L195', 'L196', 'L197']
u0 +++$+++ u2 +++$+++ m0 +++$+++ ['L198', 'L199']
u0 +++$+++ u2 +++$+++ m0 +++$+++ ['L200', 'L201', 'L202', 'L203']
u0 +++$+++ u2 +++$+++ m0 +++$+++ ['L204', 'L205', 'L206']
u0 +++$+++ u2 +++$+++ m0 +++$+++ ['L207', 'L208']
```

Figure 8.2: Sample content of the movie_conversations.txt file

As you can see in the preceding figure, this file contains line numbers, and the actual content of the conversation is present in *movie_lines.txt*. +++$+++ acts as a separator. You must definitely be eager to know how to process this dataset; just bear with me for a while and we will cover this aspect in the upcoming sections.

Now let's look at the content of the next file.

Content details of movie_lines.txt

This file contents the actual movie dialogs. You can see the sample content of `movie_lines.txt` in the following figure:

```
L197 +++$+++ u2 +++$+++ m0 +++$+++ CAMERON +++$+++ Okay... then how 'bout we try out some French
cuisine.  Saturday?  Night?
L196 +++$+++ u0 +++$+++ m0 +++$+++ BIANCA +++$+++ Not the hacking and gagging and spitting part.  Please.
L195 +++$+++ u2 +++$+++ m0 +++$+++ CAMERON +++$+++ Well, I thought we'd start with pronunciation, if
that's okay with you.
L194 +++$+++ u0 +++$+++ m0 +++$+++ BIANCA +++$+++ Can we make this quick?  Roxanne Korrine and Andrew
Barrett are having an incredibly horrendous public break- up on the quad.  Again.
```

figure 8.3: Sample content of movie_lines.txt

As you can see in the preceding figure, each line has a unique conversation line ID. This `line_id` refers to the `movie_conversations.txt` file. This file contains the same line separator and the names of the characters involved in the conversation.

If you see the both files together, then it is might make more sense to you. In the `movie_conversations.txt` file, refer to the conversations on *line_id 194, 195, 196,* and *197.* All these conversations can be found in `movie_lines.txt`. In the preceding image, you can see that *line_id 194* contains this question: *Can we make this quick? Roxanne Korrine and Andrew Barrett are having an incredibly horrendous public break- up on the quad. Again.* On the other hand, *line_id 195* contains the answer: *Well, I thought we'd start with pronunciation, if that's okay with you.*

We need to prepare the dataset in the form of a question-answer format before feeding it to the machine. We will implement the data preparation step before using it for training.

Now let's look at the bAbI dataset.

The bAbI dataset

This dataset is built by Facebook AI Research (FAIR), where AI stands for artificial intelligence. This dataset belongs to the bAbI project. You can download the dataset from `https://research.fb.com/downloads/babi/`. It is a well-maintained dataset. The goal of the bAbI project is to try to build an automatic text understanding and reasoning system. This dataset consists of the following sub datasets:

- The (20) QA bAbI tasks
- The (6) dialog bAbI tasks
- The Children's Book Test
- The Movie Dialog dataset
- The WikiMovies dataset
- The Dialog-based Language Learning dataset
- The SimpleQuestions dataset
- HITL Dialogue Simulator

We will be using only one subset here, which is the (20) QA bAbI tasks because it is the one that's most useful for building the chatbot.

The (20) QA bAbI tasks

Let's look at this subdataset in detail. Here, 20 different tasks have been performed using this (20) QA bAbI dataset. Let's see what these tasks are. These tasks give machines the capacity to perform some reasoning, and based on that, the machine can answer a question. You can refer to the task name given in the following figure:

TASK
T1. Single supporting fact
T2. Two supporting facts
T3. Three supporting facts
T4. Two arguments relations
T5. Three arguments relations
T6. Yes/no questions
T7. Counting
T8. Sets
T9. Simple negation
T10. Indefinite knowledge
T11. Basic coreference
T12. Conjunction
T13. Compound coreference
T14. Time reasoning
T15. Basic deduction
T16. Basic induction
T17. Positional reasoning
T18. Size reasoning
T19. Path finding
T20. Agent's motivation

Figure 8.4: (20) QA bAbI task details

Image source: http://www.thespermwhale.com/jaseweston/babi/abordes-ICLR.pdf

Facebook researchers Jason Weston, Antoine Bordes, Sumit Chopra, Alexander M. Rush, Bart van Merriënboer, Armand Joulin, and Tomas Mikolov published a paper in which they proposed an interesting AI-based QA system. You can refer to their research paper by visiting `https://arxiv.org/abs/1502.05698`. In this chapter, we will be attempting to achieve the results for task T1, and we will regenerate its result.

This dataset contains the corpus in two languages, English and Hindi. There are two types of folders here: the folder with the name *en* has 1,000 training examples, whereas *en-10K* has 10,000 training examples. The format for each of the task datasets is given in the following figure:

```
ID text
ID text
ID text
ID question[tab]answer[tab]supporting fact IDS.

Example:

1 John travelled to the hallway.
2 Mary journeyed to the bathroom.
3 Where is John?    hallway 1
```

Figure 8.5: Format of Single supporting QA bAbI task

The supporting facts are called a story. Based on the story, the user can ask questions to the machine, and the machine should give the logically correct answer that can be derived from the provided supporting text. This is a hard task because in this case, the machine should remember the long context that it can use as and when needed. We will use this interesting dataset soon.

Now let's start building the chatbot baseline version.

Building the basic version of a chatbot

In this section, we will be building the basic version of a chatbot. Getting data is not an issue for any company nowadays but getting a domain-specific conversational dataset is challenging.

There are so many companies out there whose goal is to make an innovative domain-specific chatbot, but their major challenge is getting the right data. If you are facing the same issue, then this basic approach can help you in that. This basic version of a chatbot is based on the closed domain and the retrieval-based approach, which uses the rule-based system. So, let's start understanding each aspect of the rule-based system.

Why does the rule-based system work?

As I mentioned earlier, a rule-based system is the way to implementing a retrieval-based approach. Now, you may wonder why we need a rule-based system. Considering that we are living in the era of Machine Learning (ML), doesn't it sound old? Let me share my personal experience with you. I closely collaborate with many start-ups. Some of them operate in the financial domain, some in the human resource domain, and some in the legal domain. In this era of chatbots, start-ups are really keen on developing domain-specific chatbots that can help users. Initially, they work on some general dataset so that the machine can learn the language and generate the logical casual answers for them, but they soon realize that they don't have enough domain-specific data to help them build a good chatbot. Let me give you an example.

I collaborated with a fintech start-up where we needed to build a chatbot. The specific requirement for the chatbot was that it should help customers who want to apply for a home loan as well as those who have already applied and need some assistance. Now, this fintech just started 1 and a half years ago. So they don't have large chat logs about the kind of queries customers may have. In short, the company doesn't have enough domain-specific data, such as what kind of queries a home loan applicant may ask and how to synchronize these customer queries to the loan procedure this fintech company follows. In this case, there are two main things that we need to focus on:

- We need to build a minimum viable chatbot that can help customers with basic FAQs
- With the help of this minimum viable chatbot, you can also come to learn what kind of questions people are asking, and based on these questions, the chatbot can be tweaked

In these kind of situations, where we don't have a domain-specific dataset, the rule-based or retrieval-based model will work for us. From the next section onward, we will explore the rule-based system and the approach of developing a basic chatbot and its architecture.

Understanding the rule-based system

In this section, we will cover the rule-based system so that you don't feel left out when we start developing the retrieval-based chatbot. The **rule-based** (**RB**) system is defined as follows: using available knowledge or rules, we develop a system that uses the rules, apply the available system rules on the corpus, and try to generate or infer the results. From the perspective of the chatbot, the RB system has all possible questions and answers and they're hardcoded. We can definitely use regular expressions and fuzzy logic to implement some kind of heuristics in order to make the RB system more accurate.

Refer to the following figure, which will give you an idea about the workflow of the chatbot using the retrieval-based approach:

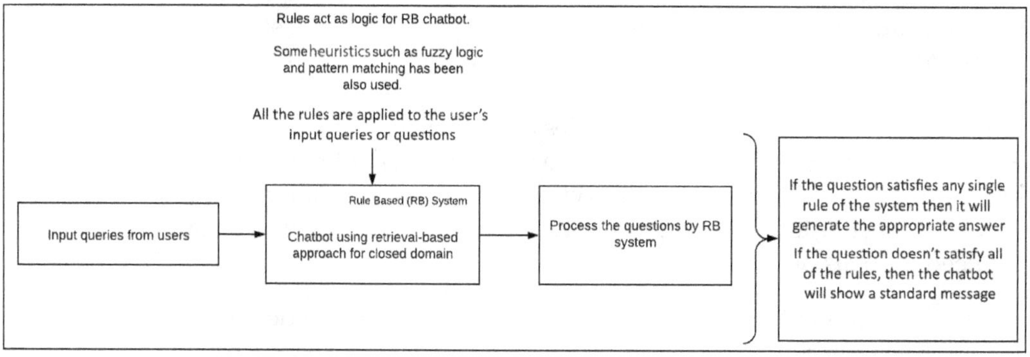

Figure 8.6: Workflow of rule-based chatbot

Based on the preceding figure, you know that in an RB system we will manually hand-code all possible questions and answers as well as implement regular expressions and fuzzy logic, which will give the chatbot the ability to generate the appropriate answers. Based on business requirements, questions can be added and deleted from this system. Now let's discuss our approach, and based on this approach we will build a basic version of the chatbot.

Understanding the approach

In this section, we will look at the steps that will help us implement the basic version of the chatbot. Here, I'm building a chatbot for the finance domain, which will help users apply for home loans. We will code some questions so that you know how a rule-based chatbot can be developed. We need to perform the following steps:

1. Listing down possible questions and answers.
2. Deciding standard messages.
3. Understanding the architecture.

Listing down possible questions and answers

First of all, we need to list all the questions that we can think of on behalf of the users. Once we decide on the questions, then one by one we need to decide the answers to these questions. Suppose we ask the user to provide their full name, email ID, phone number, and loan amount so in case the user drops in between, the customer executive can call them back. After this, we ask the user what kind of assistance they require and then they can ask their questions. They may ask for the eligibility criteria, application status, document requirements, and so on. During the first iteration, you need to add the bare minimum questions that are frequently asked by users. Once we decide the questions and answers, it will be easy for us to code them.

Say, I include the following questions in this basic version of the financial domain chatbot:

- Please let me know the eligibility criteria for getting a home loan
- Please let me know what the status of my loan application is
- Let me know the list of documents I need to submit

The answers to each of these questions will be as follows:

- We need a minimum of 3 years of job experience, 3 years of IT returns, and a minimum income of more than 3.5 lakh INR
- Your application is with our credit risk management team
- You need to submit salary slips for the last 6 months, a proof of identity, 3 years of IT returns, and the lease documents for your house.

We also need to decide some standard messages, which we will cover in the next section.

Deciding standard messages

We need to decide the standard message, for example, a welcome message from the chatbot. If the user asks a question that the chatbot cannot answer, then what message should pop up? We also need to decide the message when the user ends the chat.

These standard messages help users understand what they can and cannot ask the chatbot. Now let's look at the architectural part of the basic version of the chatbot.

Understanding the architecture

In this section, let's talk about architecture. When we are building a domain-specific rule-based chatbot, then we need to store whatever questions the users ask. We also need to build a chatbot that is fast and scalable. In this approach, we build the web services. The web service REST APIs will be easily integrated with the website and the frontend. We need a database that can store the conversations of the users. This conversation data will be helpful when we try to improvise the chatbot or use it for ML training. The libraries that I'm using are given as follows:

- Flask for implementing web services and REST APIs
- MongoDB for storing the conversations. The reason behind choosing the NoSQL database is that conversations don't have a specific format. NoSQL is a good option to store schema-less data. We need to store the raw conversations, so NoSQL is a good option.

You can refer to the following figure, which will help you understand the entire architecture and process:

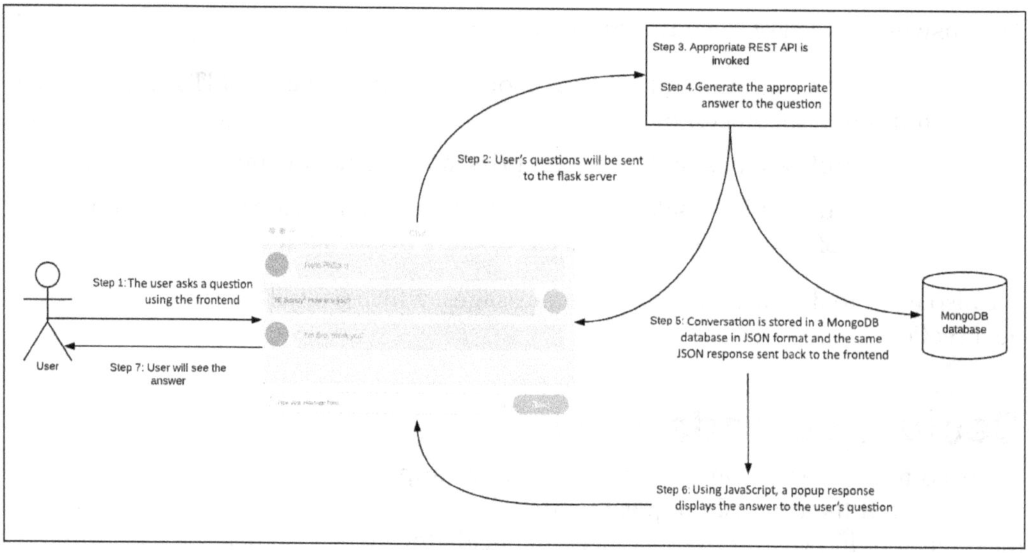

Figure 8.7: Architectural design for the basic version of a chatbot

Based on this architecture, you will find that the process flow of the basic version of a chatbot is quite simple. This flow involves seven simple steps:

1. The user will ask their questions to the chatbot.
2. The rule-based engine of the chatbot will process the question. Here, the REST API has been called to generate the response.

3. If the question that's asked is available to the RB system, then the user will get an appropriate answer.
4. If the question that's asked is not available to the RB system, then the user will not get the answer but a standard error message.
5. The conversation of the user will be stored in the MongoDB database. This response is in the JSON format.
6. The same JSON response is sent by the REST API to the frontend. At the frontend, a JavaScript parses this response and pops up the appropriate answer.
7. When the user gets their answer, they may end the chat or ask another question.

Another major point that I want to highlight is that before storing the data to MongoDB, we need to finalize the attributes of the JSON response that will actually help us when we parse the JSON response using JavaScript. You can refer to the following screenshot, which will help you learn which kind of JSON schema I have decided on:

```
{
    "current_form_action": "/welcomemsg_chat",
    "message_bot": [
        "Hi, I'm personal loan application assistant.",
        "You can apply for loan with help of mine.",
        "To keep going say Hi to me."
    ],
    "message_human": "",
    "next_field_type": "button",
    "next_form_action": "/hi_chat?msg=",
    "placeholder_text": "Hi",
    "previous_field_type": "",
    "previous_form_action": "",
    "suggestion_message": [
        "Hi"
    ]
}
```

Figure 8.8: Understanding the JSON response attribute

The usage of each of the JSON attributes is as follows:

- `current_form_action`: This attribute indicates which REST API is currently being invoked.
- `message_bot`: This field carries the answer from the bot.
- `message_human`: This field carries the query of the user.

- `next_field_type`: If we need to populate the textbox or button in the next question, this is useful for generating dynamic HTML components.
- `next_form_action`: This attribute indicates which REST API we should invoke in the upcoming request.
- `placeholder_text`: If you want to put watermark text in the textbox, then this attribute helps you with the HTML functionality.
- `previous_field_type`: This attribute keeps track of what the last field type was.
- `previous_form_action`: This attribute keeps track of what the last REST API we invoked was.
- `suggestion_message`: Sometimes, we need a message to invoke a specific rule. This is the same as when you say, *OK Google* and the Google home assistance is invoked. This attribute basically guides the user as to what they need to expect when asking their queries.

Now let's start the implementation of the rule-based chatbot.

Implementing the rule-based chatbot

In this section, we will understand the implementation of the chatbot. This implementation is divided into two parts. You can find this code by visiting: `https://github.com/jalajthanaki/Chatbot_Rule_Based`:

- Implementing the conversation flow
- Implementing RESTful APIs using flask

Implementing the conversation flow

In order to implement the conversation logic, we are writing a separate Python script, so that whenever we need to add or delete some logic it will be easy for us. Here, we create one Python package in which we put this conversation logic. The name of the file is *conversationengine.py* and it uses JSON, BSON, and re as Python dependencies.

In this file, we have implemented each conversation in the form of a function. When the user opens the chatbot for the first time, a welcome message should pop up. You can refer to the code given in the following screenshot:

```
# Welcome msg
assistant_defualt_welcome_msg = [
    "Hi, I'm personal loan application assistant.",
    "You can apply for loan with help of mine.", "To keep going say Hi to me."]


def loan_assistant_welcome_msg():
    welcome_json_obj = json.dumps({'message_human': "", 'message_bot': assistant_defualt_welcome_msg,
                                   'suggestion_message': ["Hi"], 'current_form_action': "/welcomemsg_chat",
                                   'next_form_action': "/hi_chat?msg=", 'previous_form_action': "",
                                   'next_field_type': "button", 'previous_field_type': "",
                                   "placeholder_text": "Hi"},
                                  sort_keys=True, indent=4,
                                  separators=(',', ': '), default=json_util.default)
    # welcome_json_obj = json.dumps(welcome_json_obj)
    return welcome_json_obj
```

Figure 8.9: Code snippet for the welcome message

Now the users need to type in **Hi** in order to start a conversation. When the user types **hi**, the `start_coversation_action` function will be invoked and the chatbot will ask for some information so that it can give the user a more accurate, personalized answer. First, it asks the user their name, and then it asks for their email ID and phone number. You can refer to the following screenshot:

```
def start_converation_action(humanmessage):
    START_CONV_KEYWORDS = ("hello", "hi", "Hi", "Hello")
    START_CONV_RESPONSES = [
        "Please provide me borrower's full name"]
    text = humanmessage
    start_res = ""
    if text.lower() in START_CONV_KEYWORDS:
        # start_res = random.choice(START_CONV_RESPONSES)
        start_conv_json_obj = json.dumps(
            {'message_human': text, 'message_bot': START_CONV_RESPONSES,
             'suggestion_message': ["Please provide me borrower's full name"],
             'current_form_action': "/hi_chat?msg=",
             'next_form_action': "/asking_borowers_full_name?msg=", 'previous_form_action': "/welcomemsg_chat",
             'next_field_type': "text",
             'previous_field_type': "button", "placeholder_text": "Enter borrower's full name",
             "max_length": "255"},
            sort_keys=True, indent=4,
            separators=(',', ': '), default=json_util.default)
    elif text.lower() == "" or text.lower() is None or len(text) == 0:
        start_conv_json_obj = json.dumps({'message_human': text,
                                          'message_bot': defualt_missing_data_error,
                                          'suggestion_message': ["Hi"], 'current_form_action': "/hi_chat?msg",
                                          'next_form_action': "", 'previous_form_action': "/welcomemsg_chat",
                                          'next_field_type': "", 'previous_field_type': "button",
                                          "placeholder_text": "Hi"},
                                         sort_keys=True, indent=4,
                                         separators=(',', ': '), default=json_util.default)
    else:
        start_conv_json_obj = json.dumps({'message_human': text,
                                          'message_bot': defualt_error,
                                          'suggestion_message': ["Hi"], 'current_form_action': "/hi_chat?msg",
                                          'next_form_action': "", 'previous_form_action': "/welcomemsg_chat",
                                          'next_field_type': "", 'previous_field_type': "button",
                                          "placeholder_text": "Hi"
                                          },
                                         sort_keys=True, indent=4,
                                         separators=(',', ': '), default=json_util.default)
    return start_conv_json_obj
```

Figure 8.10: Code snippet for asking basic user information

In the same way, there are the `borrowers_name_asking`, `borrowers_email_id_asking`, and `mobilenumber_asking` functions, which ask the user to provide their name, email ID, and phone number. Apart from this, there are questions that can help users learn what the status of their loan application is. If the customer is new, then they can ask questions such as *what kind of documents are needed in order to apply for a home loan?* You can find these status- and document-related questions inside the `other_cases` function. You can refer to the code for this function in the following screenshot:

```
def other_cases(user_other_query):
    text = user_other_query.lower()

    search_status = re.search(r".*\bstatus\b.*",text.lower(),re.MULTILINE|re.IGNORECASE)
    search_documents = re.search(r".*\bdocument\b.*",text.lower(),re.MULTILINE|re.IGNORECASE)

    if text.lower() !="" and search_status:
        user_other_query_json_obj = json.dumps({'message_human': text,
                                                'message_bot': [" Your application is underprocess","It is at risk management team.","It
             will take 2 working days."],
                                                'suggestion_message': ["Enter your query"],
                                                'current_form_action': "/other_chat?msg",
                                                'next_form_action': "/end_chat?msg=", 'previous_form_action': "/loan_chat",
                                                'next_field_type': "text", 'previous_field_type': "text",
                                                "placeholder_text": "Enter your query"},
                                               sort_keys=True, indent=4,
                                               separators=(',', ': '), default=json_util.default)
    if text.lower() !="" and search_documents:
        user_other_query_json_obj = json.dumps({'message_human': text,
                                                'message_bot': [" You need to submit following documents.",
                                                                "1. 3-years ITR",
                                                                "2. Identity proof.",
                                                                "3. 3-months Salary sheet",
                                                                "4. 6-months bank statement",
                                                                ],
                                                'suggestion_message': ["Enter your query"],
                                                'current_form_action': "/other_chat?msg",
                                                'next_form_action': "/end_chat?msg=",
                                                'previous_form_action': "/loan_chat",
                                                'next_field_type': "text", 'previous_field_type': "text",
                                                "placeholder_text": "Enter your query"},
                                               sort_keys=True, indent=4,
                                               separators=(',', ': '), default=json_util.default)
```

Figure 8.11: Code snippet for question related to loan application status and documents needed for applying for a home loan

As you can see in the preceding figure, we have used a regular expression here so that the chatbot can answer status- and document-related questions. This is coded purely using keyword-based logic.

Now let's look at how to build the web service with this function using flask.

Implementing RESTful APIs using flask

So far, we have only coded the function that takes the user input query and invokes the appropriate function based on that query. For better maintenance and easy integration, we need to implement RESTful APIs using flask. In order to implement this, we use the `flask`, `json`, `os`, `uuid`, `datetime`, `pytz`, and `flsk_pymongo` libraries. Flask is an easy-to-use web framework. You can find the code snippet in the following figure:

```
@app.route('/')
def hello_world():
    return 'Hello from chat bot Flask...!'


@app.route("/welcomemsg_chat")
def welcomemsg_chat():
    welcome_msg = cs.loan_assistant_welcome_msg()
    conversation_list_history.append(welcome_msg)
    db_handler = mongo.db.chathistory
    db_handler.insert({"request_user_id": request_user_id, "conversation": conversation_list_history,
                       "time": now_india.strftime(fmt)})
    db_handler.update({"request_user_id": request_user_id}, {
        '$set': {"request_user_id": request_user_id, "conversation": conversation_list_history, "time": now_india.strftime(fmt)},
        "$currentDate": {"lastModified": True}}, upsert=True)
    resp = Response(welcome_msg, status=200, mimetype='application/json')
    return resp
```

Figure 8.12: Code snippet for making a RESTful API for the chatbot

As you can see in the preceding figure, each route calls a different method that is part of the `conversationengine.py` file we covered earlier. In order to run this flask engine, we need to use the flask `app.run ()` command. You can find all APIs and their functions by visiting: `https://github.com/jalajthanaki/Chatbot_Rule_Based/blob/master/flaskengin.py`.

Now let's test this rule-based chatbot.

Testing the rule-based chatbot

In this section, we will test the basic version of the chatbot. Let's begin with basic personal information that the chatbot asks for from the user. Here, I will generate the JSON response generated by the flask RESTful API. We need a JavaScript to parse this JSON response if we are integrating these APIs with the frontend. I won't explain the frontend integration part here, so let's analyze the JSON responses.

For the welcome message, refer to the following screenshot:


```
{
    "current_form_action": "/welcomemsg_chat",
    "message_bot": [
        "Hi, I'm personal loan application assistant.",
        "You can apply for loan with help of mine.",
        "To keep going say Hi to me."
    ],
    "message_human": "",
    "next_field_type": "button",
    "next_form_action": "/hi_chat?msg=",
    "placeholder_text": "Hi",
    "previous_field_type": "",
    "previous_form_action": "",
    "suggestion_message": [
        "Hi"
    ]
}
```


Figure 8.13: JSON response for the welcome message

The JSON response when the chatbot is asking for the name of a user is given in the following figure:


```
{
    "current_form_action": "/hi_chat?msg=",
    "max_length": "255",
    "message_bot": [
        "Please provide me borrower's full name"
    ],
    "message_human": "Hi",
    "next_field_type": "text",
    "next_form_action": "/asking_borowers_full_name?msg=",
    "placeholder_text": "Enter borrower's full name",
    "previous_field_type": "button",
    "previous_form_action": "/welcomemsg_chat",
    "suggestion_message": [
        "Please provide me borrower's full name"
    ]
}
```


Figure 8.14: JSON response for asking the name of the user

If the user asks for the status of his application, then they will get the JSON response given in the following figure:


```
{
    "current_form_action": "/other_chat?msg",
    "message_bot": [
        " Your application is underprocess",
        "It is at risk management team.",
        "It will take 2 working days."
    ],
    "message_human": "what is the status of my application",
    "next_field_type": "text",
    "next_form_action": "/end_chat?msg=",
    "placeholder_text": "Enter your query",
    "previous_field_type": "text",
    "previous_form_action": "/loan_chat",
    "suggestion_message": [
        "Enter your query"
    ]
}
```


Figure 8.15: JSON response to get status-related information

If the user asks status-related questions with a blend of Hindi-English (Hinglish) and if they use the word *status* in their query, then the chatbot will generate the response. You can see the response in the following figure:

```
{
    "current_form_action": "/other_chat?msg",
    "message_bot": [
        " Your application is underprocess",
        "It is at risk management team.",
        "It will take 2 working days."
    ],
    "message_human": "meri loan application ka status kya hai?",
    "next_field_type": "text",
    "next_form_action": "/end_chat?msg=",
    "placeholder_text": "Enter your query",
    "previous_field_type": "text",
    "previous_form_action": "/loan_chat",
    "suggestion_message": [
        "Enter your query"
    ]
}
```

Figure 8.16: json response to get status-related information for the Hindi-English (Hinglish) language

If the user asks queries that are not coded, then it will generate the following json response:

```
{
    "current_form_action": "/other_chat?msg",
    "message_bot": [
        "I can't do that for you.",
        "To keep going say hi to me.",
        " You can also call to our customer-executive on 022-1111111"
    ],
    "message_human": "what kind of loan you are offering other than home loan?",
    "next_field_type": "text",
    "next_form_action": "",
    "placeholder_text": "Enter your query",
    "previous_field_type": "text",
    "previous_form_action": "/loan_chat",
    "suggestion_message": [
        "Enter your query"
    ]
}
```

Figure 8.17: JSON response for an unknown question

After testing, we come to learn that queries that have been coded are working fine, but this basic version of a chatbot is not working properly for questions that we haven't coded. I want to point out some advantages after testing the rule-based chatbot. However, there are various disadvantages of this approach too, which we will discuss in an upcoming section.

Advantages of the rule-based chatbot

You can refer to the following advantages of the rule-based chatbot:

- Easy to code.
- Needs less computation power.
- Uses the pattern matching approach so if users use English and other languages in their conversation, they will still get an answer. This is because the chatbot identifies keywords that the user provides in their question. Suppose the user asks in English, *can you provide me a list of documents that I need to submit?* And another user may ask a question in the Hindi language: *Kya aap mujhe bata sakte hain mujhe kaun se documents submit karne hain?* For this question, the chatbot will generate the answer because it finds specific keywords from user queries, and if those keywords are present, then the chatbot generates an answer irrespective of the language.

Now let's look at the problems related to this approach that we need to solve in order to improve the chatbot.

Problems with the existing approach

In this section, we will discuss the problems with the basic version of our chatbot. As we already know, for unseen queries this approach doesn't work, which means that the basic approach is not able to generalize the user's questions properly.

I have listed down some of the problems here:

- Time consuming because we need to hardcode each and every scenario, which is not feasible at all
- It cannot work for unseen use cases
- The user should process the rigid flow of conversation
- It cannot understand the long context

Most of these problems can be solved using the generative-based approach. Let's look at the key concepts that will help us improvise this approach.

Understanding key concepts for optimizing the approach

In this section, we will be discussing the key concepts that can help us improvise the chatbot basic version. The problems that we have listed down previously can be solved by using **Deep Learning** (**DL**) techniques, which can help us build a more generalized chatbot in less time.

Before proceeding ahead, we need to decide which DL technique we will use for our revised approach. DL helps us achieve great results. Here, we need to use the End-to-End DL approach that makes no assumptions about data, the structure of the dialog, and use cases. This is what we want. In order to achieve this, we will be using **Recurrent Neural Nets** (**RNN**). Now you may ask why RNN is useful. Let me explain this by way of an example. Suppose we want to classify the temperature in the hot or cold category; to do that, we will be using a feed forward neural net to classify the temperature into hot or cold, but the conversation isn't a fixed size. A conversation is a sequence of words. We need to use a neural net that can help us process the sequences of words. RNN is best for processing these kinds of sequences. In RNN, we feed data back into the input while training it in a recurring loop.

In the revised approach, we are going to use the sequence-to-sequence (seq2seq) model from TensorFlow. So, let's discuss the sequence model for a bit.

Understanding the seq2seq model

The good part of using the seq2seq model is that we don't need to perform feature engineering. Like most of the DL techniques, it generates features by its own. We will discuss the seq2seq model briefly. The seq2seq model consists of two **Long Short Term Memory** (**LSTM**) recurrent neural networks. The first neural net is an *encoder*. It processes the input. The second neural net is a *decoder*. It generates the output. Usually, the DL algorithm needs a dimensionality of the inputs and outputs to be a fixed size, but here, we are accepting a sequence of words in a sentence and outputting a new sequence of words. So, we need a sequence model that can learn data with long range memory dependencies. The LSTM architecture is best suited for this. The encoder LSTM turns the input sentence of variable length into a fixed dimensional vector representation. We can think of this as a *thought vector* or a *context vector*. The reason we are using LSTM is that it can remember words from far back in the sequence; here, we are dealing with large sequence attention mechanisms of the seq2seq model, which helps the decoder selectively look at the parts of the sequence that are most relevant for more accuracy.

You can refer to the architecture of the seq2seq model in the following figure:

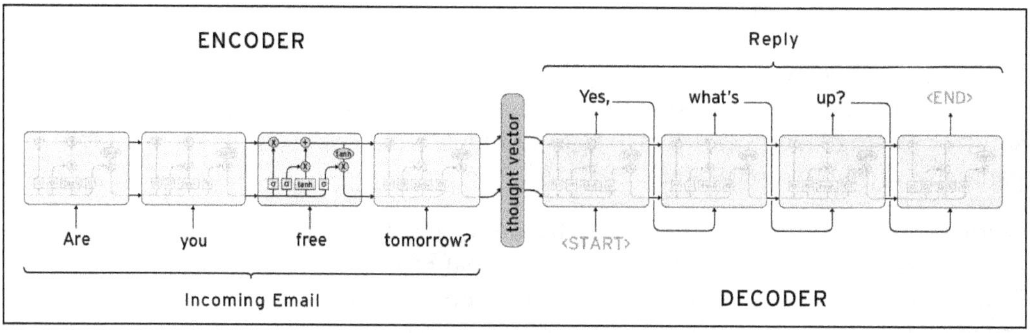

Figure 8.18: Architecture of the seq2seq model

Image source: `http://suriyadeepan.github.io/img/seq2seq/seq2seq2.png`

When we provide a large enough dataset of questions and responses, it will recognize the closeness of the set of questions and represent them as a single thought vector. This representation helps the machine to understand the intent of the questions irrespective of the structure of the sentence so the machine can recognize the questions such as "what time it is?" and "what's the time?" have the same intent, so they will fall into a single thought vector. After training, we will have a huge set of not just synapse weights but thought vectors as well. After that, we need to use additional hyper parameters along with appropriate loss functions when we train the model. Once we train the model, we can chat with it.

If you want to know more details about the seq2seq model, then you should refer to a research paper published by Google researchers titled *A Neural Conversational Model*. You can also refer to this paper at: `https://arxiv.org/pdf/1506.05869v3.pdf` and this amazing article if you want to learn more about LSTM at: `http://colah.github.io/posts/2015-08-Understanding-LSTMs/`.

Now let's implement the chatbot using the seq2seq model.

Implementing the revised approach

In this section, we will cover each part of the implementation. You can find the code by using this GitHub link: `https://github.com/jalajthanaki/Chatbot_tensorflow`. Note that here, I'm using TensorFlow version 0.12.1. I perform training on a GeForce GTX 1060 6GB GPU for a few hours. In this implementation, we don't need to generate features because the seq2seq model generates its internal representation for sequences of words given in a sentence. Our implementation part has the following steps:

- Data preparation
- Implementing the seq2seq model

Let's begin our coding.

Data preparation

During this implementation, we will be using the Cornell movie-dialogs dataset. First of all, we need to prepare data in a format that we can use for training. There is a Python script that is used to perform data preparation. You can find the script at: `https://github.com/jalajthanaki/Chatbot_tensorflow/blob/master/data/prepare_data_script/data.py`.

Data preparation can be subdivided into the following steps:

- Generating question-answer pairs
- Preprocessing the dataset
- Splitting the dataset into the training dataset and the testing dataset
- Building a vocabulary for the training and testing datasets

Generating question-answer pairs

In order to generate question-answer pairs from the Cornell movie-dialogs dataset, we are using the `movie_lines.txt` and `movie_conversations.txt` files. The `movie_lines.txt` files give us information about *line_id* of each conversation along with the real conversation, whereas `movie_conversations.txt` has *line_ids* only. In this situation, we need to generate the appropriate pair of conversations of question and answer from the dataset. For that, we will combine these two files. In Python script, there are some functions that help us combine these files. The details related to functions are as follows:

- `get_id2line()`: This function helps us spilt the data using the +++$+++ pattern. We perform splitting on the `movie_lines.txt` file. After splitting, with the help of this function, we create a dictionary in which we put *line_id* as the key and the movie dialog as the value. So, *key* = *line_id* and *value* = *text*
- `get_conversations()`: This function splits the data given in the `movie_conversations.txt` file. This will help us create a list. This list contains list of *line_ids*.
- `gather_dataset()`: This function actually generates question-answer pairs. In this function, a simple logic is applied. We take the list of *line_ids* and we know that the last element indicates the answer. So, we separate the questions and answers. With the help of the `get_id2line()` function, we search the questions and their corresponding answers. Here, we are using the value of the key to search questions and answers.

You can refer to the following screenshot to see the actual coding:

```
'''
    1. Read from 'movie-lines.txt'
    2. Create a dictionary with ( key = line_id, value = text )
'''
def get_id2line():
    #, encoding='utf-8', errors='ignore'
    lines=open('/home/jalaj/PycharmProjects/Chatbot_tensorflow/data/cornall_movie_dialog_dataset/movie_lines.txt').read().split('\n')
    id2line = {}
    for line in lines:
        _line = line.split(' +++$+++ ')
        if len(_line) == 5:
            id2line[_line[0]] = _line[4]
    return id2line

'''
    1. Read from 'movie_conversations.txt'
    2. Create a list of [list of line_id's]
'''
def get_conversations():
    conv_lines = open('/home/jalaj/PycharmProjects/Chatbot_tensorflow/data/cornall_movie_dialog_dataset/movie_conversations.txt').read().split('\n')
    convs = [ ]
    for line in conv_lines[:-1]:
        _line = line.split(' +++$+++ ')[-1][1:-1].replace("'","").replace(" ","")
        convs.append(_line.split(','))
    return convs

'''
    1. Get each conversation
    2. Get each line from conversation
    3. Save each conversation to file
'''
def extract_conversations(convs,id2line,path=''):...

'''
    Get lists of all conversations as Questions and Answers
    1. [questions]
    2. [answers]
'''
def gather_dataset(convs, id2line):
    questions = []; answers = []

    for conv in convs:
        if len(conv) %2 != 0:
            conv = conv[:-1]
        for i in range(len(conv)):
            if i%2 == 0:
                print [conv[i]]
                questions.append(id2line[conv[i]])
            else:
                answers.append(id2line[conv[i]])

    return questions, answers
```

Figure 8.19: Functions used for generating question-answer pairs

Now let's explore the data preprocessing section.

Preprocessing the dataset

Some preprocessing and filtering steps are involved here. As a part of preprocessing, we perform the following steps:

- We convert the conversation into lowercase using the inbuilt string function, `lower()`.
- We also remove the junk characters and too short or too long conversations. For this, we use a list-based approach to remove junk characters and the `filter_data()` function to remove too short or too long conversations. When we apply the `filter_data()` function on our dataset, *28%* of dataset is filtered.
- We also filter out conversations with so many unknowns. Here, *2%* of the dataset has been affected. For this, we have used the `filter_unk()` method.
- We also tokenize the sentences. In this process, we convert *list of [line of text]* into *list of [line of words]*. This tokenization is helpful because during training, the machine can process individual words of the sentence, and with the help of the word ID, data retrieval becomes much faster.

You can refer to the code given in the following screenshot:

```
# filter out unnecessary characters
print('\n>> Filter lines')
questions = [ filter_line(line, EN_WHITELIST) for line in questions ]
answers = [ filter_line(line, EN_WHITELIST) for line in answers ]

'''
 filter too long and too short sequences
    return tuple( filtered_ta, filtered_en )

'''
def filter_data(qseq, aseq):
    filtered_q, filtered_a = [], []
    raw_data_len = len(qseq)

    assert len(qseq) == len(aseq)

    for i in range(raw_data_len):
        qlen, alen = len(qseq[i].split(' ')), len(aseq[i].split(' '))
        if qlen >= limit['minq'] and qlen <= limit['maxq']:
            if alen >= limit['mina'] and alen <= limit['maxa']:
                filtered_q.append(qseq[i])
                filtered_a.append(aseq[i])

    # print the fraction of the original data, filtered
    filt_data_len = len(filtered_q)
    filtered = int((raw_data_len - filt_data_len)*100/raw_data_len)
    print(str(filtered) + '% filtered from original data')

    return filtered_q, filtered_a
```

Figure 8.20: Code snippet for preprocessing

Splitting the dataset into the training dataset and the testing dataset

After preprocessing, we will split the data into the training dataset and the testing dataset and for that, we will use the following functions:

- We can save the training and testing datasets using the `prepare_seq2seq_files()` function
- You can access the `train.enc`, `train.dec`, `test.enc`, and `test.dec` data files directly from this GitHub link: `https://github.com/jalajthanaki/Chatbot_tensorflow/tree/master/data`

Building a vocabulary for the training and testing datasets

Now it's time to generate the vocabulary from the dataset. For vocabulary generation, we will perform the following steps:

- Using the `prepare_custom_data()` function of the `data_utils.py` file, we can generate the vocabulary that we will feed into the seq2seq model while training.
- You can access the `data_utils.py` file using this link: `https://github.com/jalajthanaki/Chatbot_tensorflow/blob/master/data_utils.py`
- Note that vocabulary files are generated when we start training.
- The filenames of vocabulary files are `train.enc.ids20000`, `train.dec.ids20000`, `test.enc.ids20000`, and `test.dec.ids20000`. Here, 20000 indicates the size of the vocabulary we have provided
- You can access this file at: `https://github.com/jalajthanaki/Chatbot_tensorflow/tree/master/data`

You can see the code for the `prepare_custom_data()` function in the following screenshot:

```
def prepare_custom_data(working_directory, train_enc, train_dec, test_enc, test_dec, enc_vocabulary_size, dec_vocabulary_size, tokenizer=None):

    # Create vocabularies of the appropriate sizes.
    enc_vocab_path = os.path.join(working_directory, "vocab%d.enc" % enc_vocabulary_size)
    dec_vocab_path = os.path.join(working_directory, "vocab%d.dec" % dec_vocabulary_size)
    create_vocabulary(enc_vocab_path, train_enc, enc_vocabulary_size, tokenizer)
    create_vocabulary(dec_vocab_path, train_dec, dec_vocabulary_size, tokenizer)

    # Create token ids for the training data.
    enc_train_ids_path = train_enc + (".ids%d" % enc_vocabulary_size)
    dec_train_ids_path = train_dec + (".ids%d" % dec_vocabulary_size)
    data_to_token_ids(train_enc, enc_train_ids_path, enc_vocab_path, tokenizer)
    data_to_token_ids(train_dec, dec_train_ids_path, dec_vocab_path, tokenizer)

    # Create token ids for the development data.
    enc_dev_ids_path = test_enc + (".ids%d" % enc_vocabulary_size)
    dec_dev_ids_path = test_dec + (".ids%d" % dec_vocabulary_size)
    data_to_token_ids(test_enc, enc_dev_ids_path, enc_vocab_path, tokenizer)
    data_to_token_ids(test_dec, dec_dev_ids_path, dec_vocab_path, tokenizer)

    return (enc_train_ids_path, dec_train_ids_path, enc_dev_ids_path, dec_dev_ids_path, enc_vocab_path, dec_vocab_path)
```

Figure 8.21: Code snippet for generating the vocabulary

Now let's actually implement the seq2seq model using TensorFlow.

Implementing the seq2seq model

In this section, we chatbot development:seq2seq model, building" will be performing the actual training using the seq2seq model. We will be using TensorFlow to implement the seq2seq model. Before getting into training, let's look into the hyper parameters configuration file, which you can access using this GitHub link: `https://github.com/jalajthanaki/Chatbot_tensorflow/blob/master/seq2seq.ini`.

Duringchatbot development:seq2seq model, building" training, our script uses these files and their parameters. The following parameters are in this configuration file:

- `Mode`: This can be either train or test
- `train_enc`: This contains the path of the training dataset for the encoder.
- `train_dec`: This contains the path of the training dataset for the decoder.
- `test_enc`: This contains the path of the testing dataset for the encoder.
- `test_dec`: This contains the path of the testing dataset for the decoder.
- `Working_directory`: This is the folder where we can store our checkpoints, vocabulary, and temporary data files
- `enc_vocab_size`: This number defines the vocabulary size for the encoder. We set 20,000 as the vocabulary size.
- `dec_vocab_size`: This number defines the vocabulary size for the decoder. We set 20,000 as the vocabulary size.

- `num_layers`: This indicates the number of LSTM layers. Here, we set it as 3.
- `layer_size`: This indicates the number of layers in the seq2seq model. We set it as 256.
- `steps_per_checkpoint`: At a checkpoint, the model's parameters are saved, the model is evaluated, and results are printed.
- `learning_rate`: This indicates how fast or how slow we train our model. We set the value to 0.5 for now.

Most of the preceding parameters can be changed in order to get the best possible results. During training, we need to set the Mode as train and run the following command:

```
$ python execute.py
```

Now it's time to understand what is inside the execute.py file. You can access this file using this GitHub link: `https://github.com/jalajthanaki/Chatbot_tensorflow/blob/master/execute.py`.

In this script, we call the TensorFlow API. This script can be divided into the following parts:

- Creating the model
- Training the model

Creating the model

We are using the `Seq2SeqModel()` function from TensorFlow here. This function reads the configuration file and uses the values defined in the configuration file. In order to store the train model, we use the `saver.restore()` function, and to get the status of the checkpoints we use the `get_checkpoint_state()` function. You can refer to the code snippet given in the following figure:

```
def create_model(session, forward_only):

  """Create model and initialize or load parameters"""
  model = seq2seq_model.Seq2SeqModel( gConfig['enc_vocab_size'], gConfig['dec_vocab_size'], _buckets, gConfig['layer_size'], gConfig['num_layers'], gConfig['max_gradient_norm'],
 gConfig['batch_size'], gConfig['learning_rate'], gConfig['learning_rate_decay_factor'], forward_only=forward_only)

  if 'pretrained_model' in gConfig:
      model.saver.restore(session,gConfig['pretrained_model'])
      return model

  ckpt = tf.train.get_checkpoint_state(gConfig['working_directory'])
  # the checkpoint filename has changed in recent versions of tensorflow
  checkpoint_suffix = ""
  if tf.__version__ > "0.12":
      checkpoint_suffix = ".index"
  if ckpt and tf.gfile.Exists(ckpt.model_checkpoint_path + checkpoint_suffix):
    print("Reading model parameters from %s" % ckpt.model_checkpoint_path)
    model.saver.restore(session, ckpt.model_checkpoint_path)
  else:
    print("Created model with fresh parameters.")
    session.run(tf.initialize_all_variables())
  return model
```

Figure 8.22: Code snippet for creating seq2seq model

Training the model

We defined the `train()` method inside the `execute.py` file. This function initializes the TensorFlow session and begins training. You can refer to the code snippet given in the following screenshot:

```
def train():
    # prepare dataset
    print("Preparing data in %s" % gConfig['working_directory'])
    enc_train, dec_train, enc_dev, dec_dev, _, _ = data_utils.prepare_custom_data(gConfig['working_directory'],gConfig['train_enc'],gConfig['train_dec'],gConfig['test_enc'],
gConfig['test_dec'],gConfig['enc_vocab_size'],gConfig['dec_vocab_size'])

    # Only allocate 2/3 of the gpu memory to allow for running gpu-based predictions while training:
    gpu_options = tf.GPUOptions(per_process_gpu_memory_fraction=0.666)
    config = tf.ConfigProto(gpu_options=gpu_options)
    config.gpu_options.allocator_type = 'BFC'

    with tf.Session(config=config) as sess:
        # Create model.
        print("Creating %d layers of %d units." % (gConfig['num_layers'], gConfig['layer_size']))
        model = create_model(sess, False)

        # Read data into buckets and compute their sizes.
        print ("Reading development and training data (limit: %d)."
               % gConfig['max_train_data_size'])
        dev_set = read_data(enc_dev, dec_dev)
        train_set = read_data(enc_train, dec_train, gConfig['max_train_data_size'])
        train_bucket_sizes = [len(train_set[b]) for b in xrange(len(_buckets))]
        train_total_size = float(sum(train_bucket_sizes))

        # A bucket scale is a list of increasing numbers from 0 to 1 that we'll use
        # to select a bucket. Length of [scale[i], scale[i+1]] is proportional to
        # the size if i-th training bucket, as used later.
        train_buckets_scale = [sum(train_bucket_sizes[:i + 1]) / train_total_size
                               for i in xrange(len(train_bucket_sizes))]
```

Figure 8.23: Code snippet for training the model

Now it's time to train the model. When we execute the `python execute.py` command, you will see the output given in the following screenshot:

```
jalaj@jalaj:~/PycharmProjects/Chatbot_tensorflow$ ls
data  data_utils.py  env_setup.sh  execute.py  __init__.py  neuralconvo.ini  README.md  seq2seq.ini  seq2seq_model.py  seq2seq_serve.ini  ui  working_dir
jalaj@jalaj:~/PycharmProjects/Chatbot_tensorflow$ python execute.py
I tensorflow/stream_executor/dso_loader.cc:128] successfully opened CUDA library libcublas.so locally
I tensorflow/stream_executor/dso_loader.cc:128] successfully opened CUDA library libcudnn.so locally
I tensorflow/stream_executor/dso_loader.cc:128] successfully opened CUDA library libcufft.so locally
I tensorflow/stream_executor/dso_loader.cc:128] successfully opened CUDA library libcuda.so.1 locally
I tensorflow/stream_executor/dso_loader.cc:128] successfully opened CUDA library libcurand.so locally

>> Mode : train

Preparing data in working_dir/
Tokenizing data in data/train.enc
  tokenizing line 100000
Tokenizing data in data/train.dec
  tokenizing line 100000
Tokenizing data in data/test.enc
I tensorflow/stream_executor/cuda/cuda_gpu_executor.cc:937] successful NUMA node read from SysFS had negative value (-1), but there must be at least one NUMA node, so re
turning NUMA node zero
I tensorflow/core/common_runtime/gpu/gpu_device.cc:885] Found device 0 with properties:
name: GeForce GTX 1060 6GB
major: 6 minor: 1 memoryClockRate (GHz) 1.7085
pciBusID 0000:01:00.0
Total memory: 5.92GiB
Free memory: 5.20GiB
I tensorflow/core/common_runtime/gpu/gpu_device.cc:906] DMA: 0
I tensorflow/core/common_runtime/gpu/gpu_device.cc:916] 0:   Y
I tensorflow/core/common_runtime/gpu/gpu_device.cc:975] Creating TensorFlow device (/gpu:0) -> (device: 0, name: GeForce GTX 1060 6GB, pci bus id: 0000:01:00.0)
Creating 3 layers of 256 units.
```

Figure 8.24: Training of the seq2seq model using TensorFlow

Here, training has been performed on a GPU. I trained this model for 3 hours. I have trained this model for 15,000 checkpoints. You can refer to the following screesnhot:

```
global step 14100 learning rate 0.5000 step-time 0.12 perplexity 17.55
  eval: bucket 0 perplexity 1120.93
  eval: bucket 1 perplexity 692.78
  eval: bucket 2 perplexity 906.21
  eval: bucket 3 perplexity 962.42
global step 14400 learning rate 0.5000 step-time 0.12 perplexity 17.05
  eval: bucket 0 perplexity 349.57
  eval: bucket 1 perplexity 1054.40
  eval: bucket 2 perplexity 828.66
  eval: bucket 3 perplexity 958.57
global step 14700 learning rate 0.5000 step-time 0.12 perplexity 17.19
  eval: bucket 0 perplexity 1049.27
  eval: bucket 1 perplexity 1078.80
  eval: bucket 2 perplexity 1014.25
  eval: bucket 3 perplexity 949.07
global step 15000 learning rate 0.5000 step-time 0.12 perplexity 16.94
  eval: bucket 0 perplexity 423.88
  eval: bucket 1 perplexity 707.58
  eval: bucket 2 perplexity 1055.38
  eval: bucket 3 perplexity 952.69
global step 15300 learning rate 0.5000 step-time 0.12 perplexity 16.58
  eval: bucket 0 perplexity 915.01
  eval: bucket 1 perplexity 1094.83
  eval: bucket 2 perplexity 1001.52
  eval: bucket 3 perplexity 1000.35
```

Figure 8.25: Output of the seq2seq training

On a CPU, training will take a lot of time, so I have also uploaded pre-trained models for you to use. You can download them by using this GitHub link: `https://github.com/jalajthanaki/Chatbot_tensorflow/tree/master/working_dir`.

Now it's time to understand the testing metrics that help us evaluate the trained model.

Testing the revised approach

In this section, we will perform testing of the revised approach. Before performing actual testing and seeing how good or bad the chatbot conversation is, we need to understand the basic testing metrics that we will be using for this approach and for the best approach. These testing metrics help us evaluate the model accuracy. Let's understand the testing metrics first, and then we will move on to the testing of the revised approach.

Understanding the testing metrics

In this section, we need to understand the following testing metrics:

- Perplexity
- Loss

Perplexity

In the NLP domain, perplexity is also referred to as per-word perplexity. Perplexity is a measurement of how well a trained model predicts the output for unseen data. It is also used to compare probability models. A low perplexity indicates that the probability distribution is good at predicting the sample. Even during training, you can see that for each checkpoint, perplexity is decreasing. Ideally, when there is no change in perplexity, we need to stop the training. During the training of the seq2seq model, I stopped training after 3 hours, so when you train the model from your end you can wait till the perplexity stops decreasing further.

Perplexity is using the concept of entropy. If you want to know about perplexity, then you can refer to `https://www.youtube.com/watch?v=BAN3NB_SNHY`. Per-word perplexity is based on entropy. So, in order to understand entropy, you can refer to the following links:

- `https://www.youtube.com/watch?v=Bd15qhUrKCI`
- `https://www.youtube.com/watch?v=K-rQ8KnmmH8`
- `https://www.youtube.com/watch?v=ICKBWIkfeJ8&list=PLAwxTw4SYaPkQXg8TkVdIvYv4HfLG7SiH`

Once you understand entropy, it will be easy for you to understand the equation of perplexity. Refer to the equation given in the following figure:

$$e^{loss} = e^{-\frac{1}{N}\sum_{i=1}^{N} \ln P_{target\ i}}$$

Figure 8.26: Equation of perplexity

Image source: https://www.tensorflow.org/tutorials/recurrent

Here, N is the number of samples and P is a probability function. We are calculating entropy using the natural logarithm function. Now let's look at another testing metric.

Loss

Training loss indicates the direction in which the training progresses. Usually, when we start training, the value of loss is high and training accuracy is low, but during the training, the value of loss goes down and the training accuracy goes up. There are many error functions that are used in DL algorithms. Here, we are using cross-entropy as a loss function. Cross-entropy and log loss are slightly different depending on the context, but in machine learning, when calculating error rates between 0 and 1, they are the same thing. You can refer to the equation given in the following figure:

Code

```
def CrossEntropy(yHat, y):
    if yHat == 1:
      return -log(y)
    else:
      return -log(1 - y)
```

Math

In binary classification, where the number of classes M equals 2, cross-entropy can be calculated as:

$$-(y\log(p) + (1-y)\log(1-p))$$

If $M > 2$ (i.e. multiclass classification), we calculate a separate loss for each class label per observation and sum the result.

$$-\sum_{c=1}^{M} y_{o,c}\log(p_{o,c})$$

Note

- M - number of classes (dog, cat, fish)
- log - the natural log
- y - binary indicator (0 or 1) if class label c is the correct classification for observation o
- p - predicted probability observation o is of class c

Figure 8.27: Equation for cross-entropy

Image source: http://ml-cheatsheet.readthedocs.io/en/latest/loss_functions.html#cross-entropy

If you want to explore the cross-entropy loss function, then you can refer to: `http://neuralnetworksanddeeplearning.com/chap3.html`.

We haven't gone into great mathematical detail here because just by tracking the training process, you will get to know whether the value of loss is increasing or decreasing. If it is decreasing over the period of training time, then the training is moving in the right direction. This is applicable to perplexity as well. Initially, the perplexity value is huge, but during training it gradually falls down and at some point it neither increases nor decreases. At that time, we need to stop the training. Now let's test the revised chatbot.

Testing the revised version of the chatbot

In this section, we will be performing testing of the revised chatbot. I have trained it on a GPU for only 3 hours; now let's check how much our chatbot can tell us. For testing, we need to make a small change in the `seq2seq.ini` configuration file. We need to set *value of mode as test* and then execute the `python execute.py` command.

After executing the given command, you will get the output given in the following figure:

```
jalaj@jalaj:~/PycharmProjects/Chatbot_tensorflow$ python execute.py
I tensorflow/stream_executor/dso_loader.cc:128] successfully opened CUDA library libcublas.so locally
I tensorflow/stream_executor/dso_loader.cc:128] successfully opened CUDA library libcudnn.so locally
I tensorflow/stream_executor/dso_loader.cc:128] successfully opened CUDA library libcufft.so locally
I tensorflow/stream_executor/dso_loader.cc:128] successfully opened CUDA library libcuda.so.1 locally
I tensorflow/stream_executor/dso_loader.cc:128] successfully opened CUDA library libcurand.so locally

>> Mode : test

I tensorflow/stream_executor/cuda/cuda_gpu_executor.cc:937] successful NUMA node read from SysFS had negative value (-1), but there must be at least one NUMA node, so re
turning NUMA node zero
I tensorflow/core/common_runtime/gpu/gpu_device.cc:885] Found device 0 with properties:
name: GeForce GTX 1060 6GB
major: 6 minor: 1 memoryClockRate (GHz) 1.7085
pciBusID 0000:01:00.0
Total memory: 5.92GiB
Free memory: 5.20GiB
I tensorflow/core/common_runtime/gpu/gpu_device.cc:906] DMA: 0
I tensorflow/core/common_runtime/gpu/gpu_device.cc:916] 0:   Y
I tensorflow/core/common_runtime/gpu/gpu_device.cc:975] Creating TensorFlow device (/gpu:0) -> (device: 0, name: GeForce GTX 1060 6GB, pci bus id: 0000:01:00.0)
WARNING:tensorflow:From /home/jalaj/PycharmProjects/Chatbot_tensorflow/seq2seq_model.py:174 in __init__.: all_variables (from tensorflow.python.ops.variables) is depreca
ted and will be removed after 2017-03-02.
Instructions for updating:
Please use tf.global_variables instead.
Reading model parameters from working_dir/seq2seq.ckpt-15300
> hi
What ?
> where are you going?
I ' m going to see you .
> how are you feeling today?
I ' m fine .
> What is your name?
_UNK .
> Can you tell me where you have been?
I ' m sorry .
> tell me your favorite word
I ' m sorry .
> It's nice talking with you
You ' re a _UNK .
> What a nice whether..!

> How are you toady?
I ' m fine .
> |
```

Figure 8.28: Output of testing revised approach

If you train for a longer period of time, then you will get a more impressive result. I feel that DL algorithms help us if we want to build the chatbot using the generative-based approach. Now let's discuss how we can improvise this revised approach.

Problems with the revised approach

In this section, we will be discussing what the problems with the revised approach are. Is there any way in which we can optimize the revised approach? So first of all, let's discuss the area of improvement so that during the upcoming approach, we can focus on that particular point.

Some of the points that I want to highlight are as follows:

- In the previous version of our chatbot there was a lack of reasoning, which means the chatbot couldn't answer the question by applying basic reasoning to it. This is what we need to improve.
- Let me give you an example. Suppose I tell chatbot a story: *John is in the kitchen. Daniel is in the bathroom.* After that, say, I ask the chatbot this question: *Where is John?* The chatbot that we have built so far will not be able to answer this simple question. We as humans answer these kinds of questions well.
- We try to implement this kind of functionality in our next approach so that we can enable some features of AI in the chatbot

Let's look at the important concepts that can help us build the AI-enabled chatbot.

Understanding key concepts to solve existing problems

The Facebook AI research group published a paper that proposed a Memory Network that can prove that the machine can also answer questions that are based on reasoning. You can certainly refer to this paper titled, Towards AI-Complete question answering: A set of prerequisite toy tasks. The link is: `https://arxiv.org/pdf/1502.05698.pdf`. You can also refer to this paper on the memory network at: `https://arxiv.org/pdf/1410.3916.pdf`.

Here, we will be using the bAbI dataset and train the model based on the improvised memory network. Once training is done, we will check whether our chatbot can answer questions based on using the simple reasoning ability or not. We will be recreating the result of the Facebook research paper. Before we move to the implementation part, we need to understand what memory networks are and how we can build a system that will use logic to answer questions. So, let's look at memory networks briefly.

Memory networks

In this section, we will explore the memory network so that we can understand what is actually happening behind the scenes when we implement it in the upcoming section.

Basically, in the LSTM network, memory is encoded by using hidden states and weights. These hidden states and weights are too small for extremely long sequences of data, be that a book or a movie. So, in a language translation application, multiple LSTM stats are used along with the attention mechanism in order to choose the appropriate work for translation that fits the context. Facebook researchers have developed another strategy called a memory network that outperforms LSTMs for the question-answer system.

The basic idea behind the memory network was to allow the neural network to use an external data structure as memory storage, and it learns where to retrieve the required memory from this external memory structure in a supervised way. You can refer to the architecture of the memory network given in the following figure:

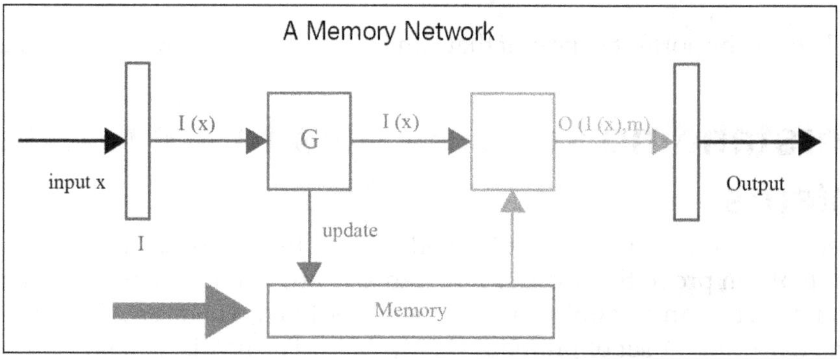

Figure 8.29: Architecture of memory network

When it came to answering questions from the little data that was generated, the information was pretty easy to handle with the memory network, but in the real world, having the data handle long dependency relations is a challenging task. On Kaggle, there was a competition called The Allen AI Science Challenge in which the winner used a special variation of the memory network called a dynamic memory network (DMN), and that is what we are using to build our chatbot.

Dynamic memory network (DMN)

The architecture of DMN is given in the following figure:

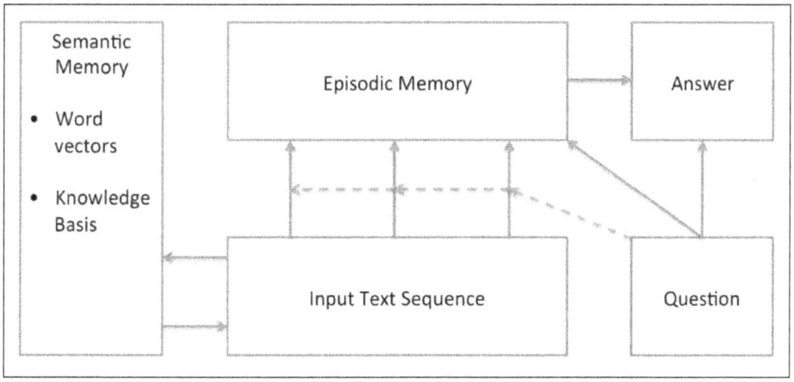

Figure 8.30: Architecture of DMN

Image source: https://yerevann.github.io/public/2016-02-06/dmn-high-level.png

The architecture of DMN defines two types of memory, which are as follows:

- Semantic memory: We are using the pre-trained glove model that will generate vectors for input data. These vectors are the input to our DMN model and are used as semantic memory.
- Episodic memory: This memory contains other knowledge. The inspiration for this memory came from the hippocampus function of our brain. It's able to retrieve temporal states that are triggered by a response, such as an image or a sound. We will see the usage of this episodic memory in a bit.

These are some important modules that we need to understand:

- Input module
- Question module
- Episodic memory module

Before I start explaining the modules, please refer to the following figure for better understanding:

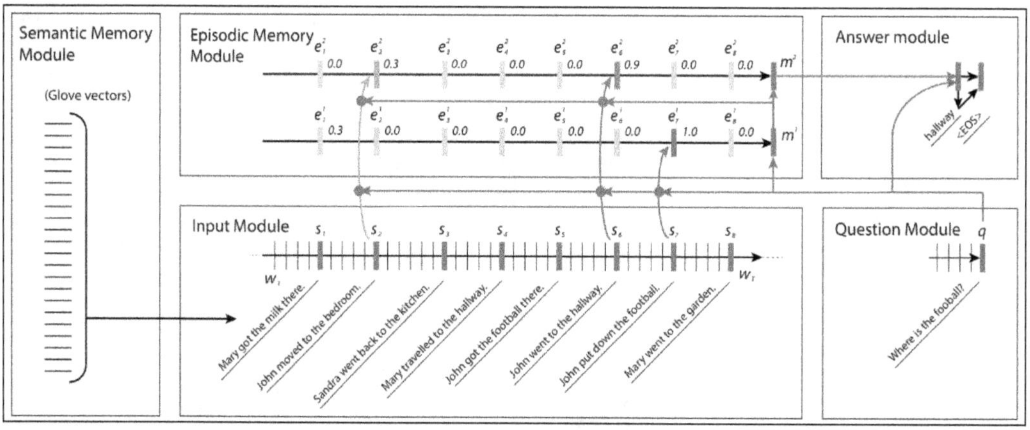

Figure 8.31: Details on each DMN module

Image source: https://yerevann.github.io/public/2016-02-06/dmn-details.png

Input module

The input module is a GRU (Gated Recurrent Unit) that runs on a sequence of word vectors. A GRU cell is kind of like an LSTM cell, but it's more computationally efficient since it has only two gates and doesn't use a memory unit. The two gates control when the content is updated and when it's erased. There are only two tasks GRU is performing: one is *Update* and the other is *Reset*. You can refer to the following figure depicting LSTM and GRU:

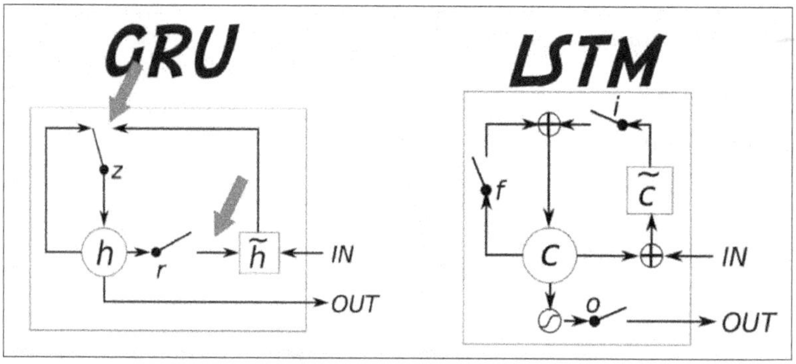

Figure 8.32: Illustration of LSTM and GRU

Image source: https://cdn-images-1.medium.com/max/1200/0*1udenjz1XCZ5cHU4

The hidden stats of the input module represent the input process in the form of a vector so far. It outputs hidden states after every sentence, and these outputs are called facts in the paper because they represent the essence of what is fed. You might want to know how the hidden state is calculated in GRU. For that, you can refer to the following equation:

Ht = GRU(Xt, ht-1)

Here, Ht is the current timestep, ht-1 is the previous timestep, and Xt is the given word vector. The preceding equation is the simple format of the GRU hidden stat calculation. You can see more detailed and complex equations in the following figure:

GRU Definition: Assume each time step has an input x_t and a hidden state h_t. We will abbreviate the below computation with $h_t = GRU(x_t, h_{t-1})$:

$$z_t = \sigma\left(W^{(z)}x_t + U^{(z)}h_{t-1} + b^{(z)}\right); \qquad r_t = \sigma\left(W^{(r)}x_t + U^{(r)}h_{t-1} + b^{(r)}\right) \quad (1)$$

$$\tilde{h}_t = \tanh\left(Wx_t + r_t \circ Uh_{t-1} + b^{(h)}\right); \qquad h_t = z_t \circ h_{t-1} + (1 - z_t) \circ \tilde{h}_t, \quad (2)$$

where $\circ$ is an element-wise product, $W^{(z)}, W^{(r)}, W \in \mathbb{R}^{n_H \times n_I}$ and $U^{(z)}, U^{(r)}, U \in \mathbb{R}^{n_H \times n_H}$. The dimensions n are hyperparameters.

Figure 8.33: Equation for calculating the hidden state in GRU

Image source: https://yerevann.github.io/public/2016-02-06/gru.png

In this equation, with the help of the given word vector and the previous timestep vector, we compute the current timestep vector. The update gave us a single layer neural network. We sum up the matrix multiplications and add bias terms to it. Then, the sigmoid squashes it to a list of values between 0 and 1, and that is our output vector. We do this twice with different sets of weights, and then we use the reset gate that will learn to ignore the past timesteps when necessary. For example, if the next sentence has nothing to do with those that came before it, the update gate is similar in that it can learn to ignore the current timestep entirely. Maybe the current sentence has nothing to do with the answer whereas previous ones did.

Question module

This module processes the question word by word and outputs a vector using the same GRU as the input module and with the same weight. We need to code for input statements (input data) and for the question that we will ask. We can code them by implementing embedding layers for them. Now we need to create an episodic memory representation for both.

Episodic memory

As I've described earlier, the concept of episodic memory derives from the hippocampus function of our brain. Both fact and question vectors extracted from the input and enter to the episodic memory module. It is composed of two nested GRUs. The inner GRU generates what are called episodes. It does this by passing over the facts from the input module. When updating its inner state, it takes into account the output of an attention function on the current fact. The attention function gives a score between 0 and 1 to each fact and so the GRU ignores facts with low scores. During training, after each full pass on all the available facts, the inner GRU outputs an episode, which is then fed to the outer GRU. We need multiple episodes so that our model can learn what part of a sentence it should pay attention to. During the second pass, the GRU realizes that something else is also important in the sentence. With the help of multiple passes, we can gather increasingly relevant information.

This is a brief explanation of DMN. You can refer to this great article as well: `https://yerevann.github.io/2016/02/05/implementing-dynamic-memory-networks/`.

Now let's look at the implementation for this.

The best approach

We have covered the entire concept that can help us implement the DMN-based chatbot. In order to implement this approach, we will be using Keras with the TensorFlow backend. Without wasting any time, we will jump to the implementation section. You can refer to the code for this approach using this GitHub link: `https://github.com/jalajthanaki/Chatbot_based_on_bAbI_dataset_using_Keras`.

Implementing the best approach

Here, we will train our model on the given bAbI task 1 dataset. First of all, we need to parse the stories and build the vocabulary. You can refer to the code in the following figure:

```
def vectorize_stories(data, word_idx, story_maxlen, query_maxlen):
    X = []
    Xq = []
    Y = []
    for story, query, answer in data:
        x = [word_idx[w] for w in story]
        xq = [word_idx[w] for w in query]
        # let's not forget that index 0 is reserved
        y = np.zeros(len(word_idx) + 1)
        y[word_idx[answer]] = 1
        X.append(x)
        Xq.append(xq)
        Y.append(y)
    return (pad_sequences(X, maxlen=story_maxlen),
            pad_sequences(Xq, maxlen=query_maxlen), np.array(Y))

try:
    path = get_file('babi-tasks-v1-2.tar.gz', origin='https://s3.amazonaws.com/text-datasets/babi_tasks_1-20_v1-2.tar.gz')
except:
    print('Error downloading dataset, please download it manually:\n'
          '$ wget http://www.thespermwhale.com/jaseweston/babi/tasks_1-20_v1-2.tar.gz\n'
          '$ mv tasks_1-20_v1-2.tar.gz ~/.keras/datasets/babi-tasks-v1-2.tar.gz')
    raise
tar = tarfile.open(path)

challenges = {
    # QA1 with 10,000 samples
    'single_supporting_fact_10k': 'tasks_1-20_v1-2/en-10k/qa1_single-supporting-fact_{}.txt',
    # QA2 with 10,000 samples
    'two_supporting_facts_10k': 'tasks_1-20_v1-2/en-10k/qa2_two-supporting-facts_{}.txt',
}
challenge_type = 'single_supporting_fact_10k'
challenge = challenges[challenge_type]

print('Extracting stories for the challenge:', challenge_type)
train_stories = get_stories(tar.extractfile(challenge.format('train')))
test_stories = get_stories(tar.extractfile(challenge.format('test')))

vocab = set()
for story, q, answer in train_stories + test_stories:
    vocab |= set(story + q + [answer])
vocab = sorted(vocab)

# Reserve 0 for masking via pad_sequences
vocab_size = len(vocab) + 1
story_maxlen = max(map(len, (x for x, _, _ in train_stories + test_stories)))
query_maxlen = max(map(len, (x for _, x, _ in train_stories + test_stories)))

print('-')
print('Vocab size:', vocab_size, 'unique words')
print('Story max length:', story_maxlen, 'words')
print('Query max length:', query_maxlen, 'words')
print('Number of training stories:', len(train_stories))
print('Number of test stories:', len(test_stories))
```

Figure 8.34: Code snippet for parsing stories and build vocabulary

We can initialize our model and set its loss function as a categorical cross-entropy with stochastic gradient descent implementation using RMSprop in Keras. You can refer to the following screenshot:

```
# the original paper uses a matrix multiplication for this reduction step.
# we choose to use a RNN instead.
#answer = LSTM(lstm_size, return_sequences=True)(answer)  # Generate tensors of shape 32
#answer = Dropout(0.3)(answer)
answer = LSTM(lstm_size)(answer)  # Generate tensors of shape 32
answer = Dropout(0.3)(answer)
answer = Dense(vocab_size)(answer)  # (samples, vocab_size)
# we output a probability distribution over the vocabulary
answer = Activation('softmax')(answer)

# build the final model
model = Model([input_sequence, question], answer)
model.compile(optimizer='rmsprop', loss='categorical_crossentropy',
              metrics=['accuracy'])

if load_model == 1:
    model = keras.models.load_model('model.h5')

if train_model == 1:
    # train, batch_size = 32 and epochs = 120
    model.fit([inputs_train, queries_train], answers_train, batch_size, train_epochs,
          validation_data=([inputs_test, queries_test], answers_test))
    model.save('model.h5')
```

Figure 8.35: Code snippet for building the model

Before training, we need to set a hyperparameter. With the help of the value of the hyperparameter script, we will decide whether to run the script in the training mode or the testing mode. You can see all the hyperparameters that we need to set during training in the following figure:

```
train_model = 1
train_epochs = 100
load_model = 0
batch_size = 32
lstm_size = 64
test_qualitative = 1
user_questions = 0
```

Figure 8.36: Hyperparameter values for training

Here we have used three hyperparameters. We can experiment with them. Let's discuss them for a minute:

- train_epochs: This parameter indicates the number of times the training examples complete a forward pass and backward pass in a neural network. One epoch means one forward pass and one backward pass of the training example. Here we are setting train_epochs 100 times. You can increase it but then the training time also increases.

- batch_size: This parameter indicates the number of training examples in one forward and backward pass. The higher batch size needs more memory so we have set this value to 32. If you have more memory available then you can increase the batch size. Please see the simple example given in the following information box.
- lstm_size: This parameter indicates the number of LSTM cells present in our neural network. You can decrease and increase the number of LSTM cells. In our case, less than 64 LSTM cells will not give us good output so I have set lstm_size to 64.

> If you have 1000 training examples and your batch size is 500 then it will take 2 iterations to complete 1 epoch.

I have trained this model on a GPU. If you are not using a GPU then it may take a lot of time. You can start training by executing this command: `python main.py`. The output of the training is given in the following figure:

```
Epoch 95/100
10000/10000 [==============================] - 1s - loss: 0.1182 - acc: 0.9581 - val_loss: 0.6518 - val_acc: 0.8330
Epoch 96/100
10000/10000 [==============================] - 1s - loss: 0.1117 - acc: 0.9612 - val_loss: 0.6448 - val_acc: 0.8350
Epoch 97/100
10000/10000 [==============================] - 1s - loss: 0.1068 - acc: 0.9608 - val_loss: 0.6427 - val_acc: 0.8440
Epoch 98/100
10000/10000 [==============================] - 1s - loss: 0.1115 - acc: 0.9627 - val_loss: 0.6643 - val_acc: 0.8280
Epoch 99/100
10000/10000 [==============================] - 1s - loss: 0.1058 - acc: 0.9649 - val_loss: 0.6466 - val_acc: 0.8300
Epoch 100/100
10000/10000 [==============================] - 1s - loss: 0.1085 - acc: 0.9640 - val_loss: 0.6606 - val_acc: 0.8440
```

Figure 8.37: Code snippet for the training output

Once we train the model, we can load and test it. There are two testing modes available:

- Random testing mode
- User interactive testing mode

Random testing mode

In this mode, the script itself will load a random story and give you its answer. You can see the value of the hyperparameters in the following figure:

```
train_model = 0
train_epochs = 100
load_model = 1
batch_size = 32
lstm_size = 64
test_qualitative = 1
user_questions = 0
```

figure 8.38, Value of hyperparameters for random testing mode.

For testing, execute the `python main.py` command and you can see the testing results. These results have been shown in the following figure:

```
Qualitative Test Result Analysis
John travelled to the hallway . Mary journeyed to the bathroom . Where is John ? | Prediction: hallway | Ground Truth: hallway
```

Figure 8.39: Result of a random testing mode

User interactive testing mode

In this mode, if the testing user can give their own story and ask their own question, the chatbot will generate the answer to that question. You just need to remember that before every word, you need to provide space. You can refer to the value of the hyperparameter for the user interactive testing mode in the following figure:

```
train_model = 0
train_epochs = 100
load_model = 1
batch_size = 32
lstm_size = 64
test_qualitative = 0
user_questions = 1
```

Figure 8.40: Values of hyperparameters for the user interactive testing mode

For testing, execute the `python main.py` command and you can see the testing results. These results are shown in the following figure:

```
--------------------------------------------------------------------------------------
Custom User Queries (Make sure there are spaces before each word)
--------------------------------------------------------------------------------------
Please input a story
John travelled to the bathroom . Mary travelled to the kitchen .
Please input a query
Where is Mary ?
['John', 'travelled', 'to', 'the', 'bathroom', '.', 'Mary', 'travelled', 'to', 'the', 'kitchen', '.'] ['Where', 'is', 'Mary', '?']
Result
John travelled to the bathroom . Mary travelled to the kitchen . Where is Mary ? | Prediction: kitchen
--------------------------------------------------------------------------------------
```

Figure 8.41: Result of the user interactive testing mode

If you want to test all other tasks, then you can use this web application: `https://ethancaballero.pythonanywhere.com/`.

This approach gives us up to 92 to 95% accuracy. This approach helps us build AI-enabled chatbots.

Discussing the hybrid approach

In a real-life scenario, in order to build the chatbot we can also combine some of the techniques described here. As per the business needs we can use a hybrid approach.

Let's take an example. Suppose you are building a chatbot for the finance domain. If a user asks for the available balance in his account then we just need a rule-based system, which can query the database and generate the account balance details for that user. If a user asks how he can transfer money from one account to the other account, the chatbot can help the user by generating step-by-step information on how to transfer money. Here, we will use the deep learning-based generative approach. We should have one system that includes a rule-based engine as well as a deep learning algorithm to generate the best possible output. In this system, a user's question first goes to the rule-based system. If that question's answer can be generated by the rule-based system, then the answer will be passed to the end user. If the answer is not generated by a rule-based system, then the question will pass further on to the deep learning algorithm and it will generate the answer. Finally, the end-user will see the response to his question.

Summary

In this chapter, we referred to a different dataset in order to make a chatbot. You learned about the rule-based approach that can be used if you don't have any datasets. You also learned about the open and closed domains. After that, we used the retrieval-based approach in order to build the basic version of a chatbot. In the revised approach, we used TensorFlow. This revised approach is great for us because it saves time compared to the basic approach. We implemented Google's neural Conversational Model paper on the Cornell Movie-Dialogs dataset. For the best approach, we built a model that used the Facebook bAbI dataset and built the basic reasoning functionality that helped us generate good results for our chatbot. Although the training time for the revised and best approaches are really long, those who want to train the model on the cloud platform can choose to do so. So far, I like Amazon Web Services (AWS) and the Google Cloud platform. I also uploaded a pre-trained model to my GitHub repository so you could recreate the results. If you are a beginner and want to make a really good chatbot, then Google's API.AI is a good chatbot development platform. It is now known as Dialogflow and is available at: `https://dialogflow.com/`. You can also refer to the IBM Watson API at: `https://www.ibm.com/watson/how-to-build-a-chatbot/`. These APIs can help you a great deal in building a chatbot; plus it requires less coding knowledge.

In the next chapter, we will be building a computer vision-based application that will help us identify named objects present in images and videos. This application will detect objects in real time. The object-detection application is used to build self-driving cars, robots, and so on, so keep reading!

9

Building a Real-Time Object Recognition App

In this chapter, we will build an application that can detect objects. This application will help us recognize the object present in an image or a video feed. We will be using real-time input, such as a live video stream from our webcam, and our real-time object detection application will detect the objects present in the video stream. We will be using a live video stream, which is the main reason why this kind of object detection is called **Real-Time Object Detection**. In this chapter, we will be using the **Transfer Learning** methodology to build Real-Time Object Detection. I will explain Transfer Learning in detail during the course of the chapter.

In this chapter, we will cover the following topics:

- Introducing the problem statement
- Understanding the dataset
- Transfer Learning
- Setting up the coding environment
- Features engineering for the baseline model
- Selecting the **Machine Learning** (ML) algorithm
- Building the baseline model
- Understanding the testing metrics
- Testing the baseline model
- Problems with the existing approach

- How to optimize the existing approach
    - Understanding the process for optimization
- Implementing the revised approach
    - Testing the revised approach
    - Understanding problems with the revised approach
- The best approach
    - Implementing the best approach
- Summary

Introducing the problem statement

In this chapter, we will be building an object detection application. We won't just be detecting objects, but we will be building the application that detects the objects in real time. This application can be used in self-driving cars, for segregation tasks in the agricultural field, or even in the robotics field. Let's understand our goal and what we are actually building.

We want to build an application in which we will provide the live webcam video stream or the live video stream as the input. Our application will use pre-trained Machine Learning models, which will help us predict the objects that appear in the video. This means that, if there is a person in the video, then our application can identify the person as a person. If the video contains a chair or a cup or a cell phone, then our application should identify all these objects in the correct manner. So, our main goal in this chapter is to build an application that can detect the objects in images and videos. In this chapter, you will also learn the concept of Transfer Learning. All our approaches are based on Deep Learning techniques.

In the next section, we will be discussing the dataset.

Understanding the dataset

In this section, we will cover the dataset on which the Deep Learning models have been trained. There are two datasets that are heavily used when we are trying to build the object detection application, and those datasets are as follows:

- The COCO dataset
- The PASCAL VOC dataset

We will look at each of the datasets one by one.

The COCO dataset

COCO stands for Common object in context. So, the short form for this dataset is the COCO dataset. Many tech giants, such as Google, Facebook, Microsoft, and so on are using COCO data to build amazing applications for object detection, object segmentation, and so on. You can find details regarding this dataset at this official web page:

`http://cocodataset.org/#home`

The COCO dataset is a large-scale object detection, segmentation, and captioning dataset. In this dataset, there are a total of 330,000 images, of which more than 200,000 are labeled. These images contain 1.5 million object instances with 80 object categories. All the labeled images have five different captions; so, our machine learning approach is able to generalize the object detection and segmentation effectively.

By using COCO Explorer, we can explore the COCO dataset. You can use the `http://cocodataset.org/#explore` URL to explore the dataset. COCO Explorer is great user interface. You just need to select objects tags such as *I want to see images with a person, a bicycle, and a bus in the picture* and the explorer provides you images with a person, a bicycle, and a bus in it. You can refer to the following figure:

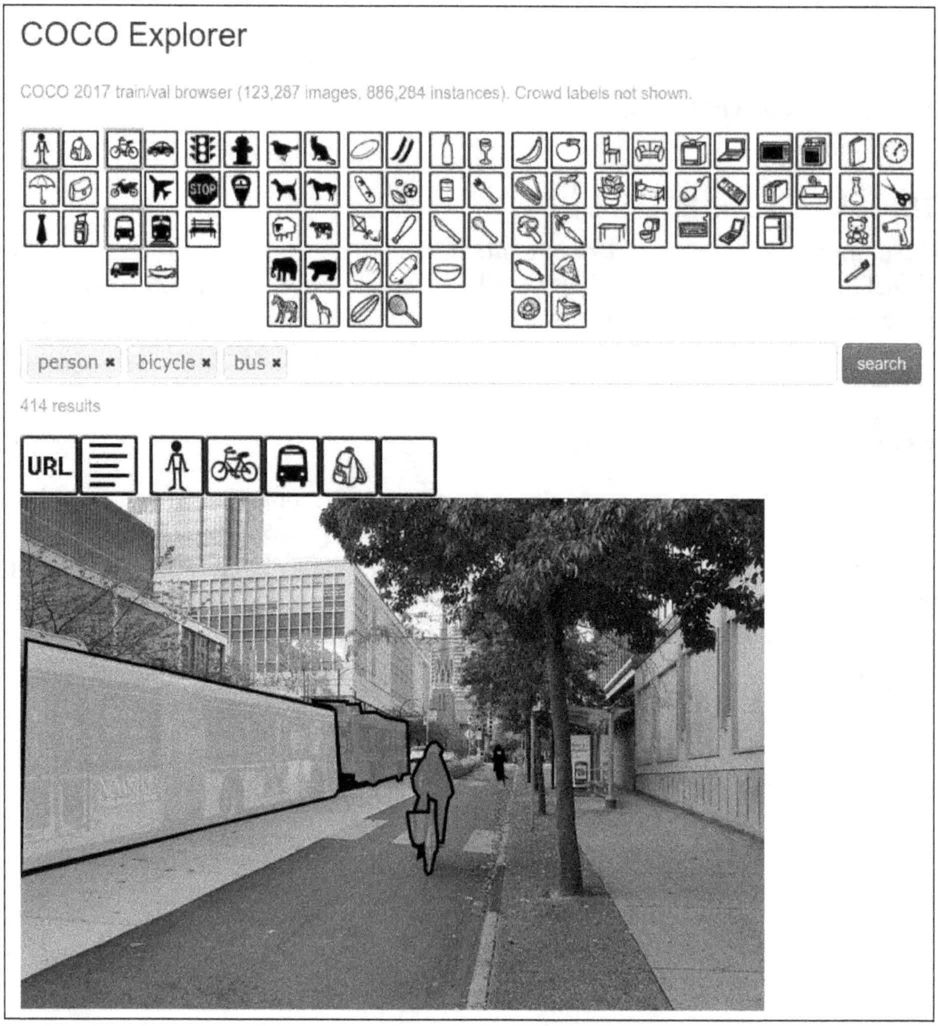

Figure 9.1: COCO Dataset explorer snippet

In each image, the proper object boundary has been provided for each of the major objects. This is the main reason why this dataset is great if you want to build your own computer vision application from scratch.

Here, we are not downloading the dataset because if we need to train the models from scratch on this dataset, then it will require a lot of time and lots of GPUs in order to get good accuracy. So, we will be using a pre-trained model, and using Transfer Learning, we will implement real-time object detection. Now let's move on to the PASCAL VOC dataset.

The PASCAL VOC dataset

PASCAL stands for Pattern Analysis, Statistical Modeling, and Computational Learning and VOC stands for Visual Object Classes. In this dataset, images are tagged for 20 classes for object detection. Action classes and person layout taster tagging are available as well. In the person layout taster tagging, the bounding box is all about the label of each part of a person (head, hands, feet). You can refer to the details of this dataset at `http://host.robots.ox.ac.uk/pascal/VOC/voc2012/index.html`.

PASCAL VOC classes

Images have been categorized into four major classes:

- Person
- Animal
- Vehicle
- Indoor

Each image is tagged with the preceding major classes, plus there are specific tags given to the objects in the images. Each of the preceding four categories has specific tags, which I have described in the following list:

- **Person**: person
- **Animal**: bird, cat, cow, dog, horse, sheep
- **Vehicle**: aero plane, bicycle, boat, bus, car, motorbike, train
- **Indoor**: bottle, chair, dining table, potted plant, sofa, tv/monitor

You can refer to the following figure, which will help you understand the tagging in this PASCAL VOC dataset:

Figure 9.2: PASCAL VOC tagged image example

As you can see in the preceding figure, two major classes have been tagged: Person and Animal. Specific tagging has been given for objects appearing in the image, that is, the person and the sheep. We are not downloading this dataset; we will be using the pre-trained model, which was trained using this dataset.

You have heard the terms Transfer Learning and pre-trained model a lot until now. Let's understand what they are.

Transfer Learning

In this section, we will look at what Transfer Learning is and how it is going to be useful for us as we build real-time object detection. We divide this section into the following parts:

- What is Transfer Learning?
- What is a pre-trained model?
- Why should we use a pre-trained model?
- How can we use the pre-trained model?

Let's start with the first question.

What is Transfer Learning?

We will be looking at the intuition behind Transfer Learning first and, then, we will cover its technical definition. Let me explain this concept through a simple teacher-student analogy. A teacher has many years of experience in teaching certain specific topics or subjects. Whatever information the teacher has, they deliver it to their students. So, the process of teaching is all about transferring knowledge from the teacher to the student. You can refer to the following figure:

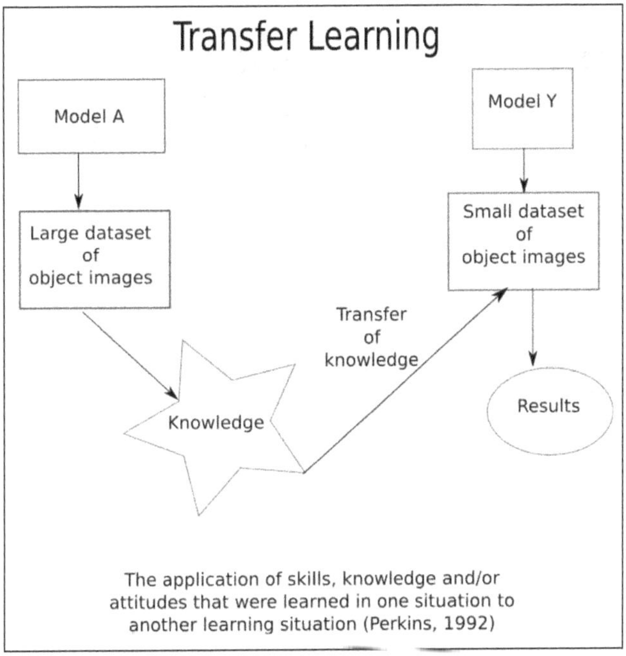

Figure 9.3: An overview of Transfer Learning

Now, remember this analogy; we will apply it to neural networks. When we train a neural network, it gains knowledge from the given dataset. This trained neural network has some weights that help it learn from the given dataset; after training, we can store these weights in a binary format. The weight that we have stored in the binary format can be extracted and then transferred to any other neural network. So, instead of training the neural network from scratch, we transfer the knowledge that the previously trained model gained. We are transferring the learned features to the new neural network and this will save a lot of our time. If we have an already trained model for a particular application, then we will apply it to the new but similar type of application, which in turn will help save time.

Now, it's time to define Transfer Learning in more technical terms. Transfer Learning is a research problem in Machine Learning that focuses on storing knowledge gained while solving a particular problem and applying it to a different but related problem. Sometimes, Transfer Learning is also called inductive transfer. Let's take a solid example to solidify your vision. If we build a Machine Learning model that gained knowledge while learning to recognize cars, it can also be applied when we are trying to recognize trucks. In this chapter, we are using Transfer Learning in order to build this real-time object detection application.

What is a pre-trained model?

I want to give you a simple explanation. A pre-trained model is one that is created and built by someone else to solve a specific problem. This means that we are using a model which has already been trained and plugging and playing with it. By using the pre-trained model, we can build new applications with similar domains.

Let me give you an example: suppose we want to create a self-driving car. In order to build it, our first step would be to build a decent object recognition system. You can spend a year or more to build the decent image and object recognition algorithm from scratch, or you can use a pre-trained model, such as the Google inception model or the YOLO model, which has been built using the PASCAL VOC dataset.

There are some advantages of using a pre-trained model, as follows:

- A pre-trained model may not give you 100% accuracy, but it saves a lot of effort.
- You can optimize the accuracy of the real problem on which you are working rather than making an algorithm from scratch; as we say sometimes, there is no need to reinvent the wheel.
- There are many libraries available that can help us save trained models, so we can load and use them easily whenever we need them.

Apart from the advantages the pre-trained models provide us, we need to understand other real reasons why we should use pre-trained models. So, let's discuss that in our next section.

Why should we use a pre-trained model?

When we are focusing on developing the existing algorithms in a different manner, our goal would be to build an algorithm that would outperform every other existing algorithm and making it more efficient. If we just focus on the research part, then this can be a nice approach to develop an efficient and accurate algorithm, but if your vision is to make an application and this algorithm is one part of the entire application, then you should focus on how quickly and efficiently you can build the application. Let's understand this through an example.

In this chapter, we want to build real-time object detection techniques. Now, my primary focus would be on building an application that would detect objects in real time. Not just that; I need to combine object detection and real-time tracking activity as well. If I ignore my primary goal and start making the new but effective object detection algorithm, then I will lose focus. My focus will be on building the entire real-time object detection application and not just a certain algorithm.

Sometimes, if we lose focus and try to build the algorithm from scratch, then it will take a lot of time. We will also waste our efforts, because some smart people in the world may have already built it for us. When we use this already developed algorithm, we will save time and focus on our application. After building a prototype of our actual application, we will have time to improvise it so that it can be used by many other people.

Let me tell you my story. I started building an image detection application that could be used in the security domain a couple of months ago. At that time, I didn't want to use a pre-trained model, because I wanted to explore how much effort it would take to build an algorithm from scratch. So, I started making one on my own. I tried several different algorithms, such as SVM, **Multilayer Perceptron** (**MLP**), and **Convolution Neural Network** (**CNN**) models, but I got really low accuracy. I lost focus on building an image-detection algorithm application that could be used in the security domain and just started focusing on making the algorithm better. After some time, I realized that it would be better if I used a pre-trained model with an optimization technique that would save my time and enable me to build a better solution. After this experience, I tried to explore the option of using Transfer Learning in problem statements I was solving, and if I found that there would be no scope for Transfer Learning, then I would make the algorithms from scratch; otherwise, I preferred using the pre-trained model. So, always explore all the options before building the algorithm. Understand the application usage and build your solution based on that. Suppose you are building your own self-driving car; then, real-time object detection would become an important part of a self-driving car, but it would be just a part of the entire application; therefore, it would be better if we were to use a pre-trained model to detect objects, so that we could use our time to build a quality self-driving car.

How can we use a pre-trained model?

Generally, a pre-trained model is in the binary format, which can be downloaded and then used in our applications. Some libraries, such as Keras, TensorFlow, Darknet, and so on, already have those pre-models that you can load and use with certain available APIs. These pre-trained networks have the ability to generalize images that are not part of the PASCAL VOC or COCO dataset via Transfer Learning. We can modify the pre-existing model by fine-tuning the model. We don't want to modify the weights too much, because it has been trained on a large dataset using lots of GPUs. The pre-trained model has the ability to generalize the prediction and classification of objects, so we know that this pre-trained model can be generalized enough to give us the best possible outcome. However, we can change some hyperparameters if we want to train the model from scratch. These parameters can be the learning rate, epochs, layer size, and so on. Let's discuss some of them:

- Learning Rate: Learning rate basically controls how much we should update the weights of neurons. We can use fixed learning rate, decreassing learning rate, momentum-based methods, or adaptive learning rates.
- Number of epochs: The number of epochs indicates the number of times the entire training dataset should pass through the neural network. We need to increase the number of epochs in order to decrease gap between the test error and the training error.
- Batch Size: For convolutional neural networks, mini-batch size is usually more preferable. A range of 16 to 128 is really a good choice to start from for convolutional neural networks.
- Activation function: As we know, activation functions introduce non-linearity to the model. ReLU activation function is the first choice for convolutional neural networks. You can use other activation functions, such as tanh, sigmoid, and so on, as well.
- Dropout for regularization: Regularization techniques are used to prevent overfitting problems. Dropout is the regularization technique for deep neural networks. In this technique, we are dropping out some of the neurons or units in neural networks. The drop out of neurons is based on probability value. The default value for this is 0.5, which is good choice to start with, but we can change the value for regularization after observing training error and testing error.

Here, we will be using pre-trained models such as the Caffe pre-trained model, the TensorFow object detraction model, and **You Only Look Once (YOLO)**. For real-time streaming from our webcam, we are using OpenCV, which is also useful in order to draw bounding boxes. So first, let's set up the OpenCV environment.

Setting up the coding environment

In this section, we will list down the libraries and equipment you need in order to run the upcoming code. You need to have a webcam that can at least stream the video with good clarity. We will be using OpenCV, TensorFlow, YOLO, Darkflow, and Darknet libraries. I'm not going to explain how to install TensorFlow, because it is an easy process and you can find the documentation for the installation by clicking on `https://www.tensorflow.org/install/install_linux`.

In this section, we will be looking at how to set up OpenCV first and, in the upcoming sections, we will see how to set up YOLO, Darkflow, and DarkNet.

Setting up and installing OpenCV

OpenCV stands for Open Source Computer Vision. It is designed for computational efficiency, with a strong focus on real-time applications. In this section, you will learn how to set up OpenCV. I'm using Ubuntu 16.04 and I have a GPU, so I have already installed CUDA and CUDNN. If you haven't installed CUDA and CUDNN, then you can refer to this GitHub link: `https://gist.github.com/vbalnt/a0f789d788a99bfb62b61cb809246d64`. Once you are done with that, start executing the following steps:

1. This will update the software and libraries: `$ sudo apt-get update`
2. This will upgrade the OS and install OS-level updates: `$ sudo apt-get upgrade`
3. This is for compiling the software: `$ sudo apt-get install build-essential`
4. This command installs prerequisites for OpenCV: `$ sudo apt-get install cmake git libgtk2.0-dev pkg-config libavcodec-dev libavformat-dev libswscale-dev`
5. This command installs optional prerequisites for OpenCV: `$ sudo apt-get install python-dev python-numpy libtbb2 libtbb-dev libjpeg-dev libpng-dev libtiff-dev libjasper-dev libdc1394-22-dev`
6. Create a directory using this command: `$ sudo mkdir ~/opencv`
7. Jump to the directory that we just created: `$ cd ~/opencv`
8. Clone the following OpenCV projects from GitHub inside the opencv directory:
    1. `$ sudo git clone https://github.com/opencv/opencv.git`
    2. `$ sudo git clone https://github.com/opencv/opencv_contrib.git`

9. Inside the opencv folder, create another directory named build: `$ sudo mkdir ~/opencv/build`
10. Jump to the build directory or folder: `$ cd ~/opencv/build`
11. Once you are in the build folder location, run this command. It may take some time. If you run this command without any error, then proceed to the next step:

```
$ sudo cmake -D CMAKE_BUILD_TYPE=RELEASE \
-D CMAKE_INSTALL_PREFIX=/usr/local \
-D INSTALL_C_EXAMPLES=ON \
-D INSTALL_PYTHON_EXAMPLES=ON \
-D WITH_TBB=ON \
-D WITH_V4L=ON \
-D WITH_QT=ON \
-D WITH_OPENGL=ON \
-D OPENCV_EXTRA_MODULES_PATH=../../opencv_contrib/modules \
-D BUILD_EXAMPLES=ON ..
```

12. Identify how many CPU cores you have by using this command.: `$ nproc`
13. Once you know the number of cores of the CPU, you can use it to process multi-threading. I have allocated four CPU cores, which means there are four threads running simultaneously. The command for this is `$ make -j4` and it compiles all of the classes written in C for OpenCV.
14. Now, execute this command for the actual installation of OpenCV: `$ sudo make install`
15. Add the path to the configuration file: `$ sudo sh -c 'echo "/usr/local/lib" >> /etc/ld.so.conf.d/opencv.conf'`
16. Check for the proper configuration using this command: `$ sudo ldconfig`

Once you have installed OpenCV successfully, we can use this library to stream real-time video. Now, we will start building our baseline model. Let's begin!

Features engineering for the baseline model

In order to build the baseline model, we will use the Caffe implementation of the Google MobileNet SSD detection network with pre-trained weights. This model has been trained on the PASCAL VOC dataset. So, in this section, we will look at the approach with which this model has been trained by Google. We will understand the basic approach behind MobileNet SSD and use the pre-trained model to help save time. To create this kind of accurate model, we need to have lots of GPUs and training time, so we are using a pre-trained model. This pre-trained MobileNet model uses **Convolution Neural Net** (**CNN**).

Let's look at how the features have been extracted by the MobileNet using CNN. This will help us understand the basic idea behind CNN, as well as how MobileNet has been used. The CNN network is made of layers and, when we provide the images to CNN, it scans the region of the images and tries to extract the possible objects using the region proposal method. Then, it finds the region with objects, uses the warped region, and generates the CNN features. These features can be the position of the pixels, edges, the length of the edges, the texture of the images, the scale of the region, the lightness or darkness of the picture, object parts, and so on. The CNN network learns these kinds of features by itself. You can refer to the following figure:

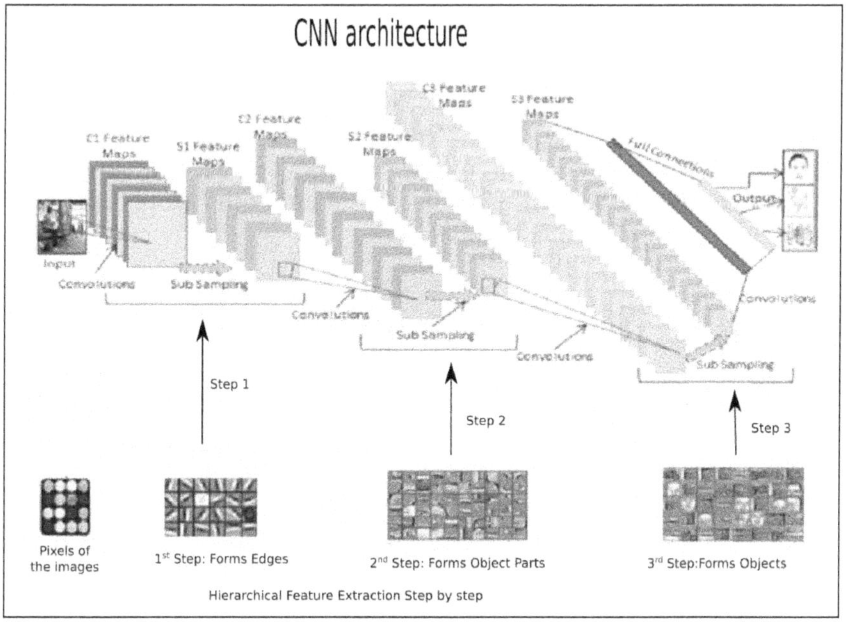

Figure 9.4: Understanding features extraction in CNN

As you can see in the preceding image, the region of the image has been scanned and the first CNN layer, made up of C1 and S1, will generate the features. These features can identify the representation of edges that eventually build the whole object. In the second stage, CNN layers learn the feature representation that can help the neural network identify parts of the objects. In the last stage, it learns all the features that are necessary in order to identify the objects present in the given input images. If you want to explore each and every aspect of the CNN network, you can refer to `http://cs231n.github.io/convolutional-networks/`. Don't worry; we will cover the overview of the CNN architecture in the upcoming section, so that you can understand how object detection will work. Now, it's time to explore CNN.

Selecting the machine learning algorithm

We already know that we are using **Convolution Neural Networks** (**CNN**) for developing this application. You might wonder why we have chosen CNN and not another neural net. You might already know the answer to this question. There are three reasons why we have chosen CNN:

- The amount of visual data present nowadays, which is carefully hand-labeled
- The affordable computation machines through which GPUs open the door for optimization
- The various kinds of architecture of CNN outperforms the other algorithms

Due to these reasons, we have chosen the CNN with SSD. During the development of the baseline model, we will be using MobileNet, which uses CNN with **Single Shot Detector** (**SSD**) techniques underneath. So, in this section, we will look at the architecture of the CNN used during the development of the MobileNet. This will help us understand the pre-trained model.

Architecture of the MobileNet SSD model

MobileNet SSD is fast and does the job of object detection in images and video well. This model is faster than **Region-based Convolution Neural Network** (**R-CNN**). SSD achieves this speed because it scans images and video frames quite differently.

In R-CNN, models performed region proposals and region classifications in two different steps, given as follows:

- First, they used a region proposal network in order to generate regions of interest
- After that, fully connected layers or positive sensitive constitutional layers classified the objects in the selected regions.

These steps are at par with the R-CNN, but SSD performs them in a single shot, which means it simultaneously predicts the bounding boxes and the classes of the objects appearing in the bounding boxes. SDD performs the following steps when an image or video streams and set of basic truth labels has been given as the input:

- Pass the images through the series of convolution layers that generate the sets of features map in the form of a different size of matrix. The output can be in the form of a 10×10 matrix, a 6×6 matrix, or a 3×3 matrix.
- For each location in each of the feature maps, use the 3×3 convolution filter in order to evaluate the small set of default bound boxes. These generated default bounding boxes are equivalent to anchor boxes, which are generated using Faster R-CNN.
- For each box, simultaneously predict the bounding box offset and the class probability for objects.
- During the training, match the ground truth box with these predicted boxes. This matching is performed by using Intersection of Union (IoU). The best predicted box will be labeled as a positive bounding box. This happens to every boundary box. An IoU with more than 50% truth value has been considered here.

Take a look at the following figure for a graphical representation. MobileNets have streamlined architecture that uses depth-wise separable convolutions in order to build light weight deep neural networks for mobile and embedded vision application. MobileNets are a more efficient ML model for computer vision application. You can also refer to the original paper for MobileNet at `https://arxiv.org/pdf/1704.04861.pdf`.

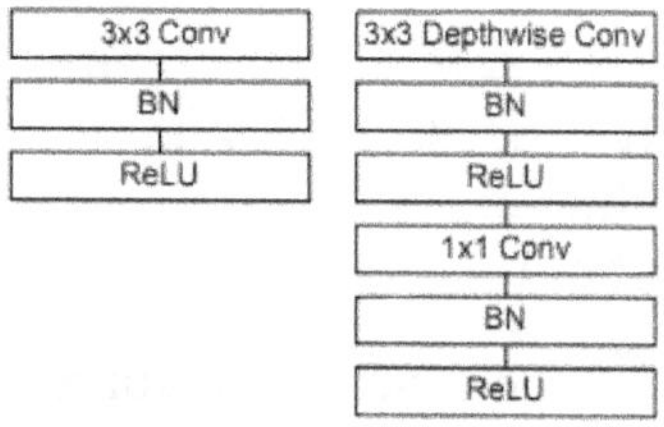

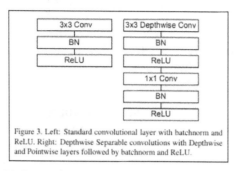

Figure 3. Left: Standard convolutional layer with batchnorm and ReLU. Right: Depthwise Separable convolutions with Depthwise and Pointwise layers followed by batchnorm and ReLU.

Figure 9.5: Basic architectural building blocks for MobileNet SSD

Image Source: https://arxiv.org/pdf/1704.04861.pdf

As you can see in the preceding figure, we used the standard convolution network with the depth-wise convolution network. MobileNet SDD used the ReLU activation function. You can refer to the following figure to get an idea about what kind of filter shape this network has:

Type / Stride	Filter Shape	Input Size
Conv / s2	3 × 3 × 3 × 32	224 × 224 × 3
Conv dw / s1	3 × 3 × 32 dw	112 × 112 × 32
Conv / s1	1 × 1 × 32 × 64	112 × 112 × 32
Conv dw / s2	3 × 3 × 64 dw	112 × 112 × 64
Conv / s1	1 × 1 × 64 × 128	56 × 56 × 64
Conv dw / s1	3 × 3 × 128 dw	56 × 56 × 128
Conv / s1	1 × 1 × 128 × 128	56 × 56 × 128
Conv dw / s2	3 × 3 × 128 dw	56 × 56 × 128
Conv / s1	1 × 1 × 128 × 256	28 × 28 × 128
Conv dw / s1	3 × 3 × 256 dw	28 × 28 × 256
Conv / s1	1 × 1 × 256 × 256	28 × 28 × 256
Conv dw / s2	3 × 3 × 256 dw	28 × 28 × 256
Conv / s1	1 × 1 × 256 × 512	14 × 14 × 256
5× Conv dw / s1	3 × 3 × 512 dw	14 × 14 × 512
5× Conv / s1	1 × 1 × 512 × 512	14 × 14 × 512
Conv dw / s2	3 × 3 × 512 dw	14 × 14 × 512
Conv / s1	1 × 1 × 512 × 1024	7 × 7 × 512
Conv dw / s2	3 × 3 × 1024 dw	7 × 7 × 1024
Conv / s1	1 × 1 × 1024 × 1024	7 × 7 × 1024
Avg Pool / s1	Pool 7 × 7	7 × 7 × 1024
FC / s1	1024 × 1000	1 × 1 × 1024
Softmax / s1	Classifier	1 × 1 × 1000

Figure 9.6, MobileNet body architecture

Image Source: https://arxiv.org/pdf/1704.04861.pdf

If you want to interpret this table, then let's consider an example. If we have an original image with a pixel sixe of 224×224, then this Mobilenet network shrinks the image down to 7×7 pixels; it also has 1,024 channels. After this, there is an average pooling layer that works on all the images and generates the vector of a 1×1×1,024 size, which is just a vector of 1,024 elements in reality. If you want to learn more about MobileNet SSD, refer to the following resources:

- `http://cs231n.github.io/convolutional-networks/`
- `https://towardsdatascience.com/deep-learning-for-object-detection-a-comprehensive-review-73930816d8d9`
- `https://medium.com/ilenze-com/object-detection-using-deep-learning-for-advanced-users-part-1-183bbbb08b19`
- `http://machinethink.net/blog/googles-mobile-net-architecture-on-iphone/`

Now, let's move on to the implementation part.

Building the baseline model

In this section, we will be looking at the coding part. You can refer to the code given at this GitHub link: `https://github.com/jalajthanaki/Real_time_object_detection/tree/master/base_line_model`.

First, download the project from the given link and install OpenCV, as per the information given earlier in this chapter. When you download this project folder, there is a pre-trained MobileNet SSD that has been implemented using the caffe library, but here, we are using the pre-trained binary model. We are using OpenCV for loading the pre-trained model as well as streaming the video feeds from the webcam.

In the code, first, we specify the libraries that we need to import and define the command-line arguments that will be used to run the script. We need to provide the parameter file and the pre-trained model. The name of the parameter file is `MobileNetSSD_deploy.prototxt.txt` and the filename for the pre-trained model is `MobileNetSSD_deploy.caffemodel`. We have also defined the classes that can be identified by the model. After this, we will load the pre-trained model using OpenCV. You can refer to the coding up to this stage in the following screenshot:

```
# USAGE
# python real_time_object_detection.py --prototxt MobileNetSSD_deploy.prototxt.txt --model MobileNetSSD_deploy.caffemodel
# import the necessary packages
from imutils.video import VideoStream
from imutils.video import FPS
import numpy as np
import argparse
import imutils
import time
import cv2
# construct the argument parse and parse the arguments
ap = argparse.ArgumentParser()
ap.add_argument("-p", "--prototxt", required=True,
    help="path to Caffe 'deploy' prototxt file")
ap.add_argument("-m", "--model", required=True,
    help="path to Caffe pre-trained model")
ap.add_argument("-c", "--confidence", type=float, default=0.2,
    help="minimum probability to filter weak detections")
args = vars(ap.parse_args())
# initialize the list of class labels MobileNet SSD was trained to
# detect, then generate a set of bounding box colors for each class
CLASSES = ["background", "aeroplane", "bicycle", "bird", "boat",
    "bottle", "bus", "car", "cat", "chair", "cow", "diningtable",
    "dog", "horse", "motorbike", "person", "pottedplant", "sheep",
    "sofa", "train", "tvmonitor"]
COLORS = np.random.uniform(0, 255, size=(len(CLASSES), 3))

# load our serialized model from disk
print("[INFO] loading model...")
net = cv2.dnn.readNetFromCaffe(args["prototxt"], args["model"])
```

Figure 9.7: Code snippet for the baseline model

Now, let's look at how we can stream the video from our webcam. Here, we are using library `imutils` and its video API to stream the video from the webcam. Using the start function, we will start the streaming and, after that, we will define the frame size. We grab the frame size and convert it into a blob format. This code always verifies that the detected object confidence score will be higher than the minimum confidence score or the minimum threshold of the confidence score. Once we get a higher confidence score, we will draw the bounding box for those objects. We can see the objects that have been detected so far. You can refer to the following figure for the video streaming of the baseline model:

```
# initialize the video stream, allow the cammera sensor to warmup,
# and initialize the FPS counter
print("[INFO] starting video stream...")
vs = VideoStream(src=0).start()
time.sleep(2.0)
fps = FPS().start()
# loop over the frames from the video stream
while True:
    # grab the frame from the threaded video stream and resize it
    # to have a maximum width of 400 pixels
    frame = vs.read()
    frame = imutils.resize(frame, width=500)
    # grab the frame dimensions and convert it to a blob
    (h, w) = frame.shape[:2]
    blob = cv2.dnn.blobFromImage(cv2.resize(frame, (300, 300)),
        0.007843, (300, 300), 127.5)
    # pass the blob through the network and obtain the detections and
    # predictions
    net.setInput(blob)
    detections = net.forward()
    # loop over the detections
    for i in np.arange(0, detections.shape[2]):
        # extract the confidence (i.e., probability) associated with
        # the prediction
        confidence = detections[0, 0, i, 2]

        # filter out weak detections by ensuring the `confidence` is
        # greater than the minimum confidence
        if confidence > args["confidence"]:
            # extract the index of the class label from the
            # `detections`, then compute the (x, y)-coordinates of
            # the bounding box for the object
            idx = int(detections[0, 0, i, 1])
            box = detections[0, 0, i, 3:7] * np.array([w, h, w, h])
            (startX, startY, endX, endY) = box.astype("int")

            # draw the prediction on the frame
            label = "{}: {:.2f}%".format(CLASSES[idx],
                confidence * 100)
            cv2.rectangle(frame, (startX, startY), (endX, endY),
                COLORS[idx], 2)
            y = startY - 15 if startY - 15 > 15 else startY + 15
            cv2.putText(frame, label, (startX, y),
                cv2.FONT_HERSHEY_SIMPLEX, 0.5, COLORS[idx], 2)
    # show the output frame
    cv2.imshow("Frame", frame)
```

Figure 9.8: Code snippet for the baseline model video streaming

In order to stop the streaming, we need to break the loop by pressing Q or Ctrl + C and we need to take care that when we close the program, all windows and processes will stop appropriately. You can see this in the following screenshot:

```
# stop the timer and display FPS information
fps.stop()
print("[INFO] elapsed time: {:.2f}".format(fps.elapsed()))
print("[INFO] approx. FPS: {:.2f}".format(fps.fps()))

# do a bit of cleanup
cv2.destroyAllWindows()
vs.stop()
```

Figure 9.9: Code snippet for ending the script

Before we run the testing of the script, let's understand the testing metrics for the object detection application. Once we understand the testing metrics, we will run the code as well as checking how much accuracy we are getting.

Understanding the testing metrics

In this section, we will cover the testing metrics. We will look at the two matrices that will help us understand how to test the object detection application. These testing matrices are as follows:

- Intersection over Union (IoU)
- mean Average Precision (mAP)

Intersection over Union (IoU)

For detection, IoU is used in order to find out whether the object proposal is right or not. This is a regular way to determine whether object detection is done perfectly or not. IoU generally takes the set, A, of proposed object pixels and the set of true object pixels, B, and calculates IoU based on the following formula:

$$IoU\left(A,B\right)=\frac{A\cap B}{A\cup B}$$

Generally, IoU >0.5, which means that it was a hit or that it identified the object pixels or boundary box for the object; otherwise, it fails. This is a more formal understanding of the IoU. Now, let's look at the intuition and the meaning behind it. Let's take an image as reference to help us understand the intuition behind this matrix. You can refer to the following screenshot:

Figure 9.10: Understanding the intuition behind IoU

The preceding screenshot is an example of detecting a stop sign in an image. The predicted bounding box is drawn in red and pixels belonging to this red box are considered part of set A, while the ground-truth bounding box is drawn in green and pixels belong to this green box are considered part of set B. Our goal is to compute the Intersection of Union between these bounding boxes. So, when our application draws a boundary box, it should match the ground-truth boundary box at least more than 50%, which is considered a good prediction. The equation for IoU is given in the following figure:

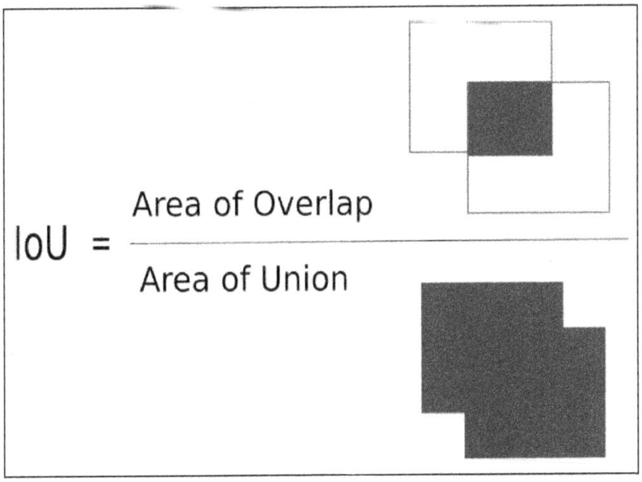

Figure 9.11: Equation of IoU based on intuitive understanding

There are few chances in reality where the (x, y) coordinate of our predicted bounding box will exactly match the (x, y) coordinates of the ground-truth bounding box. In the following figure, you can see various examples for poor, good, and excellent IoUs:

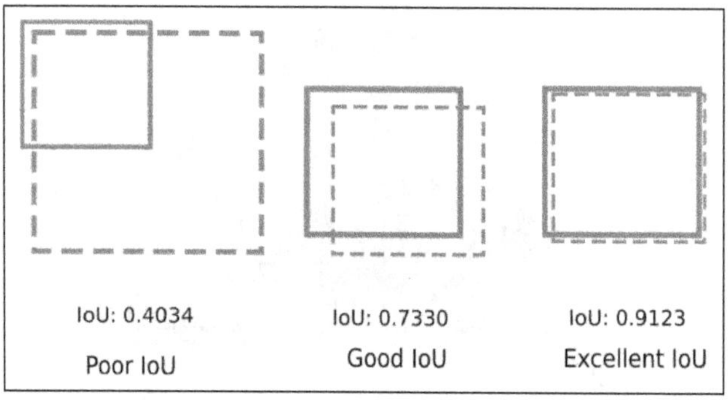

Figure 9.12: Various IoU boundary box examples

IoUs help us to determine how well the application identifies the object boundaries and differentiates the various objects from each other. Now, it's time to understand the next testing metrics.

mean Average Precision

In this section, we will cover the **mean Average Precision** (**mAP**). In object detection, first, we identify the object boundary box and then we classify it into a category. These categories have some labels, and we provide the appropriate label to the identified objects. Now, we need to test how well the application can assign these labels, which means how well we can classify the objects into different predefined categories. For each class, we will calculate the following:

- True Positive TP(c): A predicted class was C and the object actually belongs to class C
- False Positive FP(c): A predicted class was C but in reality, the object does not belong to class C
- Average Precision for class C is given by the following equation:

$$Average\,Precision\,for\,class\,c = \frac{\neq TP(c)}{\neq TP(c) + \neq FP(c)}$$

So, for all the classes, we need to calculate the mAP and the equation for that is as follows:

$$mAP = \frac{1}{|classes|} \sum_{c \in classes} \frac{\neq TP(c)}{\neq TP(c) + \neq FP(c)}$$

If we want better prediction, then we need to increase the IoU from 0.5 to a higher value (up to 1.0, which would be perfect). We can denote this with this equation: $mAP_{@p}$, where $p \in (0,1)$ is the IoU. $mAP_{@[0.5:0.95]}$ means that the mAP is calculated over multiple thresholds and then it is averaged again.

Now, let's test the baseline model and check the mAP for this implementation.

Testing the baseline model

In this section, we will run the baseline model. In order to run the script, we need to jump to the location where we put the script titled `real_time_object_detection.py` and, on Command Prompt, we need to execute the following command:

```
jalaj@jalaj:~/PycharmProjects/Real_time_object_detection/base_line_model$ ls
__init__.py  MobileNetSSD_deploy.caffemodel  MobileNetSSD_deploy.prototxt.txt  real_time_object_detection.py
jalaj@jalaj:~/PycharmProjects/Real_time_object_detection/base_line_model$ python real_time_object_detection.py --prototxt MobileNetSSD_deploy.prototxt.txt --model Mobile
NetSSD_deploy.caffemodel
[INFO] loading model...
[INFO] starting video stream...
```

Figure 9.13: Execution of the baseline approach

Take a look at the following figure. Here, I have just placed example images, but you can see the entire video when you run the script. Here is the link to see the entire video for real-time object detection using the baseline approach: `https://drive.google.com/drive/folders/1RwKEUaxTExefdrSJSy44NugqGZaTN_BX?usp=sharing`.

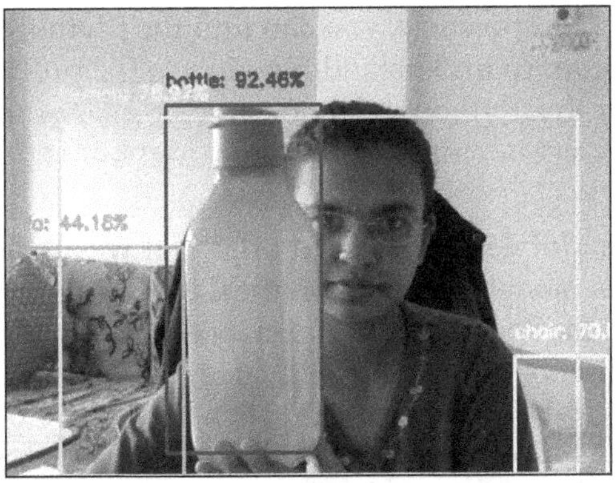

Figure 9.14: Output of the baseline approach (image is part of the video stream)

Here, the mAP for the MobileNet SSD is 71.1% . You will learn how to optimize this approach in the upcoming section. First, we will list down the points that we can improve in the next iteration. So, let's jump to our next section.

Problem with existing approach

Although the MobileNet SSD is fast and gives us good results, it still can't identify classes such as cup, pen, and so on. So, we need to use the pre-trained model that has been trained on a variety of objects. In this upcoming iteration, we need to use the pre-trained model, for example, the TensorFlow object detection API, which will able to identify the different objects compared to the baseline approach. So now, let's look at how we will optimize the existing approach.

How to optimize the existing approach

As mentioned earlier, in order to optimize the existing approach, I will be using the TensorFlow Object Detection API. You can refer to Google's TensorFlow GitHub repo for this API at the following link: `https://github.com/tensorflow/models/tree/master/research/object_detection`. This API is trained using the COCO dataset as well as the PASCAL VOC dataset; so, it will have the capability of identifying the variety of classes.

Understanding the process for optimization

The most important part for us is how to use the various pre-trained models. The steps are as follows:

1. First, pull the TensorFlow models repository using this link: `https://github.com/tensorflow/models`
2. Once you pull the repository, you can find the iPython Notebook that I have referred to in order to understand how to use the pre-trained model and to find the link for the iPython notebook at `https://github.com/tensorflow/models/blob/master/research/object_detection/object_detection_tutorial.ipynb`.
3. Here, SSD with MobileNet has been used, but we are using the detection model zoo. This model is trained on the COCO dataset and their versions are given based on the speed and performance of the model. You can download the pre-trained model from this link: `https://github.com/tensorflow/models/blob/master/research/object_detection/g3doc/detection_model_zoo.md`. I have already placed all these parts together, so it is easy for everyone to implement the code.

4. The main thing is that this model is trained using the SSD approach, but it has taken datasets such as the kitti dataset and the Open Image dataset. So, this model is able to detect more objects and is more generalized. The link for the Kitti dataset is `http://www.cvlibs.net/datasets/kitti/` and the link for the Open Image dataset is `https://github.com/openimages/dataset`.

Once we download the repository and the pre-trained model, we will load the pre-trained model. In TensorFlow, as we know, the models are saved as a .pb file. Once we load the model, we will be using OpenCV to stream the video. In the upcoming section, we will be implementing the code for the revised approach.

Implementing the revised approach

In this section, we will understand the implementation of the revised approach. You can refer to this GitHub link: `https://github.com/jalajthanaki/Real_time_object_detection/tree/master/revised_approach`, which has the pre-trained model and the TensorFlow's Object detection folder. Before we even begin with the code, I will provide information regarding the folder structure of this approach. You can refer to the following figure:

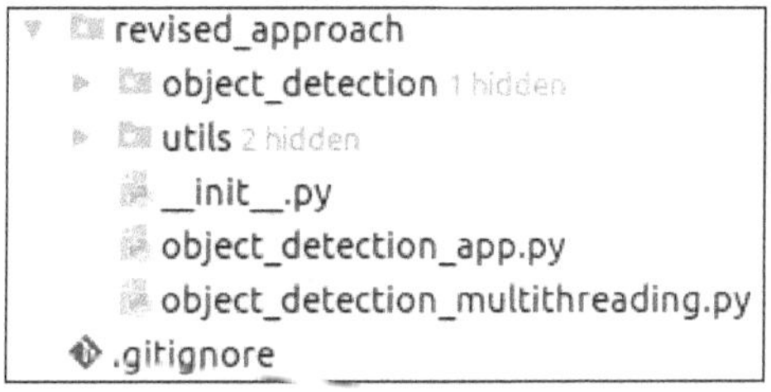

Figure 9.15: Understanding the folder structure for the revised approach

Here is the object detection folder downloaded from the TensorFlow model repository: `https://github.com/tensorflow/models/tree/master/research/object_detection`. In the `utils` folder, there are some helper functions to help us stream the video. The main script that helps us run the script is `object_detection_app.py`. The pre-trained model has been saved inside the object detection folder. The path for pre-trained model in this folder is this: `~/PycharmProjects/Real_time_object_detection/revised_approach/object_detection/ssd_mobilenet_v1_coco_11_06_2017/frozen_inference_graph.pb`.

Now, let's look at the coding implementation step by step. In the first step, we will import the dependency libraries and load the pre-trained model. You can refer to the following figure:

```
import os
import cv2
import time
import argparse
import multiprocessing
import numpy as np
import tensorflow as tf

from utils.app_utils import FPS, WebcamVideoStream

# from imutils.video import VideoStream
# from imutils.video import FPS

from multiprocessing import Queue, Pool
from object_detection.utils import label_map_util
from object_detection.utils import visualization_utils as vis_util

CWD_PATH = os.getcwd()

# Path to frozen detection graph. This is the actual model that is used for the object detection.
MODEL_NAME = 'ssd_mobilenet_v1_coco_11_06_2017'
PATH_TO_CKPT = os.path.join(CWD_PATH, 'object_detection', MODEL_NAME, 'frozen_inference_graph.pb')

# List of the strings that is used to add correct label for each box.
PATH_TO_LABELS = os.path.join(CWD_PATH, 'object_detection', 'data', 'mscoco_label_map.pbtxt')

NUM_CLASSES = 90

# Loading label map
label_map = label_map_util.load_labelmap(PATH_TO_LABELS)
categories = label_map_util.convert_label_map_to_categories(label_map, max_num_classes=NUM_CLASSES,
                                                            use_display_name=True)
category_index = label_map_util.create_category_index(categories)
```

Figure 9.16: Code snippet for loading the pre-trained model in the revised approach

In this model, there are 90 different types of objects that can be identified. Once we load the model, the next step is the `detect_objects()` function, which is used to identify the objects. Once the object is identified, the bounding boxes for that object are drawn and we simultaneously run the pre-trained model on those objects, so that we can get the identification labels for the object, whether it's a cup, bottle, person, and so on. You can refer to the following figure:

```
def detect_objects(image_np, sess, detection_graph):
    # Expand dimensions since the model expects images to have shape: [1, None, None, 3]
    image_np_expanded = np.expand_dims(image_np, axis=0)
    image_tensor = detection_graph.get_tensor_by_name('image_tensor:0')

    # Each box represents a part of the image where a particular object was detected.
    boxes = detection_graph.get_tensor_by_name('detection_boxes:0')

    # Each score represent how level of confidence for each of the objects.
    # Score is shown on the result image, together with the class label.
    scores = detection_graph.get_tensor_by_name('detection_scores:0')
    classes = detection_graph.get_tensor_by_name('detection_classes:0')
    num_detections = detection_graph.get_tensor_by_name('num_detections:0')

    # Actual detection.
    (boxes, scores, classes, num_detections) = sess.run(
        [boxes, scores, classes, num_detections],
        feed_dict={image_tensor: image_np_expanded})

    # Visualization of the results of a detection.
    vis_util.visualize_boxes_and_labels_on_image_array(
        image_np,
        np.squeeze(boxes),
        np.squeeze(classes).astype(np.int32),
        np.squeeze(scores),
        category_index,
        use_normalized_coordinates=True,
        line_thickness=8)
    return image_np
```

Figure 9.17: Code snippet for the detect_objects() function

After this, we have the `worker()` function, which helps us stream the video as well as perform some GPU memory management. You can refer to the following figure:

```
def worker(input_q, output_q):
    # Load a (frozen) Tensorflow model into memory.
    detection_graph = tf.Graph()
    ### Add by me
    config = tf.ConfigProto()
    config.gpu_options.per_process_gpu_memory_fraction = 0.33
    ### End add by me
    with detection_graph.as_default():
        od_graph_def = tf.GraphDef()
        with tf.gfile.GFile(PATH_TO_CKPT, 'rb') as fid:
            serialized_graph = fid.read()
            od_graph_def.ParseFromString(serialized_graph)
            tf.import_graph_def(od_graph_def, name='')

        sess = tf.Session(graph=detection_graph,config=config)

    fps = FPS().start()
    while True:
        fps.update()
        frame = input_q.get()
        frame_rgb = cv2.cvtColor(frame, cv2.COLOR_BGR2RGB)
        output_q.put(detect_objects(frame_rgb, sess, detection_graph))

    fps.stop()
    sess.close()
```

Figure 9.18: Code snippet for the worker() function

As you can see, we have defined the GPU memory fraction, as well as the kind of colors used when it detects the objects. Now, let's look at the main function of the script. In the main function, we define some optional arguments and their default values. The list of these arguments is as follows:

- Device index of the camera: `--source=0`
- Width of the frames in the video stream `--width= 500`
- Height of the frames in the video stream `--height= 500`
- Number of workers `--num-workers=2`
- Size of the queue `--queue-size=5`

You can refer to the implementation of the main function shown in the following figure:

```
if __name__ == '__main__':
    parser = argparse.ArgumentParser()
    parser.add_argument('-src', '--source', dest='video_source', type=int,
                        default=0, help='Device index of the camera.')
    parser.add_argument('-wd', '--width', dest='width', type=int,
                        default=480, help='Width of the frames in the video stream.')
    parser.add_argument('-ht', '--height', dest='height', type=int,
                        default=480, help='Height of the frames in the video stream.')
    parser.add_argument('-num-w', '--num-workers', dest='num_workers', type=int,
                        default=2, help='Number of workers.')
    parser.add_argument('-q-size', '--queue-size', dest='queue_size', type=int,
                        default=5, help='Size of the queue.')
    args = parser.parse_args()

    logger = multiprocessing.log_to_stderr()
    logger.setLevel(multiprocessing.SUBDEBUG)

    input_q = Queue(maxsize=args.queue_size)
    output_q = Queue(maxsize=args.queue_size)
    pool = Pool(args.num_workers, worker, (input_q, output_q))

    video_capture = WebcamVideoStream(src=args.video_source,
                                      width=args.width,
                                      height=args.height).start()
    print "executed"
    print input_q
    print output_q

    fps = FPS().start()

    while True:  # fps._numFrames < 120
        frame = video_capture.read()
        input_q.put(frame)

        t = time.time()

        output_rgb = cv2.cvtColor(output_q.get(), cv2.COLOR_RGB2BGR)
        cv2.imshow('Video', output_rgb)
        fps.update()

        print('[INFO] elapsed time: {:.2f}'.format(time.time() - t))

        if cv2.waitKey(1) & 0xFF == ord('q'):
            break

    fps.stop()
    print('[INFO] elapsed time (total): {:.2f}'.format(fps.elapsed()))
    print('[INFO] approx. FPS: {:.2f}'.format(fps.fps()))
```

Figure 9.19: Code snippet for the main function

When we run the script, we can see the output given in the upcoming figure. Here, we have placed the image, but you can see the video by using this link:

`https://drive.google.com/drive/folders/1RwKEUaxTExefdrSJSy44NugqGZaTN_BX?usp=sharing`

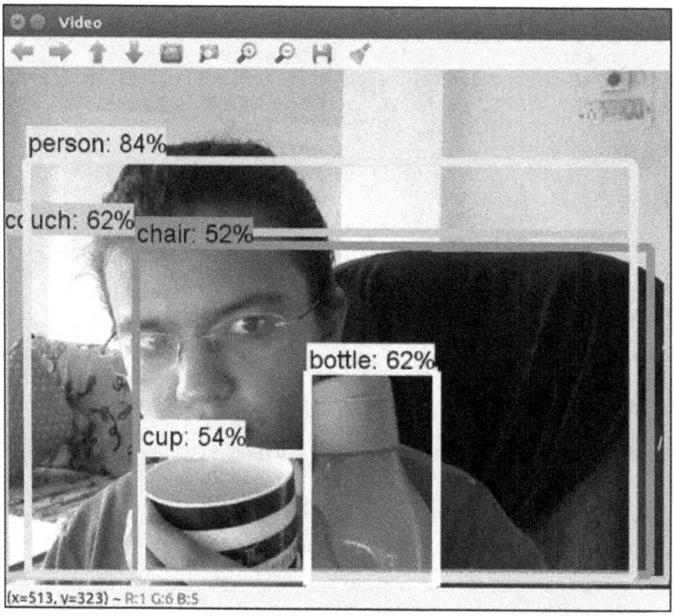

Figure 9.20: Output of the revised approach

Once we end the video, the resources and the process should end as well. For that, we will be using the code that has been provided to us through the following figure:

```
pool.terminate()
video_capture.stop()
cv2.destroyAllWindows()
```

Figure 9.21: Code snippet to release the resources once the script is terminated

Testing the revised approach

Once we have executed this approach, we can identify objects such as cups, pens, and so on. So, we can say that our baseline approach is definitely improvised and there are some modified labels, such as a sofa (in this approach, identified as a couch). Apart from this, if we talk about the mAP of this pre-trained model, then as per the documentation, on the COCO dataset, this model gets around 52.4% accuracy. In our input, we will get around 73% accuracy. This approach identifies more objects with different categories, which is a great advantage.

In the upcoming section, we will discuss the points that we can use to come up with the best possible solution.

Understanding problems with the revised approach

We have tried approaches that are fast and accurate, but we need an approach that is fast as well as accurate and optimized. These are the points we need to keep in our mind when we develop the best possible solution:

- The SSD-based approach is great, but is not that accurate when you train your own model using COCO or the PASCAL VOC dataset.
- The TensorFlow detection model zoo will have a mAP score on the COCO test dataset from 20 to 40%. So, we need to explore other techniques that can help us give a better result in terms of processing and object detection accuracy.

So, in the upcoming section, we will look at the approach that can help us optimize the revised approach.

The best approach

In this section, we will be trying the approach named **YOLO**. YOLO stands for You Only Look Once. This technique gives us good accuracy, is fast, and its memory management is easy. This section will be divided into two parts:

- Understanding YOLO
- Implementing the best approach using YOLO

In the first section, we will understand the basics about YOLO. During the implementation, we will be use YOLO with the pre-trained YOLO model.
So, let's begin!

Understanding YOLO

YOLO is a state-of-the-art, real-time object detection system. On GPU Titan X, it processes images at 40-90 FPS and has a mAP on the PASCAL VOC dataset of 78.6% and a mAP of 48.1% on the coco test-dev dataset. So, now, we will look at how YOLO works and processes the images in order to identify the objects. We are using YOLOv2 (YOLO version 2) as it is a faster version.

The working of YOLO

YOLO reframes the object detection problem. It considers the object recognition task as single regression problem, right from the image pixels to the bounding box coordinates and class probabilities. A single convolutional network simultaneously predicts multiple bounding boxes and class probabilities for those boxes. YOLO trains on full images and directly optimizes detection performance. This approach has several advantages compared to traditional methods, as follows:

- YOLO is extremely fast. This is because, in YOLO, frame detection is a regression problem, and we do not need to use a complex pipeline.
- We can simply run our neural network on a new image at the time of testing to predict detection. Our base network runs at 45 frames per second with no batch processing on a Titan X GPU and a fast version runs at more than 150 fps. This means that we can process streaming video in real time with less than 25 milliseconds of latency.

YOLO processes images globally when it makes a prediction regarding information about classes as well as their appearance. It also learns the generalization of objects.

YOLO divides the input image into an $S \times S$ grid. If the center of an object falls into a grid cell, then that grid cell is responsible for detecting the object. Each grid cell predicts the B bounding boxes and confidence scores for those boxes. These confidence scores reflect how confident the model is that the box contains an object and how accurate it thinks the box that it predicts is. So, formally, we can define the confidence mechanism for YOLO by using this notation. We define the confidence as Pr(object) * IoU. If no object exists in that cell, then the confidence scores should be zero; otherwise, we want the confidence score to equal the IoU between predicted box and the ground truth. Each bounding box consists of five predictions: x, y, w, h, and confidence. The (x, y) coordinates represent the center of the box relative to the bounds of the grid cell. The w and h represents the width and height. They are predicted in relativity to the whole image. Finally, the confidence score represents the IoU. For each grid cell, it predicts C conditional class probabilities, *Pr(Classi | Object)*. These probabilities are conditioned on the grid cell that contains an object. We predict only one set of class probabilities per grid cell regardless of the number of bounding boxes B. At the time of testing, we multiply the conditional class probabilities and the individual box confidence prediction that is defined by this equation:

$$Pr(Classi \mid Object) \times Pr(Object) \times IOU = Pr(Classi) \times IOU$$

The preceding equation gives us the class-specific confidence score for each of the boxes. This score contains both the probability of the class appearing in the box and how well the predicted box fits the object. The pictorial representation of the whole process of YOLO is shown in the following figure:

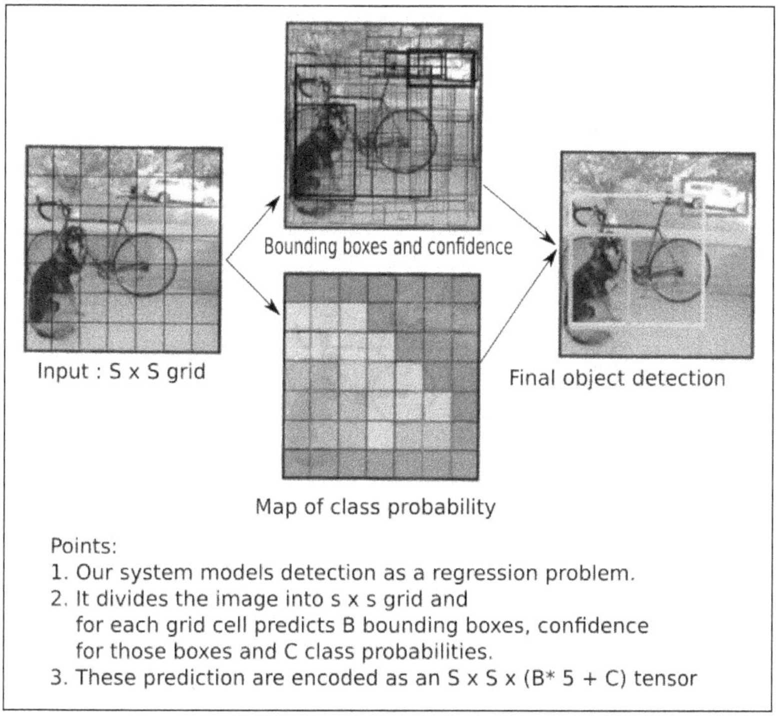

Figure 9.22: Pictorial representation of YOLO object detection

Now, let's get to basic knowledge about the YOLO architecture.

The architecture of YOLO

In this section, you will the learn basics about the YOLO architecture. In YOLO, there are 24 convolutional layers followed by two fully connected layers. Instead of the inception modules used by GoogleNet, YOLO simply uses 1×1 reduction layers followed by 3×3 convolutional layers. Fast YOLO uses a neural network with fewer convolutional layers. We use nine layers instead of 24 layers. We also use fewer filters in these layers. Apart from this, all parameters are the same for YOLO and Fast YOLO during training and testing. You can refer to the architecture in the following figure:

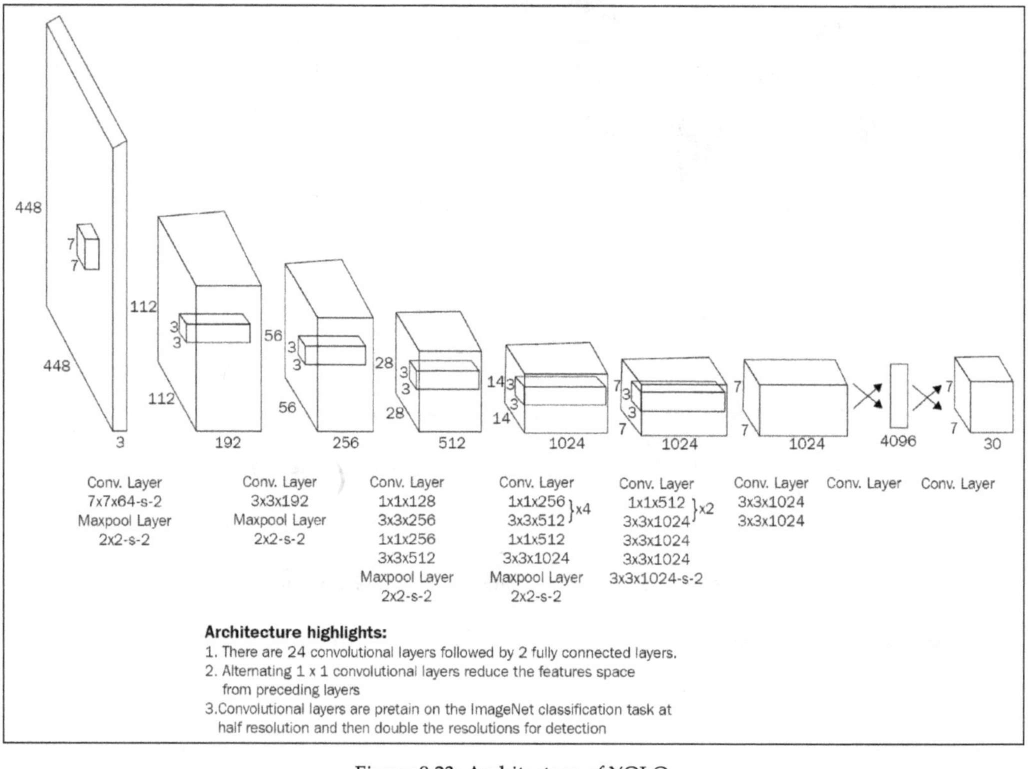

Figure 9.23: Architecture of YOLO

Now, let's move on to the implementation part.

Implementing the best approach using YOLO

In order to implement YOLO, we need to install the Cython module. Apart from that, you can use either Darknet or the Darkflow, which is the TensorFlow wrapper on Darknet. Darknet is written in C and CUDA, so it is quite fast. Here, we will be implementing both the options. Before implementation, we need to set up the environment. The implementation part should be divided into two sections here:

- Implementation using Darknet
- Implementation using Darkflow

You can refer to this GitHub repository for all the code: `https://github.com/jalajthanaki/Real_time_object_detection_with_YOLO`.

Implementation using Darknet

We are following these steps in order to implement YOLO using Darknet:

- Environment setup for Darknet
- Compile the Darknet
- Download the pre-trained weight
- Run object detection for the image
- Run object detection for the video stream

Environment setup for Darknet

In this step, we need to download the GitHub repository of Darknet. We can do that using the following command. You can download this repository at any path:

```
$ git clone https://github.com/pjreddie/darknet
```

Once you run this command, the directory named Darknet is created. After that, you can jump to the next step.

Compiling the Darknet

Once we have downloaded the Darknet, we need to jump to the directory named Darknet. After that, we need to compile the Darknet. So, we need to execute the following commands sequentially:

```
$ cd darknet
$ make
```

Downloading the pre-trained weight

Configuration files are already inside the `cfg/` subdirectory inside the darknet directory. So, by executing the following command, you can download the pre-trained weight for the YOLO model:

```
$ wegt https://pjreddie.com/media/files/yolo.weights
```

This download may take some time. Once we have the pre-trained weight with us, we can run the Darknet.

Running object detection for the image

If you want to identify the objects in the image, then you need to execute the following command:

```
./darknet detect cfg/yolo.cfg yolo.weights data/dog.jpg
```

You can refer to the output of this command in the following figure:

```
jalaj@jalaj:~/PycharmProjects/Real_time_object_detection_YOLO/best_approach_yolo/darknet$ sudo ./darknet detect cfg/yolo.cfg yolo.weights data/dog.jpg
[sudo] password for jalaj:
layer     filters    size              input                output
    0 conv     32  3 x 3 / 1   608 x 608 x   3   ->   608 x 608 x  32
    1 max          2 x 2 / 2   608 x 608 x  32   ->   304 x 304 x  32
    2 conv     64  3 x 3 / 1   304 x 304 x  32   ->   304 x 304 x  64
    3 max          2 x 2 / 2   304 x 304 x  64   ->   152 x 152 x  64
    4 conv    128  3 x 3 / 1   152 x 152 x  64   ->   152 x 152 x 128
    5 conv     64  1 x 1 / 1   152 x 152 x 128   ->   152 x 152 x  64
    6 conv    128  3 x 3 / 1   152 x 152 x  64   ->   152 x 152 x 128
    7 max          2 x 2 / 2   152 x 152 x 128   ->    76 x  76 x 128
    8 conv    256  3 x 3 / 1    76 x  76 x 128   ->    76 x  76 x 256
    9 conv    128  1 x 1 / 1    76 x  76 x 256   ->    76 x  76 x 128
   10 conv    256  3 x 3 / 1    76 x  76 x 128   ->    76 x  76 x 256
   11 max          2 x 2 / 2    76 x  76 x 256   ->    38 x  38 x 256
   12 conv    512  3 x 3 / 1    38 x  38 x 256   ->    38 x  38 x 512
   13 conv    256  1 x 1 / 1    38 x  38 x 512   ->    38 x  38 x 256
   14 conv    512  3 x 3 / 1    38 x  38 x 256   ->    38 x  38 x 512
   15 conv    256  1 x 1 / 1    38 x  38 x 512   ->    38 x  38 x 256
   16 conv    512  3 x 3 / 1    38 x  38 x 256   ->    38 x  38 x 512
   17 max          2 x 2 / 2    38 x  38 x 512   ->    19 x  19 x 512
   18 conv   1024  3 x 3 / 1    19 x  19 x 512   ->    19 x  19 x1024
   19 conv    512  1 x 1 / 1    19 x  19 x1024   ->    19 x  19 x 512
   20 conv   1024  3 x 3 / 1    19 x  19 x 512   ->    19 x  19 x1024
   21 conv    512  1 x 1 / 1    19 x  19 x1024   ->    19 x  19 x 512
   22 conv   1024  3 x 3 / 1    19 x  19 x 512   ->    19 x  19 x1024
   23 conv   1024  3 x 3 / 1    19 x  19 x1024   ->    19 x  19 x1024
   24 conv   1024  3 x 3 / 1    19 x  19 x1024   ->    19 x  19 x1024
   25 route  16
   26 conv     64  1 x 1 / 1    38 x  38 x 512   ->    38 x  38 x  64
   27 reorg              / 2    38 x  38 x  64   ->    19 x  19 x 256
   28 route  27 24
   29 conv   1024  3 x 3 / 1    19 x  19 x1280   ->    19 x  19 x1024
   30 conv    425  1 x 1 / 1    19 x  19 x1024   ->    19 x  19 x 425
   31 detection
mask_scale: Using default '1.000000'
Loading weights from yolo.weights...Done!
data/dog.jpg: Predicted in 18.448386 seconds.
dog: 82%
car: 28%
truck: 64%
bicycle: 85%
```

Figure 9.24 : Output of object detection for the image using Darknet

Now, let's implement YOLO on the video stream.

Running the object detection on the video stream

We can run YOLO on the video stream using this command:

```
./darknet detector demo cfg/coco.data cfg/yolo.cfg yolo.weights <video
file>
```

Here, we need to pass the path of the video. For more information, you can refer to this Darknet documentation: `https://pjreddie.com/darknet/yolo/`. Now, let's understand the implementation of Darkflow.

Implementation using Darkflow

In this implementation, you need to refer to the code given in the folder named Darkflow. We need to perform the following steps:

1. Installing Cython
2. Building the already provided setup file
3. Testing the environment
4. Loading the model and run object detection on the images
5. Loading the model and run object detection on the video stream

Installing Cython

In order to install Cython, we need to execute the following command. This Cython package is needed because the Darkflow is a Python wrapper that uses C code from Darknet:

```
$ sudo apt-get install Cython
```

Once Cython is installed, we can build the other setup.

Building the already provided setup file

In this stage, we will be executing the command that will set up the necessary Cython environment for us. The command is as follows:

```
$ python setup.py build_ext --inplace
```

When we execute this command, we will have to use `./flow` in the cloned Darkflow directory instead of flow, as Darkflow is not installed globally. Once this command runs successfully, we need to test whether we installed all the dependencies perfectly. You can download the pre-trained weight by using the following command:

```
$ wegt https://pjreddie.com/media/files/yolo.weights
```

Testing the environment

In this stage, we will test whether Darkflow runs perfectly or not. In order to check that, we need to execute the following command:

```
$ ./flow --h
```

You can refer to the following figure:

```
jalaj@jalaj:~/PycharmProjects/Real_time_object_detection_YOLO/best_approach_yolo/darkflow_yolo$ ./flow --h

Example usage: flow --imgdir sample_img/ --model cfg/yolo.cfg --load bin/yolo.weights

Arguments:
  --trainer          training algorithm
  --load             how to initialize the net? Either from .weights or a checkpoint, or even from scratch
  --savepb           save net and weight to a .pb file
  --demo             demo on webcam
  --labels           path to labels file
  --dataset          path to dataset directory
  --threshold        detection threshold
  --keep             Number of most recent training results to save
  --binary           path to .weights directory
  --metaLoad         path to .meta file generated during --savepb that corresponds to .pb file
  --gpuName          GPU device name
  --help, --h, -h    show this super helpful message and exit
  --imgdir           path to testing directory with images
  --json             Outputs bounding box information in json format.
  --epoch            number of epoch
  --lr               learning rate
  --saveVideo        Records video from input video or camera
  --gpu              how much gpu (from 0.0 to 1.0)
  --save             save checkpoint every ? training examples
  --config           path to .cfg directory
  --momentum         applicable for rmsprop and momentum optimizers
  --train            train the whole net
  --annotation       path to annotation directory
  --pbLoad           path to .pb protobuf file (metaLoad must also be specified)
  --batch            batch size
  --summary          path to TensorBoard summaries directory
  --queue            process demo in batch
  --verbalise        say out loud while building graph
  --model            configuration of choice
  --backup           path to backup folder

jalaj@jalaj:~/PycharmProjects/Real_time_object_detection_YOLO/best_approach_yolo/darkflow_yolo$
```

Figure 9.25 : Successful testing outcome of Darkflow

Once you can see the preceding output, you'll know that you have successfully configured Darkflow. Now, let's run it.

Loading the model and running object detection on images

We can run the Darkflow on images. For that, we need to load YOLO pre-trained weights, configuration files, and path of images so you can execute the following command:

```
./flow --imgdir sample_img/ --model cfg/yolo.cfg --load ../darknet/
yolo.weights
```

If you want to save the object detection in the json format, then that is possible as well. You need to execute the following command:

```
./flow --imgdir sample_img/ --model cfg/yolo.cfg --load ../darknet/
yolo.weights --json
```

You can see the output inside the `sample_img/out` folder; refer to the following figure:

Figure 9.26 : Output image with predicted objects using Darkflow

You can also refer to the following figure:


```
[{"topleft": {"y": 147, "x": 323}, "confidence": 0.12, "bottomright": {"y": 313, "x": 409}, "label": "tvmonitor"}, {"topleft": {"y": 145, "x": 318}, "confidence":
0.46, "bottomright": {"y": 317, "x": 423}, "label": "cup"}, {"topleft": {"y": 346, "x": 374}, "confidence": 0.37, "bottomright": {"y": 374, "x": 421}, "label": "cup"},
{"topleft": {"y": 259, "x": 464}, "confidence": 0.12, "bottomright": {"y": 357, "x": 499}, "label": "spoon"}, {"topleft": {"y": 316, "x": 419}, "confidence": 0.25,
"bottomright": {"y": 364, "x": 484}, "label": "bowl"}, {"topleft": {"y": 94, "x": 157}, "confidence": 0.88, "bottomright": {"y": 280, "x": 345}, "label": "tvmonitor"},
{"topleft": {"y": 263, "x": 123}, "confidence": 0.8, "bottomright": {"y": 371, "x": 333}, "label": "keyboard"}, {"topleft": {"y": 19, "x": 0}, "confidence": 0.49,
"bottomright": {"y": 351, "x": 130}, "label": "refrigerator"}]
```


Figure 9.27 : json output of the object detected in the image

Loading the model and running object detection on the video stream

In this section, we will run object detection on the video stream. First, we will see how to use the webcam and perform object detection. The command for that is as follows:

```
./flow --model cfg/yolo.cfg --load ../darknet/yolo.weights --demo
camera --saveVideo --gpu 0.60
```

You can refer to the following figure. You can see the video at this link: `https://drive.google.com/drive/folders/1RwKEUaxTExefdrSJSy44NuggGZaTN_BX?usp=sharing`

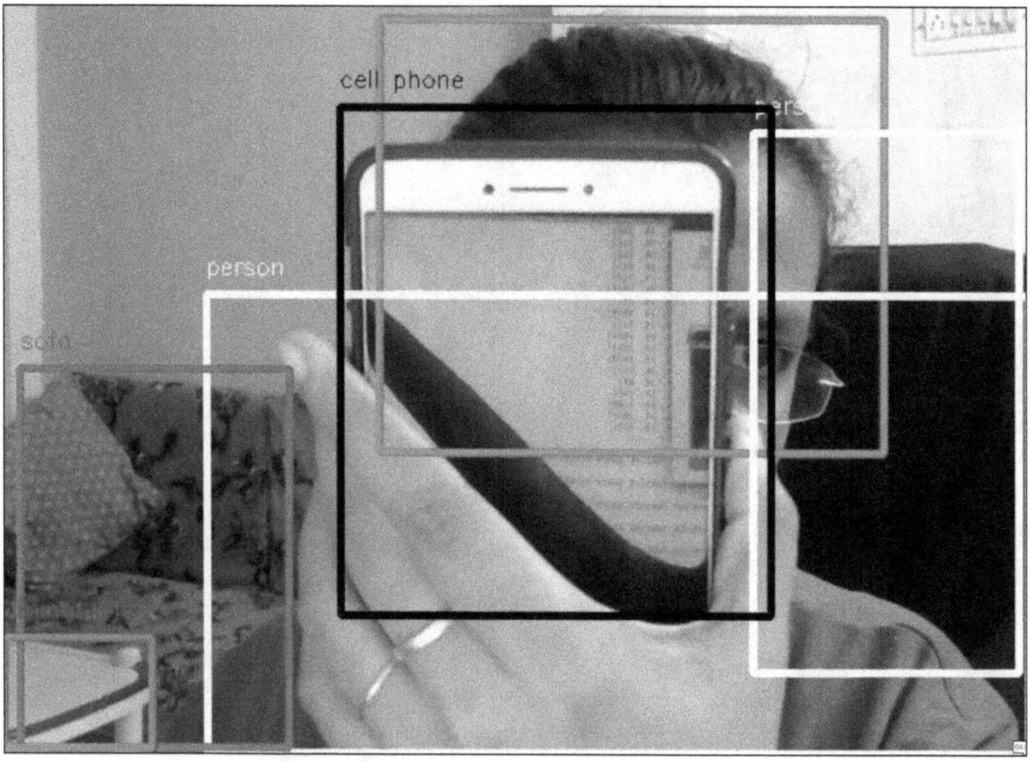

Figure 9.28 : Output of the object detection using Darkflow for the webcam video stream

We can also run the Darkflow for a prerecorded video. For that, you need to run the following command:

```
./flow --model cfg/yolo.cfg --load ../darknet/yolo.weights --demo ~/
Downloads/Traffic.avi --saveVideo --gpu 0.60
```

You can refer to the following figure. You can see the video at this link: `https://drive.google.com/drive/folders/1RwKEUaxTExefdrSJSy44NugqGZaTN_BX?usp=sharing`.

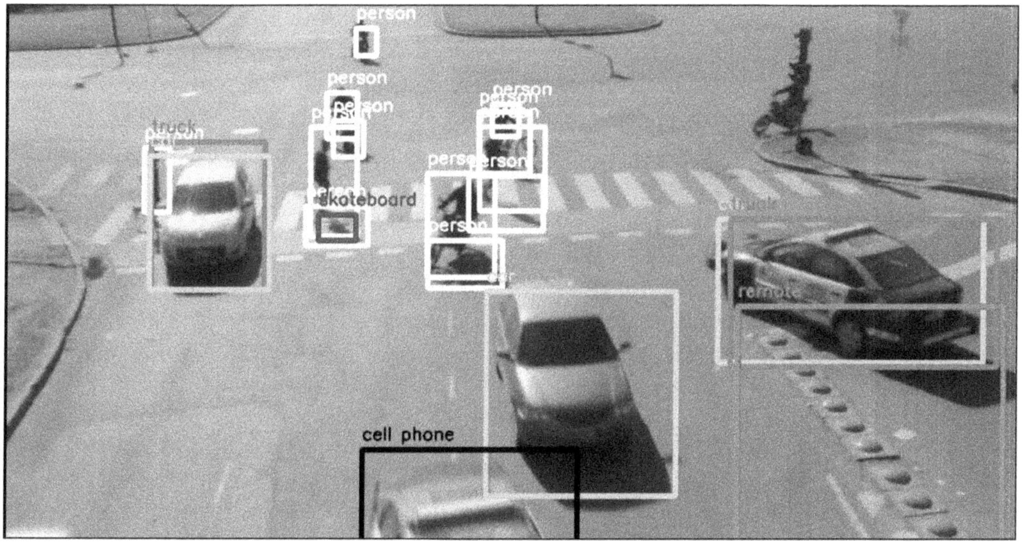

Figure 9.29 : Output of the object detection using Darkflow for the prerecorded video

In both commands we have used the – save Video flag to save the video and the – gpu 0.60 flag, which use 60% memory of GPU. Using this approach, we will get an accuracy of 78%.

Summary

In this chapter, you learned about Transfer Learning. We explored different libraries and approaches in order to build a real-time object detection application. You learned how to set up OpenCV and looked at how it is rather useful in building the baseline application. In this baseline approach, we used the model that is trained using the caffe deep learning library. After that, we used TensorFlow to build real-time object detection, but in the end, we used a pre-trained YOLO model, which outperformed every other approach. This YOLO-based approach gave us more generalized approach for object detection applications. If you are interested in building innovative solutions for computer vision, then you can enroll yourself in the VOC challenges. This boosts your skills and gives you a chance to learn. You can refer to this link for more information: `http://host.robots.ox.ac.uk/pascal/voc/` (PASCAL VOC Challenges 2005-2012). You can also build your own algorithm and check the result and compare your result with the existing approach and, if it outperforms the existing approaches, you can definitely publish the paper in reputed journals. By using the YOLO approach, we get the Mean Average Precision of 78% on the PASCAL VOC dataset and it works pretty well when you apply this model to any video or image. The code credit for this chapter goes to Adrian Rosebrock, Dat Tran, and Trieu. We defined the mAP score based on the mAP it gets for either the COCO dataset or the PASCAL VOC dataset.

In the next chapter, we will explore another application that belongs to the computer vision domain: face detection and facial expression detection. In order to build this application, we will be using Deep Learning techniques. So, keep reading!

10
Face Recognition and Face Emotion Recognition

In the previous chapter, we looked at how to detect objects such as a car, chair, cat, and dog, using Convolutional Neural Networks and the YOLO (You Only Look Once) algorithm. In this chapter, we will be detecting human faces. Apart from that, we will be looking at expressions of the human face, such as a human face seeming happy, neutral, sad, and so on. So, this chapter will be interesting, because we are going to focus on some of the latest techniques of face detection and face emotion recognition. We are dividing this chapter into two parts:

- Face detection
- Face emotion recognition

First, we will cover how face detection works, and after that, we will move on to the face emotion recognition part. In general, we will cover the following topics in this chapter:

- Introducing the problem statement
- Setting up the coding environment
- Understanding the concepts of face recognition
- Approaches for implementing face recognition
- Understanding the dataset for face emotion recognition
- Understanding the concepts of face emotion recognition
- Building the face emotion recognition model
- Understanding the testing matrix
- Testing the model

- Problems with the existing approach
- How to optimize the existing approach
    - Understanding the process for optimization
- The best approach
    - Implementing the best approach
- Summary

Introducing the problem statement

We want to develop two applications. One application will recognize human faces, and the other will recognize the emotion of the human faces. We will discuss both of them in this section. We will look at what exactly we want to develop.

Face recognition application

This application should basically identify human faces from an image or a real-time video stream. Refer to the following photo; it will help you understand what I mean by identifying faces from an image or a real-time video stream:

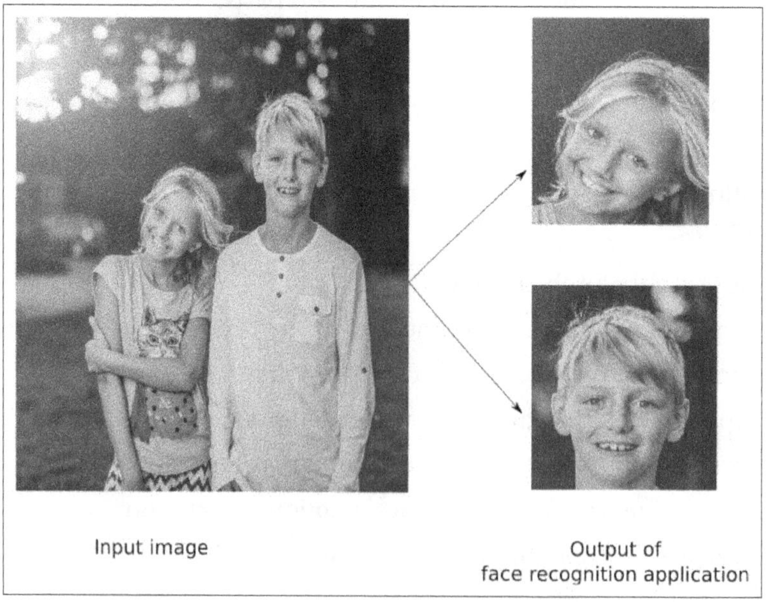

Figure 10.1: Demo output for understanding the face recognition application

Images source: https://unsplash.com/photos/Q13lggdvtVY

As you can see in the preceding figure (Figure 10.1), when we provide any image as the input, in the first step, the machine can recognize the number of human faces present in the image. As the output, we can get cropped images of the faces.

Beyond this, I also want the application to identify the name of the person based on the face. I think you are familiar with this kind of application. Let me remind you. When you upload an image on Facebook, the face recognition mechanism of Facebook immediately recognizes names of people who are part of that image, and suggests that you tag them in your image. We will develop similar functionality here in terms of the face recognition application. Now let's move on to another part of the application.

Face emotion recognition application

In this part of the application, we want to build an application that can detect the type of emotion on a human face. We will try to recognize the following seven emotions:

- Anger
- Disgust
- Fear
- Happiness
- Sadness
- Surprise
- Neutral

So, we will categorize facial emotions into these seven types. This kind of application will be helpful to know what kind of feeling the person is experiencing, and this insight will help in performing sentiment analysis, body language analysis, and so on.

Here, we will first build the face recognition application, and after that, we will move on to the face emotion recognition application.

Setting up the coding environment

In this section, we will set up the coding environment for the face recognition application. We will look at how to install dependencies. We will be installing the following two libraries:

- dlib
- face_recognition

Let's begin the installation process.

Installing dlib

In order to install the dlib library, we need to perform the following steps. We can install this library either on a Linux operating system (OS), or on macOS. Let's follow the stepwise instructions:

1. Download the source code of dlib by executing this command:

   `sudo git clone https://github.com/davisking/dlib.git.`
2. Now jump to the `dlib` directory by executing this command: `cd dlib.`
3. Now we need to build the main `dlib` library, so we need to execute the following commands stepwise:
   1. `sudo mkdir build.`
   2. `cd build.`
   3. `cmake .. -DDLIB_USE_CUDA=0 -DUSE_AVX_INSTRUCTIONS=1.`
   4. `cmake --build.`

Once the project has been built successfully, you can move to the next installation steps. You also need to install **OpenCV**. The installation steps for OpenCV have already been given in *Chapter 10, Real-Time Object Detection*.

Installing face_recognition

In order to install the `face_recognition` library, we need to execute the following commands:

```
$ sudo pip install face_recognition (This command is for python 2.7)
$ sudo pip3 install face_recognition (This command is for python 3.3+)
```

The preceding commands install the `face_recognition` library only if we have a perfectly installed `dlib`.

Once the preceding two libraries have been installed, we can move on to the next section, in which we will be discussing the key concepts of face recognition.

Understanding the concepts of face recognition

In this section, we will look at the major concepts of face recognition. These concepts will include the following topics:

- Understanding the face recognition dataset
- The algorithm for face recognition

Understanding the face recognition dataset

You may wonder why I haven't discussed anything related to the dataset until now. This is because I don't want to confuse you by providing all the details about the datasets of two different applications. The dataset that we will cover here is going to be used for **face recognition**.

If you want to build a face recognition engine from scratch, then you can use following datasets:

- CAS-PEAL Face Dataset
- Labeled Faces in the Wild

Let's discuss them in further detail.

CAS-PEAL Face Dataset

This is a huge dataset for face recognition tasks. It has various types of face images. It contains face images with different sources of variations, especially Pose, Emotion, Accessories, and Lighting (PEAL) for face recognition tasks.

This dataset contains 99,594 images of 1,040 individuals, of which 595 are male individuals and 445 are female individuals. The captured images of the individuals are with varying poses, emotions, accessories, and lighting. Refer to the following photo to see this. You can also refer to the following link if you want to see the sample dataset: `http://www.jdl.ac.cn/peal/index.html`.

Figure 10.2: CAS-PEAL Face Dataset sample image

Image source: http://www.jdl.ac.cn/peal/Image/Pose_normal/NormalCombination-9-Cameras.jpg

You can download this dataset from the following link: `http://www.jdl.ac.cn/peal/download.htm`

Labeled Faces in the Wild

This dataset is also referred to as the LFW dataset. It is used in the `face_recognition` library. We will be using this library to build our face recognition application. This dataset contains more than 13,000 images of faces collected from the web. Each face is labeled with the name of the person pictured. So, the dataset is a labeled dataset. There are 1,680 people pictured with two or more distinct face images in the dataset. You can refer to the sample dataset using the following diagram:

Figure 10.3: Sample images from the LFW dataset

Image source: http://vis-www.cs.umass.edu/lfw/person/AJ_Cook.html

> You can find out more about this dataset by clicking on `http://vis-www.cs.umass.edu/lfw/index.html`. You can also download the dataset by using the same link. You can refer to the Caltech 10,000 web faces dataset as well by clicking on `http://www.vision.caltech.edu/Image_Datasets/Caltech_10K_WebFaces/`. You should also refer to the INRIA Person Dataset, which will be quite useful. The link for the INRIA Person Dataset is `http://pascal.inrialpes.fr/data/human/`.

In order to build the face recognition application, we will be using the `face_recognition` library. We are using the pre-trained model provided by this library via its API. We will certainly explore the algorithm and the concept behind this pre-trained model and library. So let's begin!

Algorithms for face recognition

In this section, we will look at the core algorithm that is used for face recognition. The name of the algorithm is **Histogram of Oriented Gradients** (**HOG**). We will see how HOG is used in face recognition tasks. A face recognition (FR) task is basically a classification task, as we are detecting the face from the image as well as trying to identify the person's name with the help of the person's face. HOG is a good option to try out.

The other approach is to use the Convolutional Neural Network (CNN). In this section, we will also cover CNN for the FR task. So, let's start out with HOG!

Histogram of Oriented Gradients (HOG)

The HOG algorithm is one of the best approaches for state-of-the-art results for face recognition. The HOG method was introduced by Dalal and Triggs in their seminal 2005 paper, available at `http://lear.inrialpes.fr/people/triggs/pubs/Dalal-cvpr05.pdf`. The HOG image descriptor and a linear Support Vector Machine can be used to train highly accurate classifiers that can classify human detectors. So, HOG can be applied to an FR task as well. First, we will cover the basic intuition behind the algorithm.

HOG is a type of feature descriptor. A feature descriptor is a representation of an image that simplifies the image by extracting useful information and ignoring the information. Here, our focus will be on the faces only. So, we will be ignoring other objects, if there are any. The LWF dataset has less noise, so the task of generating an accurate feature descriptor is comparatively easy. The step-by-step process is as follows:

Step 1: In order to find the faces in image, we will start by converting our color image into black and white, because we don't need color data to recognize the face. Refer to the following diagram:

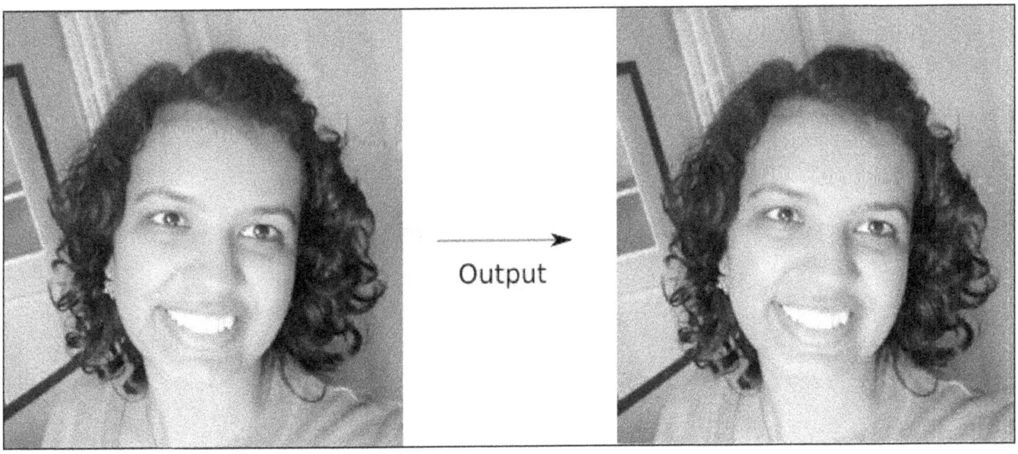

Figure 10.4: Converting a color image to a black and white image

Step 2: In this step, we will look at every single pixel in our image at a time. For every single pixel, we want to look at pixels that directly surround it. Refer to the following diagram:

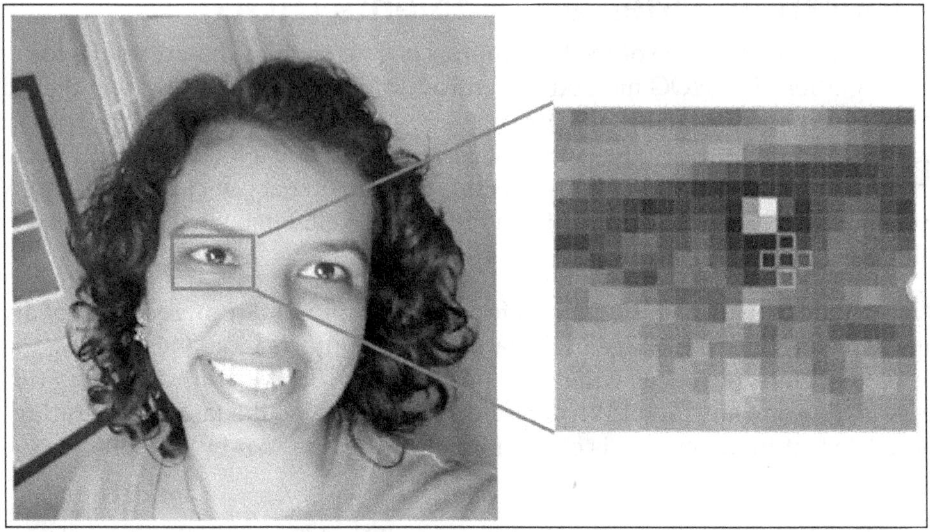

Figure 10.5: Process of scanning every single pixel of the image

Step 3: Here, our goal is to find out how dark the current pixel is with respect to the pixels directly surrounding it. We need to draw an arrow that indicates the direction in which the pixels of the image are getting darker. In order to achieve this, we scan the entire image. Refer to the following diagram:

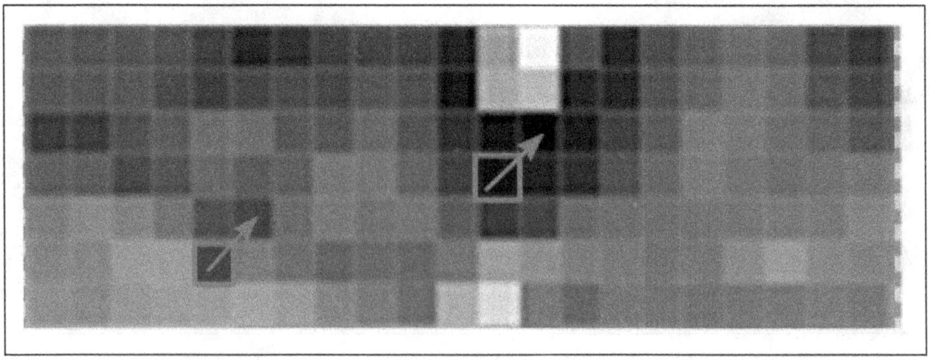

Figure 10.6: An arrow direction from a light pixel to a dark pixel

As you can see in the preceding diagram, we have considered a pixel and the other pixels surrounding it. By looking at the pixels, we can easily figure out that the arrow head is pointing toward the darker pixel.

Step 4: If we repeat this process for every single pixel in the image, then we will end up with every pixel being replaced with arrows. These arrows are called *gradients*. These *gradients* show the flow from light to dark pixels across the entire image. Refer to the following diagram:

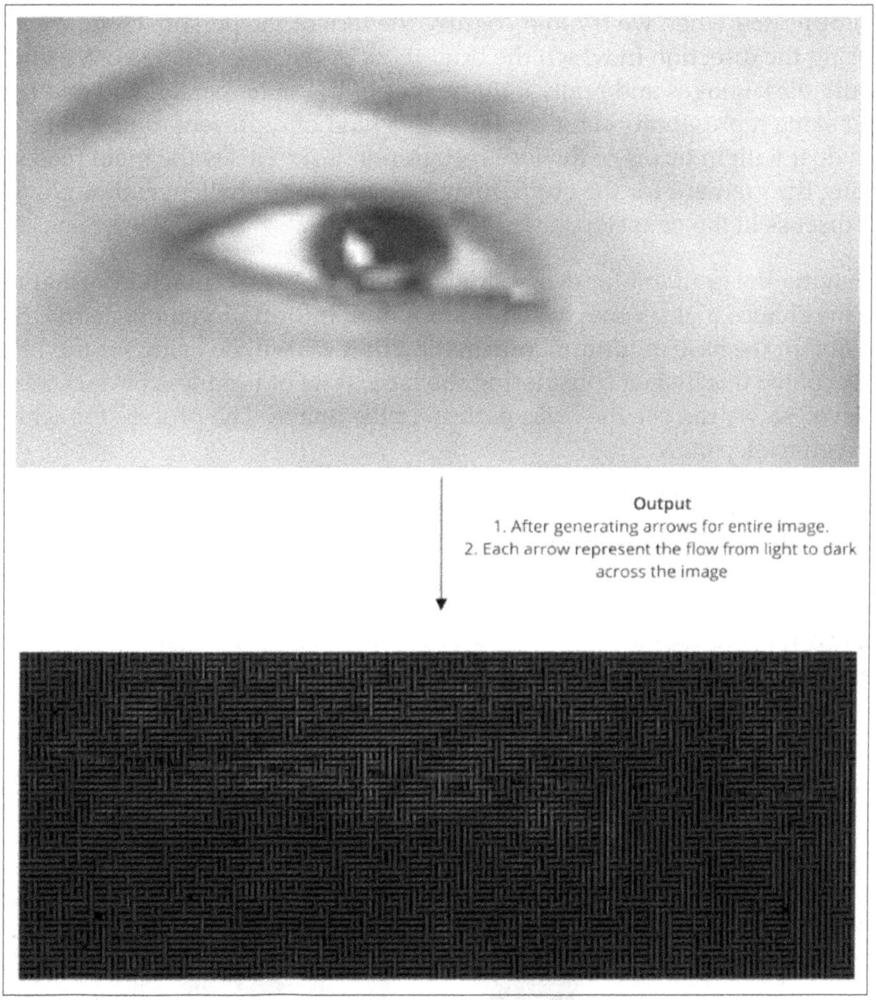

Figure 10.7: Gradient arrows for the entire image

In the preceding diagram, you can see the kind of output we get after generating a gradient for the input image. The scanning of the entire image might seem like a random thing to do, but there is a reason for replacing the pixels with gradients. If we analyze the original pixel values directly, then really dark images and really light images of the same person will have totally different pixel values, which make things more complicated when we try to recognize the face of the person. Here, we are considering the direction in which the brightness of the pixel changes. We find that both really dark images and really light images of the same person will end up with the exact same representation for the face. This kind of representation will be easy for us to deal with in terms of the face recognition task. This is the main reason for generating the gradient for the entire image. There is one challenge, though, which we will discuss in the next step.

Step 5: Saving the gradient for every single pixel gives us too much information, and there is the chance that we may use this amount of information inefficiently. So, we need to obtain the bare minimum information that we will be using for the FR task. We will achieve this by just considering the basic flow of lightness or darkness at a higher level, so we can see the basic pattern of the image. The process for achieving this is given in step 6.

Step 6: We will break up this image into small squares of 16 x16 pixels each. In each square, we will count the number of gradient points in each major direction, which means we will count how many arrows point up, point down, point right, point left, and so on. After counting this, we will replace that square in the image with the arrow directions that were the strongest. The end result is that we convert the original image into a simple representation that captures the basic structure of a face. Refer to the following diagram:

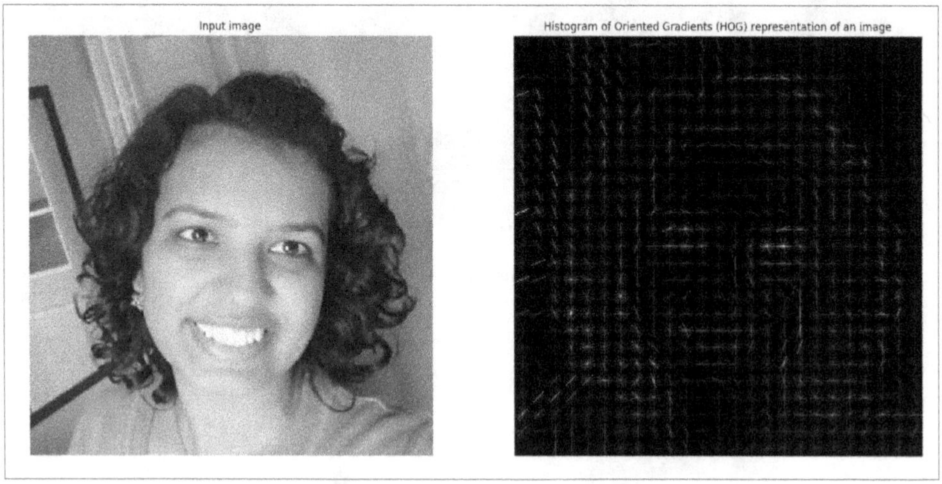

Figure 10.8: Simple face representation in the HOG version

This kind of representation is easy to process for the FR task; it's called the HOG version of the image. It represents the features that we will consider in the FR task, and that is why this representation is referred to as an HOG features descriptor.

Step 7: In order to find out the faces in this HOG image, we have to find out the part of our image that looks the most similar to a known HOG pattern that was extracted from a bunch of other training faces. Refer to the following diagram:

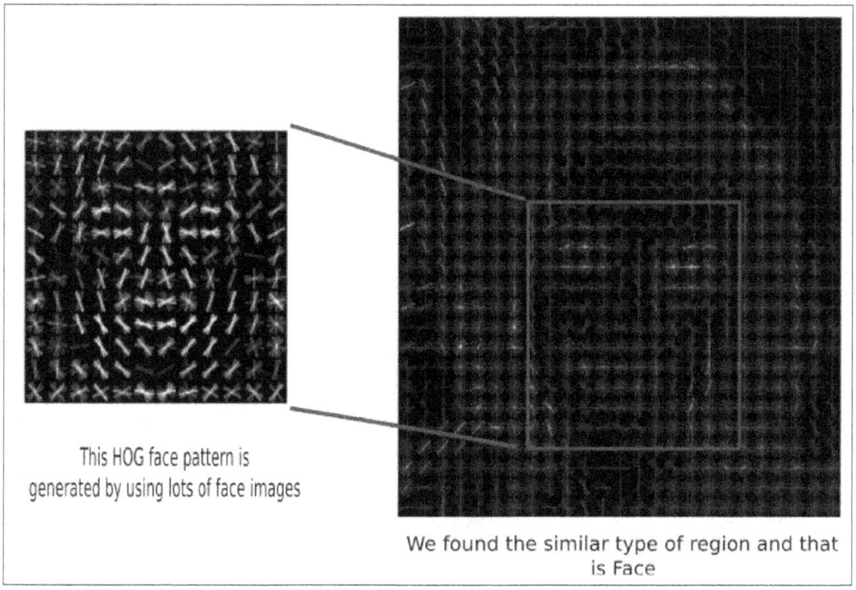

This HOG face pattern is
generated by using lots of face images
We found the similar type of region and that
is Face

Figure 10.9: Process of recognizing a face using the HOG version of our image

Using this technique, we can easily recognize the faces in any image.

Convolutional Neural Network (CNN) for FR

In this section, we will look at how a CNN can be used to recognize the faces from the images. This section is divided into two parts:

- Simple CNN architecture
- Understanding how a CNN works for FR

Simple CNN architecture

I don't want to get too deep into how a CNN works, as I have already provided most of the necessary details in *Chapter 9, Building Real-Time Object Detection*; however, I want to remind you about some necessary stuff regarding CNN. First, refer to the following diagram:

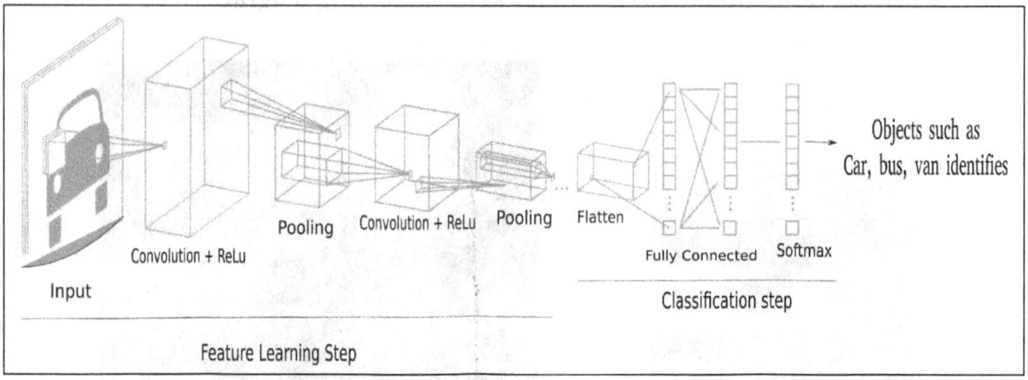

Figure 10.10: The CNN architecture

As you can see in the preceding diagram, there is a convolutional layer, a pooling layer, a fully connected layer, and an output layer. There are different activation functions, penalties, and SoftMax functions involved. This is high-level information. For this FR task, we can use three convolutional and pooling layers with ReLU as activation functions. You can add more layers, but it will become more computationally expensive to train.

Understanding how CNN works for FR

Intuitively, the CNN model performs the following steps in order to build a good FR application. The basic process is as follows:

Step 1: Look at a picture. Crop the images that contain only faces.

Step 2: Now, in this step, we focus on a face and try to understand that even if a face is turned in a weird direction, or an image is taken in bad lighting, we need to identify the proper placement of the face in this kind of image. Step 3 will give us a solution.

Step 3: In order to identify the face from any image, whether that image is taken in bad lighting conditions, or the orientation of the face seems totally weird, we need to identify the face. To achieve that, we pick out unique features of the face that can be used to tell us something unique about the person's face. With the help of these unique features, we can identify the face of the same person, as well as the face of the different persons. These features can include how big the eyes are, how long the face is, and so on. There are 68 specific points that should be considered; and they are called landmarks. These points are defined based on the face landmark estimation. Refer to the following paper to get more details about this: `http://www.csc.kth.se/~vahidk/papers/KazemiCVPR14.pdf`. Take a look at the following diagram:

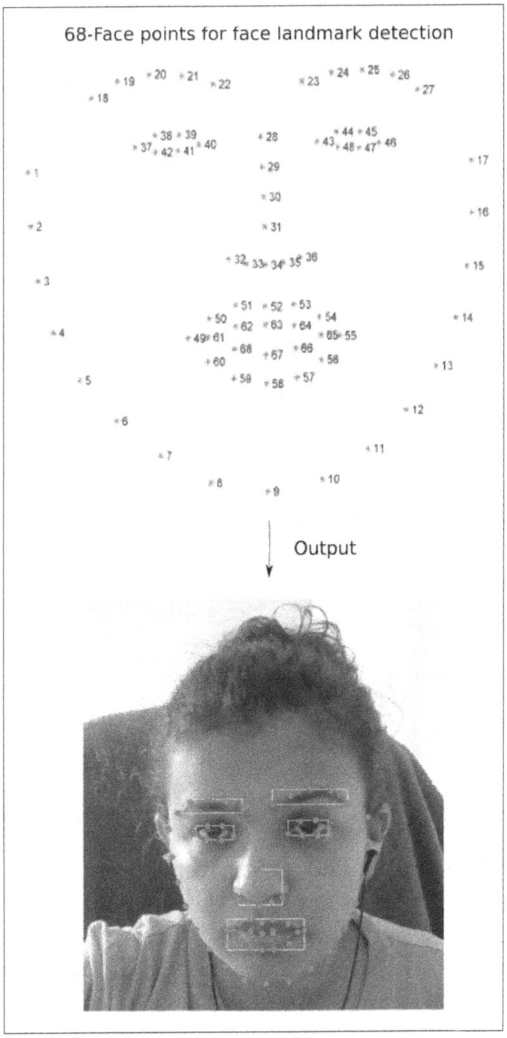

Figure 10.11: 68 points for face landmark estimation

Step 4: We need to identify the person's face with their name, so in order to achieve this, we will compare the unique features of that face with all the people we already know in order to determine the person's name. Suppose you have added the images for Bill Gates, Barack Obama, and so on. You have generated the unique features for their faces, and now we will compare their unique facial features with these already generated facial features, and if the features are similar, then we get to know the name of the person, which is Barack Obama or Bill Gates in the given image. The identification of the person based on their facial features is a classification problem, which can easily be solved by CNN. We are generating a face embedding vector of size 128 measurements. As an input, we should provide this face embedding vector. Once we complete the training, our application will be ready to identify the person's name.

Step 5: The trained model looks at all the faces we have measured in the past, and looks at the person who has the closest measurements to our faces' measurements. That is our match.

The preceding approach is for our CNN-based FR and real-time face recognition task. We have covered the basic concepts and the idea behind the algorithms that are used in the FR task. Now let's start the implementation.

Approaches for implementing face recognition

In this section, we will be implementing the FR application. We are using the `face_recognition` library. We have already configured the environment for that. We will be implementing the following approaches here:

- The HOG-based approach
- The CNN-based approach
- Real-time face recognition

Now let's start coding!

Implementing the HOG-based approach

In this approach, we are using the HOG algorithm to find out two things: the total number of faces in the image, and the paces. We are using the API of the `face_recgnition` library. You can find the code by clicking on the following GitHub link: `https://github.com/jalajthanaki/Face_recognition/blob/master/face_detection_example.py`. The code snippet is provided in the following diagram:

```
from PIL import Image
import face_recognition

# Load the jpg file into a numpy array
image = face_recognition.load_image_file("./img/1.png")

# Find all the faces in the image using the default HOG-based model.
# This method is fairly accurate, but not as accurate as the CNN model and not GPU accelerated.
# See also: find_faces_in_picture_cnn.py
face_locations = face_recognition.face_locations(image)

print("I found {} face(s) in this photograph.".format(len(face_locations)))

for face_location in face_locations:

    # Print the location of each face in this image
    top, right, bottom, left = face_location
    print("A face is located at pixel location Top: {}, Left: {}, Bottom: {}, Right: {}".format(top, left, bottom, right))

    # You can access the actual face itself like this:
    face_image = image[top:bottom, left:right]
    pil_image = Image.fromarray(face_image)
    pil_image.show()
```

Figure 10.12: Code snippet for the HOG-based approach for FR

In the preceding diagram, we have given an image as input, and with the help of the API of the `face_recognition` library, we can find the pixel location of the face in an image. Here, we will also count how many faces there are in an image, and with the help of the `Image` library, we can crop the faces from the given image. You can find the output of this script in the following figure:

```
/usr/bin/python2.7 /home/jalaj/PycharmProjects/Face_recognition/face_detection_example.py
I found 1 face(s) in this photograph.
A face is located at pixel location Top: 139, Left: 124, Bottom: 268, Right: 253

Process finished with exit code 0
```

Figure 10.13: Output of the HOG-based approach for FR

Refer to the cropped face output in the following screenshot:

Figure 10.14: Cropped face output

As you can see in the last output diagram with the help of a simple API, we can build a simple face recognition application. This approach is kind of a baseline approach for us.

Now let's move on to the CNN-based approach. The HOG-based approach is less accurate compared to the CNN-based approach. If we use GPU for the CNN-based approach, then we can train the model in a less amount of time. Now let's look at the code for the CNN-based approach.

Implementing the CNN-based approach

In this approach, we will be using the `face_recognition` library, where we specified the name of the model. Our model's name is `cnn`. This particular approach will load the pre-trained model via the `face_recognition` API, and we can generate a more accurate output. You can find the code by clicking on the following GitHub link: `https://github.com/jalajthanaki/Face_recognition/blob/master/face_detection_GPU_example.py`. Refer to the code snippet given in the following figure:

```
from PIL import Image
import face_recognition

# Load the jpg file into a numpy array
image = face_recognition.load_image_file("./img/3.jpg")

# Find all the faces in the image using a pre-trained convolutional neural network.
# This method is more accurate than the default HOG model, but it's slower
# unless you have an nvidia GPU and dlib compiled with CUDA extensions. But if you do,
# this will use GPU acceleration and perform well.
# See also: find_faces_in_picture.py
face_locations = face_recognition.face_locations(image, number_of_times_to_upsample=0, model="cnn")

print("I found {} face(s) in this photograph.".format(len(face_locations)))

for face_location in face_locations:

    # Print the location of each face in this image
    top, right, bottom, left = face_location
    print("A face is located at pixel location Top: {}, Left: {}, Bottom: {}, Right: {}".format(top, left, bottom, right))

    # You can access the actual face itself like this:
    face_image = image[top:bottom, left:right]
    pil_image = Image.fromarray(face_image)
    pil_image.show()
```

Figure 10.15: Code snippet for the CNN-based approach for FR

Here, the implementation code is almost the same as earlier, but the difference is that we have provided the model name as `cnn` during the API call. You can see the output of this implementation in the following diagram:

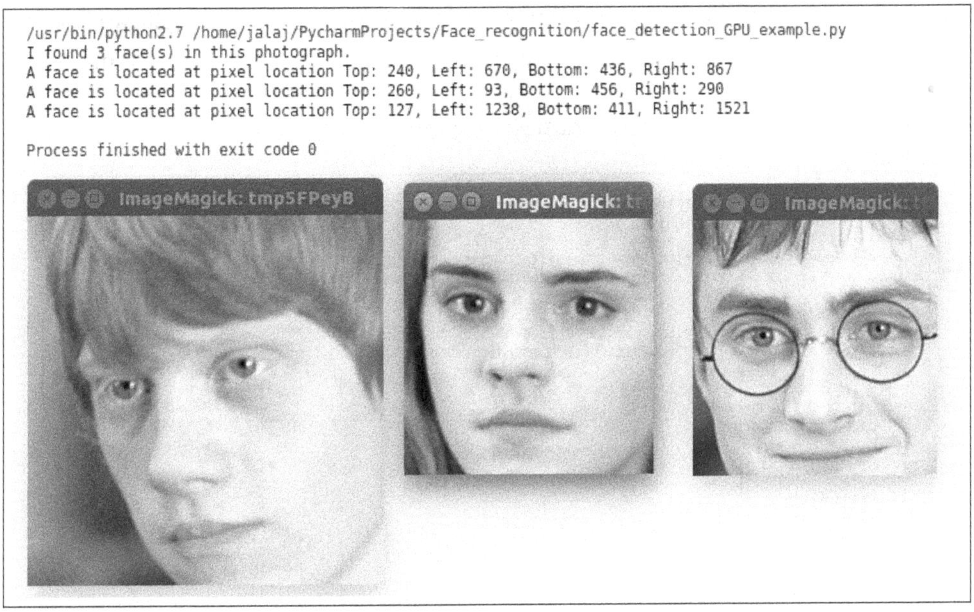
/usr/bin/python2.7 /home/jalaj/PycharmProjects/Face_recognition/face_detection_GPU_example.py
I found 3 face(s) in this photograph.
A face is located at pixel location Top: 240, Left: 670, Bottom: 436, Right: 867
A face is located at pixel location Top: 260, Left: 93, Bottom: 456, Right: 290
A face is located at pixel location Top: 127, Left: 1238, Bottom: 411, Right: 1521
Process finished with exit code 0
ImageMagick: tmp5FPeyB
ImageMagick:
ImageMagick:

Figure 10.16: Output of the CNN-based approach for FR

The output of this implementation is the same as the last one. This version of the implementation is fast, and has better accuracy. Now let's try to implement the FR task for a real-time video stream.

Implementing real-time face recognition

In this section, we will implement the FR task for a real-time video stream. We will try to identify the name of the person who has appeared in the video. Doesn't that sound interesting? Let's begin. You can find the code by clicking on the following GitHub link: `https://github.com/jalajthanaki/Face_recognition/blob/master/Real_time_face_detection.py`.

Again, we are using the API of the `face_recognition` library. We are using `OpenCV` as well. First of all, we need to feed the sample image of the person with the person's name, so that the machine can learn the name of the person and identify it during the testing. In this implementation, I have fed the image of Barack Obama and Joe Biden. You can add your image as well. If the face features are familiar and match with the already-fed images, then the script returns the name of the person, and if the face features are not familiar to the given image, then that person's face is tagged as *Unknown*. Refer to the implementation in the following diagram:

```
video_capture = cv2.VideoCapture(0)

# Load a sample picture and learn how to recognize it.
obama_image = face_recognition.load_image_file("./img/obama.jpg")
obama_face_encoding = face_recognition.face_encodings(obama_image)[0]

# Load a second sample picture and learn how to recognize it.
biden_image = face_recognition.load_image_file("./img/biden.jpg")
biden_face_encoding = face_recognition.face_encodings(biden_image)[0]

# Create arrays of known face encodings and their names
known_face_encodings = [
    obama_face_encoding,
    biden_face_encoding
]
known_face_names = [
    "Barack Obama",
    "Joe Biden"
]

# Initialize some variables
face_locations = []
face_encodings = []
face_names = []
process_this_frame = True

while True:
    # Grab a single frame of video
    ret, frame = video_capture.read()

    # Resize frame of video to 1/4 size for faster face recognition processing
    small_frame = cv2.resize(frame, (0, 0), fx=0.25, fy=0.25)

    # Convert the image from BGR color (which OpenCV uses) to RGB color (which face_recognition uses)
    rgb_small_frame = small_frame[:, :, ::-1]

    # Only process every other frame of video to save time
    if process_this_frame:
        # Find all the faces and face encodings in the current frame of video
        face_locations = face_recognition.face_locations(rgb_small_frame)
        face_encodings = face_recognition.face_encodings(rgb_small_frame, face_locations)

        face_names = []
        for face_encoding in face_encodings:
            # See if the face is a match for the known face(s)
            matches = face_recognition.compare_faces(known_face_encodings, face_encoding)
            name = "Unknown"

            # If a match was found in known_face_encodings, just use the first one.
            if True in matches:
                first_match_index = matches.index(True)
                name = known_face_names[first_match_index]

            face_names.append(name)

    process_this_frame = not process_this_frame
```

Figure 10.17: Implementation of real-time FR

As you can see in the preceding code, I have provided sample images of Barack Obama and Joe Biden. I have also provided the names of the people whose images I'm feeding to my script. I have used the same face recognition API for detecting and recognizing the face in the video stream. When you run the script, your webcam streams your real-time video and this script detects the face, and if you provide the image of the person that the machine knows, then it identifies it correctly this time as well. Refer to the following diagram:

Figure 10.18: Output of the real-time FR

As you can see, I have not provided my image to the machine, so it identifies me as **Unknown**, whereas it can identify Barack Obama's image. You can also find the animated image by clicking on `https://github.com/jalajthanaki/Face_recognition/blob/master/img/Demo.gif`.

We are finished with the first part of the chapter, which entails developing an application that can recognize human faces, as well as identify the name of the person based on their face. We implemented three different variations of FR.

In the upcoming section, we will look at how to develop a face emotion recognition (FER) application. We need different kinds of datasets to build this application, so we will start by understanding a dataset for FER.

Understanding the dataset for face emotion recognition

To develop an FER application, we are considering the `FER2013` dataset. You can download this dataset from `https://www.kaggle.com/c/challenges-in-representation-learning-facial-expression-recognition-challenge/data`. We need to know the basic details about this dataset. The dataset credit goes to Pierre-Luc Carrier and Aaron Courville as part of an ongoing research project.

This dataset consists of 48x48 pixel grayscale images of faces. The task is to categorize each of the faces based on the emotion that has been shown in the image in the form of facial expressions. The seven categories are as follows, and for each of them there is a numeric label that expresses the category of the emotion:

- `0` = Anger
- `1` = Disgust
- `2` = Fear
- `3` = Happiness
- `4` = Sadness
- `5` = Surprise
- `6` = Neutral

This dataset has the `fer2013.csv` file. This csv file will be used as our training dataset. Now let's look at the attributes of the file. There are three columns in the file, as follows:

- **Emotion**: This column contains the numeric label of the facial expression. For fear, this column contains the value `2`; for sadness, this column contains the value `4`, and so on.
- **Pixels**: This column contains the pixel values of the individual images. It represents the matrix of pixel values of the image.
- **Usage**: This column contains the general tag about whether the particular data record will be used for training purposes or for testing purposes. There are three labels that are part of this column, and those are *Training*, *PublicTest*, and *PrivateTest*. For training purposes, there are 28,709 data samples. The public test set consist of 3,589 data samples, and the private test set consists of another 3,589 data samples.

Now let's cover the concepts that will help us develop the FER application.

Understanding the concepts of face emotion recognition

We are using Convolutional Neural Network (CNN) to develop the FER application. Earlier, we looked at the basic architecture of CNN. In order to develop FER applications, we will be using the following CNN architecture and optimizer. We are building CNN that is two layers deep. We will be using two fully connected layers and the SoftMax function to categorize the facial emotions.

We will be using several layers made of the convolutional layer, followed by the ReLU (Rectified Linear Unit) layer, followed by the max pooling layer. Refer to the following diagram, which will help you conceptualize the arrangement of the CNN layers. Let's look at the working of CNN. We will cover the following layers:

- The convolutional layer
- The ReLU layer
- The pooling layer
- The fully connected layer
- The SoftMax layer

Understanding the convolutional layer

In this layer, we will feed our image in the form of pixel values. We are using a sliding window of 3 x 3 dimension, which slides through the entire image. The area that is chosen by the sliding window is called the *receptive field*. It is the patch of the image. A sliding window is just the matrix of a 3 x 3 dimension, and it can scan the entire image. By using the sliding window, we scan nine pixel values of the image using the matrix of a 3 x 3 dimension. This receptive field or a piece of the image is the input of the convolutional network.

Refer to the following diagram:

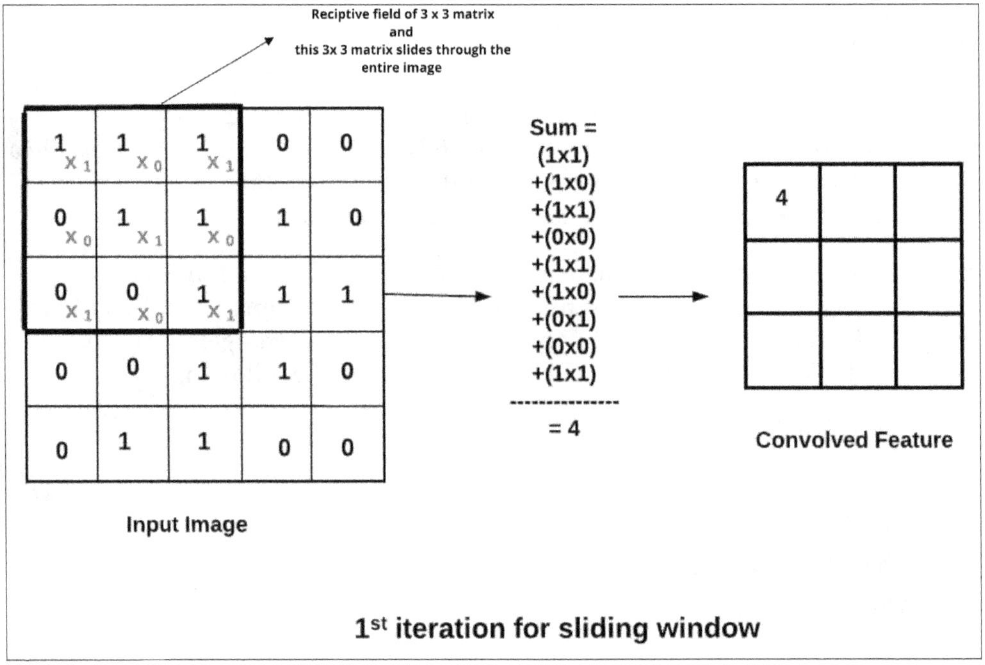

Figure 10.19: Sliding window and receptive field

This receptive field carries the values in the form of pixel values of the input image. These pixel values are called feature maps, features, filter, weight matrix, or kernel. We already had a matrix of 3 x 3, which is referred to as the feature map. The size of the feature map is one of the hyperparameters. We can take the n x n matrix, where n >=1. Here, we have considered a 3 x 3 matrix to understand the operation. Now it's time to perform a simple math operation, the steps for which are as follows:

Step 1: Get the feature map. Here, the feature map means the image patch that is generated in the form of a receptive field.

Step 2: We need to perform the dot product between the feature map and the entire image. Again, we scan the entire image using the sliding window, and generate the value of dot products.

Step 3: We need to sum up all the values that we get from obtaining the dot product.

Step 4: We need to divide the value of the summation for the dot product by the total number of pixels in the feature. In this explanation, we have a total of nine pixels, so we will divide the sum by 9. As an output, we get the image that is referred to as a feature image.

Refer to the following diagram:

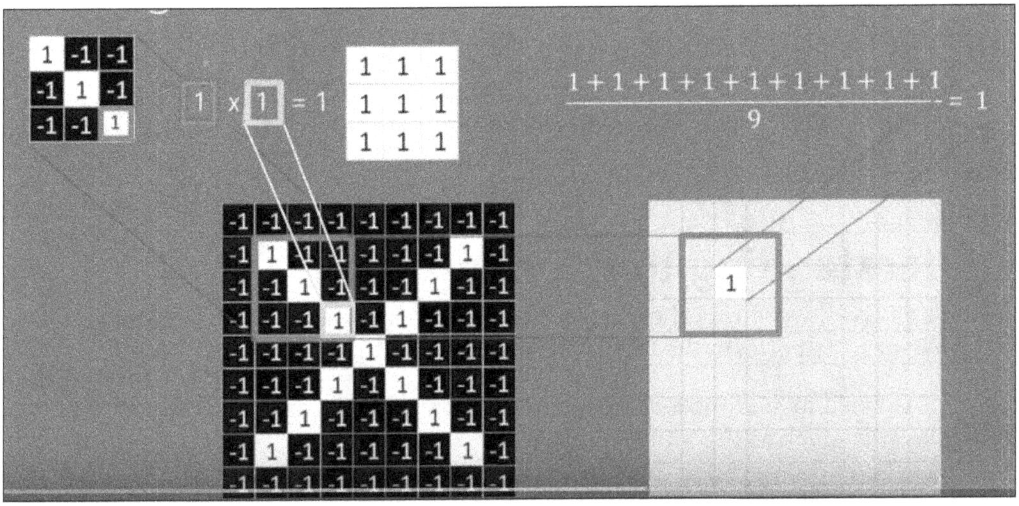

Figure 10.20: Math operation for the convolutional layer

We will repeat this operation for almost all the possible positions of the image, and we will try out all the possible combinations, which is the reason why this operation is referred to as convolutional. Now let's look at the ReLU layer.

Understanding the ReLU layer

This layer basically introduces nonlinearity to the convolutional network. Here, we need to use the `activation` function. For this application, we have chosen the Rectified Linear Unit as the activation function. This layer performs some sort of normalization to our feature map. Let's see what it does to our feature map:

Step 1: This layer takes the feature map as the input that is generated by the convolutional layer.

Step 2: This layer just converts the negative values into zero.

Refer the following diagram:

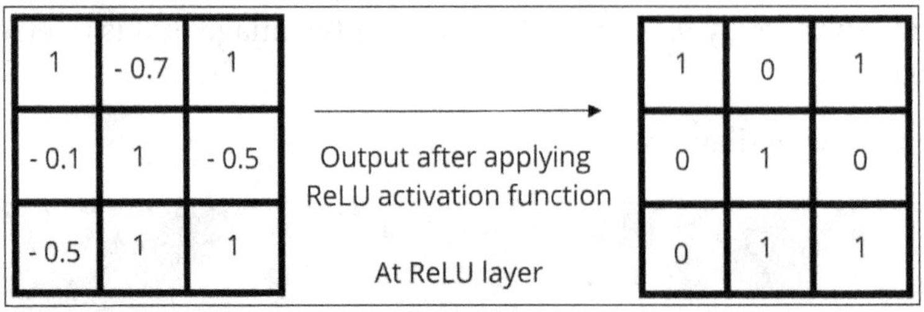

Figure 10.21: Operations performed by the ReLU layer

Now it is time to look at the pooling layer.

Understanding the pooling layer

Using this layer, we shrink the image. We will be using the max pooling operation here. We need to perform the following steps:

Step 1: We need to feed the feature map as the input, and this time, the output of the ReLU layer is given as the input to this layer.

Step 2: We need to pick up the window size. Generally, we pick up the size of 2 x 2 pixels or 3 x 3 pixels. We will be taking 2 x 2 as our window size.

Step 3: We scan the entire image based on this window size, and we will take the maximum value from four pixel values.

You can understand the operation by referring to the following diagram:

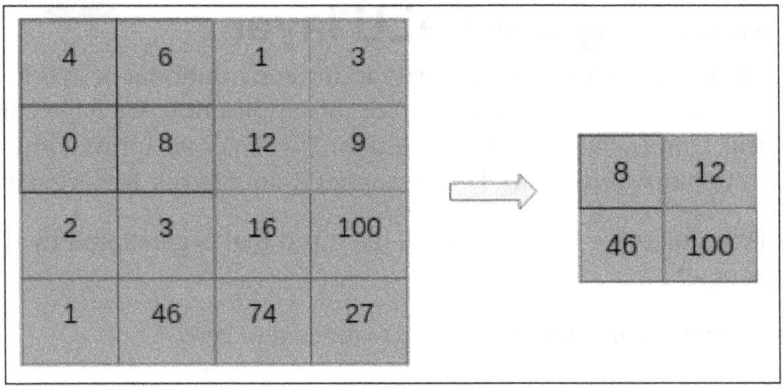

Figure 10.22: Operations performed by the max pooling layer

We can do deep stacking of these layers as deep as we need. You can repeat the convolutional, ReLU, and pooling layers an n number of times in order to make CNN deep.

Understanding the fully connected layer

The output of all the layers is passed on to the fully connected layer. This layer has a voting mechanism. All image patches are considered for votes. The image patches of 2 x 2 matrices are arranged in a horizontal way. The vote depends on how strongly a value predicts the face expression. If certain values of this layer are high, it means they are close to 1, and if certain values of this layer are low, it means they are close to 0. For each category, certain cell values are close to 1 and others are 0, and this way, our network will predict the category. Refer to the following diagram:

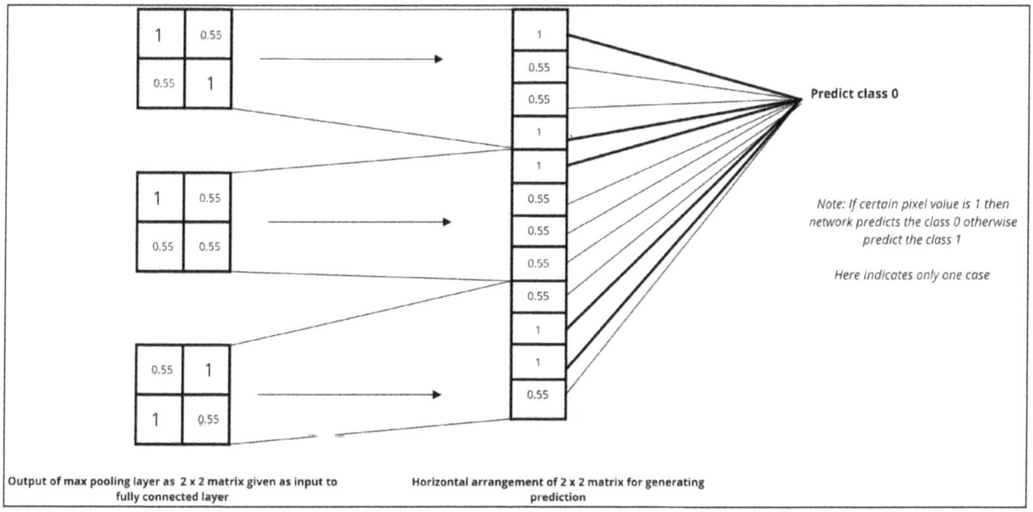

Figure 10.23: Intuitive understanding of the fully connected layer

There is only one math operation that's been performed here. We are taking average values. As you can see in preceding diagram, the first, fourth, fifth, tenth, and eleventh cells of the fully connected layer are predicting one category, so we need to sum up all the values present in those cells and find their average. This average value tells us how confident our network is when it predicts the class. We can stack up as many fully connected layers as we want. Here, the number of neurons is the hyperparameter.

Understanding the SoftMax layer

We can also use the SoftMax layer, which converts the feature's values into the probability value. The equation for this is as follows:

$$S(yi) = \frac{e^{yi}}{\sum_j e^{yj}}$$

Figure 10.24: The SoftMax equation

This layer takes the feature values, and using the preceding equation, it generates the probability value. Refer to the following diagram:

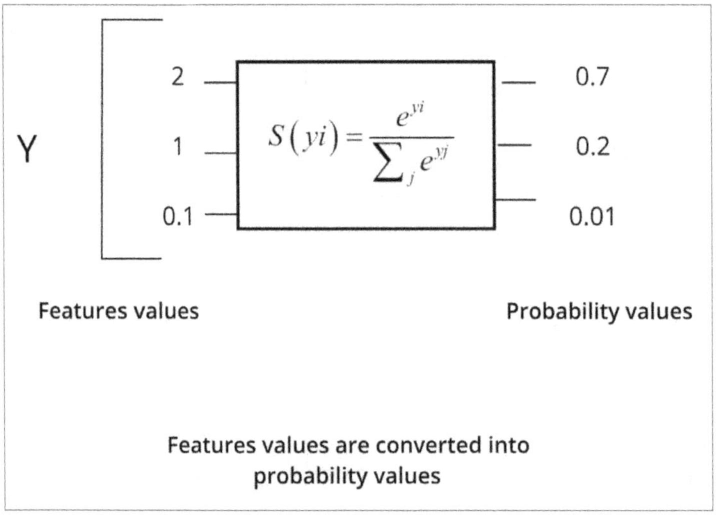

Figure 10.25: Process of calculating the SoftMax function

Updating the weight based on backpropagation

The weight of the CNN network has been updated based on the backpropagation technique. We will measure the difference between our predicted answer and the actual answer. Based on this error measurement, we calculate the gradient for the loss function, which tells us whether we should increase the weight or decrease it. If the predicted answer and the actual answers are the same then there will be no change in weights.

We have understood most of the core concepts of CNN that we will be using for developing face emotion recognition model.

Building the face emotion recognition model

In this section, we will implement the application of FER using CNN. For coding purposes, we will be using the `TensorFlow`, `TFLearn`, `OpenCV`, and `Numpy` libraries. You can find the code by using this GitHub link: `https://github.com/jalajthanaki/Facial_emotion_recognition_using_TensorFlow`. These are the steps that we need to follow:

1. Preparing the data
2. Loading the data
3. Training the model

Preparing the data

In this section, we will be preparing the dataset that can be used in our application. As you know, our dataset is in grayscale. We have two options. One is that we need to use only black and white images, and if we are using black and white images, then there will be two channels. The second option is that we can convert the grayscale pixel values into RGB (red, green, and blue) images and build the CNN with three channels. For our development purposes, we are using two channels as our images are in grayscale.

First of all, we are loading the dataset and converting it into the `numpy` array. After the conversion, we will save it as a `.npy` format so that we can load that dataset as and when needed. We are saving actual data records in one file and the labels of their data records in another file. Our input datafile name is `fer2013.csv`. Our output file that contains the data is `data_set_fer2013.npy`, and labels are present in the `data_labels_fer2013.npy` file. The script name that performs this task is `csv_to_numpy.py`. You can refer to its code using this GitHub link: `https://github.com/jalajthanaki/Facial_emotion_recognition_using_TensorFlow/tree/master/data`

Refer to the code snippet for loading the dataset in the following diagram:

```
FILE_PATH = './fer2013.csv'
data = pd.read_csv(FILE_PATH)


labels = []
images = []
index = 1
total = data.shape[0]

for index, row in data.iterrows():
    emotion = emotion_to_vec(row['emotion'])
    image = data_to_image(row['pixels'])
    if image is not None:
        labels.append(emotion)
        images.append(image)
        #labels.append(emotion)
        #images.append(flip_image(image))
    else:
        print "Error"
    index += 1
    print "Progreso: {}/{} {:.2f}%".format(index, total, index * 100.0 / total)

print "Total: " + str(len(images))
np.save('data_set_fer2013.npy', images)
np.save('data_labels_fer2013.npy', labels)
```

Figure 10.26: Code snippet for loading the dataset

The code for the `helper` function is given in the following diagram:

```
cascade_classifier = cv2.CascadeClassifier(CASC_PATH)

def format_image(image):
  if len(image.shape) > 2 and image.shape[2] == 3:
    image = cv2.cvtColor(image, cv2.COLOR_BGR2GRAY)
  else:
    image = cv2.imdecode(image, cv2.CV_LOAD_IMAGE_GRAYSCALE)
  gray_border = np.zeros((150, 150), np.uint8)
  gray_border[:,:] = 200
  #gray_border[((150 / 2) - (SIZE_FACE/2)):((150/2)+(SIZE_FACE/2)), ((150/2)-(SIZE_FACE/2)):((150/2)+(SIZE_FACE/2))] = image
  gray_border[(int(150 / 2) - int(SIZE_FACE / 2)):(int(150 / 2) + int(SIZE_FACE / 2)),
  (int(150 / 2) - int(SIZE_FACE / 2)):(int(150 / 2) + int(SIZE_FACE / 2))] = image
  image = gray_border

  faces = cascade_classifier.detectMultiScale(
    image,
    scaleFactor = 1.3,
    minNeighbors = 5
  )
  # None is we don't found an image
  if not len(faces) > 0:
    #print "No hay caras"
    return None
  max_area_face = faces[0]
  for face in faces:
    if face[2] * face[3] > max_area_face[2] * max_area_face[3]:
      max_area_face = face
  # Chop image to face
  face = max_area_face
  image = image[face[1]:(face[1] + face[2]), face[0]:(face[0] + face[3])]
  # Resize image to network size

  try:
    image = cv2.resize(image, (SIZE_FACE, SIZE_FACE), interpolation = cv2.INTER_CUBIC) / 255.
  except Exception:
    print("[+] Problem during resize")
    return None
  print image.shape
  return image


def emotion_to_vec(x):
    d = np.zeros(len(EMOTIONS))
    d[x] = 1.0
    return d

def flip_image(image):
    return cv2.flip(image, 1)

def data_to_image(data):
    #print data
    data_image = np.fromstring(str(data), dtype = np.uint8, sep = ' ').reshape((SIZE_FACE, SIZE_FACE))
    data_image = Image.fromarray(data_image).convert('RGB')
    print data_image
    data_image = np.array(data_image)[:, :, ::-1].copy()
    data_image = format_image(data_image)
    return data_image
```

Figure 10.27: Code snippet for the helper function

Now let's look at how we can load the data that we have saved in the `.npy` format.

Loading the data

In this section, we will look at how we are going to use the dataset we have prepared so that we can use it for training. Here, we create a separate script to help us load the data. In this, we define a test dataset that we will be using during testing.

This is a simple and straightforward code. You can find the code snippet in the following figure:

```
import ...

class DatasetLoader(object):

  def __init__(self):
    pass

  def load_from_save(self):
    self._images      = np.load(join(SAVE_DIRECTORY, SAVE_DATASET_IMAGES_FILENAME))
    self._labels      = np.load(join(SAVE_DIRECTORY, SAVE_DATASET_LABELS_FILENAME))
    #self._images_test = np.load(join(SAVE_DIRECTORY, SAVE_DATASET_IMAGES_TEST_FILENAME))
    #self._labels_test = np.load(join(SAVE_DIRECTORY, SAVE_DATASET_LABELS_TEST_FILENAME))
    self._images      = self._images.reshape([-1, SIZE_FACE, SIZE_FACE, 1])
    self._images_test = self._images.reshape([-1, SIZE_FACE, SIZE_FACE, 1])
    self._labels      = self._labels.reshape([-1, len(EMOTIONS)])
    self._labels_test = self._labels.reshape([-1, len(EMOTIONS)])

  @property
  def images(self):
   return self._images

  @property
  def labels(self):
    return self._labels

  @property
  def images_test(self):
    return self._images_test

  @property
  def labels_test(self):
    return self._labels_test

  @property
  def num_examples(self):
    return self._num_examples
```

Figure 10.28: Code snippet for the data loader script

This class and its methods will be used when we write the script for training. You can see the code of this script using this GitHub link: `https://github.com/jalajthanaki/Facial_emotion_recognition_using_TensorFlow/blob/master/dataset_loader.py`.

Training the model

In this section, we will look at how to train the model, so that it can recognize the facial emotion. These are the steps that we will be performing. You can find the code for this training step by referring to this GitHub link: `https://github.com/jalajthanaki/Facial_emotion_recognition_using_TensorFlow/blob/master/emotion_recognition.py`.

Loading the data using the dataset_loader script

Here, we are loading the dataset with the help of the script that we have written and understood in the last section. You can find the code snippet in the following figure:

```
from __future__ import division, absolute_import
import re
import numpy as np
from dataset_loader import DatasetLoader
import tflearn
from tflearn.layers.core import input_data, dropout, fully_connected, flatten
from tflearn.layers.conv import conv_2d, max_pool_2d, avg_pool_2d
from tflearn.layers.merge_ops import merge
from tflearn.layers.normalization import local_response_normalization
from tflearn.layers.estimator import regression
from constants import *
from os.path import isfile, join
import random
import sys

class EmotionRecognition:

  def __init__(self):
    self.dataset = DatasetLoader()
```

Figure 10.29: Loading the data during the training of the model

Now let's build the CNN that is actually used for training.

Building the Convolutional Neural Network

In this step, we will be building the CNN that will be used for training purposes. Here, we have three layers of the convolutional network, the ReLU layer, and the pooling layer. The first two layers have 64 neurons, and the last one has 128 neurons. We have added the dropout layer. For some neurons, the dropout layer sets the value to zero. This layer selects the neurons that have not changed their weight for a long time, or have not been activated for a long time. This will make our training more effective. We have two fully connected layers, and one fully connected layer using the SoftMax function to derive the probability for the facial emotion class. We are using the `momentum` function for performing the gradient descent. Here, our loss function is categorical cross-entropy. Refer to the code snippet in the following diagram:

```
def build_network(self):
  # Smaller 'AlexNet'
  # https://github.com/tflearn/tflearn/blob/master/examples/images/alexnet.py
  print('[+] Building CNN')
  self.network = input_data(shape = [None, SIZE_FACE, SIZE_FACE, 1])
  self.network = conv_2d(self.network, 64, 5, activation = 'relu')
  #self.network = local_response_normalization(self.network)
  self.network = max_pool_2d(self.network, 3, strides = 2)
  self.network = conv_2d(self.network, 64, 5, activation = 'relu')
  self.network = max_pool_2d(self.network, 3, strides = 2)
  self.network = conv_2d(self.network, 128, 4, activation = 'relu')
  self.network = dropout(self.network, 0.3)
  self.network = fully_connected(self.network, 3072, activation = 'relu')
  self.network = fully_connected(self.network, len(EMOTIONS), activation = 'softmax')
  self.network = regression(self.network,
    optimizer = 'momentum',
    loss = 'categorical_crossentropy')
  self.model = tflearn.DNN(
    self.network,
    checkpoint_path = SAVE_DIRECTORY + '/emotion_recognition',
    max_checkpoints = 1,
    tensorboard_verbose = 2
  )
  self.load_model()
```

Figure 10.30: Code snippet for building CNN

Now let's see how to perform training.

Training for the FER application

In this step, we need to start training so that our model can learn to predict facial emotions. In this step, we will be defining some hyperparameters for training. Refer to the code snippet in the following diagram:

```
def start_training(self):
  self.load_saved_dataset()
  self.build_network()
  if self.dataset is None:
    self.load_saved_dataset()
  # Training
  print('[+] Training network')
  self.model.fit(
    self.dataset.images, self.dataset.labels,
    validation_set = (self.dataset.images_test, self.dataset._labels_test),
    n_epoch = 100,
    batch_size = 50,
    shuffle = True,
    show_metric = True,
    snapshot_step = 200,
    snapshot_epoch = True,
    run_id = 'emotion_recognition'
  )
```

Figure 10.31: Code snippet for performing training

As you can see in the preceding diagram, we have set the epoch to `100`. The training batch size is `50`. We can see the `shuffle` parameter, which acts as the flag. The value of this parameter is `true`, which indicates that we are shuffling our dataset during training.

The command to start training is `$ python emotion_recognition.py train`.

Predicting and saving the trained model

In this step, we are defining the `predict` method. This method helps us generate a prediction. We have also defined the method that can help us save the trained model. We need to save the model, because we can load it as and when needed for testing. You can find the code snippet in the following diagram:

```
def predict(self, image):
  if image is None:
    return None
  image = image.reshape([-1, SIZE_FACE, SIZE_FACE, 1])
  return self.model.predict(image)
```

Figure 10.32: Code snippet for predicting the class

Refer to the code snippet in the following diagram:

```
def save_model(self):
  self.model.save(join(SAVE_DIRECTORY, SAVE_MODEL_FILENAME))
  print('[+] Model trained and saved at ' + SAVE_MODEL_FILENAME)
```

Figure 10.33: Code snippet for saving the trained model

Now it's time to look at the testing matrix. After that, we need to test our trained model. So, before testing our model, we should understand the testing matrix.

Understanding the testing matrix

In this section, we will look at the testing matrix for the facial emotion application. The concept of testing is really simple. We need to start observing the training steps. We are tracking the values for loss and accuracy. Based on that, we can decide the accuracy of our model. Doesn't this sound simple? We have trained the model for 30 epochs. This amount of training requires more than three hours. We have achieved 63.88% training accuracy. Refer to the code snippet in the following diagram:

```
Training Step: 6440  | total loss: 1.20367 | time: 565.402s
| Momentum | epoch: 023 | loss: 1.20367 - acc: 0.5683 | val_loss: 1.01957 - val_acc: 0.6349 -- iter: 13974/13974
--
Training Step: 6600  | total loss: 1.01954 | time: 319.599s
| Momentum | epoch: 024 | loss: 1.01954 - acc: 0.6343 | val_loss: 1.05124 - val_acc: 0.6175 -- iter: 08000/13974
--
Training Step: 6720  | total loss: 1.13529 | time: 560.962s
| Momentum | epoch: 024 | loss: 1.13529 - acc: 0.5888 | val_loss: 0.99228 - val_acc: 0.6383 -- iter: 13974/13974
--
Training Step: 6800  | total loss: 1.07410 | time: 161.562s
| Momentum | epoch: 025 | loss: 1.07410 - acc: 0.6070 | val_loss: 1.02039 - val_acc: 0.6302 -- iter: 04000/13974
--
Training Step: 7000  | total loss: 1.17867 | time: 562.285s
| Momentum | epoch: 025 | loss: 1.17867 - acc: 0.5687 | val_loss: 1.01229 - val_acc: 0.6302 -- iter: 13974/13974
--
Training Step: 7200  | total loss: 1.05028 | time: 400.865s
| Momentum | epoch: 026 | loss: 1.05028 - acc: 0.6123 | val_loss: 1.01683 - val_acc: 0.6257 -- iter: 10000/13974
--
Training Step: 7280  | total loss: 0.94902 | time: 562.776s
| Momentum | epoch: 026 | loss: 0.94902 - acc: 0.6567 | val_loss: 0.96527 - val_acc: 0.6513 -- iter: 13974/13974
--
Training Step: 7400  | total loss: 0.99141 | time: 241.778s
| Momentum | epoch: 027 | loss: 0.99141 - acc: 0.6341 | val_loss: 0.95987 - val_acc: 0.6536 -- iter: 06000/13974
--
Training Step: 7560  | total loss: 1.17840 | time: 563.996s
| Momentum | epoch: 027 | loss: 1.17840 - acc: 0.5967 | val_loss: 0.97300 - val_acc: 0.6522 -- iter: 13974/13974
--
Training Step: 7600  | total loss: 1.07340 | time: 82.192s
| Momentum | epoch: 028 | loss: 1.07340 - acc: 0.6053 | val_loss: 0.96578 - val_acc: 0.6502 -- iter: 02000/13974
--
Training Step: 7800  | total loss: 1.00146 | time: 482.759s
| Momentum | epoch: 028 | loss: 1.00146 - acc: 0.6295 | val_loss: 0.97425 - val_acc: 0.6455 -- iter: 12000/13974
--
Training Step: 7840  | total loss: 1.17828 | time: 565.771s
| Momentum | epoch: 028 | loss: 1.17828 - acc: 0.5956 | val_loss: 0.94325 - val_acc: 0.6632 -- iter: 13974/13974
--
Training Step: 8000  | total loss: 0.96527 | time: 321.324s
| Momentum | epoch: 029 | loss: 0.96527 - acc: 0.6391 | val_loss: 0.96504 - val_acc: 0.6528 -- iter: 08000/13974
--
Training Step: 8120  | total loss: 1.04503 | time: 561.649s
| Momentum | epoch: 029 | loss: 1.04503 - acc: 0.6174 | val_loss: 0.93508 - val_acc: 0.6637 -- iter: 13974/13974
--
Training Step: 8135  | total loss: 0.99740 | time: 29.484s
| Momentum | epoch: 030 | loss: 0.99740 - acc: 0.6388 -- iter: 00750/13974
```

Figure 10.34: Training progress for getting an idea of training accuracy

This is the training accuracy. If we want to check the accuracy on the validation dataset, then that is given in the training step as well. We have defined the validation set. With the help of this validation dataset, the trained model generates its prediction. We compare the predicted class and actual class labels. After that, we generate the validation accuracy that you can see in the preceding diagram. Here, `val_acc` is 66.37%, which is great. To date, this application has been able to achieve up to 65 to 70% accuracy.

Testing the model

Now we need to load the trained model and test it. Here, we will be using the video stream. The FER application will detect the emotion based on my facial expression. You can refer to the code using this GitHub link: `https://github.com/jalajthanaki/Facial_emotion_recognition_using_TensorFlow/blob/master/emotion_recognition.py`.

You can find the code snippet for this in the following figure:

```
  def load_model(self):
    if isfile(join(SAVE_DIRECTORY, SAVE_MODEL_FILENAME)):
      self.model.load(join(SAVE_DIRECTORY, SAVE_MODEL_FILENAME))
      print('[+] Model loaded from ' + SAVE_MODEL_FILENAME)


def show_usage():
  # I din't want to have more dependecies
  print('[!] Usage: python emotion_recognition.py')
  print('\t emotion_recognition.py train \t Trains and saves model with saved dataset')
  print('\t emotion_recognition.py poc \t Launch the proof of concept')

if __name__ == "__main__":
  if len(sys.argv) <= 1:
    show_usage()
    exit()

  network = EmotionRecognition()
  if sys.argv[1] == 'train':
    network.start_training()
    network.save_model()
  elif sys.argv[1] == 'poc':
    import poc
  else:
    show_usage()
```

Figure 10.35: Code snippet for loading the trained model and performing testing

In order to start testing, we need to execute the following command:

```
$ python emotion_recognition.py poc
```

This testing will use your webcam. I have some demo files that I want to share here. Refer to the following figure:

Figure 10.36: Code snippet for FER application identifying the emotion of disgust

Also refer to the the following figure:

Figure 10.37: tThe FER application identifying the happy emotion

Refer to the code snippet in the following figure:

Figure 10.38: Code snippet for the FER application identifying the neutral emotion

Refer to the code snippet given in the following figure:

Figure 10.39: Code snippet for the FER application identifying the angry emotion

Now let's look at how we can improve this approach.

Problems with the existing approach

In this section, we will list all the points that create problems. We should try to improve them. The following are things that I feel we can improve upon:

- If you find out that class sampling is not proper in your case, then you can adopt the sampling methods
- We can add more layers to our neural network

We can try different gradient descent techniques.

In this approach, training takes a lot of time that means training is computationally expensive. When we trained the model, we used GPUs even though GPU training takes a long time. We can use multiple GPUs, but that is expensive, and a cloud instance with multiple GPUs is not affordable. So, if we can use transfer learning in this application, or use the pre-trained model, then we will achieve better results.

How to optimize the existing approach

As you have seen in the previous section, because of the lack of computation hardware, we have achieved a 66% accuracy rate. In order to improve the accuracy further, we can use the pre-trained model, which will be more convenient.

Understanding the process for optimization

There are a few problems that I have described in the previous sections. We can add more layers to our CNN, but that will become more computationally expensive, so we are not going to do that. We have sampled our dataset well, so we do not need to worry about that.

As part of the optimization process, we will be using the pre-trained model that is trained by using the `keras` library. This model uses many layers of CNNs. It will be trained on multiple GPUs. So, we will be using this pre-trained model, and checking how this will turn out.

In the upcoming section, we will be implementing the code that can use the pre-trained model.

The best approach

We have achieved approximately a 66% accuracy rate; for an FER application, the best accuracy will be approximately 69%. We will achieve this by using the pre-trained model. So, let's look at the implementation, and how we can use it to achieve the best possible outcome.

Implementing the best approach

In this section, we will be implementing the best possible approach for the FER application. This pre-trained model has been built by using dense and deep convolutional layers. Because of the six-layer deep CNN, and with the help of the stochastic gradient descent (SGD) technique, we can build the pre-trained model. The number of neurons for each layer were 32, 32, 64, 64, 128,128, 1,024, and 512, respectively. All layers are using ReLU as an activation function. The 3 x 3 matrix will be used to generate the initial feature map, and the 2 x 2 matrix will be used to generate the max pooling. You can download the model from this GitHub link: `https://github.com/jalajthanaki/Facial_emotion_recognition_using_Keras`

You can look at the code by referring to the following diagram:

```
import ...

##Satart Section
''' Keras took all GPU memory so to limit GPU usage, I have add those lines'''

import tensorflow as tf
from keras.backend.tensorflow_backend import set_session

config = tf.ConfigProto()
config.gpu_options.per_process_gpu_memory_fraction = 0.1
set_session(tf.Session(config=config))
''' Keras took all GPU memory so to limit GPU usage, I have add those lines'''
## End section

faceCascade = cv2.CascadeClassifier('haarcascade_frontalface_alt2.xml')

video_capture = cv2.VideoCapture(0)
model = load_model('keras_model/model_5-49-0.62.hdf5')
model.get_config()

target = ['angry', 'disgust', 'fear', 'happy', 'sad', 'surprise', 'neutral']
font = cv2.FONT_HERSHEY_SIMPLEX
while True:
    # Capture frame-by-frame
    ret, frame = video_capture.read()

    gray = cv2.cvtColor(frame, cv2.COLOR_BGR2GRAY)

    faces = faceCascade.detectMultiScale(gray, scaleFactor=1.1)

    # Draw a rectangle around the faces
    for (x, y, w, h) in faces:
        cv2.rectangle(frame, (x, y), (x + w, y + h), (0, 255, 0), 2, 5)
        face_crop = frame[y:y + h, x:x + w]
        face_crop = cv2.resize(face_crop, (48, 48))
        face_crop = cv2.cvtColor(face_crop, cv2.COLOR_BGR2GRAY)
        face_crop = face_crop.astype('float32') / 255
        face_crop = np.asarray(face_crop)
        face_crop = face_crop.reshape(1, 1, face_crop.shape[0], face_crop.shape[1])
        result = target[np.argmax(model.predict(face_crop))]
        cv2.putText(frame, result, (x, y), font, 1, (200, 0, 0), 3, cv2.LINE_AA)

    # Display the resulting frame
    cv2.imshow('Video', frame)

    if cv2.waitKey(1) & 0xFF == ord('q'):
        break

# When everything is done, release the capture
video_capture.release()
cv2.destroyAllWindows()
```

Figure 10. 40: Code snippet for using the pre-trained FER model

In the preceding code, we loaded the pre-trained `keras` model. We are providing two provisions. We can use this script for detecting the facial expression from the image as well as by providing the video stream.

If you want to test the facial expression present in any image, then we need to execute the `$ python image_test.py tes.jpg` command. I have applied it to this model on the `tes.jpg` image. You can see the output image as follows:

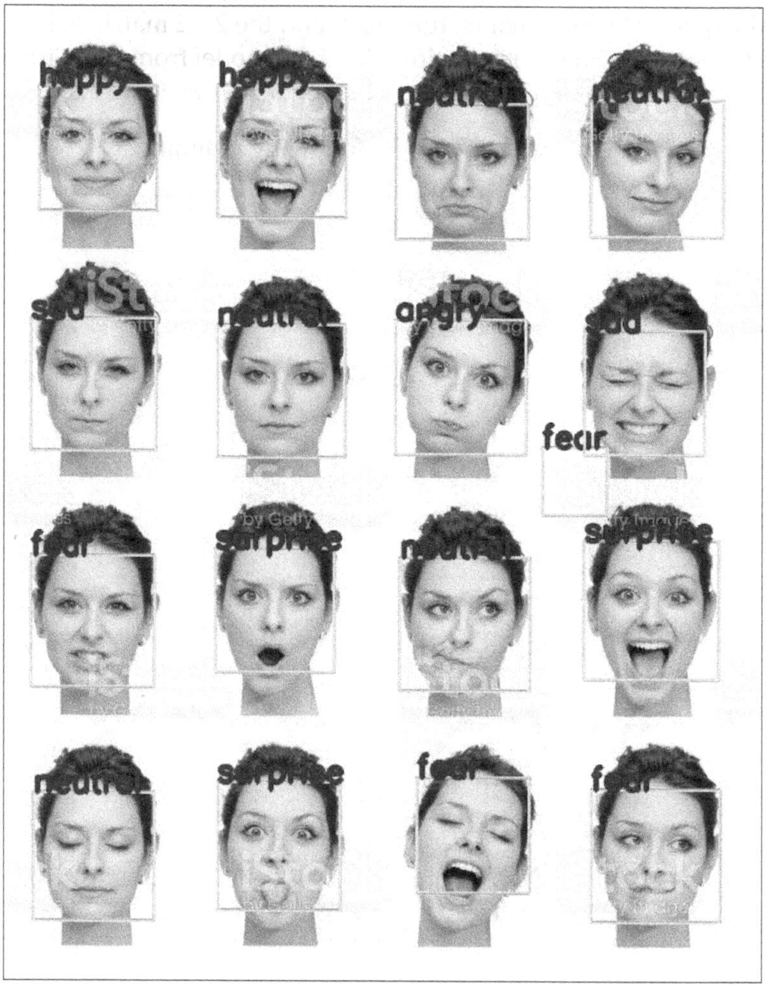

Figure 10.41: Output of the FER application for the image

If you want to test the model for the video stream, then you need to execute this command: `$python realtime_facial_expression.py`.

Refer to the output in the following figure:

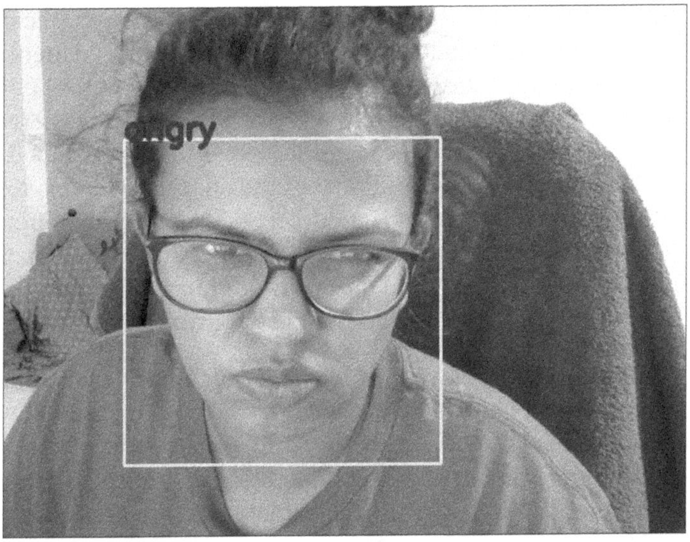

Figure 10.42: Output of the FER application for the video stream

You can find the output file in the following figure:

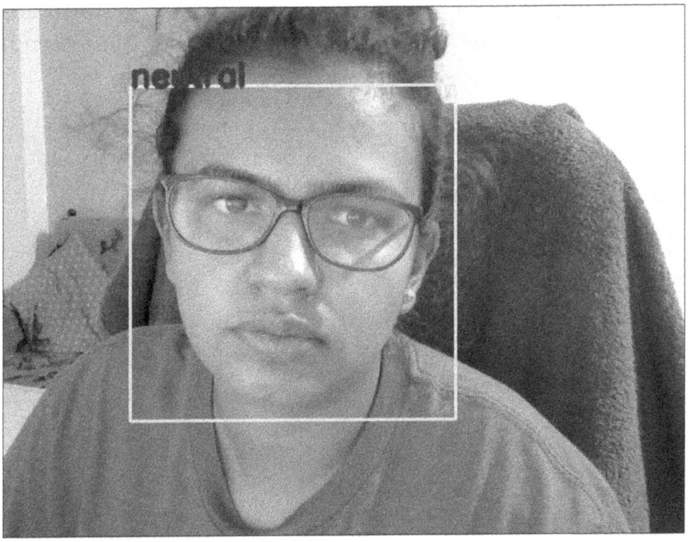

Figure 10.43: Output of the FER application for the video stream

This application provides us with approximately 67% accuracy, which is great.

Summary

In this chapter, we looked at how to develop the face detection application using the `face_recognition` library, which uses the HOG-based model to identify the faces in the images. We have also used the pre-trained convolutional neural network, which identifies the faces from a given image. We developed real-time face recognition to detect the names of people. For face recognition, we used a pre-trained model and already available libraries. In the second part of the chapter, we developed the face emotion recognition application, which can detect seven major emotions a human face can carry. We used `TensorFlow`, `OpenCV`, `TFLearn`, and `Keras` in order to build the face emotion recognition model. This model has fairly good accuracy for predicting the face emotion. We achieved the best possible accuracy of 67%.

Currently, the computer vision domain is moving quickly in terms of research. You can explore many fresh and cool concepts, such as `deepfakes` and 3D human pose estimation (machine vision) by the Facebook AI Research group. You can refer to the `deepfakes` GitHub repository by clicking here: `https://github.com/deepfakes/faceswap`. You can refer to the paper on 3D human pose estimation by clicking on this link: `https://arxiv.org/pdf/1705.03098.pdf`. Both the concepts are new and fresh, so you can refer to them and make some fun applications.

The next chapter will be the last chapter of this book. In the course of the chapter, we will try to make a gaming bot. This chapter will heavily use reinforcement learning techniques. We will be developing a bot that can play Atari games on its own. So keep reading!

11
Building Gaming Bot

In previous chapters, we covered applications that belong to the computer vision domain. In this chapter, we will be making a gaming bot. We will cover different approaches to build the gaming bot. These gaming bots can be used to play a variety of Atari games.

Let's do a quick recap of the past two years. Let's begin with 2015. A small London-based company called DeepMind published a research paper titled Playing Atari with Deep Reinforcement Learning, available at `https://arxiv.org/abs/1312.5602` In this paper, they demonstrated how a computer can learn and play Atari 2600 video games. A computer can play the game just by observing the screen pixels. Our computer game agent (the computer game player) will receive rewards when the game score increases. The result presented in this paper is remarkable. The paper created a lot of buzz, and that was because each game has different scoring mechanisms and these games are designed in such a way that humans find it difficult to achieve the highest score. The beauty of this research paper is that we can use the concept and given model architecture without any changes to learn different games. This model architecture and algorithm are applied to seven games, and in three of them, the algorithm performed way better than a human! This is a big leap in the field of AI because the hope is that we can build a single algorithm that can master many tasks, as well as build a General Artificial Intelligence or Artificial General Intelligence (AGI) system at some point in the next few decades. You can read more about AGI at: `https://en.wikipedia.org/wiki/Artificial_general_intelligence`. We all know that DeepMind was immediately acquired by Google.

In 2017, Google DeepMind and OpenAI achieved a major milestone, which gives us hope that AGI will happen soon. Let's start with Google DeepMind first; you must have heard that Google DeepMind 's AlphaGo AI (a gaming bot) won a three-match series against the world's best Go player. Go is a complex game because it has a huge number of permutations and combinations for a single move. You can watch the video for this game by clicking on this YouTube video: `https://www.youtube.com/watch?v=vFr3K2DORc8`. Now let's talk about OpenAI. If this is the first time you have heard about OpenAI, this is a short introduction. OpenAI is a non-profit AI research organization, cofounded by Elon Musk, which is trying to build AI that will be safe and ensure that the benefits of Artificial Intelligence (AI) systems are widely and evenly distributed as far as possible. In 2017, OpenAI's gaming bot beat the world's best Dota 2 players. You can watch this YouTube video for reference: `https://www.youtube.com/watch?v=7U4-wvhgx0w`. All this was achieved by AGI system environments created by tech giants. The goal of making an AGI system is that a single system can perform a variety of complex tasks. The ideal AGI system can help us solve lots of complex tasks in the fields of healthcare, agriculture, robotics, and so on without any changes to its algorithm. So, it is better for us if we can understand the basic concepts in order to develop the AGI system.

In this chapter, just to start with, we will be trying to make a gaming bot that can play simple Atari games. We will achieve this by using reinforcement learning.

In general, we will be covering the following topics in this chapter:

- Introducing the problem statement
- Setting up the coding environment
- Understanding reinforcement learning (RL)
- Basic Atari gaming bot for pathfinder
    - Understanding the key concepts
- Implementing the basic version of the gaming bot
- Building the Space Invaders gaming bot
    - Understanding the key concepts
- Implementing the Space Invaders gaming bot
- Building the Pong gaming bot
    - Understanding the key concepts
- Implementing the Pong gaming bot
- Just for fun - implementing the Flappy Bird gaming bot
- Summary

Introducing the problem statement

We know we are trying to develop a gaming bot: a program that can play simple Atari games. If we provide enough time and computation resources, then it can outperform humans who are experts at playing certain games. I will list down some famous Atari games so that you can see which types of games I'm talking about. You must have played one of these games for sure. Some of the famous Atari games are Casino, Space Invaders, Pac-man, Space War, Pong (ping-pong), and so on. In short, the problem statement that we are trying to solve is how can we build a bot that can learn to play Atari games?

In this chapter, we will be using already built-in gaming environments using `gym` and `dqn` libraries. So, we don't need to create a gaming visual environment and we can focus on the approach of making the best possible gaming bot. First, we need to set up the coding environment.

Setting up the coding environment

In this section, we will cover how to set up a coding environment that can help us implement our applications. We need to install the gym library. These are the steps that you can follow. I'm using `Ubuntu 16.04 LTS` as my operating system:

- Step 1: Clone the gym repository from GitHub by executing this command: `$ sudo git clone https://github.com/openai/gym.git`
- Step 2: Jump to the gym directory by executing this command: `$ cd gym`
- Step 3: Execute this command to install the minimum number of required libraries for `gym`: `$ sudo pip install -e`
- Step 4: Install the gaming environment for Atari games by executing this command: `$ sudo pip install gym[atari]`
- Step 5: This step is optional. If you want to install all the gaming environments, then you can execute the following commands:
    - `$ sudo apt-get install -y python-numpy python-dev cmake zlib1g-dev libjpeg-dev xvfb libav-tools xorg-dev python-opengl libboost-all-dev libsdl2-dev swig`
    - `$ sudo pip install gym[all]`

This is how you can install the `gym` machine learning library, which we will be using to develop the gaming bot. We will be using the TensorFlow implementation of the `dqn` library, so there will be no need to install `dqn` separately, but you can definitely refer to this installation note: `https://github.com/deepmind/dqn`.

As we are ready with the environment setup, we need to move on to our next section, which will help us understand the techniques that will be useful in order to develop the gaming bots. So let's begin!

Understanding Reinforcement Learning (RL)

In this chapter, we are making a gaming bot with the help of reinforcement learning techniques. The motivation behind reinforcement learning is simple. RL gives the machine or any software agent a chance to learn its behavior based on the feedback this agent receives from the environment. This behavior can be learned once, or you can keep on adapting with time.

Let's understand RL with a fun example of a child learning to speak. These are the steps a child will take when they are learning how to speak:

- Step 1: The first thing is that the child starts to observe you; how you are speaking and how you are interacting with him or her. The child listens to the basic words and sentences from you and learns that they can make a similar sound too. So, the child tries to imitate you.
- Step 2: The child wants to speak full sentences or words but they may not understand that even before speaking sentences, they need to learn simple words! This is a challenge that comes while they are trying to speak. Now the child attempts to make sounds, some sounds are funny or weird, but they are still determined to speak words and sentences.
- Step 3: There is another challenge that the child faces, which is that they need to understand and remember the meaning behind the words they are trying to speak. But the child manages to overcome this challenge and learns to speak their first few words, which are very simple words, such as *mama, papa, dadda, paa, maa*, and so on. They learn this task by constantly observing their surroundings.
- Step 4: The real challenge begins with how to use a particular word, when to use which word, and remembering all the words they hear for the first time. Try to feed the meaning of all the words and the context in which the child needs to use them. Sounds like a challenging task, doesn't it?

For a child, it is a difficult task, but once it starts understanding the language and practices the sentences, then it will become a part of the child's life. Within 2-3 years, the child could have enough practice to start interacting easily. If we think of ourselves speaking, it is an easy task for us because we have learned enough about how to interact within our environment.

Now, let's try to connect the dots. With the help of the preceding example, we will try to understand the concept of Reinforcement Learning. The problem statement of the given example is speaking, where the child is the agent who is trying to manipulate the environment (which word the child speaks first) by taking an action (here, the action is speaking), and they try to speak one word or the other. The child gets a reward—say, a chocolate—when they accomplish a submodule of the task, which means speaking some words in a day, and will not receive any chocolate when they are not able to speak anything. This is a simplified description of reinforcement learning. You can refer to the following diagram:

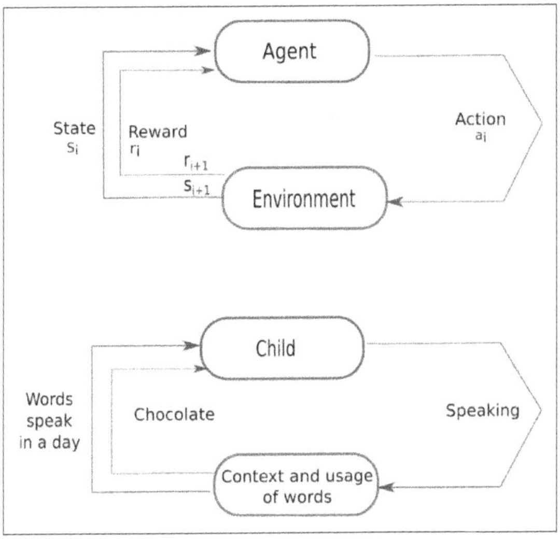

Figure 11.1: Pictorial representation of the basic concept of RL

So basically, RL allows machines and software agents to automatically determine the ideal and best possible behavior within a specific task or within a specific context in order to maximize the performance of software agents. Simple reward feedback is required for the agent to learn its behavior, and this is known as the reinforcement signal. Every time the software agent tries to take the kind of actions that lead it to gain maximum rewards. Eventually, it learns all the actions or moves that lead the agent to the optimum solution of the task so that it becomes the master of it. The algorithms for RL learn to react to an environment.

In order to build the gaming bot, RL algorithms are the perfect choice, and there is a reason behind it. Suppose there are many slot machines with random payouts and you want to win the maximum amount of money. How do you win the maximum amount of money? One naive approach is to just select a single machine and pull its lever all day long, and it might give you some payouts. If you are lucky enough, then you may hit the jackpot. There are chances that in order to try this approach, you may lose some money. This approach is called a *pure exploitation approach*. It is not an optimal approach.

Let's take another approach. In this approach, we will pull the lever of every single slot machine and pray that at least one of them hits the jackpot. This too is a naive approach. In this approach, we need to keep pulling the lever all day long. This approach is called a *pure exploration approach*. This approach is not optimal as well, so we need to find a proper balance between these two approaches in order to get maximum rewards. This is referred to as the exploration versus exploitation dilemma of RL. Now we need to solve this issue. Well, for that, we need a mathematical framework that can help us achieve the optimal solution, and that mathematical approach is *Markov Decision Process (MDP)*. Let's explore this.

Markov Decision Process (MDP)

Markov Decision Process uses the following parameters:

- Set of states, S
- Set of actions, A
- Reward function, R
- Policy, π
- Value, V

In order to perform transition for one state to the end state *(S)*, we have to take an action *(A)* or a series of actions. We will get rewards *(R)* for each action we take. Our action can provide us either a positive reward or a negative reward. The set of actions that we take define our policy *(π)*. The rewards that we get in return after performing each action define our value *(V)*. Our goal is to maximize the rewards by choosing the correct policy. We can do that by performing the best possible action. Mathematically, we can express this as shown in the following screenshot:

$$E\left(r_t \mid \pi, s_t\right)$$

Figure 11.2: Mathematical representation of Markov Decision Process

We will be applying the preceding equation for all possible values of *S* for a time t. We have a set of states and actions. We need to consider these states, actions, and rules for transitioning the agent from one state to another. When we perform an action that changes the state of the gaming agent, the the agent will get rewards for doing that. This entire process of state, action, and getting rewards makes up Markov Decision Process (MDP). One round of a game is considered *one episode* of MDP. This process includes a finite sequence of states, actions, and rewards. Take a look at the following equation for a representation of the process: :

$$S_0, a_0, r_1, s_1, a_1, r_2, s_2, a_2, r_3, \ldots, s_{n-1}, a_{n-1}, r_n, s_n$$

Here, s_i represents the state, ai is the action, and r_{i+1} is the reward that we will get after performing the action. sn indicates that a particular episode ends with a terminal state, and this happens when the **game over** screen appears. A Markov Decision Process is based on the Markov assumption, the probability of the next state s_{i+1} depends on the current state s_i and the performed action ai and does not depend on the preceding states or actions.

Discounted Future Reward

In the long term, if we want our gaming agent to do well, then we need to take into account the immediate rewards, but we also need to consider the future awards that our agent will get. How should we approach this scenario? Well, the answer lies in the concept of discounted future rewards.

Given one run of MDP, we can calculate the *total rewards* for one episode by using the following equation:

$$R = r_1 + r_2 + r_3 + \ldots + r_n$$

Based on the preceding equation, we can calculate the *total future rewards* from time stamp *t* onward, and that can be expressed by the given equation:

$$R_t = r_t + r_{t+1} + r_{t+2} + r_{t+3} + \ldots + r_n$$

Here, we are dealing with a gaming environment that is random, and we cannot be sure whether we will get the same rewards the next time we perform the same actions to play a specific game. The more you think about the future, the more it will get diverged. For that reason, it is better that we use *discounted future rewards* instead of total rewards:

$$R_t = r_t + \gamma r_{t+1} + \gamma_2 r_{t+2} + \ldots + \gamma_{n-1} r_n$$

Here, γ is the discount factor. Its value is between *0 to 1*. It is easy to understand that the discounted future reward at particular time step t can be expressed with the help of the rewards of the current stare plus rewards at time step *t+1*:

$$R_t = r_t + \gamma\,(r_{t+1} + \gamma\,(r_{t+2} + \ldots)) = r_t + \gamma R_{t+1}$$

Now let me tell you what the practical meaning of tuning this discount factor is: if we set the value of the discount factor $\gamma = 0$, then our strategy of plying will be short-sighted and we take our gaming decision just based on the immediate rewards. We need to find a balance between immediate rewards and future rewards, so we should set the value of the discount factor to something more than 0.7.

For example, we can set the value as $\gamma = 0.9$. If our gaming environment is deterministic and we know that the same actions always lead us to the same reward, then we can set the value of the discount factor $\gamma = 1$. A good strategy for a gaming agent would be to always *choose an action that maximizes the discounted future reward.*

We have covered the basics of RL. From now onward, we will start implementing our gaming bot. So let's get ready for some fun!

Basic Atari gaming bot

In this chapter, we are trying a hands-on approach to building some basic gaming bots. We are choosing some famous Atari games that nearly everybody has played at some point in their lives. We choose Atari games because we know how to play them, and that makes our life easy because we can understand what kind of action our bot should perform in order to get better over a period of time.

In this section, we are building our own game. This game is simple, so we can look at how we can apply the Q-Learning algorithms. Here, we will be designing the game world on our own. Let's begin!

Understanding the key concepts

In this section, we will be looking at a lot of important aspects that will help us while coding, so here, we will be covering the following topics:

- Rules for the game
- Understanding the Q-Learning algorithm

Rules for the game

Before we begin with the basic concepts or algorithms, we need to understand the rules of the game that we are building. The game is simple and easy to play. The rules for this game are as follows:

- *Rules of the game:* The gaming agent means a yellow box has to reach one of the goals to end the game: it can be either a green cell or a red cell. This means the yellow box should reach either the green cell or the red cell.
- *Rewards:* Each step gives us a negative reward of - 0.04. If our gaming agent reaches the red cell, then the red cell gives us a negative reward of - 1. If our gaming agent reaches the green cell, then the green cell gives us a positive reward of +1.
- *States:* Each cell is a state for the agent that it takes to find its goal.
- *Actions:* There are only four actions for this game: Up direction, Down direction, Right direction, Left direction.

We need the `tkinter` library to implement this approach. I have already provided a description about how to install it at this GitHub link: `https://github.com/jalajthanaki/Q_learning_for_simple_atari_game/blob/master/README.md`.

Now let's look at the Q learning algorithm that we will use during this chapter to build the gaming bot.

Understanding the Q-Learning algorithm

This algorithm was originally published by DeepMind in two papers. The first one was published with the title *Playing Atari with Deep Reinforcement Learning* on NIPS 2013. The link for the paper is `https://arxiv.org/pdf/1312.5602.pdf`. The second one was published with the title *Human-level control through deep reinforcement Learning* on Nature in 2015. The link for this paper is `http://www.davidqiu.com:8888/research/nature14236.pdf`. You should definitely read these papers. I have simplified the main concepts of these papers for you.

In Q-learning, we need to define a *Q (s, a)* function that represents the discount factor reward when we perform action *a* in state *s*, and it continues optimally from that point onward. You can see the equation that helps us choose the maximum reward in the followingscreenshot:

$$Q(s_t, a_t) = max_\pi R_{t+1}$$

Figure 11.3: Equation for Q-function

We can think of the Q (s, a) function as giving us the best possible score at the end of the game after performing action *a* in the particular state *s*. This function is the Q function because it indicates the *quality* of a certain action in a certain given state.

Let me simplify this for you. Suppose you are in state *s* and are thinking about whether you should perform action *a* or *b*. You really want to win the game with a high score. So, in order to achieve your goal, you want to select the action that gives you the highest score at the end of the game. If you have this Q-function with you, then the selection of actions become quite easy because you just need to pick the action that has the highest Q-value. You can see the equation that you can use to obtain the highest Q-value in the following screenshot:

$$\pi(s) = argmax_a Q(s,a)$$

Figure 11.4: Equation for choosing the maximum rewards using the Q-function

Here, π represents the policy. The policy indicates the rules of the game and the action. With the help of the policy, we can choose what kind of typical actions are available in each state. Our next step is to obtain this Q-function. For that, we need to concentrate on just one transition. This transition is made of four states: < *s, a, r, s'* >. Remember the discount factor reward, where we can express the Q-value of the current state *s* and the current action *a* in terms of the Q-value of the next state *s'*. The equation for calculating rewards is provided in the following screenshot:

$$Q(s,a) = r + \gamma max_{a'} Q(s',a')$$

Figure 11.5: The bellman equation for calculation rewards

The preceding equation is called the Bellman equation, and it is the main idea behind the Q-learning algorithm. This equation is quite logical, and it indicates that the maximum future rewards for this state and action are the summation of the immediate rewards and the maximum future reward for the next state.

The main intuition is that with the help of the *n number of iterations followed by approximation* step, we can generate the values for the Q-function. We will achieve this by using the *Bellman equation*. In the simplest case, the Q-function is implemented in the form of a table where states are its rows and actions are its columns. The pseudo steps of this Q-learning algorithm are simple. You can take a look at them, as follows: at them, as follows:

- Step 1: Initialize Q [number of states, number of actions] arbitrarily
- Step 2: Observe initial states

- Step 3: Repeat

```
Select and perform an action a
Observe two things: reward r and new state s'
Q [s, a] = Q [s, a] + α (r + γmaxa' Q [s', a'] - Q [s, a])
s = s'
```

- Until terminated

We need to follow these steps, where α is the learning rate. The learning rate verifies the difference between the previous Q-value and the newly proposed Q-value. This difference value is taken into account so that we can check when our model will converge. With the help of the learning rate, we can regulate the speed of training in such a way that our model won't become too slow to converge or too fast to converge in a way that it cannot learn anything. We will be using *maxa'Q [s', a']* to update *Q [s, a]*In order to maximize the reward. This is the only operation that we need to perform. This estimation operation will give us the updated Q-value. In the early stages of training, when our agent is learning, there could be a situation where our estimations may go completely wrong, but the estimations and updated Q-values get more and more accurate with every iteration. If we perform this process enough times, then the Q-function will converge. It represents the true and optimized Q-value. For better understanding, we will implement the preceding algorithm. Refer to the code snippet given in the following screenshot:

```
#Initialize table with all zeros
Q = np.zeros([env.observation_space.n,env.action_space.n])
# Set learning parameters
lr = .8
y = .95
num_episodes = 2000
#create lists to contain total rewards and steps per episode
#jList = []
rList = []
for i in range(num_episodes):
    #Reset environment and get first new observation
    s = env.reset()
    rAll = 0
    d = False
    j = 0
    #The Q-Table learning algorithm
    while j < 99:
        j+=1
        #Choose an action by greedily (with noise) picking from Q table
        a = np.argmax(Q[s,:] + np.random.randn(1,env.action_space.n)*(1./(i+1)))

        #Get new state and reward from environment
        s1,r,d,_ = env.step(a)
        #Update Q-Table with new knowledge
        Q[s,a] = Q[s,a] + lr*(r + y*np.max(Q[s1,:]) - Q[s,a])
        rAll += r
        s = s1
        if d == True:
            break
    #jList.append(j)
    rList.append(rAll)
```

Figure 11.6: Code snippet for building and updating the Q-table

You can see the output in the form of a Q-table in the following screenshot:

```
print("Final Q-Table Values")
print(Q)

Final Q-Table Values
[[2.25094571e-01 7.84023714e-03 6.40285120e-03 6.00414870e-03]
 [1.03573258e-03 1.12538441e-04 5.02409717e-04 1.76579501e-01]
 [3.63221924e-03 2.16355699e-03 5.75539049e-03 2.79143850e-01]
 [2.03956110e-04 1.34670361e-03 3.27968892e-04 2.20072554e-02]
 [3.86180668e-01 7.83072895e-05 6.97186941e-04 1.74695343e-05]
 [0.00000000e+00 0.00000000e+00 0.00000000e+00 0.00000000e+00]
 [3.74351418e-04 2.02811376e-06 1.18782770e-01 2.90052094e-05]
 [0.00000000e+00 0.00000000e+00 0.00000000e+00 0.00000000e+00]
 [1.37229498e-03 0.00000000e+00 1.19306209e-03 3.38309382e-01]
 [1.84143217e-03 3.99062039e-01 0.00000000e+00 0.00000000e+00]
 [1.08084678e-01 1.19488819e-03 2.41984186e-04 1.03772879e-03]
 [0.00000000e+00 0.00000000e+00 0.00000000e+00 0.00000000e+00]
 [0.00000000e+00 0.00000000e+00 0.00000000e+00 0.00000000e+00]
 [0.00000000e+00 0.00000000e+00 3.91024796e-01 0.00000000e+00]
 [0.00000000e+00 0.00000000e+00 0.00000000e+00 6.03141321e-01]
 [0.00000000e+00 0.00000000e+00 0.00000000e+00 0.00000000e+00]]
```

Figure 11.7: Q-table value

You can see the implementation of the preceding algorithm by referring to this GitHub link: `https://github.com/jalajthanaki/Q_learning_for_simple_atari_game/blob/master/Demo_Q_table.ipynb`.

Now let's start implementing the game.

Implementing the basic version of the gaming bot

In this section, we will be implementing a simple game. I have already defined the rules of this game. Just to remind you quickly, our agent, yellow block tries to reach either the red block or the green block. If the agent reaches the green block, we will receive + 1 as a reward. If it reaches the red block, we get -1. Each step the agent will take will be considered a - 0.04 reward. You can turn back the pages and refer to the section Rules for the game if you want. You can refer to the code for this basic version of a gaming bot by referring to this GitHub link: `https://github.com/jalajthanaki/Q_learning_for_simple_atari_game`.

For this game, the gaming world or the gaming environment is already built, so we do not need to worry about it. We need to include this gaming world by just using the import statement. The main script that we are running is `Lerner.py`. The code snippet for this code is given in the following screenshot:

```
discount = 0.3
actions = World.actions
states = []
Q = {}
for i in range(World.x):
    for j in range(World.y):
        states.append((i, j))

for state in states:
    temp = {}
    for action in actions:
        temp[action] = 0.1
        World.set_cell_score(state, action, temp[action])
    Q[state] = temp

for (i, j, c, w) in World.specials:
    for action in actions:
        Q[(i, j)][action] = w
        World.set_cell_score((i, j), action, w)


def do_action(action):
    s = World.player
    r = -World.score
    if action == actions[0]:
        World.try_move(0, -1)
    elif action == actions[1]:
        World.try_move(0, 1)
    elif action == actions[2]:
        World.try_move(-1, 0)
    elif action == actions[3]:
        World.try_move(1, 0)
    else:
        return
    s2 = World.player
    r += World.score
    return s, action, r, s2


def max_Q(s):
    val = None
    act = None
    for a, q in Q[s].items():
        if val is None or (q > val):
            val = q
            act = a
    return act, val
```

Figure 11.8: Code snippet for the basic version of the gaming bot - I

As you can see in the preceding code, we are keeping track of the agent's states and actions with the help of the code given in loops. After that, we will define the four possible actions for this game, and based on that, we will calculate the reward values. We have also defined the `max_Q` function, which calculates the maximum Q value for us. You can also refer to the following screenshot:

```
def inc_Q(s, a, alpha, inc):
    Q[s][a] *= 1 - alpha
    Q[s][a] += alpha * inc
    World.set_cell_score(s, a, Q[s][a])


def run():
    global discount
    time.sleep(1)
    alpha = 1
    t = 1
    while True:
        # Pick the right action
        s = World.player
        max_act, max_val = max_Q(s)
        (s, a, r, s2) = do_action(max_act)

        # Update Q
        max_act, max_val = max_Q(s2)
        inc_Q(s, a, alpha, r + discount * max_val)

        # Check if the game has restarted
        t += 1.0
        if World.has_restarted():
            World.restart_game()
            time.sleep(0.01)
            t = 1.0

        # Update the learning rate
        alpha = pow(t, -0.1)

        # MODIFY THIS SLEEP IF THE GAME IS GOING TOO FAST.
        time.sleep(0.1)


t = threading.Thread(target=run)
t.daemon = True
t.start()
World.start_game()
```

Figure 11.9: Code snippet for basic version of gaming bot - II

As you can see in the preceding code snippet, the helper function uses the `inc_Q` method in order to update Q. By using the `run` function, we can update Q values so that our bot will learn how to achieve the best solution. You can run this script by executing this command:

```
$ python Learner.py
```

When you run the script, you can see the following output window, and within 1-2 minutes, this bot will find the optimal solution. You can find the bot's initial state and final state output in the following screenshot:

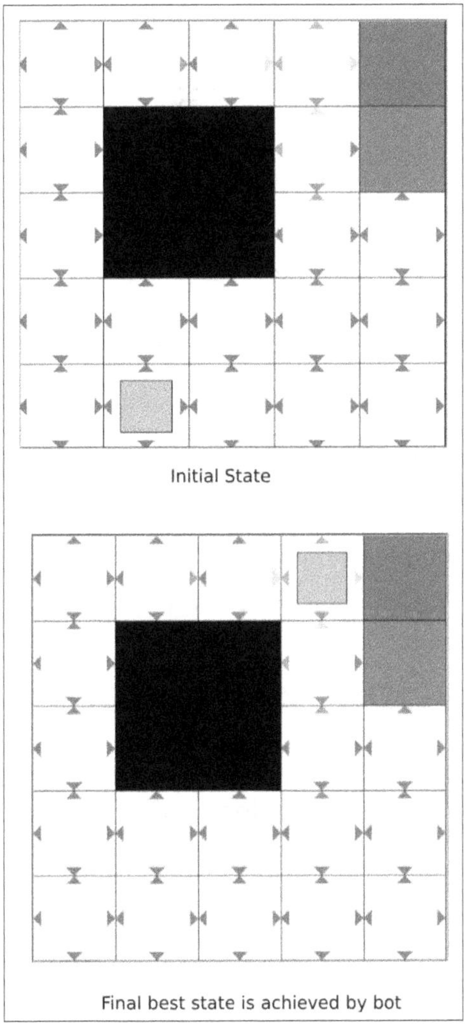

Figure 11.10: Output of the basic version of the gaming bot

You can track the progress of the bot by using the reward score. You can refer to the following screenshot:

```
Fail! score:  -2.72
Fail! score:  -1.16
Success! score:  0.32
Success! score:  1.04
Fail! score:  -6.66133814775e-16
Success! score:  1.08
Success! score:  0.64
Success! score:  1.48
Success! score:  1.16
Success! score:  1.52
Success! score:  1.36
Success! score:  1.48
Success! score:  1.72
Success! score:  1.56
Success! score:  1.72
Success! score:  1.72
Success! score:  1.68
Success! score:  1.48
Success! score:  1.72
Success! score:  1.72
Success! score:  1.72
Success! score:  1.72
Success! score:  1.72
```

Figure 11.11: Tracking the progress of the gaming bot

As you can see, during the initial iteration, the gaming bot didn't perform well after some iterations bot started learning how to take action based on the experience it gained. We stopped the code when there was no significant improvement in the reward scores. That is because our gaming bot was able to achieve the best solution.

Now let's build a more complex gaming bot; we will be using a deep Q-network for training. So let's begin.

Building the Space Invaders gaming bot

We are going to build a gaming bot that can play Space Invaders. Most of you may have played this game or at least heard of it. If you haven't played it or you can't remember it at this moment, then take a look at the following screenshot:

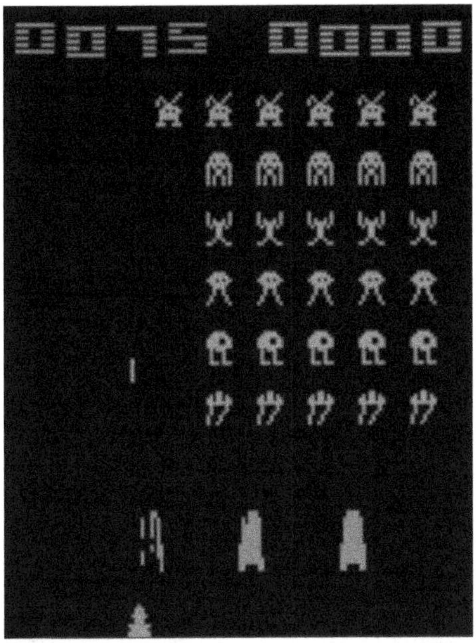

Figure 11.12: Snippet of the Space Invaders game

Hopefully you remember the game now and how it was played. First, we will look at the concepts that we will be using to build this version of the gaming bot. Let's begin!

Understanding the key concepts

In this version of the gaming bot, we will be using the deep Q-network and training our bot. So before implementing this algorithm, we need to understand the concepts. Take a look at the following concepts:

- Understanding a deep Q-network (DQN)
- Understanding Experience Replay

Understanding a deep Q-network (DQN)

The deep Q-network algorithm is basically a combination of two concepts. It uses the Q-learning logic for a deep neural network. That is the reason why it is called a deep Q-network (DQN).

Every gaming world has a different environment. So, say, Super Mario looks different from Space Invaders. We can't feed the entire gaming environment for an individual game every time, so first of all, we need to decide on the universal representation of all games so that we use them as input for the DQN algorithm. The screen pixels are the obvious choice for input because clearly they contain all the relevant information about the game world and its situation. Without the help of the screen pixels we cannot capture the speed and direction of the gaming agent.

If we apply the same preprocessing steps to the game screens as mentioned in the DeepMind paper, then we need to follow these steps:

Step 1: We need to consider the last four screen images of the game as the input.

Step 2: We need to resize them to 84 x 84 and convert them into grayscale with 256 gray levels. That means we would have $256^{84x84x4}$, which is approximately 10^{67970} possible gaming states. This means we have 10^{67970} rows in our imaginary Q-table, and that is a big number. You could argue that many pixel combinations or states never occur so we can possibly represent it as a sparse matrix. This sparse matrix contains only visited states. However, most of the states are rarely visited. So, it would take a long time for the Q-table to converge. Honestly, we would also like to take a good guess for Q-values for states we have never seen before by the agent so that we can generate a reasonably good action for the gaming agent. This is the point where deep learning enters the picture.

Step 3: Neural networks are quite good for generating good features for highly structured data. With the help of the neural network, we can represent our Q-function. This neural network takes the states, which means four game screens and actions, as input and generates the corresponding Q-value as output. *Alternatively, we could take only game screens as the input and generate the Q-value for each possible action as output.* This approach has a great advantage. Let me explain. There are two major things that we are doing here. First, we need to obtain the updated Q-value. Second, we need to pick up the action with the highest Q-value.

So if we have Q-values for all possible actions, then we can update the Q-value easily. We can also pick the action with the highest Q-value with a lot of ease. The interesting part is that we can generate the Q-values for all actions by performing a forward pass through the network. After a single forward pass, we can have a list of Q-values for all possible actions with us. This forward pass will save a lot of time and give the gaming agent good rewards.

Architecture of DQN

You can find the optimal architecture of a deep Q-network represented in the following diagram:

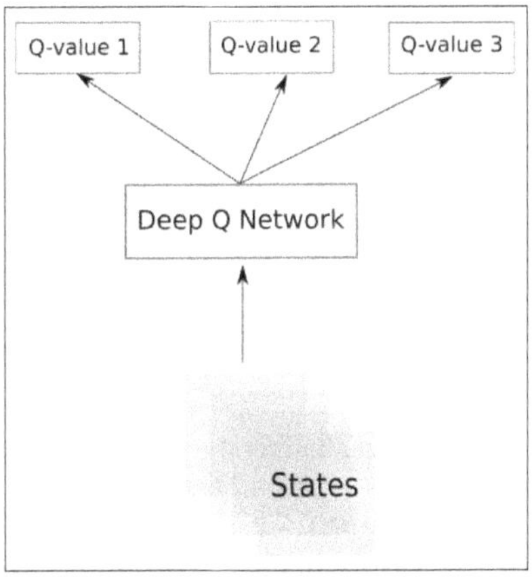

Figure 11.13: Architecture of DQN

The preceding architecture is used and published in a DeepMind paper. The architecture for the neural network is shown in the following screenshot:

Layers	Input	Filter size	Stride	Num filters	Activation	Output
conv1	84x84x4	8×8	4	32	ReLU	20x20x32
conv2	20x20x32	4×4	2	64	ReLU	9x9x64
conv3	9x9x64	3×3	1	64	ReLU	7x7x64
fc4	7x7x64			512	ReLU	512
fc5	512			18	Linear	18

Figure 12.14: The DQN architecture

The provided architecture uses a classic convolutional neural network (CNN). There are three convolutional layers followed by two fully connected layers that we have seen in the CNN architecture for object detection and face recognition CNN with pooling layers. Here, there are no pooling layers. That is because the main motive behind using pooling layers is that they make the neural network insensitive to the location. This means that if we use the pooling layer, then the placement of the objects in the image is not considered by the neural network. This kind of location insensitivity makes sense for a classification task, but for games, the location of the objects in a gaming environment is important. They help us determine the action as well as potential rewards, and we wouldn't want to discard this information. So, we are not using pooling layers here.

Steps for the DQN algorithm

Let's see the steps for DQN algorithm:

Input of network: Four 84 x 84 grayscale game screen pixels.

Output of network: As output, we will generate Q-values for each possible action. Q- values take any real number, which means it can be any real number you can possibly imagine, and that makes it a regression task. We know we can optimize the regression function with a simple squared error loss. The equation of the error loss is shown in the following screenshot:

$$L = \frac{1}{2}\left[r + \gamma max_{a'} Q(s', a') - Q(s, a)\right]^2$$

Figure 11.15: Equation for the error loss function

Q-table update step: There's the transition $< s, a, r, s' >$, but this time, the rules for updating the Q-table are not the same as Q-learning. There are some changes. So, the steps for updating the Q-table are as follows:

- Step 1: We need to perform a feedforward pass for the current state s in order to get predicted Q-values for all actions.
- Step 2: Perform a feedforward pass for the next sate s' and calculate the maximum over all network output $maxa'Q(s', a')$.
- Step 3: Set a Q-value target for action a to $r + \gamma maxa'Q(s', a')$. Here, we can use the $maxa'Q(s', a')$ value that we have already calculated in step 2. For all other actions, set the Q-values that are originally from step 1, making the error zero for those outputs.
- Step 4: We need to update the weights of the neural network using backpropagation.

Now let's look at the concept of experience replay.

Understanding Experience Replay

We are estimating the future rewards in each state using two concepts. We use Q-learning and approximate the Q-function using a convolutional neural network. Here, the approximation of Q-values is done using a nonlinear function, and this function is not very stable for converging the model. So, we need to experiment with various hyperparameters. This takes a long time: almost a week on a single GPU to train the gaming bot.

We will be using a concept called experience replay. During the training, all the experiences < s, a, r, s' > are stored in a replay memory. When we perform training, the network will use random samples from the replay memory instead of the most recent transition. This way, the training time will be less, plus there is another advantage. With the help of the experience replay, our training task will become more similar to the usual supervised learning. Now we can easily perform debugging and testing operations for the algorithm. With the help of the replay memory, we can store all our human experiences of gameplay and then train the model based on this dataset.

So, the steps for the final Q-learning algorithm used in DQN will be as follows. This algorithm takes from the original DQN paper, which is available at `https://arxiv.org/pdf/1312.5602.pdf`:

- Step 1: We need to initialize the replay memory D
- Step 2: We need to initialize the action-value function Q with random weights
- Step 3: Observe value of the initial states
- Step 4: Repeat

```
Choose an action a
with probability ε we need to select a random action
otherwise we need to select a = argmaxa'Q(s,a')
Perform action a
Check reward r and new state s'
store the gameplay experience <s, a, r, s'> in replay memory D
sample random transitions <ss, aa, rr, ss'> from replay memory D
calculate target for each minibatch transition
if ss' is terminal state then tt = rr
otherwise tt = rr + γmaxa'Q(ss', aa')
We need to train the Q network using (tt - Q(ss, aa))^2 as loss
s = s'
until terminated
```

We are using Q-learning and DQN to implement the Space Invaders gaming bot. So let's start coding.

Implementing the Space Invaders gaming bot

In this section, we will be coding the Space Invaders game using DQN and Q-learning. For coding, we will be using the `gym`, `TensorFlow`, and `virtualenv` libraries. You can refer to the entire code by using this GitHub link: `https://github.com/jalajthanaki/SpaceInvaders_gamingbot`.

We are using a convolutional neural network (CNN). Here, we have defined the CNN in a separate file. The name of this file is `convnet.py`. Take a look at the following screenshot: at the following figure:

```
def __init__(self, params, trainable):
    self.shape = [None, params.width, params.height, params.history_length]
    self.x = tf.placeholder(tf.float32, self.shape)
    self.in_dims = self.shape[1]*self.shape[2]*self.shape[3]
    self.out_dims = params.actions
    self.filters = [32, 64, 64] # convolution filters at each layer
    self.num_layers = 3 # number of convolutional layers
    self.filter_size = [8, 4, 4] # size at each layer
    self.filter_stride = [4, 2, 1] # stride at each layer
    self.fc_size = [512] # size of fully connected layers
    self.fc_layers = 1 # number of fully connected layers
    self.trainable = trainable
```

Figure 11.16: Code snippet for Convnrt.py

You can refer to the code using this GitHub link: `https://github.com/jalajthanaki/SpaceInvaders_gamingbot/blob/master/convnet.py`.

We are defining the DQN algorithm in the `dqn.py` script. You can refer to the code snippet shown in the following screenshot:

```
def __init__(self, env, params):
    self.env = env
    params.actions = env.actions()
    self.num_actions = env.actions()
    self.episodes = params.episodes
    self.steps = params.steps
    self.train_steps = params.train_steps
    self.update_freq = params.update_freq
    self.save_weights = params.save_weights
    self.history_length = params.history_length
    self.discount = params.discount
    self.eps = params.init_eps
    self.eps_delta = (params.init_eps - params.final_eps) / params.final_eps_frame
    self.replay_start_size = params.replay_start_size
    self.eps_endt = params.final_eps_frame
    self.random_starts = params.random_starts
    self.batch_size = params.batch_size
    self.ckpt_file = params.ckpt_dir+'/'+params.game

    self.global_step = tf.Variable(0, trainable=False)
    if params.lr_anneal:
        self.lr = tf.train.exponential_decay(params.lr, self.global_step, params.lr_anneal, 0.96, staircase=True)
    else:
        self.lr = params.lr

    self.buffer = Buffer(params)
    self.memory = Memory(params.size, self.batch_size)

    with tf.variable_scope("train") as self.train_scope:
        self.train_net = ConvNet(params, trainable=True)
    with tf.variable_scope("target") as self.target_scope:
        self.target_net = ConvNet(params, trainable=False)

    self.optimizer = tf.train.RMSPropOptimizer(self.lr, params.decay_rate, 0.0, self.eps)

    self.actions = tf.placeholder(tf.float32, [None, self.num_actions])
    self.q_target = tf.placeholder(tf.float32, [None])
    self.q_train = tf.reduce_max(tf.multiply(self.train_net.y, self.actions), reduction_indices=1)
    self.diff = tf.subtract(self.q_target, self.q_train)
```

Figure 11.17: Code snippet for dqn.py

For training, we have defined our training logic in `train.py`. You can refer to the code snippet shown in the following screenshot:

```
sample_success = 0
sample_failure = 0
print "\nstart training..."
start_time = time.time()
for i in xrange(self.agent.train_steps):
    # annealing learning rate
    lr = self.agent.trainEps(i)
    state, action, reward, next_state, terminal = self.agent.observe(lr)

    if len(self.agent.memory) > self.agent.batch_size and (i+1) % self.agent.update_freq == 0:
        sample_success, sample_failure, loss = self.agent.doMinibatch(sess, sample_success, sample_failure)
        total_loss += loss

    if (i+1) % self.agent.steps == 0:
        self.agent.copy_weights(sess)

    if reward == 1:
        successes += 1
    elif terminal:
        failures += 1

    if ((i+1) % self.agent.save_weights == 0):
        self.agent.save(self.saver, sess, i+1)

    if ((i+1) % self.agent.batch_size == 0):
        avg_loss = total_loss / self.agent.batch_size
        end_time = time.time()
        print "\nTraining step: ", i+1,\
              "\nmemory size: ", len(self.agent.memory),\
              "\nLearning rate: ", lr,\
              "\nSuccesses: ", successes,\
              "\nFailures: ", failures,\
              "\nSample successes: ", sample_success,\
              "\nSample failures: ", sample_failure,\
              "\nAverage batch loss: ", avg_loss,\
              "\nBatch training time: ", (end_time-start_time)/self.agent.batch_size, "s"
        start_time = time.time()
        total_loss = 0
```

Figure 11.18: Code snippet for train.py

At last, we import all these separate scripts to the main `atari.py` script, and in that script, we define all the parameter values. You can refer to the code snippet given in the following screenshot:

```
parser = argparse.ArgumentParser()
envarg = parser.add_argument_group('Environment')
envarg.add_argument("--game", type=str, default="SpaceInvaders-v0", help="Name of the atari game to test")
envarg.add_argument("--width", type=int, default=84, help="Screen width")
envarg.add_argument("--height", type=int, default=84, help="Screen height")

memarg = parser.add_argument_group('Memory')
#memarg.add_argument("--size", type=int, default=100000, help="Memory size.")
memarg.add_argument("--size", type=int, default=1000, help="Memory size.")
memarg.add_argument("--history_length", type=int, default=4, help="Number of most recent frames experiences by the agent.")

dqnarg = parser.add_argument_group('DQN')
dqnarg.add_argument("--lr", type=float, default=0.00025, help="Learning rate.")
dqnarg.add_argument("--lr_anneal", type=float, default=20000, help="Step size of learning rate annealing.")
dqnarg.add_argument("--discount", type=float, default=0.99, help="Discount rate.")
dqnarg.add_argument("--batch_size", type=int, default=32, help="Batch size.")
dqnarg.add_argument("--accumulator", type=str, default='mean', help="Batch accumulator.")
dqnarg.add_argument("--decay_rate", type=float, default=0.95, help="Decay rate for RMSProp.")
dqnarg.add_argument("--min_decay_rate", type=float, default=0.01, help="Min decay rate for RMSProp.")
dqnarg.add_argument("--init_eps", type=float, default=1.0, help="Initial value of e in e-greedy exploration.")
dqnarg.add_argument("--final_eps", type=float, default=0.1, help="Final value of e in e-greedy exploration.")
dqnarg.add_argument("--final_eps_frame", type=float, default=1000000, help="The number of frames over which the initial valu
dqnarg.add_argument("--clip_delta", type=float, default=1, help="Clip error term in update between this number and its negat
dqnarg.add_argument("--steps", type=int, default=10000, help="Copy main network to target network after this many steps.")
#dqnarg.add_argument("--train_steps", type=int, default=500000, help="Number of training steps.")
dqnarg.add_argument("--train_steps", type=int, default=50000, help="Number of training steps.")
dqnarg.add_argument("--update_freq", type=int, default=4, help="The number of actions selected between successive SGD update
#dqnarg.add_argument("--replay_start_size", type=int, default=50000, help="A uniform random policy is run for this number of
 memory.")
dqnarg.add_argument("--replay_start_size", type=int, default=5000, help="A uniform random policy is run for this number of f
 memory.")
#dqnarg.add_argument("--save_weights", type=int, default=10000, help="Save the mondel after this many steps.")
dqnarg.add_argument("--save_weights", type=int, default=1000, help="Save the mondel after this many steps.")
```

Figure 11.19: Code snippet for atari.py

You can start training by executing the following command:

```
$ python atari.py --game SpaceInvaders-v0 --display true
```

Training this bot to pass human level performance requires at least 3-4 days of training. I have not provided that amount of training, but you can definitely do that. You can take a look at the output of the training in the following screenshot: the following figure:

```
starting 50000 random plays to populate replay memory

memory size: 10000
Successes:  132
Failures:  13

memory size: 20000
Successes:  266
Failures:  26

memory size: 30000
Successes:  391
Failures:  41

memory size: 40000
Successes:  541
Failures:  54
```

Figure 11.20: Output snippet of training step - I

You can refer to the code snippet for the gaming environment initial score by referring to the following screenshot:

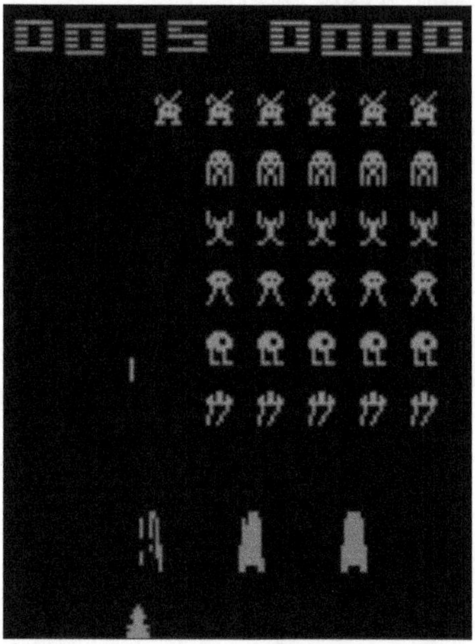

Figure 11.21: Code snippet of the score for the initial few games from the gaming bot

To stop the training, there will be two parameters: either we can end our training when our loss function value becomes constant for a few iterations, or we complete all the training steps. Here, we have defined 50,000 training steps. You can refer to the code snippet of the output of training in the following screenshot :

```
Training step:  27488
memory size:  1000
Learning rate:  0.9752617
Successes:  448
Failures:  45
Sample successes:  3059
Sample failures:  314
Average batch loss:  4.30831181575e-06
Batch training time:  0.0332949012518 s

Training step:  27520
memory size:  1000
```

Figure 11.22: Code snippet for the training log

You can see the score of the gaming bot after 1,000 iterations by taking a look at the following screenshot:

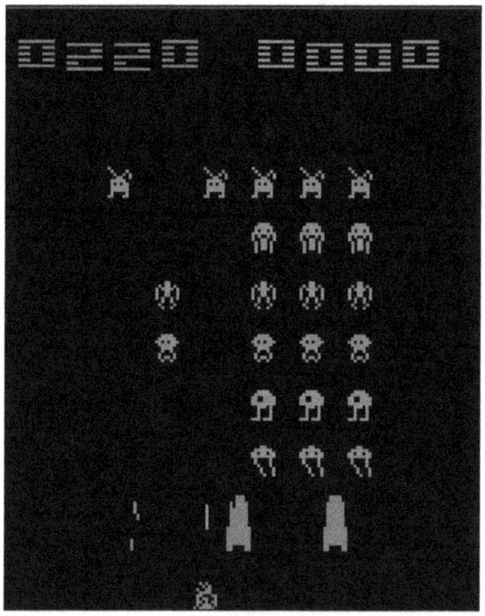

Figure 11.23: Code snippet for the gaming bot after 1,000 iterations

I have already upload the pre-trained model for you. You can download it by using this GitHub link: `https://github.com/jalajthanaki/SpaceInvaders_gamingbot/tree/master/model`.

Now it's time to build the gaming bot for the Pong game. If you train this bot for a week using a single GPU, it can beat the AI rules that are written by the gaming manufacture team. So, our agent will surely act better than the computer agent.

Building the Pong gaming bot

In this section, we will be looking at how we can build a gaming bot that can learn the game of Pong. Before we start, we will look at the approach and concepts that we will be using for building the Pong gaming bot.

Understanding the key concepts

In this section, we will be covering some aspects of building the Pong game bot, which are as follows:

- Architecture of the gaming bot
- Approach for the gaming bot

Architecture of the gaming bot

In order to develop the Pong gaming bot, we are choosing a neural-network-based approach. The architecture of our neural network is crucial. Let's look at the architectural components step by step:

1. We take the gaming screen as the input and preprocess it as per the DQN algorithm.
2. We pass this preprocessed screen to an neural network (NN.)
3. We use a gradient descent to update the weights of the NN.
4. Weight [1]: This matrix holds the weights of pixels passing into the hidden layer. The dimension will be [200 x 80 x 80] – [200 x 6400].
5. Weight [2]: This matrix holds the weights of the hidden layer passing into the output. The dimension will be [1 x 200].

You can refer to the following diagram:

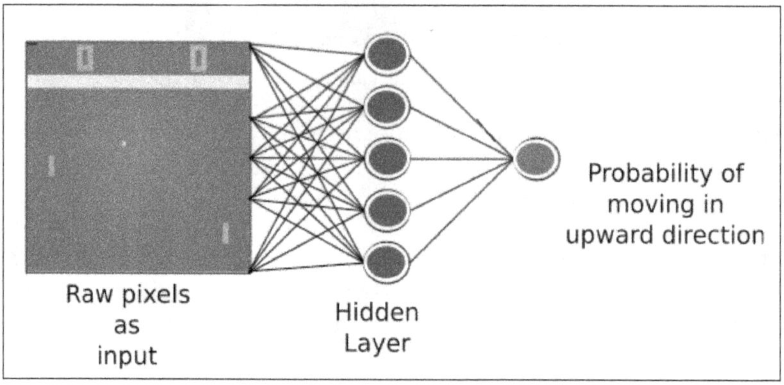

Figure 11.24: Architecture of NN for the Pong gaming bot

The tasks for each component of the NN make more sense when we see the detailed approach for this gaming bot.

Approach for the gaming bot

In order to build the Pong gaming bot, we will be using the following approach:

- For implementation, we are using the preprocessed image vector, which is a [6400 x 1] dimension array.
- With the help of NN, we can compute a probability of moving up.

- With the help of that probability distribution, we will decide whether the agent is moving up or not.
- If the gaming round is over, it means that the gaming agent as well as the opponent missed the ball. In this case, we need to find out whether our gaming agent won or lost.
- When the episode finishes, which means if either of the players scores 21 points, we need to pass the result. With the help of the loss function, we can find out the error values. We applied the gradient descent algorithm to find out the direction in which our neural network's weight should be updated. Based on the backpropagation algorithm, we propagate the error back to the network so that our network can update the weights.
- Once 10 episodes have finished, we need to sum up the gradient, and after that, we update the weights in the direction of the gradient.
- Repeat this process until our networks weights are tuned and we can beat the computer.

Now let's cover the coding steps.

Implementing the Pong gaming bot

These are the implementation steps that we need to follow:

- Initialization of the parameters
- Weights stored in the form of matrices
- Updating weights
- How to move the agent
- Understanding the process using NN

You can refer to the entire code by using this GitHub link: `https://github.com/jalajthanaki/Atari_Pong_gaming_bot`.

Initialization of the parameters

First, we define and initialize our parameters:

- `batch_size`: This parameter indicates how many rounds of games we should play before updating the weights of our network.
- `gamma`: This is the discount factor. We use this to discount the effect of old actions of the game on the final result.

- `decay_rate`: This parameter is used to update the weight.
- `num_hidden_layer_neurons`: This parameter indicates how many neurons we should put in the hidden layer.
- `learning_rate`: This is the speed at which our gaming agent learns from the results so that we can compute new weights. A higher learning rate means we react more strongly to results, and a lower rate means we don't react much to each result.

You can refer to the code snippet shown in the following screenshot:

```
# hyperparameters
episode_number = 0
batch_size = 10
gamma = 0.99 # discount factor for reward
decay_rate = 0.99
num_hidden_layer_neurons = 200
input_dimensions = 80 * 80
learning_rate = 1e-4

episode_number = 0
reward_sum = 0
running_reward = None
prev_processed_observations = None
```

Figure 11.25: Initialization of parameters

Weights stored in the form of matrices

The weights of the neural network are stored in the form of matrices. The first layer of NN is a 200 x 6400 matrix that represents the weights for our hidden layer. If we use the notation $w1\_ij$, then that would mean that we are representing the weight of the ith neuron for the input pixel j in layer 1. The second layer is a 200 x 1 matrix representing the weights. These weights are the output of the hidden layer. For layer 2, element $w2\_i$ indicates the weights placed on the activation of the ith neuron in the hidden layer.

You can refer to the code snippet given in the following screenshot:

```
weights = {
    '1': np.random.randn(num_hidden_layer_neurons, input_dimensions) / np.sqrt(input_dimensions),
    '2': np.random.randn(num_hidden_layer_neurons) / np.sqrt(num_hidden_layer_neurons)
}
```

Figure 11.26: Weight matrices

Updating weights

For updating the weight, we will be using RMSprop. You can refer to this paper in order to understand more details about this function:

`http://sebastianruder.com/optimizing-gradient-descent/index.html#rmsprop`. Refer to the following figure for the following figure.

$$E\left[g^2\right]_t = 0.9E\left[g^2\right]_{t-1} + 0.1g_t^2$$

$$\theta_{t+1} = \theta_t - \frac{\eta}{\sqrt{E\left[g^2\right]_t + \varepsilon}} g_t$$

Figure 11.27: Equation for RMSprop

The code is shown in the following screenshot:

```
def update_weights(weights, expectation_g_squared, g_dict, decay_rate, learning_rate):
    """ See here: http://sebastianruder.com/optimizing-gradient-descent/index.html#rmsprop"""
    epsilon = 1e-5
    for layer_name in weights.keys():
        g = g_dict[layer_name]
        expectation_g_squared[layer_name] = decay_rate * expectation_g_squared[layer_name] + (1 - decay_rate) * g**2
        weights[layer_name] += (learning_rate * g)/(np.sqrt(expectation_g_squared[layer_name] + epsilon))
        g_dict[layer_name] = np.zeros_like(weights[layer_name]) # reset batch gradient buffer
```

Figure 11.28: Code snippet for updating weights

How to move the agent

With the help of the preprocessed input, we pass the weight matrix to the neural network. We need to generate the probability of telling our agent to move up. You can refer to the code snippet shown in the following screenshot:

```
def preprocess_observations(input_observation, prev_processed_observation, input_dimensions):
    """ convert the 210x160x3 uint8 frame into a 6400 float vector """
    processed_observation = input_observation[35:195] # crop
    processed_observation = downsample(processed_observation)
    processed_observation = remove_color(processed_observation)
    processed_observation = remove_background(processed_observation)
    processed_observation[processed_observation != 0] = 1 # everything else (paddles, ball) just set to 1
    # Convert from 80 x 80 matrix to 1600 x 1 matrix
    processed_observation = processed_observation.astype(np.float).ravel()

    # subtract the previous frame from the current one so we are only processing on changes in the game
    if prev_processed_observation is not None:
        input_observation = processed_observation - prev_processed_observation
    else:
        input_observation = np.zeros(input_dimensions)
    # store the previous frame so we can subtract from it next time
    prev_processed_observations = processed_observation
    return input_observation, prev_processed_observations
```

Figure 11.29: Code snippet to move the agent

We are done with all the major helper functions. We need to apply all this logic to the neural network so that it can take the observation and generate the probability of our gaming agent for going in upward direction.

Understanding the process using NN

These are the steps that can help us generate the probability for our agent so that it can decide when they should move in upward direction

- We need to compute hidden layer values by applying the dot product between weights [1] and `observation_matrix`. Weight [1] is a 200 x 6400 matrix and `observation_matrix` is a 6400 x 1 matrix. The dimension of the output matrix is 200 x 1. Here, we are using 200 neurons. Each row of Q-function represents the output of one neuron.
- We apply a nonlinear function ReLU to the hidden layer values.
- We are using hidden layer activation values in order to calculate the values for the output layer. Again, we performed dot product between `hidden_layer_values` [200 x 1] and weights [2] [1 x 200]. This dot product gives us single value [1 x 1].
- Finally, we apply the sigmoid function to the output value. This will give us the answer in terms of probability. The value of the output is between 0 and 1.

You can refer to the code snippet shown in the following screenshot:

```
def apply_neural_nets(observation_matrix, weights):
    """ Based on the observation_matrix and weights, compute the new hidden layer values and the new output layer values"""
    hidden_layer_values = np.dot(weights['1'], observation_matrix)
    hidden_layer_values = relu(hidden_layer_values)
    output_layer_values = np.dot(hidden_layer_values, weights['2'])
    output_layer_values = sigmoid(output_layer_values)
    return hidden_layer_values, output_layer_values

def choose_action(probability):
    random_value = np.random.uniform()
    if random_value < probability:
        # signifies up in openai gym
        return 2
    else:
         # signifies down in openai gym
        return 3

def compute_gradient(gradient_log_p, hidden_layer_values, observation_values, weights):
    """ See here: http://neuralnetworksanddeeplearning.com/chap2.html"""
    delta_L = gradient_log_p
    dC_dw2 = np.dot(hidden_layer_values.T, delta_L).ravel()
    delta_l2 = np.outer(delta_L, weights['2'])
    delta_l2 = relu(delta_l2)
    dC_dw1 = np.dot(delta_l2.T, observation_values)
    return {
        '1': dC_dw1,
        '2': dC_dw2
    }

def update_weights(weights, expectation_g_squared, g_dict, decay_rate, learning_rate):
    """ See here: http://sebastianruder.com/optimizing-gradient-descent/index.html#rmsprop"""
    epsilon = 1e-5
    for layer_name in weights.keys():
        g = g_dict[layer_name]
        expectation_g_squared[layer_name] = decay_rate * expectation_g_squared[layer_name] + (1 - decay_rate) * g**2
        weights[layer_name] += (learning_rate * g)/(np.sqrt(expectation_g_squared[layer_name] + epsilon))
        g_dict[layer_name] = np.zeros_like(weights[layer_name]) # reset batch gradient buffer
```

Figure 11.30: Code snippet for the process happens using NN

To run this code, you need to execute the following command:

```
$ python me_Pong.py
```

If you want to build a bot that can beat the computer, then you need to train it for at least three to four days on a single GPU. You can refer to the output of the bot in the following screenshot:

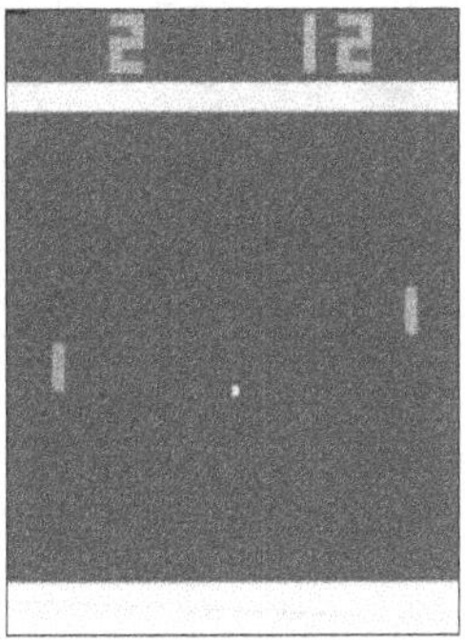

Figure 11.31: The Pong gaming bot output

You can see the training log in the following screenshot:

```
resetting env. episode reward total was -21.000000. running mean: -21.000000
```

Figure 11.32: Training log for Pong gaming bot

Now let's build a gaming bot just for fun. This bot uses the Flappy Bird gaming environment.

Just for fun - implementing the Flappy Bird gaming bot

In this section, we will be building the Flappy Bird gaming bot. This gaming bot has been built using DQN. You can find the entire code at this GitHub link: `https://github.com/jalajthanaki/DQN_FlappyBird`.

This bot has a pre-trained model, so you test it using the pre-trained model. In order to run this bot, you need to execute this command:

```
$ python deep_q_network.py
```

You can see the output in the following screenshot:

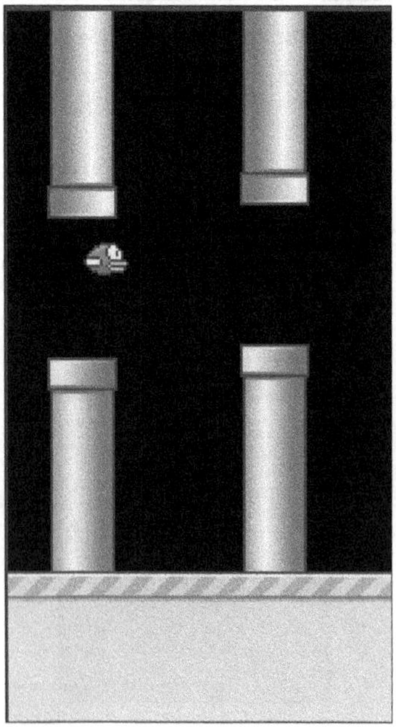

Figure 11.33: Output of the Flappy Bird gaming bot

You can see the combination of all the concepts that we have studied so far in this implementation, so make sure you explore this code. Consider this your exercise for the chapter.

Summary

Congratulations, readers; you have made it to the end! We covered basic concepts related to reinforcement learning in this chapter. You learned about the various concepts and algorithms of building the gaming bot. You also learned how the Deep Q Learner algorithm works. Using the `gym` library, we loaded the gaming world. By using the `dqn` library, we will be able to train the model. Training a gaming bot that can defeat human level experts takes a lot of time. So, I trained it for a few hours only. If you want to train for more hours, you can definitely do that. We tried to build a variety of simple Atari games, such as a simple pathfinder gaming bot, Space Invaders, Pong, and Flappy Bird. You can expand this basic approach to the bigger gaming environment. If you want to get yourself updated and contribute, then you can take a look at the OpenAI GitHub repository at: `https://github.com/openai`. Deep Mind news and the blog section are at this link: `https://deepmind.com/blog/` .

In the following section, you will find an appendix that can help you gain some extra information. This extra information will help you when you are building Machine Learning (ML) applications or taking part in a hackathon or other competitions. I have also provided some cheat sheets that can help you when you are building ML applications.

A
List of Cheat Sheets

This appendix basically helps you to get access to the cheat sheets for different Python libraries that we have used throughout this book. Apart from that, I have already provided information for installing the Python dependencies for each and every application. You can find those installations related information in the README section of each application.

So, let's jump to the cheat sheets related information.

Cheat sheets

I have put all the cheat sheets on GitHub, so you can refer them at any point of time, as and when needed. I have included following cheat sheets:

- Basic Linux OS commands
- Python for data science
- NumPy
- scipy
- pandas
- flask
- scikitlearn
- TensorFlow
- Keras
- pyspark
- Important mathematical concepts
- Visualization libraries: Bokeh and matplotlib
- Git commands

You can also provide your valuable feedback if you want to add a cheat sheet for any other library. You can raise your request and ask your questions by joining this slack channel: `https://jalajthanaki.slack.com`.

All cheat sheets are available at this GitHub link: `https://github.com/jalajthanaki/cheat_sheets_of_python_libraries`.

Summary

In this appendix, we have seen the list of the cheat sheets which you can explore. An installation guide has been already provided for each and every chapter in their respective GitHub repository under their corresponding README file. Apart from that, if anyone wants to clear their doubts then they can join the given slack channel.

In Appendix B, I will cover different aspects of how you can make effective strategies in order to win the hackathons. I also want to let you know how you can update yourself because, right now, Data Science related fields are moving so fast. So, keep reading guys!

B
Strategy for Wining Hackathons

This appendix is really interesting because here we are discussing two important aspects. Those two aspects are as follows:

- Strategy for winning hackathons
- Keeping up to date

So let's begin.

Strategy for winning hackathons

If you want to win hackathons or any Kaggle competition, then these are the things to keep in mind:

- Try to start as soon as you encounter the competition.
- Do exploratory data analysis properly. This will really help you build a good solution.
- Try to achieve a base-line model in the first five iterations.
- Track your own progress as well as track progress of others by checking out public and private leaderboards.
- Try different approaches and be innovative.
- Ask appropriate questions in forums but don't waste too much of your time.
- If you feel that in order to win you need to form a team, then ask other members to join you.

- When you create your team does matter. You need to form a team at least 15 days before the deadline of the competition so your team can work together and come up with the best possible approaches.
- The selection of team members also plays an important role. You should team up with those who have a complementary skill set so you can take advantage of each other's knowledge.
- Understand your team member's solutions and discuss approaches in depth.
- Your team members should know each other's strengths and weaknesses so it is easy to collaborate.
- Your team should discuss opportunities--meaning, you need to discuss other possible approaches in order to try them if possible.
- If you lose the competition, don't get disheartened. Try harder next time and learn what went wrong this time. List those things that went wrong and next time you won't make those kinds of mistakes. Try to improve those things. You will definitely win.

Keeping up to date

Data science and artificial intelligence (AI) related techniques and applications move at a fast pace so you need to stay up to date. The best way to update yourself is by following the research blogs of tech giants. Social media platforms such as Twitter, LinkedIn, and Slack will really help you. You must know who to follow so you can ask them appropriate questions. Be a part of the various communities in which you are interested. Try to explore some YouTube channels. You can also use education platforms such as Udacity, Coursera, and so on. You can also contribute on Quora. Be a part of open source projects. Update your work on GitHub. You should also read or subscribe to blogs and news. I'm listing some blogs that will help you update your knowledge:

- `https://www.datasciencecentral.com/`
- `https://research.googleblog.com/`
- `https://deepmind.com/blog/`
- `https://www.kdnuggets.com/websites/blogs.html`
- `https://medium.com/`
- `https://www.kaggle.com/blog`
- `https://www.library.cornell.edu/`
- `https://arxiv.org/`

Summary

In this appendix, we have discussed some tips and tricks that can help you to understand strategies for hackathons related to data science, as well as listed some learning resources that can really help you in order to get an idea of what is happening currently in the field of AI. Remember, always be open and curious in order to learn new things, and if you know something then share your knowledge with others.

Other Books You May Enjoy

If you enjoyed this book, you may be interested in these other books by Packt:

Machine Learning with TensorFlow 1.x
Quan Hua, Shams Ul Azeem, Saif Ahmed

ISBN: 9781786462961

- Explore how to use different machine learning models to ask different questions of your data
- Learn how to build deep neural networks using TensorFlow 1.x
- Cover key tasks such as clustering, sentiment analysis, and regression analysis using TensorFlow 1.x
- Find out how to write clean and elegant Python code that will optimize the strength of your algorithms
- Discover how to embed your machine learning model in a web application for increased accessibility
- Learn how to use multiple GPUs for faster training using AWS

Python Machine Learning - Second Edition
Sebastian Raschka, Vahid Mirjalili

ISBN: 9781787125933

- Understand the key frameworks in data science, machine learning, and deep learning
- Harness the power of the latest Python open source libraries in machine learning
- Master machine learning techniques using challenging real-world data
- Master deep neural network implementation using the TensorFlow library
- Ask new questions of your data through machine learning models and neural networks
- Learn the mechanics of classification algorithms to implement the best tool for the job
- Predict continuous target outcomes using regression analysis
- Uncover hidden patterns and structures in data with clustering
- Delve deeper into textual and social media data using sentiment analysis

Leave a review - let other readers know what you think

Please share your thoughts on this book with others by leaving a review on the site that you bought it from. If you purchased the book from Amazon, please leave us an honest review on this book's Amazon page. This is vital so that other potential readers can see and use your unbiased opinion to make purchasing decisions, we can understand what our customers think about our products, and our authors can see your feedback on the title that they have worked with Packt to create. It will only take a few minutes of your time, but is valuable to other potential customers, our authors, and Packt. Thank you!

Index

A

B

C

D

E

F

G

H

I

J

K

L

O

P

R

www.ingramcontent.com/pod-product-compliance
Lightning Source LLC
Chambersburg PA
CBHW060637060326
40690CB00020B/4427
* 9 7 8 1 7 8 8 3 9 0 0 4 0 *